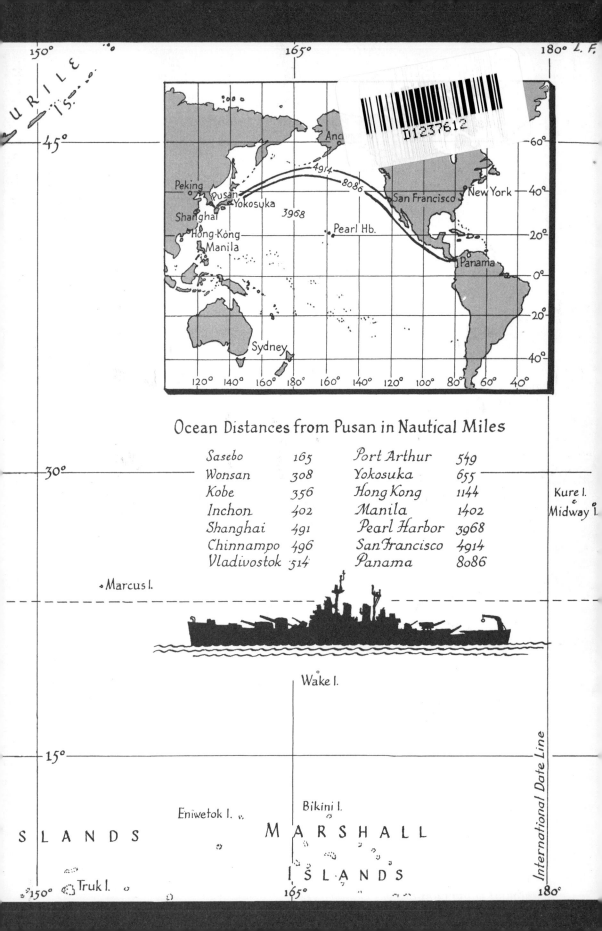

Ocean Distances from Pusan in Nautical Miles

Sasebo	165	Port Arthur	549
Wonsan	308	Yokosuka	655
Kobe	356	Hong Kong	1144
Inchon	402	Manila	1402
Shanghai	491	Pearl Harbor	3968
Chinnampo	496	San Francisco	4914
Vladivostok	514	Panama	8086

All hail, thou western world! by heaven design'd
Th' example bright, to renovate mankind.
Soon shall thy sons across the mainland roam;
And claim, on far Pacific shores, their home;
Their rule, religion, manners, arts, convey,
And spread their freedom to the Asian sea. . . .
O'er morn's pellucid main expand their sails,
And the starr'd ensign court Korean gales.

—TIMOTHY DWIGHT,
Greenfield Hill, 1794.

. . . I am convinced that Corea could be made to understand not only the policy of a treaty with the United States, but its absolute necessity as a matter of protection against the aggression of surrounding powers. Corea would in fact be the battlefield of any war between China and Russia or Japan in whichever way these nations might confront each other.

—COMMODORE R.W. SHUFELDT, USN,
13 October 1880.

The practices of dispatching naval fleets and air wings from one part of the world to another . . . cannot, naturally, be recognized as normal methods in international relations.

—N. S. KHRUSHCHEV,
7 September 1958.

History of United States Naval Operations

KOREA

by
JAMES A. FIELD, Jr.

with a foreword by
REAR ADMIRAL ERNEST McNEILL ELLER, USN (Retired)
Director of Naval History

WASHINGTON : 1962

L.C. Card 62–60083

For sale by the Superintendent of Documents, U.S. Government Printing Office
Washington 25, D.C. – Price $4.25

Foreword

CONTROL OF THE SEA has been one of the United States' greatest blessings. As Washington repeatedly pointed out, without superiority on the sea the American Revolution could not have been won. Three generations later seapower was decisive in preserving the Union in the Civil War, was overwhelming at sea, fundamental to victory ashore. In the twentieth century it has been indispensable for victory in the giant world wars that have shaken our times. In the Korean War it was the foundation for successes and repeated salvation against disasters.

The far possibilities inherent in control of the sea were highlighted at Inchon when General MacArthur signaled, "The Navy and Marines have never shone more brightly than this morning." Yet even the brightest victories are but a fragment of the vast and far-reaching influence of power based at sea—a power that has been growing in leaps and bounds with the growth of science and technology.

As the industrial revolution gathered momentum generations ago, it began to have profound effects upon navies. One result was the remarkable increase in power not only for operations afloat but in attack against forces ashore. Several of the many revolutions that changed navies last century, such as the internal-combustion engine, combined to make possible at about the same time both an effective submarine and a practical airplane. Thus navies began to go under the sea and into the air to gain new dimensions and potentialities unlimited. Neptune's trident had gained three prongs and become a true trident indeed.

Most of the ever-expanding technological revolutions have increased the capacity of balanced navies both to control the sea and to operate against the land. Hence the last generation has witnessed an unprecedented increase in amphibious capacity which wrote a remarkable record of consistent success against island and continent in World War II. It was America's great fortune that this amphibious capability, though mutilated in the years immediately after World War II, nevertheless by remnants and improvisation could still serve well in Korea.

Americans think of the Korean War as death and hardship in the bitter hills of Korea. It was certainly this, and for those who fought this is what they generally saw. Yet every foot of the struggles forward, every step of the retreats, the overwhelming victories, the withdrawals and last ditch stands had their seagoing support and overtones.

v

The spectacular ones depended wholly on amphibious power—the capability of the twentieth century scientific Navy to overwhelm land-bound forces at the point of contact.

Yet the all pervading influence of the sea was present even when no major landing or retirement or reinforcement highlighted its effect. When navies clash in gigantic battle or hurl troops ashore under irresistible concentration of shipborne guns and planes, nations understand that seapower is working. It is not so easy to understand that this tremendous force may effect its will silently, steadily, irresistibly even though no battles occur.

No clearer example exists of this truth in war's dark record than in Korea. Communist-controlled North Korea had slight power at sea except for Soviet mines. So beyond this strong underwater phase the United States Navy and allies had little opposition on the water. It is, therefore, easy to fail to recognize the decisive role navies played in this war fought without large naval battles.

The United States and the United Nations stopped aggression (and could have won clear cut victory) through the sound exercise of control of the sea. This power is, of course, only one facet of national power and itself, alone, could not assure victory in the Korean War, if in any war; yet loss of it would have assured certain defeat.

These facts stand out repeatedly in the following graphic account of the interweaving of sea based strength in land conflicts. They point out again the old lesson to America of the importance of the sea to her destiny—an importance that grows rather than lessens with transoceanic missiles, Polaris submarines, nuclear power and space satellites.

In the writing of this history the author has been given a free hand. All of the large body of documents then accumulated in the custody of the Division of Naval History in preparation for this history, and all of any classification that could subsequently be obtained, were assembled, organized, and made available to him under the able direction of Miss Loretta I. MacCrindle, Head of the Classified Archives Branch of this Office, and after 1958 by her most capable successor, Mr. Dean Allard. In this work, they had the extremely valuable assistance of Miss Barbara A. Gilmore and Mrs. Mildred D. Mayeux. Special searches were conducted far and wide for missing documents. Microfilms of dispatches of the period were researched when they were not available in their original form. Personal papers of Admiral Joy and others were made available and leading participants were interviewed or sent pertinent portions of the manuscript for comment. Admiral A. D. Struble in particular worked hard over the manuscript and devoted many days to interviews and discussion with Mr. Field and with this office. Except for a few missing items it is doubtful that a more complete United States naval record of original sources can ever be assembled.

The manuscript was read in its various stages by Captain F. K. Loomis, Assistant Director of Naval History, and myself. We did not hesitate to make a number of criticisms, general and specific, but the author made only the changes he thought justified. Hence the book bears no censorship in any way, neither is it a Navy Department publication to express an official view. It is the work of an experienced historian given the facts to tell the story as he saw it.

Korea is but one chapter in the hot and cold war pressed by those who would destroy democracy. These pages show the influence of the sea in small and large ways throughout the Korean War. In a broader sense they reflect the state of the whole·free world—a confederacy of the sea joined in united strength only if the sea is held and made one by those who love freedom.

These nations find that their life blood and liberty itself flow in the sea.

In this book, the author writes that the presence of the United States Navy in the Far East has been "the alpha and omega of Korean-American relations." It has also been, and seems certain to continue to be through the unknown future, the Alpha and Omega of all United States-world relations.

E. M. ELLER,
Rear Admiral, USN (Ret.),
Director, Naval History Division.

Preface

PERHAPS THE SIMPLEST WAY to describe the Korean War is to say that it was different, for it fell, or seemed to fall, outside the pattern of all previous American experience. It was a surprising war in a surprising place at a surprising time, and one which imperatively called for answers to neglected problems of national defense. It was begun as a police action; it developed rapidly into an undeclared war of no small magnitude; it ended as an unpopular and seemingly profitless stalemate. It was conducted, at least in theory, less as a national enterprise in defense of an easily apprehended national interest than as an exercise in collective security under the aegis of the United Nations. And while partial precedents can doubtless be discerned in battles long ago, the package was a new and unsettling one.

In addition to differences such as these in the nature of the war itself, there were others which bear upon the historian. Since the enemy had no navy, the conflict lacks the drama inherent in the clash of fleets. Since the focus of action was always on land, the three services were pretty constantly mixed up in each other's affairs, and simple single-service history becomes an impossibility. The chronology of the struggle, in which a year of violent and dramatic action was followed by two of deadlock, poses problems of selection and emphasis and makes for injustice to those who came late on the scene. The absence, in notable contrast to the situation of 1945, of any appreciable quantity of enemy records, constitutes a further obvious difficulty.

Nevertheless, an attempt to tell the story of United States naval operations in Korea has seemed worthwhile. If many of the specific lessons of the conflict are now obsolete, the general principle remains: that for those who have abjured the offensive, the main problem is how to prepare for the unexpected, or more cynically, how to be surprised at least cost. If war is to remain a political act, the Korean experience seems worth contemplating for its demonstration that the neglected problems of stalemate may at times be as important as those of advance and retreat. If the absence of contending fleets detracts from the excitement of the story, it also emphasizes the fact that since all war is an exercise in persuasion, naval activity has always been ultimately directed against the far shore. And finally, one may hope that caution will help to counteract the one-sided nature of the available source material.

To the puzzling question of how far to treat the actions of the other services, I have found no wholly satisfactory answer. I have attempted throughout to keep before the reader a general picture of the campaign, but

to deal in detail with Army and Air Force operations only when they interacted with those of the Navy. But while this standard has seemed the only
one possible, it should be made plain that it distorts the picture. For the
Army it means that emphasis is on the hard times when help was called
for, rather than on periods of prosperity when things were moving well;
for the Air Force the vexed question of tactical support receives considerable
attention, while the work of Bomber Command and of the fighter pilots
up by the Yalu is scanted.

In some cases this procedure gives rise to questions of a certain delicacy.
The Korean War took place at a time when the new defense establishment
was suffering growing pains; the course of the conflict was such that divergent and strongly held views were put to the test; interpretation of the consequences is unavoidably controversial. Although I have not thought it
possible to gloss over these matters, I cannot hope that my conclusions will
please everyone. Perhaps, indeed, they will satisfy none: the manuscript
has been read by those connected in one way or another with Army, Navy,
and Air Force alike, all of whom (happily for different reasons) have dis-
agreed with certain of the views expressed. In this connection it may be
worth stating, for those who wonder how "official" this history is, that I have
had full liberty to express my own opinions, and that there have been no
deletions from the manuscript on security or other grounds.

One final caveat. Throughout the book I have referred to General
MacArthur, and to his successors in supreme command, by their United States
short title, CincFE, rather than as CincUNC, Commander in Chief United
Nations Command. This usage has been employed as a matter of euphony
only, and in no way indicates a desire on my part to deemphasize the international nature of the campaign.

No one ever writes a book alone, and like all authors I have incurred
heavy debts. I am grateful to those individuals, in and out of the armed
services, who have been generous of their time in discussing the war and in
criticizing the manuscript, and to others who on other occasions have contributed to my education in these matters. I must record my thanks to the
administration of Swarthmore College for the grant of a leave of absence
without which completion of the book would have been long delayed.
Throughout the enterprise Rear Admiral E. M. Eller, USN (Ret.), the Director of Naval History, and his staff have been most helpful. Erwin Raisz
has been both skillful and patient in working through the complex specifica-
tions for the maps which illustrate the volume. Karlene Madison's contribution went far beyond the military fortitude with which she typed and retyped.
My wife and children have shown great forbearance.

JAMES A. FIELD, JR.

Swarthmore, Pennsylvania

Contents

List of Photographs

List of Maps

List of Tables

CHAPTER I

To Korea By Sea

1. The Commodore's Treaty

As the sun rose from behind the Korean hills all was in readiness for the assault. On the warships lying off Inchon plans and preparations were complete. As morning wore on the boats were brought alongside and the landing force was embarked. Upstream from the transport area *Monocacy* and the gunboats were already engaging enemy strong points, and toward mid-day, with the flooding tide, the landing craft left the anchorage and headed north. At 1330, under cover of the continuing bombardment, the signal was given and the boats went in. By 1345 the first wave of Marines was ashore and moving forward, while the boat crews and other members of the landing force struggled to get supporting weapons through the thick Korean mud and onto hard ground. So effective had been the bombardment that initial objectives on the heights overlooking the beaches were overrun without difficulty. By 1645 the artillery had been brought up, outposts were placed, the lines tied in, and the force settled down to get such rest as it could prior to resuming the advance at first light. It was the 10th of June, 1871.

The event is of some importance, if only for its illumination of the fact that the presence of the United States Navy in the Far East has been the alpha and omega of Korean-American relations. American naval activity was responsible for the opening of this distant nation and for its incorporation into the international system. When the decline of American interest resulted in naval withdrawal; Korean independence proved shortlived. In mid-20th century the Navy's return to the Western Pacific was the precondition of Korean liberation from Japanese control; a second such return permitted the preservation of the Republic of Korea from Communist domination. Only through free access by sea can the United States wield influence upon this distant peninsula. When access is disputed only naval power can ensure it. The history of American relations with Korea has been in large degree a function of the availability of such power.

The attack on the Korean forts in the summer of 1871 was one of the last acts of pre-industrial outward-looking America, the product of a pattern of oversea activity which dated back to the earliest days of the republic. The importance of maritime trade to the young nation had led to the growth of a merchant marine second only, and barely so, to that of Great Britain, and had governed the development and activities of the United States Navy. Created to defend American commerce against the pirates of Algiers, the Navy developed into a police force for the seven seas, an instrument of scientific discovery, and a spearhead of western influence in distant places. Campaigns against pirates were fought in the Mediterranean, the West Indies, and in China seas. Exploring expeditions ranged the globe. Naval diplomats sought commercial treaties from the princes of Barbary and the Sultan of Turkey, and the Mediterranean activities of Commodores Preble and Rodgers were followed by more famous efforts on the far side of the globe. As early as 1815 Commodore David Porter had proposed an expedition to the Pacific to open Japan, China, and surrounding territories to American commerce. The suggestion was premature, and in China, at least, the merchants got there first without government help. But the voyage of Edmund Roberts in *Peacock,* the activities of Commodore Kearny in China, and Perry's opening of Japan nevertheless bore witness to a naval and commercial policy of a remarkably forward nature for what was then one of the minor powers of the world.

Although the period of the Civil War brought the effective liquidation of the American merchant marine and a corresponding concentration on internal development, the old interest in the oceans and in what lay beyond them did not immediately disappear. The decade after Appomattox, which brought the attack on the Korean forts, was an active one overseas. These years saw the purchase of Alaska in the northwest, and proposals for the acquisition of Greenland and Iceland in the eastern approaches; interest was evidenced in the acquisition of a North African naval base; a reciprocity treaty was negotiated with Hawaii, and in Samoa an American agent became prime minister of that most beautiful of all kingdoms. *Divitis indiae usque ad ultimum sinum,* the motto of the town of Salem, had been the operating motto of American merchants and sea captains and of the American Navy, and now at the end of a century of independence the uttermost gulf had been reached. Across the Pacific, beyond the great bulge of the China coast and sheltered by the island screen that runs from Formosa to the empire of Japan, lay the Yellow Sea. On its eastern shore, at the mouth of the River Han, stood the forts which guarded the capital of Korea, last of the isolated civilizations of earth.

A generation before, Edmund Roberts had suggested that a Japanese treaty might lead to trade with Korea. In the 1840's a resolution had been introduced in Congress urging the establishment of commercial relations with both countries. But these proposals were nugatory, and in Korea, as so often elsewhere, the ultimately effective impulse to governmental action came not from home, but from the oversea activities of merchant marine and Navy. In 1866 the American merchantman *General Sherman* was destroyed, and its crew massacred, in the Taedong River below Pyongyang. The report of this tragedy brought the dispatch of a ship of the Asiatic Squadron, the U.S.S. *Wachusett,* Commander Robert W. Shufeldt, to investigate the affair, and to communicate with the King of Korea.

Shufeldt's mission proved fruitless, but the *General Sherman* incident led two successive commanders of the Asiatic Squadron, Rear Admirals Stephen C. Rowan and John Rodgers, to interest themselves in the possibility of a Korean treaty. The latter's proposal of a naval expedition, modelled on that of Commodore Perry, brought government action, and the American minister to China was designated to carry out the negotiation in cooperation with the Squadron Commander. Preparations were made, a force was assembled at Nagasaki, and on 30 May 1871 five United States ships of war, totalling 85 guns, dropped anchor off the mouth of the Han.

For this procedure the Perry expedition was not the only precedent: in just such a manner an earlier John Rodgers had extorted a favorable treaty from the contumacious Bey of Tunis. But the capital of the King of Korea, unlike that of the Bey, was upstream and beyond the range of naval guns; unlike the forces of the Bey, and indeed unlike the Japanese on the occasion of Perry's arrival, the Koreans opened fire; although Rodgers had strength enough to capture the forts he lacked that necessary to capture a treaty. On 3 July, honor having been satisfied, the expedition withdrew.

Nine years were to elapse before congressional pressure to obtain a treaty and the ambition of another naval officer to conclude it led to a second effort. In 1880 Commodore Shufeldt, who 14 years before had carried the first letter to the Korean King, returned to the Orient in the U.S.S. *Ticonderoga* with authority to treat. Efforts to communicate with the Koreans through the government of Japan were unproductive, but in mid-summer an offer of assistance came from the Chinese viceroy Li Hung-chang. China and Japan were currently at odds; as had been the case with other rulers subject to outside pressures, Li was desirous of American aid in developing his navy; in exchange for technical assistance he undertook to forward negotiations with Korea. Shufeldt proceeded to China, advice and advisors were provided the Chinese, and talks with Li were begun. In these discussions between Commodore and Viceroy may be seen some of the abiding realities of the situation: 71 years later, under very different circumstances, another American flag officer was to find himself negotiating with the Chinese concerning the future of Korea.

Two years of complicated intrigue were required before Shufeldt could attain his goal. But at last, on 22 May 1882, a treaty arranged in Tientsin by the Chinese Viceroy was signed on the Korean shore within view of the U.S.S. *Swatara.* By this instrument, which provided for perpetual peace and friendship and for the exchange of diplomatic and consular representation, American citizens were granted trading rights, extraterritoriality, and most-favored-nation treatment. The aims of commerce were satisfied and, as Shufeldt reported, the United States had brought "the last of the exclusive countries within the pale of western civilization."

The movement to open Korea, with its inevitable impact on the equilibrium of eastern Asia, has been described as America's most important action in the Far East prior to the occupation of the Philippines. Be this as it may, it was the last such action, and as such marked the end of an era both for the Navy and for the nation. Industrialism was bringing the end of the period of free exchange of goods, the development of internal resources was replacing foreign trade as a prime source of wealth. As nations became industrialized so did their navies, and the new complexities of maintenance, together with the new fuel problem, forced the fleets of the world to retire on their bases. With the development of new nationalisms the naval function shifted from one of exploring, opening, and policing to one of fighting. Shufeldt had opened Korea, but although the Secretary of the Navy in 1884 urged the establishment of a naval station at Port Hamilton, off the southern Korean coast, and although it appears that such facilities were offered by the Korean government, nothing was done. The next important American naval action in Asiatic waters came in 1898 in the Battle of Manila Bay.

2. *The American Link*

The country launched by the American Commodore upon the seas of international life had dwelt for centuries in isolation. Although Europe had long traded with China and the Spice Islands, it was only with the 19th century that western ships in increasing number visited the Korean coasts. There, as earlier elsewhere, the history of exploration came to be written on the Admiralty charts of the world: Russian interest was memorialized in such places as Port Lazaref and Kornilov Bay; French designs in Eugénie Island and the Prince Imperial Archipelago; British discovery in Broughton Bay and Port Hamilton; the arrival of the Americans in Washington Gulf, Maury Island, and Monocacy Bay.

But while discoveries could be made and recorded, efforts to penetrate beyond the Korean shoreline were long unsuccessful. Within the peninsula the first important western contact was that of Christianity, which filtered in by way of China, and which in the 1830's brought French missionary priests to the Hermit Kingdom. But many were martyred, and nature as well as the natives was hostile to foreign interference. In 1846 the French frigates *Gloire* and *Victorieuse,* sent to investigate a massacre of missionaries, grounded on uncharted shoals; the extreme tidal range of the Yellow Sea left them high and dry, the crews were taken off by a passing English ship, and the frigates abandoned to the elements. In 1866, the year of the loss of the *General Sherman,* another French expedition was defeated at the mouth of the Han River, and five years later Admiral Rodgers was frustrated in his purpose. Yet the influence of the west was growing: conversions to Christianity continued, by mid-century there were some 15,000 Korean Catholics, and in the 1860's the first Protestant missionary effort was begun.

Through her centuries of isolation Korea had maintained a special, if somewhat vague, relationship with China. This relationship, which the Koreans apparently felt not disadvantageous, was conceived of in Confucian terms. Governed not by law but by standards of propriety, it required a deferential attitude, such as that of younger toward elder brother, on the part of Korea in her relations with the Middle Kingdom. Put forward by the Koreans as the reason they could have no dealings with outsiders, and concurred in by the Chinese with the proviso that Korean actions were none of their concern, this familial relationship seemed to legalistic westerners a piece of sublime mysticism and nonsense. For Korea, however, it had at least the utility of providing some freedom of maneuver, and of delaying by a few years the inevitable arrival of the barbarians. Only in 1876, when Japan did for Korea what Perry had done for her, did the Hermit Kingdom accept relations with an outside power. Only with the Shufeldt treaty did she accept them with a non-Asiatic people. Oddly enough, despite Chinese assistance in both negotiations, neither treaty made mention of Korean dependence on China, and this apparent admission of sovereignty had considerable impact on the outer world. Although the Commodore's accomplishment went largely unnoticed at home, such was not the case abroad, where Britain, Germany, France, and Russia hastened to make treaties on the Shufeldt model.

Inevitably all this raised serious questions about the ancient relationship with China. But here the basic issue was the vitality of China herself, and at this point in history the Middle Kingdom was a doubtful proposition. Things being what they were in the 1880's, it would have taken a very vigorous elder brother to preserve the peace of a peninsula which divides the waters between China and Japan, and which dangles from the Asiatic mainland where Manchuria and the Maritime Provinces meet. The treaty with the United States, with its emphasis on Korean independence, may have hastened the coming of trouble, but hardly more than that. Long before the treaty was concluded Shufeldt had written that "Corea would in fact be the battlefield of any war with China and Russia or Japan in whichever way these nations might confront each other," and his prediction was speedily borne out.

Without preparation for the diplomatic rough and tumble of the outer world, situated between three stronger powers in a time of rapid change, the little kingdom found itself subjected to increasing pressures, and the winds blew ever stronger from north, east, and west. In the old Confucian family there had been the easy traditional relationship of father and son, or of elder and younger brother. In the new family of nations into which Korea had been welcomed there were three competing volunteers for a big brother role construed in more modern terms.

China was attempting to reassert her historic dominance, Russia to move southward into ice-free ports, and Japan to gain control of the peninsula as a springboard for continental expansion. All urged their chosen advisers upon the Korean King, and the triple pressure from without was reflected in serious strains within. Torn by the inevitable factionalism of a people emerging from isolation, the country found itself divided between nationalists and reactionaries, between a progressive party desirous of acquiring foreign skills and methods and a traditional pro-Chinese faction. In this situation America and the Americans, although far away and preoccupied with other things, had for the progressive group of Koreans a special meaning.

The United States had been the first of the western powers to make a treaty with Korea. It was for some time the only such power to send a minister to the Korean court. A provision of the Shufeldt treaty stated that "if other powers deal unjustly or oppressively with either government, the other will exert their good offices . . . to bring about an amicable arrangement." Together with the traditional American sympathy for a society attempting to modernize itself, all this seemed full of promise for the new era and inevitably placed the United States in a conspicuous position. The King, on the arrival of the first American minister, is reported to have danced with joy.

But in Washington, and in the United States generally, small attention was paid to Korean matters. From the viewpoint of the America of the 1880's the treaty was but a last echo of the period of maritime greatness and the product of Shufeldt's personal diplomacy. Yet however little the provision for good offices may have meant to the American government, America had from the beginning given sympathy and support to the independence of small nations. It remained willing, if asked, to issue sound advice. Since, in the last analysis, self-determination means self-defense, it would provide, although dilatorily, assistance in military organization. Nor was the importance of the United States limited to the actions of its government: American businessmen would bring their skills across the sea; the American religious community would send forth missionaries bearing, along with the Protestant word, western education and western techniques. Somehow the Koreans seem to have sensed a disinterested benevolence in the distant republic, and to have founded great and indeed excessive hopes upon it: in 1897, in an audience with the American minister, the Korean King was to remark, "We feel that America is to us as our Elder Brother."

Reality, unfortunately, did not live up to expectations. The conclusion of the Shufeldt treaty had reversed the roles of Korea and the United States, and the Hermit Kingdom was now the petitioner. Desiring to consolidate his new-found independence, the King cleared out his Chinese and Russian advisers in the hope of replacing them with Americans. But the response of the American government was disappointing. Although internal disorder in 1882 brought the arrival of the U.S.S. *Monocacy* with instructions to offer good offices, and although the United States created a ministerial post at Seoul equal in rank to those at Tokyo and Peking, the instructions of Lucius H. Foote, the first incumbent, reflected the non-participating sympathy so often evident in American policy in distant places. Foote was authorized to tender advice to the King, but unless covered by specific instructions this advice was to be considered personal rather than official, and such instructions rarely came. Korean requests for advisers in foreign affairs, for military instructors, and for school teachers remained unfulfilled, and the American minister found his dispatches unanswered by a lethargic State Department and his grade reduced by an economizing Congress.

Resentful of these indignities and of the apparent indifference of the home government, Minister Foote resigned his post. But lack of official interest in Washington did not prevent further development of non-governmental relations. As the negotiation of the treaty had been largely an individual enterprise on the part of Shufeldt, so relations between the two countries became increasingly personal and unofficial. From China came an American to be Inspector-General of Korean Customs; a former United States consul at Tientsin assumed the post of vice-president of the Foreign Office. In 1884, following the departure of Foote, custody of the legation fell to a young naval officer, Ensign George Foulk, who became deeply concerned with the future of Korea and for three years struggled to uphold both the integrity of that country and the dignity of the United States. By the time of his recall Foulk had gained the highest favor, and the desire of the Korean King to name him personal adviser in foreign affairs was frustrated only by heavy pressure from the Chinese government.

Despite this victory for Chinese influence the American connection continued strong. Munitions for the army were ordered from the United States. Under the leadership of General William M. Dye, the military mission which the King had earlier requested finally arrived in 1888. Dye, a veteran of Vicksburg and the Red River campaign who had later served in the army of Egypt, took over the military academy, published a tactical manual in Korean, and produced a body of highly trained troops. But the Korean noblemen proved unamenable to discipline, and that part of the army not subject to his personal influence continued to suffer from faction and intrigue.

In economic development, too, there was progress. With the passing of years American businessmen followed the Navy's trans-Pacific lead to found a Korean-American bank, to operate Korea's most important gold mine, and to build a street railway system for the capital. In Seoul there arose the Astor House hotel, and over the Yalu River a bridge, built by American engineers, which in the fullness of time would be knocked down by American naval aviators.

The final, and increasingly the most important link between the two countries, was that of the missionary effort. The 19th century had seen a great expansion of Protestant missions in which Americans had played a leading part. Throughout the non-European world these pioneers had been active in bringing the gospel and the gifts of western civilization to those who dwelt in darkness, and in beginning a revolutionary undermining of the static societies of Asia. Typically, although influential in worldly things, the missionaries had accomplished few conversions, but in Korea, where Christianity had already taken root, their success was greater. By 1885 both Presbyterians and Methodists had arrived from America and begun their work, profiting from the esteem in which their country was held. By the end of the decade a dozen stations had been established, running from Kanggye far in the north through Pyongyang, seven-gated Kaesong and Seoul, and southward to Taegu and Pusan.

Schools, colleges, and hospitals were established by the missionaries, in their efforts to assist the people, and in time an important Christian community developed. By 1910 there were some 72,000 Korean Catholics and almost 180,000 Protestants. Yet things move slowly in the Orient: at least as late as the First World War the missionaries in Pyongyang could enjoy the sight, at one of the city gates, of the anchor and chain from the *General Sherman,* preserved in commemoration of that successful encounter with the outer world.

Their obvious concern for Korean welfare, and their open support of Korean independence, quickly brought the missionaries into close relations with government as well as people. The medical missionary Horace N. Allen established a government hospital, was appointed court physician, and served both as a Korean emissary to the United States and as American minister at Seoul. Horace B. Underwood, translator of the gospel into the Korean tongue, became an unofficial adviser to the King, and his wife the Queen's physician. The link between missionary activity and the Navy, so strong in Ottoman regions, reappeared in Korea: when the King, despite strong Chinese opposition, moved to establish a legation in Washington, Allen accompanied the emissaries, who eluded the Chinese warships sent to intercept them by taking passage in the U.S.S. *Ossipee.* Although these intimate connections proved at times embarrassing to the American government, to the Koreans they seemed a very present help. In the dark days of 1895, following the Japanese-instigated murder of the Queen, the missionaries rallied to the King, giving him moral support and safeguarding his food supply. In 1905 Korean confidence in the selfless strangers was again demonstrated when, in a last desperate effort to avoid Japanese domination, the Emperor secretly sent Allen and Homer Hulbert, another distinguished missionary, to seek the assistance of the United States.

Great changes came with the Japanese occupation, but in time the older pattern was repeated. In 1945 the United States Navy again sailed the coasts of Asia, and its return was followed by a new opening of Korea and a new period of American influence. Where earlier Americans like Foulk and Allen had advised the Korean King, American Military Government now supervised the creation of a new state; where American entrepreneurs had brought the techniques of the West there now came ECA aid; where General Dye had commanded the palace guard there appeared the Korean Military Advisory Group. Again the missionaries arrived, to renew their efforts, and Homer Hulbert, the American interpreter of Korean culture and the Emperor's personal emissary in the crisis of 1905, returned to end his days in this distant country.

3. The Dominance of Japan

All this lay hidden in the future as the 19th century ended. Korea was small and far away, its opening seemed the last effort of an age that was past, and the treaty provision for good offices was to prove less meaningful than the dancing king had hoped.

For Korea the years following the conclusion of the Shufeldt treaty brought internal chaos and increasing Chinese influence. By 1894, despite the presence of American and other foreign advisers and despite the best efforts of the Japanese, Chinese dominance had been thoroughly reestablished. But the triple pressure continued, and while the Middle Kingdom could dominate her younger brother she was unable to withstand her stronger neighbor. The position so carefully retrieved by Li Hung-chang was to be suddenly destroyed by war with Japan.

In the summer of 1894 anti-foreign rebellion broke out in the southern provinces of Korea. A request from the King for the assistance of Chinese troops was somewhat reluctantly acceded to, but by the time these arrived the revolt had been put down. Japan, meanwhile, on the pretext of protecting her nationals and property, had sent troops of her own, and despite the restoration of peace continued to increase these forces until they greatly outnumbered those of the Chinese. Efforts by the American minister and others to compose the differences and secure the withdrawal of troops proved unsuccessful. There followed a coup in which the Japanese seized the King and installed his father-in-law as Regent. Chinese troopships bringing reinforcements were sunk by the Japanese, and in August war was declared.

The Sino-Japanese war, which eliminated Chinese influence in the Korean peninsula for more than half a century, was a sufficiently one-sided affair. Politically it is noteworthy as the first step in a Japanese expansion which would only be checked at Midway and Guadalcanal. Militarily it was important for the Battle of the Yalu, the first major engagement between ironclads, which marked the opening of the era in which the world's strategic pattern depended upon the new navies of industrialism. For the United States this engagement demonstrated that a policy based on a belief in self-determination may have its difficulties, and that one people's self-determination may be another's poison. While the Japanese Navy, victors at the Yalu River, had benefited from American advice and assistance, the Chinese battleship *Chen Yuen* was fought in this engagement by Philo McGiffin, a Naval Academy graduate of the Class of 1884.

By the Treaty of Shimonoseki of 1895 Japan acquired Formosa and the Pescadores, and so gained strategic control of the approaches to North China and to Peking; the treaty also ensured Korean independence of Chinese domination. The Japanese had expected that it would ensure still more, and would give them control of Korea's foreign relations and internal communications, but their position was greatly compromised by their murder of the Korean Queen, which excited both Korean nationalism and foreign interference.

Although the attitude of the American government remained one of strict neutrality and abstention, Americans in Korea were gravely concerned by the prospect of Japanese control. This concern was demonstrated by the actions of the American minister, John M. B. Sill, who maneuvered against the Japanese; by missionary support of the King; and by an attempt of Korean patriots, with the assistance of certain Americans, to rescue the King from Japanese control. On the failure of the effort some of the Koreans were given asylum in the American legation, and Sill asked for a warship to convey them to safety. But his request was refused by the State Department and his actions on behalf of Korean independence were censured.

The resultant power vacuum was quickly filled. The King took refuge in the Russian legation, temporary Russian dominance of Korean affairs ensued, and at Russian suggestion the Kingdom of Korea was translated into the Empire of Dai Han. But in their turn the Russians overreached themselves, and in 1898, at the request of the Emperor, their advisers were withdrawn. There followed, briefly, a period of apparent Korean independence, marked by resurgent Japanese economic penetration, by Korean misgovernment and confusion, and by tension between Russia and Japan which led shortly to a second war.

War with Russia brought further triumphs to the Japanese. A second Battle of the Yalu, fought this time on land, resulted in the first great triumph of an Asiatic army over a European one, and the repercussions of this notable event, reinforced by the naval victory of Tsushima and the course of the subsequent campaign, reached through India to the heart of Africa. Yet though the fighting was with Russia, Japanese operations were aimed at Korea. Two days before declaring war the Japanese seized the capital and the palace of the Emperor, and within a month an agreement was signed in which Japan guaranteed the integrity of Korea and the Koreans promised to take none but Japanese advice.

The vigor with which the Japanese pressed their advantages proved irresistible by the faction-ridden inhabitants of the peninsula. Korean confidence in the promise of American good offices had been strengthened by the assurances of their American friends, internal reform had been neglected, and no steps had been taken—if indeed any could have been taken—to improve the position of Korea. Seeing his country becoming a Japanese protectorate, the Emperor in September 1904 appealed for American help in maintaining its integrity, and in the next year urgent efforts were made to communicate secretly with President Roosevelt through the American missionaries and through a young Korean patriot named Syngman Rhee.

The hopes founded on the American elder brother proved delusive. Although the treaty ending this war on the Asiatic mainland was signed on the eastern seaboard of the United States, this geographical oddity reflected Theodore Roosevelt's concern with larger matters than Korean independence. Already the President had made his attitude clear, observing that "we cannot possibly interfere for the Koreans against Japan. They could not strike a blow in their own defense." And Korea's future, so far as the United States was concerned, was settled by the Taft-Katsura conversations of 1905, in which the Secretary of War expressed the view, immediately confirmed by the President, that Japanese suzerainty would contribute to the peace of the Orient.

So Korea became a Japanese protectorate and acquired a new and unwished for elder brother. Ironically enough, when the Japanese took over the management of Korea's foreign relations, it was the United States, the country whose good offices had been promised in case of unjust treatment, which was the first to remove its legation from Seoul. But while the loss of Korean independence was distressing to those Americans, diplomatic and missionary, who were on the spot, it can hardly be denied that President Roosevelt correctly construed the feeling of the country. The victories of Japan, it seemed, proved the Japanese to be America's foremost pupils, and testified retrospectively to the importance of Commodore Perry's mission.

Despite difficulties over Japanese immigration and landholding, a general admiration for the accomplishments of the Japanese nation had developed in America, as indicated by a spate of juvenile novels with such unlikely titles as *With Togo to Tsushima, or, Two American Boys in the Navy of Japan.*

Yet there were deeper forces affecting the conduct of the United States than the transitory admiration for Japanese progress in western ways. If somewhat absent-mindedly, the United States had also participated in the new imperialism. With the overseas holdings acquired in the War with Spain came new responsibilities. The new realism in foreign affairs, manifested in the policies of Theodore Roosevelt, was part of the price of empire.

In the development of this new realism, as in that of the New Navy which had won the victories at Santiago and Manila Bay, the writings of an American naval officer were of great influence. To Alfred Thayer Mahan, as he sat in the English Club at Lima perusing Mommsen's *History of Rome,* there had been vouchsafed a vision of the meaning of command of the seas. Building upon this vision Mahan developed a gospel of sea power and, as his evidence was drawn from the great 18th century wars for empire, his message was well suited to the new imperial age. Hailed throughout the world, and particularly by the rising naval powers of Germany and Japan, his writings became a potent influence in burying the strategic concepts of the old Navy in which he had served so long and a strong stimulus to the navalism of the early 20th century.

Rapidly, in these years, the strategic geography of the world changed and became compartmented, and not least as a result of the rise of Japan and of Japanese adherence to the doctrines of the American naval officer. Where Shufeldt had brought Korea "within the pale of western civilization," Mahan provided a philosophic framework for Japan's effort to make East Asia her exclusive sphere. Where detachments of western navies had policed the Asiatic seas on behalf of the international commercial community, there now developed an oriental battle fleet. For the United States, with its flag planted in the Philippines some 7,000 miles from home, the development was a significant one and elicited a double response. In 1908 the Great White Fleet set forth across the Pacific on its cruise around the world; in 1910 Japan annexed Korea with the approval of the American government. The protectorate was ended, the Emperor pensioned off, and the country opened by the American commodore disappeared from the map. Where Shufeldt had seen commercial opportunity, Americans now thought of Korea, if they thought of it at all, as a picturesque and distant land of topknots and horsehair hats. All that remained of the period of independence was the missionary link, now weakened and harassed by the Japanese rulers of the peninsula, and a scattered and impotent band of Korean nationalist conspirators.

4. Return to Asia

The lot of Korea under Japanese rule was hard. In a consistent effort to subjugate the populace the Japanese took over the administration, the control of education, and the police. A directed economy was imposed, with the aim of ending Korean self-sufficiency and of integrating the country into the imperial economy of Japan. Investment in Korean plant was not inconsiderable, but the benefits flowed back across the sea, and the inhabitants of the peninsula were reduced to hewers of wood and drawers of water for their alien overlords.

Despite the best efforts of the conquerors, however, the independence movement remained alive. Those who had struggled to save their country from alien control became the nucleus of a continued resistance which made Korea the Ireland of the East. The quiet of the Land of the Morning Calm was a quiet imposed from above, but from time to time the pressures broke through in riots and uprisings, and in 1919 there came an echo of the past. In Paris President Wilson was laboring to remake the world on principles derived from the older America; his emphasis on the self-determination of peoples and the rights of small nations had repercussions even in Korea, where the resisters, hoping to draw attention to their country's plight, issued a Proclamation of Independence.

But Japan had fought with the Allies. The Proclamation got no response, the protesters were driven underground or into exile, and the sole accomplishment of their effort was the formation of a Korean Provisional Government at Shanghai. Yet even here there were traces of the American connection: the presidency of this government was conferred upon Syngman Rhee, who had been educated by American missionaries, who had studied at Woodrow Wilson's Princeton, who on returning to Korea had escaped arrest through the assistance of a missionary bishop, and who was living in Hawaii.

Yet while the influence of American ideas was still potent, American policy remained one of continuing abstention. Japanese annexation of Korea had not been questioned. American participation in the League of Nations was defeated by the Senate. When crisis threatened with Japan the solution was found in the Washington treaties, which by restrictions on warship construction and on base development effectively trisected the Pacific Ocean and left the Japanese unchallenged in their sphere. A growing inclination to disengage from the Orient brought the grant of prospective independence to the Philippines.

This retirement from the outer world, which culminated in the extreme isolationism of the late thirties, was ended by the new dictatorships. For while these did not immediately menace the security of the country, they did endanger the continued existence of that minimum degree of world order which seems necessary to the United States. With Munich the withdrawal stopped, while the fall of France and the threat to Britain brought a forward diplomacy in the Atlantic and a sizable rearmament program. With the Japanese attack on Pearl Harbor new emphasis was placed on the Pacific. There followed, in due course, a second advance to the shores of Asia, and one in force such as had never before been seen. The United States Pacific Fleet, which by summer of 1945 was dominant in Japanese home waters, was a far cry from the five ships and 85 guns with which John Rodgers had attacked the Korean forts.

To the captive Koreans the outbreak of war in the Pacific brought new hope. Repeated efforts between the wars to gain the attention of the powers had met with no success. Various uprisings in the thirties had been repressed, and in 1940 an organized non-cooperation movement had been vigorously put down. In China the advance of the Japanese armies forced the Korean Provisional Government to flee inland to Chungking. But Pearl Harbor changed the shape of things, and on 11 December 1941 the government in exile declared war on Japan.

Somewhat surprisingly, perhaps, despite the ancient friendship and the missionary link, the Korean question remained long neglected by the United States. The Provisional Government was ignored, and attempts by Syngman Rhee to win recognition gained no countenance from the State Department. By 1943, however, American thinking with regard to Korea had advanced to the point of contemplating that liberation from Japan would be followed by an international trusteeship. The communique of the Cairo Conference promised Korean independence "in due course," and both at Yalta and at Moscow discussion of the trusteeship idea resulted in apparent general agreement.

But while agreement on trusteeship came easily in talk and in paper planning, the realities of the Korean situation remained much as before. Geography, at least, had not changed. The Japanese elder brother was facing expulsion, but Russia and China were still much in the picture, and so, once again, was the United States. Although Korean nationalism was undiminished, the strains which had beset the Korean kingdom persisted and the independence movement was itself a divided one. Syngman Rhee, the President of the Provisional Government, was in the United States, where important Korean groups existed in Hawaii and in Washington. In China, and under Chinese Nationalist influence, was the greater part of the Provisional Government, along with some army divisions supported by the regime of Chiang Kai-shek. The other China of Mao Tse-tung boasted its own Korean adherents, and as early as 1939 had created a so-called Korean Volunteer Army. Large numbers of Koreans had taken refuge in the Soviet Maritime Provinces, and many had served in the Russian armies. And finally, Koreans of all factions urgently desired immediate independence, and took a poor view of qualifying phrases such as "in due course."

In this situation events took charge. The sudden end of the war in the Pacific found the United States unprepared, its attentions focused on the projected invasion of the Japanese homeland. Hasty efforts in Washington to cope with the issues of Japan's surrender resulted in a directive which provided, with Soviet concurrence, that Japanese forces in Korea north of the 38th parallel would surrender to the Russians, and those south of that line to the United States. In time, of course, this decision on the mechanics of surrender was to divide Korea in rigid and illogical fashion, but it also saved the southern half of the country from Communist control. On 12 August, with American forces still 600 miles and almost a month away, Russian troops entered Korea against negligible Japanese resistance.

The moment of victory in the Pacific found the United States suffering from a shortage of sea power in the midst of plenty. The defeat of Japan was one thing; the simultaneous occupation of key points all along the Asiatic littoral was quite another. Since all available amphibious lift was needed for the occupation of the Japanese islands, peripheral areas had to wait. But in time ships did become available. Lieutenant General John R. Hodge's XXIV Corps was embarked at Okinawa, and on 8 September 1945 a group of Seventh Fleet transports steamed up the Inchon approaches and prepared to land the troops. The second coming had taken place. The wheel that Rodgers and Shufeldt had set in motion had come full circle.

CHAPTER II

Policy and Its Instruments

1. Divided Korea

IN ONE IMPORTANT sense the second coming of the Americans resembled the first. Again the arrival marked the culmination of a great thrust overseas; again, even as the shores of Korea were reached, the tide was beginning to turn. Shufeldt's treaty had been greeted with massive disinterest by an America absorbed in internal development; by the time Hodge led his corps ashore at Inchon demobilization had begun and domestic concerns were again uppermost in the American mind. For the next five years American policy in Korea would be dominated by the desire to fulfill the wartime commitments as quickly and economically as possible, and to get out and go home.

The Cairo Declaration had promised a unified, free, and democratic Korea. The 38th parallel, however, promised some difficulties in the achievement of these aims. Although originally proposed as an administrative convenience to facilitate the surrender of Japanese forces this arrangement soon acquired other overtones. In view of the interallied frictions which had already developed in Europe the dividing line seemed to derive virtue as a barrier to further Soviet advance, as a cover for the American position in Japan, and as providing the United States with a position of strength from which to press for Korean independence. In this last context, a country which habitually saw the resolution of political disputes as a function of voting strength could look with satisfaction on the fact that almost two-thirds of Korea's thirty million inhabitants lived south of the parallel.

But whatever the virtues of the 38th parallel, division of the country between the two new elder brothers created a situation which called for serious diplomatic preparation. This, however, seems not to have been forthcoming. In the State Department the question of the divided peninsula appears to have been looked upon as little more than a minor nuisance, while for American public opinion the question hardly existed. The democratizing of Japan under the shining leadership of General MacArthur effectively monopolized the public consciousness; compared with this the liberation of Korea by a simple corps commander excited little interest.

16

No political guidance and little information had been provided General Hodge. No military government teams were available to accompany his corps. Whether the Koreans were to be regarded as liberated friends or as the inhabitants of a corner of a conquered empire remained obscure. In this situation Hodge and his officers had to improvise policy as best they could, maintain order, and somehow administer the country, while awaiting directives from home. American Military Government was consequently imposed on South Korea, and a successor Korean government which had sprung up in the wake of the Japanese defeat was refused recognition. But this policy, reminiscent of the wartime trusteeship proposals, antagonized important native elements and made the position of the American command more difficult.

The end of the war found Korea approaching economic collapse. The country was beset by a spiralling inflation, and by acute shortages of raw materials, tools, and capital. A generation of Japanese occupation in which all managerial posts had been retained in the hands of the conqueror had resulted in a woeful lack of administrative personnel. To add to the difficulties of an exploited economy, now suddenly bereft of its managerial staff, the division at the 38th parallel had separated fields on the south from fertilizer in the north, and the larger cities and the majority of the population from the sources of hydroelectric power and of coal.

Obvious first steps in reconstruction were to permit freedom of movement between the two zones, and to unify at least the administration of the Korean economy. Proposals to this effect were made by General Hodge, but the Russian commander was unresponsive. The problems of unification were perforce transferred to a higher plane, and at Moscow, in December 1945, a joint U.S.-U.S.S.R. committee was established to prepare, in consultation with the Koreans, for a democratic government of Korea. At the moment, perhaps, this step appeared promising; in fact it merely marked the disappearance of the Korean question into those proliferating procedural jungles which, in the post-war period, so obfuscated points at issue between Russia and her western allies. The details of the work of the Joint Committee need not concern us here: suffice it to say that disputes over terminology concerning the proposed trusteeship led to adjournment in May 1946. Some progress had by this time been made by the two military commands in accomplishing a limited exchange of certain commodities. But on political matters progress was nil and Korea remained divided.

It was possible of course to consider that the Korean question should be settled on its own merits. Such presumably was the view of the Koreans, such had been the viewpoint of Americans in the eighties and nineties, and such was the attitude of General Hodge and of others on the spot. But Korea was but one facet of the world-wide problem of adjustment between the Soviets and the West which followed the collapse of Germany and

Japan. Difficulties had developed even before the shooting stopped, as in the problem of the Polish boundary; as the months went by the situation was exacerbated by squabbles over German reparations and the communization of the Balkan states; internal strife in China made it evident that the defeat of Japan had not ended the war for East Asia. In March 1946, the month that the Korean Joint Committee convened to begin its deliberations, the darkening picture was dramatically presented in Winston Churchill's speech at Fulton, Missouri. In these circumstances only an extreme optimist could conceive of a resolution of the Korean question in simple local terms.

Throughout the year interallied relations remained difficult, and spring of 1947 came in an atmosphere of increasing crisis. The month of March brought the breakdown of the Moscow Conference and the signing of the Treaty of Dunkirk. It brought also, as a result of Soviet pressures on Turkey and of Communist guerrilla warfare in Greece, the enunciation of the Truman Doctrine. In June the depressing possibilities presented by the economic dislocation of western Europe produced the Marshall Plan for cooperative reconstruction with American support. One month later an influential American periodical published a disillusioned article on "The Sources of Soviet Conduct" under a pseudonym carefully selected to make unmistakable the official nature of the analysis.

In such an atmosphere of hardening American policy it was unlikely that much would come of bilateral discussion of Korean problems. Following a second abortive effort by the Joint Committee in the summer of 1947 the United States proposed a four-power conference on Korea, and advanced procedural suggestions which were extremely sensible if considered simply from the Korean point of view. But the Russians declined to cooperate. The fact that the great majority of the Korean population lived within the American zone, that South Korea had the votes, had come to mean that unification on any democratic basis would be equivalent to an American victory and to a retreat of the Soviet frontier. If a way existed of compromising this question while maintaining a decent regard for the Koreans themselves, it was not discovered. With Russian rejection of the American proposals all serious effort to reach a solution through negotiation came to an end.

But to the United States the occupation of South Korea was a costly and troublesome business. The expenses of relief were high; the continuation of military government lent itself to propaganda about fascism and colonialism. In September 1947 a Joint Chiefs of Staff study concluded that Korea was of little strategic importance, and that in view of the current shortage of operating forces the divisions locked up in the peninsula would be better employed elsewhere. As in the earlier period of Foote and Foulk and Sill the cost of a forward policy in Korea seemed greater than any promised reward, and as frustration increased the search for a solution to Korea's problems gave way to an attempt to disengage.

The upshot was a new departure in American policy, and a decision to transfer the Korean question to the United Nations. This step, part of a developing effort to use this organization to mobilize pressure against the Soviets, was in some respects highly appealing. It promised to divest the United States of an expensive and onerous burden and to focus attention on Russian obstruction of Korean unification; it put those countries critical of the American administration of South Korea in a position where they would have to take some responsibility. Like so many American decisions in the years following the Second World War it appeared to answer the felt needs for economy while maintaining at least verbal adherence to previously stated goals. But unless one seriously believed in the effectiveness of "world public opinion," the transfer of the Korean question to the U.N. hardly represented a harmonizing of ends and means. No serious effort was made to gain Soviet approval of an agreed procedure, or to develop a program acceptable to all concerned. Yet the Soviets had clearly demonstrated their concern, and Russian forces still occupied North Korea.

On 17 September 1947 the United States placed the question of Korean independence on the agenda of the General Assembly, and in the next month discussion began. The trusteeship concept had by this time disappeared, and had been replaced by a plan for United Nations midwifery of an independent nation. The American proposal called for the creation of a U.N. commission to supervise the organization of an all-Korean government with representation on the basis of population; in reply the Soviets insisted that representatives of North and South Korea should participate in these discussions as equals. The General Assembly, having taken up the question under American initiative, in November adopted a modification of the American plan. A Temporary Commission on Korea was established composed of representatives of nine countries, including the Ukraine but not the United States, which would observe elections, assist the elected representatives in the formation of a Korean government, and help to arrange the withdrawal of the occupying powers.

In January 1948 the Temporary Commission, less its Ukrainian representative, reached Seoul to be greeted by cheering crowds. But no cheers came from north of the parallel, and the inability of the Commission to secure Soviet cooperation, or even to gain access to North Korea, raised the question of whether to hold elections in South Korea alone. This prospect, generally opposed by Korean politicos, was supported by the American military command. It was also supported by certain Korean leaders, of whom Syngman Rhee, now returned to his homeland and chairman of the National Association for the Rapid Realization of Korean Independence, was most prominent.

Doubtful both as to its mandate under these conditions and of the possibility of free elections in South Korea, the Commission sought counsel of the General Assembly's interim committee. Despite large scale riots organized by Korean Communists it was decided to proceed with supervised elections, and with the formation of a National Assembly in which one-third of the seats would be reserved for a North Korean delegation. This decision, which promised to bring closer the time of possible evacuation, and to liquidate the military commitment without abandonment of the political aims, was gratifying to the United States.

Elections in South Korea were consequently scheduled for May. The preparatory tasks of the Temporary Commission were complicated by more riots in March and April, by ostentatious firing exercises and fortification building along the northern side of the 38th parallel, and by "unification conferences" staged by the North Korean authorities in a further attempt to undermine the electoral procedure. Nevertheless the elections went off on schedule, with large popular participation and few noticeable irregularities. Four days later the reply from the north arrived as the Communists pulled the switches on the power lines, a move countered by the dispatch of two U.S. Navy power barges to furnish electricity until the output of South Korean steam plants could be increased.

There now followed, in both zones, a race to set up governments. On 1 May 1948 a new constitution had been promulgated in North Korea. In the south the National Assembly chose Syngman Rhee as chairman at the end of May, drafted a constitution and elected him President in July, and completed the formation of a government in early August. On 9 August President Rhee requested the occupation authorities to turn over the administration of South Korea and on the 15th his wish was granted. Ten days later an election was held in North Korea, observed only by the occupying power, and was followed by rapid ratification of a constitution. On 7 September the government of the People's Republic was established under a person calling himself Kim Il Sung, and on the 19th the Soviets announced that Russian forces would be out by year's end. Below the parallel withdrawal of American troops began in September, but this movement was shortly halted as a result of representations by President Rhee, and a regimental combat team was retained in South Korea until June of 1949.

With the establishment of an independent and freely elected South Korean government it could be argued that the decision to refer the Korean question to the United Nations had been largely justified. On the other hand, it was at least possible that disengagement and the withdrawal of occupying forces had increased rather than diminished the danger of conflict. If North Korea was a Soviet puppet, South Korea depended for its continued existence upon the United States, and there was no guarantee that these antagonistic client states would prove as responsible and as restrained as their protectors. Saber-rattling had already gone on in the north, while below the parallel President Rhee had not been backward in expressing his willingness to unify by force. The Korean situation, always an inflammable one, was now certainly no less so. Where Korea's geography had made it the oriental equivalent of the Low Countries, and its resistance to Japanese rule had given it the aspect of an Asiatic Ireland, its new situation, to those who could remember the 1930's, gave some promise that it would become a far eastern Spain.

2. *Unified Defense*

The year 1948 opened with the United Nations overseeing the birth of the Republic of Korea and the Russians that of the North Korean People's Republic. Elsewhere the new year brought a series of crises in the relations between east and west which seemed even more dangerous than those of the previous spring. In Czechoslovakia, a country closely linked in its origins with the United States, and one whose abandonment at Munich had profoundly moved Americans, the government was taken over by the Communists, and the coup shortly followed by a second defenestration of Prague. Following close upon this tragedy an ominous dispatch from General Lucius D. Clay, USA, the American commander in Germany, reported a new atmosphere of menace in his dealings with the Russians. Where economic dislocation in Europe and civil war in Greece had earlier seemed susceptible to treatment by financial grants and military missions, these events raised the specter of full-scale war.

Bestirring itself to counter the threat so dimly foreseen, the government found that the national defense cupboard was bare: the reasoning which had impelled the Joint Chiefs of Staff to urge withdrawal of Army units from Korea was reemphasized in the discovery that a call for more than one division would require partial mobilization. Faced with this situation, President Truman on 17 March 1948 called upon the Congress for an immediate increase in armed strength. But the summons to arms was complicated by the issue of universal military training and by lack of any firm program: only as the congressional debate began did the armed services, now six months unified in the new National Military Establishment, undertake for the first time since the war a serious consideration of the relation between policy and its instruments.

Three years earlier the United States had possessed the greatest military machine in history. Across the Atlantic, in the spring of 1945, its ground forces were reaching far into Europe; on the far side of the Pacific they were landing in strength on the island of Okinawa. Over Germany and Japan American bombers with long-range fighter escort penetrated almost at will. On the seas the United States operated an irresistible navy, which had destroyed its Japanese adversary and had demonstrated its ability to land troops against whatever opposition. But by spring of 1948 all this had gone. The armed forces had done their job too well. Since human institutions are created to answer human needs, the most successful are presumably self-obsoleting, and the American people had paid their Army and Navy the supreme compliment of assuming that the requirements which had called them into being had been fulfilled. As the shooting ended demobilization became the order of the day, and with the same vigor with which they had fought the war the armed services proceeded to disband. Within a year there was very little left.

Yet while disarming themselves along with their former enemies, the American people also undertook to reorganize their armed services in the interests of efficiency and economy by a unification of these forces in a single department of defense. Much of the pressure for this change came from the long-held Army belief in the efficacy of a single command, much from the desire of the Army Air Force for equal status, but there were other factors at work. The failure of intelligence and coordination at Pear Harbor had led many to see a solution in terms of command unified in Washington as well as in the field; there was a widespread impression that unified procurement and planning would produce appreciable economies. In any event the pressures were strong, and the apparent lessons of the immediate past were given great, perhaps too great weight. It is proverbial that generals always prepare for the last war, but in this instance the generals had strong popular support. With the enactment of unification legislation in 1947 the presumed dominance of the heavy bomber in the Second World War was institutionalized in an independent Department of the Air Force.

This step, seemingly so natural and right, and which as a practical matter was surely unavoidable, had large implications. Although the greatest wartime successes of the air weapon had been tactical in nature, the doctrinal emphasis, based on formulations a generation old, continued to stress the centrality of strategic air warfare. Yet while emphasizing the long-range bombing function, with its implication of the separateness of air war, the theorists also insisted on the indivisibility of air power. This situation, deriving from a long standing equation of means and ends, of vehicle and mission, presented interlocking technical and administrative problems.

Revolutionary advances in military technology, the product of Mars' forcing-house, had brought the piloted bomber close to the end of the road. If World War II was not "the last war of the pilots"—the phrase was General Arnold's—it was pretty close to it, for the bomber fleets which darkened the skies over Germany and Japan ended the war in double jeopardy. At the home base the threat was of replacement by guided missiles, of which the V-2 was but the early forerunner; over the target the danger came from new antiaircraft weapons and from the jet interceptor. For a time, doubtless, it would still be possible to produce an airplane that could get through, though at a cost which could only be justified, for the bomber no less than for the prospective long-range missile, by the employment of nuclear weapons.

While technology was undermining the theory of war based on the piloted bomber, the unitary nature of that theory posed difficulties in the organizational sphere. Indubitably there were areas of aircraft employment—reconnaissance, tactical operations with ground and naval forces, air transport—where discrimination as well as guidance was necessary, and where the pilot was less easily replaced by the gadget. But while these operations, interlocking with those of the surface forces, were precisely those in which the advocates of separate air war were least interested, the monopoly theory which lumped all activities of winged vehicles together still seemed to require their assignment to the separate air force.

Clearly there were puzzles here. Improvements in air defense had made the future of strategic bombardment, and so implicitly that of the independent air force, dependent upon the use of a weapon which the United States was attempting to place under international control. The monopoly theory posed serious problems for the Army, bereft as it would be of control over instruments vital to its mission; if followed out strictly it would raise great difficulties for the Navy as well. And finally, as the development of the missile gained momentum, Army and Air Force would face difficult metaphysical questions as to the precise range at which this ceased to be the analogue of an artillery shell but became, for administrative purposes, an airplane.

If the future was thus replete with paradox, so was the path to unification. Within the military it was the Army, which had never wholly succeeded in integrating its air and ground components, which led the parade. The Army's desire for a single staff and a single command as an extension of its own organizational practices was natural enough, but its willingness to divest itself of its air arm is more difficult to understand. Some, indeed, opposed this move: in 1945 a board of Army officers recommended against the abandonment of tactical and transport aviation. But history had passed them by: a generation of Air Corps pressure for autonomy had been capped by a four-year partnership with the RAF, with concomitant representation on the Joint and Combined Chiefs of Staff; the genie was out of the bottle, and the proposal was overruled.

The attitude of the Army Air Force, both traditional and understandable in that unification promised its best hope of independence, was perhaps extreme, calling as it did for triplication in the name of unity and for the creation of a separate service whose cardinal strategic principle was that of freedom from outside control. The Navy, historically the most successful in the coordination of diverse forces, and which had operated surface and undersea components, aviation, and the Marine Corps in reasonable harmony and with great success, approached the wedding with reluctance.

The ardent agreement between Army and Army Air Force, earlier so long at odds, as to the desirability of unifying first and facing the problems afterward, was unnerving to the Navy. Widespread rumors that the Army hoped to abolish the Marine Corps were not reassuring. Evidence of Air Force desires to absorb naval aviation raised the frightening possibility that the fate which had overtaken the Royal Navy in 1919, and which had proved so costly when war came again, might be repeated here. To some, at least, in the naval establishment, questions of intelligence, procurement, resources planning, and the integration of military and diplomatic policy seemed of primary importance, and not simply soluble by the establishment of a single command. But the basic reason for naval reluctance lay in the fear expressed by Admiral King that the contemplated organization would permit the reduction of American "sea power" by those unfamiliar with its potentialities. Since the reorganization provided for two services whose primary concern was with war on and over great land masses, the fear was perhaps not wholly unreasonable. Since representatives of one of these services, from the time of General Mitchell, had gone repeatedly on record regarding the inutility of navies, apprehensions were not diminished.

A further reason for these apprehensions, and one largely the fault of the Navy itself, stemmed from a serious failure in communications both with the public and with the other services. Somehow, it seemed, the Navy had never fully succeeded in putting its case across, and in explaining itself and its needs even to those who were, or ought to have been, its best and most sympathetic customers. Those who, in Admiral King's phrase, were unfamiliar with these matters had been permitted to remain that way. The silent service had been too silent for its own good.

To a degree this fact is understandable, for naval warfare is to some extent mysterious. An image, of a sort at least, of land or air war is easily put before the public: the advance of the armies is visible on the map; the flattening of cities is easily understood. But on the ocean there are no frontiers, negative results may be as valuable as positive ones, and the operations which maintain and exploit control of the seas are frequently invisible. That the presence of armies in a foreign theater and of aircraft in foreign skies testifies to a completed naval task is not always appreciated. Great successes are often obtained by a minimum of fighting, though with a maximum of effort, but to dramatize and explain this effort is a sophisticated and difficult problem. Regrettably, in an age of violence, such commodities as pressure and movement and maneuver have less public appeal than shock.

As in all human affairs there was in the unification controversy a mixture of wisdom and foolishness, and of selfishness with disinterested patriotism. If there were cannibals in the Army and Air Force who cast hungry eyes at the Marine Corps and at naval aviation, there were also naval officers who saw all future conflict in the image of the war against Japan. Nevertheless, in due course, a compromise was reached and an act was passed. And while the fact of unification reflected the initiative of those outside the Navy Department, the form of the legislation was in considerable degree the product of those within. The services, now three in number, were federated rather than merged; the same act that reordered the military establishment also created the National Security Council, the Central Intelligence Agency, and the National Security Resources Board. In the autumn of 1947 the Secretary of the Navy, James V. Forrestal, became the first Secretary of Defense.

The passage of the National Security Act of 1947 did not, of course, solve all problems of form and function. Not all gears could mesh at once. There were, for example, important differences in the systems of staff and command. The Army and Air Force, conditioned to large-scale continental operations, had developed highly centralized systems of management of forces in the field. But while Air Force doctrine placed the locus of command at the highest possible level, and while the Army's basic tactical unit was the division, to the Navy the part was almost as important as the whole. Naval operations were far more atomistic, and called now for a large fleet, now for a small force, now for a single ship. The lack of shipboard accommodations for large managerial organizations, the need to maintain radio silence at sea, and the necessity for continual separation and reassembly of various units for various tasks made necessary a delegation of responsibility and a decentralization of authority on the basis of agreed doctrine. And both in Washington and in the field these morphological differences had serious implications for the planning and conduct of joint operations.

Nor was this all. Under the new roof there dwelt not only different services and different practices, but also different histories. All services, in the years following the war, faced an unavoidable problem of rethinking roles and missions, and in some ways this was hardest for the Navy. The Army had gone through its period of reorientation in the late thirties, when the Nazi threat brought an end to the concept of hemispheric defense. Now, with their recent experience of the war against Germany, Army commanders made an easy transition to the new policies of coalition, containment, and the defense of Europe. The Air Force, enjoying its original monopoly of the nuclear weapon, was enabled to renew its ancient promises of quick and decisive war. But the Navy's experience was dominantly that of the war against Japan; Pacific veterans held the top positions in the Navy Department; and while the Navy's performance in the Pacific had on the whole been brilliant, that war was perhaps not the most obvious source of precedent for the situation of mid-century. It is, after all, hard to reach Moscow by boat.

Finally, in a sense, the successes of wartime came to tell against the Navy in peace. No strong hostile navy presented an obvious menace. To commanders who had crossed the seas as passengers, the passage and the amphibious assault presented no great difficulty, but were simply the prelude to the real campaign; to those whose responsibility it was to get them there the situation appeared otherwise. As in the Second World War certain leaders of the RAF had never fully understood their dependence on victory over the submarine, so now American ground and air officers would willingly deploy their forces overseas with little thought as to how their support could be assured should the new weapons not produce a quick decision. Busily at work on the superstructure of strategy, they could either neglect or assume its foundation. Concentrating as they did on the defense of Europe, possibilities elsewhere could be ignored.

In these divergent attitudes there was nothing fundamentally irreconcilable. But under the conflicting pressures of strategic need and budgetary possibility, the interservice differences became increasingly acute. In January 1948 the first budget subsequent to unification was sent up to the Congress, with a request for $11 billion for the National Military Establishment. But February, when the hearings began, was also the month of the Czech coup and of the discovery that the Army had but one uncommitted division, and March brought the telegram from General Clay. With the President's appeal for more armed strength, the military, already deeply involved in the complexities of reorganizing their vast establishment, found themselves faced with the problem of expansion. But since neither in the armed services nor in the State Department was there agreement as to the armaments needed for the support of policy, competition for the new appropriations inevitably developed. Such competition, of course, had always existed, but in the time of separate departments it had gone on in the light of day, in hearings before congressional committees. Under the new dispensation the service chiefs had to deal not with the Congress but with each other; across the table the legislator had been replaced by a competitor; the triangular nature of the new establishment promised great rewards from an alliance policy which would set two services against one.

In this situation the Navy was at a disadvantage. In the Joint Chiefs of Staff it was the minority member: although there were differences a-plenty between Army and Air Force, they were successfully plastered over. In strategic formulations based on the threat to Europe it seemed to have little more than a supporting function. Increasingly it found itself forced back on the defense of its organizational integrity. And as the Air Force pressed steadily for the dominant role in the military establishment, and as competition for funds became competition for public support, open quarrelling broke out in the public press. In an attempt to head off the in-fighting, the Secretary of Defense convened a conference of the Joint Chiefs at Key West in March 1948. But although he there persuaded the sovereignties to recognize each other's legal existence, no real meeting of minds was gained in the areas where functions and weapons interlocked, and the high command of the Air Force remained opposed to the existence of naval aviation. Outside the military there had also been interest in these matters, and the report of the President's Air Policy Commission on "Survival in the Air Age," which effectively equated the future of warfare with the large-scale delivery by the Air Force of weapons of mass destruction, had further exacerbated the situation. Thus early in 1948 the argument was already off center, and had focussed on the air question, with emphasis on nuclear bombardment, to the detriment of any rounded approach to the development of instruments of policy. After a fashion, at least, the problems of a short and big war were being faced, but those of a small and long one had been forgotten.

Where wisdom lay among these conflicting viewpoints is doubtless a matter for the philosopher rather than the historian. At all times, inevitably, differing service preconceptions give rise to different strategic views, and a changing world will emphasize the virtues first of one outlook and then of another. But what can be noted, and indeed almost postulated as a law, is the tendency for the minority view to become the correct one. Defense planning is, after all, merely a preliminary form of strategic deployment, and strategy is a two-sided game. This fact, too often forgotten, ensures that whatever the formulations of the moment the enemy will work to circumvent them, and in time may make progress in this effort.

Despite all difficulties within the Defense Department, a program of a sort was worked out and presented to Congress at the end of March. This program, greatly scaled down by Secretary Forrestal from the original desires of the service chiefs, and dissented from by the Air Force, called for an increase of $3 billion in expenditures over the $11 billion already budgeted for the coming year. In the end, after the services, the Congress, and the Budget Bureau had all had their say, the decision was made by the President. No program would be undertaken which would bring future annual costs above $15 billion.

Under this presidential ceiling, in the autumn of 1948, the planning for fiscal 1950 was begun. But by now the military had begun to worry. Even allowing for the human tendency to pad the budget, the first estimates from the Joint Chiefs of Staff, which called for $30 billion, would have seemed to indicate that capabilities and intentions were out of phase. By September, however, the Joint Chiefs had developed a war plan, and had painfully reduced their requests by almost half. Down to about the $20 billion mark agreed solutions were forthcoming, both in allocation of funds and in strategic planning, but at lower figures these were not obtainable. The final request for $16.9 billions, which was accompanied by the statement that the presidential limit would support only an atomic counteroffensive from the British

Isles and would entail abandonment of the Mediterranean in case of war, was the product of a split vote. In this difficult situation the Secretary of Defense, who had thus far displayed a notable concern for balanced forces, now turned to concentrate upon strategic air. Under the circumstances this was wholly logical, for if the air riposte was all that could be managed it was surely desirable to strengthen it as much as possible. But the budget ceiling remained firm, and a request for additional funds for the Air Force was refused.

This presidential decision was of great importance. What had begun as a year of crisis was ending as an election year, and the complications overseas were fading from the public mind. Except for the reenactment of Selective Service, the proposed expansion of the armed forces, trumpeted in the spring of 1948, was over by fall without having proceeded very far. American military capabilities, vis-à-vis the Soviet Union, remained limited to the atomic counteroffensive; American capabilities in other contexts had hardly been considered. But the rigidity of this military posture, so out of line with diplomatic policy, was disguised by the still sizable dollar sums allotted the Army and Navy, which while insufficient for serious wartime operations preserved a mobilization base and some appearance of a balanced establishment.

By mid-summer of 1948 two facts had become obvious. The first was that rearmament would be severely restricted by the President in terms of dollars. The second was that in the competition for these dollars the Air Force, with its long-range nuclear bombing function, enjoyed the larger measure of public and congressional support. Yet June 1948 saw the commencement of the Berlin blockade, a maneuver not easily countered by strategic bombing. It was clear that the outside world remained both dangerous and unpredictable. It was less clear that the weapons best suited to win the battle of the budget were those most useful in support of other aspects of national policy.

Throughout the year, as the Secretary of Defense and Joint Chiefs grappled with their problems, the interservice propaganda war continued with the Air Force well in the lead. Although the Secretary of the Navy and the Chief of Naval Operations were committed to the support of Forrestal's program, the Secretary and Chief of Staff of the Air Force remained vigorously partisan, calling at every opportunity for special treatment. Since the justification for such treatment rested upon the nuclear weapon, Navy claims to share in its delivery did nothing to calm the atmosphere. In the fall the Air Force Association, the civilian auxiliary, violently attacked the whole concept of naval aviation, and in reply an aviation admiral attacked the Air Force. Throughout these months a series of articles, bitterly critical of the Navy and of naval aviation, were being prepared with Air Force cooperation for publication in a national magazine; these would appear between November 1948 and April 1949, at the time the 1950 budget was scheduled to come before the Congress. In this atmosphere of tension the new year began, and in April the House Appropriations Committee reported out a bill providing large sums for the Air Force and reduced support for the Navy.

Increasingly, as the months passed, the defense establishment was developing along lines unsuited to a maritime strategy and alarming to senior naval officers. Increasingly, also, military policy was diverging from that of the Department of State. In diplomacy the effort was toward an ever closer grouping of alliances, especially with regard to Europe. In military matters the emphasis was tending toward the development of a capability for independent action by investment in intercontinental bombing at the expense of ground and naval strength. But to suggestions from State that this overlooked the chance of localized conflict, the reply was returned that increased surface forces were financially impossible.

In the spring of 1949 Secretary Forrestal left the Military Establishment and was replaced by Louis Johnson. There was now a firm, tactless, and economical hand at the helm, and a bill in Congress to amend the National Security Act promised that the hand would become firmer. In April, less than a month after the arrival of the new Secretary, the ax first hit the Navy, with cancellation of the construction of the aircraft carrier *United States,* a step supported by Army and Air Force, but on which neither the Secretary of the Navy nor the Chief of Naval Operations was consulted.

It would have been hard to think of a more dramatic blow at the naval establishment. This first post-war carrier had been designed, on the basis of wartime experience, in anticipation of the newer and heavier aircraft coming into operation, and with an eye to the use of the new weapons. Its construction had been approved by the Congress, and other projects had been abandoned to permit it to go forward under the budgetary limitations. But although the impact of the cancellation within the Navy was tremendous, it was little felt outside. The Secretary of the Navy resigned at once in vigorous protest, but Congress and public seemed little disturbed.

Once more the Navy had failed to make its case. Whatever its primary purpose, the usefulness of the great carrier would far transcend the single function of strategic bombing. But the debates on military policy had become so centered on this type of operation that the ship had been drawn into the quarrel, and suspicion of an intent to invade Air Force prerogatives was increased by a symbolism which some read into the name *United States.* The subject, indeed, was raised in congressional hearings, where the naval witnesses unfortunately failed to remember that a frigate of the same name had been one of the first ships of the old Navy. There was also, perhaps, a failure of subtlety here, for among the early frigates there had also been a *Congress* and a *President,* either of which names, it would seem, might have served as better defensive armament.

Within the naval establishment the fact and manner of the cancellation revived the fears that the transfer of naval aviation to the Air Force and the abolition of the Marine Corps were imminent. These apprehensions were compounded by the events of the next few months. In July a new ceiling of $13 billion was placed over the defense budget, and the scalpels of the economizers were soon poised over the carriers of the *Essex* class, of which the Navy wanted to maintain eight in operation, the Army considered four sufficient, and the Air Force wished all mothballed. In August the Secretary of Defense halved the strength of naval and Marine aviation by ordering a reduction of operating carriers from 8 to 4, of carrier air groups from 14 to 6, and of Marine Corps squadrons from 23 to 12. This was followed by efforts to prepare for the next fiscal year by a reduction of current expenditures, and in September the Navy was instructed to trim its current budget by $353 million, a step possible only through drastic cutbacks in the procurement of new aircraft.

By this time the tension between the services had reached an extraordinary pitch. Although the Air Force, riding the tide of success, now moderated its propaganda activities, bitterness within the Navy continued to grow. Having been abused in the press, having been consistently outvoted in the Joint Chiefs of Staff, finding themselves subjected to an antagonistic Secretary of Defense and to a doubtfully sympathetic Secretary of the Navy, many senior naval officers felt that their worst fears of unification were coming true. It seemed, as Admiral King had prophesied, that American sea power was being reduced by those who did not understand it, and the country's safety committed to an unsound theory of war.

These interservice tensions led in the latter part of 1949 to some remarkable developments. An anonymous document, produced in the Navy Department, which alleged that Air Force procurement policies were dominated by the financial interests of those in authority, was brought to the attention of the Congress. The Secretary of Defense charged in a speech at the National War College that the Navy was waging a "campaign of terror" against unification. There were reports in the press of naval officers being shadowed by detectives hired by the Department of the Air Force. In September a well-known naval aviator declared publicly that the Navy was being purposely eliminated as a factor in the defense establishment. In October the press received through unorthodox channels a copy of a letter in which a prominent flag officer expressed to the Secretary of the Navy his fear that the country's security was being jeopardized by acceptance of the theory of quick victory through strategic bombing, stated that "the morale of the Navy is lower today than at any time since I entered the commissioned ranks in 1916," and urged a congressional investigation of the fundamentals of national security. Publication of the letter forced the investigation.

In October 1949, in an atmosphere somewhat sobered by the report of an atomic explosion within the Soviet Union, the congressional hearings were begun. In these hearings the Navy labored under serious handicaps. Its new secretary was hostile to the dissidents' case, while the Chief of Naval Operations, in this extremely difficult situation, was endeavoring to mediate between his subordinates and higher authority. Preparation of the Navy brief consequently lacked official sanction and the assistance that such sanction could give, while the emotional involvement of the naval witnesses made it difficult to identify the enemy and to plan a coherent campaign. The result was that the naval testimony was somewhat scattered and uncoordinated, imperfectly prepared, and at times tactically ill-advised.

Although the basic issues went far deeper, the October hearings were an outgrowth of an earlier investigation of procedures used in procurement of the B–36 intercontinental bomber, and the B–36 remained prominent as a subject of discussion. Whatever the technical merits or demerits of this giant of the skies, it had become a symbol of current difficulties, and to most naval officers seemed to have grown horns and a tail. Yet the approach to the question was a narrow one, with too much of the naval case concentrated on the B–36 as airplane and too little on the B–36 as symbol—symbol of a strategy, symbol of domestic propaganda, and symbol of future budgetary troubles. On the other hand much naval testimony seemed retrospective, centering on the war against Japan, while clarification of the current implications of naval and amphibious capabilities was hampered by general acceptance of the concept that Russia was the one possible enemy and Europe the one possible theater. The result was that to many the arguments seemed either a disagreement of experts on technical matters or a simple case of hurt feelings; it was even possible to suggest that the Navy was aggrieved merely because the Air Force had developed a bomber of astonishingly long range. Nevertheless the hearings presented an impressive and disturbing spectacle: as the congressional committee observed, nearly the entire high command of the United States Navy appeared to protest the current policies of the Department of Defense.

Two points emerged fairly clearly from the testimony of the naval witnesses. The fact that the type of armed force embodied in the Navy and the Marine Corps was being whittled down to a dangerous level, emphasized in the testimony of three major fleet commanders, the Commandant of the Marine Corps, and the Chief of Naval Operations, was forcefully developed. A second point, repeatedly made, was that the Navy was not accepted as an equal partner in the unification process, and while the documentation was unnecessarily weak, this contention received strong if surprising confirmation in the bitter and partisan rebuttal delivered by General Omar N. Bradley, USA, Chairman of the Joint Chiefs of Staff.

Some matters of central importance, however, were not made wholly clear. The fact that the budget ceiling imposed by the President on the defense establishment was too low to permit effective support of the commitments assumed by the President and the State Department was obscured by the attack on the Air Force. Perhaps the point could not have been well made under any circumstances. It is difficult to take issue with civilian judgment without seeming to attack civilian control; an outright appeal for funds opens the military man to undesirable accusations; in their economic thinking the military incline to the conservative, and to unquestioning acceptance of statements that the economy can only stand so much. In any event it was the members of the congressional committee, rather than the military witnesses, who showed the most concern over the adequacy of appropriations.

A second subject which remained somewhat obscure, and one always difficult to explain clearly, was the relationship between armament and foreign policy, and between types of armament and strategic flexibility. The discussion did indeed involve the importance of relating strategy to war aims, of differentiating when dealing with tyrants between the rulers and the ruled, and of maintaining insofar as possible the fabric of civilization in the interest of the post-war world. The implications of an intercontinental bombing strategy for a diplomatic policy of alliance, and the inconsistencies implicit in simultaneous efforts to create a North Atlantic Treaty Organization and a weapons system independent of foreign bases were touched on. Salutary emphasis was laid on the need for tactical air strength to attack enemy forces in being and their lines of communication, and for immediately available forces, with ground and air components trained and packaged together, ready for quick deployment. But the course of the hearings was such as to deprive these matters of their merited consideration.

Consideration, nevertheless, would soon be given them, although less as the result of the efforts of naval officers than of those of the North Korean People's Army. For this unforeseen war in an unexpected theater was to pose in excruciating form the strategic and tactical problems the defense establishment had not been permitted to meet. As if to emphasize the problems of balanced forces and limited war brought forth in the hearings, the Korean conflict would see the naval witnesses occupying crucial posts: Commander in Chief Pacific Fleet and Chairman of the Joint Chiefs of Staff; Commander of the Fast Carrier Task Force in Korean waters and Chief of Staff and acting Commander Naval Forces Far East; Commanding General of the First Marine Aircraft Wing. The nature of the war would raise an imperative but unanticipated need for close interservice cooperation, and would keep the problem of roles and missions, so long a bone of contention in Washington, steadily to the fore. And finally, the course of the struggle on that distant peninsula would do much—at least temporarily—to redress the military imbalance of 1949.

For the moment, however, the "revolt of the admirals" was inconclusive. The rebuttal testimony of representatives of the Army and Air
Force was generally moderate in tone: controversial issues were skirted, sin
was denied, and the Navy chided for not accepting unification. In the
sequel the Navy lost one Chief of Naval Operations with the removal of
Admiral Louis E. Denfeld, and gained another in the person of Admiral
Forrest P. Sherman. The escape of steam during the hearings diminished
pressures inside the Pentagon and produced a period of comparative interservice moderation. The report of the congressional committee was
in many respects a model discussion of a highly complex matter: whatever the public thought, and despite the diffuseness of the naval presenta-
tion, the members had not missed the points at issue. Within the National
Security Council, where the Russian atomic explosion had led to a review
of military policy, the naval arguments may have had some weight. But
so far as the all-important question of the budget was concerned, the hearings were of no effect. The ceiling for fiscal 1951 remained at $13 billion,
reduction of naval strength continued apace, and even the Air Force found
its plans cut back. Within the House of Representatives efforts were begun
to provide the Navy with funds for new construction, although not for a
new *United States,* but the attitude of the executive branch remained
unchanged.

Yet what in retrospect seems most striking about the hearings of 1949,
and what presumably would have most impressed an observer from beyond
the Iron Curtain, was less the evidence of difficulties between the services than
the emerging picture of American strategic thought. Almost all witnesses,
of whatever service, agreed that there was but "one possible enemy." Almost
all focussed their attention on the defense of Europe. Just as some of the
naval testimony was nostalgic in nature, so was that of the dominant Army-
Air Force wing, although with a different bias stemming from a different past.
The next war, it seemed clear beyond peradventure, would begin like the last
with a massive enemy surprise attack; just as in World War II, except for the
use of bigger and better weapons, the reply would take the form of a strategic
air offensive; the end would come on the ground with a new V–E Day.
Whether the Russians were equally convinced of this was a question raised
by none.

Repeated emphasis on "the" strategic plan and on the importance of
long-range nuclear bombardment, together with the contemplated reductions in naval and amphibious capabilities, promised a steady diminution
in ability to reply to pinpricks, or to police non-Russian aggression, or to act
with strength and speed outside the European theater. The capabilities
and intentions of the United States were plain. There had grown up, in
effect, a mirror-image concept of strategy: the United States thinks Europe
is important and has created NATO; therefore the Russians must think

Europe important, and be planning to invade it. An equal rigidity on the part of the enemy was assumed, all capacity for subtlety or maneuver was denied him, and the upshot would seem to have been an invitation to war by proxy in distant places.

The situation which the hearings thus exposed was a remarkable one even for a nation not noted for flexibility or sophistication in strategic thought. The lack of clarity in the area of grand strategy evinced by the naval witnesses can doubtless be explained as a result of their immediate troubles, and of the intellectual difficulties they faced in trying to harmonize a traditionally more flexible outlook with the rigidities of the agreed strategic plan. Implicit, if not explicit, in some of their testimony, there can be found a very different point of view. But to account for the attitude of those within the military establishment who professed themselves satisfied with the situation is more difficult, for they were wrong on any reading of history. Essentially, it would seem, the fact that able and devoted men could agree along such lines stemmed from the fear of defeat by bankruptcy, and the historian of this episode must conclude that if war is too important a matter to be left to the military, it is also too important to be subjected to the budgetary treatment of 1948–50. Those skilled in the mysteries of economics had told the service heads that their country could spend no more in time of peace, and peace presumably existed until the shooting began. The President had imposed a firm ceiling, and orders were orders. Accepting the $13 billion limit and the force that this could purchase as the nation's maximum capability, the dominant members of the Joint Chiefs could think only as they did. In no other way could they continue to carry their heavy responsibilities. A broader outlook on possibilities was too agonizing to be endured.

3. *The Estimate of the Situation*

In contrast to the alarms and crises of preceding years the early months of 1950 brought an appearance of stability in the world at large. Within the Defense Department things were quieter. In Europe Tito's defection from the Russian bloc had been followed by termination of the civil war in Greece. The Berlin blockade had ended, West Berlin remained free, and the development in the autumn of 1949 of two German governments amounted to an acknowledgement that for the foreseeable future the German question would remain insoluble. In Asia the Chinese civil war was over, the Mandate of Heaven had been withdrawn from Chiang Kai-shek, the Generalissimo with his remaining forces had retired to Formosa, and the Chinese People's Republic had been proclaimed. In Korea, as in Germany, agreement to disagree had been institutionalized in the formation of two governments. Although the state of the world was not one to bring entire satisfaction to American policy makers, things appeared to be settling down.

In many respects, moreover, it could be said that the United States had responded brilliantly to the challenge with which it had been faced. Far from withdrawing from a degenerate outer world, the American government had reacted with extraordinary fertility of imagination, and had accomplished some notable acts of statecraft. The Truman Doctrine had marked the turning point, and had signalled a determination to face up to the problems of mid-century, but the Truman Doctrine by no means stood alone. The vision of Secretary Marshall's Harvard speech had borne fruit in the European Recovery Program, which began operations in the summer of 1948. The North Atlantic Treaty Organization, the diplomatic reply to the Czech coup and the Berlin blockade, became operative in 1949, as did a Mutual Defense Assistance Program designed to give arms to those who manned the frontiers of freedom. Enactment of the Point Four program, intended to make freedom worth defending where needs were more material than conceptual, seemed in early prospect. Progress in rationalizing the defense establishment had been less obvious, but it could be maintained that the military had met with great success their only test of strength: the work of the Air Force, assisted by Navy and RAF transport squadrons, in maintaining the Berlin airlift, had not only led to diplomatic triumph but had presented to the world a picture of a United States that was determined, restrained, and possessed of extraordinary operational capabilities.

Nevertheless it should be noted that the successes of American policy were largely European: in Asia the settling dust revealed a situation at variance with all earlier hopes. The principal effects of Communist success in China were perhaps two: to increase the importance of Japan as the pivot of American policy in the Orient and, since Europe seemed more amenable as well as more important, to reemphasize the European orientation of diplomacy. Two countries, Germany and Korea, were divided by the frontiers of the divided world, yet while American divisions were held in Germany the last American troops were withdrawn from Korea in June 1949. That the defense of South Korea was now a matter for the South Koreans themselves could be assumed from the tendencies in American military policy brought out in the October hearings, as well as from speeches by General MacArthur and Secretary of State Acheson which drew the American strategic frontier through the Korean Strait.

Despite the transfer of responsibility for Korean unification to the United Nations and the withdrawal of American troops, the Republic of Korea remained a problem for American policy makers. Since 1945 American aid to Korea had annually exceeded the sum of $100 million, and the economy of the Republic was wholly dependent on congressional appropriation and the ECA. Similar circumstances doubtless obtained above the parallel, but the steady southward flow of refugees, which did nothing to simplify the eco-

nomic problems of the Republic, gave evidence of a less tactful and less generous protecting power.

There was also a military problem. In the north the Russians had
set up a military academy in 1945, and three years later had activated the
North Korean People's Army, three divisions strong. In the course of time
the North Koreans were provided with Soviet tanks; by 1949 three more
infantry divisions had been activated; a rapid expansion in the spring of
1950 raised NKPA strength to ten infantry divisions, a number of infantry
regiments, and an armored brigade. An aviation unit had been created in
1946; in 1948 the obsolete Japanese aircraft used for training began to be
replaced by newer types received from Russia; by 1950 the number on hand
was approaching the hundred mark. The People's Republic boasted a
navy of some 45 small craft, including a few 60-foot aluminum-hulled
Russian torpedo boats; at Najin, in the northeast, the Russians administered
a training program for Korean naval personnel; there and at Chongjin and
Unggi the Soviet Navy enjoyed the use of base facilities.

In the Republic of Korea the situation was otherwise. Following the
withdrawal of American fighting forces the United States had provided,
at the request of the Korean government, a small Korean Military Advisory
Group, and military supplies for a force of 50,000 men were left behind.
But while an impressive quantity of small arms, vehicles, ammunition, and
artillery was transferred, along with some 20 training planes, and while
further deliveries were scheduled under the Mutual Defense Assistance
Program, the capabilities of the South Korean Army remained somewhat
limited. As a result of the belligerence of Syngman Rhee, who seemed
quite prepared to attempt a forcible unification of the peninsula, this army
was given no tanks, no medium or heavy artillery, and no military aircraft.

By 1950 the strength of the ROK Army was approaching the 100,000
mark and eight divisions had been organized. Small unit training had
made good progress, but experience in large-scale maneuvers was lacking
and there had been no training in defense against tanks. Nevertheless,
the Military Advisory Group was optimistic, and its confidence that ROK
forces could handle the threat from the north was apparently accepted on
the higher levels.

The Republic's navy, somewhat larger than its northern counterpart,
had been established in 1948 on the foundation of the coast guard set up
during the American occupation. Its strength in 1950 was something over
7,000 men; its headquarters were in an office building in Seoul and its principal base facilities at Chinhae on the south coast; its ships were largely
ex-United States YMS types and ex-Japanese minesweepers and picket boats.
Some advice and assistance had been provided in the early years by former
United States Coast Guard personnel attached to the KMAG, but money
and material had been sadly lacking, ships had been kept in operation only

by cannibalizing, morale had been low, and defections had taken place. In 1949, however, prospects had brightened with the receipt of a shipment of spare parts from the United States, and Rear Admiral Sohn Won Il, ROKN, the Chief of Naval Operations, had gone to America to bring back four ex-U.S. Navy 173-foot steel-hulled PCs. Something, too, had happened to morale, for the money to purchase one of these vessels had been provided by subscription of the officers and men, an unusual event in any navy.

So the Far East still presented problems, and not only in Korea. The Communist success in China had become a major subject of domestic political dispute; a large proportion of American ground strength remained on occupation duty in Japan; inevitably the American posture in the Orient was kept under review. General J. Lawton Collins, USA, the Army Chief of Staff, had visited Japan in the autumn of 1949, and June of 1950 saw a renewal of high-level travel to the Far East. The Secretary of Defense and the Chairman of the Joint Chiefs of Staff flew to Manila for discussions with Vice Admiral Arthur D. Struble, Commander Seventh Fleet; John Foster Dulles, consultant to the Secretary of State, paid a visit to Korea; all then proceeded to Japan for talks with General MacArthur. While at Seoul Mr. Dulles had addressed the Korean National Assembly, and had assured his audience of the strength and resolution of the free world and of the support of the American people. Intended as a diplomatic counter to North Korean threats, the speech proved unsuccessful, and photographs of Mr. Dulles peering across the 38th parallel were shortly featured in the Communist press as it hailed him as the strategist of South Korean aggression.

By the time these visitations took place the ostentatious military preparations in the north had alarmed the Rhee government, and had led the U.N. Commission to establish a system of border observers. For some time, also, reports of increasing North Korean strength had been available to the intelligence section of the Far East Command in Tokyo. An appreciation of December 1949, which considered it axiomatic that the Russians would be unwilling to permit the survival of a non-Communist Korean state, had commented on the arrival of reinforcements from Manchuria and suggested that spring would bring a period of danger. In January it was reported that March and April had been designated as the time for an attack on South Korea. In March it was noted that recent evidence pointed to an invasion in June. Subsequent information indicated that the inhabitants were being evacuated from the border zone north of the parallel, and that North Korean regular divisions had been deployed along the dividing line. In the last weeks of peace word was received of minor clashes along the parallel, of conferences of North Korean commanders, of guerrilla infiltration of South Korea, and of North Korean receipt of Soviet aircraft. But all this information received negative evaluation in the Far East Command: the March report of a prospective June invasion was forwarded with the comment that civil war was unlikely, although the reasons for this view remained unstated, and this judgment was repeated in subsequent appreciations.

One of the principal conclusions of the Pearl Harbor investigating committee had concerned the failure of evaluation and action despite the availability of intelligence, and this aspect of that tragedy had provided one of the chief arguments for postwar efforts to coordinate diplomatic, military, and intelligence activities. Yet this war like the last was to begin with a failure of intelligence, and if the immediate damage to the United States was less, the performance of the new apparatus seems if anything to have been worse than that of the old. Once again the information was available, this time in even more detail, but the ability to use it was still more notable in its absence. Once again it was clear how imprisoned men are in their own frames of reference, and how difficult it is to believe in unpleasant possibilities. Again, perhaps, there can here be seen the influence of the agreed strategic plan. Whatever the secret agents say, the evaluating authorities will believe only what they wish to believe.

CHAPTER III

War Begins

1. The Decision to Intervene

ON 25 JUNE 1950, at 0400 in the morning, the North Korean People's Army, with seven infantry divisions and one armored brigade in the line, and with two more infantry divisions in reserve, struck south across the parallel. In Korea it was Sunday, a favored day for starting modern wars.

In Washington, half a world away and half a day behind in time, it was the middle of a summer Saturday. President Truman was out of town, visiting his family in Missouri. In the offices of government, in the State Department in Foggy Bottom and in the Pentagon across the river, only duty personnel were at work. As evening came, press rumors of a Korean crisis drifted into the State Department, and then, at twenty-six minutes past nine, a dispatch reporting the invasion was received from Ambassador John J. Muccio in Seoul. Around the town the telephones began to ring. Echelon by rising echelon the officers of the Department of State were summoned. Before midnight came the Secretary of State had reached the President by telephone, and the Secretary General of the United Nations had been notified of the emergency.

Sunday in Washington was a day of frenzied activity. Two hours after midnight Secretary Acheson again telephoned the President, the decision to seek action of the Security Council was made, and at three in the morning the request was formally presented to Secretary Lie. Hastily summoned, the members of the Security Council met at three that afternoon, but with the Soviet delegate in self-imposed absence. By this time a report of the invasion had been received from the United Nations Commission on Korea, and the United States had prepared a resolution on this breach of the peace which called upon the North Korean People's Republic to desist from aggression. By a vote of nine to nothing, Yugoslavia alone abstaining, the resolution was approved.

While these measures were in train at Lake Success the United States government was in emergency action. Throughout the morning the Secretary of State, the Secretary of the Army, and the military chiefs were in conference at the Pentagon. In the afternoon, in response to another call from Secretary Acheson, President Truman flew back to the capital. In the evening the President and his military and diplomatic advisers held a meeting at Blair House which began with dinner and which lasted until 11 o'clock. Here the first decisions leading to American commitment in Korea were taken.

The situation which confronted the United States that Sunday evening was sufficiently obscure. Aggression had been committed. The cold war had become hot. But the aggression was local, the general emergency had not begun, and along the rest of the cold war's battleline prospects were unpredictable. At Blair House the discussion ranged from Korea to Formosa, to the implications of the invasion for Japan and the Philippines, and to the strength of Russian forces in the Far East. The possibility of Russian or Chinese intervention in Korea was raised, but to those present seemed remote. Over and above these concrete questions, to which concrete answers could at least be hazarded, there weighed heavily on the minds of all the memories of the 1930's. All present had lived through the agonizing series of crises which had marked the world's descent into the second great war, and whose very names—Manchuria, Ethiopia, the Rhineland, Munich—had become emotional symbols. If, as seems quite possible, Stalin was encouraged in the Korean venture by memories of democratic impotence in the Manchurian crisis, he overlooked one factor of central importance: his principal antagonist in 1950, the man from Missouri, was also a student of history.

In the light of these memories, and with the overpowering feeling that aggression, once unchecked, might sweep all before it, certain preparatory decisions were taken. American civilians and dependents were to be evacuated from Korea by sea and air; to cover this evacuation air and naval action in defense of the Korean capital, of the harbor of Inchon, and of Kimpo airfield was authorized. The Seventh Fleet was to be started north from the Philippines so as to be more readily available should things get worse. Shipment to Korea of ammunition and of military hardware under the Mutual Defense Assistance Program would be expedited by all available means. Shortly after eleven the meeting broke up, and the military chiefs hastened to the Pentagon to communicate the decisions to General of the Army Douglas MacArthur, USA, Commander in Chief, Far East Command.

Monday the 26th was another day of action. Around the world, outside the Iron Curtain, the news of the invasion of South Korea had shocked governments and peoples alike. But although feelings were both indignant and apprehensive, few saw any likelihood of direct action; the salvation of the Republic of Korea was up to the South Koreans. In the morning President Truman announced the decision to expedite arms aid to the Rhee government under the MDA Program, but no mention was made of the movements of American armed forces. In the evening a second conference of the military and civilian chiefs took place. On the far side of the globe, as the meeting began, ships and aircraft were evacuating Americans from Korea and the Seventh Fleet Striking Force had sortied from its bases in the Philippines and was steaming north.

The decisions taken at this second Blair House meeting were far-reaching. The Secretary of State had come with positive recommendations. His suggestion that air and naval support be given the Republic of Korea under sanction of the Security Council resolution of the day before, that increased military aid be extended to the Philippines and Indo-China, and that Formosa be neutralized, met with general approval. The need for rapid action made this use of force appear imperative; the continuing overestimate of the ROK Army, and the confidence that neither Soviets nor Chinese would intervene, made it appear sufficient. Little thought seems to have been given the question of whether to commit ground forces. The recommendations were accepted by the President, and a directive was at once sent General MacArthur authorizing him to use his air and naval forces against the invading army south of the 38th parallel, and instructing him to neutralize Formosa by the use of the Seventh Fleet.

This news was made public at noon on Tuesday the 27th. Following an earlier meeting with congressional leaders at the White House, the President announced that pursuant to the action of the Security Council he had ordered naval and air support of the Republic of Korea, and that he had instructed the Seventh Fleet to prevent either an attack on Formosa from the mainland or an invasion of China by the forces of Chiang Kai-shek. The mood of other governmental bodies matched his own: the House of Representatives extended the Selective Service Act by a vote of 315 to 4; in the Senate the action was unanimous. In the afternoon the Security Council met again at Lake Success to vote on an American-sponsored resolution which called upon members of the United Nations to assist the Republic of Korea in repelling the attack. Action was for a time delayed while the Indian and Egyptian delegates sought vainly to obtain instructions from their governments, but in the evening the vote was taken and the resolution passed.

Following so rapidly upon the President's announcement of American action, this move by the United Nations led to an extraordinary rise in spirit throughout the western world. For the first time within memory the democracies seemed to have produced a leader who would stand fast in time, and little heed was paid to Soviet denunciation of the U.N. action as illegal. But while hearts were high the news was increasingly bad: the forces of the Republic of Korea were disintegrating, the invaders were advancing almost unopposed, the capital of Seoul had fallen. On Thursday the 29th the gloom increased. The armies of the Korean Republic were proving weaker than anyone had expected and those of North Korea stronger;

the threat of American air and naval action was clearly ineffective. In the afternoon the National Security Council met at the White House; inevitably, since the show of force seemed to have accomplished nothing, the discussion turned to the question of whether to commit ground troops. Here, in unexpected form, was the prospect of that war on the mainland of Asia against which all military authorities had warned. For such a war there were no plans, no detailed estimates of the forces required. These, indeed, could only be guessed at, although doubtless it was still possible to postulate a distinction between policing a minor power like North Korea and warring with a more serious opponent. Although the discussion seems to have drifted in the direction of commitment, decision was deferred pending the receipt of further information from General MacArthur, who had flown to Korea for a personal reconnaissance of the battle front.

Shortly after midnight the report from the Supreme Commander came in. In a telecon discussion in the first hours of Friday morning General MacArthur stated that the line could not be held without American help, and recommended the immediate movement of one regimental combat team to the Korean front as nucleus for a possible build-up to two divisions for early offensive action. This in time would prove a notable underestimate of the required force, but the view that the invaders would cease and desist, once confronted by U.S. Army contingents, was shared in Washington. In any event the highest authority on the spot, the man who would be responsible for conducting the campaign, had spoken. The decision could not be deferred. A little before five in the morning the Secretary of the Army telephoned the President to tell him what General MacArthur had reported. The President said to send the troops.

Here was the full commitment, although its ultimate magnitude was as yet unforeseen. On the morning of Friday, 30 June, after meeting with the Secretaries of State and of Defense, the Joint Chiefs of Staff, and congressional leaders, President Truman made public the new decisions. General MacArthur was authorized to bomb north of the 38th parallel as governed by military necessity, a naval blockade of North Korea would be proclaimed, and "certain supporting ground units" would be committed to action.

2. The Far East Command

Despite optimistic statements issuing from the upper levels, the readiness of the United States for war in the summer of 1950 was very doubtful. For the war with which the country found itself confronted, this was the more the case. The Army had a total of ten combat divisions, all but one understrength. The Marines had two, both undermanned. The Navy was in the process of being cut down and even the Air Force, despite public and congressional favor, had been forced to narrow its focus and channel its capabilities.

The interaction of budget ceiling and strategic plan had led to emphasis on long-range bombardment and the European theater, an emphasis reflected in the deployment of American strength. The ground forces were divided between the continent of Europe, the continental United States, and occupation duty in Japan. The Navy's larger half was in the Atlantic. The weight of the Strategic Air Command and of other Air Force units lay at home and in the forward European bases. On the assumption that the first and most important Communist objective was Western Europe, it may be said that this deployment proved itself. No war came there. But for the war that did come this posture was more than a little awkward.

American forces in the Orient in 1950 were organized into the presumably unified command of General MacArthur, Commander in Chief Far East Command, who was also, as Supreme Commander for the Allied Powers,

Table 1.—THE FAR EAST COMMAND, JUNE–AUGUST 1950

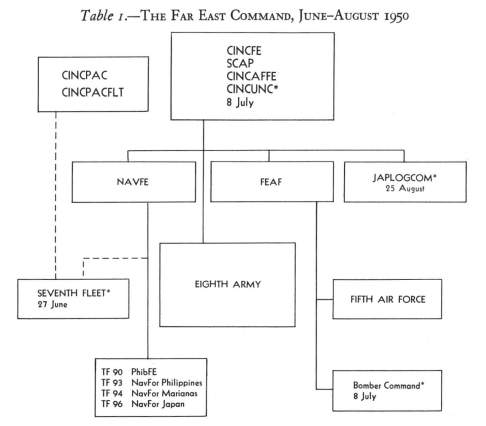

*Commands assigned or created subsequent to commencement of Korean hostilities.

responsible for the occupation of Japan. Occupation responsibilities bulked large at Headquarters, but in addition to these duties General MacArthur was charged with the defense of Japan, Okinawa, the Marianas, and the Philippines. To enable him to carry out these missions, forces of all three services had been assigned CincFE.

Notwithstanding the European orientation of strategy, the needs of the Japanese occupation had brought a large proportion of American ground strength to the Far East. On paper, Army Forces Far East was not unimpressive: its four divisions—the 7th, 24th, and 25th Infantry Divisions, and the dismounted 1st Cavalry Division—organized as the United States Eighth Army, were commanded by Lieutenant General Walton H. Walker, USA, who had been one of Patton's corps commanders in France. But all of Walker's divisions were understrength, with only two battalions to a regiment, and were undertrained and underequipped as well. No Army theater headquarters had been established, but the functions of such an organization were carried out by CincFE's staff.

The Far East Air Forces, the air component of General MacArthur's command, were commanded by Lieutenant General George E. Stratemeyer, USAF. In June 1950 FEAF contained five fighter and two bomber wings, a transport wing, and miscellaneous support units making up a total of some 1,200 aircraft. The principal mission of the Far East Air Forces, the air defense of Japan, Okinawa, Guam, and the Philippines, was reflected in the order of battle: of the 553 aircraft in organized units, 365 were F-80C jet fighters. These aircraft, which had recently replaced the piston-engined F-51 Mustang, had, as befitted their intended purpose, comparatively high performance. But their combat radius without external fuel tanks was limited to 100 miles; with external fuel no bombs could be carried, and their operation required sizable modern airstrips. The efficiency of General Stratemeyer's command suffered from certain deficiencies of materiel, its engineering support was inadequate, and training had been restricted by budget cuts.

Joint training by the Army and Air Force in Japan had been minimal, in part owing to the defensive nature of their missions, in part to the emphasis in all American military planning on strategic rather than tactical air operations. The Air Force, it should be said, had indeed proposed some exercises at the division level which would involve a working out of the mechanics of air support, and had suggested the creation of a Joint Operations Center. But occupation duties and the lack of suitable maneuver areas had adversely affected ground force readiness, and the Army, not wishing to sacrifice its program of small-unit training, had declined the offer. The result was that such joint exercises as were held were small in scale, and formal and cut and dried in nature.

Despite these limitations, the main strength of the Far East Command lay on the ground and in the air. Only a little over a third of the Navy's active strength was in the Pacific, only a fifth of that was in the Far East, and the naval component under Vice Admiral C. Turner Joy was very small. But although Naval Forces Far East was largely a housekeeping command, ComNavFE did control, in Task Force 96, a small amount of fighting strength, and in Task Force 90 the nucleus of an amphibious force.

The combat units of Task Force 96, Naval Forces Japan, were fast and able ships, but none mounted anything larger than a 5-inch gun. *Juneau,* Captain Jesse C. Sowell, flagship of Rear Admiral John M. Higgins' Support Group, was a younger sister and namesake of the light antiaircraft cruiser sunk by a Japanese submarine in 1942 while retiring after the Battle of Guadalcanal. With a designed displacement of 6,000 tons, she had a speed of better than 33 knots and mounted a main battery of 16 5-inch dual purpose guns. The four ships of Captain Halle C. Allan's Destroyer Division 91—*Mansfield, De Haven, Collett,* and *Swenson*—were 2,200-ton, 35-knot ships of the *Sumner* class, completed in 1944 and mounting six 5-inch guns each.

Table 2.—NAVAL FORCES IN JAPANESE WATERS, 25 JUNE 1950

TASK FORCE 90. AMPHIBIOUS FORCE, FAR EAST.   REAR ADMIRAL J. H. DOYLE.

Mount McKinley (F)	1 AGC
Cavalier	1 APA
Union	1 AKA
LST 611	1 LST
Arikara	1 ATF

TASK FORCE 96. NAVAL FORCES, JAPAN.   VICE ADMIRAL C. T. JOY.

Task Group 96.5. Support Group.   Rear Admiral J. M. Higgins.

Task Unit 96.5.1. Flagship Element.   Captain J. C. Sowell.
Juneau (F) .... 1 CLAA.

Task Unit 96.5.2. Destroyer Element.   Captain H. C. Allan, Jr.
Destroyer Division 91: *Mansfield* (F), *De Haven, Collett, Lyman K. Swenson* .... 4 DD.

Task Unit 96.5.3. British Commonwealth Support Element.
Comdr. I. H. McDonald, RAN.
HMAS *Shoalhaven* .... 1 PF.

Task Unit 96.5.6. Submarine Element.   Lt. Comdr. L. V. Young.
Remora [1] .... 1 SS.

Task Group 96.6. Minesweeping Group.   Lt. Comdr. D. V. Shouldice.
Mine Squadron 3:
Mine Division 31: *Redhead, Mocking Bird, Osprey, Partridge, Chatterer, Kite* .... 6 AMS.
Mine Division 32: *Pledge* (F),[2] *Incredible,*[3] *Mainstay,*[3] *Pirate* [3] ... 4 AM.

[1] On loan from Seventh Fleet.   [2] In reduced commission.   [3] In reserve.

In addition to this small fighting force, ComNavFE controlled a variety of auxiliary ships. The most important of these were those of Amphibious Group 1, Rear Admiral James H. Doyle: the command ship *Mount Mc-Kinley*, the attack transport *Cavalier* and the attack cargo ship *Union, LST 611,* and the fleet tug *Arikara.* This group, which held the tactical designation of Task Force 90 in the Naval Forces Far East organization, had recently arrived in Japan to conduct a program of amphibious training with units of the Eighth Army.

A third category of force at Admiral Joy's disposal consisted of the units of Mine Squadron 3, which were engaged in check-sweeping World War II minefields. Minron 3 contained six 136-foot, wooden-hulled, diesel-engined craft, and four 184-foot, twin-screw *Admirable* class AMs; but three of the latter were in caretaker status and the fourth, *Pledge,* in reduced commission. Finally, ComNavFE controlled a number of Japanese-manned ships belonging to the Shipping Control Administration, Japan—Scajap—which were employed in logistic support of the occupation and in repatriation of former Japanese prisoners of war from the continent of Asia.

The activities of Admiral Joy's headquarters, like those of the forces it controlled, had been limited to the peaceful routine of an occupation force. The staff totaled only 28 officers and 160 enlisted men. There were four officers in the operations section, five in plans, four in communications. Since the activities of naval aviation in the Western Pacific were centralized at Guam, the NavFE staff had no air or aerology departments. Although two officers qualified in mine warfare were authorized, none was aboard. Like everyone else in the armed services, Commander Naval Forces Far East had based his plans on the assumption of a major conflict with the Soviets which would be centered elsewhere. The operation plans in effect in June of 1950 were concerned with such matters as passive defense, security under air attack, and the evacuation of American citizens in emergency.

Naval base facilities in Japan were minimal. There was no logistic command, no representative of Service Forces Pacific Fleet to plan, coordinate, or procure. At Fleet Activities, Yokosuka, there was a minor ship repair facility which could perform routine upkeep, but which lacked specialized shops for torpedoes or for electronics repair; a supply section adequate to the support of the roughly 5,000 naval personnel and dependents in Japan and Japanese waters; an ordnance facility with some 3,000 tons of ammunition; and a naval hospital whose capacity had recently been reduced to 100 beds. At Sasebo in western Kyushu, where the Imperial Japanese Navy had formerly maintained a major base, there was an excellent harbor with extensive drydocking facilities. But other equipment was at a minimum, and the on-board complement was only 5 officers and 100 enlisted men. And neither Yokosuka nor Sasebo was well supplied with the material for underwater harbor defense.

The single naval air base in Japan was the Naval Air Facility, Yokosuka, which supported two or three flying boats loaned by the Seventh Fleet for search and rescue missions. NAF Yokosuka had been but recently commissioned, rehabilitation of the buildings was still underway, only about five percent of the area of the former Japanese seaplane base was Navy-controlled, and Eighth Army was using the landing strip as a park for vehicles. As for land-based naval aviation, its total strength in Japan consisted of one target tow plane for antiaircraft gunnery training.

Fortunately, however, Task Force 90 and Task Force 96 were not the only naval units in Asiatic waters. Based in the Philippines, 1,700 miles to the southward, and under the command of Vice Admiral Arthur D. Struble, there lay the Seventh Fleet, the principal embodiment of American naval power in the Western Pacific. Yet while rejoicing in the title of fleet, Struble's command, in Second World War terms, amounted to little more than a few small task units. There was a carrier "group" with its screen, a submarine group, the two patrol plane squadrons of Fleet Air Wing 1, an evacuation group concerned with the safety of American citizens in emer-

Table 3.—SEVENTH FLEET, 25 JUNE 1950

SEVENTH FLEET	VICE ADMIRAL A. D. STRUBLE.
Task Group 70.6. Fleet Air Wing 1.	Captain E. Grant.
VP 28	9 P4Y-2.
VP 47	9 PBM-5.
Task Group 70.7. Service Group.	Captain J. R. Topper.
Piedmont (F)	1 AD.
Navasota	1 AO.
Karin	1 AF.
Mataco	1 ATF.
Task Group 70.9. Submarine Group.	Comdr. F. W. Scanland.
Segundo (F), *Catfish, Cabezon,*[1] *Remora*[2]	4 SS.
Florikan[3]	1 ASR.
TASK FORCE 77. STRIKING FORCE.	VICE ADMIRAL A. D. STRUBLE.
Task Group 77.1. Support Group.	Captain E. L. Woodyard.
Rochester (FF)	1 CA.
Task Group 77.2. Screening Group.	Captain C. W. Parker.
Destroyer Division 31 less *Keyes* and *Hollister* plus *Radford* and *Fletcher: Shelton, Eversole, Radford, Fletcher*	4 DD.
Destroyer Division 32: *Maddox, Samuel L. Moore, Brush, Taussig*	4 DD.
Task Group 77.4 Carrier Group.	Rear Admiral J. M. Hoskins.
Valley Forge (F)	1 CV.

[1] Relieved by *Pickerel* 11 July.   [2] On loan to Naval Forces Japan.   [3] Relieved by *Greenlet* 30 June.

gency, and a variety of minor supporting units. The logistic group, which contained a small station reefer, a destroyer tender, and an oiler on shuttle service, constituted the total mobile fleet support in the Western Pacific, and was hard pressed to supply even the small Seventh Fleet.

The Fleet's principal base of operations was on the island of Luzon, where the Navy, following the war, had developed new facilities at Subic Bay and an airfield at Sangley Point. Peacetime operations of the Seventh Fleet were under the control of Commander in Chief Pacific Fleet, Admiral Arthur E. Radford, but standing orders provided that, when operating in Japanese waters or in the event of an emergency, control would pass to Commander Naval Forces Far East. There were, however, certain problems implicit in this arrangement: Admiral Radford's area of responsibility included potential trouble spots outside the limits of the Far East Command; lacking an aviation section on his staff, the control of a carrier striking force and of patrol squadrons would present problems for ComNavFE; Admiral Struble was senior to Admiral Joy.

Although early postwar policy had called for the maintenance of two aircraft carriers in the Western Pacific, the reductions in defense appropriations had made this impossible: for some time prior to January 1950 no carrier had operated west of Pearl; current procedure called for the rotation of single units on six-month tours of duty. In these circumstances Admiral Struble's Seventh Fleet Striking Force, Task Force 77, was made up of a carrier "group" containing one carrier, a support "group" containing one cruiser, and a screening group of eight destroyers. The duty carrier in the summer of 1950 was *Valley Forge,* an improved postwar version of the *Essex* class, completed in 1946, with a standard displacement of 27,100 tons, a length of 876 feet, and a speed of 33 knots. Flagship of Rear Admiral John M. Hoskins, Commander Carrier Division 3, *Valley Forge* had reported in to the Western Pacific in May, at which time her predecessor, *Boxer,* had been returned to the west coast for navy yard availability. The 25th of June found *Valley Forge,* with the destroyers *Fletcher* and *Radford,* in the South China Sea, one day out of Hong Kong en route to the Philippines. Admiral Struble was in Washington; Admiral Hoskins, upon whom command of the Seventh Fleet had devolved, was at Subic Bay; the carrier's commanding officer, Captain Lester K. Rice, was acting as ComCarDiv 3.

The air group of *Valley Forge,* Carrier Air Group 5, Commander Harvey P. Lanham, was the first in the Navy to attempt the sustained shipboard operation of jet aircraft. Its complement of 86 planes was made up of two jet fighter squadrons with 30 Grumman F9F–2 Panthers; two piston-engined fighter squadrons equipped with the World War II Vought F4U–4B; and a piston-engined attack squadron of 14 Douglas Skyraider AD–4s. Over and above these five squadrons the group contained 14 aircraft, principally

ADs, which were specially equipped and modified—"configurated" in current Navy jargon—for photographic, night, and radar missions. The fighter squadrons had enjoyed considerable jet experience prior to receiving their Panthers and moving aboard ship; the group as a whole had conducted extensive training in close support of troops with the Marines at Camp Pendleton, California.

The submarine force under the operational control of Commander Seventh Fleet, administratively organized as Task Unit 70.9, consisted of four fleet submarines and a submarine rescue vessel; its principal activity had been in antisubmarine warfare training exercises with units of the Fleet and of Naval Forces Far East. One of the four boats, *Remora,* was at Yokosuka on loan to ComNavFE; *Cabezon* was at sea en route from the Philippines to Hong Kong; *Segundo,* with Commander Francis W. Scanland, the task unit commander, was at Sangley Point in the Philippines; *Catfish* was at Subic Bay. The submarine rescue ship *Florikan* was at Guam, where she was about to be relieved by *Greenlet.* No submarine tender was stationed in the Western Pacific, but limited quantities of spare parts and torpedo warheads were available from the destroyer tender *Piedmont* at Subic Bay.

Patrol plane activity in the Western Pacific, another Seventh Fleet monopoly, was centralized at Guam under control of Commander Fleet Air Wing 1, Captain Etheridge Grant, who served also as Commander Task Unit 70.6 and Commander Fleet Air Guam. For long-range search and reconnaissance in the theater Captain Grant had at his disposal two squadrons of patrol aircraft. Patrol Squadron 28, a heavy landplane squadron with nine P4Y–2 Privateers, the single-tailed Navy modification of the Liberator, was based at Agana, Guam. At Sangley Point, Luzon, Patrol Squadron 47 operated nine Martin PBM–5 Mariner flying boats. In addition to these two squadrons and their supporting organizations, Fleet Air Wing 1 had a small seaplane tender, *Suisun,* which on 25 June was moored in Tanapag Harbor, Saipan.

For Captain Grant the impending crisis would not prove wholly unfamiliar, for the outbreak of war in December 1941 had found him commanding a seaplane tender in the Philippines. But his situation on 25 June was a somewhat scrambled one, for a second Mariner squadron, VP 46, was moving into the area as relief for VP 47, and the take-over process had already begun. Homeward bound, their tour in distant parts completed, the PBMs of VP 47 were widely dispersed. Two were at Yokosuka on temporary duty with Commander Naval Forces Far East, two were at Sangley Point, two were in the air and on their way, and three had already reached Pearl Harbor.

Such then was America's Western Pacific naval strength in June of 1950. Combat units assigned to ComNavFE and Commander Seventh Fleet totalled one carrier, two cruisers, three destroyer divisions, two patrol squadrons, and a handful of submarines. Not only was this a limited force with which to support a war on the Asiatic mainland: its southward deployment, with the principal base facilities at Guam and Luzon, made it ill-prepared for a campaign in Korea.

Yet if forces, bases, and plans alike seemed inadequate to the challenge of Communist aggression, there were certain mitigating factors. To employ force, whether for police action or for war, on the far side of an ocean, is to conduct an exercise in maritime power for which fighting strength, bases, and shipping are essential. Unplanned for though the emergency was, a sufficient concentration was still possible. The occupation forces in Japan contained a large fraction—four of ten Army divisions—of American ground strength. FEAF's air strength was by no means inconsiderable. Naval forces in the Far East could be reinforced, from the west coast in the first instance, in time from elsewhere. Limited though the fleet bases were in the narrow sense, in the larger context the base was Japan, and the metropolis of Asia offered many advantages in the form of airfields, staging areas, industrial strength, and skilled labor. Additionally, and by no means least, there existed and was available a sizable Japanese merchant marine, which could help to provide the carrying capacity without which control of the seas is meaningless, and which could be employed to project the armies and their supplies to the far shore.

The war in Korea, moreover, was in a sense a suburban war, and one must go back to 1898 to find in the American experience a parallel to this proximity of base and combat areas. The distances between Key West and Cuba and between Sasebo and Pusan are much the same. It could be argued, perhaps, that Admiral Joy's situation presented certain parallels to that of Admiral Cervera, but there was at least one notable difference: in 1950, despite the withdrawal of the entire occupation force, the populace of Japan proved reliable; in 1898, despite the presence of a Spanish army, the populace of Cuba did not. Doubtless to the Communists Korea seemed the most promising spot for aggression. In many ways it was also the area where the United States could best extemporize a reply.

3. *First Days of Naval Action*

The main thrust of the Communist invasion, three infantry divisions with armored and air support, was directed initially toward the capital at Seoul. Poorly disposed for defense and considerably outnumbered at the scene of action, the Army of the Republic of Korea broke under the weight of the attack; the government fled to Taejon; Seoul fell. As the enemy pressed southward down the road toward Suwon the South Korean Army appeared to be in the process of dissolution. On 30 June, after describing its heavy losses of supplies and equipment, General MacArthur had concluded that it was no longer capable of united action, and that only by commitment of American ground forces could the Han River line be held.

At sea the invasion was accompanied by a number of small unopposed landings along the east coast, which were magnified by rumor both as to number and as to location. These maritime efforts, which extended as far south as Samchok, would end with the arrival of United Nations naval forces, but in the first crucial hours of the war they were confronted only by the Navy of the Republic of Korea.

This Navy had its principal establishment at Chinhae, just west of Pusan, where the Japanese during their occupation had developed a considerable naval base with docks, barracks, petroleum storage, and a marine railway. Next in importance was the base at Inchon, seaport of the capital city, and rudimentary facilities had been established at Mukho and Pohang on the east coast, at Pusan and Yosu on the south, and at Mokpo and Kunsan on the shore of the Yellow Sea. At Inchon, on 25 June, there were four YMS, two steel-hulled ex-Japanese minecraft (JML), and the ROK Navy's single LST. At Mokpo, at the southwestern tip of the peninsula, there were two YMS and some small craft. Nine YMS were in the Pusan-Chinhae area along with some small craft, as was also the recently arrived *PC701, Bak Du San,* purchased by subscription of naval personnel. Three other PCs had been obtained from the United States, but these were still in the Hawaiian Islands, and so was the Chief of Naval Operations.

With all ships on the western and southern coasts, no strength was immediately available to oppose the east coast landings. Nevertheless the ROK units at once put to sea, and on the evening of the 25th there took place the most important surface engagement of the war. Northeast of Pusan *PC 701,* Commander Nam Choi Yong, ROKN, encountered a 1,000-ton armed steamer with some 600 troops embarked, and sank it after a running fight. Since Pusan, the only major port of entry available for the movement of supplies and reinforcements to South Korea, was at the time almost wholly defenseless, the drowning of the 600 was an event of profound strategic importance.

In Tokyo the 25th of June found the headquarters of Naval Forces Far East settled down for a normal peacetime weekend. Then the telephone rang, and when the Lieutenant Colonel of Marines who was Staff Duty Officer that day picked up the receiver he found himself talking to the Military Attaché at Seoul. This conversation put an end to holiday routine. Within minutes the headquarters had shifted to a state of readiness, and overnight it became clear that war, at least of a sort, was at hand.

The unexpected nature of the Korean involvement and the speed with which the crisis broke meant that most NavFE planning, like that of other military headquarters, had to be thrown out the porthole. But it was at least possible to salvage so much of it as was concerned with the evacuation of American citizens. On the 25th, as American civilians and their dependents were ordered out of the Seoul area by Ambassador Muccio, ComNavFE instructed Admiral Higgins to send *Mansfield* and *De Haven* to cover the exodus from the port of Inchon. The evacuation was an interservice affair: on the 26th, as the destroyers were steaming west to cover the departure from Inchon, Air Force fighters orbited over the harbor; on the 27th loading of refugees was also commenced at Pusan, FEAF transport aircraft began to fly personnel out of the capital's airfield at Kimpo, and Air Force fighters destroyed seven enemy aircraft in the area of Seoul.

After getting the civilians out the next step was to get some ammunition in, under the accelerated MDA Program ordered by President Truman on the 25th. During the days of their imperial greatness the Japanese had talked of constructing a tunnel under the Korean Strait, but this grandiloquent scheme never reached the stage of action and the road to Korea remained, as in the days of Hideyoshi, a sea road. Ammunition from stocks available in Japan was therefore hastily loaded onto two ships bearing the agreeably symbolic names of *Sergeant Keathley* and *Cardinal O'Connell*. The operation order covering this movement was sent out by Admiral Joy's headquarters in the early hours of the 27th, and in the course of the next two days sergeant and prelate sailed forth to war.

The decision to give air and naval assistance to the Republic of Korea was made at Blair House on the evening of Monday the 26th, Washington time, midday of the 27th in the Far East. At 2015 that evening Admiral Joy's Operation Order 5–50, the basic order of the Korean naval campaign, was issued. In this dispatch ComNavFE informed his forces that President Truman had ordered the fullest possible support of South Korean units south of the 38th parallel "to permit these forces to reform," and had instructed the Seventh Fleet to take station to prevent either a Communist invasion of Formosa or the use of that island for operations against the mainland. Task Group 96.5, composed of *Juneau* and the four destroyers of Desdiv 91, was designated the South Korea Support Group, instructed to base at Sasebo, and ordered to patrol Korean coastal waters, oppose hostile landings and destroy vessels engaged in aggression, provide fire support to friendly forces, and cover shipping engaged in evacuation or in carrying supplies to South Korea. Five and a half hours later the order was amplified to designate as primary targets for the attention of the task group the coast and off-lying islands from Tongyong, west of Pusan, to Ulsan on the east, and the east coast sector between Samchok and Kangnung.

On the evening of the 27th, when ComNavFE's operation order was promulgated, Admiral Higgins' Support Group was widely dispersed. The flagship *Juneau,* with the task group commander embarked, was leaving Sasebo to investigate a reported North Korean landing on the island of Koje Do, southwest of Pusan; in the Yellow Sea *De Haven* was escorting a Norwegian freighter with the first evacuees from Inchon, while *Mansfield* awaited the sailing of a second load in a Panamanian ship; *Collett* and *Swenson* had been ordered down from Yokosuka to Sasebo. Early on the 28th *Juneau* anchored off the southeastern shore of Koje Do, a party was sent ashore by whaleboat, difficulties in communication with the inhabitants were somehow surmounted, and the fact established that the island remained peaceful and undisturbed. Following this check on his southern area of responsibility, Higgins headed north, and in the afternoon put the landing party ashore at Ulsan with similar result. With evening *Juneau* again got underway, and continued up the coast to patrol the area between Samchok and Kangnung, which was reported to have been occupied by the enemy.

In Korea the situation was shrouded in uncertainty, and available intelligence was both fragmentary and confusing. False reports had caused the investigation of Koje Do and Ulsan, and a more tragic instance of misdirected effort was now to follow. At 0203 on the morning of the 29th, in 37°25' N, *Juneau* detected two groups of surface ships by radar. Since the South Korean Navy was reported to have retired south of 37°, fire was opened, one target sunk, and the others dispersed. But the information, unfortunately, was in error: the ROK retirement was still in progress, the sunken target was the South Korean *JML 305,* and the action gave rise to Korean reports of a Russian cruiser in the Samchok area.

On the 29th, as *Juneau* continued her patrol, Admiral Higgins ordered *Swenson,* which had now reached Sasebo, to rendezvous with *Mansfield* in the Yellow Sea. During the day *De Haven* joined the flagship, and at 2311 *Juneau* commenced firing the first bombardment of the war. At Mukho half an hour's deliberate shooting, conducted with searchlight illumination and with target advice from an ROKN lieutenant, brought the expenditure against enemy personnel of 16 rounds of influence-fused 5-inch and more than 400 rounds of 5-inch antiaircraft common, with what were felt to be excellent results.

The invasion of South Korea found Admiral Doyle's Amphibious Group busy with its training duties. On the morning of the 25th Task Force 90 got underway from Yokosuka, with elements of the 35th Regimental Combat Team embarked, to conduct landing exercises outside Tokyo Bay. Although operations were carried out on the 26th and 28th, in accordance with the training order, the attention of both teachers and pupils was progressively distracted by reports of happenings in Korea. During the second landing observers from the Far East Air Forces were ordered back to their stations; on completion of the exercise the ships returned at once to Yokosuka to debark the troops. On 30 June, as a movement of ground forces into Korea appeared increasingly probable, all ships of the Amphibious Group were placed on four-hour notice for getting underway.

No reports of enemy mining had as yet come in, although in time there would be plenty, but there was no lack of tasks for the small ships of Minron 3. The eight AMS were at once deployed on picket duty, harbor defense, and convoy escort. In this they were joined by *Pledge,* the only operational AM, while at Yokosuka the work of activating the other ships of Mindiv 32 was at once begun.

It was late on the 30th, Tokyo time, that President Truman approved the commitment of American troops. Early the next afternoon Admiral Joy's headquarters issued its Operation Order 7–50 assigning 16 Scajap LSTs to Admiral Doyle, and instructing him to lift the 24th Infantry Division, Major General William F. Dean, USA, from Fukuoka and Sasebo to Pusan. Pursuant to this order CTF 90 got underway at once with *Mount McKinley, Cavalier,* and *Union,* escorted by HMS *Hart,* and headed for Sasebo. The uncertainty which still existed as to the dimensions of this war was not diminished during the journey. Two doubtful sound contacts on submarines were reported by *Hart,* depth charges were dropped, and at midday of the 3rd, while rounding the southwestern tip of Kyushu, visual sighting of a surfaced submarine was made.

Admiral Doyle's ships reached Sasebo on the afternoon of the 3rd, only to find that the 24th Division had already begun its move. Two infantry companies with supporting artillery had been flown to Pusan on the 1st, and the rest of the division was hastily loading in locally available shipping to follow by sea. Since the situation seemed under control, the ships of Task Force 90 were retained at Sasebo for other employment.

While the few American naval units in Japanese waters were being committed to the support of the Korean Republic, Admiral Joy's command was increasing in size. Following the decision at the first Blair House meeting to start the Seventh Fleet toward Japan, a dispatch from the Chief of Naval Operations had directed its commander to send his carrier striking force, his submarines, and necessary supporting units, to report to ComNavFE at Sasebo. This order reached Admiral Hoskins on the 26th as the *Valley Forge* group was entering Subic Bay. At 0515 on the 27th, after emergency replenishment, the Striking Force sortied, accompanied by *Piedmont* and *Navasota,* and headed north. On the afternoon of the same day Admiral Joy assumed operational control, but feeling that Sasebo, in the rapidly developing circumstances, was a little close to the Russian air concentration at Vladivostok, diverted the force to Okinawa.

ComNavFE's Operation Order 5–50, issued that evening, instructed the Seventh Fleet to conduct surface and air operations to neutralize Formosa. On the morning of the 29th, pursuant to these instructions, Admiral Hoskins made his presence felt by flying 29 F4Us and ADs up Formosa

Strait. At 0630 in the morning of 30 June Task Force 77 reached Okinawa and dropped anchor in Nakagusuku Wan, now known as Buckner Bay in honor of the commanding general of the Tenth Army, killed in June 1945 in the moment of victory. At this base, strategically located between Korea and Formosa, the fleet did have the protection of distance, but there were no antisubmarine defenses other than those provided by the force's own destroyers, and no stocks of ammunition.

The Seventh Fleet submarines, in the meantime, were also moving northward. *Segundo* and *Catfish* took on full loads of torpedo warheads from *Piedmont* at Subic Bay on the 26th, and on the next day sailed for Sasebo. *Cabezon* made a fast turnaround at Hong Kong and joined with the others on the 28th off the northern tip of Luzon. Revised orders from Commander Seventh Fleet changed their destination also from Sasebo to Okinawa, and there they arrived on 30 June, to be joined next day by the submarine rescue vessel *Greenlet* from Guam. At Buckner Bay new orders were received, and on the 3rd *Greenlet* and her three charges sailed in company for Yokosuka.

The hasty redeployment of the Seventh Fleet also affected the patrol planes, and the homeward voyage of Patrol Squadron 47, so recently begun, was destined not to be completed. The two Mariners at Yokosuka were at once assigned to local antisubmarine patrol; those en route and those which had reached Pearl Harbor were recalled to the Western Pacific. One plane was lost in an accident at Guam, when it missed its buoy, grounded, and sank, but by 7 July six PBMs were operating out of Yokosuka. Two for the moment remained in the Philippines, but these would shortly fly north to Japan, as aircraft from the incoming VP 46 reached Sangley Point and Buckner Bay.

With the transfer of Seventh Fleet forces to his operational control, Admiral Joy acquired all immediately available American naval strength. Considering the unpredictable responsibilities of his situation this was little enough, and a most helpful addition soon came in the form of British Commonwealth units commanded by Rear Admiral Sir William G. Andrewes, KBE, CB, DSO, RN, Flag Officer Second in Command, Far Eastern Station. On 29 June, following the vote of the Security Council for military assistance to the Republic of Korea, the British Admiralty placed Royal Navy units in Japanese waters at the disposition of ComNavFE; on the next day similar action was taken by the Australian government; in Canada three destroyers were ordered to prepare to sail; from New Zealand came promise of the early dispatch of two frigates.

Commonwealth naval strength in Japanese waters was by no means inconsiderable. Andrewes' command included *Triumph,* a 13,000-ton light carrier, completed in 1946 and operating about 40 aircraft; two 6-inch gun cruisers, heavily armored *Belfast,* the largest cruiser in the Royal Navy, and

Jamaica; three destroyers and four frigates. The hospital ship *Maine,* soon to be added to the force, was for some time to be the only such vessel available for the evacuation of casualties from Korea. In the absence of American naval air bases in Japan the Royal Australian Air Force seaplane base at Iwakuni on the Inland Sea, which was at once made available, was to be of great assistance.

Table 4.—COMMONWEALTH NAVAL FORCES, 30 JUNE 1950

TASK GROUP 96.8. BRITISH COMMONWEALTH FORCES.

REAR ADMIRAL SIR W. G. ANDREWES, RN.

HMS *Triumph*	1 CVL.
HMS *Belfast* (F), HMS *Jamaica*	2 CL.
HMS *Cossack,* HMS *Consort,* HMAS *Bataan*	3 DD.
HMS *Black Swan,* HMS *Alacrity,* HMS *Hart,* HMAS *Shoalhaven*	4 PF.

On the evening of the 29th ComNavFE requested Admiral Andrewes to send *Jamaica* and the frigates to join Admiral Higgins' Support Group, and to proceed with his flagship *Belfast,* the carrier *Triumph,* and the two British destroyers to Okinawa and report to Commander Seventh Fleet. Early in the morning of the 30th Admiral Joy assumed operational control of Andrewes' forces, and in the evening modified Operation Order 5–50 to include the Commonwealth units for Korean operations only, thus exempting them from the neutralization of Formosa and the Pescadores, which remained a purely American affair.

With these augmented but by no means extravagant forces Admiral Joy confronted his tasks. He was required to evacuate American citizens, support the Republic of Korea, blockade the North Korean coastline, and at the same time to remain prepared for the unpredictable in connection with Formosa, the protection of his flanks, and a possible expansion of the conflict. And as his responsibilities and his forces grew, further difficulty was presented by the inadequacy of his staff and of those of subordinate commands. The total strength, officer and enlisted, of the NavFE staff at the end of June was 188; by November it would have reached 1,227. But in the first weeks, before reinforcements arrived, the job had to be done with what was on hand. Rarely in the history of 20th century warfare can so many have been commanded by so few.

It was not done without effort. The Plans Section went to heel and toe watches, 12 hours on and 12 off. The Operations Officer moved in a cot and did such sleeping as he could in his office; his people found themselves working a 12-hour day, with an additional four-hour night watch four days out of five. For Communications the situation became a nightmare as high-precedence traffic skyrocketed; in the first days the load of encrypted messages went up by a factor of 15, and was further complicated by great quantities of interservice and United States-British dispatches.

Somehow they made do. Even as anguished requests were sent off to Washington for more personnel, the round the clock efforts of those on the spot were accomplishing the reorganization and redeployment of available naval strength. To Naval Forces Japan had now been added the Seventh Fleet and British Commonwealth units; with these accessions Admiral Joy had gained all that would be available until reinforcements could come from afar. This strength was organized in three principal groups: Naval Forces Japan, the Seventh Fleet, and the Amphibious Force.

Table 5.—NAVAL OPERATING COMMANDS, 25 JUNE–20 JULY 1950 (NavFE OpOrds 5–50 (revised), 8–50)

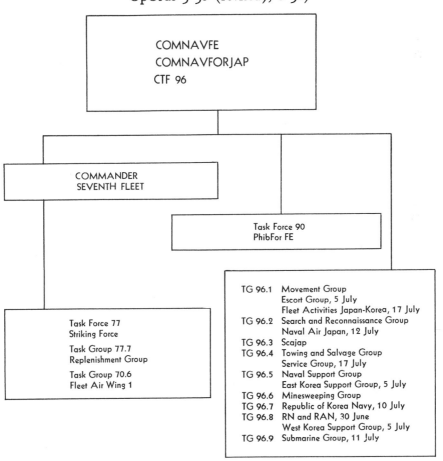

COMNAVFE
COMNAVFORJAP
CTF 96

COMMANDER
SEVENTH FLEET

Task Force 90
PhibFor FE

Task Force 77
Striking Force

Task Group 77.7
Replenishment Group

Task Group 70.6
Fleet Air Wing 1

TG 96.1   Movement Group
           Escort Group, 5 July
           Fleet Activities Japan-Korea, 17 July
TG 96.2   Search and Reconnaissance Group
           Naval Air Japan, 12 July
TG 96.3   Scajap
TG 96.4   Towing and Salvage Group
           Service Group, 17 July
TG 96.5   Naval Support Group
           East Korea Support Group, 5 July
TG 96.6   Minesweeping Group
TG 96.7   Republic of Korea Navy, 10 July
TG 96.8   RN and RAN, 30 June
           West Korea Support Group, 5 July
TG 96.9   Submarine Group, 11 July

Of these, Admiral Doyle's Amphibious Force Far East, Task Force 90, had been moved forward from Yokosuka to Sasebo, where it was awaiting instructions. Under the direct control of ComNavFE, Task Force 96, Naval Forces Japan, was engaged in various tasks. The long range aircraft of VP 47 had been organized as the Search and Reconnaissance Group, Task Group 96.2, under Captain John C. Alderman, Chief of Staff to Commander Fleet Air Guam, who had been on leave in Japan at the onset of hostilities and found himself shanghaied for this purpose. In Korean waters the Support Group, Task Group 96.5, originally consisting of *Juneau* and Destroyer Division 91, had been reinforced by *Jamaica, Shoalhaven,* and *Black Swan,* and *Alacrity* was about to join up. Although Admiral Andrewes' ships had received the designation of Task Group 96.8, these for the moment were divided between the Support Group and the Seventh Fleet Striking Force, which had reached Okinawa on 30 June. Joined on the next day by *Triumph, Belfast, Cossack,* and *Consort,* Task Force 77 remained for the moment poised between Korea and Formosa.

No less difficult than the problems of concentration and control of forces were those of their support. The shore activities of Naval Forces Japan had been centralized at Fleet Activities Yokosuka, with the secondary base at Sasebo in what approximated caretaker status. But although the workload at Yokosuka was at once increased, as activation of reserve minesweepers and frigates was begun, war in Korea soon reversed the roles of the two bases. Sasebo is more than 500 miles closer to Pusan, a fact of obvious importance and one emphasized by the original orders from the Chief of Naval Operations to the Seventh Fleet. At Sasebo an immediate expansion was undertaken, and effort made to provide more personnel; the lack of antisubmarine defenses brought urgent action to provide at least a token patrol off the entrance, and this was accomplished on the 29th.

Two more organizational problems faced Admiral Joy in the first hectic days: the provision of some sort of escort for shipping en route to Pusan, and the establishment of the blockade of North Korea, recommended by the Chief of Naval Operations on 30 June and ordered by the President next day. These matters were dealt with by ComNavFE in Operation Order 8-50, promulgated on 3 July and effective on the 4th, which made further refinements in the organization of Task Force 96.

Escort of shipping between Japan and Korea had so far been on a wholly catch-as-catch-can basis: *Arikara* and *Shoalhaven* had been so used on 1 and 2 July, *Jamaica* and *Collett* on the 3rd. But now provision was made for an Escort Group, Task Group 96.1, with a commander and units to be assigned when available. Shortly the job would be turned over to the frigates under Captain A. D. H. Jay, DSO, DSC, RN, commanding officer of *Black Swan.*

Blockade and inshore work south of latitude 37° was assigned the ROK Navy, shortly to become Task Group 96.7, with such assistance as might become available from the Far East Air Forces and from any NavFE units that happened by. For the coastline north of 37° separate East and West Coast Support Groups were established: in the east the job was entrusted to Admiral Higgins' Task Group 96.5, in the west to the Commonwealth units of Task Group 96.8. The northern limits of the blockade were set at 41° on the east coast and at 39° 30′ in the west, well south of the northern frontiers, and the precaution implicit in these boundaries was emphasized by a specific admonition to all units to keep well clear of Manchurian and Russian waters. Important though this statement of policy was, it remained for some time of purely academic importance, for emergency calls for gunfire support along the coast were such as to limit the blockading forces to only intermittent sweeps north of the 38th parallel.

4. Air Strikes, Coastal Bombardment, Flank Patrols

With supplies and troops on the move, and with gunnery ships converging on the Korean coast, it remained to reach inland by air. Air strikes could destroy the North Korean Air Force. Air strikes could harass the invading formations, interrupt their supply, and so help in the ground battle which was about to be joined. Air supremacy, indeed, seemed the key to modern war: without it victory was impossible; with it victory followed as the night the day. Its attainment was a matter of utmost urgency.

The Far East Air Forces had been committed, along with the Navy, to the support of the Korean Republic on 27 June; like the Navy they had already seen action. On the first day of the invasion Air Force fighters on patrol over the Sea of Japan had been fired on south of the parallel by a small North Korean convoy; two days later transport planes had flown American nationals out of Kimpo and fighters covering the evacuation had destroyed some enemy aircraft; the first missions in support of the ROK Army had been dispatched on the 28th.

Like the rest of the defense establishment, FEAF had planned on a different war. The 19th Bombardment Group at Guam, the only such unit in the Far East, was trained for strategic attack. The equipment and training of the fighter groups stationed in Japan had been tailored to the mission of air defense, a responsibility which the coming of war in Korea did little to diminish, and which, for a time, it promised perhaps to emphasize. Nevertheless the decision to commit American forces was followed by a rapid movement of the bombers to Okinawa, whence they flew their first missions against the invader, and by concentration of available fighter strength in the Fukuoka area in Kyushu, where the Fifth Air Force, Lieutenant General Earle E. Partridge, USAF, set up an operations center. But although these Kyushu airfields were the closest available to Korea, the limited endurance of the F–8oC permitted it to remain only very briefly in the target area, and effective operations waited upon the establishment of Korean bases, the manufacture of new wing tanks, or a change in aircraft type.

Lack of target information for the bombers and the limited capabilities of Air Force fighters placed great premium upon carrier-borne aviation. Never, perhaps, had the virtues of free movement upon the face of the waters shone so brightly, even to those who had long derided this instrument of war. On 29 June, as his Seventh Fleet Striking Force was approaching Buckner Bay, Admiral Struble flew into Tokyo from Washington. By presidential proclamation and NavFE operation order the mission of the Seventh Fleet was the neutralization of Formosa, but the rapid deterioration of the situation in Korea raised pressing questions concerning its employment there. Early on the 30th Struble queried his staff by dispatch as to how soon *Valley Forge* and *Triumph* could conduct a first strike in the area of the 38th parallel, and in a conference with General MacArthur, Admiral Joy, and General Stratemeyer, the decision was reached to strike objectives in the Pyongyang area. First emphasis would be given to the airfield complex of the North Korean capital, second priority to the railroad yards and to the bridges over the Taedong River. Following these discussions Struble flew on to Okinawa to rejoin his force, and early in the evening ComNavFE promulgated Operation Order 6–50 governing the employment of the carrier striking force.

The prospect of operating this mixed force presented some problems, owing to the differences between British and American aircraft types and to the fact that *Triumph's* maximum speed of 23 knots was 10 knots slower than that of *Valley Forge*. But the British were eager to go; many of their officers had had experience in joint operations in the Second World War and the two forces had recently held joint maneuvers; the advantages outweighed the difficulties. Although obscurity still surrounded the intentions of Communist submarines, Seventh Fleet forces had already reported two contacts, one some distance off Okinawa, one at the entrance of Buckner Bay; the Seventh Fleet submarine commander was therefore drafted as antisubmarine warfare adviser to ComCardiv 3. On the evening of 1 July Task Force 77, now enlarged to two carriers, two cruisers, and ten destroyers, sortied from Buckner Bay and headed northwest and north toward the launching area in the Yellow Sea.

Along the Korean coastline, following the Mukho bombardment of the evening of the 29th, *Juneau* and *DeHaven* had continued on patrol. The British cruiser *Jamaica* had reported to Admiral Higgins by radio at 1940, and had requested a rendezvous, and on the next day *Black Swan* also checked in by dispatch. But radio communications had become clogged, owing to the sudden expansion of high-precedence traffic, and communications with the British were for the moment worst of all: the instructions for a rendez-vous never reached the British ships, and his allies had to seek out Admiral Higgins by intuitive means.

Nevertheless the clans were gathering. On the west coast, where *Swenson* had joined *Mansfield* on 30 June, the patrol of areas Yoke and Zebra continued without contact with the enemy. On the east coast, following conferences with southbound ROK naval personnel, *Juneau* returned to Mukho to expend a further 43 rounds of 5-inch VT against troop positions and a shore battery. *Collett* came up from Pusan, where she had embarked ROK interpreters, signalmen, and liaison officers for distribution throughout the force, and at 2200 *Jamaica* joined. On the 1st, *Alacrity* and *Black Swan* arrived, and the day was spent in patrolling the coast and reorganizing the Support Group. *DeHaven* and *Collett* were detached to Sasebo to fuel and to escort troopships to Pusan; *Alacrity* was ordered into the Yellow Sea to relieve *Mansfield* in Area Yoke; *Juneau, Jamaica,* and *Black Swan* continued on east coast patrol.

On the morning of 2 July the South Korean Support Group returned to action. At 0615 bow waves were sighted close inshore, and investigation disclosed four torpedo boats and two motor gunboats heading north from Chumunjin, whither they had escorted ten motor trawlers loaded with ammunition. As the cruisers put on speed to intercept the enemy, the tor-pedo boats, with more bravery than discretion, turned to attack. Fire was opened at 11,000 yards, and by the time the range had closed to 4,000 one PT had been sunk and one stopped, a third was heading for the beach, and the fourth was escaping seaward. The final score of the engagement was three torpedo boats and both gunboats destroyed, and two prisoners taken by *Jamaica.* Following this first engagement with the North Korean Navy, also in effect the last, the cruisers bombarded shore batteries at Kangnung, and late in the day *Jamaica* was sailed for Sasebo to fuel.

The 3rd of July saw a number of dispersed skirmishes around the Korean coastline. Along the convoluted western shore Communist activities had extended far south of the formal battleline, and in the evening the ROK *YMS 513* caught and sank three small boats unloading military supplies at Chulpo. On the east coast *Juneau* finished off the ammunition trawlers at Chumunjin, and the British frigate *Black Swan* was subjected to the first enemy air attack of the war.

Although the North Korean Air Force, in the first days of conflict, had performed useful services in demoralizing ROK troops, its strength in any serious terms was small. Estimates of its composition as of the outbreak of hostilities varied between some 75 and 130 aircraft, none of very recent types. But on 2 July ComNavFE had alerted the Support Group against possible air attack, and at 2012 on the 3rd two enemy fighters, thought to have been Stormoviks, came in on *Black Swan* from over the land and out of the haze, inflicted minor structural damage, and escaped without being hit. Fortunate in their evasive action, these pilots were doubly fortunate in their assignment that day, for their colleagues back at Pyongyang had just received a thorough working over by the aircraft of Task Force 77. In any event such attacks were not to be soon repeated: the efforts of Seventh Fleet and Fifth Air Force fighters and the airfield attacks by Bomber Command speedily demobilized the North Korean Air Force. *Black Swan's* experience remained for some time unique, and not until 23 August did another U.N. ship undergo attack from the air.

Since the evening of 1 July Task Force 77 had been steaming north from Buckner Bay, and by early morning of the 3rd Admiral Struble's Striking Force had reached the designated launching point. There, in the middle of the Yellow Sea, the force was some 150 miles from the target area, but only 100 miles from Chinese Communist airfields on the Shantung Peninsula and less than 200 miles from the Soviet air garrison at Port Arthur. The air defense problem, therefore, was potentially somewhat larger than the size of the North Korean Air Force would indicate; like the submarine situation, it required a certain investment in defensive measures. At 0500 *Valley Forge* launched combat and antisubmarine patrols; beginning at 0545 *Triumph* flew off 12 Fireflies and 9 Seafires for an attack on the airfield at Haeju, and 15 minutes later *Valley Forge* commenced launching her strike group. Sixteen Corsairs loaded with eight 5-inch rockets each, and 12 Skyraiders carrying 1,600-pound bombloads were launched against the Pyongyang airfield. When the propeller-driven attack planes had gained a suitable headstart, *Valley Forge* catapulted eight F9F-2 Panthers, whose higher cruising speed would bring them in first over the target area.

No serious opposition was encountered by the American jets as they swept in over the North Korean capital. Two Yaks were destroyed in the air, another was damaged, and nine aircraft were reported destroyed on the ground. For the enemy, this sudden appearance of jet fighters more than 400 miles from the nearest American airfield was both startling and salutary. Quite possibly, as one American commander observed, it may have deterred a sizable commitment of aircraft to North Korean bases.

Following the Panthers in, the Corsairs and Skyraiders bombed and rocketed hangars and fuel storage at the airfield. Both at Pyongyang and at Haeju enemy antiaircraft opposition was negligible, and no plane suffered serious damage. In the afternoon aircraft from *Triumph* flew a second strike, and a second attack was launched by *Valley Forge* against the marshalling yards at Pyongyang and the bridges across the Taedong River. Considerable damage was reported inflicted on locomotives and rolling stock, but the bridges survived this effort.

In view of the Formosan commitment, the carrier strikes had been originally planned as a one-day affair. But this had been modified during the

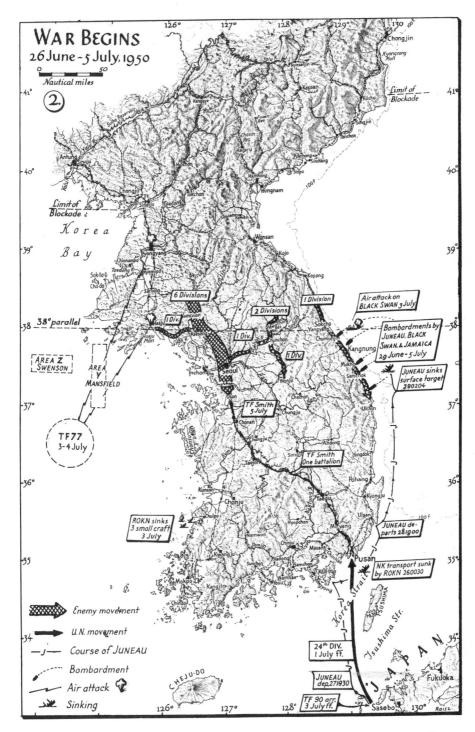

WAR BEGINS
26 June – 5 July, 1950

Nautical miles

②

Limit of Blockade

Korea Bay

Limit of Blockade

38° parallel

AREA Z SWENSON

AREA Y MANSFIELD

TF 77 3-4 July

6 Divisions

1 Div.

2 Divisions

1 Div.

1 Division

1 Div.

Air attack on BLACK SWAN 3 July

Bombardments by JUNEAU, BLACK SWAN, & JAMAICA 29 June-5 July

JUNEAU sinks surface target 290204

TF Smith 5 July

TF Smith One battalion

JUNEAU departs 281900

ROKN sinks 3 small craft 3 July

NK transport sunk by ROKN 260030

24th DIV. 1 July ff.

JUNEAU dep.271930

TF 90 arr. 3 July ff.

Korea Strait

Tsushima Str.

JAPAN

CHEJU-DO

Enemy movement

U.N. movement

Course of JUNEAU

Bombardment

Air attack

Sinking

63

First strike in the west: Marshalling yard and rail bridges at Pyongyang under attack by Valley Forge aircraft. 3 July 1950. (USN 417144)

approach, owing to the "rapidly deteriorating Korean situation," and General MacArthur had authorized the attack to continue as practicable beyond the first day. Targets for the second day, selected by CincFE, were designated by dispatch on the night of the 2nd, with first priority given the railroad facilities and bridges in the neighborhood of Kumchon, just north of the parallel on the main line from Pyongyang to Seoul, second priority to similar installations at Sariwon, halfway between the two capitals, and third priority to those near Sinanju, where the main road and rail lines from Manchuria cross the Chongchon River.

With a fine disregard of these instructions Task Force 77 celebrated the Glorious Fourth with further attacks on Pyongyang. This time a break was made in one of the Taedong River bridges, some locomotives were destroyed, and some small ships in the river were attacked. Antiaircraft opposition had increased somewhat over that of the previous day, four ADs were damaged, and one, unable to lower its flaps, landed fast and bounced over the barrier, destroying three planes and damaging six more. With completion of flight operations the Striking Force retired southward. On the 5th Admiral Andrewes, with *Belfast, Cossack,* and *Consort,* was detached to join the blockading forces in compliance with orders from ComNavFE, Admiral Struble flew to Tokyo by carrier plane, and Task Force 77 continued on to Buckner Bay. There it arrived on 6 July, and there it was retained until the 16th.

On the east coast, on 4 July, *Juneau* and *Black Swan* worked up and down the shore between Samchok and Chumunjin, firing on bridges and on the coastal road. On the 5th *Jamaica* returned from Sasebo, *Juneau* retired to replenish fuel and ammunition, and for the next few days the bombardment duty was left in the hands of the British.

The 5th of July, which saw Task Force 77 retiring southward and *Juneau* completing her second tour of firing at coastal targets, saw also the beginning of the ordeal of the American foot soldier. As early as 27 June an Advance Command Group under Brigadier General John H. Church, USA, had been established at Suwon, some 25 miles south of Seoul, to help in reorganizing ROK forces and to expedite logistic assistance. But events soon demonstrated the optimism of this assignment, and on 30 June, with the arrival of the North Korean People's Army momentarily expected, this group was withdrawn to the southward. As ADCOM was retiring the first units of the 24th Infantry Division were being flown into Korea, and as the rest of the division was hastily embarking in Japan this advanced element, two infantry companies with supporting artillery under Lieutenant Colonel Charles B. Smith, USA, began its northward movement from Pusan. On the 5th Task Force Smith made contact with the enemy at Osan, south of Suwon, where it ran into an entire North Korean infantry division with armored support. From 0800 to 1500 the fight went on, at which time the survivors, outmaneuvered, outflanked, and most of all outnumbered, withdrew with the loss of all equipment save small arms.   Twelve miles back down the road a larger force underwent the same fate, and the Americans were forced back on Chonan, where they would hold to 8 July.

The war was now ten days old.   American citizens had been evacuated; a carrier air strike had been made against the enemy capital and the enemy air force; the east coast invasion route was under fire from naval guns.   In the air the Far East Air Forces were putting forth their best efforts.   On the ground the Army had engaged the enemy.   Across the Korean Strait a stream of shipping was flowing into Pusan where, prior to the arrival of an Army port company, the unloading of 55 ships with 15,000 troops and 1,700 vehicles was handled by two ECA employees, Alfred Meschter and Milton Nottingham.   In Korea the situation was being dealt with to the limit of the abilities of the forces available.   There remained the problem of the northern and southern flanks.

What the dimensions of this problem might be, no one knew.   If the invasion of South Korea had surprised the United States, and had shown how wrongly intelligence had been evaluated, what faith could be put in estimates of Communist intentions elsewhere?   Suddenly capabilities became important.   The State Department had warned all hands on 26 June of the possibility that Korea was but the first of a series of coordinated moves; the military forces of the United States had gone on world-wide alert; in the Mediterranean the Sixth Fleet had put to sea.   In the immediate theater of operations, no less than on the world scene, possibilities were unpleasant and visibility poor.   The Joint Chiefs, it is true, had estimated that there would be no Soviet or Chinese intervention, but there was plenty of history, including a day at Pearl Harbor, to teach the outpost commander that estimates make poor weapons.

What of the northern neighbor, whose airfields at Vladivostok and Port Arthur flanked the Korean peninsula and were less than two hours flying time from Japan?   What of the estimated four-score submarines based in the Vladivostok area?   For the air threat, which had caused Admiral Joy to divert the Seventh Fleet to Buckner Bay, FEAF's fighter strength provided some counter, but the submarine situation was less satisfactory.   The excitement of the first week of conflict had brought forth eight reports of submarine sightings, ranging from Okinawa to the Sea of Japan, and while most were doubtless in error they at least posed serious questions.   Harbor defense equipment was lacking in the Far East, and the shortage of antisubmarine units was acute: of the three American destroyer divisions in the theater, two were needed to provide a minimum sound screen for *Valley Forge*.   Of necessity, therefore, the patrol planes of VP 47 were employed on local antisubmarine patrol and in the escort of shipping, and long range search had to await the coming of reinforcements.

What were the intentions of the Communist Chinese? In Korea their capabilities could for the moment be largely disregarded, but ComNavFE had been instructed to use the Seventh Fleet to neutralize Formosa, and to prevent attack in either direction across Formosa Strait. Here Chiang's forces presented no problem, but the Communists had the capability, and both the Generalissimo and Admiral Struble thought an August effort wholly possible. The implications of such a development, added to the situation in Korea, greatly outweighed Admiral Joy's new accretions of force, and he may well have wondered what tools he was supposed to use to do this job. Some show of muscle, at least, had been made by *Valley Forge* as she steamed north, when she flew an air parade over Formosa Strait and the city of Taipei. But the chance that more would be required, as well as problems of logistic support, had made it necessary, following the Pyongyang strikes, to return Task Force 77 to Okinawa.

If Formosa was to be defended, coordinated planning was obviously necessary, and the state of Nationalist morale was such as to require stiffening. Arriving in Tokyo on the afternoon of 5 July, Struble had proposed a prompt resumption of carrier strikes, this time from the Sea of Japan. But decision on these was delayed, the talk turned to the Formosa problem, and the suggestion of a visit to that island was approved by General MacArthur. On the 6th, Commander Seventh Fleet flew back to Buckner Bay, and on the next day boarded a destroyer for a high-speed run to Taipei and two days of talks with the Generalissimo and the Nationalist military. Another few days would see the Formosa Strait under reconnaissance by planes of Fleet Air Wing 1, but the question of a surface patrol was more difficult. With the gunnery ships committed up to their ears in Korea, and with the situation there calling ever more urgently for Task Force 77, all that remained were the submarines of the Seventh Fleet. On 18 July *Catfish* was sailed from Yokosuka for a reconnaissance of the China coast, and was followed on the next day by *Pickerel*.

Finally, the northern sector, so great in undisclosed potentialities, was also brought under surveillance. On 7 July the first patrol plane reinforcements reached the Far East, and the long range P2V Neptunes of VP 6 were at once assigned to search in the Sea of Japan. On the 23rd the submarine *Remora,* escorted by *Greenlet,* headed north from Yokosuka for a patrol of La Pérouse Strait.

CHAPTER IV

Help on the Way

1. The Strategic Problem

ON BOTH SIDES of the Pacific the invasion of South Korea was followed by a period of violent activity. Along its western rim the forces of the Far East Command, so suddenly committed, were bending every effort to evacuate friendly nationals, to support the Republic of Korea, to check the North Korean invaders, and to guard the flanks. Far to the eastward the government of the United States, hastily gathering reinforcements and preparing to move them across the world's largest ocean to the scene of action, girded itself for an effort to influence history by sea power.

For this effort, however unexpected, there was no lack of precedent: if less all-embracing than some of its disciples have thought, the influence of sea power has still been one of profound importance. Seven-tenths of the earth's surface is wet, and the capability of moving goods and services, including armies, across this surface, and of restricting such movements on the part of others, is a very considerable one. Since most civilized activities involve the movement of goods, the history of civilization is in large degree the history of transport routes, and of those who have controlled them. Through their private Mediterranean and their unmatched roads the Romans controlled the ancient world; through their domination of medieval trade routes the castled barons placed their impress upon their times; in recent centuries much history has revolved around the story of the oceans.

With the development of sailing ship technology the states of western Europe entered upon a great age of competitive expansion, which by the 18th century saw the nations of the Atlantic littoral locked in struggle for control of overseas wealth. The upshot of these wars was the dominance of Great Britain, an island nation difficult to invade, located to windward across the western approaches to the continent, and with bases scattered at the narrow places of the extra-European world. So situated, the British could withstand all comers, and could bring down mighty enemies through policies of alliance and subsidy, assisted by the freedom of action conferred by sea control which made possible descent at will along the European coastline. It is a commonplace that the peaceful world order of the 19th century rested in large measure upon the Royal Navy.

But the influence of history upon sea power has also been profound, and even as this classic period was celebrated by its historian the foundations were shifting. With the improvement of land communications the inner regions of Europe developed rapidly in population, wealth, and power. Effective and economical movement of goods was no longer a maritime monopoly, and land transport increasingly approximated that in a fluid medium. In Europe there followed an inward displacement of the disturber of the peace, from Napoleon to the Kaiser, from Hitler to Stalin, while across the oceans new power centers arose with the industrialization of the United States and of Japan. These developments led to the new strategic formulations of the 20th century, while at the same time the developments of the new technology powerfully modified the nature and conduct of war.

In place of the world of the sailing ship there developed a world based on the possibilities of coal and oil. In place of overseas empire internal development was emphasized. In place of the single European power center there now existed three, and in warfare there developed a third dimension. Faced in these changing circumstances by threatening new rivals, and struggling to maintain the world they knew, the maritime powers of Europe now looked overseas for essential supplies and reinforcements, and to the New World to redress the balance of the Old. Off the coast of Asia the adaptable, prolific, and xenophobic Japanese gazed southward toward the resources of the Indies. If the changes of the industrial age had downgraded the oceans as the source of commercial wealth and had produced new inland concentrations of power, they gave added emphasis to ocean highways as sources of salvation construed in mundane terms of money, men, and oil. As defense of the rimlands against the interior superseded the struggle for distant colonies, the unique importance of the battle fleet was modified, the set-piece battle declined in importance, and the far shore replaced the enemy fleet as the focus of operations. But the continuing struggle for the control of ocean routes remained the most important of all. It became also one of the costliest: between 1939 and 1945 more than 72,000 lives were lost in the Battle of the Atlantic.

To the western powers, therefore, the two wars with Germany fell in the same strategic mold: initial resistance to the prepared aggressor while strength was mustered in the rear and preparation made to fight things through. The time required for this evolution had, of necessity, to be bought by those on the line: by Britain's contemptible little army and the taxis of the Marne, by the RAF and the Royal Navy, and in both wars, be it said, by mighty Russian formations on the eastern front. In some senses the war against Japan was different, yet this last great struggle for overseas empire followed the same sequence of expansion, containment, and return. For the nations of the west, for those who liked the world as it was and resisted violent change, this pattern clearly posed three requirements. The line had to be held against disaster; control of the seas had to be gained and maintained; these things having been done, it was necessary to mobilize and move in the reserve. Failure in one of these requirements meant failure in all.

There was thus imposed upon the west a maritime strategy in which final victory on land resulted from the exploitation of the seas. Even in the second war this remained true. Hitler's advance stopped at the Channel; Rommel's African operations were a function of the struggle for the central Mediterranean. Control of the seas gave access to the resources which sustained and the reinforcements which strengthened Great Britain. British and American maritime power kept Russia in the war, forced the Germans to disperse their defenses, and delivered a concentrated and irresistible assault. Naval force severed the Japanese from their essential resources, brought the bombers to Saipan, and prepared the invasion it made unnecessary.

The end of the second war found the United States the dominant maritime power of the world. In many respects its position approximated that of Great Britain in the 19th century. It possessed the world's largest navy; it maintained bases and forces in being at various points about the globe. If the American flag merchant marine was not, like that of Britain at an earlier date, the world's greatest, Americans controlled a very large tonnage sailing under foreign flags and had access for emergency use to most of the world's shipping. Along with these trappings of power the United States had also inherited the responsibilities, together with such lessons concerning the conduct of these affairs as history seemed to teach.

Chief of these lessons, it seemed, was that of the chronic unpreparedness of the western powers. Minimum forces in the line, inadequate naval strength, and unmobilized reserves had twice brought them close to catastrophe. The appearance of a new aggressor, therefore, had been followed by the deployment to the Mediterranean of the Sixth Fleet, reinforcement of the Strategic Air Command, and the creation of the North Atlantic Treaty Organization. On one side of the world, at least, and within the limits of presumed budgetary capabilities, it seemed the lessons had been learned. So far as the peninsula of Europe was concerned the defenses were going up.

Then, shockingly, the same strategic problem was presented on a smaller and more distant peninsula. Once again the race was on to manipulate the variables of space, time, and movement capacity so as to check the invader and turn defeat into victory. Once again, after the first few days of optimism, the outcome of the race seemed unpredictable. The North Koreans had tanks and aircraft, the South Koreans did not. The North Koreans, their armies loaded with veterans of the Chinese Civil War and with even a few who had fought at Stalingrad, had experienced combat leadership; the South Koreans did not. The Communist powers of Asia had military stockpiles far exceeding those available to the government of Syngman Rhee. Yet even these stockpiles were not limitless: the industrial base of Communist aggression lay far to the west in European Russia, and the capacity of the trans-Siberian railway was only some 17,000 tons a day, less than that of the port of Pusan, much less than that of Pacific Ocean shipping.

Having taken up the challenge of the 25th of June, the maritime world for the third time in a century faced excruciating problems of time and distance. From the 38th parallel north of Seoul, where the main invading force came down across the border, the airline distance to Pusan is some 225 miles. From Pusan to San Francisco by the great circle route is 4,914 miles, and by way of Pearl Harbor a thousand more. The task which faced the United States in mid-summer 1950 was that of equalizing these distances.

It was on this mission of equalization that Task Force Smith flew to Pusan and entrained for the north. It was not an impressive force: two companies of infantry, one company of field artillery, two mortar platoons and one of recoilless rifles, six rocket launching teams. The emergency which brought it to Korea was one for which it had neither planned nor trained. Others, however, had gone before it on a similar errand. Like the British Expeditionary Force of another generation at Mons, like the RAF in the September sky ten years before, like the Americans and Filipinos at Bataan, the navies in the Java Sea, and the carrier pilots at Midway, Task Force Smith and those who followed were put in to hold the line. Whether this commitment would be justified depended on the speed with which help came. To come, it had to cross the seas.

2. *Troops and Supplies*

The troops and supplies, so urgently needed in Korea, could come in the first instance only from within the Far Eastern theater. In the first days of war ammunition had been sent in on the *O'Connell* and *Keathley,* and Admiral Doyle's Amphibious Group had been ordered down to Sasebo. On 1 July, as Task Force Smith was flown to Pusan, the rest of the 24th Division had begun a hurried embarkation, at Sasebo and Inland Sea ports, in vessels belonging to the Shipping Control Administration, Japan. Escort for the priceless cargo carried by these Scajap ships was provided by the fleet tug *Arikara,* a somewhat limited screening force to represent the greatest naval power on earth.

The Scajap fleet, Japanese manned and Japanese supported but operating under occupation force control, held the designation of Task Group 96.3 in the organization of Naval Forces Japan. In the emergency of 1950 its 12 freighters and 39 LSTs were to prove a priceless asset, and beginning with the movement of the 24th Division the Scajap ships would be used to the limit in intra-area lift. But the principal responsibility for over-water transportation, both by statute and by order of CincFE, fell upon the Military Sea Transportation Service.

The Military Sea Transportation Service is a unified logistic organization, established within the Navy Department to provide, under a single authority, the necessary sea transport for Defense Department cargo and personnel, save only that handled by the fleet itself. As such it had absorbed the old Naval Transportation Service and the ships and seagoing functions of the Army Transportation Corps. Headed by a vice admiral responsible to the Chief of Naval Operations and administered through a naval command structure, but staffed largely by civil service personnel, the Service was designed to function both as a scheduling and as an operating agency. In the first capacity MSTS chartered from commercial operators the space required for the greater portion of Defense Department sea lift. In the second, in addition to its commissioned and Navy-manned (USS) and civil service-manned (USNS) transports and cargo ships, MSTS came to own and control a tanker fleet operated under contract by private companies for the Military Petroleum Supply Agency, the unified petroleum procurement agency of the Department of Defense. In emergencies for which space charter and the MSTS fleet were together inadequate, the Service could resort to time charter of merchant shipping.

MSTS had been created in October 1949 by directive of the Secretary of Defense, pursuant to the National Security Act of 1947. In the following months it developed into a world-wide operating agency, with major area commands in London, New York, San Francisco, and Tokyo. The first Deputy Commander for the Western Pacific reached Tokyo in January 1950 to organize his command, activation of which was scheduled for 1 July. On that date, in accordance with plan, Captain Alexander F. Junker assumed his responsibilities as DepComMSTS WestPac to find himself faced by an emergency of wholly unexpected dimensions.

The first problem was to find the shipping for an immediate large-scale lift of troops and supplies. That under Captain Junker's own control—the MSTS "owned" shipping in the area—was initially limited to 25 intra-area support ships inherited from the Army. Not all of these were of types useful to the task, but there were ten 175-foot, 500-ton capacity cargo ships (AKL) of Army design, the two 340-foot coastal transports (T–APc) *Sergeant Keathley* and *Sergeant Muller* each normally carrying 100 troops, and six LSTs. Three LSTs and two AKLs had been inactivated, but work on them was quickly put in hand, and the LSTs were operating by the 8th.

A second source of shipping was, of course, to be found in the Scajap fleet, which was immediately made available and which continued to be employed in close connection with MSTS. A third expedient was to retain and employ MSTS transports and cargo ships which, like the aircraft transport *Cardinal O'Connell,* had reached the Far Eastern theater on normal trans-Pacific runs. Finally, most fortunately and most importantly, there was the possibility of charter of Japanese merchant ships.

By 10 July the MSTS-controlled fleet in or en route to the Western Pacific had risen from 25 to 70 vessels, not counting the 50-odd ships belonging to Scajap. But not all had reached the Far East and some, for reasons of size or type or availability, were unsuited to the work at hand: of the total of 70 vessels, 52 were available for emergency movements to Korea. Of these, Japanese vessels on charter on 10 July accounted for 29 bottoms and 74,000 measurement tons; five days later this number would have increased to 40. In addition to the *Maru*s and to the ships inherited from the Army, Captain Junker had two AKAs and three T–APs which had reached Japan and which had been retained to lift men and material to Pusan.

The 24th Infantry Division had completed its movement to Korea by 6 July. Hard on its heels the 25th Division began to move, its first elements loading at Moji on Shimonoseki Strait on the 8th, and subsequent echelons at Inland Sea ports and at Sasebo; for this movement Japanese time-chartered ships were extensively used. The third major Army unit to be lifted from Japan was the 1st Cavalry Division, and this, since handling facilities at Pusan were clogging from overload, was put in over the beaches. This movement was accomplished by Admiral Doyle's Amphibious Group, temporarily augmented by the loan from MSTS of two AKAs, three T–APs, one ocean tug, five LSTs, and four time-chartered Japanese *Maru*s. Late in July the final intra-theater movement of the initial phase brought in two battalions of the 29th Infantry Regiment from Okinawa. On the 16th MSTS assigned two Japanese passenger vessels and a cargo ship to this lift, and on the 24th these troops were landed at Pusan.

Thus the job was done. By mid-July all Army forces in the Far East had been committed or were scheduled for commitment, with the single exception of the 7th Division, held back to provide a skeleton garrison for Japan. And while the emergency movements within the Far Eastern theater were going on, others were in preparation elsewhere. In Hawaii the Mid-Pacific branch of MSTS was assembling shipping to lift the 5th Regimental Combat Team west. On the west coast planning for the movement of the 2nd Division was in progress, and urgent efforts to project supplies forward across the ocean highways were underway.

In the United States the logistic agencies of all three services were struggling with a flood of emergency requisitions for medical and hospital supplies, for equipment in general, and above all for ammunition. All along the west coast naval ammunition facilities which had been operating in reduced or maintenance status were expanded. In June, Port Chicago in San Francisco Bay had a normal weekly handling capacity of 1,250 tons of naval ammunition. On the 28th CincPacFleet called for operations on a three-shift basis, extra personnel was laid on, and within a month Port Chicago was outloading more than 9,000 tons a week for both Navy and Army. On 8 July activation of facilities at Fallbrook and Seal Beach, California, was begun, and Bangor Annex, at Keyport in Puget Sound, was made available for the outloading of Army and Air Force ammunition.

For all services requirements skyrocketed. The planned overseas movement of Army ammunition alone was to rise from zero to 77,000 tons for the month of August, a growth paralleled by increased calls for general stores, refrigerated provisions, and for personnel. The Military Sea Transportation Service had prepared for a predicted movement of 66,000 tons of cargo to the Far East in July; in fact it ended up moving 312,000 tons and 30,000 passengers. More tonnage was urgently required and was being hastily assembled by Captain William R. Thayer, Deputy Commander MSTS Pacific; by the third week in July the transports under his control had increased from 20 to 31, and 12 commercial vessels had been taken on under time charter.

3. *Fighting Ships*

Like all conflicts, that in Korea had its strange and unpredictable characteristics. One of these was the fact that, so far as control of the seas was concerned, the war started with the exploitation phase. It was never necessary to fight the convoys through. But of this no one could at first be sure, and with men and supplies in very large quantity committed to the ocean highways, and with the extent of opposition doubtful, insurance was necessary. To maintain sea control, should new enemy forces choose to dispute it, further combatant strength was needed.

Yet almost all the fighting ships west of the continental United States had already been committed. Statistically speaking, the division of the Pacific Fleet in June between ships operating in home waters and those to the westward was roughly an even one. One hundred and twenty-five naval vessels of all types were based on the west coast while another 128 were scattered between Alaska, the Hawaiian Islands, the trust territories, and the Western Pacific. But the statistics are deceptive, including as they do auxiliaries, small craft, and local forces, and the distribution of major combatant types was very different. Of 86 active units, three-quarters were based on the west coast of the United States.

Of the three large aircraft carriers in the Pacific Fleet, one was with Task Force 77 and two were in the San Diego area, where the Fleet's two escort carriers also based. The Fleet contained no active battleship. Two cruisers were already at work in Far Eastern waters and the remaining four were on the west coast. Of a total of 57 destroyer types and 30 submarines, 12 and 6 respectively were operating outside of continental waters, 12 and

4 were operating under ComNavFE. Quite clearly any naval reinforcement had to come a long way.

The first forward movement concerned the long-range patrol planes. On 26 June the seaplane tender *Gardiner's Bay,* which had completed fitting out for a tour in the Western Pacific, sailed from San Diego for Yokosuka, where she arrived on 12 July. On 28 June Patrol Squadron 6, a medium landplane squadron operating nine P2V–5 Neptunes, was deployed forward from Barber's Point, Oahu. By the 7th the squadron had reached Japan where, in the absence of any suitable naval air station, it operated out of Johnson Air Force Base at Tachikawa.

The two heavy *Baltimore*-class cruisers of Cruiser Division 3, moored in Long Beach when the Korean War broke out, had arrived only two weeks before from an eight-month cruise in the Western Pacific. These ships, *Helena* and *Toledo,* completed in 1945, had a standard displacement of 13,600 tons, a speed of 33 knots, a main battery of nine 8-inch guns and a secondary battery of twelve dual-purpose 5-inch. Alas, the delights of civilization were to be but briefly tasted, and the expected period of rest, recreation, and upkeep was to be brutally cut short. On 29 June the division commander, Rear Admiral Charles C. Hartman, received orders to prepare to head back west again with a departure date a week away. All leaves were at once cancelled by telegram, emergency repairs were hastened, and supplies quickly loaded aboard.

At San Diego there were two *Essex*-class aircraft carriers: *Boxer,* Captain Cameron Briggs, back from her tour in the Western Pacific, was waiting to enter a navy yard for repairs; *Philippine Sea,* Captain Willard K. Goodney, had just arrived from the Atlantic Fleet and was preparing for an October departure for the Far East as relief for *Valley Forge.* The air group designated for this deployment, Carrier Air Group 11, Commander Raymond W. Vogel, was similar in composition to Air Group 5, being composed of two F9F jet fighter squadrons, two squadrons of F4Us, one of ADs, and a mixed bag of specially configured Corsairs and Skyraiders. Its training, however, was considerably less advanced than that of the *Valley Forge* group. The jet squadrons had been handicapped by shortage of aircraft and the pilot situation was highly unstable: many of the younger officers had received orders for separation on 30 June, and many of their replacements were not yet up to fleet standards. Difficult as the situation was, it would have been much worse had the North Koreans appreciated the strategic importance of accounting periods and delayed their attack until the end of the fiscal year. As it was, emergency action by the Bureau of Naval Personnel made it possible to avoid forced separations from the service and to minimize dislocation.

With the outbreak of hostilities in Korea all plans and schedules were scrapped. Loading for the Western Pacific was put on a high speed basis, considerable gear was transferred from *Boxer* to her sister carrier, and the air group was embarked under emergency orders. On 6 July *Philippine Sea* got underway from San Diego for Pearl Harbor, where she arrived on the 14th to commence a ten-day period of accelerated training exercises.

The remaining carrier strength of the Pacific Fleet, Carrier Division 15, consisted of the escort carriers *Sicily,* another recent immigrant from the Atlantic, and *Badoeng Strait.* These were ships of the postwar CVE 105 type, modelled on the old *Sangamon* class of converted tankers which had seen so much service in the war against Japan. Based at San Diego and normally assigned to antisubmarine warfare duty, the ships of Cardiv 15 were also from time to time employed to give carrier refresher training to Marine fighter squadrons from El Toro. The outbreak of war found *Badoeng Strait* en route to Pearl Harbor on a summer training cruise, with a Marine fighter squadron, 223 reserve midshipmen, and five visiting professors of disciplines ranging from economics to forestry on board.

All this was quickly changed and the division disassembled to solve some urgent problems. *Badoeng Strait* landed her professors at Pearl and returned hastily to San Diego, where she disgorged the trainees and began loading more Marine aircraft and aircrews on a 24-hour basis. *Sicily,* alerted on 2 July, was sailed on the 4th for Pearl Harbor and Guam, to strengthen the antisubmarine capabilities of Western Pacific forces. The division commander, Rear Admiral Richard W. Ruble, was ordered forward with his staff by air to help handle the rapid build-up of naval air strength in Japan. On 10 July admiral and staff reached Tokyo, and two days later Ruble took over command of Task Group 96.2, Naval Air Japan.

The three Canadian destroyers, earlier alerted, sailed from the west coast on 5 July. On the 6th, in accordance with his orders of a week before, Rear Admiral Hartman sortied his cruisers from Long Beach, joined up with four fleet oilers, six destroyers, and five submarines, and headed for Pearl Harbor. This westward deployment of submarines had been ordered by CincPacFleet as a precautionary measure, in view of the possible commitment of Russian naval units to the Korean conflict. But this fear was to prove groundless, none of these boats was moved west of the islands, and submarine strength in the Western Pacific was increased only by the submarine transport *Perch,* requested by the Marines for special raiding purposes.

Admiral Hartman's force was only a day out of Long Beach when *Toledo* was ordered forward at best speed, and two days later *Helena* and Destroyer Division 111 were detached from the task group with orders to hurry onward. Thus scattered by the need for haste the ships steamed west: *Toledo* reached Pearl Harbor on the 9th and left on the 11th; the *Helena* group arrived on the 11th and left on the 13th; the tankers, the submarines, and the two remaining destroyers pressed on behind. For destroyers en route to the Far East the distances west of Pearl posed problems of fuel consumption: steaming at 24 knots would save a day in transit, as compared to steaming at economical speed, but would also necessitate refuelling. But the oilers with which they had left the coast were far behind, none was available at Pearl for forward deployment, and the facilities at Midway Island, on the direct route westward, had been deactivated in May on instructions from the Department of Defense.

The budgetary ceiling had thus affected not only the strength of the Pacific Fleet but also its mobility in time of crisis. Reactivation of Midway was clearly in the cards, but for the moment extemporization was necessary. Two chief petty officers, recent graduates of the Service Force Petroleum School, were rounded up and embarked on the first destroyer as it was leaving Pearl Harbor. On arrival at Midway the chiefs activated the fuelling system and replenished two of the destroyers from the oil which remained in the tanks, while *Helena* refueled the others.

With the war still in its second week very considerable reinforcements were on their way. Three days after American troops first entered action, naval fighting strength equal to the original Western Pacific deployment had set sail from the continental United States. But the departure of these units from the west coast found the Pacific Fleet approaching the bottom of the barrel. On 8 July, in order to provide some slight reserve for new contingencies, the Chief of Naval Operations authorized the activation of certain units of the mothball fleet.

4. Naval Logistics

The westward movement of so large an increment of naval strength posed urgent problems of logistic support. The naval population of the Western Pacific, which on 25 June approached 11,000, was to more than triple in the space of five weeks. To plan and organize in one month's time for the support of such a force 6,000 miles from home is no mean problem, the more so when, in addition to food and clothing, these individuals are busily consuming fuel, ammunition, equipment, and spare parts at an accelerated rate.

Overseas stocks of the countless items needed to support a modern fighting force were limited. At Pearl Harbor a supply officer could find everything, or almost everything, but to the westward the situation was spotty. At Yokosuka, by good fortune, there were fairly sizable supplies of general materials and nucleus stocks of technical spares. But Guam, which had supported very large naval forces during the war against Japan, had nothing: the island's mission of fleet support had been cancelled in 1947. At Subic Bay in the Philippines there were small quantities of various items, but Subic, originally planned as a major fleet base, had been reduced to partial ·maintenance status in January. All this had been done in the name of economy; it had been rationalized by the stated intention of providing mobile support for any forces west of Pearl Harbor; such support was now called for with a vengeance.

The concept of mobile support for the fighting ships of the U.S. Navy has a long history. In its origins it dates back to the War with Tripoli when the frigate *John Adams,* with reduced armament, was assigned to shuttle service between the Chesapeake and the Mediterranean carrying drafts of men and shipments of supplies for Commodore Preble's squadron. But provision of the spare spars and cordage, the pease and salt meat, which the *Adams* brought out, was simplicity itself compared to the problem of supporting a modern navy. Long before the electronic age the progress of technology had threatened to restrict the radius of fleet action, in the first instance in the fundamental question of fuel.

The fuel problem and the other logistic complications which came with mechanization first faced the United States in connection with the Civil War blockade of Gulf coast ports. They arose again following the War with Spain, as the immense distances of the Pacific came to be realized, and were emphasized over the years by increasing possibilities of trouble with Japan. As early as 1904 Civil Engineer Andrew C. Cunningham had put forward the idea of a floating base; efforts at mobile support of naval forces in Europe had been made during the First World War; and by the middle twenties the concept of the mobile base had become the accepted one for support of the fleet at sea. Following Pearl Harbor performance caught up with precept, and in the later stages of the Pacific War great fleets of tenders, repair ships, and floating drydocks moved westward from atoll to atoll in attendance on the striking forces.

The concept of mobile support had abundantly proved itself as both economically sound and strategically effective. But its wartime embodiment, the vast collection of men and material which made up Service Squadron 10, was no more. The total roster of Service Force ships assigned to the Western Pacific on 25 June consisted of one destroyer tender, one reefer, a fleet oiler on shuttle duty for the Seventh Fleet, a fleet tug, and an LST on loan to Task Force 90 for training purposes. There had been no prior planning for a minor war, or indeed for anything short of full mobilization. In the sphere of fleet logistics, as elsewhere, the response to the North Korean invasion was to be an exercise in extemporization.

Responsibility for the logistic support of the Pacific Fleet and of other Pacific naval activities lay with the Service Force Pacific Fleet, commanded by Rear Admiral Francis C. Denebrink, whose headquarters were at Pearl Harbor. Like everyone else the Service Force had felt the impact of the fiscal year just ending. Not only in the Western Pacific had mobile support been reduced to a bare minimum: the only hospital ship and the only fleet stores issue ship in the Pacific Fleet had been decommissioned, and the lone dock landing ship in Admiral Denebrink's command had escaped this fate only as a result of the requirements of Operation Greenhouse, the atomic test series then pending at Eniwetok.

The total strength of the Pacific Fleet Service Force, as of the end of June, came to 91 auxiliaries of various types. The largest share of these mobile support units, 47 ships, was organized in Service Squadron 1, Captain Bernard L. Austin. This command was responsible for the logistic support of fleet units in the Eastern Pacific, including Alaska; most of its units were located in west coast ports. At Pearl Harbor, under the direct control of ComServ-Pac, were the 26 auxiliaries of the Logistic Support Group, whose area of responsibility included fleet units and bases in the Western, Central, and South Pacific. The 18 remaining units were assigned to Service Division 51, a subordinate echelon of the Logistic Support Group, located at Guam and charged with the administration of Service Force responsibilities in the Marianas and Carolines.

In the first days of hostilities uncertainty as to the identity of the enemy and the extent of the underwater threat had led ComNavFE to call for additional small craft for offshore patrol. In response to this request Admiral Denebrink recommended to CincPacFleet the reactivation of the three minesweepers in caretaker status at Yokosuka, and of five subchasers and three fleet tugs. At the same time the Service Force staff turned its attention to the urgent problems of logistic support for the forces going into action in the Far East.

Ammunition came first. At Yokosuka, under the control of Commander Fleet Activities Japan, there was a small stock of some two or three thousand tons of various types, but with one surprising deficiency: there was no antisubmarine ordnance in Japan. Ammunition in the Philippines was negligible; at Guam there were some 6,000 tons. Necessarily, therefore, the supply of items lacking at Yokosuka and Guam, and the replacement of expenditures from these stocks, had to be made from the Hawaiian Islands, more than 3,000 miles away, where there were wartime leftovers in massive quantities. To lift ammunition to the forward area, ComServPac had available a single ammunition ship, *Mount Katmai,* at Port Chicago, and an assortment of cargo types which, with special sheathing of the holds, could be made to do.

Lacking word from Admiral Joy as to the pattern of anticipated needs, and lacking also a subordinate Service Force commander in the forward area to coordinate requirements, the staff at Pearl Harbor undertook at once, by deduction and by intuition, an estimate of what was required. This work was expeditiously done. The estimate was ready by the night of 26–27 June in the form of a revised loading plan for *Mount Katmai,* and was at once promulgated by dispatch for comment. Within two days the views of the operational commanders concerned had been received and integrated and a detailed loading list was on its way by air to the west coast.

But *Mount Katmai's* arrival was weeks away, and in the next few days, as special requests came in from ComNavFE, ammunition was moved forward from Guam by cargo ship. In the absence of underwater ordnance in Japan, and with the submarine problem still unclarified, depth charges were given priority: on 13 July a shipload reached Yokosuka, followed on the next day by another of 5-inch and 40-millimeter ammunition. By this time also a load of 8-inch cruiser ammunition was at sea en route from Guam to Sasebo, and another ship had been sailed for Buckner Bay with aircraft ordnance for Task Force 77.

The second problem of immediate and overriding importance was that of fuel. In the Pacific the responsibility for petroleum supply was a divided one: Commander Service Force, as logistic agent for CincPac, was responsible for the Pacific Area outside of General MacArthur's command, while the Area Petroleum Office at CincFE's headquarters was charged with procurement for the forces of the Far East Command. Throughout the Pacific POL inventories were low, in consequence of directives based on budgetary restrictions; this situation was potentially most dangerous in aviation gasoline, production of which is inelastic and not susceptible to rapid expansion. Anticipating a rapid increase in consumption, ComServPac's Petroleum Office made early requests for larger allocations, and fortunately so. The timely arrival of these from the continental United States would provide adequate stocks for the trans-Pacific pipeline, and make it possible to help out the Far East Command, where serious shortages developed owing to lack of similar foresight.

The need for aviation gasoline was matched by that for black oil for the naval forces moving westward. Of the ten fleet oilers assigned to the Service Force, two were on shuttle duty serving the Seventh Fleet and the mid-Pacific, eight were in west coast ports. Four of these—*Cimarron, Cacapon, Caliente,* and *Platte*—were immediately ordered forward and sailed in company with Admiral Hartman's cruisers and destroyers. Three were routed onward from Pearl to Okinawa and Japan, while *Caliente,* on 24 July, discharged 65,000 barrels of fuel oil at Midway Island to keep that newly reactivated base in business.

The emphasis on floating support for fleet units, made necessary by the limited base facilities in the Western Pacific, was desirable for other reasons as well. A prime virtue of naval power is its mobility; if the bases can also move this virtue is increased. For reasons of economy, and to obviate the need for an extensive shore establishment in Japan which would itself be logistically costly and complicating, mobile support was also desirable. But complete floating support for the fleet was well beyond the capabilities of the Service Force as then constituted, or indeed under any circumstances short of pretty complete mobilization. Again it is worth emphasizing how fortunate it was for this campaign that the resources and productive facilities of the Japanese base were close to hand. In the Second World War almost complete support for forces overseas had been provided from the continental United States. But now at midcentury the effort was made to live off the land, and the foraging party reappeared, not in the form of the sergeant with his squad, but in that of the supply officer armed with contract and fountain pen.

Yet however helpful, the Japanese economy could not support the war alone, and two questions called for immediate answers from Admiral Denebrink and his staff. What Service Force units would be required in the operating areas to support the fleet? What shipping would be necessary, over and above that provided by MSTS, to keep the 6,000-mile Pacific pipeline full? A study of anticipated needs led to requests on 5 and 8 July for the activation of two gasoline tankers and the assignment of another ammunition ship, and then on the 9th the full bill was presented in a memorandum to CincPacFleet which called for the activation of 58 auxiliaries in 16 categories ranging from destroyer tenders down to tugs.

By this time the redeployment of Service Force units was well underway. Seven auxiliaries were headed north from the Marianas and the Carolines, six were on their way from Pearl Harbor, and another seven from the west coast of the United States. This very considerable movement into the forward area consisted of two destroyer tenders, two reefers, three cargo ship types, three fleet oilers, two gasoline tankers, two repair ships, five fleet tugs, and a dock landing ship. So much activity required a coordinating authority and so, at ComServPac's request, the Chief of Naval Operations on 10 July established Service Squadron 3 as the Navy's principal logistic agent in the Western Pacific. Captain Austin was transferred from Service Squadron 1 to take command of this new force, which was gathering at Buckner Bay.

5. The Marine Brigade

The first few days of combat had made it evident that the North Korean People's Army was not going to be frightened home again either by United Nations resolves or by the intervention of token American forces. Shortly it seemed doubtful whether the commitment of all available Far Eastern strength would stop the invaders. Further reinforcements became increasingly urgent, and these, necessarily, had to come from outside the theater. Although foreign help had been promised, its arrival was some time off. But in Hawaii the Army was preparing a regimental combat team for sailing, on the west coast a division had been alerted, and MSTS was assembling the shipping for these lifts. And the Marines, too, were on their way.

In addition to the ten Army combat divisions in existence in 1950 the United States could also call on the two divisions of the Fleet Marine Force.

616779 O—62——7

Total Fleet Marine Force strength at this time was about 28,000 men, of whom 12,000 were in FMF Pacific, in the 1st Marine Division and its attached 1st Marine Aircraft Wing, and the balance of almost 16,000 in FMF Atlantic, the 2nd Marine Division and MAW 2. Headquarters of the Fleet Marine Force Pacific were at Pearl Harbor; the 1st Marine Division was at Camp Pendleton, California; Marine Air Wing 1 was at nearby El Toro. Like all branches of the armed forces the Marines had suffered from austerity: all units were understrength, and the 1st Marine Division was operating with two platoons to a company and two companies to a battalion.

The United States Marines have landed on many foreign shores since Lieutenant O'Bannon and his immortal six set out from Alexandria to march on Tripoli. But in the middle of the 20th century their special claim to fame, and the basis of their mission as defined in the National Security Act, rested on their development of the techniques of amphibious warfare. The success of the Corps in developing workable techniques for assault from the sea against defended objectives, considered by some the most far-reaching tactical innovation of the Second World War, was achieved in the face of overwhelming expert opinion that such attacks were no longer possible. Contemplating the sad spectacle of Gallipoli, a distinguished naval historian of the interwar period had commented that while Great Britain might perhaps survive another war, she could never survive another Churchill. In fact, however, she did both, while the Navy and Marines destroyed the presumed basis for this judgment by spearheading the amphibious advance from Guadalcanal to Okinawa, an advance in which they suffered no single check.

The United States now found itself confronted with difficulties in Korea, a peninsula with a long shoreline and located on the far side of an ocean. A priori, one would assume this a made to order theater for the Marines, and the responsible Commander in Chief had already shown his interest: early in 1950, in connection with his mission of defending Japan, General MacArthur had requested instructors to train his occupation forces in amphibious warfare. Navy and Marine training specialists had consequently been provided, along with Admiral Doyle's Amphibious Group, and had just begun to hold school in Japan when the invasion broke.

Yet amphibious warfare, in 1950, was out of favor with many due to strategic preconceptions, and the Marines with others for other reasons. In the congressional hearings on the unification troubles the Chairman of the Joint Chiefs of Staff had described the amphibious landing as a thing of the past, and had observed that anyhow he had taken part in the two greatest amphibious operations of history and the Marines had not. The prediction awaited the test of time; the statement, certainly correct, might well have been amplified to point out that the Army troops which stormed the beaches of Europe did so in accordance with doctrine developed by the

Marine Corps and the Navy. Even in war the pen and the guiding brain are at times as significant as the sword.

Quite apart from their amphibious specialty, there were other advantages to be derived from the commitment of the Marines to Korea. What was needed was needed fast; the Corps lives with its bags packed. While the requirement to go anywhere at short notice had made the Marines mobile, the requirements of the assault from the sea had led to the development of an extremely powerful package of strength. Man for man there was probably no more powerful force in existence anywhere. The ground elements made up a heavily armed and highly professional outfit in which every individual could handle a rifle. The air-ground team, long hoped for but delayed by World War II requirements, had by the end of that war become a fact, and the Marines had no need to wheedle their necessities in the upper regions out of a separate force with separate preoccupations. All their pilots had had infantry training; all were carrier qualified, and could operate from decks offshore until airstrips became available. With these capabilities, and with this understanding of the requirements on the surface of the earth, they commanded and deserved the confidence of the riflemen below.

Again, the Fleet Marine Force was well trained. As a small organization, the Marines had found it possible to maintain recruiting without recourse to trade and travel propaganda; since their withdrawal from North China they had been able to attend to business without the distractions of occupation duty. Between December and June the units of FMF Pacific had gone through two field exercises of regimental size or larger, an amphibious demonstration, and various lesser drills involving submarines, helicopters, and the seizure of San Nicholas Island by an airlifted battalion.

A further factor of importance, and one again suggestive of the realism of the Corps, was its readiness for movement. Naval movement plans, it is true, are almost automatic, but for other forces preparations are necessary, and the Marines appear to have been the only people in the armed services with concrete arrangements for anything less than that Armageddon euphemistically known as a "general emergency." In 1948 plans had been worked out for the rapid movement of a regimental combat team and a Marine air group from the west coast to any point in the Pacific, and the materiel bureaus of the Navy Department were on ten-day notice to provide the necessary mounting-out equipment.

Finally, Marines are volunteers both in fact and by temperament. Their inbred highly competitive attitude had been strengthened by the post-war atmosphere within the Pentagon, with its repeated rumors of plans for the abolition of the Corps or for its limitation to guard duty. At Corps headquarters, where there hangs a painting of the Korean landing of 1871, there was little question as to involvement in this war, and on 28 June the Commandant of the Marine Corps, General Clifton B. Cates, USMC, recommended to the Chief of Naval Operations employment of the Fleet Marine Force in Korea. Three days later Admiral Sherman queried CincPacFleet as to the time necessary to move out a battalion landing team or a regimental combat team. Admiral Radford's reply, received on Sunday the 2nd, stated that a BLT could be loaded in four days and sailed in six, and an RCT loaded in six and sailed in ten. CNO at once advised Admiral Joy by dispatch that a Marine regimental combat team could be made available to CincFE if desired, and this offer, relayed to General MacArthur by ComNavFE in person, was accepted with enthusiasm. Before this busy Sunday was over the 1st Marine Division had been alerted and Admiral Sherman, with JCS approval, had ordered CincPacFleet to move an RCT with appropriate attached air strength to the Far East for employment by CincFE.

Three days after these orders to Admiral Radford, Fleet Marine Force Pacific issued its operation plan. This prescribed the task organization of the force, designated the 1st Provisional Marine Brigade (Reinforced), which was to be built around the 5th Marines from Camp Pendleton and Marine Aircraft Group 33 from El Toro. Command of the brigade was assigned Brigadier General Edward A. Craig, USMC, assistant commander of the 1st Marine Division, while Brigadier General Thomas J. Cushman, USMC, deputy commander of the 1st Marine Aircraft Wing, became both deputy brigade commander and commanding general of the wing's forward echelon. In an age of specialization this flexibility, which could be matched by no other ground force in any country, is worth remark: the routine step of making the aviator the second in command of the brigade was another promise of close teamwork between ground and air.

From the time of the warning order, division and wing staffs had been hard at work on the problems of mounting out the brigade. The task of bringing the various components up to authorized war strength was complicated by the fact that the summer period of leave and transfer had begun, and by a directive of 3 July from the Commandant of the Corps which required that all sergeants and below whose enlistments would expire before March be transferred and left behind. But leaves were cancelled and transfers rescinded, and not all of the enlisted personnel were willing to accept this high-handed treatment by headquarters.

By 7 July, when the brigade was formally activated, shortages were being filled by personnel from the Marine Barracks at Camp Pendleton and from west coast stations. Supplies and gear were moving from Pendleton and from the storage center at Barstow in the California desert to the staging areas. The time from receipt of the alert had been well employed, but the speed with which the brigade moved out owed much to earlier planning, and to the ten-day readiness stocks of material which had been maintained for both ground forces and the air group. By the 9th, when the first ships became available, embarkation plans had been completed and loading could be begun.

The brigade had been built around the infantry strength of the 5th Marines, with 132 officers and 2,452 enlisted men. The next largest ground component, the artillery, was provided by the 1st Battalion of the 11th Marines, 44 officers and 474 enlisted men. To these were added motor transport, medical, shore party, engineer, tank, and amphibious tractor companies; detachments of signal, ordnance, service, reconnaissance, and military police units; an amphibious truck platoon; and the organic observation squadron, VMO 6, with eight OY observation planes and four HO3S-1 Sikorsky helicopters. The air strength of the brigade, the forward echelon of the 1st Marine Aircraft Wing, was made up of MAG 33's two day fighter squadrons, totaling 48 F4U-4B aircraft, and one night fighter squadron of F4U-5Ns.

The responsibility for producing the shipping to lift the Marine Brigade fell upon Rear Admiral Francis X. McInerney, acting commander of the Amphibious Force, Pacific Fleet. To provide this lift a supply expedition which was preparing to sail for Point Barrow, Alaska, was hastily modified, and its commanding officer, Captain Louis D. Sharp, Jr., was designated Commander, Provisional Transport Group. All available ships were incorporated in the Transport Group, and the capacity thus made available was almost enough. Except for some motor transport everything was taken along, but this deficiency would be remedied on the far shore, by capture from the enemy or the Army.

Ground forces of the brigade embarked at San Diego in the three attack transports of Captain Sharp's Task Group 53.7, *George Clymer, Henrico,* and *Pickaway;* in the attack cargo ships *Whiteside* and *Alshain;* and in the LSDs *Gunston Hall* and *Fort Marion.* Air group personnel and equipment boarded the transport *General A. E. Anderson* and the attack cargo ship *Achernar* at Terminal Island; aircraft and aircrews were embarked on *Badoeng Strait.* On 12 July, exactly ten days after the receipt of the warning order, the LSDs sailed from San Diego with the tanks and the amphibious tractor companies, and two days later the rest of the convoy followed.

General Craig and General Cushman had remained behind to tidy up administrative detail. On the 15th they departed by air from El Toro to Japan, where they arrived on 19 July. Another Marine, however, had preceded them to Tokyo. The Commanding General of the Fleet Marine Force Pacific, Lieutenant General Lemuel C. Shepherd, Jr., USMC, had flown west on the 7th, and on the 10th conferred with General MacArthur. On the same day, as a result of this discussion, CincFE asked the Joint Chiefs for the entire 1st Marine Division.

6. *Air Transport and Air Reinforcement*

No aspect of armed force has received more emphasis in our time than the military employment of the airplane. First conceived of as a means by which the commander could tell what was going on on the other side of the hill, aircraft have had their principal impact in two other areas: as long-range gun, extending the distance at which blows may be aimed and delivered, and as flying vehicle, capable of the rapid movement of goods regardless of obstacles on the surface of the earth. With ground and surface reinforcements headed westward, it remains to consider the air aspect of the trans-oceanic deployment in support of the Korean campaign.

This, it need hardly be said, was no independent phenomenon. The use of the air is intimately connected with the course of affairs below. In reconnaissance as in transport, whether of explosives, troops, or supplies, the mission of the airplane is defined by the course of events on land and sea. And while in all these functions the airplane has developed tremendous capabilities, in all it depends on surface logistic support. If, as has so often been said, communications dominate war, the aerial capability has both solved old requirements and imposed new ones in this controlling field.

Command of the air, so essential to western-style war, depends in a trans-oceanic theater on command of the seas. Like the Army, the Air Force is projected, supported, and sustained by surface shipping. In some sense this fact has been neglected as the result of what may be described as optical illusion. Aircraft in flight, indeed, resemble air theorists on paper in their apparent independence of logistic problems. But although the flexibility of the airplane is extraordinary, within its limits of range and performance, it is equally true that the logistic requirements of a modern air force are immense. Where bases do not exist they must be constructed; where they do exist they must be supported; the appetite for fuel and ammunition, spare parts, shops and tools, runway surfacing, buildings and personnel, which is evinced by any considerable deployment of air strength is a very impressive one. The plane in the air on its mission is the end product of an elaborate, costly, and highly developed organization.

Yet given the base facilities and the aircraft, it is possible to deliver across great distances not only ammunition to the ultimate consumer but much else besides. In the Second World War the possibilities of airborne operations were dramatically demonstrated by the German conquests of Norway and Crete, and by the Allied airdrop into Normandy in 1944. Equally if not more important were the logistic feats accomplished through air supply: in Burma the British planned a whole campaign around this capability; in France, although insufficient air tanker capacity halted Patton's tanks in 1944, the final advance into Germany saw the airlift bringing up half a million gallons of gasoline a day. Nothing so colossal was to supervene in

Korea, although air supply would prove a priceless asset, but from the beginning air transport was called on to assist the overseas deployment.

Since air transport offered the quickest method of alleviating critical shortages, the call for help was urgent. From all services requests came flooding in for vitally needed gear and personnel. For Naval Forces Far East, communicators to handle the dispatch load, boat crews for undermanned amphibious shipping, individuals of all ranks and rates were hurried west to build up personnel to something approaching wartime complement, to staff the expanding base facilities, and perhaps most urgent of all, to staff the staffs. The result of this overwhelming demand was to force an extremely rapid expansion upon the air transport facilities of the armed services, the Military Air Transport Service and the Fleet Logistic Air Wing.

The Military Air Transport Service, operated by the Air Force, is the aerial counterpart of MSTS. Established as a unified logistic organization pursuant to the National Security Act, MATS operates what is in effect a scheduled airline between major traffic generating points around the world. To supplement this schedule by providing feeder service to dispersed naval activities, the flexibility of non-scheduled operations, and something to fall back on in a general emergency when MATS would be pretty well mortgaged to other activities, the Navy had set up its Fleet Logistic Support Wings. Of these there had originally been two, one on each coast, but the passion for centralizing which had afflicted the Defense Department had led to their merger, despite objections from the fleet commanders, into a single Fleet Logistic Air Wing, responsible to the Chief of Naval Operations and with headquarters at Patuxent River, Maryland.

At the outbreak of hostilities three Navy air transport squadrons were employed in the Pacific to supplement the regular MATS schedule. One, under the operational control of CincPacFleet, was operating six R5Ds from Barber's Point, Oahu; the second was flying four JRM Martin Mars flying boats out of Alameda; the third, with five R5Ds and two R6Os was at Moffett Field. This capacity was speedily to prove inadequate.

On 28 June CincPacFleet asked the Chief of Naval Operations for operational control of the west coast squadrons, and two days later the request was granted. On 1 July, in his capacity as CincPac, Admiral Radford requested the commander of the Pacific Division of MATS to double his lift within ten days. On the 4th, as CincPacFleet, he ordered the Commander 14th Naval District to establish facilities for transport aircraft at Midway, and called upon Patuxent River for an additional increment of planes. Three more R5Ds were at once assigned the Moffet Field squadron, but backlogs were piling up on the west coast, more were urgently needed, and on the 7th the Fleet Marine Force Pacific was asked to contribute ten more transport aircraft.

All this was little enough. Air transport is not always the economical way of moving men and goods, but its expediency in time of crisis creates irresistible pressures. Despite the transfer of additional equipment to the Pacific run, and despite creation of a west coast coordinating office to make some sense out of priorities inflated beyond all meaning, the jam increased. By mid-July personnel awaiting transportation totalled nine times FLAW's maximum weekly lift, the cargo backload was seven times maximum, and MATS, in a similar situation, was chartering commercial planes. Nor had the theoretical virtues of centralization held up in the emergency: Patuxent River was too far away, and before the month was out CNO had established the Fleet Logistic Air Wing Pacific under the control of CincPacFleet.

By the end of July all available Navy and Marine R5Ds in the continental United States had been appropriated, some had been taken off the Port Lyautey run, and the number flying the Pacific had increased from 11 to 56. This build-up, while speeding vital cargoes, brought its own problems of surface logistics in the need for fuel, parts, and administrative personnel along the route westward through Oahu, Johnston, Kwajalein, and Guam, and in the requirement for the reactivation of facilities at Midway.

In Korea, in the meantime, the air war had begun. Like the war at sea, it began in the exploitation phase. But while command of the air was not seriously contested, there were still logistic and operational problems to solve. To ensure uninterrupted maintenance, both of air transport and air action against the enemy, ComServPac had already requested increased allocations of aviation fuel. To keep the Air Force bombers supplied with ammunition the west coast loading facilities had been reactivated. Happily, there was no need to construct bomber fields in the Far East. The capacity of Air Force bases in Japan and Okinawa exceeded the forces available, and shortly after the commencement of hostilities two B–29 bombardment groups were flown out from the United States to make up, with the 19th Group already there, the Bomber Command of the Far East Air Forces.

Unfortunately the Superforts, so rapidly deployed, were not the weapons best suited to repel the North Korean invasion. Major General Emmet O'Donnell, USAF, who headed up the Bomber Command, wanted to "go to work on burning five major cities in North Korea to the ground, and to destroy completely every one of about 18 major strategic targets." Here once again was the ancient belief, so often disproven and so often reaffirmed, that the flattening of cities will speedily end a war. But the burning process, vetoed in Washington, was somewhat inconsistent with the early concept of police action, and only a confirmed North Korean booster could have discovered 18 major strategic targets in that country. In this war the supplies came from over the border, while the target of priority was the invading army.

Yet if the B–29 was not the ideal weapon to provide what was required, the jet fighters assigned to the defense of Japan were, in the first instance, hardly better. The cycle of strategic planning and weapons design, predicated upon the big war, had all but priced the Air Force out of the kind of operations which were now so urgently needed. Emphasis on the Sunday punch, natural enough under budgetary restrictions which meant that something had to go, had largely eliminated the workaday measures of limited war. But once again, under pressure of emergency, the Air Force demonstrated its notable ability to act with vigor in time of crisis against all its peacetime preachment. In the first week of July the crucial needs of the ground forces brought the decision to reconvert back again, and to abandon the jets for the F–51 Mustang with its superior endurance, lifting capacity, and ability to operate from rudimentary Korean airstrips. The next step was to get more planes.

The obvious imminence of increased aircraft attrition had led the Chief of Naval Operations to include, in his orders of 8 July to the Reserve Fleet, instructions to activate two transport aircraft carriers. But to get these moving would take time, and while there were a few Mustangs in Japan, FEAF's need for more was urgent. *Boxer,* recently returned from the Western Pacific and awaiting overhaul, had the capacity and the speed, and was ordered into the breach. After emergency repairs at San Diego, she sailed for Alameda, where on the 8th she began to load. The Air Force got the planes to the docks and on the 14th, carrying 145 F–51s and six L–5s for the Air Force, 19 Navy planes, a Marine GCA unit, and a capacity load of fuel, ammunition, and personnel, *Boxer* steamed out the Golden Gate and headed west.

By mid-July the waters of the Pacific and the air above them were again bearing westward a great burden of military traffic. Fighting ships and their numerous auxiliaries, Army troops and the Marine Brigade, planes for the Air Force, food, fuel, and ammunition for all were converging upon the Far Eastern theater. Hour by hour the 6,000-mile distance was decreasing. If a line could be held into August a wholly new order of force would be available to stem the Communist aggression. But distances in Korea were decreasing too. By 15 July North Korean forces had covered half of the 225-mile journey to Pusan. The foothold was not yet secure. Whether it could be held depended on the course of events in the Korean hills, in the Korean air, and along the Korean coasts.

CHAPTER V

Into the Perimeter

1. The Korean Theater

ALTHOUGH the conduct of war is always, in large measure, an exercise in applied geography, in Korea this was more than usually the case. On land, at sea, and in the air, the movements of forces and the employment of weapons were greatly affected by the nature of the arena.

The Korean peninsula, divided by the fortunes of international politics, itself divides the Yellow Sea from the Sea of Japan. S-shaped, and with its long axis oriented generally north and south, the country lies between the parallels of 34° and 42° North, and spans the latitude between Los Angeles and central Oregon, or between North Carolina and the southern New Hampshire border. Although Korean territory extends for almost 600 miles from north to south, the distance between eastern and western coasts nowhere exceeds 200 miles, and in places is little more than half that distance. One consequence of this geographical configuration is of striking military importance: with a total area of some 83,000 square miles, or of 85,000 if all the islands are included, only a small strip along the northern border is more than 100 miles from the sea.

But although Korea is surrounded by sea, its situation to leeward of the greatest of continents has given it a climate of extremes. While summer in the north is temperate the mountain winter is extremely bitter: even on the seacoast the mean January temperature at the Russian border is but 15° Fahrenheit. In southern Korea, by contrast, the climate is warm enough to permit the growing of cotton; summer temperatures reach the nineties, and the rains of June and July produce an exhausting combination of heat and humidity; at the peninsula's southwestern tip winters are frost-free and the August mean is 80°. Summer is also the season of typhoons, which form in the Marianas and move northwestward toward the East China Sea. Typically, they recurve in time to pass over southern Japan or through the Straits of Tsushima, with only their fringes affecting southeastern Korea; sometimes, however, they recurve late and cross the peninsula; always their approach brings problems for the navigator and the strategist.

For five years prior to the outbreak of war the 38th parallel had divided Korea into roughly equal parts. But the division was an illogical one, resulting in such oddities as the isolation of the Ongjin peninsula in the west, and the separation of the city of Haeju from its port facilities; still more important was its separation of the populous and agricultural south from the complementary industrial economy of the north. Yet the parallel was not the country's sole internal barrier, for long before geographers drew lines on maps, nature had divided this peninsula and subdivided it again.

Much of Korea is mountainous. In all the peninsula there are no true flatlands or plains. Like Italy with its Alps, Korea is protected from the continental land mass to the north by high mountains which fill the triangular area above the mouth of the Yalu River, and extend beyond the border to the Manchurian plain. Much of this triangle lies above 3,000 feet; peaks of over 6,000 feet are not uncommon; only along the coast does the altitude drop below 1,500 feet. The Yalu and Tumen Rivers, which separate Korea from Manchuria and from the Russian Maritime Provinces, have their origins in the Pai Shan range, which towers above 9,000 feet and is capped by perpetual snow.

Only three significant routes of access to the peninsula penetrate this formidable terrain. Of these the most important is the western corridor, along the lower reaches of the Yalu, through which the Japanese advanced in 1905 against the Russians and through which Communist Chinese forces would move against the United Nations. But there is also a gap in the mountains in central North Korea, formed by the valleys of the Tongno and Chongchon Rivers, while in the extreme northeastern corner of the country narrow valleys and a coastal strip lead down from eastern Manchuria and the Vladivostok region.

From the northern mountain mass a rocky cordillera runs southward, paralleling the eastern coast; along this shore, except in the embrasure at the head of the Korean Gulf between the seaport cities of Wonsan and Hungnam, the mountains descend steeply to the sea. North of Wonsan the coast is somewhat indented, with a number of harbors and towns; to the southward it is almost unbroken and the Korean divide, running within ten miles of the Sea of Japan, hems in a narrow and isolated ribbon of land where population is sparse, towns are small, and ports are few. Behind the coastal range the mountain spine recurves to.the southwest, diminishes for a time in altitude, and then rises again in the south central region to form an isolated massif with peaks of five and six thousand feet. From the axial range, throughout the length of the peninsula, razorbacked spurs run off to west and southwest, compartmenting the country.

These mountain spurs and isolated masses divide the populous western part of Korea into a series of river basins, draining into the Yellow Sea and the Korean Strait, which in earlier times formed the principal geographic

and economic units of the country.   Although not navigable by ocean-going
ships, these rivers remain of considerable internal importance: the principal
Korean ports lie at their mouths, and the capitals of North and South Korea
only a short way upstream.   Five of these rivers, two north and three south of
the 38th parallel, deserve the attention of the student of the Korean War.

The Chongchon River, northernmost of the strategically important west
coast streams, is blocked to ocean shipping by drying mud banks which extend far offshore.   But the central rail and road route to the north runs down
its valley; the town of Sinanju, near the river's mouth, is important as the
junction of the western and central routes from Manchuria; and the bridges
across the river are vulnerable to air attack.

Sixty miles to the southward the Taedong River, scene of the massacre of
the crew of the *General Sherman,* empties into the Yellow Sea.   Near its
mouth lies Chinnampo, a city of some 90,000, seaport of the important northern mining and industrial region.   Fifteen miles upstream the city of Kyomipo
contains Korea's largest iron and steel works; 30 miles to the northeastward
lies the North Korean capital of Pyongyang.   Once the ancient capital of the
country, Pyongyang contains the tombs of long-dead monarchs, including
that of Kija, legendary inventor of the topknot.   In the Sino-Japanese War
it was the scene of considerable fighting; early in the century it became the
last abode of the deposed emperor.   Under the Japanese it developed into a
considerable manufacturing city, with industry based on the neighboring
coal mines, and in due course, as the largest city in the north, became the
capital of the People's Republic.   Like the bridges over the Chongchon at
Sinanju, those which cross the Taedong at Pyongyang are of strategic
significance.

Most important of Korea's rivers is the Han, whose basin extends 150
miles from north to south and half that distance from east to west.   With its
principal tributaries, the Imjin and the Pukhan, the Han drains a major
portion of the country on both sides of the 38th parallel.   Rising only a few
miles from the east coast, these streams wind through the central mountains
before joining to pass the capital of Seoul and empty into the Yellow Sea near
the principal west coast port of Inchon.   For some 60 miles above its estuary
the lower Han runs in a more or less east-west line, cutting the western lowlands and forming a potentially important and defensible military position.

South of the Han basin and west of the coastal range the country is
drained by two important rivers.   Some 90 miles below Inchon the Kum
descends from the central massif to empty into the Yellow Sea; at its mouth
lies Kunsan, a principal shipping center for the agricultural regions of southwestern Korea.   In the southeastern corner of the peninsula, between the
coastal range and the central highlands, the Naktong River flows southward for 100 miles or so, then east, then south again to empty into the Korean
Strait.   Near the mouth of the Naktong is the excellent harbor of Pusan,

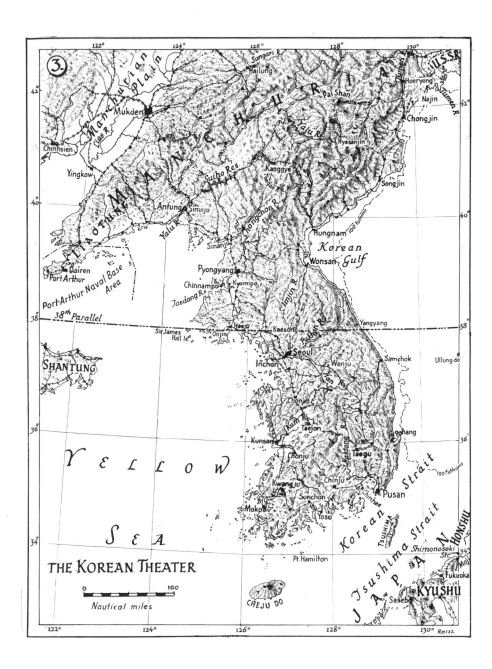

THE KOREAN THEATER

0   100

Nautical miles

93

second city of the country and port of ingress from Japan. To the north
the Naktong basin is divided from that of the Han by mountains more
than 3,000 feet high; on the west it is separated from the Kum by the
southern massif. Between these mountain masses the divide between the
Naktong basin and those of the Han and Kum diminishes in altitude;
through this gap runs the main line of Korean communications, linking
Japan and Pusan with the areas of heaviest population and agricultural
production and with the capital at Seoul.

The geography of Korea, in sum, is dominated by three main features:
a north blocked by high mountains; an east coast strip isolated by the mountain spine; and a broken piedmont to the west and south divided into a series
of river basins. Upon this pattern industrial man, in the person of the
Japanese, imposed his own geography. But although railroads, like faith,
can sometimes move mountains, in Korea this movement was only a partial
one. A traffic pattern could be developed which would unite the river basins,
but the linking of eastern and western provinces remained incomplete. The
mountain framework, broken, jumbled, and forbidding, continued to dominate the life of the country and to impose a north-south orientation which
made division at the 38th parallel the more painful.

The first Korean railroad, built early in the century by the Japanese,
linked the port of Pusan with the capital at Seoul. Although its construction
required 99 bridges and 22 tunnels, it was completed by the time of the
Russo-Japanese War. During that war its northward extension, from Seoul
to Sinuiju on the Yalu River, was rushed to completion for strategic purposes. But a decade elapsed before the coasts were linked by a line through
the mountain gaps between Seoul and Wonsan, and still longer until the construction of the east coast railroad, leading south from Siberia, began the
transformation of fishing villages into industrial towns.

By 1950 the main structure of rail and road communications had assumed an X-shaped pattern, with the crossing at Seoul. From Manchuria
in the northwest a line of double track spanned the Yalu at Sinuiju and ran
southeast to Sinanju. There it was joined by a line which crossed the
border below the Suiho reservoir, and by one coming from the upper reaches
of the Yalu by way of the Tongno-Chongchon gap. From Sinanju, where
these lines merged, the double track ran south to Pyongyang, Seoul, and
beyond. On the far side of the mountain masses, widely separated from
this west coast network, another rail line came south from the Vladivostok
complex. One coastal spur extended from the lower Tumen River to Najin
near the Russian border; farther inland, the main line ran south to Chongjin,
along the shore to the new manufacturing cities of Hungnam and Wonsan,
and on through the mountains to Seoul. On the east coast south of Wonsan
the track extended as far as Yangyang, just above the 38th parallel, but from

Yangyang to Pohang, 65 miles above Pusan, movement depended on road and sea.

The routes from the north thus converged at the Korean capital. Below this hub the railroad lines spread out again through South Korea. Two ran southeastward to the Pusan area, one leading directly from the valley of the Han into that of the Naktong, while the main line, now doubletracked, passed westward through Taejon in the Kum basin. From the latter, branches extended to the southwestern ports of Kunsan, Mokpo, and Yosu, but there was no south coast line, and rail traffic between Pusan and the southwestern ports had to be detoured northward around the central mountain massif.

To this extent the mountains remained unconquered. The lack of lateral communication remained the dominant feature of the transportation nets, road and rail alike. Of intercoastal rail links there were but two, one running north and south between Seoul and Wonsan, and one east and west, connecting the Wonsan-Hungnam region to Sinanju and Pyongyang. The Korean transport system thus rested upon three focal points, the Wonsan area on the east coast, the Pyongyang-Sinanju complex on the west, and Seoul. This situation sufficiently explains the strategic importance of these regions, for while the Korean road net was much more extensive than that of the railroad, and permitted access to most of the mountain regions, the roads were generally poor, unimproved, and unsuited to heavy mechanized equipment, and the anatomy of the highway system followed that of the rail lines.

Inevitably the scheme of maneuver adopted by the North Korean army for the conquest of this corrugated country was governed by the orientation of transport routes. The war had begun with a four-pronged invasion. The principal attack, delivered by the North Korean 3rd and 4th Infantry Divisions and the 105th Armored Brigade, and with two more divisions in reserve, was aimed south toward Seoul along the valley line from Wonsan. To the west the North Korean 6th Division overran the isolated Ongjin peninsula, and then joined with the 1st Division to move southeast, along the main line from Pyongyang, through Kaesong to the capital. In the central mountains the 2nd and the newly organized 7th Divisions attacked southward to Chunchon, terminus of a branch rail line from Seoul, after which the 2nd Division moved southwesterly down the railroad toward the capital while the 7th marched southward over mountain roads toward Wonju and the eastern of the two rail lines to Pusan. On the east coast beyond the divide, in a theater all its own, the North Korean 5th Division advanced southward along the shore road, leapfrogging ahead with small-scale amphibious operations.

Four prongs became three as the mass of the invading troops converged upon the capital's transportation nexus. In this second phase the 5th Division continued its independent operations east of the mountain spine, while in the central mountains the 7th Division, supported by constabulary troops, threaded its way southward through Wonju in the direction of Andong.

But the overwhelming bulk of the North Korean army, five first-line infantry divisions, two divisions of recent conscripts, and the armored brigade, had to be funneled through the Seoul complex. Once through the capital three divisions were peeled off to the southeast, and sent by rail and road to Wonju and Chungju to join the troops coming south through the mountains, while the remaining five moved down the main road. It was the advance guard of this massive force that Task Force Smith had run up against on 5 July.

By the end of the second week of war the American 24th Division had been driven out of Chonan and was retiring on Taejon. Somewhat surprisingly, despite its overwhelming numerical strength, the North Korean army now slowed its advance: a full week was to pass before the battle of Taejon began. Although not apparently appreciated at the time, this was the first evidence of the logistic limitations which forced the enemy to conduct his offensives in a series of massive lunges, and which prevented the maintenance of continuous pressure during an advance. Only on 20 July, after a bitter three day fight in which General Dean, the division commander, was captured, was Taejon lost and the 24th Division forced once again to retreat.

By this time the invasion was again a four-pronged affair. Unknown to the Americans, the North Korean army had split its main force a second time, and had sent the 6th Division with attached troops southward to Kunsan, which it entered on the 16th, and toward the southwestern tip of the peninsula. In pursuit of the retiring 24th Division the enemy main body, now seven divisions strong, pressed southeastward from Taejon along the main road and rail line toward the saddle which gives access to the Naktong Basin. Five divisions were moving through the mountains to the Andong area, while on the east coast the 5th Division continued its solitary southward course.

Although this east coast threat was opposed only by the ROK 3rd Division, it was accessible to bombardment from the sea. ROK forces were also operating on the northern mountain front in the Andong-Chungju area, and the U.S. 25th Division was moving up from Pusan to Hamchang, north of Taegu, to block this enemy advance. It was the plan of General Walker, who assumed command of all ground forces in Korea on 13 July, to employ the 1st Cavalry Division to reinforce the 24th Division on the main enemy route of advance, and to push the 29th Infantry, which was coming from Okinawa, west from Pusan to a blocking position south of the central hill mass. But by mid-July North Korean forces had covered more than half the distance to Pusan, and had occupied the line Chonju-Taejon-Yongjin-Yongdok, while the 1st Cavalry and the 29th Infantry had not yet arrived.

As Korean physiography and the Korean transportation net governed the land scheme of maneuver, so the hydrography of the area profoundly affected naval capabilities. The Korean coastline, generally straight along the Sea of Japan but deeply convoluted on south and west, has a length of some 5,400 miles. The steepness of the east coast, where the mountains rising from the sea confine road and railroad to a narrow coastal strip, has its underwater counterpart: except in the Gulf of Korea, off Wonsan and Hungnam, the 100-fathom curve runs close to shore, coastal shipping is exposed, and warships can get within gun range of land communication facilities. But in the south and west conditions are very different, and the countless islands and deeply indented bays which mark the disappearance of the mountain ranges into the sea provide shelter for coastal traffic. The operations of major fighting ships are restricted, and effective supervision of coastal shipping calls for small craft of shallow draft. On the western shore further complications arise from the extraordinary hydrographic conditions of the Yellow Sea: whereas the tidal range in the Sea of Japan is of the order of a foot or two, here it ranges from 20 to 36 feet; currents are considerable and the water turbid; nowhere are there depths greater than 60 fathoms, and the 20-fathom line runs ten miles offshore. Extending far from land and exposed at low tide, the mud banks which trapped the French frigates a century ago remain a hazard for the unwary.

These hydrographic facts of life and the very limited forces available combined to dictate the early activities of the Navy. Task Force 77 had been withdrawn to Okinawa, and the period from 5 to 17 July saw naval effort concentrated on the movement of troops and supplies into Pusan, gunfire support of ROK forces resisting the enemy east coast advance, and the planning of future operations.

2. 5–17 July: East Coast Bombardment

Off Korea's eastern shore, on 5 July, *Jamaica* relieved *Juneau* of her bombardment duties, and Admiral Higgins' flagship headed for Sasebo to replenish. On the same day the British cruiser, accompanied by *Black Swan,* fired on the road and bridge in 37° 16′ N, where the coastal route runs close to the sea, and on the 6th shot up oil tanks, bridges, and shipping, and silenced a shore battery at Chumunjin. On the 7th, as *Black Swan* was relieved by *Hart,* the British cruiser destroyed an oil tank north of Ulchin, cruised northward firing at the cliff roads, and ended the day with an effective bombardment of Yangyang, the end of the coastal rail line from the north, where more oil tanks were destroyed.

While *Jamaica* was at work, the reinforcement and reorganization of the South Korea Support Group was underway in accordance with ComNavFE's Operation Order 8–50. These instructions had been promulgated while the carriers were striking Pyongyang, and as Task Force 77 retired southward Admiral Andrewes was detached to join the Support Group; with *Belfast,*

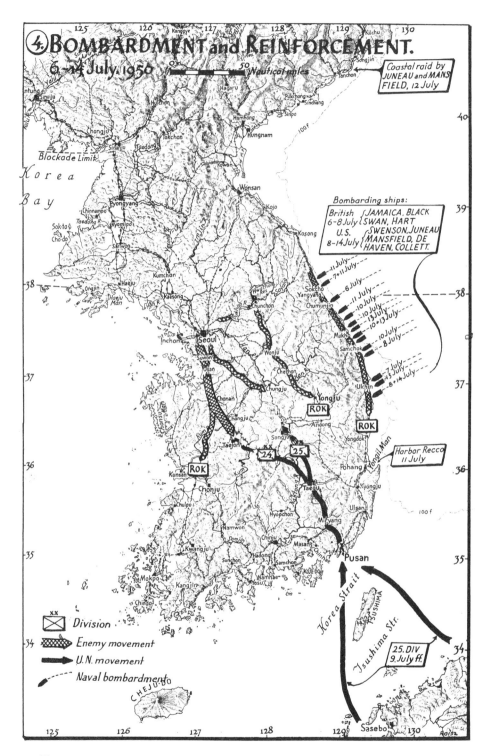

4. BOMBARDMENT and REINFORCEMENT.
6–14 July. 1950   0   50 Nautical miles

Coastal raid by
JUNEAU and MANS
FIELD, 12 July

Bombarding ships:
British { JAMAICA, BLACK
6–8 July { SWAN, HART
U.S.   { SWENSON, JUNEAU
8–14 July{ MANSFIELD, DE
         { HAVEN, COLLETT.

Harbor Recco
11 July

25. DIV
9. July ff.

Blockade Limit

Korea
Bay

XX
⊠ Division
▨▨▨ Enemy movement
➤ U.N. movement
- - - Naval bombardment

ROK
ROK
ROK
XX 24
XX 25

98

Cossack, and *Consort,* he proceeded to Sasebo where *Juneau* was replenishing. On 6 July Higgins and Andrewes flew to Tokyo to consult with Admiral Joy on the reorganization of the force and on problems of coordination with the Army in Korea and with the ROK Navy. An additional matter of importance, which had formed the subject of a dispatch from ComNavFE the previous day, was the question of the rail line on the northeast coast of Korea between Chongjin and Wonsan. Interruption of this line, both vital and vulnerable, would force the enemy to move rail traffic from the Vladivostok region by a circuitous route through Manchuria and down the west coast. Such interruption was urgently desired by Admiral Joy.

On the east coast 8 July saw *Jamaica* and *Hart,* now joined by *Swenson,* operating in the neighborhood of 37°. There, where the highway skirts the water's edge, road traffic was taken under fire, enemy shore batteries were engaged, and the British cruiser received a hit from a 75-millimeter shell which killed four and injured eight. Late in the day an alarm from Pohang brought *Jamaica, Hart,* and *Swenson* south at speed, while *Mansfield* broke off her escort duties and *Juneau* got underway from Sasebo. All five ships joined off Pohang on the morning of the 9th, but although the situation ashore was serious it was not yet out of control.

Since the threatened encirclement of the Korean forces north of the town remained only a threat, *Jamaica* was relieved and ordered to Sasebo, the destroyers were left to provide fire support, and *Juneau* proceeded to Pusan. There Admiral Higgins spent the day in conference with Korean and U.S. Army authorities, and in attempts to round up more interpreters and to obtain some solid information on the situation ashore. With evening the cruiser proceeded north again, and from 0200 to 0330 of the 10th bombarded the port of Samchok, following which she headed south to check once more on the situation at Pohang. But another more northerly mission was now brewing.

On the 10th a dispatch from ComNavFE instructed Higgins to extend his blockade as far north as practicable, and reemphasized the importance of the coastal tunnels on the Chongjin-Wonsan railroad. With these targets in mind equipment had already been procured and plans worked out to land a demolition party, and following another night on coastal patrol and a dawn bombardment of Yangyang and Sokcho, *Juneau* and *Mansfield* headed north for the region between Tanchon and Songjin.

At 2000 on the 11th the ships slowed and the demolition party, a lieutenant and four enlisted Marines and four gunner's mates, led by Commander William B. Porter, *Juneau*'s executive officer, transferred from the cruiser to *Mansfield.* Moving onward through the darkness the two ships reached the target area, ten miles south of Songjin, at midnight. *Mansfield* closed to within 1,000 yards of the beach, hove to and lowered her whaleboat, and the demolition party went on in. The landing was without incident, no opposition was encountered, and after considerable scrambling around the precipitous terrain the party managed to locate the tunnel and rig two 60-pound charges for detonation by the next train.

Although the results of the enterprise were unobserved, later reports of broadcasts by the North Korean radio seemed to indicate that the scheme had worked. By 0330 Commander Porter's party was back aboard, safe and sound, and with the distinction of having been the first members of the armed forces of the United States to invade Korea north of the 38th parallel. With their mission completed *Juneau* and *Mansfield* headed south again, and by noon of 12 July had rejoined *Swenson* on patrol between 37° and 38°.

The North Korean 5th Division had by this time reached south of the 37th parallel, and on the 12th the Army called for naval bombardment of the cliff road in 36°50'. On the 13th *De Haven* came up from Pusan with an artillery major for Admiral Higgins' staff and, although air and ground observers were still unavailable, communications were established with the 25th Division artillery detachment which was supporting the eastern front. Coastal fog on the 13th made targets hard to distinguish, but *Juneau* and *De Haven* nevertheless spent a busy day shooting at the cliff road in response to the Army request, at troops in Ulchin, at Mukho, at a railroad yard on the local line which leads back into the mountains, and at POL storage in the harbor of Samchok. The shooting was good, but the distressing ineffectiveness of 5-inch shells against roads and bridges made the arrival of 8-inch gunned cruisers from the United States appear increasingly urgent.

No requests from ashore were received on the 14th, and visibility remained poor, but with evening *Juneau* let off a few rounds against truck headlights on the road south of Ulchin. On the 15th, however, the cruiser and *De Haven* had a big day on the 20-mile stretch between 36°34' and 36°52' where the road runs generally close to the sea. For the first time an Army liaison plane was available to provide air spot, and a total of 645 rounds of 5-inch ammunition, expended against troops, shore batteries, and other targets, included a little night work against road traffic with the aid of star shell illumination. Joined by *Mansfield* on the next day, Higgins covered the coast between 36°30' and 37°15', and the three ships fired 173 rounds against targets of opportunity along the highway.

The 17th found *Juneau* fueling at Pusan while Admiral Higgins conferred with representatives of the Korean Navy. In the absence of the flagship, *Mansfield* and *De Haven* fired more than 400 rounds at miscellaneous targets in the same coastal area, and the British returned to the business of coastal bombardment with the cruiser *Belfast* and the destroyer *Cossack*. All this was useful, but the next day brought wholly unprecedented activity along the east coast in the form of an amphibious landing and a strike by the Seventh Fleet carrier force.

East coast bombardment: Juneau, flagship of Admiral Higgins' Support Group, rearming at Sasebo.   6 July 1950.
(USN 417996)

3. 3–30 July: The Pohang Landing

In the course of the first week of July American infantrymen had made contact with the enemy, the 24th Division had completed its movement to Korea, and the 25th Division had begun its embarkation. The Air Force had carried out attacks against the invading army and against targets of opportunity. A carrier strike had been flown against the North Korean capital, and the gunnery ships of Naval Forces Japan, augmented by British units, had continued their bombardment of the enemy's east coast invasion route. This week saw also the commencement of planning for the first amphibious operation of the campaign.

Admiral Doyle had brought his ships into Sasebo on 3 July only to find that his prospective passengers had already departed. Next day, on orders from Admiral Joy, he flew back to Tokyo with members of his staff to work on a plan for the landing of two regimental combat teams of the 1st Cavalry Division on the west coast of Korea. For this operation CincFE's preferred objective was Inchon, seizure of which would give access to the Seoul transportation complex and would cut the enemy's main supply route; alternatively, it was proposed to land the cavalrymen at Kunsan, at the mouth of the river Kum, whence they could strike inland toward Taejon and the enemy's right flank. The concept of a landing at Inchon was certainly strategically appealing, and was the germ of the operation which in September would put the enemy to ignominious flight. Its proposal in early July was evidence of early confidence in the efficacy of American intervention. But a few short days sufficiently demonstrated the visionary aspects of the idea, and even Kunsan, a much more modest alternative, was soon seen to be an impossibility. Almost at once the problem came to be not one of throwing the 1st Cavalry Division against the enemy's flank, but of getting this force into Korea while there remained some Korean territory to get into.

For four days Doyle's staff struggled with the Inchon and Kunsan problems. But although these objectives were discarded on the 8th, the work was not wholly wasted, for the need for an amphibious operation remained. Not only was it necessary to get the troops into Korea at the earliest possible moment, but to do so if possible without putting them through Pusan. By 6 July that port had handled 55 ships, more were on the way, and although the Army had set up a Pusan Logistical Command on the 4th, the port facilities were overloaded and in danger of being swamped.

Thus the situation called for a landing on the southern or eastern coast. The problem was to find an objective with easy access to the interior, north or west of Pusan and south and east of the advancing enemy. On 10 July Admiral Doyle's suggestion of Pohang was accepted, planning proceeded at an accelerated rate, and the activity was legalized on the 12th when Commander Naval Forces Far East issued his Operation Order 9–50. The affair was christened with the code name "Bluehearts."

The town of Pohang, which would shortly receive these visitors from overseas, had some 50,000 inhabitants. Located about 65 miles north of Pusan, it lies on the western shore of Yongil Man, a bay about six miles wide. To the southeast Yongil Man is protected by a high peninsula; on the west it is bordered by dunes, with sand hills beyond; the bottom affords good holding ground. At Pohang there were two long jetties with ten feet of water alongside where landing craft could unload; from Pohang rail and road communications ran south to Pusan and, more important for the purpose of the moment, west through the mountains to Taegu; there was an airstrip of sorts nearby. All in all, the choice of objective was both obvious and sound.

The speed with which the operation was planned and mounted was remarkable. Normal lead time for an amphibious operation is measured in weeks if not in months, but this objective was selected on 10 July, the expedition sailed on the 14th and 15th, and the landing was made on the morning of the 18th. Such an unprecedented schedule gave little time to collect information and to plan, train personnel, and assemble and modify gear. That these dates were met must be reckoned a considerable feat.

There were, it is true, certain favoring circumstances. The Amphibious Group was a good outfit, and knew its business; although the 1st Cavalry Division lacked amphibious experience its men were willing and put their backs into the work. As a consequence of CincFE's plan for amphibious training of occupation troops there were present in Japan, in addition to Doyle's ships, detachments from the Pacific Fleet Amphibious Training Command, including an Air and Naval Gunfire Liaison Company or "Anglico," which could be assigned to the Cavalry Division's staff to help with the conduct of the operation. All concerned, Army and Navy alike, were cheek by jowl in Tokyo, so that written communications could be eliminated and the business got on with by high-speed conversation.

But there were also major problems. The first of these, and one which would recur throughout the war, was the problem of intelligence: nobody knew much about Pohang. If one proposes to put landing craft up on the beach in order to get troops ashore it is desirable to know the underwater characteristics of the objective area, but although American forces had occupied South Korea, and had undertaken to conduct a mapping program, Korean beach gradients and much else remained a mystery. This, it may be observed, was no new experience; the same situation had prevailed in the Philippines after 40 years of American occupation. In January 1945, when American attack forces set forth for Lingayen Gulf and the reconquest of Luzon, information concerning those beaches, which other Americans had previously defended against the Japanese, was conspicuous by its absence. Yet experience had not taught convincingly the need for basic intelligence studies, and so far as South Korea was concerned the lack of information, as Admiral Doyle remarked, "was appalling."

Fortunately there was a solution. Pohang was still in friendly hands. On 10 July U.S. troops were reported guarding the airstrip, an aviation engineer unit was landed by LST, and Fifth Air Force was preparing to move in a fighter squadron. On the 11th some officers from the Amphibious Group and Cavalry Division staffs were flown to Pohang, to return two days later with useful and previously unavailable information. On the 15th a second group flew across to make such preparations for the landing as were possible, and to keep the command informed of enemy progress down the coastal road.

There was also a problem of shipping. The Amphibious Group had been sent westward for training purposes, and the four vessels available— a command ship, an attack transport, an attack cargo ship, and an LST— were wholly inadequate to the contemplated task. Fifteen more LSTs were procured from Scajap, and two attack cargo ships, *Oglethorpe* and *Titania,* were borrowed from the Military Sea Transportation Service for the assault phase. For the follow-up echelons shipping was also provided by MSTS, in the amount of three transports, a dozen Scajap LSTs, and four Japanese time-charter vessels.

Although *Oglethorpe* and *Titania* had retained the classification of AKA while assigned to MSTS, their equipment and personnel had been radically reduced. The first problem was met by Fleet Activities Yokosuka, where landing craft, boat fittings, and much miscellaneous gear including slings, nets, and the like were installed. At the same time an emergency air movement of boat crews and other specialized personnel from the west coast helped to strengthen the crews, but the two ships were still below peacetime complement when the force set sail, and far below that of wartime.

The load imposed on Fleet Activities Yokosuka in preparation for "Bluehearts" was not limited to the modification of the AKAs. To assist in unloading at the objective half a dozen LSUs were reactivated; the proposal to tow these to Pohang by LST superimposed a requirement for the manufacture of towing gear. Both in this high-speed shipyard work and in the loading of the Attack Force there was reason to be grateful for Japanese facilities and Japanese labor. The larger ships, which carried an average of 138 vehicles and 575 tons of bulk cargo, were loaded in little over a day, and the vehicle-laden LSTs in only four hours. Despite all difficulties the sailing date was somehow met.

The employment of Scajap LSTs in both the assault phase and the follow-up echelons, and the use of chartered Japanese merchant ships, created an unusual situation. Seldom, indeed, do men embark for war in ships manned and navigated by enemy aliens. Since control of the Scajap fleet was exercised through the Civilian Merchant Marine Committee, an agency of the Japanese Government, its administration was somewhat unwieldy. Always, of course, there was the language problem. But the most important complications were of a military nature. If sailed independently, the only contact with these ships was through Japanese radio channels, cumbersome and presenting difficult questions of security. Even when sailing in company, problems arose in communicating with units which could not be issued classified publications. Placing of Navy radiomen and quartermasters aboard, while answering some difficulties gave rise to others, not least in the manifestation at meal time of cultural differences between east and west. Yet these problems, if not overcome, were mitigated by various expedients, and the Scajap LSTs gave yeoman service throughout the war.

Table 6.—POHANG ATTACK FORCE

TASK FORCE 90. ATTACK FORCE.   REAR ADMIRAL J. H. DOYLE.

Task Force 91. Landing Force.   Major General Hobart Gay, USA.

Task Group 90.1. Tactical Air Control Group.   Comdr. E. Moore.
Tacron 1.

Task Group 90.2. Transport Group.
1 AGC, 1 APA, 3 AKA.

Task Group 90.3. Tractor Group.   Captain N. W. Sears.
1 USN LST, 15 Scajap LST, 2 ATF, 1 ARS, 6 LSU.

Task Group 90.4. Protective Group.   Lt. Comdr. D. V. Shouldice.
2 DD, 1 AM, 6 AMS.

Task Group 90.7. Reconnaissance Group.   Lt. Comdr. J. R. Wilson.
1 APD, 1 UDT detachment.

Task Group 90.8. Control Group.   Lt. Comdr. C. E. Allmon.
1 APD,[1] 1 ATF.[2]

Task Group 90.9. Beach Group.   Lt. Comdr. J. L. Lowentrout.
1 Beachmaster Unit detachment, 1 UDT detachment.

Task Group 90.0. Follow-up Shipping Group.   Captain D. J. Sweeney.
3 AP, 12 Scajap LST, 4 *Maru*.

Task Group 96.5. Gunfire Support Group.   Rear Admiral J. H. Higgins.
1 CLAA, 3 DD,[3] 1 RAN DD.

Close air support from Seventh Fleet; deep air support from FEAF; patrol aircraft from Task Group 96.2.

[1] From Task Group 90.7.   [2] From Task Group 90.3.   [3] 2 DD from Task Group 90.4.

First landing: The attack transport Cavalier unloading at Pohang during the movement of the 1st Cavalry Division. 18 July 1950. (CARL MYDANS—LIFE)

106

Although the Pohang operation was a comparatively small one, and although plans and preparations were made in record time, the organization of the Attack Force followed standard amphibious practice. The landing force, commanded by Major General Hobart Gay, USA, consisted of the 5th and 8th RCTs of the 1st Cavalry Division, an artillery group of three battalions, and minor attached units. These were transported to the objective area in the large vessels of the transport group, in the 16 LSTs of the tractor group, and in follow-up shipping. The Attack Force also included a minesweeping group of one AM and six AMS; a gunfire suport group made up of *Juneau,* the American destroyers *Kyes, Higbee,* and *Collett,* and the Australian *Bataan;* and units assigned for reconnaissance, control purposes at the objective, administration of the beaches, and the like. Deep air support was the responsibility of the Air Force, which by this time had a fighter squadron on the Pohang air strip; close air support at the objective, should the natives prove unfriendly, would be provided by the Seventh Fleet, which was coming up from Okinawa for the occasion.

On the 14th, as the minesweepers started work in Yongil Man, the tractor group of LSTs, towing the LSUs and with two fleet tugs as escort, sailed from Tokyo Bay, to be followed on the morrow by the transport group. The route was south along the coast of Japan, then north by Bungo Strait through which *Yamato,* mightiest battleship in the world, had sortied on her final cruise in vain attempt to strike the American fleet off Okinawa. Turning westward through the Inland Sea, the force steamed past Shimonoseki, where almost a century before the U.S.S. *Wyoming* had engaged the forces of the Daimyo of Choshu, and into the Korean Strait. Early in the morning of the 18th, tractor and transport groups joined, and the ships moved into Yongil Man. Fighting had been reported only a few miles north of Pohang, but the ROK 3rd Division still held the road, and at 0559 Admiral Doyle made the signal to "Land the Landing Force" in accordance with the plan for an unopposed operation. Task Force 77 and *Juneau* were released from their support commitments, and only a small combat air patrol from *Valley Forge* was retained overhead to protect the shipping of the Attack Force.

Although peaceful, the scene at Pohang on the 18th was a busy one. From the ships of the transport group at anchor in Yongil Man, troops and vehicles were shuttled ashore. Nine of the LSTs disgorged their cargo along the jetty wall and on the beaches of Yongil Man, along with the smaller landing craft; seven were ordered out to Kuryongpo around the point to unload vehicles. Landing was begun at 0715; general unloading commenced at 0930; except for *Cavalier,* all major ships had been emptied by midnight, while the LSTs had discharged all personnel, all vehicles, and more than half their bulk cargo. More than 10,000 troops and 2,000 vehicles, and almost 3,000 tons of cargo had been put ashore.

There is no landing better than an unopposed landing. Since the ROK troops were still holding out to the northward, the cavalry division had been greeted at Pohang not by the enemy but by General Walker, and by trains ready-formed to carry them to the front. To some, however, this came as a disappointment. As the first sizable planned naval operation of the war, "Bluehearts" had drawn the attention of the press, and 26 correspondents were embarked in the command ship *Mount McKinley*. At Pohang the lack of correlation between public interest and strategic worth, always a problem for the armed services in a democracy, reappeared in the report of the public information officer that "the fact that the landing was unopposed detracted a great deal from the news value." But however saddened the scribes, the bloodless and expeditious nature of the operation was to the military a matter for rejoicing.

At noon on the 19th General Gay assumed command ashore. In the afternoon, with unloading completed, ships of the Attack Force shifted to heavy weather anchorages as Grace, the first typhoon of the season, was reported heading for Korea Strait. On the 22nd Grace came up the coast, bringing gusts of 50 knots to Yongil Man and delaying the arrival of the second echelon of shipping. This had been scheduled to come in on the 21st, but the MSTS units reached Pohang only on the 23rd, and the chartered Japanese freighters the next day. The LSTs of the third echelon arrived on the 26th and 29th.

For a variety of reasons, unloading of the follow-up shipping was somewhat slow. The MSTS transports suffered from their shortages of personnel; the Japanese freighters lacked trained hatch crews and unloading gear, and the ever-present language problem complicated supervision; after two days of continuous labor the shore party was getting tired. Nonetheless the work proceeded. On the 23rd the commanding officer of a Navy LST was directed by Admiral Doyle to take over the duties of senior officer present, and late in the evening the force commander sailed in *Mount McKinley*, with *Union, Kyes,* and *Diachenko,* for Tokyo. A week later it was all over, and CTF 90 was able to report the completion of operations at Pohang and the withdrawal of all shipping from Yongil Man. But this report was by way of formality, for the strategic rewards of the operation had long since been apparent. On 22 July, four days after the initial landing, the 1st Cavalry Division had relieved the battered 24th Division southeast of Taejon.

4. 10–31 July: Seventh Fleet Operations

At Buckner Bay, 600 miles to the southward, Admiral Struble's staff had been working on ways to deal with the Seventh Fleet's Formosan responsibilities while planning with Admiral Hoskins for further carrier strikes in Korea.

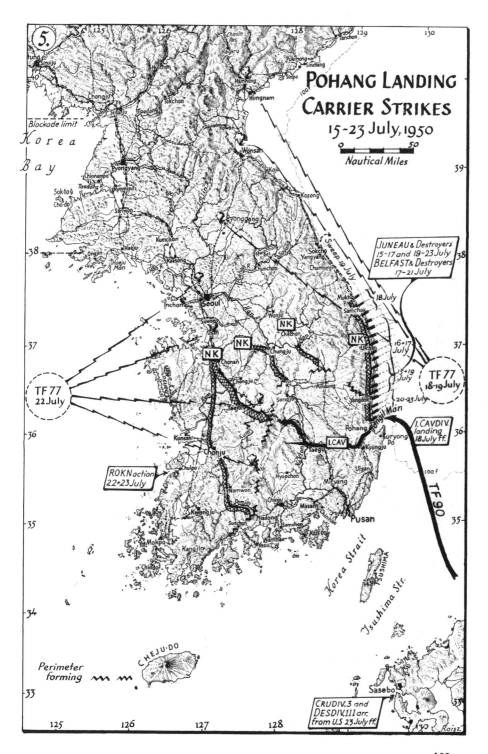

5.

POHANG LANDING
CARRIER STRIKES
15-23 July, 1950

0 _____ 50
Nautical Miles

Korea Bay

Blockade limit

JUNEAU & Destroyers
15-17 and 19-23 July
BELFAST & Destroyers
17-21 July

TF 77
22 July

NK

NK

NK

NK

18 July

16·17
July

15·19
July

TF 77
18-19 July

20-23 July

TF 77
22 July

ROKN action
22·23 July

1.CAV

1. CAV DIV.
landing
18 July ff.

TF 90

Korea Strait

TSUSHIMA

Tsushima Str.

CHEJU-DO

Perimeter
forming

Sasebo

CRUDIV.3 and
DESDIV.111 arr.
from U.S 23 July ff.

Raisz

In Formosa, where some expected an invasion attempt before mid-August by a force of up to 200,000, rivalries and dissension on the upper levels and low morale below raised the prospect of rapid collapse in the event of a landing in strength. Seventh Fleet control of the Strait was consequently the crucial factor; with the Seventh Fleet involved in Korea, warning of attack was essential; on 10 July, therefore, as Struble returned from his visit to Taipei, redeployment of the Seventh Fleet patrol planes was begun. VP 28, a P4Y squadron, was moved up from Guam to Okinawa; VP 46, a Mariner squadron with units at Sangley Point and Buckner Bay, was ordered forward to the Pescadores along with the tender *Suisun;* Commander Fleet Air Wing 1 was relieved of responsibilities at Guam and instructed to advance his headquarters to Okinawa.

These movements were expeditiously completed. Captain Grant had his wing headquarters in operation at Naha Air Force Base by the 15th; on the next day VP 28 began daily patrols of the China coast and northern Formosa Strait; by 17 July VP 46 was flying searches in the southern sector. On the basis of this forward deployment Commander Seventh Fleet proposed on the 16th that General MacArthur announce the imminent commencement of naval air reconnaissance of Formosa Strait. The proposal was approved the same day, and having brandished the weapon of publicity against the Chinese Communists, Admiral Struble sailed from Buckner Bay to employ his Striking Force against the North Koreans.

In Korea his presence was urgently desired. On 9 July General Dean, then commanding all Army units in Korea, had inquired hopefully about the possibility of carrier air support. In response Struble next day advised Admiral Joy of his willingness to help out either with close support or with further strikes on west coast targets, while noting that until ammunition reached Okinawa on the 18th he would be limited to two days of close support operations. For effective work in support of troops the front line communications problem was governing: if the Tactical Air Control Squadron from *Mount McKinley* could be made available, all would be well; if not, Seventh Fleet could supply a small control team, although equipment would have to be provided it. Subject to these considerations Struble proposed to sail from Buckner on the 11th for operations on the 13th and 14th.

The offer, however, was not accepted. Admiral Joy's reply stated that he knew of no plans for carrier close support, and that the Tacron was not designed for shore employment. The limitations on Seventh Fleet endurance, moreover, made him want to hold it in reserve to cover the landing of the 1st Cavalry Division, and on the 12th a dispatch operation order instructed Admiral Struble to provide objective air cover at Pohang, support of the landing force, and such additional effort as might be directed. Two days later Struble again flew to Tokyo for talks with Admiral Joy and General Stratemeyer: a schedule was worked out which called for two days in support of the landing and in northward strikes against the enemy, a day for replenishment, and two more days of operations; an east coast area was cleared with FEAF for strikes on the 18th and 19th. On 16 July, as the Seventh Fleet started north to cover the Pohang landing, Admiral Joy issued Operation Order 10–50 governing the conduct of carrier attacks against the North Korean forces.

The planning for these operations had seen the emergence of the first of a series of problems concerning carrier employment which was to trouble naval commanders throughout the campaign. So far as support of the Pohang landing was concerned there was no difficulty: this was a conventional naval task in which all hands felt quite at home. But attack on the North Korean forces and installations beyond the beachhead raised problems of coordination with the Air Force. Subsequent to the first carrier attack on Pyongyang, General Stratemeyer had requested the Seventh Fleet to confine its further strikes to northeastern Korea, north of the 38th parallel and east of 127° E, with target priorities beginning with rail and highway cuts and running down through petroleum facilities to airfields. Yet such an employment of carrier aviation, however desirable in the situation of the moment, was certainly not envisaged in the existing unification agreements. The roles and missions papers for the armed forces, worked out during the painful period of unification, made interdiction of enemy land power and communications an exclusive Air Force function in which the Navy could participate only after a complicated bureaucratic procedure of authorization. The fact that naval air was not to be so used had been one of the reasons advanced in support of the cancellation of construction of the carrier *United States*.

It had, of course, been recognized that in an emergency the instruments at hand and the urgency of the situation would take precedence over paper agreements. But there was the further difficulty that the employment of carrier aviation in interdiction was not contemplated in current naval thinking. On the one hand the interdiction of land communications calls for continuous effort; on the other, it was felt that logistic considerations and the dangers of air and submarine attack made it undesirable for carriers to operate for more than two days in the same location. By autumn, when concern over air and submarine opposition had greatly subsided and when underway replenishment had improved, the carriers would be operating for protracted periods in the same locality. But autumn was far away, and in the intervening period of emergency things would become worse before they became better.

This triple conflict between legislation, doctrine, and the exigencies of the situation was to prove the less manageable owing to difficulties in coordination with the Air Force. Although these, stemming both from doctrinal differences and from technical difficulties in communication, were never to be completely solved, some steps had already been taken. On 8 July General Stratemeyer had advised CincFE that it was essential that he have "operational control" of all naval aircraft in the theater. To the Navy, quite apart from doubts as to FEAF's technical capability to handle this effort, the implications of the request appeared excessive, involving as they did the authority to control carrier movements as well as to assign targets, and after some discussion a CincFE letter of the 15th delegated "coordination control" to the commanding general of FEAF.   It was on the basis of this agreement that Struble had cleared with FEAF his plans to strike northward from Pohang and that Joy issued his operation order of 16 July.

Morning of the 18th found *Valley Forge, Triumph,* and their screening ships in the southern Sea of Japan, some 60 miles northeast of Pohang.   At dawn local antisubmarine and combat air patrols were launched by *Triumph,* and *Valley Forge* sent off a target combat air patrol and a support group of attack planes to assist the landing.   No alternative targets seem to have been given the support group; the location of the front line and the needs of the ROK 3rd Division were apparently unknown; and when the landing proved unopposed and the task force was released from its air commitments the support group jettisoned its load.

Except for the requirement of a combat air patrol over Pohang, the *Valley Forge* air group was now available for attacks on North Korean targets.   On the 18th and 19th, therefore, strikes were flown against railroad facilities, industrial plants, and airfields from Pyonggang and Wonsan north through Hungnam and Hamhung.   In the two days of attacks two aircraft were lost, but both pilots were recovered.   About 50 grounded aircraft were sighted, of which more than half were destroyed and the remainder damaged, while flights north along the railroad on the 19th exploded four locomotives.   But the biggest explosion was at Wonsan.

This seaport city, located at the head of the Korean Gulf and at the east coast focus of Korean rail communications, had grown rapidly under the Japanese regime.   Its population, now of the order of 150,000, had tripled within a generation.   It was the site of a number of manufacturing plants, and the center of a considerable complex of petroleum installations, developed to support Japanese continental expansion, which included the largest refinery in Korea.   Following the arrival of the Russians in 1945 this refinery had for some time been inactive, but in 1947 a joint Russian-North Korean enterprise had been formed to operate it, Soviet supervisors had been provided, and late in the next year crude oil began to arrive in Soviet tankers for processing.

On the afternoon of the 18th *Valley Forge* jets reported that the refinery appeared in full operation, and at 1700 a strike group of 11 Skyraiders and 10 Corsairs was launched, the former armed with 1,000 and 500-pound bombs and the latter with high velocity aircraft rockets.   As the group came in over the city the Corsairs went down first, firing their rockets and 20-millimeter guns, and were followed by the ADs with their bombs.   The results were spectacular, with large fires and so much smoke that photographic damage

First strike in the east: The Wonsan oil refinery burning after attack by Valley Forge *aircraft. 18 July 1950. (USN 707876)*

assessment was difficult. On the next day a *Valley Forge* flight passing in the neighborhood observed the refinery still burning vigorously, while the smoke, rising to 5,000 feet, was visible to the force at sea.

The attack on the Wonsan refinery gave rise to an interservice conflict of claims. Air Force planes had attacked the city between 6 and 13 July. There then followed the carrier attack of the 18th, on the basis of which the Navy reported the destruction of the refinery. On 10 August another heavy raid was made by B–29s, after which a FEAF communique claimed total destruction of the refinery, which had been attacked on the basis of "reconnaissance photographs [which showed] that only a small portion . . . had been damaged in the previous small air strikes."

Interrogation of supervisory personnel by Marine Corps officers in the autumn elicited the statement that although the early raids had had adverse effects on employee morale, and had stimulated the removal of bulk petroleum products, no bomb had hit in any vital area. The *Valley Forge* attack of the 18th was reported to have destroyed 12,000 tons of refined products, saturated every vital area in the refinery, and caused it to be declared a total loss. What remained of the plant had been flattened by the bombing of 10 August, and in early October, as ROK forces approached Wonsan, the Russian supervisors had headed north for the border.

Apart from the question of who hit what, the strikes of 18 and 19 July raise questions as to target selection in a police action. The objectives were, of course, in accordance with the desires expressed by FEAF concerning attacks by Seventh Fleet aircraft on North Korean targets. But the aspect of strategic air warfare which emphasizes attack on industrial plant is slow to have effect at the battleline; the real strategic targets were outside Korea, and destruction of North Korean facilities as of this date would seem merely to have promised difficulties in reconstruction, assuming U.N. success in the campaign. Overshadowed though it was by the refinery quarrel, it seems probable that the destruction of grounded aircraft by the *Valley Forge* air group was the most important result of the two-day operation; together with some similarly successful sorties by Air Force jets on the 19th, this pretty well liquidated the North Korean Air Force. But habits are hard to break, and just as the carrier commanders were reluctant to undertake continuous operations in the same area, so others found it difficult to divest themselves of strongly held notions on air warfare: on 31 July a message from the Joint Chiefs urged the strategic bombing of North Korean industrial targets.

It may be conceded, in this context, that the case of the Wonsan refinery is not entirely clearcut. Despite the handcarrying nature of the North Korean army the destruction of 12,000 tons of petroleum products may have had valuable consequences, so great is the importance of oil to modern war. And inevitably, the course of the Korean conflict being what it was, the policeman's attitude developed into that of the warrior. But in these early weeks, at least, it would seem that the police action should have been conducted as such. Rioters are quelled with nightsticks, not by turning off the gas and water at their homes. Had it been possible in the early days to deliver, in accordance with Army desires and naval capabilities, well-controlled and well-coordinated close air support at the front, the effect on the ground situation would have been more immediate. It was on the ground that the emergency lay.

Two days of east coast strikes had gone off well, but nature now intervened to change the schedule. Concerned by the time involved in commuting between Okinawa and the scene of action, Commander Seventh Fleet had been expediting arrangements for underway replenishment and was contemplating a shift of base forward to Sasebo; the plans of the moment called for the force to fuel at sea on the 20th in preparation for two more days of operations. But the approach of Typhoon Grace forced postponement, and with completion of flight operations on the 19th all ships set

Typhoon Condition One and prepared for the worst in the way of weather. On the 20th, in winds of up to 40 knots, the force cruised the Sea of Japan, and late in the day headed south through Tsushima Strait to get clear of Grace's skirts and gain an operating position off the west coast of Korea. On the 21st *Triumph* was detached with *Comus* for a ten-day period of availability at Sasebo.

Admiral Struble had advised ComNavFE on the afternoon of the 20th that he hoped to conduct a one-day strike on west Korea on the 22nd, spend a day in refueling and rearming his force, and return on the 24th and 25th for further attacks against west coast targets. But this schedule depended on factors beyond his control, on weather and on the availability of replenishment ships. The tanker *Navasota* was by this time on hand to fuel the force, but for rearming the situation was less clear, and depended on whether the AK *Grainger*, which had reached Okinawa on the 18th with a load of aircraft ammunition from Guam, could rearm the force at sea. Failing in this it would be necessary to proceed to Sasebo, with consequent delay.

At dawn on the 22nd, from a location in the Yellow Sea northwest of Kunsan, *Valley Forge* launched her air group. Although his force was now down to a single carrier, Struble undertook the double mission of support of troops and attack on northern targets: the propeller-driven ADs and F4Us were sent off to the eastward to work under airborne controllers from Fifth Air Force in close support of the ground forces; the jets headed north to attack targets beyond Seoul. The air support mission, first of the Korean War, went awry as the strike aircraft, unable to reach the controllers on the prescribed radio frequencies, resorted to attacks on secondary targets in the area of the capital. In the afternoon a second effort met with similar results, and after recovery of the strike group the force headed southward to rendezvous with *Navasota*. By this time *Valley Forge* was down to a little less than a one-day supply of aviation gasoline.

Rendezvous with the tanker was made late in the morning of the 23rd to the southward of Cheju Do, but *Grainger* and the ammunition were not there. On completion of refueling, therefore, Task Force 77 headed for Sasebo where it arrived on the morning of the 24th. The delay in resuming operations, which Admiral Struble had feared, had been forced upon him.

In the meantime the events of the 22nd had prompted a review of the mission of the Seventh Fleet. The waste of effort consequent to the inability of his strike groups to reach the controllers had led Struble to look for more profitable employment elsewhere. Casting his eyes northward, he proposed to ComNavFE a change of schedule which would call for two days of strikes against east coast targets from Chongjin southward, coupled with cruiser and destroyer bombardment between 40° and 41°, and asked for detailed target information. But by this time a new emergency was developing in Korea. The Pohang landing had been successful, the main front had been reinforced, but west of the central hill mass the advance of the North Korean 6th Division had continued unopposed. The entire southwestern region had been overrun, and the invaders were moving eastward with nothing to block their path. On the 23rd, while *Valley Forge* was refueling, an emergency dispatch from Eighth Army advised all major commanders that an "urgent requirement" existed for the employment of naval air in the west coast area beginning that very day, and requested information as to naval capabilities in close and general support.

From both Joy and Struble this dispatch brought prompt reply. The former observed that subject to the primary mission of the neutralization of Formosa, and to the undesirability of protracted operations in one spot, no great difficulty was expected in coordinating Seventh Fleet and Air Force operations, provided only that successful joint communications were established. But to Commander Seventh Fleet the situation appeared more complicated. While observing that Eighth Army's urgent requirement could be met beginning on the 26th, he emphasized the fact that present methods of coordination were unsatisfactory, and that in addition to the communications problem there was an urgent requirement for personnel trained in the control of close support aircraft. To fill this need Struble repeated his proposal of 10 July that either the Tactical Air Control Squadron from Admiral Doyle's Amphibious Group be sent to Korea, or that the Seventh Fleet itself supply a small but experienced control team.

The need for some competent control group to handle close support had already received consideration. Four days earlier EUSAK—Eighth U.S. Army in Korea—had requested that the Anglico which had been attached to the 1st Cavalry Division for the Pohang landing be assigned on completion of that operation to assist the Joint Operations Center in control of naval gunfire and naval air. The request had been approved by Admiral Joy's headquarters, and Admiral Doyle was so instructed on the 20th. But by then the Anglico was returning to Yokohama by sea, and by the time of its arrival it had come to seem more profitable to retain it in Japan to train Army and Air Force personnel.

So things stood when the crisis in the west and Eighth Army's call for help led Struble to renew his suggestion for the employment of the Tacron or of a Seventh Fleet control party. These proposals also were to prove abortive. The plan for the Seventh Fleet tactical air control party, worked up at Buckner Bay, had contemplated a pooling of *Valley Forge* and *Triumph* material and personnel, but the sortie on the 16th had interrupted preparations. The recommended employment of the Tacron was vetoed at the instance of Admiral Doyle, who felt its personnel would be spread unprofitably thin. The upshot was that efforts to increase the yield of carrier operations in close support were limited to attempts, themselves badly needed,

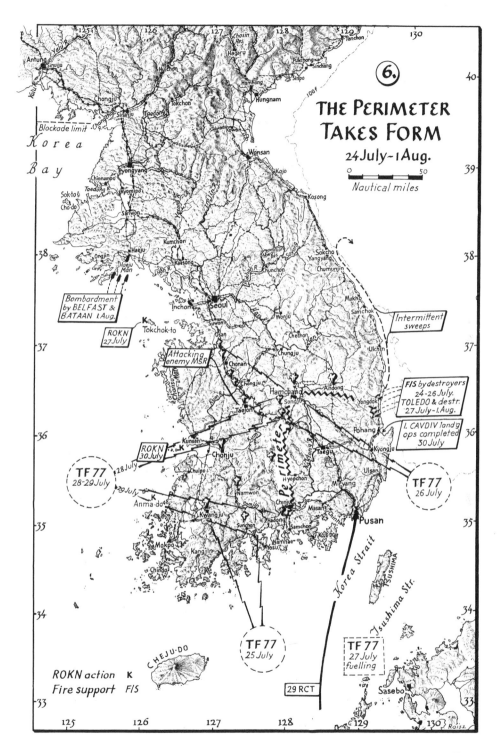

THE PERIMETER TAKES FORM
24 July–1 Aug.

6.

Nautical miles
0   50

Korea Bay

Blockade limit

Korea Strait

Tsushima Str.

Bombardment
by BELFAST &
BATAAN I.Aug.

ROKN
27 July

Attacking
enemy MSR

Intermittent
sweeps

FIS by destroyers
24-26 July.
TOLEDO & destr.
27 July-I.Aug.

I. CAVDIV land'g
ops completed
30 July

ROKN
30 July

TF 77
28-29 July

TF 77
26 July

TF 77
25 July

TF 77
27 July
fuelling

29 RCT

ROKN action   K
Fire support   FIS

CHEJU-DO

Pusan

Sasebo

TSUSHIMA

Raisz

117

to improve radio communications between the Seventh Fleet Striking Force and the JOC.

At Sasebo rearming of *Valley Forge* had begun on the morning of the 24th. But replenishment was to be cut short by the rapid deterioration of the ground situation in the west. Early in the afternoon an emergency dispatch was received from ComNavFE, cancelling existing plans and assigning Task Force 77 the area south of the Kum and west of the line Kunsan-Chonju-Namwon-Kwangju. This region was believed to contain a major concentration of North Korean forces: according to the dispatch the "total area is considered enemy." Commander Task Force 77 was adjured to search carefully and to destroy all armor, bridges, traffic, troop concentrations, and barges up to the limit of his capabilities. The only restrictions on his operations were to beware of Korean Navy YMS types operating inshore, and to "hit only military targets" at Kunsan, where preservation of port facilities seemed desirable in view of possible future amphibious operations. As the dispatch emphasized the critical situation of the ground forces and urged immediate efforts, *Valley Forge* broke off her rearming before completion, and *Triumph,* whose yard period had barely begun, rejoined the force. At midnight on the 24th Task Force 77 was again underway from Sasebo, headed north.

The carriers launched at 0800 on the 25th from a position south of Korea, and for the remainder of the day maintained planes in the air over the front line. Once again, however, results were disappointing: pilots returning from the morning strikes reported that air controllers had more planes than they could handle and that radio channels were overcrowded; these factors, together with the lack of common charts and procedures, had prevented controlled attacks, with the result that the "free opportunity" area assigned in the west had been liberally used to dispose of ammunition.

Early in the afternoon Admiral Struble reported that owing to lack of targets the morning sweeps had been of very minor effect. In point of fact it appears that ComNavFE's intelligence was stale, and that the North Korean 6th Division had by this time passed through the country assigned the carriers and was concentrated about Sunchon. The region so menacingly described in the emergency dispatch from Admiral Joy turned out to be a peaceful agricultural area populated principally by donkey carts and men working in rice paddies. Although he announced that he would continue with afternoon attacks, the effort seemed unfruitful to Commander Seventh Fleet, and once again he emphasized the need of proper communications with commanders in the field.

In view of the unproductive nature of the day's work the *Valley Forge* air group had flown pilots to Taegu to arrange for targets and communications for the 26th. The result was an assignment to close support at the front, attack on miscellaneous targets as directed by the Joint Operations

Center, and deep support strikes in the region between Taejon and Seoul. In the evening these intentions were reported by Commander Seventh Fleet to ComNavFE, and the Striking Force turned northeast and headed for the Korean Strait and for a morning position off Pohang.

Admiral Struble's dispatch stating his plans for 26 July produced an immediate howl from Tokyo. No new area for carrier operations had been arranged with FEAF headquarters in Japan, and Admiral Joy requested immediate information as to Commander Seventh Fleet's intentions. Prior to the 25th arrangements for carrier strikes had been made on the upper levels, between ComNavFE and the commanding general of FEAF, on a basis of general area coordination, but with the commencement of efforts to use carrier planes in support of troops this system began to break down. Struble's reply described the arrangements which had been made directly with EUSAK and JOC, and since difficulties were still being experienced in direct communication, followed up with a request that ComNavFE clear with FEAF for operations as far north as Suwon. On the 27th a message from ComNavFE implicitly endorsed the procedure of coordinating operations with the JOC in Korea, and from this time on such coordination was increasingly attempted.

Within the force, morning of the 26th was marked by an extremely convincing submarine contact, but the early strikes led to little more than the destruction of some trucks on the enemy main line of communications. But in the afternoon, despite congestion of aircraft in the target area, one flight of four ADs at last found adequate control. The result was the reported destruction of 70 percent of Yongdong, a junction town just west of the saddle where two highways and the railroad come together, and two later flights of eight Corsairs applied more effort to this pressure point by striking troop concentrations in the region between Yongdong and Taejon.

On conclusion of the operations of the 26th, which at least represented some improvement over earlier efforts in suport of Eighth Army, the task force withdrew to refuel. CincFE had expressed his enthusiasm over the effect of the carrier air attacks, and on the 27th the Fifth Air Force JOC, after politely describing the attacks of the 26th as "invaluable and much appreciated," inquired as to their results, requested information as to future operations, and stated it could handle as many flights as could be provided. But a report from Admiral Doyle on the state of Army and Air Force control of tactical air seemed to indicate a need for basic reorganization and training before adequate standards could be obtained, while the Seventh Fleet, despite the compliments, remained unsatisfied with the results of its work.

By now, too, there were signs that a crisis was making up in Formosa Strait. On the 21st a reported sighting of between 500 and 1,500 junks by the master of a British merchantman had led to special searches by Fleet Air Wing 1. These proved negative, but on the 26th a VP 28 patrol plane was attacked by two fighters in the northern part of the Strait. In this situation, and as continuation of the support effort seemed of doubtful value, Struble recommended to ComNavFE that the Seventh Fleet move south to the Buckner-Formosa area for a possible sweep of the Strait.

This proposal, however, was disapproved. The needs of Eighth Army remained paramount, other units were dispatched to the southward, and on 28 July Task Force 77 returned to the attack, operating in the area northwest of Mokpo. The strikes of propeller-driven aircraft on the 28th were again concentrated around Yongdong, and in the neighborhood of Hamchang at the northwest corner of the perimeter. Attacks were made on troop concentrations, trucks, and tanks, and although one jet flight to the Naktong River front failed to contact a controller and returned without result, control arrangements were reported somewhat improved.

In an attempt to make them even better, by improvement of communications between the task force and the JOC and by simplification of the complicated control procedures then in effect, another mission was flown to Taegu. This visit bore fruit in the establishment of a direct communications link, and helped to minimize some operating problems by making JOC personnel aware of what the carrier force could and could not do. The previous overloading of airborne controllers was partially rectified by the assignment, for the 29th, of a defined section of the front line and of specific Mosquito aircraft to the planes of Task Force 77. Within the force, with similar ends in view, another move to organize a tactical air control party with *Valley Forge* and *Triumph* personnel had begun, but the early permanent detachment of the British carrier was to prevent fruition.

On the 29th the Corsairs and Skyraiders shifted their efforts to the Hadong-Sunchon region of the south coast, from which a battalion of the 29th Regiment, moved west from Pusan to block the passage south of the central hill mass, had just been driven by the North Korean 6th Division. Here pilots reported destruction of a score or more trucks and a couple of tanks and damage to bridges and rolling stock, and described control procedures as varying from very good to very bad. To the northward, on the Naktong River front, a morning strike of eight Panther jets found a controller who was at least frank to admit that he was overloaded and could not work them: four were detached on armed reconnaissance to the northward while the others, although unable to make radio contact, showed their initiative by following an F-80 flight in a strafing run on enemy troops.

With the end of the day's operations the Striking Force retired. Carrier operations during July, limited though they were by logistic problems and frustrated by difficulties in control, had been reasonably successful, but they had not been free from cost. In addition to the aircraft destroyed in the deck crash of 4 July, two F9Fs, three F4Us, and a helicopter had gone into the water, and on the 22nd an AD had crashed and burned, taking its pilot down with it. Most downed personnel, however, had been fished out of the sea by screening ships; one pilot had been recovered 80 miles from the force by *Triumph's* amphibian plane; another, shot down behind enemy lines, had been picked up by an Army helicopter which in turn had gone down from fuel exhaustion, but both pilots ultimately had made contact with friendly forces. Perhaps the most remarkable loss of the period had occurred on the 28th when a *Triumph* fighter pilot on combat air patrol, vectored out to investigate a radar contact which showed unfriendly, had somewhat absent-mindedly closed a B–29 only to find himself shot down west of Anma Do in the Yellow Sea. But he too was recovered by a destroyer.

Following the operations of the 29th five ADs were launched with pilot passengers to pick up replacement aircraft which had reached Japan in *Boxer*; *Triumph* and *Comus* were detached to Japan for further assignment to the west coast blockading force; Admiral Struble boarded a destroyer and headed for Sasebo in anticipation of a flying trip to Formosa with CincFE; *Valley Forge* and her screen steamed south for Buckner Bay. There they anchored on the 31st and there, on the next day, Task Force 77 received a welcome accession of strength with the arrival of the carrier *Philippine Sea*.

5. 7 July–2 August: Patrol Planes and Gunnery Ships

Through the hectic weeks of July, as the U.N. Command struggled to stem the enemy advance, naval operations fell into three interrelated categories. To support the campaign in the peninsula a steady stream of shipping was flowing into Pusan, while the Pohang landing, carried out by Task Force 90, permitted the rapid reinforcement of the front by the previously uncommitted 1st Cavalry Division. At the same time Task Force 77, the U.N.'s long-range weapon, worked over North Korean air strength and communications, attacked targets of opportunity like the Wonsan refinery, and attempted to support the western front against the pressure of the numerically superior enemy. As troops and supplies were fed into Korea, and as Struble's force struck northward and struggled with problems of communications and control, the units of Naval Forces Japan were busy on both sides of the peninsula. While patrol planes covered the maritime flanks, the gunnery units escorted shipping, bombarded enemy positions, and gave fire support to the ROK forces holding the east coast road.

Like everyone else, the Fleet Air Wing 1 detachment had more jobs than it could easily handle. To perform the multitudinous duties of antisubmarine patrol, escort of convoy, weather reconnaissance, and shipping search, Captain Alderman had a total of eight PBM Mariner flying boats and nine P2V Neptunes. Shortly after their arrival in Japan the PBMs of VP 47 moved from Yokosuka to the RAAF base at Iwakuni, near Hiroshima on the Inland

Sea. Messed, housed, and supported by the hospitable Australians, the squadron managed to extemporize a seadrome and to maintain an antisubmarine patrol of the Korean Strait, and on the 15th the arrival of the seaplane tender *Gardiner's Bay* brought more ample logistic assistance.

Meanwhile the Neptunes of VP 6, which had reached Japan on 7 July and were operating out of Johnson Air Force Base at Tachikawa, were flying daily reconnaissance of the Korean east coast between 37° and 42°, and of the Yellow Sea and west coast as far north as 39°30'. But the lack of enemy seaborne traffic made the flights unproductive, while coordination with surface units was hindered by the remoteness of Johnson AFB from other naval activities. There were also certain difficulties in communications: on 20 July a VP 6 pilot spent three hours inside Typhoon Grace looking for a convoy he had been instructed to escort, only to discover on his return that the weather had kept the ships in port. On the 29th, however, the opportunities open to the Neptunes were enlarged by authorization to attack enemy shipping and installations, and two at once complied by destroying, with rockets and 20-millimeter fire, a train on the east coast line near Chongjin.

The arrival of Rear Admiral Ruble, Commander Carrier Division 15, and of his staff, enabled Admiral Joy to rationalize his air command. The Search and Reconnaissance Group was united with the other naval aviation activities in a new command, Naval Air Japan, which assumed responsibility for squadrons, aircraft, logistics, and bases. But while this improved the administrative situation, it in no way lightened the load for the 17 patrol planes and their crews, and when at the end of the month three RAF Sunderland flying boats reached Iwakuni from Hong Kong, they were most welcome.

On the east coast, day after day, bombardment of the enemy invasion route continued. Coordination with the troops ashore was improving steadily, Korean interpreters had been assigned the ships, an artillery officer had been attached to Admiral Higgins' staff, and spotting planes were at least intermittently available.

On 18 July, as the 1st Cavalry was landing at Pohang, *Mansfield* and *De Haven* were working the coastal road in the vicinity of Samchok, while *Belfast* and *Cossack* were patrolling at the 38th parallel. In the morning, as *Juneau* was released from her support commitments, the others came south to join the flagship off Yongdok, where the day was spent firing on targets of opportunity and where a reported "full-scale" enemy offensive was broken up. In the afternoon, parties of American and British naval officers went ashore to confer with the KMAG group attached to the ROK 3rd Division and to pass out radio sets in the interest of improved communications. That evening Admiral Higgins instituted a new technique, and while the main body operated off the battleline a single destroyer was detached nightly to prowl northward along the coast, seeking out and shooting up promising targets.

For the next two days *Juneau, Belfast,* and the destroyers operated off Yongdok, between 36°17′ and 36°30′, and although the spotting planes were grounded by the passage of Grace, the gunners' efforts met with great success. Two days of shooting up the valley at troop concentrations in Yongdok cost the ships some 1,300 rounds and got them a radio station, more than 400 enemy troops "by actual count," and enthusiastic reports from the shore fire control personnel.

But at Yongdok, as all around the perimeter, pressure continued to be severe, information scanty, and communications inadequate. The forces defending the town had lost contact with General Walker's headquarters: a EUSAK message advising that the general situation was critical and that the line had to be held reached the Army ashore only after relay by *Juneau.* Admiral Doyle, too, was in the dark, and on the 20th, with his second echelon scheduled to reach Pohang the next day, asked for information on the situation and prospects at Yongdok. Again the whaleboat was called away, and information brought back from shore indicated that landing operations could be safely continued, and that the ROK forces were planning the recapture of Yongdok on the morrow.

Temporarily, at least, this operation was successful. At 0600 on the 21st, after a 15-minute bombardment of the town, two star shells from *Juneau* gave the signal for the attack, and by 0717 the South Koreans had overrun Yongdok. Firing in support of the advance continued throughout the day, and *Juneau, Belfast,* and the destroyers expended more than 800 rounds. In the afternoon *Belfast* and *Mansfield* retired to Sasebo while *Juneau,* with *Swenson* and *Higbee,* continued close off Yongdok. On the 22nd, in preparation for further advance, 243 rounds were fired by the cruiser, but this time things went badly. The enemy counterattacked in force, the artillery observer was forced to retire, communications broke down, and weather had again grounded the spotting planes. On the 23rd, as the southward retirement of friendly forces continued, the responsibility for fire support was turned over to the destroyers and Higgins sailed for Sasebo, where early on the 24th *Juneau* moored alongside a new arrival, the heavy cruiser *Toledo.*

The growing strength of Naval Forces Japan had already brought changes in the organization of Task Force 96. ComNavFE's operation order of early July had been modified by the addition of Task Group 96.7, the ROK Navy, and of Task Group 96.9, the submarines acquired from the Seventh Fleet. With the arrival of Admiral Ruble all aviation activities had been consolidated into Naval Air Japan, Task Group 96.2. Logistic support at Sasebo was shortly to be improved by the establishment of Service Division 31, Captain Joseph M. P. Wright, with the designation of Task

Group 96.4. But before this last event took place the arrival of new gunnery strength from the United States made possible a reorganization of the Support Groups.

The first of the units sailed from the west coast reached Japan on 23 July as Rear Admiral Hartman, Commander Cruiser Division 3, arrived at Yokosuka with *Helena* and Destroyer Division 111, while *Toledo,* which had been ordered ahead, entered Sasebo. On reporting to ComNavFE, Admiral Hartman was instructed to take over command of all naval forces engaged in escort, support, and blockade, with the exception of the ROK Navy. Pursuant to these orders *Helena* and the destroyers sailed at once

Table 7.—NAVAL OPERATING COMMANDS, 21 JULY–11 SEPTEMBER 1950

(NavFE Opord 5–50, revisions of 21 July ff)

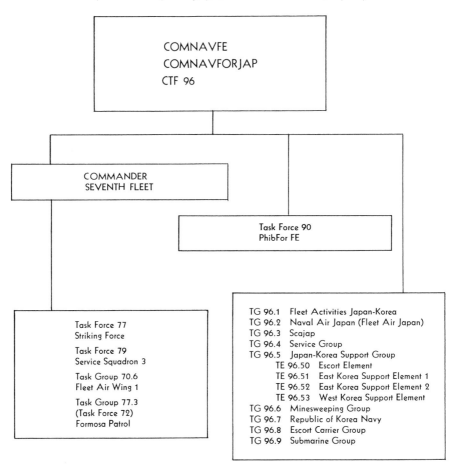

for Sasebo, where they arrived on the 25th and where not only *Toledo,* but *Belfast* with Admiral Andrewes and *Juneau* with Admiral Higgins were awaiting them.

At Sasebo, on the 25th, a conference was held between Admirals Joy, Hartman, Higgins, and Andrewes, and other officers of the force. The Support Groups and the Escort Group were reorganized and consolidated into Task Group 96.5, the Japan-Korea Support Group, under command of Com-Crudiv 3. On the basis of Admiral Higgins' reports of the ineffectiveness of 5 and 6-inch gunfire against reinforced concrete bridges it was decided to use the 8-inch cruisers for bombardment and fire support; *Juneau* was scheduled for transfer to the Seventh Fleet, and Higgins shifted his flag to *Toledo.* The new organization of Task Group 96.5, as here worked out, involved the creation of four subordinate units: two rotating East Coast Support Elements were set up, one under Admiral Hartman with *Helena* and Destroyer Division 111, the other under Admiral Higgins with *Toledo* and Desdiv 91; Captain Jay was given command of the Escort Element, to which the four frigates were assigned; command of the West Coast Support Element, composed of British Commonwealth ships and the Dutch destroyer *Evertsen,* remained with Admiral Andrewes. In addition to his responsibility for Yellow Sea and west coast operations, Admiral Andrewes was charged with the supervision of all non-American United Nations naval forces, for which purpose he set up an administrative headquarters in a frigate at Sasebo.

Early on the morning of the 26th Admiral Hartman assumed command of the Support Group, sortied from Sasebo with Cruiser Division 3 and Desdiv 111, and headed north to bombard the Korean coast. But his plans were to be rudely interrupted by the developments to the southward which had concerned Admiral Struble. At 1500 a dispatch came in ordering Hartman to proceed with *Helena* and the destroyers to Formosa at best speed. These instructions placed ComCrudiv 3 in a somewhat complicated situation, for he now found himself commanding two task groups in two different fleets, and charged with two missions separated by 15 degrees of latitude.

Operational control of Korean affairs was turned over to Admiral Higgins in *Toledo,* who was ordered to join the fire support ships off Yongdok; *Helena* and the destroyers reversed course and disappeared over the southern horizon; *Toledo* continued onward alone. But although only one of the heavy cruisers reached Yongdok, the arrival of 8-inch guns with their greater hitting power was helpful. From the 27th to the 30th, in rainy, windy weather, *Toledo, Mansfield,* and *Collett* operated off the battle line. Troops and other targets made for good shooting, and both shore and air spot were available; starshell illumination by the ships aided the artillery ashore; the destroyers continued to alternate days' duty in running north along the shoreline to bombard targets between Yongdok and the parallel. By month's end the pressure was diminishing.

The arrival of reinforcements and the reorganization of Task Group 96.5 greatly increased the strength available for operations in the Yellow Sea, where in the early days *Alacrity* had patrolled alone. Although Admiral Andrewes had assumed command of the West Coast Support Group in early July, the greater needs and opportunities of the east coast situation had made heavy demands upon his ships. Now, however, he had under his control the light cruisers *Jamaica, Kenya,* and *Belfast,* the British destroyers *Cossack, Cockade,* and *Charity,* the Australian *Bataan,* and the Netherlands *Evertsen.* On 30 July his command was further enlarged by the arrival of the three Canadian Tribal class destroyers, *Cayuga, Athabaskan,* and *Sioux,* and on 8 August the West Coast Element acquired its own air strength when *Triumph,* her yard period completed, reported in with *Comus* to Andrewes' control. The availability of *Triumph* was of particular importance in view of the hydrography of the west coast, which restricted the movement of heavy ships and so made aircraft the more useful. Destroyers and cruisers could bombard, and could check traffic passing around the headlands, but the important inshore patrol had thus far been largely left to the ROK Navy.

This force had done good work. The action off Pusan at the outbreak of war had been of profound importance, and other engagements had followed. On the east coast, on 2 July, the Pohang Naval Base Detachment exterminated a small enemy force that had landed near Ulsan. In the west, where the invaders were attempting the forward movement of supplies and personnel by sea, *YMS 513* sank three enemy small craft off Chulpo, south of Kunsan.

But invasion had brought disorganization: Admiral Sohn, the Chief of Naval Operations, had not yet returned from the United States, and naval headquarters at Seoul had been quickly overrun. Since a functioning Korean Navy was of prime importance, both for its resources of local knowledge and for its monopoly of types capable of inshore operations, ComNavFE moved quickly to restore cohesion. Arriving by air from the United States, Commander Michael J. Luosey found himself designated Deputy Commander, Naval Forces Far East, and put on the first plane for Korea. On 9 July, with Lieutenant David C. Holly and five enlisted men, Luosey arrived at Pusan and assumed operational control of the Korean Navy. Six days later President Rhee formally turned over command of the ROK armed forces to General MacArthur, and on 17 July Admiral Sohn arrived with the other two PCs.

Luosey's first days were spent in extemporizing logistic support at Pusan for U.N. ships, in establishing liaison with the Army, and in gaining the confidence of the Koreans. On the 15th, inshore patrol sectors were established along both coasts south of 37°, and a detachment of Korean Marines was sailed for Kunsan by LST in an attempt to hold that port. On the next day the Marines were landed, and a large store of government rice evacuated, but possession of Kunsan was brief. Heavily engaged on the 17th by an entire North Korean regiment, the 600-odd Marines were lifted out two days later to begin a minor epic of landings, forced marches, engagements, and retreats, which by the end of the month had brought the survivors to Chinju.

Little by little order emerged from chaos. By late July coordination with the British west coast element had been established and the Korean Navy was back in effective action. On the 22nd *YMS 513* repeated her earlier exploit by sinking three more enemy vessels off Chulpo, and the next day *YMS 301* had a brush with small craft in the same area. On the 27th a more important encounter took place to the northward as the newly acquired *PC*s *702* and *703* bombarded Palmi Do and Wolmi Do in Inchon harbor, and then, during their retirement, encountered a flotilla of southbound sampans loaded with ammunition and proceeded to sink 12 of them.

The increased strength of the West Coast Support Element now permitted more ambitious efforts. On 1 August Admiral Andrewes took *Belfast* and *Bataan* into the Haeju Man approaches to bombard the shore batteries guarding this potential source of enemy seaborne supply. And by this time ComNavFE had ordered a bombardment of the Mokpo area by British warships, with patrol plane spot from Naval Air Japan.

Such a bombardment is no child's play, for it involves a 30-mile approach through a constricted and tortuous channel where the currents at ebb and flood exceed ten knots. But on the 1st a promise of big business arrived, with a report from FEAF of large ships and many small craft in Mokpo harbor, and on the next day the destroyers *Cockade* and *Cossack* steamed in to the attack. Docks and railroad sidings were bombarded with satisfactory results, but the FEAF dispatch appears to have been in error: after an hour over the target the spotters in the VP 6 Neptune reported that one sunken steamer constituted the only shipping present.

6. *The Marines Arrive*

In the spring of 1950, when war in Korea was still just a war of nerves, the North Koreans had put forward a unification scheme which called for all-Korean elections on 5 August. In Moscow, *Izvestia* had informed the Communist world that the unification of Korea was expected to take place in time to permit elections on that date. On 25 June, in military array, large numbers of would-be voters had crossed the 38th parallel headed south. But contrary, doubtless, to plan, this one-sided enlargement of the electorate had not continued unopposed. Non-Communist guardians of the polls had been hastily sent forward by sea, and as July ended and the scheduled date drew near, the Far Eastern theater had been considerably reinforced.

Boxer had reached Yokosuka on 23 July with her cargo of Mustang fighters for the Fifth Air Force, having established a new trans-Pacific record by steaming from San Francisco to Tokyo Bay in eight days and 16 hours. The carrier *Philippine Sea* had left San Diego on the 6th; after ten days concentrated training in the Hawaiian area she had steamed westward at speed to reach Buckner Bay on 1 August. Admiral Hartman's cruisers and destroyers had reported in to ComNavFE, and although *Helena* and the destroyer division had been sent to Formosa, this detachment was only temporary. Since 8-inch guns were more useful in action in Korea than on patrol in Formosa Strait, Admiral Struble formed Task Group 77.3, composed of *Juneau,* the destroyers *Moore* and *Maddox,* and the oiler *Cimarron,* and sent it south to relieve the *Helena* group. On 1 August, after five days in the Formosa area, Admiral Hartman headed north again, and on the 7th was bombarding the North Korean coast.

In still other categories the situation was improving. As an offshoot of Captain Austin's Service Squadron 3, a second logistic command had been created in Service Division 31, which opened for business at Sasebo on 1 August and which would steadily grow in strength. And other United Nations ships were coming in: in addition to those incorporated in Admiral Andrewes' west coast element, one French and two New Zealand frigates arrived on 1 August to reinforce the escort group.

By now, too, the air and ground components of the 1st Provisional Marine Brigade were approaching the theater of action. The ships of Task Group 53.7, which had been assembled by the Pacific Fleet Amphibious Force to lift this contingent, had sailed from southern California ports on 12 and 14 July. During the following two weeks, as fighting in Korea increased in intensity, the task group had steamed steadily westward across the Pacific. Steadily, that is, except for a pair of near-serious mishaps. One day out of San Diego the well deck of the LSD *Fort Marion* had accidentally flooded, and salt water had damaged a number of tanks and a quantity of ammunition. The transport *Henrico* had developed serious mechanical difficulties and had been forced to put back to Oakland for repairs. Three days of urgent effort were required to put *Henrico* back in commission, but on the 18th she steamed out the Golden Gate and headed west at best speed in the hope of overtaking the task group.

With the brigade on its way, General Craig and General Cushman flew westward, reaching Tokyo on 19 July. There in conference with the Commander in Chief they learned the plans for their employment. It was the hope of CincFE to mount an amphibious counterstroke, and by a September landing at Inchon to seize the Seoul transportation complex and sever the invaders from their source of supply. To carry out this plan he had asked for the entire 1st Marine Division. The brigade would be held in Japan until the rest of this force arrived.

Headquarters had intended to base the ground elements of the Marine Brigade at Sasebo, and the air echelon near Kobe, some 350 miles to the eastward on the Inland Sea. In his interview with the Supreme Commander, General Craig had placed special emphasis on the importance of maintaining the integrity of his air-ground team, and had secured the promise that it would remain intact. To keep it so, and to avoid the administrative and training problems which dispersion would impose, the Marine generals proposed to base the entire force in the Kobe-Osaka area, and on the 23rd secured approval of this arrangement. But the 23rd was also the day of EUSAK's emergency call for carrier air support, and the developing crisis made it impossible to retain the brigade for the September landings. In the north the enemy was already inside the Naktong basin; the central front was under heavy pressure; on the west the North Korean flanking movement had reached Hadong, only 75 miles from Pusan. Nothing could now be held back. All available force had to be committed. The ships containing the Marine air echelon would continue on to Kobe to unload, but on the 25th orders went out to Task Group 53.7 to land the ground force at Pusan.

If the Marine Brigade was to be committed at once the air group had to be quickly made operational, and this required some unscrambling. The escort carriers of Cardiv 15 had been separated at the start of the emergency: *Sicily,* with her antisubmarine squadron, had been ordered to Guam, while *Badoeng Strait* had embarked the aircraft of MAG 33 and sailed in company with the transports carrying the ground personnel. *Sicily* reached Guam on 20 July; as the submarine menace had not materialized she there disembarked her squadron and sailed for Yokosuka, where she arrived on the 27th. Four days later, on 31 July, *Badoeng Strait* and the transports entered Kobe.

With the arrival of his carriers Rear Admiral Ruble was relieved of his temporary chores as Commander Naval Air Japan and began a fancy juggling act. On the 31st he put his staff aboard *Sicily* at Yokosuka and sailed her for Kobe to rejoin her consort. There she loaded ground personnel, spare parts, and ammunition for VMF 214, and on the afternoon of 1 August sailed for the southern tip of Kyushu to rendezvous with the destroyers *Doyle* and *Kyes*. On the same afternoon *Badoeng Strait* got underway from Kobe to fly off aircraft to the Itami airbase; this was completed the next day, whereupon the carrier returned to port to replenish. On the 2nd, as *Sicily* was joining her escorts in Van Diemen Strait, Admiral Ruble went aboard *Badoeng Strait*. On the 3rd the Corsairs of VMF 214 took off from Itami, landed aboard *Sicily* early in the afternoon, and then, as the ship steamed toward Tsushima Strait, flew off their first air strike in support of ground forces in Korea. *Badoeng Strait,* with the division commander on board, also got underway on the 3rd, escorted by destroyers *Endicott* and *Thomas,* to spend the next two days in refresher training for her squadron, while *Sicily* moved into the Yellow Sea to strike targets on the Korean west coast.

While the units of Carrier Division 15 were performing these gyrations, efforts were being made to provide the communications and control facilities so essential to the effective cooperation of air and ground components. Marine Tactical Air Control Squadron 2 was split, the air defense section moving to Itami, where the night fighters of VMFN 513 were to base, while the air support section was sailed for Pusan by LST, along with ground personnel of the observation squadron. On the 2nd, four helicopters and four spotting planes of VMO 6 were flown from Japan to Pusan, and then onwards to Chinhae on the 4th, as the LST with the ground crews reached Pusan.

In the meantime the ground forces were arriving. *Henrico,* the tail-end transport, just made it. On the morning of 2 August she overtook the rest of Task Group 53.7 in Tsushima Strait, and in the afternoon the ships carrying the Marine Brigade steamed into Pusan. Around the Korean perimeter the situation was so bad that decisions were being made on a minute-to-minute basis, and it was not until almost midnight that General Craig learned his destination. An all-night effort by all hands got the supplies ashore and deposited with the Pusan Base Command, additional transport was borrowed from the Army, and by 0700 the troops were moving toward the perimeter. By evening of the 3rd the Marines were deployed defensively west of the town of Changwon.

By 5 August communications had been established between the brigade's air support control personnel and the escort carriers at sea. On the 6th *Sicily* and *Badoeng Strait* rendezvoused off the southwestern tip of Korea, Admiral Ruble's staff joined him by breeches buoy, and air and ground forces were ready to operate as a unit.

It was high time. Changwon is less than 30 miles from Pusan. Six miles or so beyond Changwon lies the town of Masan, and beyond Masan was the North Korean 6th Division. Distances in Korea, in early August, were very small.

CHAPTER VI

Holding the Line

1. The Perimeter Takes Form

AUGUST opened in an atmosphere of crisis. All early estimates of the Korean problem had been invalidated, anticipations of speedy victory were dead, and the U.N. Command faced the excruciating question of whether it would be able to hold on the Korean peninsula, or whether its forces would be thrown into the sea. Space had been previously traded off for time, but both commodities were now in short supply. One natural defensive line remained, the line of the Naktong River. When this was reached it would be time to turn and fight.

There were now available to General Walker five reconstituted ROK divisions, the better part of four U.S. Army divisions, and the Marine Brigade. Although contemporary estimates gave the North Koreans a heavy numerical superiority, it appears in fact that U.N. combat strength already slightly exceeded that of the enemy. But it was the estimates that formed the picture, and in any event there was a critical shortage in reserves: where the North Korean People's Army, holding the initiative and with victory in sight, could afford to accept heavy losses in exchange for important gains, for EUSAK any loss was a matter of grave concern.

Only at sea and in the air did the U.N. have important advantages. If proper employment of Air Force, Navy, and Marine aircraft, and of the fire support ships could offset the enemy's presumed superiority of numbers, it was possible that with skill and bravery the line could be held. To accomplish more was for the moment out of the question. Even the holding mission seemed problematical enough. Yet while to those in the line the problem of chasing the enemy home again was for the moment of no concern, on higher levels it was being given active consideration.

To General MacArthur it seemed that a landing at Inchon followed by seizure of the Seoul area, the hub of the Korean communications network, promised the best hope of a speedy decision. To carry out this landing, and to amputate the invaders from their sources of supply, amphibious shipping and a trained amphibious assault force were required. Repeated requests by CincFE for the early dispatch of the 1st Marine Division were finally answered in late July: the division would sail from the west coast in mid-August. But while this marked a considerable step toward the desired goal, other difficulties remained.

The objective on which General MacArthur had set his heart, however desirable strategically, presented serious tactical difficulties. The tidal range of the Yellow Sea and the hydrography of Inchon Harbor were limiting factors: to bring in and beach LSTs with supplies for the assault force required a tidal range of 29 feet, and spring tides of such a magnitude are limited to one three-day period a month. Thus strategy depended upon astronomy, and the future of the war upon the phases of the moon. One period of high tides would come in mid-September, and this date set the double problem for the United Nations Command. The Korean foothold had to be held for the intervening six weeks. The Marine Division had to arrive in time.

By early August the perimeter in which Eighth Army was to make its stand had assumed pretty much its final form. Through the latter part of July the North Korean invaders had continued their four-pronged advance, with one column in the east coast strip, two moving southeast along the main routes from Seoul, and a flanking force on the right skirting the central hill mass. Tardy discovery of this last movement, which was opposed only by small ROK detachments, had brought the misdirected call for carrier strikes in the region east of Kunsan, and the movement of a battalion of the 29th Regiment westward from Pusan to Hadong on the south coast.

The week from 29 July to 5 August saw the American and ROK forces retiring on all fronts. In the northwest the Communist armies advanced some 35 miles, streaming over the mountain wall and down into the Naktong Valley, to reach the river opposite Waegwan. In the northern hill sector the enemy pushed forward 15 to 20 miles, from Yongju to Andong on the upper Naktong. In the south, at Hadong, affairs went badly: the American battalion and associated ROK troops were overrun and, while about 100 survivors were evacuated by ROK small craft from the Chinhae Naval Base and others escaped overland, casualties exceeded 50 percent.

At the start of the week United Nations positions had run northward from Hadong to the divide between the Kum and Naktong basins, northeasterly to Yongju, and southeast to the coastal town of Yongdok. As the week ended U.N. forces held only about a seventh of the territory of the Republic of Korea, and had been compressed into an area measuring some 100 miles from north to south, and slightly more than half of that from east to west. From Chindong-ni on the south coast the line ran north along the Naktong River, and east through Andong to Yongdok, where ROK forces supported by naval gunfire still held fast.

Although the withdrawals of the previous week had diminished the area to be defended, they had complicated the problems of the defenders; paradoxically, the shrinkage of the perimeter had extended the fighting front. During the retreat phase the tactical problem had been to slow the North Korean advance along the principal communication routes. But now, with the enemy well inside the Naktong basin, his spearheads were no longer constricted by the hill masses and his freedom of maneuver was increased. In the north the advance to Andong, which brought him down into the lowlands and to an east-west highway leading to Yongdok, was followed by the eastward movement of the 12th Division to strengthen the attack on Pohang. In the northwest the descent from the saddle toward Waegwan opened lateral communications east of the central hill mass, and permitted a southward displacement of Communist strength which brought pressure along the whole Naktong River line. It also posed a serious threat to Taegu, where the South Korean government had established itself, where there was an important airstrip, and where the Fifth Air Force had set up its Joint Operations Center. With the enemy inside the landing circle the Air Force was obliged to remove its planes to Japan and the JOC to Pusan, with all the complications in communication and control that such movements entail. How agreeable a prospect this situation afforded when viewed from the north is evidenced by a North Korean I Corps operation order of 3 August, which called for the capture of Taegu and Pusan by the 6th.

In this the enemy was to be disappointed. But the more extensive road system now available permitted him to redeploy his strength and, as August wore on, to exert heavy pressure at four points around the perimeter. Two of the crucial areas were inland, at Waegwan on the main line of communications, and on the Naktong front west of Yongsan. Two were on the flanks, at Pohang on the eastern shore, and in the south between Masan and Chinju. It was in this southern area, where the enemy flanking movement seemed to pose the most immediate threat to Pusan, that General Walker planned his first counteroffensive. It was for this spoiling attack that the Marine Brigade had been ordered forward, and had been combined with two RCTs of the 25th Division into Task Force Kean.

2. 26 July–13 August: Coastal Bombardment, the Problem of Carrier Air, and the Southern Spoiling Offensive

While this southern counterattack was in preparation, U.N. naval and air forces pressed their efforts against the enemy's lengthening lines of communication. Carried on by coastal patrol and blockade, by bombardment from the sea, and by air attack, this work would continue in increasing strength. Air Force as well as naval reinforcements were coming in, and FEAF's daily sorties were rapidly increasing in number. In the last days of July General Stratemeyer persuaded CincFE to release some of his bombers from work below the parallel, and the B-29s were preparing to strike north against the enemy's urban complexes and against his transportation net.

As July ended Task Force 77 retired to Okinawa for logistics, and naval responsibility for air support of the perimeter devolved upon the escort carriers. Of these *Sicily* was first in action. On 2 August she picked up her screening ships south of Kyushu, and on the next day the aircraft of VMF 214 arrived on board from Itami. That afternoon a first strike was flown off against North Korean troop concentrations near Chinju in the south and on the central Naktong front. On the 4th further strikes were flown against the enemy in the Chinju area, and with evening the *Sicily* group steamed into the Yellow Sea and headed northward.

There on the 5th an international three-dimensional evolution took place. Screened by *Charity* and *Cossack,* the cruisers *Belfast* and *Kenya* steamed up the hazardous approaches to Inchon, where with spot provided by a Neptune from VP 6 they bombarded oil storage, factories, warehouses, and gun positions. Fighter cover for the spotting plane was given by some of *Sicily's* Corsairs, while others attacked transport and industrial facilities in the Inchon-Seoul region. The Marine Brigade was not yet in action and close support activity had not begun, but close reconnaissance was now put into practice. His suspicion aroused by the antiaircraft defenses of an Inchon factory, one pilot buzzed past at 50 feet, peered in the windows to observe a concentration of vehicles, and returned to deal with the situation by putting a napalm bomb into the building. On the 6th the *Sicily* group moved southward to strike targets at Kunsan and Mokpo and troops on the south coast, and to rendezvous with *Badoeng Strait* and her attendant destroyers.

On the east coast the last echelon of Pohang shipping was completing its unloading when Admiral Higgins arrived with *Toledo* on 26 July. There the arrival of the heavy cruiser proved a useful addition to the destroyers on duty offshore, and to the field artillery battalion and the F–51 fighter-bomber squadron which had already reinforced this isolated theater. For the aviators, as for the contending ground forces, these east coast operations constituted a private war: lacking communications with the JOC at Taegu the squadron operated from the Pohang airstrip on its own. Despite all difficulties coordination with the east coast naval forces was reasonably good, but there were still surprises: in August *Helena's* helicopter and a destroyer would fish two downed F–51 pilots out of the Sea of Japan, neither of whom was aware that the ships off Yongdok were friendly.

On 27 July 8-inch guns were used for the first time against the invading army, as *Toledo* fired on troop concentrations, supplies, and revetments by day, and by night illuminated the battleline with star shell. By careful conservation of ammunition this support was continued for 11 days, and so effective was the shooting of the cruiser and the destroyers, assisted by a

24th Division fire control party and by air spot, that only here did the battleline remain stable. Cruising generally some 7,000 yards offshore, exchanging liaison personnel with the forces ashore by whaleboat, covering the seaborne arrival of supplies for frontline troops, and making arrangements for possible evacuation, the ships of Higgins' element found their days full. On 4 August good work was done at a village near Yongdok in cooperation with rocket-firing Air Force fighters: troops were dispersed, large fires were started, and when clearing smoke revealed the fire-fighters at work the process was repeated. On the 5th, after shooting with air spot at enemy front line positions, gratifying compliments were received from both ground and airborne spotting personnel.

By this time, indeed, the situation seemed sufficiently stabilized so that Admiral Higgins, who felt 8-inch gunfire somewhat wasted in harassing troops, could request and receive permission to look for something better. The 7th of August was therefore spent 70 miles to the northward, in the neighborhood of Samchok, where the task element ranged along a 25-mile stretch of coast, firing on targets selected from aerial photographs. A bridge across a small river was destroyed, road junctions were plowed up, embankments were knocked down across the highway, and two tunnels sealed by bombardment and landslide.

Admiral Hartman's *Helena* group had meanwhile been cruising Formosa Strait, where it was joined by *Juneau* on 30 July. Two cruisers and a destroyer division are a small force with which to prevent a large-scale invasion, especially one embarked in a fleet of almost unsinkable junks. But the issue did not arise, and in any case the Seventh Fleet Striking Force remained on call. On 1 August the task group was dissolved, Admiral Hartman headed his ships back northward, and after three days at Sasebo for logistics sailed once again for the northeastern coast of Korea, where air sightings had reported a thousand railroad cars in the region between 40° and 42° N. This time he got there.

The bombardment of the town of Tanchon in 40°28′, carried out by *Helena* and Destroyer Division 111 on 7 August, marked the furthest north for U.N. surface forces since *Juneau's* early raid. Located a couple of miles up an estuary at the point where two rivers join, Tanchon offered tempting rail and highway bridge targets, a marshalling yard, and some minor industrial facilities. With a VP 6 spotting plane overhead, the force shot up boxcars in the yard and the town power plants, and inflicted a satisfactory 75 percent damage on the railroad bridge. The only excitement of the day was provided by the late arrival of a four-plane combat air patrol from Fifth Air Force, which showed no IFF and was only identified visually after batteries had been released. Having applied this pressure to the northeastern artery, the *Helena* group came southward during the night, and on the next day dropped a highway and a rail bridge near Sokcho, just above

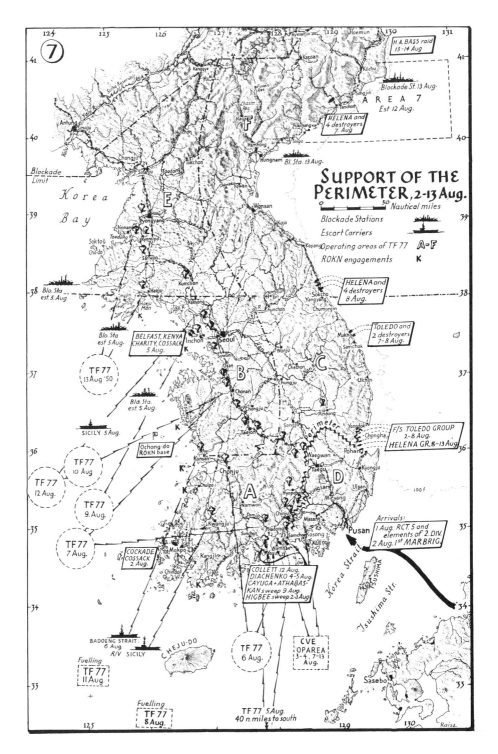

the 38th parallel. This work completed, Admiral Hartman relieved Admiral Higgins of his fire support responsibilities off Yongdok, and the *Toledo* group headed for Sasebo to replenish.

On the west coast of Korea Admiral Andrewes' element, now divided into three rotating sections of a cruiser and two or more destroyers each, was carrying out its duties of bombardment and blockade. Here the land war had swept past and no fire support was required, but the numerous islands and the shoal waters which fringe the coast made the interdiction of communications a sufficient task. On the 5th, on instructions from Com-NavFE, the British commander established three barrier stations off the western headlands, between 38°08′ and 36°45′, which were kept manned as availability of ships permitted. Inshore work steadily improved as cooperation with the reviving ROK Navy was developed, and the blockade became increasingly effective.

In the south, however, new problems were arising. There on 28 July CincFE had ordered a round-up of small craft to deny them to the invader, and on 1 August, in consequence of the enemy advance and the defeat at Hadong, ComNavFE had instructed Admiral Higgins' task element and Commander Luosey's ROKN units to harass and disrupt land and water movement in the neighborhood of Namhae Island. On the 8th the importance of this task was emphasized by high level estimates which indicated that the enemy had reached the end of his supply line, that he was especially short of gasoline for tanks and trucks, and that efforts at seaborne supply were to be anticipated.

The Korean Navy, however, was already fully occupied in the west. On 3 August the ROK *YMS 502* sank seven sailboats which were loading off Kunsan; four days later and 30 miles to the northward she sank two motorboats, while other Korean units destroyed four small junks in the Haeju Man approaches above Inchon. On the 9th an important step was taken in support of west coast operations as an LST was sailed for Ochong Do, an island 40 miles off Kunsan, to establish an advanced ROKN supply base which would eliminate the 300-mile round trip to Pusan.

Since the Koreans were busy elsewhere, U.S. and Commonwealth units were made available in the south. On 2 and 3 August the destroyer *Higbee* patrolled the Namhae area but encountered no enemy movement. On the night of 4–5 August underwater demolition personnel from the fast transport *Diachenko* attempted to blow bridges north of the railroad town of Yosu, a natural jumping-off place for enemy shore-to-shore movement. But the landing force was repelled by a North Korean patrol, which arrived inopportunely by handcar, and *Diachenko* had to content herself with a 40-minute bombardment of the railroad yards. Four days later an imaginative B-29 report of heavy junk concentrations near Yosu brought the Canadian destroyers *Cayuga* and *Athabaskan* on a flank speed sweep of the south coast, but with negative results. On the 12th the destroyer *Collett,* from Admiral Higgins' task element, steamed into Yosu Gulf to bombard the town.

For the first few days of August, while these coastal activities were in progress, the Seventh Fleet Striking Force lay at anchor in Buckner Bay. During this interval Admiral Struble visited Formosa, in company with General MacArthur, to perfect planning and liaison against the chance of a Communist invasion; the carrier *Philippine Sea* arrived from the United States, and Rear Admiral Edward C. Ewen, Commander Carrier Division 1, flew in from Pearl and reported aboard. In Tokyo, in the meantime, further efforts were being made to accomplish a workable coordination of the operations of the Air Force and of naval air.

The first step toward meshing naval and Air Force activities had been taken when FEAF requested strikes in northeastern Korea. A second shortly followed, with General Stratemeyer's request for "operational control" of all aircraft in the theater and with CincFE's letter delegating "coordination control" to the commanding general of FEAF; by early August further measures were in train. On the 3rd, while General MacArthur and Admiral Struble were in Formosa, a conference was held in Tokyo in which FEAF deployed four generals and a colonel to face one captain, two commanders, and two lieutenant commanders. The result was a memorandum providing that first priority for carrier operations would be in close support, second priority would go to interdiction south of the 38th parallel, and third priority to strikes on Bomber Command targets beyond that line. Coordination for attacks south of 38° was to lie with Fifth Air Force; attacks on Bomber Command targets required clearance from FEAF. Six plans, designated by letter, were devised for carrier employment, and the peninsula divided into six corresponding operating areas. Plans A through C called for the use of half the available aircraft in support of troops and half in interdiction in the designated area; plans E and F involved area attacks alone; plan D called for everything on close support.

This emphasis on the support of troops inevitably meant that the operations of carrier aircraft would fall in large degree under the control of FAFIK, Fifth Air Force in Korea, and of its Joint Operations Center. On the face of it there was nothing illogical about the arrangement, which would presumably have been successful had it only worked, and similar conditions were shortly laid upon the escort carriers by ComNavFE. But just as the problem of interdiction had raised command problems on the upper level, in the question of operational versus coordination control, so the commitment to close support was to bring almost insoluble difficulties in the tactical handling of aircraft over the lines, as doctrinal differences and the inadequacy of control mechanisms combined to frustrate the best efforts of the Striking Force. Close support turned out to work best when least needed, and when the Seventh Fleet could most profitably be employed against northern bridges and other communications targets; in times of crisis around the perimeter it worked poorly or not at all. Faced with so wasteful an employment of his very considerable strength, and not having been consulted regarding the agreement, Admiral Struble declined to accept its definition of roles and missions, and the Seventh Fleet was soon attempting to break away from the perimeter. By mid-month the primacy of close support had become a dead letter; the movements of the Seventh Fleet were being designated by periodic dispatches from CincFE; and the concepts of plan and area, set forth in the memorandum of 3 August, were tending to separate, with the letter designation indicating only the area to be attacked.

For the moment, however, the effort was to be in support of the front. On 4 August Admiral Struble issued an operation order which called for strikes on targets previously selected and coordinated with FEAF, instructed the carrier task group to establish direct communications with the JOC at Taegu and attack enemy troops and targets in the forward areas, and established a fueling rendezvous with the oiler *Cacapon* for the 7th. Late in the afternoon of the 4th the strengthened Seventh Fleet sortied from Buckner Bay and headed north once more "to conduct air operations in support of ground forces."

On the morning of the 5th the force launched from a position south of Korea. Pilots from *Philippine Sea,* entering action for the first time, were assigned specific targets in southwestern Korea, with the emphasis on the rail and highway bridges at Iri, east of Kunsan, where cuts would hamper movement of supplies to the enemy's southern flank. *Valley Forge* planes were sent off on close support missions, and while the weight of effort was concentrated on troops, supplies, and bridges in the dangerous northern sector, two Corsairs attacked enemy personnel west of Taegu and five ADs inflicted heavy casualties on troops behind the central front. But these Skyraiders reported poor control, and an eight-plane jet sweep never did succeed in reaching its assigned controller.

Dissatisfied with the operation of control procedures, Admiral Hoskins now sent four *Valley Forge* pilots to Taegu, for liaison purposes and to help in the direction of support aircraft. In the hope of reducing congestion the front was divided into four sectors, each of which was provided with both an Air Force and a Navy airborne controller. Although the original intention of having Navy controllers handle Navy flights gave way under pressure, and all hands took whatever came along, the sharing of the burden and the increased number of radio frequencies which resulted from the use of Navy planes led to considerable improvement. But periods of saturation continued, as incoming flights arrived in large batches instead of scheduled driblets, and while this congestion was particularly difficult in the case

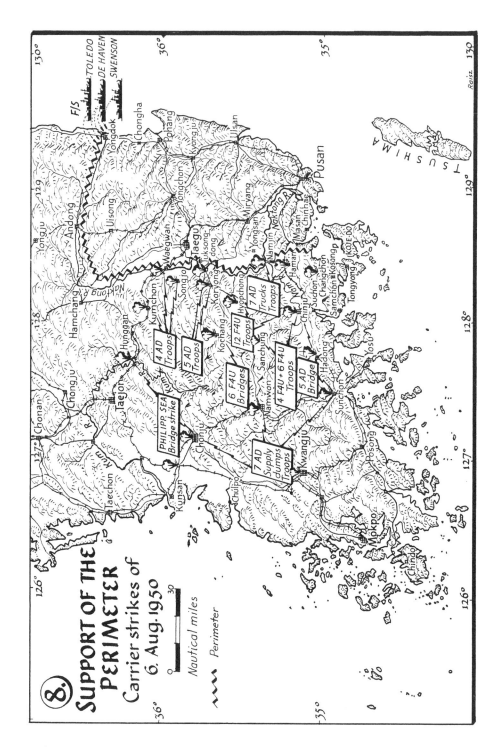

8. SUPPORT OF THE PERIMETER

Carrier strikes of 6. Aug. 1950

Nautical miles

Perimeter

of Air Force planes, operating at maximum range from their Japanese bases, it affected the work of the carrier aircraft as well.

The 6th of August saw the task force still south of Korea, attacking objectives assigned by air controllers and bridge and highway targets from Yosu north to Hwanggan. Once again *Philippine Sea* concentrated her efforts on transportation facilities, while *Valley Forge* flew 24 Corsair and 22 Skyraider sorties under JOC control. The emphasis, as on the previous day, was on the Chinju assembly area and on enemy lines of communication behind it; but attacks were also made on troop and transportation targets behind the central Naktong front, in the Waegwan area, and in the important neighboring junction town of Kumchon. Claims for the day included destruction of a large supply dump, five trucks, two jeeps, and a tank, damage to a number of bridges, and many troop casualties; the distribution of effort represented a useful attempt at close interdiction, if not at close support of troops in combat.

With the day's work completed and with pilots' reports at hand, the situation was discussed by Admiral Struble and his carrier division commanders. To Admiral Ewen the results of the effort in close air support appeared quite simply "negligible." Admiral Hoskins felt the work handicapped by the cumbersome centralization of JOC control, which required excessive expenditure of time in checking in and securing target assignments, and by the tendency of Eighth Army to call for maximum effort and so bring saturation of control facilities. The upshot of the discussion was a pair of dispatches from Commander Seventh Fleet to ComNavFE, in which he reported an urgent request from JOC for "close support" of ground operations on the next day, expressed his doubts as to the value of such an effort, proposed that the escort carriers be given the whole job on the 8th, and stated his desire to strike the important west bridge at Seoul.

During the night the force moved into the Yellow Sea, and on the 7th, from a position west of Mokpo, swept airfields and flew strikes against bridges, warehouses, rail yards, and vehicles in the region south of the 38th parallel. The realities of civil war were emphasized this day when the fleet, steaming some 70 miles offshore, passed through water containing many floating bodies, tied together in bundles and with their hands lashed behind their backs. At mid-day, in response to the JOC request, an effort at support of the perimeter was made by eight Corsairs and nine ADs flown in from *Philippine Sea*. These planes found a controller who had two tanks as a target, but who was unable to turn them over to the Navy flight as some F–80s from Japan required immediate handling. No controlled attacks, whether in close support or in interdiction, were therefore made.

The apparent wastefulness of these efforts in support of the perimeter, together with the availability of the escort carriers, now led both ComNavFE and Commander Seventh Fleet to consider springing the force loose for strikes to the northward. An afternoon dispatch from Admiral Joy suggested that, subject to especially urgent need for close support, the carriers strike coastal targets in Area F, between Chongjin and Hungnam, where many trains and much rolling stock had been recently reported, and where *Helena* was currently shooting up Tanchon. This message crossed one from Admiral Struble in which he reported that after fuelling on the 8th he hoped to strike northward in Area E on the 9th, returning to Area B the next day; should however the Army require support at the perimeter, the force would fly missions in Area B on the 9th and in A on the 10th.

These hopes, however, were to be deferred by a dispatch from Com-NavFE, received on the afternoon of the 8th as the force was fuelling from *Passumpsic* and *Cacapon* to the south of Cheju Do. Concern for the safety of Eighth Army had led CincFE to order the entire carrier air effort placed on close support and close interdiction from 8 to 17 August. With this order the southward displacement of Seventh Fleet operations, developing ever since FEAF's first request for attacks in the northeastern quadrant of Korea, reached its ultimate conclusion. For the next ten days, it appeared, the carriers were to be frozen in support of the perimeter. Close support, in this context, meant support of Army units under JOC control: the Marine Brigade, with its organic Tactical Air Control Squadron and with its own aircraft operating from the escort carriers, was well cared for. But the Army needed everything it could get: the North Koreans had forced the Naktong, and had a regiment across the river at the big bend west of Yongsan.

Admiral Struble's plan to hit targets in Area E was now perforce abandoned. The 9th of August again found the carriers west of Mokpo, flying strikes against the Inchon-Seoul area. There, for the first time, antiaircraft fire of moderate intensity was encountered; there, at Air Force request, the three-span bridge over the Han at Seoul was attacked and hit with 1,000-pound bombs. West of Taegu a four-plane flight, sent in to the perimeter from *Valley Forge,* discovered adequate control and destroyed a tank. At sea the larger sphere of relations between east and west was illustrated when a screening destroyer recovered five friendly floating Koreans, one of whom claimed U.S. citizenship.

On the 10th, operations continued in the same pattern, with continued emphasis on interdiction of the Inchon-Seoul complex. This was *Philippine Sea's* day in close support, and 4 six-plane flights were sent in at three-hour intervals. But all were forced to attack targets of opportunity, none was used in support of troops, and two failed entirely to contact a controller owing to overloaded radio channels.

Within the force the search went on for ways and means of improving the close support situation. On the 8th, on the basis of reports from liaison pilots returning from Taegu, Admiral Hoskins identified the principal problems as the "understandable" ignorance of carrier capabilities at Fifth Air

Force headquarters, the inadequate communications set-up there, and the Seventh Fleet's desire to maintain radio silence when possible. As remedies he proposed the immediate assignment of a captain aviator, experienced in carrier and close support operations, as liaison officer with Fifth Air Force in Korea, and the establishment of communications channels which would permit, and of policies which would ensure, a continuous two-way flow of information. On the next day Admiral Ewen listed as major deficiencies the absence of reliable communications, both between the carriers and JOC and at the scene of action, and the oversaturation of aircraft at the objective. Stating that less than 30 percent of the fleet's potential was being used in close support, he suggested that Admiral Struble tell ComNavFE "the whole story," and urged the assignment to the air control function of aircraft with adequate endurance and reliable radio gear, and the employment of the *Mount McKinley* air support party to improve communications in the perimeter.

Commander Seventh Fleet told "the whole story," or at least a good deal of it, on the night of 9–10 August in a message to ComNavFE with information copies to CincFE, EUSAK, FEAF, and Fifth Air Force. This dispatch pointed out the "urgent and continuing need of air support for our ground forces," described the problems of control of aircraft at the objective, and reported "only partial employment" of aircraft sent in to Taegu. Recognizing that the air controllers were operating under great difficulties, and that the Navy ought to assist in any way it could with officer personnel and communications arrangements, Admiral Struble noted that the Seventh Fleet remained prepared to contribute control aircraft as it had previously done, and once again suggested that "possibly" *Mount McKinley* air control personnel could help out.

Although no specific mention was made of the problem of interforce communications, or of Hoskins' proposed assignment of a qualified and senior liaison officer, there were possibilities here if only they were acted on. But none of the commanders to whom the dispatch was addressed seems to have followed it up, and ComNavFE's response was not entirely helpful. Apparently as a result of semantic confusion, Admiral Struble's report had been interpreted not as "partial employment" in close support, but as indicative of failure to expend ordnance, and the reply observed that this was "not understood" in view of the number of interdiction targets available in the south. Employment of the *Mount McKinley* Tacron was refused on the ground that it was engaged in training operations, and the other suggestions were passed back to the operating commanders. Commander Seventh Fleet was instructed to furnish airborne controllers as arranged with JOC; the Commanding General Fifth Air Force was invited to state any needs for personnel and communications assistance.

This exchange of generalities seems merely to have strengthened Admiral Struble's desire to get away from the perimeter and strike northward. For although he at once requested information on interdiction targets from all hands, his revised intentions for the future called for strikes in Area B on the 12th, followed by a move north to attack the region between Sinanju and Pyongyang. This dispatch elicited a request from Fifth Air Force, received on the 12th as the carrier bombers struck marshalling yards near Seoul and as jet fighters swept airfields and communication lines, which indicated that all effort was still wanted in Area B. Although undertaking to comply if necessary, Commander Seventh Fleet observed in reply that he had been cleared by GHQ to strike northward the next morning, and would do so if his efforts could be spared. Apparently they could. The prospective ten-day freeze had actually lasted five, and on the 13th aircraft from both carriers ranged north of the parallel, attacking transportation targets at Pyongyang, Chinnampo, Haeju, and way stations with good results, especially in the destruction of locomotives. On conclusion of this day's operations the force retired southward, passed *Triumph* and her escorts who were steering north to take over the Yellow Sea duty, and headed for Sasebo to replenish.

While the Seventh Fleet Striking Force was struggling with the problems of close support of the perimeter, the Marine Brigade had begun its first offensive. To contain the enemy's south coast advance, General Walker had decided to attack westward from Masan, toward Chinju, some 30 miles beyond. Army forces were to move west along the main highway; the Marines were assigned the task of cleaning out the left flank along the coastal road through Kosong and Sachon. On the 5th, as aircraft from the fast carriers struck enemy forces near Chinju, orders were issued for an attack to begin on the 7th.

On that day, the eighth anniversary of the landing on Guadalcanal, the Marine Brigade attacked westward. In this peninsula, as on that island, the weather was hot, humid, and exhausting. Three days of heavy and confused fighting followed while the hills controlling the road junction at Chindong-ni were cleared. But coordinated employment of brigade artillery and of Marine aircraft commuting in from the escort carriers broke up the enemy formations and chased them back into the hills. Tanks, vehicles, and guns were destroyed by the aviators from Admiral Ruble's task group, and napalm and strafing helped to clear the heights. By evening of the 9th the Marines were on the move, with orders to capture Paedun-ni, five miles down the coastal road, before daylight.

On the 10th General Craig pushed his brigade down the road to the southwest. *Sicily* had retired to Sasebo for two days, but *Badoeng Strait* did the work of two with 44 sorties. Paedun-ni was seized early in the morning, and indications of enemy confusion brought orders to press on with all speed. In early afternoon, a couple of miles beyond the town, the van entered an ambush at Taedabok Pass. Tanks were brought forward, the Corsairs reported in, and the pass was cleared; the force bivouacked for the night on the far side of the cut and two-thirds of the way to Kosong, the first major objective. Elsewhere, however, things were more ominous: on the 8th, during the fighting at Chindong-ni, the North Koreans built up their Naktong bridgehead to regimental strength, and by the 10th the enemy 4th Division was across the river.

At 0800 on the morning of the 11th the advance on Kosong was resumed. A few shells lobbed into the town flushed an estimated hundred vehicles which headed westward out of town at high speed. Overhead a division of Corsairs from *Badoeng Strait* observed trucks retreating so fast that some missed the turns and rolled down the embankments; making the most of this agreeable opportunity with rockets and 20-millimeter fire, the aviators piled up rolling stock in wholesale quantity. By 1000 the town had been taken, a hill to the southward was shortly secured, and the Marines headed onward toward Sachon with their observation planes and Corsairs overhead and their tanks out front.

By this time things were going well for the brigade. The enemy road-blocks had been broken, momentum had been gained, enemy casualties were estimated as approaching the 2,000 mark, and the North Koreans appeared increasingly disorganized. Marine air and ground forces were working in harmony, and the advance was being paralleled in the third element. A Scajap LST and some ROKN landing craft had been brought forward from Pusan to issue supplies and receive casualties, and General Craig had requested a destroyer to provide call fire in support of the coastal advance. But in other sectors the situation was degenerating. To the north-ward American counterattacks had failed to eliminate the Naktong bulge, while in the Marines' rear the enemy had reemerged from the hills at Chindong-ni, and had cut the main supply route for Army troops advancing on Chinju. At noon on the 12th, as the Marines were nearing Changchon, the brigade was ordered to return one battalion and a battery of artillery to clean up this road block.

Afternoon of the 12th saw the Marines fighting on two fronts for the first, if not for the last time in this war. At Changchon the 1st and 2nd Battalions encountered another ambush, but the attempted envelopment brought heavy casualties to the enveloper. While this fight was going on the 3rd Battalion was being trucked back to Chindong-ni, where it arrived in late afternoon and where before dark it carried its first objective, a hill ridge commanding the main supply route.

This singular situation, in which two of the brigade's battalions were fighting at Changchon while the third was engaging 25 road miles to the rear, was ended by orders to withdraw. On the 13th, as the 3rd Battalion continued its clean-up of hills around Chindong-ni, the others disengaged and headed back to rejoin. Although it was disappointing to be pulled back after an advance of 26 miles in four days, and after inflicting heavy damage on superior forces, there were serious reasons behind the decision. The situation in the Naktong bulge was very nearly out of control.

3. 6–20 *August: East Coast Interdiction, Pohang, and First Naktong*

For the moment, at least, the threat to the southern end of the perimeter had been ended by the advance of Task Force Kean. On the coast the Marines had repelled the enemy with heavy loss; inland the 35th Infantry had briefly regained the heights along the Nam River east of Chinju. In this region North Korean units now faced difficult problems of reorganization and reequipment, and their long supply line was suffering increasingly from the cumulative effects of interdiction strikes.

As the second week of August was ending, the critical sectors of the perimeter were on the Naktong front west of Yongsan, in the northwest beyond Taegu, and on the east coast in the vicinity of Pohang. The response to this altered situation was quickly evident in the redeployment of U.N. naval forces. Admiral Joy had been directed to carry out demolition raids on the Korean coast, and as the Marine Brigade moved northward to the Naktong bulge the weight of naval effort shifted to the northeast and to the enemy's coastal line of communications with the Soviet Maritime Provinces.

North of the 40th parallel the Korean coastline is precipitous, with mountains rising steeply from the sea. Constricted by this geography, the railroad for more than 40 miles runs close to the shore, and is thus accessible to naval gunfire and to landing parties. Here in the first weeks of war *Juneau* had carried out her raid; this vulnerable area was now to be brought under all forms of naval attack.

Execution of this work was facilitated by the arrival from San Diego of the fast transport *Horace A. Bass,* Lieutenant Commander Alan Ray, a destroyer escort conversion carrying four LCVPs and with a capacity of 162 troops. On 6 August a group of underwater demolition and Marine reconnaissance personnel was assigned to *Bass,* and the resultant package designated the Special Operations Group. Two days later a new weapon became available for raids from the sea as the submarine transport *Perch,* a conversion capable of carrying 160 troops and with a cylindrical deck caisson providing stowage for landing equipment, reached Yokosuka from Pearl Harbor. A British offer of a squad of Royal Marines provided *Perch*'s raiding personnel, and brought immediate preparations for attacks on the east coast transportation line.

To this planned schedule of raiding activity Admiral Joy now added carrier strikes. On 7 August he had noted that reports of enemy rail traffic promised useful employment for Task Force 77 in Area F; a week later, as the task force was returning to Sasebo, the continued influx of such intelligence brought similar recommendations from Fifth Air Force Headquarters in Korea. Pressure on the northern front, naval and Air Force intelligence which emphasized the importance of the east coast route, and the suggestions of the naval liaison officer led on the 13th to a request from FAFIK for carrier interdiction of Area C on the 16th, to be followed by attacks on rail and other transport facilities in Area F, between Wonsan and Chongjin.

After obtaining the views of the naval commanders CincFE ordered the execution of this plan. Task Force 77 was to strike from the Sea of Japan on the 16th and 17th, refuel on the 18th, and strike again for two days. In order further to reduce the pressure on the northern front, FEAF was instructed to put its maximum bomber effort on the Waegwan area on the 16th, while the carrier planes were striking Area C. On the 17th, as proposed by Fifth Air Force, Task Force 77 would move northward to operate against Area F.

In the meantime Admiral Joy's surface forces had begun to converge on North Korea's eastern shore. On 7 August the *Helena* group, en route to relieve off Yongdok, had bombarded Tanchon. On the 13th, in response to reports of enemy shipping at Wonsan, Admiral Hartman established blockading stations in 39°50′ and 40°50′. Enemy movement on shore was also receiving attention: between 13 and 16 August, while the ship employed the daylight hours in bombardment of rail targets, the raiders from *Horace A. Bass* carried out three night landings between 41°28′ and 38°35′ which resulted in the destruction of three tunnels and two bridges. In anticipation of future attacks by *Perch,* ComNavFE had by this time established a joint zone for surface and submarine operations, Area 7, between 40° and 41° on the Korean east coast. On the 14th, as *Perch* and her Royal Marines began their training program, the submarine *Pickerel* was sailed to procure periscope photographs of selected objectives.

But while these preparations and efforts to saw up the coastal supply line were being made, a crisis had developed at Pohang. There the ROK 3rd Division had done well. With its KMAG liaison group, with artillery and fire control personnel from the 24th Division, and with the support of naval gunfire and the Pohang-based F-51s, it had held the road longer than might have been expected, and long after the cavalry division had landed and moved inland. But by now the fire control party had been transferred to another sector, while to the westward the enemy advance had uncovered lateral communications between the North Korean 5th Division and units on the inland front.

Such an eventuality had been foreseen, and preliminary planning for a water evacuation of Pohang was underway. Three LSTs were ordered up to take out Air Force ground personnel, and on the 8th the removal of heavy equipment from the Pohang airstrip was begun. By 10 August the ROK 3rd Division, outflanked on its landward side, had been forced to hole up at Chongha, ten miles north of Pohang, where it was surrounded. Having bypassed the South Koreans, the enemy advance now gained momentum, and on the 11th heavy demands were made upon the fire support ships south of Yongdok. *Helena* got four tanks this day, as her helicopter was flying KMAG personnel to Pohang to confer with General Walker, but naval gunfire was not enough. On the 12th, tank-led troops of the North Korean 5th Division fought their way into the town, where they were joined on the next day by elements of the 12th Division, switched eastward from the northern mountain front.

Little beyond naval gunfire and strikes by Air Force planes remained available for the defense of Pohang. Yet although the former was handicapped by the withdrawal of fire control personnel ashore, and although the latter were preparing to evacuate that very day, the intensity of these efforts forced the enemy to retire temporarily on the afternoon of the 13th. But so serious was the Communist threat that an emergency call was made for reinforcements. To defend the airfield American tanks and infantry and an ROK regiment were hurried north; to prevent a major breakthrough, much of EUSAK's scant reserve was ordered up to Kyongju. But the advancing columns became entangled on the way with infiltrators disguised as refugees, and progress was slow.

Such, however, was the importance attached to the east coast railroad that, in the midst of the Pohang crisis, *Helena* and two destroyers were withdrawn to bombard the bridges and tunnels at Sinchang in the north. There on the 14th the expenditure of 170-odd rounds of 8-inch and 100 rounds of 5-inch by *Helena* and *Chandler* destroyed a train and damaged two bridges. But further word on conditions at Pohang, and rumors of an enemy landing at Kuryongpo, brought Admiral Hartman back at 25 knots.

On 15 August, following reports from KMAG of the critical condition of the ROK 3rd Division, General Walker ordered its evacuation by sea. To permit the ROKs to hold their little perimeter until shipping could be assembled, fire support was essential. This support was effectively given by the *Helena* task element, which also provided medical supplies by helicopter, and motor gasoline, brought up by destroyer from Pusan, by whaleboat. Further assistance to the besieged division came from Task Force 77, which got underway once more from Sasebo on the afternoon of the 15th, and during the night steamed north to the Sea of Japan for its scheduled operations against Areas C and F.

The first strikes on the morning of the 16th were sent off, as planned, against bridges and supply dumps in Area C. But increasing pressure on the big perimeter around Taegu and on the little one at Chongha led to a switch to close support. A morning strike of eight ADs and seven F4Us from *Philippine Sea* was diverted in the air, only to have communication problems frustrate all efforts to provide the desired services. At 1115, at the request of Fifth Air Force, all strikes were put on close support. At 1445 information on the scheduled Chongha evacuation was received on board, the major objective became the protection of the ROK division, and although two later *Valley Forge* flights destroyed trucks, supplies, and gasoline in the Taegu area, the weight of effort was at Pohang. A noon flight of 15 planes from *Philippine Sea* bombed and strafed North Korean troop concentrations, and between 1230 and 1730 *Valley Forge* flew 12 AD and 11 Corsair sorties into the Pohang area.

There remained some difficulties in control. In late afternoon an 18-plane strike from *Phillippine Sea* aborted, owing to inability to reach an air controller, and *Valley Forge* pilots returning from the Pohang region reported that their controller seemed inexperienced. But if all was not perfect the results were good enough: the attacks against targets beyond the range of naval gunfire continued throughout the day, the ROK division maintained its perimeter, and by evening, when the Striking Force turned north, the evacuation had been organized.

On the chance that rescue shipping might not reach Chongha in time, Admiral Hartman had prepared an evacuation plan which contemplated removing the Korean troops on rafts towed by whaleboats and transferring them to naval vessels offshore; fortunately such heroic measures proved unnecessary. At Pusan Commander Luosey had managed to rustle up four more LSTs, one manned by Koreans and three by Japanese. These reached the evacuation area on the evening of the 16th, and were met and led in by the destroyer *Wiltsie,* to beach with the aid of jeep headlights ashore. Throughout the night, as embarkation proceeded, the support ships maintained a planned schedule of harassing fire, and beginning at 0415 the LSTs cleared the beach. By breakfast time all 5,800 ROKs, the members of the KMAG liaison group, and 1,200 civilian refugees had been evacuated, along with some 100 vehicles.

This first amphibious operation in reverse of the Korean War was thus a signal success. The ROK 3rd Division, following its ordeal, was treated to a relaxing 30-mile sea voyage to Kuryongpo, where Admiral Doyle's LSTs had landed Cavalry Division gear a month before, and where in the afternoon the rescue ships beached to put the Koreans back in the fight. By this time relieving forces from the south had fought their way through the pseudo-refugees, ROK and American units went over to the offensive, and on 18 August the enemy was again chased out of Pohang.

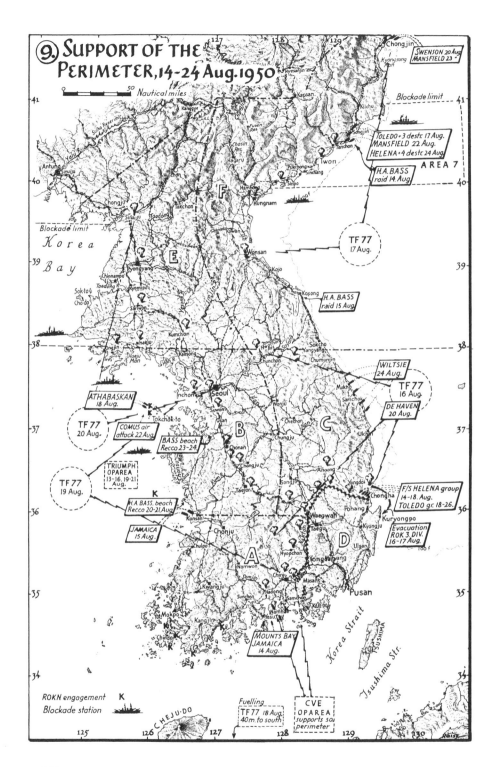

⑨ SUPPORT OF THE PERIMETER, 14-24 Aug. 1950

Nautical miles

SWENSON 20 Aug
MANSFIELD 23 "

Chongjin

Kyongsong
Han

Blockade limit

Kilchu

41

TOLEDO +3 destr. 17 Aug.
MANSFIELD 22 Aug.
HELENA +4 destr. 24 Aug.

AREA 7

Chong

Tanchon

H.A.BASS
raid 14 Aug.

Iwon

Sinpo

Hamhung

Hungnam

F

Tokchon

Taedong

Chongju

Sinuiju

Antung

Hagaru

Fuen
Res.

Chasin
Res.

Pukchong

Sinchang

Kapsan

Hyesanjin

Kangge

Suiho Reservoir

40

Blockade limit

Korea
Bay

39

Pyongyang

E

Wonsan

Kojo

TF 77
17 Aug.

Chinnampo

Sariwon

Kyemipo

Taedong

Sok-to
Cho-do

H.A. BASS
raid 15 Aug.

Kosong

Kumchon

Sokcho
Yangyang

38

Ongjin

Haeju

Kaesong

Haeju
Man

Chunchon

Chumunjin

WILTSIE
24 Aug.

TF 77
16 Aug.

ATHABASKAN
18 Aug.

Inchon

Seoul

Suwon

Wonju

Osan

Mukho
Samchok

DE HAVEN
20 Aug.

37

TF 77
20 Aug.

COMUS air
attack 22 Aug

Tokchok-to

BASS beach
Recco 23-24.

B

Chonan

Chongju

Chungju

Chechon

C

Ulchin

Andong

TRIUMPH
OP AREA
13-16, 19-21
Aug.

TF 77
19 Aug.

K

Taejon

Sangju

Yongdok

F/S HELENA group
14-18. Aug.
TOLEDO gr. 18-26.

H.A. BASS. beach
Recco 20-21, Aug.

Kunsan

Chongha

Pohang

Kuryongpo

36

JAMAICA
15 Aug.

Chonju

Chulpo

Waegwan

Taegu

Kyongju

Evacuation
ROK 3. DIV.
16-17 Aug.

A

Namwon

Hyopchon

Chinju

Ulsan

D

Yongchon

Kwangju

Sunchon

Hadong

Samchon

Masan

Yongyang

KOJE DO

Pusan

35

Mokpo

Kangjin

Chindo

Namhae

Yosu

MOUNTS BAY
JAMAICA
14 Aug.

Korea Strait

TSUSHIMA

Tsushima Str.

34

ROKN engagement   K
Blockade station

CHEJU-DO

Fuelling
TF77 18 Aug.
40 m. to south

CVE
OP AREA
supports so
perimeter

125   126   127   128   129   130

While all this was in progress at Pohang, activity was being stepped up in the north. By the 17th, when the ROK division was taken out of Chongha, *Bass* had completed her three raids and had departed the area. But *Pickerel* now arrived to begin her photographic work; the *Toledo* group, on its way to relieve off Pohang, stopped by to bombard; for the first time in a month Task Force 77 had a chance to strike northeastern Korea.

With *Mansfield, Collett,* and *Swenson* as screen, with patrol plane spot, and with a combat air patrol from Task Force 77, *Toledo* cruised the 40-mile stretch of coast, from Songjin south to Iwon, where the railroad runs close to the sea. Targets were plentiful, and the 297 rounds of 8-inch HC expended against three railroad bridges and several hundred freight cars were considered to have been profitably invested. At the same time the two carriers of Task Force 77 were flying strikes against rail facilities and such minor coastal shipping as could be discovered between the 38th and 42d parallels; in the course of this work one jet sweep found an ammunition train, and exploded it so effectively as to bring back tangible proof in the form of fragments embedded in the fighters' wings. On conclusion of the day's operations both carrier and gunnery forces headed southward, Admiral Higgins to relieve the fire support group off Pohang, and the carriers to pass through Tsushima Strait en route to their fuelling rendezvous south of Korea.

Some semblance of order had by now been reestablished at Pohang, but elsewhere the perimeter was under heavy pressure. Although the close support efforts of Task Force 77 on the 16th had been concentrated in the east, a fair number of sorties had been sent to the Waegwan front northwest of Taegu. This area had also benefited from the attentions of the FEAF Bomber Command, which on orders from GHQ had put 850 tons of explosives into enemy assembly areas in a carpet-bombing operation reminiscent of Saint Lô. But despite all efforts heavy enemy attacks on the 17th penetrated the ROK lines north of Taegu, and only the quickest of counter-measures succeeded in restoring the situation.

The Marine Brigade in the meantime had been moving north, first to Miryang and then westward to Yongsan, to confront the crisis in the Naktong bulge. Seven miles west of Yongsan the river curves to the westward, then south, then east again toward Pusan, to enclose an area some three miles in each dimension, commanded by a central hill mass, and protected on the eastward by ridges running north and south across its entrance. Having crossed the river on 6 August, the enemy in the space of four days had expanded his lodgment to include the larger part of the 4th Division, the unit which Task Force Smith had run up against on 5 July. Counterattacks on the 11th and on the 14th and 15th had failed to dislodge the three North Korean infantry regiments which, with artillery and tank support, now held the eastern ridges and were debouching onto the Yongsan road.

The danger was great. If the penetration could not be contained the lowland river valley route to Pusan would lie open to the enemy. The three Army regiments in the bulge, less than half-strength at the time the enemy crossed the river, had been heavily engaged for ten days. Nor were the Marines in much better case. To confront the crisis and restore the balance, three under-strength battalions were to be committed against perhaps twice their number; no replacements had reached the brigade since its arrival in Korea; the losses suffered in the Kosong offensive had not been made good; the battalions still lacked their third companies. But one British observer, watching the Marines as they moved up through Miryang, was emboldened to hope, though with "no valid reason," that the tragedy which threatened the entire Korean foothold might yet be averted.

Army units already in the area included a battalion in blocking position on the left, two battalions north of the Yongsan road, and two regiments under orders to attack from the northeast. The Marines, on their arrival, were ordered to attack westward along the road at 0800 on the 17th, with Obong-ni Ridge, running northwest-southeast across the entrance to the bulge, as their first objective. Shortage of transport had delayed the arrival of the brigade and had adversely affected the artillery preparation; a misunderstanding with the Army unit on the right led to a lack of flank support; the air strike from the escort carriers was 15 minutes late, so that the 18 Corsairs had only half their intended time to work over enemy positions. The advance uphill, against a numerically superior and entrenched enemy, was carried out with great bravery but at heavy cost: of the 240 men of the 2nd Battalion which led the attack, 142 had become casualties by mid-day. But the enemy, too, was suffering, and with the commitment of the 1st Battalion at 1300 the forward movement continued. By evening the northern end of the ridge had been taken and a counterattacking tank force destroyed; north of the road Army troops had moved up to parallel the brigade's advanced position; in the northern hills troops of the 24th Division had reached their objectives.

Strong enemy counterattacks during the night brought bitter fighting along Obong-ni Ridge, but the North Koreans proved unable to exploit their gains, and with morning the advance was resumed. Held up by a heavy machine gun nest less than 100 yards ahead, the Marines called for help from the air. Under ground control a dummy run, a target marking run, and a strike were completed within nine minutes, and a 500-pound bomb, deposited squarely upon the nest, eliminated this obstacle and panicked enemy troops. By 0830 the ridge had been cleared.

Already the crisis had been passed. Even before the ridge line had been taken the failure of his night counterattack had led the enemy commander to order withdrawal across the river. This movement was expedited by the Marines' seizure of their second objective, a commanding elevation half a mile to the westward, which was taken shortly after midday. With the North Koreans in disorganized retreat, artillery fire was directed at the river crossings, fighters from the escort carriers strafed troops on the banks and in the water, and the muddy Naktong ran red with blood.

While this notable slaughter was in progress the 3rd Battalion pressed forward toward the final objective, the dominating height within the bulge. Well advanced when operations were halted for the night, this attack was resumed at dawn. At 0645 on the 19th the hill was taken and the bulge secured, while west of the Naktong spreading waves of confusion, radiating outward from this setback, were expanded by attacks of strike groups from *Philippine Sea* against troop concentrations and supply dumps between Hyopchon and the river. Its task completed, the Marine Brigade was detached on the next day, assigned to Eighth Army reserve, and moved back to the Masan area. There the infantry bivouacked in a bean patch, and undertook a training program for Korean Marines, while the artillery was sent back to work at Chindong-ni, where enemy pressure had again begun to be apparent.

In the three days fighting in the bulge the Marines had captured 22 pieces of artillery and large amounts of other materiel; estimates of enemy personnel losses varied between 2,500 and 4,500. Marine casualties, in contrast, totaled 345, of whom 66 were killed and one missing, an extraordinary disproportion which testifies to what professionalism can do, and to what command of the air can accomplish when exploited by a unitary air-ground force. For the invaders the elimination of the Naktong bulge and the destruction inflicted on the 4th Division constituted the greatest defeat thus far. For the U.N. the time gained by the action was beyond all price: ten days were to go by before the enemy succeeded in reestablishing this bridgehead across the Naktong.

While the forces of the United Nations were grappling with the crises at Pohang and on the Naktong, the southern end of the perimeter remained quiescent. The Kosong spoiling attack had been a success, and the enemy was licking his wounds. But while land action had diminished, activity in coastal waters was on the rise: the increasing unpleasantness of highway travel had stimulated diligent efforts by the Communists to improve their seaborne logistics, and between 13 and 20 August the Korean Navy fought five engagements in the arc between Kunsan and the peninsula's southwestern tip. The most considerable of these took place on the 15th, a day of widespread action on western and southern coasts, when *YMS 503* encountered 45 small craft in the gut between the end of the peninsula and the offshore islands, captured 30, and sank 15.

Much of this overwater movement seemed to originate at the port of Kunsan, attacks against which had been earlier prohibited by CincFE with a view to the preservation of harbor facilities. But these restrictions had by now been lifted, and on 15 August the cruiser *Jamaica,* returning from patrol, bombarded factories and docks with satisfactory results. On the same day a third blow was struck against enemy south coast capabilities when Yosu, previously attacked by *Diachenko* and *Collett,* was bombarded so thoroughly by HMS *Mounts Bay* and HMCS *Cayuga* that no worthwhile targets were deemed to remain.

By this time the activities of ROK naval forces were no longer limited to inshore blockade. Evacuation of refugees from the south coast, and by raft and barge from the Naktong Valley, was calling forth a major effort, and on the 17th, 600 Korean Marines were landed on the Tongyong peninsula south of Kosong. There, by seizing and holding the isthmus north of Tongyong city, the ROK Marines effectively bottled enemy troops in on the landward side, and prevented their movement across the narrow water to the island of Koje, below Chinhae. And concurrently, at ROKN headquarters, plans were being made to carry the war back north.

At sea, meanwhile, the Seventh Fleet remained busy. After helping out at Chongha the carriers had moved north on the 17th to strike Area F. On the next day, prior to giving similar treatment to the west coast, Task Force 77 fuelled from *Passumpsic* and *Cacapon,* and rearmed from *Mount Katmai,* the first ammunition ship to reach the Far East. The 19th saw Admiral Struble's force again in the Yellow Sea, giving support to the perimeter and striking targets in Areas A and B, while *Triumph,* operating independently, sent her aircraft against objectives to the southward. *Philippine Sea's* interdiction strikes this day were concentrated on the vital railroad bridge at Seoul, which had survived repeated attacks by FEAF and carrier aircraft. Nine ADs with two 1,000-pound bombs each and nine F4Us with 500-pounders were sent against this target; the job was done, and photographs showed a span resting in the water, but at the cost of the loss of Commander Vogel, the air group commander.

Close support duty on the 19th also fell upon *Philippine Sea,* and the morning launch of 18 planes brought satisfactory results. Although radio channels continued crowded, tactical air controllers were contacted as planned, and effective attacks ensued. In five separate areas between Hyopchon and the front lines large fires were started with gratifying effect, as numerous personnel ran out into the open where they could be strafed. This exploitation of the success in the Naktong bulge also accomplished the destruction of six troop-laden trucks, and of two command cars which were chased into a warehouse and there burned.

On the next day the force had another chance at the type of operation favored by Admirals Joy and Struble. From a launching point west of the Tokchok Islands strikes were flown against transport facilities and warehouses along the line Sinanju-Pyongyang-Kaesong in Area E. On the evening of the 20th the carriers turned southward and headed for Sasebo, where they arrived at 1400 on the 21st.

However satisfactory to the naval commanders, this northward diversion of carrier effort was only reluctantly accepted by EUSAK. So frequent and urgent, indeed, had been the calls from Eighth Army and the JOC that Admiral Joy had asked CincFE to remind all interested commands of the complex chain through which the services of the Seventh Fleet were properly to be requested. On the 20th, in denying an Eighth Army request for permanent assignment of one of the fast carriers to the defense of the perimeter, CincFE spelled out the intended employment of naval force. *Triumph* and the gunnery strength of Task Group 96.5, and the escort carriers of Task Group 96.8, were at EUSAK's disposition. But except in great emergency the large carriers were not to operate singly; future plans made necessary a replenishment period for Task Force 77; its subsequent employment would be communicated when known.

4. 21–31 *August: Coastal Operations and Carrier Strikes*

In the last ten days of August a lull descended upon the Korean perimeter. Repulse in the south and defeat in the Naktong bulge had forced important North Korean units to break off and reorganize, and enemy losses had also been heavy in the fighting around Waegwan and Pohang. But by now Communist preparations to renew the attack were faced with circumstances of increasing difficulty. A campaign planned for ten days was approaching the end of its second month, the informal logistic procedures of the invaders were becoming increasingly inadequate, and attempts to live off the country were producing a half-starved soldiery. Supply of more specifically military items, unavailable through confiscation, had broken down as a result of naval and Air Force attacks on lines of communication. Despite resort to hand carriage, horse and ox transportation, and movement by night, the enemy's best efforts were insufficient to permit the maintenance of the offensive. Not only was he checked in his advance but his morale was suffering, and the growing effectiveness of U.N. operations was evidenced by the increasing number of prisoners taken.

By now, too, the question of who was encircling whom had become meaningful. In Korea there had developed the extraordinary spectacle of two contending armies, each nearly surrounded by hostile forces and each nourished from afar. For while the enemy controlled by far the greater part of the Korean peninsula, the sea around him and the air above remained the uncontested domains of the U.N. While he pressed against the Pusan perimeter, his own flanks and communications were under continuous attack.

Night and bad weather were the happiest times for the NKPA, but U.N. soldiers could walk upright by day; the supply lines to the north were suffering, but Pusan was a booming port.

In this situation both sides were racing against time. To the invaders the arrival of U.N. reinforcements, with more in prospect, meant that they must win quickly or they would not win at all. For the U.N. the problem was to hold its own perimeter until the counterstroke could be prepared, and then to draw the noose and explode the Pusan beachhead. The last ten days of August, which saw the North Koreans feverishly attempting to solve their logistic problems, were marked in Tokyo by important high level decisions, followed by all-out efforts to mount an amphibious attack at Inchon by the time of the September tides. General MacArthur had taken the advice of the psalmist, to strike the enemy in his hinder parts and put him to perpetual reproach. But delivery of the blow depended upon the timely arrival of the 1st Marine Division, and upon the speed with which it could be committed.

Throughout this period of lull the work of the blockading forces continued unabated. Neither the lessened tempo of action around the perimeter nor the problems of preparing the counterstroke affected the operations of east and west coast groups and of the ROK Navy. Off the front line at Pohang fire support continued, with a heavy cruiser and a destroyer division always on duty, and with the nightly northward dispatch of a destroyer to shoot up enemy supply dumps in the rear. Yet while this work went on the coastal supply line was not forgotten, two destroyers were maintained on northern blockading stations, and the attack from the sea against enemy communication centers was again extended northward by a bombardment of the iron and steel center of Chongjin.

This city of 200,000, fifty miles beyond the northern limit of the blockade and an equal distance south of the Soviet frontier, is one of the key strategic positions on the western shore of the Japan Sea. Located on a bay which opens to the southward, Chongjin had inner harbors protected by breakwaters and equipped with railroad sidings, cranes, and warehouses. In 1945 it had been captured by Russian marines in the only amphibious assault of the Soviet's short war against Japan; current information indicated that it was frequently visited by Russian ships, that Soviet naval units were stationed there, and that the port was a Soviet restricted area. Now, however, its prior exemption was cancelled out and Russian security regulations were breached. On the 19th Chongjin was bombed by FEAF B-29s, and on the 20th the destroyer *Swenson,* from the northern barrier patrol post, arrived offshore and put 102 rounds into iron works, harbor installations, railroad yards, and radio stations, starting flames that were visible for 18 miles to seaward.

Two days later the destroyer *Mansfield* shot up Songjin, just south of 41°, and in a night bombardment inflicted apparently severe damage on the docks, railroad facilities, and bridges of this mineral and lumber export center. The 23rd saw *Mansfield* off Chongjin, compounding with 180 rounds of 5-inch the damage previously inflicted by *Swenson*. On the 24th Admiral Hartman, with *Helena* and four destroyers, arrived off Tanchon, undisturbed since the *Toledo* group's bombardment of the 7th. Railroad cars and warehouses were worked over with the aid of helicopter spotting, after which the group proceeded northward to Songjin, where on the next day heavy damage was inflicted on marshalling yards and railroad cars.

Back on the line at Pohang a period of comparative quiet was followed, on the 22nd, by increased enemy pressure. On the next day a conference with Army representatives on board *Toledo* led to improved procedures in air spotting. These paid off on the 24th, as the cruisers' gunners had the gratifying experience of putting an 8-inch shell in one end of a tunnel reported to contain a supply dump, and of observing smoke come out of the other. The 25th was a day of variety as enemy tanks and guns were taken under fire, and as the North Koreans in their turn attempted an amphibious movement against the town by the use of motorboats and sailboats. But this effort was beaten off by small units of the ROKN, and when Admiral Hartman and the *Helena* group arrived to relieve next day Pohang was still in U.N. hands. Aircraft from Task Force 77 took off some pressure on the 26th, reinforcements were again moved in by EUSAK, and from the 28th to the 31st close support was provided by the Marine airmen from *Sicily*. The last day of August saw friendly forces making sizable gains.

In the Yellow Sea, throughout this period, Admiral Andrewes' units continued to man the west coast barrier stations and to interdict enemy traffic around the headlands. Here the principal excitement was the appearance of two enemy aircraft, the first in more than a month, one of which surprised and damaged the British destroyer *Comus* on the 22nd and the other an ROK vessel the next day. The attack on *Comus* produced a call for air cover from the escort carriers, which otherwise spent most of their effort during the latter part of the month in close support of Army forces on the perimeter. Despite the difficult hydrographic conditions in the west, the blockade here, as in the east, appears to have been effective: no traffic was moving south around the headlands patrolled by British units, and on 28 August Admiral Andrewes conducted a photographic reconnaissance of the entire coastline with satisfactorily negative results.

But while the enemy had abandoned his endeavors to bring supplies down from the north by sea, in the south and southwest he was vigorously attempting the forward movement of materiel and troops by small boat. This effort to improve the logistics of his southern flank led to a crescendo in the inshore operations of the ROK Navy.

Off Chindo, the island prolongation of Korea's southwestern tip, the ROK *YMS 503* found considerable activity on 20 and 21 August. Three enemy motorboats of between 30 and 100 tons were engaged, and one captured, one sunk, and the third damaged. For a few days there were only minor contacts, but the 25th brought seven engagements with enemy coastal shipping. At Pohang the North Korean attempt at a landing was repelled. Twenty miles off Inchon *PC 701* sank a large sailboat. In a small estuary east of Chindo *YMS 512* sank one 100-ton motorboat and another of 70 tons, and drowned full loads of enemy troops on both. Off Namhae Island on the south coast *YMS 504* damaged 14 of 15 small sailboats encountered. But the big work of the day was done by *YMS 514,* which in three separate engagements in less than three hours sank three enemy vessels and damaged eight. Once again excitement diminished for a time, but on the 31st *PC 702* sank two large motorboats and damaged another near Chindo.

Together with increasing enemy activity on the southern front, and with ComNavFE's previously expressed concern about inshore traffic near Namhae Island, these south coast actions led to the inauguration of a new fire support station in Chinhae Man, a bay which, reaching in to Chindong-ni and Masan, gave water access to the southern end of the perimeter. On 26 August the destroyer *Wiltsie* was assigned to duty there in support of the 25th Infantry Division, and this service was continued by various ships in rotation until late September. Since the 25th Division had trained fire control parties, in contrast to the somewhat catch-as-catch-can arrangements at Pohang, this Chinhae effort paid off handsomely.

From 21 to 25 August, while the perimeter continued generally quiet and the coasts busy, Task Force 77 was replenishing at Sasebo. On the 22nd Admiral Sherman, the Chief of Naval Operations, and Admiral Radford, Commander in Chief Pacific Fleet, arrived by air, following a brief trip to Pusan, to visit the force and to apprise Commander Seventh Fleet of his appointment to command the Inchon operation. On the 25th, as Admiral Struble left the fleet, command of the Fast Carrier Task Force devolved on Rear Admiral Ewen, Commander Carrier Division 1.

Inevitably, this period in port involved further consideration of fast carrier employment. ComNavFE had by now switched over completely to the semi-strategic party and on the 22nd, in a dispatch to CincFE, argued that best results would come from strikes north of 38°, where many "extremely lucrative and profitable targets" existed, even though the effect at the front would be felt with "some delay." This recommendation was accepted by General MacArthur, and a new schedule was promulgated which called for a sequence similar to that of the previous sortie: two days on the east coast commencing on the 26th, a day in fuelling and in transit, and two days of attacks in the west. On each coast the effort of the first day would be divided between close support and interdiction; throughout the operation first priority in interdiction would be given to railroad and other transportation targets. This dispatch was followed by another in which CincFE, "in view of current planning," expressed concern about a possible enemy air buildup, as evidenced by the attack on *Comus*; FEAF and Task Force 77 were adjured to emphasize interdiction of air facilities, and while avoiding damage to runways, to refuse the enemy the use of airfields south of 39°. Finally, a request from FEAF for cooperation in the destruction of specified North Korean bridges was approved by ComNavFE, insofar as not inconsistent with previous arrangements.

Some consolation was provided EUSAK by the assignment of a quarter of the total effort to the support of the perimeter. But the autonomy of the carrier force was emphasized in a ComNavFE dispatch of the 24th, which reported CincFE's decision to give freedom of action in the northern areas, both as to date of attacks and as to targets, to the task force commander. Thus by the end of August the frustrations of the perimeter and the attractions of interdiction had had their combined effect. Except in situations of real emergency, close support had been abandoned by the fast carriers, and within the context of the Korean conflict Task Force 77 had become an independent striking force.

Shortly after noon on 25 August Admiral Ewen sortied his ships from Sasebo for operations in the Japan Sea. As another consequence of the *Comus* episode, antiaircraft practice was conducted during sortie, but a submarine contact, later evaluated as false, brought an abrupt termination of the exercise. On the 26th enemy lines of communications were swept, attacks on targets of opportunity were carried out, and another attempt was made to provide support for the ground forces.

Three *Valley Forge* flights of F4Us and ADs attacked troops, tanks, and trucks with good results, and two reported that despite crowded radio channels the work of the controllers was satisfactory. For Air Group 11 in *Philippine Sea* the day started with a jet sweep which attacked troops in a tunnel north of Pohang, which was followed up by a strike of Corsairs and Skyraiders on a vehicle concentration west of the Naktong. It ended with another jet sweep led by Commander Ralph Weymouth, the air group's new commander, which reported good results: in the hills northwest of Pohang an attack in battalion strength had been broken up by strafing; west of the town a competent airborne controller had directed rocket and strafing runs within a hundred yards of friendly forces. Air operations were thus successfully routine, but as the force cruised the neighborhood of Ullung Do the sonarmen on the destroyers were kept jumping by numerous contacts attributed to the whales which frequent the neighborhood of that island.

During the night the carriers steamed northward, and on the 27th launched against transportation and other targets in the Wonsan-Chongjin

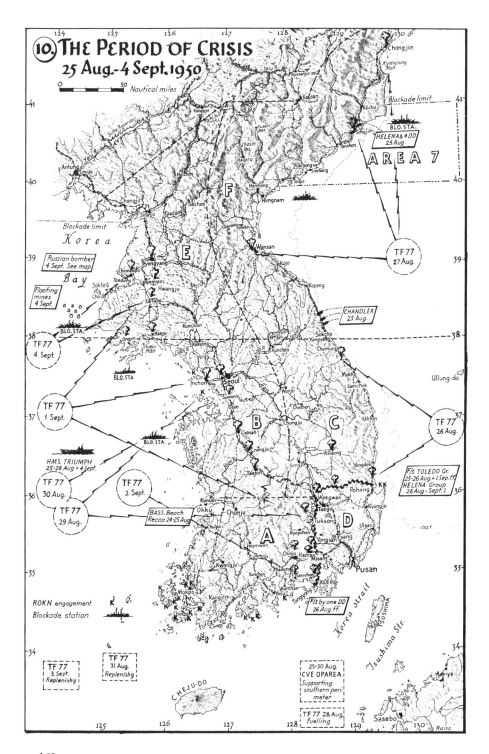

10. THE PERIOD OF CRISIS
25 Aug.-4 Sept. 1950

0 ___ 50 *Nautical miles*

AREA 7

Blockade limit

BLO.STA.
HELENA & 4 DD
25 Aug.

TF 77
27 Aug.

Blockade limit

Korea

Russian bomber
4 Sept. See map

Bay

Floating
mines
4 Sept.

CHANDLER
25 Aug.

BLO.STA.

TF 77
4. Sept.

Ullung-do

TF 77
1 Sept.

TF 77
26 Aug.

HMS. TRIUMPH
25-26 Aug. + 4 Sept.

BLO.STA.

F/s TOLEDO Gr.
25-26 Aug.+ I.Sep.ff
HELENA Group
26 Aug.- Sept. I.

TF 77
30 Aug.

TF 77
2 Sept.

TF 77
29 Aug.

BASS. Beach
Recco 24-25 Aug.

100 f

ROKN engagement
Blockade station

F/s by one DD
26 Aug. ff.

Korea strait

Tsushima Str.

TF 77
3. Sept.
Replenish'g

TF 77
31 Aug.
Replenish'g

25-30 Aug.
CVE OP AREA
Supporting
southern peri-
meter

CHEJU-DO

TF 77 28 Aug.
fuelling

Sasebo

160

coastal strip and shipping in Wonsan harbor. These strikes were described by the task force commander as more profitable than the previous day's work in support of troops. Quite possibly they were, but the comments on the support effort appear to have stemmed largely from memories of earlier chaos: although pilot reports indicated improved results in routine support missions, the effort was characterized as ineffective, owing to inadequate communications, poor radio discipline, and poor control.

On the 28th, as Task Force 77 was fuelling south of Korea and recovering replacement aircraft flown out from Japan, another list of bridges was received from FEAF and a schedule for future operations from ComNavFE. The planned activities on the west coast would now be but the start of a second sequence: fuelling on the 31st would be followed by two more days of strikes, a day in replenishment, and strikes on 4–5 September.

The trend away from the perimeter was continuing. Where CincFE's dispatch of the 23rd had called for such close support on the 29th as was desired by JOC, ComNavFE's new message called merely for strikes on that day. In fact, no support missions were flown, and the attacks of the 29th were directed against railroad bridges, airfields, and highways in the Seoul-Inchon region and to the southward. FAFIK had hoped for more than this, and had requested four-plane sorties at 20-minute intervals throughout the day, but its dispatch, delayed by communication failure, was received too late to permit compliance. On the 30th, still enjoying their new-found freedom, the fast carriers attacked bridges, docks, shipping, and the waterworks at Chinnampo and Pyongyang, and road and rail targets to the northward, and on conclusion of these operations steamed south to refuel and rearm off southwestern Korea.

Along the perimeter the operations of the 31st were on a diminished scale, as both sides continued to prepare for the future. Increased strength and diminishing pressure had permitted General Walker to relieve the 24th Division for a well-earned rest. In the bean patch at Masan the Marine Brigade was enjoying its tenth day of respite from combat, and was busying itself with the training of South Korean marines and with preparations for the next operation. At sea, activity was of a routine nature: the fire support ships at Pohang and Chinhae remained busy, the ROK Navy was fully engaged, but bombardment of the northeastern supply line had temporarily ceased. Air strength available for the support of the perimeter had also declined, as a result both of decreased enemy pressure and of the requirements of the planned invasion of Inchon. The Fifth Air Force was still operating from Japanese bases, and its daily total of support sorties had dropped well below that of early August; *Sicily,* after four days in support at Pohang, was en route to Sasebo, whither *Badoeng Strait* had preceded her and where both were scheduled to remain until 5 September; Admiral Ewen's plans for Task

Force 77 contemplated spending the next four days on railroad targets in the northwest in order to isolate the future battlefield.

But all the plans were changed and all the schedules scrapped by the development of the biggest crisis so far.

5. *1–5 September: The Enemy's Big Blast*

Late on the night of 31 August the enemy launched his greatest effort. Around the entire perimeter from Pohang to Haman heavy attacks began, very great forces were committed to the Naktong River front, and almost at once it was obvious that a major emergency was at hand. All troops were ordered out of reserve, all air support was urgently called for. At 0810 in the morning of 1 September the Marine Brigade was alerted, and shortly after ten o'clock the Joint Operations Center got off an emergency message to Task Force 77:

MAJOR ENEMY ATTACK LAUNCHED ACROSS RIVER FROM TUKSONGDONG SOUTH TO COAST X ALL AVAILABLE EFFORT FOR CLOSE SUPPORT REQUIRED SOUTHERN SECTOR IMMEDIATELY X SITUATION CRITICAL X REQUEST ARMED RECCO FROM BEACH NORTH TO TUKSONGDONG TO DEPTH OF TEN MILES WEST OF BOMB LINE X REQUEST IMMEDIATE ACKNOWLEDGMENT.

Two hundred and seventy-five miles to the northwest, in the center of the Yellow Sea, the carriers had launched that morning at 0800 against transportation facilities in the Seoul complex and to the northward. *Valley Forge* aircraft had dropped a span of the rail bridge below Sariwon and had attacked transportation targets near Hwangju and on the Ongjin peninsula; *Philippine Sea's* bombers had struck the Pyongyang railroad bridge and marshalling yards, and cars and equipment along the tracks to the northward; the sighting in the course of this activity of flatcars loaded with steel girders gave evidence of the effectiveness of previous bridge attacks. At 0935 jet sweeps from both carriers had been sent against airfields in the Seoul-Suwon region and against the harbor of Chinnampo. The fighters returned aboard at 1120, just after a second propeller strike group was flown off against North Korean bridges and marshalling yards.

Fifteen minutes after the fighters had been landed aboard, the JOC's scream for help was received. The response was immediate. Admiral Ewen at once turned his force to the southeast and built up speed to 27 knots. Strike missions in the air north of Seoul were recalled at 1155, and the combat air patrol was vectored out to help them find the fleet in its new position. At 1233 Commander Task Force 77 advised the JOC by flash message that his first strike would be on station at 1430, and at 1315 the planes began to lumber off the decks: 12 ADs carrying three 1,000-pound bombs apiece, and 16 Corsairs, each with one 1,000-pounder and four rockets. Ten minutes later the aircraft that had been recalled from the north were landed on. At 1344 a second flash message to JOC described the composition of the first strike group, and advised that it would be followed an hour later by a second of identical composition and armament.

As the task force drove southeastward, and as the strike group flew toward the perimeter, the Marine Brigade was moving north to Miryang and to the Naktong bulge. Higher levels were also bestirring themselves: at 1231 CincFE had ordered all-out support for Eighth Army, and as the carriers were completing their preparations for the second launch a dispatch relaying this information was received from ComNavFE. In Tokyo, in the course of the afternoon, FEAF informed Admiral Joy's headquarters that as of 1245 the critical situation was in the 2nd Division sector at the Naktong bulge, asked emergency action to put both the aircraft of Task Force 77 and *Badoeng Strait*'s squadron, then shore-based at Ashiya, on close support, and suggested sending any required liaison officers to the JOC at Pusan and the operation of Navy control aircraft from Taegu.

At 1630 ComNavFE passed these suggestions on to Admiral Ewen; ten minutes later the Marines were ordered to deploy *Sicily*'s squadron to Ashiya next day to reinforce the effort in Korea. At 1800 FEAF was advised by courier that the fast carrier aircraft were already in action and that all else had been provided for. In the meantime another emergency call from JOC had requested all available effort on the 2nd against continuing enemy pressure on the Naktong front, and shortly after 1900 Admiral Joy instructed Admiral Ewen to comply.

Within the perimeter, in the meantime, the old troubles in control had again arisen to plague the close support effort. On its arrival over the lines the 14-plane strike group from *Philippine Sea* was instructed to attack a tank concentration east of the bombline; the flight leader made a preliminary low pass, observed white stars on the vehicles and no attempt to take shelter by the personnel, and called off the attack; the group then foraged for targets on its own and attacked troop concentrations and a bridge on the Naktong River. *Valley Forge*'s aircraft, instructed to orbit because the controller had no targets, spent 45 minutes circling while the Mosquito called in a flight of F-51s on an enemy troop concentration. Deprived of this target, so suitable to their 1,000-pound instantaneous and VT-fused bombs, the group was finally directed to attack villages along the Naktong front.

Both carriers had launched again at 1430. This time the planes from *Valley Forge* did useful work on the 25th Division front, destroying much of the town of Haman, burning trucks on the road nearby, and flattening an enemy-occupied ridge west of the town. But *Philippine Sea*'s group again failed to find a controller and was obliged to seek its own targets along the river.   Both ships launched jet sweeps at 1615 and again at 1745 with similar results: *Valley Forge* fighters, failing to find controllers, attacked small boats in the river and trucks along the roads; those from *Philippine Sea*, equally uncontrolled, returned without firing a shot.

The response to the all-out emergency was thus in large part wasted, and conditions over the perimeter were back to what they had formerly been. Not a single plane from *Philippine Sea* had been used in controlled attacks, and of a task force total of 85 sorties, 43 had attacked without positive control. JOC's emergency call had received an emergency response, but the total of about 280 Air Force and Navy sorties flown on the 1st in support of the emergency along the Naktong was more than could be handled, and by afternoon, when the carrier planes reported in, the system had been over-whelmed and had collapsed.   Intentions had been good, and the effort commendable, and at 1800 ComNavFE sent the force a "well done" for its prompt response and for its support of the 25th Division.   Equally, how-ever, the situation was susceptible of improvement, and the suggested dis-patch of liaison officers worth acting upon.   The last event of the day within the force was the launch of a night aircraft, with Commander Weymouth, *Philippine Sea*'s air group commander, embarked as passenger for Pusan.

The difficulties over the perimeter had greatly exasperated Admiral Ewen, with the result that he ordered his pilots to spend no more than five minutes in attempting to gain contact with JOC or with control air-craft before proceeding to pre-briefed targets outside the bombline. Fortunately, however, the need for this procedure was considerably di-minished by the efforts of Weymouth and the JOC personnel to improve communications and control: the Navy would supply the controllers for the 2nd Division front, and so get a clear radio channel; the Air Force would waive the requirement of checking all planes in through JOC.   On the next day, despite deteriorating weather, the carriers sent in 127 close support sorties, to which Fifth Air Force and the Ashiya-based Marines added 201.   Ninety-nine of the carrier sorties received positive direction, and the troubles of most of the other 28 were attributable to a morning ground fog over the target area.

Once the fog lifted things went well.   *Valley Forge* aircraft destroyed 3 tanks, 12 trucks, and 3 barges, and successfully attacked 7 troop concen-trations; *Philippine Sea* strike groups claimed 2 trucks and a tank, and many casualties in attacks on 11 troop concentrations.   Communications with con-trol planes were good, the controllers were complimentary about the attacks, the commanding officer of *Philippine Sea* reported that "the operation was a success," and the pilots were cheered by the thought that they were getting into the war.   The last strike of the day was directed against enemy troops retreating across the Nam River south of the bulge, and in this sector at least things seemed to be looking up.

The Marine Brigade, in the meantime, had been on the move, northward to Miryang on the 1st, and westward to Yongsan on the 2nd, prior to attacking once more into the Naktong bulge. There the situation was even worse than a month before: the better part of two Communist divisions was now across the river, and the enemy had broken out of the bulge and advanced about four miles eastward along the Yongsan road. Local Army commanders wanted the Marines to attack at once, but General Craig, not wishing to commit his force until all troops had reached their assembly points or until his air control personnel had arrived, resisted an afternoon advance.

Not only were the controllers unavailable on the afternoon of the 2nd but the whole air situation was somewhat problematical. Fifth Air Force had asked ComNavFE to continue all available effort between Tuksongdong and the coast, but Sunday the 3rd was fuelling day for the task force, which was scheduled to meet the replenishment group west of Mokpo, and both of the escort carriers were now at Sasebo. At 2205 a dispatch from FAFIK informed Admiral Ruble that the Marines desired his air effort on the 3rd and inquired as to his availability; the message was forwarded with emergency precedence to Ashiya Air Base where both VMF 214 and VMF 323 were now located. But Typhoon Jane was nearing Japan, and at Ashiya the weather was very bad.

At Yongsan the enemy struck first on the morning of the 3rd, and a heavy attack launched at first light penetrated the Marines' intended line of departure, a ridge occupied by the 9th Infantry about a half mile west of the town. As the brigade detrucked and moved forward the North Koreans were coming through the American lines, snipers were encountered as the troops marched through Yongsan, and as they emerged west of the town the Marines came under moderate enemy fire.

As the Army troops pulled back, heavy fire by Marine artillery, tanks, and automatic weapons halted the North Korean advance. The brigade then began to press westward from Yongsan, to clear the hills controlling the road junction and the road leading onward to Obong-ni Ridge and to the bulge. The terrain was difficult and fighting was hard, but by noon the initial objectives were in hand.

But there was no Marine air overhead for close support: Jane was centered over southern Honshu, and the fighter squadrons at Ashiya were weathered in. At 1231 General Craig sent an urgent message to ComNavFE:

NO REPEAT NO CAS A/C FROM 0900 TO 1200 X REQUEST NAVAL A/C SUPPORT THIS COMMAND X NEED EIGHT ON STATION VICINITY YONGSAN.

Eighth Army, too, was in trouble, and at 0935 had called directly upon CincFE for the earliest possible return of the fast carriers. At 1342, in response to this plea, ComNavFE instructed Task Force 77, then refuelling and rearming southwest of Mokpo, to give all practicable support to the

Army since the Marine planes had been grounded by weather; at 1404 General Craig's message was relayed to the force. Once again all hands on the carriers doubled to flight stations, and at 1547 Admiral Ewen reported that his first strike would be off in an hour, with arrival over the lines at about 1745.

Although their arrival had not been anticipated by Fifth Air Force, these flights, like those of the 2nd, found comparatively good communications and control. Twenty-two planes from *Philippine Sea* worked over troops in the Masan area in close proximity to American positions. *Valley Forge* sent in 24 aircraft in four flights, some of which attacked Kwangju and Samchonpo, and some of which, despite bad weather, had considerable success under Marine control near Masan, where six Corsairs destroyed 2 tanks and 15 fieldpieces, damaged 2 other tanks, and strafed troops.

At Yongsan, despite the absence of air support, the Marines had continued their advance westward on the afternoon of the 3rd. By nightfall the originally scheduled line of departure had been gained or surpassed and the enemy, disorganized by the shock of this unexpected engagement, was retiring. But the front was a long one, recurving into a deep salient north of the road, and the night was made miserable by cold, driving rain.

At sea, despite the improved results in close support, the task force was again trying to shake itself loose. In preparation for the proposed landing at Inchon Admiral Struble had established and ComNavFE had promulgated a new series of carrier aircraft operating areas, M through Q, along the west coast of Korea, and had called for operations in Areas P and Q, north of 38°, on the 4th, and in O and P, between 37° and 39°, on the 5th. Pursuant to these instructions Admiral Ewen's dispatch reporting his launch on the afternoon of the 3rd had stated that unless otherwise directed he intended to operate north of the parallel next day.

Within the perimeter, however, life was still hard, and all possible support was desired. At 2201 on the 3rd General Craig evinced his concern in another emergency dispatch in which he reported the "situation intense," and in view of the state of affairs at Ashiya requested eight carrier planes on station throughout the 4th. But ComNavFE had already confirmed the proposed operations in Areas P and Q, and although he instructed the task force to be ready to provide support on order, his answer to General Craig reported a favorable weather forecast for Japan and stated that the fast carriers were committed to other areas.

Fortunately, the fighting on the 3rd appears to have turned the tide west of Yongsan. Although fresh from garrison duty, the North Korean 9th Division, which led the advance, was deficient in training in comparison with the enemy's original front line units and was unable to stand up to the Marine Brigade. Early morning attacks along the road to the bulge moved rapidly forward, resistance was slight, and groups of fleeing Communists were cut down by artillery and Marine air. By mid-day the advance had covered a mile and a half, much destroyed and abandoned equipment had been overrun, and much U.S. gear recaptured. Further advance was authorized, afternoon brought the gain of another mile, and by evening the Marines were dug in on the hill from which, 18 days before, they had launched their first attack in the first battle of the Naktong.

Action on the 5th started with an enemy counterattack against Army troops north of the road, which was dissolved by automatic weapons fire. Preparations were then made to continue the move westward, and during the morning, despite heavy rain and fog which hampered air operations, the Marines moved out into position for an attack on Obong-ni Ridge. But at mid-day the attack was cancelled. Although the bulge had not been cleared the situation was vastly improved; D-Day at Inchon was approaching and the brigade was needed there. On receipt of this order the Marines formed up defensively along ridges south of the road, and during the evening were relieved by elements of the 2nd Infantry Division. Shortly after midnight the brigade marched back through the rain to load into trucks and move to the Pusan staging area.

While the Marines were pressing westward from Yongsan, Task Force 77 had moved north again into the Yellow Sea. This body of water, from the viewpoint of a carrier force commander, is a somewhat restricted one. As a result of the commanding position of the Shantung Peninsula, no part of the Yellow Sea is more than 200 miles from a Communist shore; above the latitude of Seoul the operating area, less than 100 miles from Shantung, comes within progressively easier bomber range of the Soviet-occupied Port Arthur Naval Base Area. And for a carrier force dependent on the lee gauge, geography is compounded by meteorology: the prevailing light summer winds, of a mean velocity of six knots and from the northerly semicircle, do nothing to help the commander fight his way out if brought to action.

The approach to this area, therefore, had necessarily been somewhat tentative. Early strikes on North Korea had been launched from south of 37°, and operations against southern targets had been conducted from the waters west of Mokpo. But the tendency had been northward: on 20 August aircraft had been flown off in about 37°, and now on the night of 3 September Admiral Ewen took his force into the pocket, through the narrows between the Shantung Peninsula and Korea's western tip, to launch on the morning of the 4th from a position on the 38th parallel against targets in the Pyongyang-Chinnampo region.

Morning operations were routine, but the day was to offer its full share of excitement. At 1329 the destroyer *Herbert J. Thomas,* on picket duty some 60 miles north of the force, made radar contact on unidentified aircraft closing from the direction of the Russian base, and reported this to

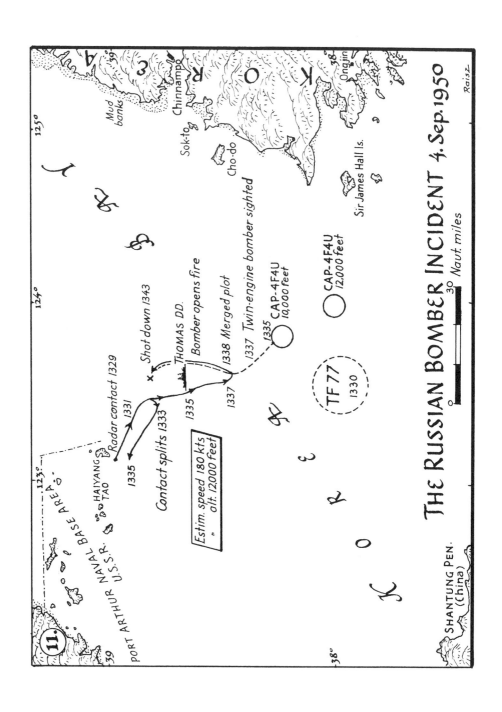

THE RUSSIAN BOMBER INCIDENT 4. Sep. 1950

Raisz

CAP-4F4U
10,000 feet

CAP-4F4U
12,000 feet

TF77
1330

Twin-engine bomber sighted
1337 1335

1338 Merged plot

Bomber opens fire

THOMAS DD.

Shot down 1343

Radar contact 1329

1331

Contact splits 1333

1335

Estim. speed 180 kts
alt. 12,000 feet

PORT ARTHUR NAVAL BASE AREA
U.S.S.R.

HAIYANG TAO

SHANTUNG PEN.
(China)

Mud banks

Chinnampo

Sok-to

Cho-do

Sir James Hall Is.

Ongjin

Naut. miles

Valley Forge planes passing overhead. Shortly the carrier herself made contact at a range of 60 miles, controllers on *Fletcher* were ordered to intercept, and a division of Corsairs which was orbiting northeast of the force was vectored out. The raid was by now estimated on course 160°, speed 180 knots, altitude 12–13,000 feet; as the fighters turned to meet it, it separated into two parts, with one retiring in the direction whence it came. Six minutes later and 30 miles north of the force the Corsairs intercepted the closing bogey and split into sections to box it in.

Here the intruder made a mistake. On sighting the fighters he nosed down, increased speed, and began evasive action, but in turning away turned eastward toward Korea rather than westward toward China. As the division leader, Lieutenant (j.g.) Richard E. Downs, flew over him in an attempt to identify, and reported a twin-engined bomber with red star markings, the intruder made a second mistake and opened fire. This was reported to base; permission to return the fire was granted. From his awkward position over the bogey the division leader made his run and missed; turning in from the starboard, his wing man made his and hit; as the port section in its turn began to roll inward a wing came off the bomber and it went down burning in a flat spin.

By now the force had gone to general quarters and was launching more fighters. On *Thomas,* where the bogey had been tracked southward and the merged plot then followed east and north, topside observers sighted an explosion and column of smoke in the sky followed shortly by a second explosion on the surface. Proceeding to the spot, the destroyer recovered the body of a Russian aviator, but artificial respiration continued for a full hour brought no sign of life.

Before the implications of this startling event could be digested, another emergency supervened. *Thomas* was still picking up debris from the downed aircraft and tension within the force was still high when another urgent call for help was received from the Joint Operations Center, asking 100 sorties a day and offering decentralized control and two VHF radio channels. Once again all strike groups were recalled, the force was turned to the southeast, speed was increased, and preparations were rushed to launch missions in support of the perimeter. But this time the emergency was cancelled out by higher authority, as ComNavFE informed the JOC that Cinc-FE had committed the fast carriers to other business, and that the Navy was unable to provide more support than that given by the Marine squadrons at Ashiya. Late in the afternoon a second flash from Fifth Air Force requested, with the concurrence of EUSAK, 100 sorties on the 5th and 50 percent of naval air effort until further notice, and asked for a representative from the task force to assist in the coordination and planning of close support. But the reply from ComNavFE to this second appeal merely referred the originator to his earlier answer to the JOC.

On the 5th, as an early morning weather flight disclosed unfavorable conditions over North Korea, Admiral Ewen turned his force southward and headed for Japan. *Sicily* was still in the yard at Sasebo, but *Badoeng Strait* was getting underway for the Yellow Sea. On the east coast a new crisis was developing with heavy enemy pressure against Pohang. At 1120 the KMAG detachment ashore asked the fire support unit to call for Navy air support to check an attack which had reached within half a mile of the town; an emergency dispatch to this effect reached ComNavFE shortly after noon and was at once relayed to Task Force 77, to Admiral Ruble, and to FEAF, with the request that all practicable help be given. But the fast carriers were 300 miles away, and bad weather left behind by Jane prevented flight operations by *Badoeng Strait*.

The immediate threat was checked by the fire support ships. Five-inch rapid fire from *Toledo* and *De Haven* broke up a tank attack and destroyed enemy artillery, while the destroyer provided further help by vectoring Fifth Air Force aircraft onto useful targets. But heavy enemy attacks continued, Pohang was lost again the next day, and by the 7th North Korean forces had gained the Hyongsan River south of the town, although still failing to reach the airfield. Further inland, things were still more threatening, and a North Korean thrust which reached almost to Kyongju forced the commitment of 24th Division units from EUSAK's strained reserve.

But while fighting was still heavy as the first week of September ended, the forces of the Far Eastern theater had done the job. Only in the north, in the region farthest from Pusan, had the enemy's all-out offensive made important gains; although there were still North Korean units east of the Naktong and south of Pohang, pressure was again diminishing. By the second week of September it was clear that CincFE's first essential had been accomplished. Despite all difficulties Eighth Army had succeeded in holding the perimeter. All now rested upon the landing at Inchon.

CHAPTER VII

Back to the Parallel

1. 10 July–11 September: Preparing the Counterstroke

FROM THE first days of war General MacArthur had hoped to deliver a counterstroke directed at the Inchon-Seoul region, the strategic solar plexus of Korea. Early in the fighting he had conceived the idea of landing the 1st Cavalry Division at Inchon, and from 4 to 8 July the staff of Amphibious Group 1 had grappled with this problem. But the rapid advance of the enemy, which forced abandonment of this scheme in favor of the decision to land the cavalrymen at Pohang, made it plain that translation of idea into actuality would involve an assault landing, and posed a requirement for amphibiously trained troops. Not unnaturally, therefore, the 10th of July, the day the Pohang landing was decided upon, was also the day of CincFE's first request for an entire Marine division.

Twice repeated in the days that followed, this request bore fruit on 20 July, with JCS approval of the movement to Korea of the 1st Marine Division, Major General Oliver P. Smith, USMC, with an arrival scheduled for November or December. But on the next day a most urgent request from CincFE for a reconsideration of this date was accompanied by his statement that its arrival by 10 September was "absolutely vital . . . to accomplish a decisive stroke." And on the 25th General MacArthur was informed that the 1st Marine Division, with attached air but less one RCT, had been ordered to prepare for a departure between 10 and 15 August.

That this commitment was met was in itself an extraordinary administrative accomplishment. Starting with a total Fleet Marine Force strength of 28,000, less than half of which was in FMF Pacific, it took some doing to provide a division of more than 20,000 men, not to mention the 4,000 or so additional personnel of the 1st Marine Aircraft Wing, without complete disorganization of the Fleet Marine Force Atlantic, and of the supporting establishment. Only the President's decision of 19 July to call up the Marine Corps Reserve enabled the Joint Chiefs to promise the division; only Marine confidence that an expedited arrival was both desirable and feasible produced the advanced departure date; only the availability of sufficient amphibious lift permitted this confidence. By such interlocking circumstances

171

CincFE was enabled to plan for a mid-September operation, but late July and early August was inevitably a time of controlled frenzy at Camp Pendleton, as security detachments, personnel from FMFLant, and reserves were processed and integrated into the violently expanding force. Difficult enough in itself, this work was further complicated by the need to provide replacements for the brigade in Korea, a requirement which was met beginning in mid-August by a series of troop movements flown west by MATS. Yet despite all obstacles loading of the division was begun on 8 August, two days ahead of schedule.

Up to this time the division promised General MacArthur consisted merely of a second RCT, the 1st Marines, plus supporting and headquarters troops and the balance of the 1st Marine Aircraft Wing. But on 10 August, as the brigade was attacking through Taedabok Pass and as the second embarkation was beginning at San Diego, the third RCT was provided and a third mobilization begun by orders to activate the 7th Marines.

The arrival of this regiment in the theater of action would constitute a striking demonstration of what can be accomplished by a force with a high degree of readiness when provided with advanced forms of transportation. One-third of the regimental strength was taken from the 2nd Marine Division on the Atlantic Coast, one-third was made up of Marine Corps Reserves summoned to active duty, and the remainder was provided by a battalion of the 6th Marines, then in the Mediterranean, and by personnel from miscellaneous posts throughout the United States. Five weeks and two days after its formal activation on 17 August, this regiment was in contact with the enemy, and the convergence upon Camp Pendleton of personnel from all over the United States had been followed by a convergence through 260° of longitude, westward from the Atlantic coast and eastward from Crete, upon Inchon. The critical days of mid-August which saw the Marine Brigade rushed northward toward the Naktong, the departure from the west coast of the first elements of the division, and the flight westward over the Pacific of the division commander and his staff, saw also the sailing from the Mediterranean of the AKA *Bexar* and the APA *Montague* with the 7th Marines' prospective 3rd Battalion.

By now some intellectual order had been made out of the Korean chaos, at least on the upper levels of command, by the imposition of a three-phase concept upon the operations in the peninsula. The first of these phases involved the halting of the North Korean advance, the second the reinforcement of U.N. forces in the perimeter to permit offensive action, the third the amphibious counterstroke. Yet these phases were not wholly separable: planning for phase three had to begin before the success of phase one was assured; the requirements of the first two phases had serious implications regarding the availability of forces for the Inchon landing.

This had been conceived of as a two-division operation, with the 1st Marine Division leading the assault. The timely presence of this unit in the Far East now seemed certain, but one of its RCTs was fully committed within the perimeter and one would not arrive in time for the initial landings. Given the continued shortage of forces in the theater, certain specific problems required solution before the planning could go forward. The availability of the Marine Brigade had to be assured; another division had to be found to follow the Marines across the beaches; a corps headquarters was needed to supervise the post-assault conduct of the campaign.

As to the first requirement, release of the brigade was promised by CincFE and the bad news communicated to General Walker. The follow-up assignment was given the 7th Infantry Division, Major General David G. Barr, USA, the last of the pre-war divisional units of the Far East Command, which had been first skeletonized to fill the ranks of units committed to Korea and then strengthened by the integration of some 8,600 South Korean recruits. To solve the command problem it was proposed either to borrow a ready-made organization from the staff of Fleet Marine Force Pacific, at Pearl Harbor, or to create a provisional corps headquarters from personnel available in Japan. Although the Marines were eager, the decision of CincFE was that the organization of a provisional X Corps Headquarters would be accomplished locally; command of the corps would be entrusted to Major General Edward M. Almond, USA, Chief of Staff of the Far East Command.

With the landing force provided for, it remained to get it there and put it ashore. This would be the job of the naval components of Joint Task Force 7, the combined force of which X Corps formed a part, command of which was assigned to Admiral Struble. The mission of Commander JTF 7 was to land the X Corps on D-Day at H-Hour on the west coast of Korea in order to seize and secure Inchon, Kimpo airfield, and Seoul, and sever North Korean lines of communication. This accomplished, the harvest would follow as X Corps, in conjunction with a planned offensive by Eighth Army and with the help of theater air and naval forces, would destroy the North Korean Army south of the line Inchon-Seoul-Ulchin.

Much of this preliminary planning was water over the dam by 22 August when the commander of the 1st Marine Division reached Tokyo. CincFE had published his directive for "Chromite" on the 12th, and Com-NavFE's derivative operation plan had been issued on the 20th. General Smith had previously heard only rumors of his task, but now he got the word. Two hours after his arrival, following a hasty fill-in by the Navy planners in Tokyo, the Marine commander had an audience with General MacArthur at which CincFE communicated his vision of the inevitable victory.

Table 8.—Far East Command Organization, Inchon and Wonsan Landings

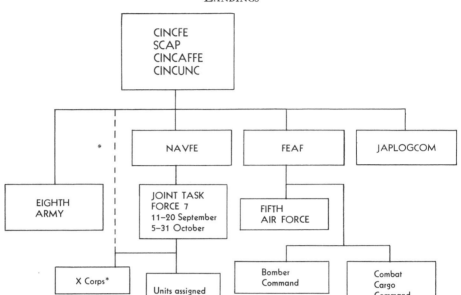

*When Commanding General assumes command ashore, X Corps reverts to the direct control of CincFE and Joint Task Force 7 is dissolved.

There followed two days of conferences of an extraordinary nature. Two members of the Joint Chiefs, Admiral Sherman and General Collins, had flown out from Washington; Admiral Radford and General Shepherd had flown in from Pearl; Admiral Joy and Admiral Doyle were there, along with numerous high-ranking officers from CincFE's headquarters. In these discussions it speedily became clear that in Tokyo the amphibious techniques which Navy and Marines had brought to high perfection, and which dominant Washington opinion considered obsolete, were held in the greatest esteem. The situation, indeed, was almost embarrassing, for without denying the strategic importance of Seoul or the desirability of its capture, naval and Marine planners could not forget the extraordinary tides and currents of the Yellow Sea, the mud banks which restricted and the islands which pockmarked the long approach to Inchon, and the absence of suitable landing beaches at the objective. Not since Admiral Rodgers sent them against the Han River forts had the Navy or Marines undertaken such a maneuver; Rodgers, at least, had not sent his landing force into the heart of a city; the

last such effort, the British raid on Dieppe, had not proven an experience
of a sort to inspire confidence in this type of assault.

Although the rule book says that what is tactically impossible can never
be strategically desirable, the doubts of the experts were of no avail. The
Commander in Chief was firm, both as to the amphibious assault and as
to the objective, while the headquarters staff, seeing the strategic desirability
clear, seemed to feel that tactical obstacles could be solved by the issuance
of orders. Naval reservations were brushed aside, and increasingly the
conferences took on the air of the attack on stout Horatius, when

> . . . those behind cried, "Forward!"
> And those before cried, "Back!"

Navy doubts about the proposed operation had developed well before
General Smith's arrival, and had led ComNavFE's staff to investigate some
possible alternatives. In the search for a better objective the fast transport
Horace A. Bass had been sent into the Yellow Sea and provided with fighter
cover by *Badoeng Strait;* there between 20 and 25 August, and despite the
presence of a full moon, her raider and UDT group had conducted night
reconnaissance of possible beaches north and south of Kunsan, and of one
in Asan Man, 38 miles below Inchon. But these efforts came to naught. Although preliminary plans had been developed for Kunsan, and although
Admiral Sherman and General Collins both favored a landing in this area,
the suggestion was ruled out by CincFE. Even General Shepherd, whose
early support of Inchon had helped in the materialization of the Marine Division, had by now developed second thoughts, but his plea for the Asan Man
alternative suffered the same fate.

Having felt themselves somewhat in the dark, the dignitaries from
Washington had come out to see what was going on. Now they knew. At
the final conference the best that Admiral Doyle could say about Inchon
was that it was "not impossible." There the situation rested. None would
gainsay CincFE. And while formal approval of the Joint Chiefs had still
to be obtained, Admiral Sherman's agreement to support the plan and the
appointment of Admiral Struble to command the operation had already
shifted the emphasis from debate to action.

At Sasebo, having learned of his large impending responsibilities, Struble
had been expanding his staff. A squadron commander was lifted from the
destroyers, an air planner from Admiral Hoskins' staff, and on the 25th,
leaving his flagship to follow him, Commander Seventh Fleet flew to Tokyo.
There, where all principal commanders were now united, there was plenty
of work for all. The west coast contingent of the Marine Division was expected to reach Kobe on the 29th. The first elements of the Attack Force
were scheduled to sail on 9 September. D-Day was only 20 days away.

But the Amphibious Group's studies of Inchon provided a basis for planning, the Marine Division staff had already moved aboard *Mount McKinley,* and with the arrival of the commander of the joint force decisions could be made.

With no time for rehearsal, with only the minimum time for combat loading, Joint Task Force 7 was responsible for the execution of an extremely audacious plan. Far larger forces had been committed to far smaller objectives during the war against Japan: at Iwo three divisions had been employed and at Okinawa four; and while the opposition on those islands was of course far stronger than that anticipated at Inchon, naval strength had made it possible to isolate the objective and to deny the enemy all hope of reinforcement. At Inchon some measure of isolation of the battlefield was indeed possible, as a result of command of the sea and air and of the effort previously expended in the knocking down of bridges. But while trains and ships and even trucks might be excluded, there was no guarantee that large numbers of unfriendly pedestrians might not be concentrated by night marches against the beachhead.

Eighty years earlier Admiral Rodgers had estimated that 5,000 troops would suffice to capture a treaty. Since then things had changed. Where formerly the only signs of habitation had been the scattered fishing huts of Chemulpo there had now developed a sizable city, while the events of the preceding weeks had sufficiently demonstrated that the enemy had modernized his military techniques. The task of the 1st Marine Division, which with attached Army and Korean units would reach a D-Day strength of 25,000, was to land in and capture a city with a population of some 250,000 souls, and then advance without loss of momentum to seize Kimpo airfield, 12 miles inland, by D plus 2. The area involved was roughly comparable to that of Saipan, where three divisions had been committed to the attack with another held in reserve, where there were no great cities, where hydrographic difficulties were slight, and where the flanks of the assault force were protected by the vastness of the Pacific Ocean and the power of the Pacific Fleet.

Reinforced, beginning on D plus 2, until it would attain a strength of almost 70,000, X Corps was to press onward to capture Seoul, capital and largest city of the country, and then hold until contact was made with Eighth Army forces coming up from the southward. How long this would take was problematical in view of the great depth of the turning movement. The distance between the point of landing and the beleaguered forces in the perimeter was some 140 miles airline, roughly comparable to that from Philadelphia to Washington, more than twice that at Anzio beachhead where the link-up took four months.

Although the risks inherent in the introduction of so small a force into so large a land mass at so great a distance from supporting units could perhaps be discounted, given the wear and tear inflicted on the North Korean People's Army and its commitment far to the south, the Inchon landing still presented some appalling tactical problems for the naval forces which had to bring it off. These difficulties stemmed principally from the extraordinary hydrography of the objective region and from the configuration of Inchon harbor. Shallow water at Inchon limited the date of a possible attack to a short three-day period each month; the rise and fall of the tide limited the time of attack to two short periods each day; the narrow and tortuous entrance channels restricted the movement of shipping for the last 34 miles of the approach, made daylight entry almost imperative for vessels of low power and poor maneuverability such as transport, cargo, and LST types, and prevented the normal night retirement of amphibious shipping from the objective area.

These hydrographic conditions had limited the development of this Korean Piraeus. Although the second port of South Korea, Inchon's ability to sustain an army corps was marginal. The navigational hazards of the approach and the tidal silting which had bordered the city with drying mud flats had kept its cargo handling capacity small: where Pusan could handle 25,000 tons a day, Inchon could manage less than half of that. Piers were lacking, and the five berths in the tidal basin compared unfavorably with the 30 alongside berths at Pusan. Nor was the outer anchorage of a sort that could conveniently accommodate an invasion armada: at Inchon this measures about seven miles from north to south and a mile or less from east to west. Only some 50 ships can anchor here; a tidal current of two to three knots sets in and out along the long axis.

Yet before the problems of post-assault logistics could be faced, some means had to be found to get the troops ashore. This too was difficult: not only did the lack of maneuvering room within the harbor complicate the ship-to-shore movement and restrict the possibilities of the fire support ships, but there was a notable absence of suitable assault landing points.

Of these only two could be found which were in any sense adequate, Blue Beach in the southeastern section of the city and Red Beach on its western shore, and they could be called beaches only by courtesy. Located at opposite ends of the town, they were separated by a four-mile water distance; lined with piers and seawalls, their assault required scaling ladders; reentrant in contour, they were subject to enfilading fire. Nor was this the sum of the difficulties, for from between these landing points there protruded from the Inchon waterfront a causeway leading to the small island of Wolmi Do, known anciently as Isle Roze in commemoration of the French admiral whose unsuccessful assault on the forts marked the first arrival of western civilization. This island, which with its smaller satellite Sowolmi dominated and divided the Inchon outer anchorage, was known to have been fortified by the Communist invaders. Before an assault into the city could be contemplated its capture was essential.

The necessity of first reducing this strong point and the constricted nature of the entrance channels ruled out a night approach by the transport groups and eliminated the possibility of surprise. Since an attack in two phases was required, it was decided to send a small force in on the morning tide to seize Wolmi Do and then, after the waters had receded and risen again, to bring in the main part of the Attack Force for a late afternoon assault into the city. Nor was the warning to the enemy limited to this inter-tidal period. The need for pre-invasion bombardment of Wolmi's fortifications, which would extend the alert period, reemphasized the fact that the attack was being directed not against an isolated island but against an area which could be reinforced.

The final impact of the Inchon tides appeared in the planning for logistic support. Only small craft could negotiate Blue Beach at the southern edge of the city; only at Red Beach in the north and at Green Beach on Wolmi Do could LSTs be brought in, and there only during the high tides between D-Day and D plus 2. At low tide nothing could be landed, and behind its ramparts of yielding ooze the city lay secure. To supply the assault forces during the night of D-Day, it was decided to run LSTs ashore at Red Beach and leave them through the inter-tidal interval, accepting the possible loss of these vessels in the interests of adequate troop support. For the LSTs, high and dry and with cargoes composed largely of explosive and inflammable materials, the prospect was not enviable, but a scheme of maneuver was worked out which emphasized the fastest possible clearing of Red Beach in order to ensure, so far as possible, the survival of these ungainly vehicles and of their priceless contents.

Such were the known generalities of the situation, but again, despite American occupation of Korea, intelligence was lacking and the specifics were unknown. Would the mud banks of Inchon support tracked vehicles? The answer was available in Rodgers' report of 80 years before, but this was safely filed in the National Archives and no recent information was at hand. How high were the seawalls? What were their implications for the lowering of ramps of landing craft, or for troops attempting to get ashore? Would scaling ladders in fact be necessary? Which piers, if any, would support heavy vehicular traffic? In the effort to acquire reliable information Army personnel who had served in Inchon were rounded up and quizzed, photographic missions were laid on, the Air Force flew some photo interpreters out from the United States, and on 1 September a naval officer, Lieutenant Eugene F. Clark, was put ashore with two interpreters, a radio, and some small arms on the friendly-held island of Yonghung Do, 15 miles below Inchon.

In the meantime, and on the basis of such intelligence as was available, the work of the planners continued. On his arrival in Tokyo Admiral Struble was briefed by Doyle's staff on the problems of Inchon, issued orders for concurrent planning, and undertook to give oral decisions as needed as the work went on. The flagship *Rochester,* on her arrival, was berthed alongside *Mount McKinley* to keep the staffs in close proximity. On the 30th Andrewes, Ruble, Higgins, and Austin flew up from Sasebo for a conference of prospective task force commanders. And while the planning proceeded the preliminary operations were begun: new operating areas and operating schedules, intended to ensure adequate preparation of the objective without an overconcentration which would alert the enemy, were made up by Struble's staff for broadcast by ComNavFE to the carrier forces at sea.

So the concept of the operation took form. In early September, and again in the days preceding the landing, the three carrier units of Joint Task Force 7—Admiral Ewen's fast carriers, Admiral Ruble's escort carriers, and the British light carrier *Triumph*—would work over the west coast with their efforts gradually converging toward Inchon. Prior to D–Day a destroyer and cruiser bombardment of Wolmi Do would be carried out. On the early morning tide of 15 September a battalion landing team of the 5th Marines would assault Wolmi in order to secure that commanding position. On the afternoon tide, at about 1700, the main attack into the city would be carried out by the 5th Marines' remaining two battalions and by the 1st Marines. While the two Marine regiments moved rapidly to expand their holdings to Kimpo airfield and the Han River line, the 7th Infantry Division (Reinforced) and corps troops would be landed administratively and would then operate as ordered by the corps commander. Throughout the operation bombardment and fire support would be provided by cruisers and destroyers, and air cover, air strikes, and close support by carrier aviation. So far as the air was concerned Joint Task Force 7 was self-sufficient: complications of coordination or control during the landing phase were fended off by the proviso that except at the request of Admiral Struble no FEAF aircraft would operate in the objective area subsequent to D minus 3, while for the later stages of the campaign X Corps was provided with its own Tactical Air Command, composed of Marine aircraft and commanded by a Marine brigadier general.

Such was the plan for the operation as worked out by the staffs of Seventh Fleet, the Amphibious Group, and the Marine Division. For Inchon, as for Pohang, the planning was necessarily carried out in violation of all the rules and in record time. By 2 September, when the Joint Task Force operation plan and the Amphibious Group's operation order were issued, Marine planning was nearing completion, and on the next day Admiral Doyle and General Smith sailed in *Mount McKinley* for Kobe, where the bulk of the Marine Division had just arrived from the United States.

This speed in planning, essential as it was, also brought its problems. There was no time for joint training, no possibility of rehearsal. Division and Attack Force staffs had to plan for lower echelons without benefit of comment or opinion from the subordinates, and completed plans made their appearance as hand-outs to the regimental and task unit commanders involved. The risks of high speed concurrent planning for so complex an enterprise were illustrated by difficulties in shipping allocation: owing to lack of information on the characteristics of available vessels, the 34 transport and cargo types which MSTS WestPac had been requested to nominate for the invasion turned out to be too few, and on 9 September, D minus 6, Captain Junker was called upon for a further 11 ships. Yet despite the necessarily authoritarian nature of the procedure, and the pressures under which it was carried out, there were few mistakes. On 7 September Admiral Struble flew to Sasebo and Kobe to confer with his principal subordinates and to tidy up loose ends. The most important of these, an overly ambitious commitment of the fast carrier air effort, was rectified in the 40-minute briefing which was all that could be given Admiral Ewen on his part in the operation.

Although two divisions were a small force with which to enter a large enemy-controlled land mass, the Inchon landing was nevertheless an operation of a certain magnitude. To transport, protect, and put ashore a force

Table 9.—Joint Task Force 7: Inchon

JOINT TASK FORCE 7. VICE ADMIRAL A. D. STRUBLE.

  TASK FORCE 90. ATTACK FORCE. REAR ADMIRAL J. H. DOYLE.
    1–2 AGC, 1 AH, 1 AM, 6 AMS, 3 APD, 1 ARL, 1 ARS, 1 ATF, 2 CVE, 2 CA, 3 CL (1 USN, 2 RN), 1 DE, 12 DD, 5 LSD, 3 LSMR, 4 ROKN PC, 1 PCEC, 8 PF (3 USN, 2 RN, 2 RNZN, 1 French), 7 ROKN YMS, 47 LST (30 Scajap), plus transports, cargo ships, etc., to a total of approximately 180.

  TASK FORCE 91. BLOCKADE AND COVERING FORCE.
    REAR ADMIRAL SIR W. G. ANDREWES, RN.
    1 CVL, 1 CL, 8 DD.

  TASK FORCE 92. X CORPS. MAJOR GENERAL E. M. ALMOND, USA.
    1st Marine Division, Reinforced; 7th Infantry Division, Reinforced; Corps Troops.

  TASK FORCE 99. PATROL AND RECONNAISSANCE FORCE.
    REAR ADMIRAL G. R. HENDERSON.
    2 AV, 1 AVP, 3 USN and 2 RAF Patrol Squadrons.

  TASK FORCE 77. FAST CARRIER FORCE. REAR ADMIRAL E. C. EWEN.
    2–3 CV, 1 CL, 14 DD.

  TASK FORCE 79. SERVICE SQUADRON. CAPTAIN B. L. AUSTIN.
    2 AD, 1 AE, 2 AF, 1 AK, 3 AKA, 3 AKL, 4 AO, 1 AOG, 1 ARG, 1 ARH, 1 ARS, 1 ATF.

of this size calls for a considerable investment in shipping and in personnel, and "Chromite," despite the expected absence of air and sea opposition, placed a heavy load upon the Navy. The total strength of Joint Task Force 7 amounted to some 230 ships of all shapes and sizes, from APDs of 2,100 tons full load displacement to transports of ten times that size. Except for a few gunnery ships held back to support the flanks of the perimeter, it included all combatant units available in the Far East. Fifty-two ships were assigned to the Fast Carrier, Patrol and Reconnaissance, and Logistic Task Forces; the remainder went to make up the Attack Force, Task Force 90, under Admiral Doyle. Of these, more than 120 were required to lift X Corps, while the rest were involved in gunfire and air support, screening, minesweeping, and miscellaneous other duties.

That so sizable an amphibious lift could be so rapidly assembled was remarkable, the more so in view of the preexisting policies of economy and of down-grading the amphibious function. In 1945 the assembly of such a force would have seemed simple enough; by 1952 it would have become quite feasible; but 1950, the year that it was needed, was the year of the drought. Inevitably, therefore, the armada that eventuated was a somewhat heterogeneous one, and of the 120-odd units assigned to lift X Corps less than half were commissioned vessels of the U.S. Navy. Thirty of the LSTs assigned the operation were Scajap ships, manned by the hardworking and loyal enemy aliens, and, of the vessels collected by MSTS WestPac, 13 were MSTS-owned, 26 were American cargo ships on time charter, and four were chartered Japanese *Marus*.

With completion of the planning phase, a stage in the operation had ended. Shipping was available, and a movement schedule had been worked out to lift X Corps to the objective area; a scheme of maneuver had been developed to overcome the natural difficulties of Inchon; supporting forces were on hand to deal with foreseeable contingencies. One minute after midnight on 11 September the Joint Task Force 7 plan was placed in effect for operations. Some of the slower shipping had already set sail.

But any military plan is based on certain assumptions, and "Chromite" was no exception. Underlying the basic concept were not only the postulates that phases one and two of the Korean campaign would be completed, but also that there would be no important change in the disposition of enemy forces, and that the greater portion of the invading army would remain committed to the Pusan perimeter. That this should be the case was fundamental to CincFE's plan, which could be described in the words of Wee Willie Keeler as to "hit 'em where they ain't," or in the more martial analogy employed by General MacArthur himself, to follow the example of Wolfe in his approach to the Plains of Abraham.

By early September these assumptions appeared to have been fulfilled. The perimeter was holding, Eighth Army had been reinforced, and the

North Korean People's Army was deep in South Korea. Large and effective though this force had proven itself to be, it possessed the defects of its virtues. Chief of these was an inflexibility in the realm of movement and logistics, which had by now been greatly accentuated by the effect of air and naval attacks on the Communist supply lines. The North Koreans could still push hard against the perimeter, but the problems of rapid and flexible redeployment were almost insuperable.

Last and in some ways most important of CincFE's assumptions was the postulate that the enemy would receive no important reinforcement. In Korea the intervention of the United Nations had wholly changed the strategic picture, and had first delayed and then threatened with frustration a campaign planned as a walk-over. The assumptions of the invader had already proven false, and agonizing reappraisal had been thrust upon the planners in North Korea, and in the regions beyond the Yalu and the Tumen. To press on with the offensive, in the hope of driving the U.N. armies into the sea before the situation could be stabilized, had been the natural first reaction. But the arrival of important naval forces and the known amphibious capabilities of the U.S. Navy must necessarily have raised the specter of a landing in the rear, forced a review of the situation, and emphasized the desirability of further assistance from the Communist elder brothers.

There was thus at least a possibility that these, in their turn, would raise the struggle to a higher level, by providing the North Koreans with ground reinforcements, or with air or submarine strength. As regards the former, however, Russian ground intervention seemed hardly probable, while the concentration of Chinese Communist Forces opposite Formosa had left them poorly deployed for rapid action. And while air and submarine strength was available in quantity in the Soviet Maritime Provinces, its employment was fairly plainly fraught with risk. In the air, perhaps, the Far East Command's air and naval contingents could have withstood a Communist offensive, but with regard to undersea warfare the situation was very different. Given the length of the seaborne supply line and the shortage of escort vessels, a serious submarine offensive would have faced the United States with a choice of accepting defeat or resorting to high-yield weapons. Quite possibly this situation was appreciated by the other side.

Since no such step was taken by the Communists, this problem was not posed, and CincFE's assumptions were almost totally borne out. The enemy offensive was not weakened to guard against an amphibious counterstroke; although the Chinese had begun a northward redeployment, no ground reinforcements were provided the North Koreans; no aerial or undersea auxiliaries made their appearance. But on a lower level, and unknown to the U.N. commanders, a rapid reaction had already taken place in the form of a minelaying campaign designed to threaten U.N. naval forces and make Korean coastal waters untenable.

As early as 10 July shipments of mines were rolling southward down the east coast railway from the Vladivostok region. One week later Soviet naval personnel had reached Wonsan and Chinnampo and were holding mine school for their North Korean friends. This reaction, which wholly justified Admiral Joy's concern with the northeastern railroad route, was sufficiently rapid to get the mines through before the limited Seventh Fleet and NavFE forces could be brought to bear. Some 4,000 mines were quickly passed through Wonsan, and by 1 August mining had been begun at that port and at Chinnampo. In time Russian naval officers ventured as far south as Inchon, shipments of mines were trucked down from Chinnampo to Haeju, and before the bridges were knocked down consignments had reached Inchon, Kunsan, and Mokpo by train.

This effort to counteract U.N. control of the sea went undetected. In mid-August search planes had reported enemy barges and patrol craft at Wonsan and Chinnampo, but while in retrospect these were believed to have been engaged in minelaying, the intelligence was not so interpreted at the time. The operation plans of ComNavFE, Commander Seventh Fleet, and Commander Attack Force, while crediting the enemy with limited mining capabilities at Inchon, stated that available information indicated no minefields in that area.

2. *15 August–21 September: North to Inchon*

While "Chromite" was still in preparation the return to the north had begun. Although heavily engaged along the coast and busy with refugee evacuation, the ROK Navy had been able to mount offensive operations. Commander Luosey, who as CTG 96.7 operated this inshore fleet, was not privy to the Inchon planning, but the basic strategic situation was as clear to those in Pusan as it was to those in Tokyo, and the increasing probability that the perimeter would be held emphasized the value of deep flanking positions, whether for raids, landings, or the infiltration of agents. On 15 August, therefore, CTG 96.7 advised ComNavFE of his intention, if not otherwise directed, of seizing the Tokchok Islands in the Inchon approaches as a base for intelligence activities and future operations.

No countermanding instructions were received, help was promised by the west coast Commonwealth units, and on the 17th Operation Lee, named for the commanding officer of *PC 702,* was begun. With two YMS in company Lee put a 110-man force ashore on Tokchok To; on the next day *Athabaskan* turned up to support the effort and the island was secured. On the 19th Lee's force landed on Yonghung Do, in the Inchon approach channel, and in the days that followed expanded its control to other islands in the west coast bight. On the 20th a landing party from *Athabaskan*

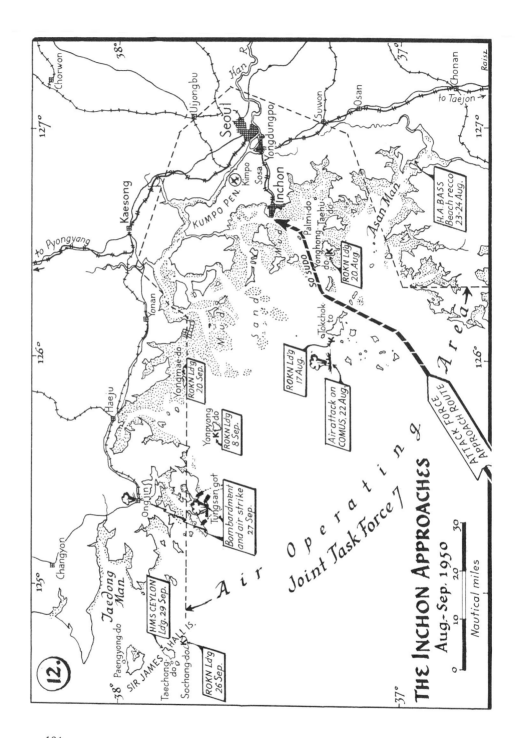

12.

THE INCHON APPROACHES
Aug.- Sep. 1950

Nautical miles
0   10   20   30

Air Operating
Joint Task Force 7

ATTACK FORCE
APPROACH ROUTE

Chorwon
38°
to Pyongyang
Kaesong
127°
Ujongbu
Han R.
Seoul
Yongdungpo
Suwon
Osan
to Taejon
127°
Chonan
Raisz
37°

Kumpo
Kumpo Pen.
Sosa
Inchon
Palmi-do
Taehu-do
Yonghong-do
Asan Man.

Onan
Haeju
126°
Muu-a
Sand
So Sudo
Tokchok-to
ROKN Ldg 20 Aug.
H.A.BASS Beach recco 23-24 Aug.

Yongmae-do
ROKN Ldg 20 Sep.
Yonpyong-do
ROKN Ldg 8 Sep.
ROKN Ldg 17 Aug.
Air attack on COMUS, 22 Aug.

Ongjin
Tungsan got
Bombardment and air strike 27 Sep.

Changyon
Jaedong Man.
125°
38°
Paengyong-do
SIR JAMES HALL Is.
HMS CEYLON Ldg. 29 Sep.
Taechong-do
Sochang-do
ROKN Ldg 26 Sep.
37°

destroyed the radio gear in the lighthouse on Palmi Do at the mouth of Inchon harbor. By 1 September, when Lieutenant Clark arrived at Yong-hung Do, considerable information concerning the defenses of Inchon had been collected by intelligence teams under Lieutenant Commander Ham Myong Su, ROKN. And reports from the British indicated that the seizure of Yonghung Do had caused the enemy to shift forces southward to guard against a possible mainland landing.

So far, so good, but on 1 September, as the invasion plans were moving to completion, there came the enemy's last and greatest effort to crush the Korean beachhead. In this hour of crisis Eighth Army needed all the help that it could get, and again phase one threatened to interfere with phase three. Not only did enemy pressure bring emergency calls for the retention of Task Force 77 in close support; it also threatened to make the Marine Brigade unavailable for the Inchon landing. Previous orders to release the brigade on 4 September were cancelled on the 1st, and for the second time the Marines were committed to the Naktong front.

Faced with the danger that EUSAK's needs might prevent the release of the brigade, General Almond proposed to replace it at Inchon by a regiment of the 7th Division. To the Navy and Marine commanders the assignment of this unit, untrained in amphibious operations and with a large infusion of South Korean recruits, would force abandonment of the two-beach assault for one in which the infantry would be landed in column behind the 1st Marines, with all the implications that this might have for the success of the operation. But the issue was fortunately resolved by Admiral Struble who, while insisting on the release of the brigade, observed that Eighth Army's need for a reserve could be met by embarking a regiment of the 7th Division and moving it to Pusan, where it could be either landed in support of the perimeter or sailed to rejoin its parent organization at Inchon.

On this basis it was settled. Release of the brigade was rescheduled for evening of the 5th. The requests for Task Force 77 were turned down by ComNavFE. For all of its magnitude the Communist offensive had succeeded neither in breaking the perimeter nor in diverting important forces from the impending counterstroke.

Although the fast carriers had withdrawn to Sasebo on 5 September, following the strikes against the Pyongyang area, naval activity continued along Korea's western shore. Between Kunsan and the 38th parallel, aircraft from *Triumph* and *Badoeng Strait* scoured the land, concentrating on railroad bridges, rolling stock, and electrical transformer stations. While continuing to interdict coastal traffic, Admiral Andrewes' surface ships found opportunity to bombard Inchon on the 5th and Kunsan the next day. On the 7th, *Triumph* departed to the east coast for two days of operations off Wonsan, but with the arrival of *Sicily* on the 8th two-carrier operations were resumed. On the 10th, the last day on station prior to departure for replen-

With ten rounds of 8-inch HC, Helena drops two spans of bridge at Kanggu Hang, 23 miles north of Pohang. View looks southeast and downstream; river mouth is a mile beyond bridge. 9 September 1950. (USN 422474)

ishment, Admiral Ruble's Marine squadrons were ordered to burn off the western half of Wolmi Do. Double loads of napalm, to a total of 95,000 pounds, were ferried in during the course of the day, with resultant destruction of 90 percent of the top cover in the designated area, and presumable discouragement of the garrison.

It might be thought that an attack of such unprecedented nature against a terrain feature of such localized strategic importance would have alerted the enemy to what was in prospect and given him five days for emergency redeployment. Perhaps it did, but his capabilities in this direction were limited, and in any case the larger security picture for the Inchon landing was problematical at best. In Japan, where there were plenty of enemy agents and no censorship, the situation was a highly compromising one, and the arrival of the Marines and the assembly and loading of troops were matters of common knowledge.

Some efforts to delude the Communists were indeed carried out. *Triumph* was briefly shifted to the east coast. After dropping a bridge on the 9th at Kanggu Hang, below Yongdok, *Helena* and her destroyers ran north to 40° to shoot up shipping and trenches at the island of Mayang Do. At Pusan the Marine Brigade was lined up and given a semi-public lecture on the hydrography of Kunsan; after replenishment at Sasebo, *Triumph* would concentrate her efforts in the vicinity of that port, as would the Fifth Air Force; in this region, where *Bass'* earlier beach survey had been detected by the enemy, a raid was scheduled by an Anglo-American force embarked in HMS *Whitesand Bay*. But the basic cover and deception appears to have been accomplished by CincFE himself, by his insistence on so improbable an objective and by his pressure for speed. The enemy, it would seem, concurred in the views of those who questioned the depth of the turning movement and the hydrography of Inchon. South of 38° the heaviest days of his mining effort were at Mokpo and Kusan on the west coast, and in the neighborhood of Chumunjin in the east. At Inchon the effort was too little and too late.

In Japan, meanwhile, the skill and devotion of the implementers had succeeded within the allotted time in matching the vision of the strategist. While Wolmi Do was burning on the 10th the slower elements of the Attack Force were getting underway. A portion of the pontoon movement group, with gear for the expansion of Inchon's port facilities, had already departed Yokohama, as had the rocket ships which would bombard the beaches. The tractor movement elements of LSTs and accompanying ships were getting underway from Kobe. At Kobe, at Sasebo, and at Pusan, the transports were preparing to set sail in accordance with the movement schedule. Shipping from Yokohama and Kobe would pass south around Kyushu and then steer to the northwest, to be joined south of Cheju Do by units from Sasebo and Pusan. Passing through predetermined points at predetermined intervals, the pieces that made up Task Force 90 would be reordered and reshuffled, moved onward into the Yellow Sea, and funneled into the Inchon approaches according to a rigidly determined plan. Once begun, so elaborate an operation is difficult to postpone or modify, and at Inchon the tides forbade delay. No delay, it is true, was anticipated from hostile action, and in any case precautions against such interruptions had been taken. What could not, however, be planned for was the hostility of the elements.

From a meteorological point of view, a war in Korea presents a problem to the maritime power, for most of the peninsula's weather is manufactured over the continental land mass. Yet there is some compensation in the fact that the typhoons which afflict the area, and which provide the greatest single threat to military operations, are of oceanic birth, and can be tracked in their passage northwestward from the Marianas. Their season, which begins in June and extends to mid-September, had thus far precisely coincided with the war. Grace, who had caused some difficulties at the time of the Pohang landing, had been followed by two milder sisters, but September brought more trouble. On the 3rd, Jane had forced the evacuation of patrol squadrons from Japan to Okinawa, and had slashed through Kobe bringing gusts of up to 10 knots, damaging ships and gear assigned to the Marine Division, taking a full day from an already tight loading schedule, and depriving the brigade of air support from Ashiya. One week later, as the Attack Force was preparing to sortie, Kezia was reported moving up from the Marianas, with a predicted arrival in Tsushima Strait on the 12th or 13th, just as the amphibious shipping was scheduled to cross her path.

Since the loss of the Duke of Medina Sidonia's Armada, the influence of weather on great naval operations has profoundly affected the history of the west; in the Orient an equally illustrious precedent is provided by the Kamikaze, the Divine Wind of 1281, which threw back the second Mongol invasion of Japan. That modern fleets are also vulnerable to such hazards was made evident in the Second World War: in the invasion of North Africa Admiral Hewitt had to balance advice from his force meteorologist against pessimistic reports from afar; the landings in Sicily were complicated by weather; "Overlord" itself had to be postponed; and two typhoons caused serious trouble for Admiral Halsey's Third Fleet. Now the same question faced Admiral Struble, and in even more excruciating form: Admiral Hewitt had been provided with alternative invasion beaches inside the Mediterranean, but here there were no alternatives; General Eisenhower had been able to put off "Overlord," but the Inchon tides permitted no postponement. On the assumption, perhaps better on the hope, that the storm would recurve, Struble ordered the assault shipping out of Kobe a day ahead of schedule, and in the early morning darkness of the 11th sortied in *Rochester* from Yokosuka. Later in the morning Admiral Doyle sailed from Kobe in *Mount McKinley* and headed southwestward for Van Diemen Strait. In

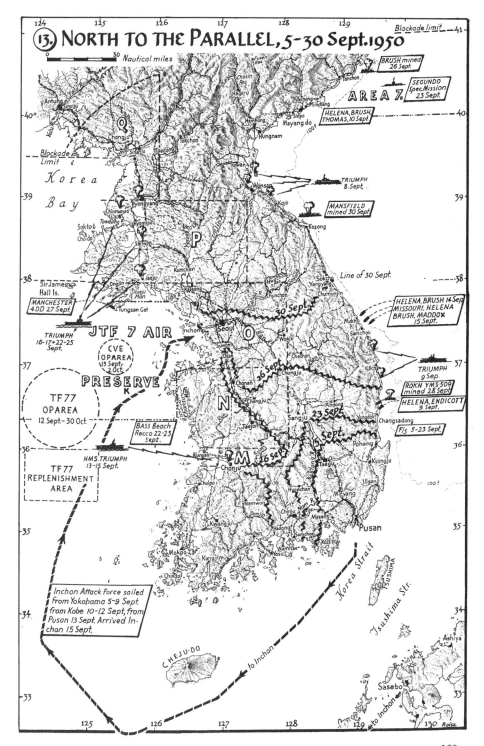

0   50
Nautical miles

124   125   126   127   128   129   Blockade limit   41

BRUSH mined
26 Sept.

AREA 7.

SEGUNDO
Spec. Mission
23 Sept.

HELENA, BRUSH,
THOMAS, 10 Sept.

Korea
Bay

TRIUMPH
8. Sept.

MANSFIELD
mined 30 Sept.

Blockade
Limit

Line of 30 Sept.

HELENA, BRUSH 14 Sep
MISSOURI, HELENA
BRUSH, MADDOX
15 Sept.

SirJames
Hall Is.

MANCHESTER
4 DD 27 Sept.

TRIUMPH
16-17+22-25
Sept.

JTF 7 AIR

CVE
OPAREA
15 Sept.
2 Oct.

PRESERVE

TRIUMPH
9 Sep.

TF 77
OPAREA
12 Sept.-30 Oct.

ROKN YMS 509
mined 28 Sept.

HELENA, ENDICOTT
9. Sept.

BASS Beach
Recco 22-23
Sept.

F/s 5-23 Sept.

HMS TRIUMPH
13-15 Sept.

TF 77
REPLENISHMENT
AREA

100 f

Korea Strait

TSUSHIMA

Inchon Attack force sailed
from Yokohama 5-9 Sept.
from Kobe 10-12 Sept, from
Pusan 13 Sept. Arrived Inchon 15 Sept.

Tsushima Str.

Ashiya

CHEJU-DO

to Inchon

Sasebo

to Inchon   Raisz

125   126   127   128   129   130

the evening, while passing east of Kyushu in heavy seas, Doyle learned that the Transport Group had reversed course to the eastward; this was promptly countermarched again in order to outrun the storm, while *Mount McKinley* headed for Sasebo to pick up CincFE and the other GHQ spectators. Prospects were still unclear, however, for on the morning of the 12th the light cruiser *Manchester,* proceeding singly from the United States, located the typhoon center 150 miles south of Kyushu, and radar tracking showed it moving at seven knots in the direction of the Yellow Sea. But fortune favored the brave. Kezia did indeed recurve, and by the time she passed over the southeast corner of Kyushu on the afternoon of the 13th the Attack Force was well clear.

The departure of the escort carriers after the burning of Wolmi Do had left the waters off Inchon tenanted only by Commonwealth and ROK blockading forces, and by a single patrol plane which, being relieved on station, maintained 24-hour supervision of the Yellow Sea. But the ROK Navy remained busy: Operation Lee was continuing; *PC 703* sank a mine-laying sailboat off Haeju on the 10th, and on the 12th got three more small craft in the Inchon approaches. And now, as the Attack Force plowed forward through heavy seas and the Marines in the troop compartments cursed their fates, the tempo of operations in the objective area began to increase.

Even here Kezia had made herself felt, for the Japan-based patrol planes had been evacuated to Okinawa, and where plans called for increased antisubmarine search around the approaching Attack Force, no such sorties could in fact be flown. But the 12th, D minus 3, saw Task Force 77 back at work in the Yellow Sea, operating in an area 120 miles west by south of Inchon. On the 12th and 13th strikes designed to seal off the objective area were flown against ground installations and lines of communication in Area O, while the jets swept airfields to the northward. On the 13th, D minus 2, a special combat air patrol was provided for the Wolmi Do bombardment group.

On the 14th, as Transport and Tractor Groups were approaching the objective and as the bombardment of Wolmi Do continued, carrier-borne aircraft were in operation and on call along the entire western coast of South Korea. *Triumph* was working over the Kunsan region while maintaining four fighters ready for immediate launching as combat air patrol for transports south of 36°. Carrier Division 15 was back on station, and in addition to keeping fighters on call to cover shipping north of 36° was providing spotting aircraft and combat air patrol for the Wolmi Do bombardment ships. From the middle of the Yellow Sea the fast carriers maintained a tactical air coordinator over the Inchon area from dawn to dusk, and provided him with three strikes, morning, midday, and afternoon, of 16 ADs apiece.

The little island of Wolmi Do, the object of much of this solicitude, forms an equilateral triangle slightly more than half a mile on a side, with its eastern edge running north and south, and with a spit extending from the northern corner. From the base of the spit a 900-yard causeway leads northeastward to the Inchon shore; from the western corner another of roughly equal length runs southward to the islet of Sowolmi. Wolmi Do was known to be defended by enemy artillery, and was thought to be heavily so. Although much of the top cover had been burned off by the Marine pilots of Cardiv 15, and although very considerable air strength was available to support the assault, preparation by naval gunfire was deemed essential.

If the war in the Pacific had demonstrated anything, it was the virtue of naval gunfire in preparation for an assault against a defended objective. Given the nature of Japanese island fortifications, no substitute existed for slow, deliberate, aimed fire directed at specific targets and delivered at short-range, and from Tarawa on progress in this technique was notable. So far as the assault troops were concerned, the longer the preparation the better, but in any given operation the time available for such preliminaries was subject to various and often conflicting considerations. At Inchon this was again the case: in view of the mainland nature of the objective it was at least possible that more time in preparation would mean more resistance subsequent to landing. A preliminary decision for a single day of effort was followed by further discussion among the parties concerned, and on the 10th Struble modified his operation plan by dispatch. Bombardment would commence on D minus 2, and would be repeated the next day if necessary.

The operation plan assigned the responsibility for this bombardment to Admiral Higgins' Gunfire Support Group, Task Group 90.6; the narrow waters of Inchon harbor placed the main burden on Captain Allan's destroyers. Hydrographic conditions also led to the decision to come in with the flooding tide and anchor, so that the ships would lie head to sea during the bombardment, and retirement in the event of damage would be simplified. At 0700 on the 13th the destroyers started up the channel in column, *Mansfield* in the lead, followed by *De Haven, Swenson, Collett, Gurke,* and *Henderson.* Behind the destroyers came the cruisers: *Rochester* with Admiral Struble embarked, *Toledo* with Admiral Higgins, *Jamaica,* and *Kenya.* Overhead there orbited a combat air patrol from Task Force 77, while to seaward that force was preparing to launch a strike which would hit the island shortly before the arrival of the destroyers. At 1010 the Support Group entered the approaches to Inchon outer harbor.

The decision to come in on the flooding tide proved advantageous in more ways than one, for at 1145 a string of watching mines was sighted off the port bow, in the area from which the British cruisers had bombarded the port ten days before. Here was a threat for which the bombardment

Five destroyers file up the channel for the bombardment of Wolmi Do. On the right smoke rises from the island following an air strike. 13 September 1950. (USN 419905)

group was ill-prepared. The first positive mine sightings had been made on 4 September, southwest of Chinnampo, by the destroyer *McKean;* three days later British units heading north through these same waters had encountered many floaters; on the 10th the Korean *PC 703* had sunk a minelayer off Haeju and had reported that the mouth of Haeju Man had been mined. In Tokyo, on that same day, Admiral Struble had discussed the mine problem with CincFE: if contact mines had been placed in the Inchon approaches, it was the opinion of Commander Joint Task Force 7 that the Attack Force could be pushed through; if the approaches had been salted with modern influence mines the situation was more doubtful; all that could be done was to go on up and see. A conference with ComNavFE led to a recommendation to CincPacFleet for the earliest possible reactivation of more AMS; on the next day Admiral Radford passed this request to CNO and himself started additional sweepers to the Far East.

But reinforcements would be long in arriving, the invasion had to go forward, no sweep had been planned, and the seven minesweepers present in the theater were two days astern with the Transport Group. Before nightfall they would be ordered to the objective area at best speed, but for the moment the best that could be done was to make do. There might be more mines further up the channel; there was no way of knowing. *Henderson,* the tail end destroyer, was detached to sink as many as she could by gunfire before the tide covered them, and the other destroyers continued on toward Wolmi Do.

It was just past noon, and the air strike was still on, as *Mansfield* and her followers moved through the harbor to their assigned positions, some less than half a mile from the fortified island. Anchoring at short stay, the ships swung around to head southward, into the flooding current, and trained their batteries out to port. There was boat traffic in the harbor, activity in the city was visible, but on Wolmi Do there was no sign of life.

Shortly before 1300 the five destroyers commenced deliberate fire on the island's batteries and on the Inchon waterfront. Some minutes of undisturbed bombardment followed, and then the enemy batteries opened up. Communist fire was concentrated on *Swenson, Collett,* and *Gurke,* the ships nearest the island, and in the course of the next 20 minutes scored on all three. *Collett* received the heaviest damage, taking nine 75-millimeter hits, one of which disabled her computer and forced her to fire in local control. Three hits were made on *Gurke;* a near miss killed an officer on *Swenson;* total casualties were one killed and five wounded. For nearly an hour the engagement continued until at 1347, after the expenditure of about a thousand 5-inch shells, the destroyers weighed and proceeded down channel. Five minutes later the cruisers opened from the lower harbor against the Wolmi batteries, and with one intermission for an air strike continued shooting until 1640, when the task group retired seaward.

Wolmi Do under bombardment. Sowolmi Do at the right; buildings in Inchon visible across the causeway. 13 September 1950. (USN 420044)

The bombardment had been a destructive one. On the other hand the enemy had been alerted: during the day U.N. headquarters had intercepted a North Korean dispatch which reported the bombing of Wolmi Do, the approach of naval vessels, and "every indication that the enemy will perform a landing." The response of Wolmi's defenders had been vigorous, and the island's gunners were still firing as the destroyers departed. For Captain Allan's ships this persistent opposition merely implied another trip in next day for a repeat performance, but for some in the higher echelons news of the enemy reaction proved unsettling. On board the command ship *Mount McKinley,* now steaming northward through the Yellow Sea, one highly placed observer noted that among those who had counted on an unopposed or lightly opposed landing "a certain measure of pessimism appeared."

Up front, however, the problems were problems of detail. In the evening Higgins and Allan went aboard *Rochester* for a conference with Admiral Struble. The decision was taken to do it again the next day. *Collett* was detached because of her damage, and told off along with the tug *Mataco* to finish the destruction of the mines. Some crystal trouble with aircraft radios, which had made difficulties for air spotting and air coordination, was dealt with by a change in the frequency plan. Otherwise all was routine, and in the morning the other four destroyers, joined by *Henderson* and supported by the cruisers, again filed up the channel.

At 1050, as an air strike against the Wolmi Do and Inchon gun emplacements was beginning, the cruisers anchored in the lower bombardment area. Twenty minutes later they commenced firing on Wolmi Do, and shortly after noon the destroyers were deployed to their anchorages in Inchon harbor. There, following another air strike, they began their pointblank bombardment of the island, firing from 1255 to 1422, and expending some 1,700 rounds. Another strike from Task Force 77 came in as the destroyers moved down channel; for another hour the cruisers continued their work. Enemy fire, this time, was late, sparse, and inaccurate, and no ship was hit. Air spotting had been considerably improved, and the itemized claims of destruction and damage inflicted by the two-day effort were encouraging. Together with the work of Task Force 77, the gunfire appeared to have done the job. Wolmi Do was ready for the Marines.

Two approaches from the Yellow Sea lead inward to Inchon, So Sudo or Flying Fish Channel to the westward, and Tong Sudo or East Channel close inshore. Although its currents are the stronger, reaching four and a half knots on a rising tide and almost seven on the ebb, So Sudo offers fewer hazards to navigation, and had been selected as the route of approach for the Attack Force. Shortly after midnight on the 15th the Gunfire Support Group again entered So Sudo and headed north, accompanied this time by the Advance Attack Group, Captain Norman W. Sears, with the 3rd BLT, 5th Marines, embarked. Following the destroyers came

THE INCHON ASSAULT, 15 Sept. 1950

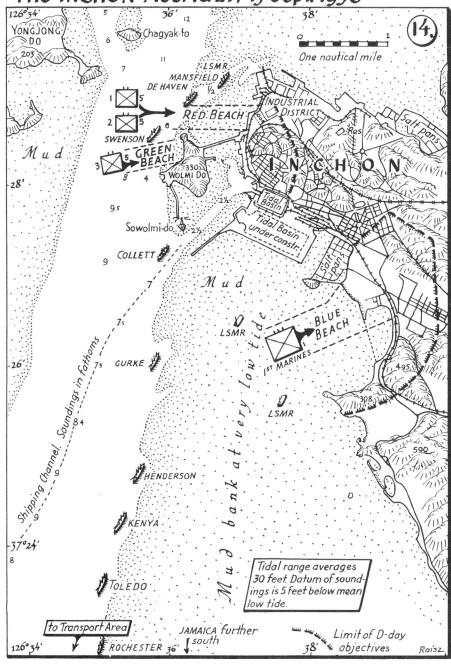

YONGJONG·DO
203
Chagyak-to
One nautical mile

LSMR
MANSFIELD
DE HAVEN
SWENSON
RED BEACH
INDUSTRIAL DISTRICT
Res
Salt pans

Mud
GREEN BEACH
WOLMI DO
330
INCHON

Sowolmi-do
COLLETT
Tidal Basin
Tidal Basin under constr.
Salt pans

Mud
LSMR
BLUE BEACH
1ST MARINES
495

GURKE
308

HENDERSON
LSMR
590

KENYA

Shipping Channel. Soundings in fathoms

Mud bank at very low tide

TOLEDO

Tidal range averages 30 feet. Datum of soundings is 5 feet below mean low tide.

to Transport Area
JAMAICA further south
ROCHESTER
Limit of D-day objectives
Raisz

the LSD *Fort Marion,* with three tank-loaded LSUs in her capacious maw, and the fast transports *Bass, Diachenko,* and *Wantuck;* the cruisers, now joined by *Mount McKinley,* again brought up the rear.

As the ships coasted in on the flooding tide, navigating by radar up the tortuous passageway, the light at the harbor's mouth went on: having found the beacon on Palmi Do still operative, Lieutenant Clark had heeded the Oriental proverb that it is better to light a candle than to curse the darkness. Offshore in the pre-dawn gloom, Task Force 77 flew off the first of the combat air patrols, barrier patrols, and deep-support strikes which it was to provide throughout the day, while Admiral Ruble's group launched ten Corsairs for the pre-landing attack on Wolmi Do. The gunfire spotter, the combat air patrol, and the deep support group were all on station by 0528, when the first strike group reported in to the Air Direction Center in *Mount McKinley.*

By this time the Advance Attack Group had reached its destination in Inchon inner harbor, and Wolmi, no longer a menace, was put to constructive use: anchoring with the island between them and the city's shore batteries, Captain Sears' ships were able to boat their troops undisturbed. The signal "Land the Landing Force" was executed at 0540, and by 0600 the assault troops had been embarked and the landing craft were circling while awaiting the coming of L-Hour. High overhead the leader of the first air strike rolled his plane over and started down.

L-Hour, set for 0630, was preceded by 45 minutes of bombardment. To the north of Wolmi Do *Mansfield, De Haven,* and *Swenson* fired on the island and on the northern shore of Inchon; south of the island *Collett, Gurke,* and *Henderson* concentrated on Wolmi, Sowolmi, and on the city's southern shore. From the southern fire support area *Toledo* and *Kenya* divided their efforts between northern Inchon and the Blue Beach area, while *Rochester* and *Jamaica* took the region behind Blue Beach and on the right flank. Any enemy reaction at the Inchon end of the Wolmi Do causeway would be dealt with by *De Haven* and *Collett,* who were assigned to cover this region with VT-fused ammunition.

While the bombardment continued Marine Corsairs from the escort carriers bombed and rocketed the island. At 0615, L minus 15, the three rocket ships, each with an allowance of 1,000 5-inch spin-stabilized rockets, moved past Green Beach on Wolmi's northern tip and let go. At 0628, as the three LSMRs moved clear, the first wave of landing craft crossed the line of departure and headed in, while the cruisers and two of the destroyers ceased fire to permit the pre-landing beach strafe by the Corsairs.

At 0633 the first troops were ashore in a scene of smoke, dust, and devastation, and were moving forward against negligible resistance. Thirteen minutes after the first wave had touched down, the three LSUs from *Fort Marion* reached the beach with supplies for the assault force, and began to disgorge their ten tanks. Thirty minutes after the initial landing the northern half of the island was controlled by the Marines.

Admiral Struble was just going over the side for a small boat reconnaissance of the situation when a visual signal was received: "The Navy and the Marines have never shone more brightly than this morning. MacArthur." Pausing only to relay the message to the fleet, the force commander boarded his boat, stopped by at *Mount McKinley* to pick up CincFE, and proceeded into the inner harbor to survey Wolmi Do. The day was warm and pleasant, everything was going well, no action was needed. By 0807 the dominating heights on Wolmi had been secured; before mid-day Sowolmi had been assaulted across the narrow causeway and had been taken with the aid of an air strike from the orbiting Corsairs. Total Marine casualties were 17 wounded; the small price paid for this essential objective, with its 400-man garrison and its fairly elaborate system of defensive works and armament, reflects the effectiveness of the advance preparation.

By noon, then, the objective had been secured and fighting had ceased. By noon, too, the waters had receded. On Wolmi Do, in the September sunshine, the Marines gazed across the half-mile causeway and the mudflats toward the silent city and its invisible garrison. In the approach channels the Transport and Tractor Groups were moving in, bearing the forces for the main assault. But until the moon brought back the tides no further advance was possible.

Yet though ground action had been halted by the intertidal lull, the supporting arms were still at work. In the outer harbor the hastily summoned minesweepers were busy checking the anchorage areas. Over the harbor, from dawn to dusk, circled two tactical air observers from the escort carriers, keeping the commanders informed. Throughout the day, at 90-minute intervals, eight Marine Corsairs reported in to process the Inchon defenses with napalm and 500-pound bombs. From the fast carriers there arrived, again at 90-minute intervals, 12-plane deep support strikes which, after delivering their armament, relieved their predecessors as barrier patrol. To this effort, in the two hours preceding the landing, Task Force 77 would add three formidably armed strikes, each composed of eight ADs. In one flight the aircraft would carry three 500-pound bombs, in the second three 1,000-pound bombs, in the third two 500-pounders plus a napalm tank, and all had maximum loads of high velocity aircraft rockets.

Fire support was also an all-day proposition. The interval between the morning and afternoon landings had been divided into two periods, the first extending to H minus 25 and the second to H minus 5, for which roughly equivalent ammunition allowances were provided. Target assignments were similar to those of the morning, but with the weight of fire shifted inland: *Toledo's* main battery was responsible for northern Inchon, *Rochester* had the area north of the tidal basin and Blue Beach, *Kenya* and

DeHaven in fire support station with guns trained out as LCVPs start in. Fires burning at the northern tip of the Inchon waterfront. Red Beach is beyond the right-hand margin. (USN 423226)

Jamaica were given the region to the south and east of the zones assigned their sisters. From the enfilading peninsula north of Red Beach through the tidal basin, the salt pan, and on beyond Blue Beach, the water front was assigned to the destroyers and to the cruisers' secondary batteries.

Not least of the problems stemming from the decision to land at Inchon was the difficulty of avoiding non-military damage to the city and injury to the population. Destruction of necessity there was, but Admiral Struble had enjoined the utmost accuracy and had warned against unnecessary devastation. All air strikes were controlled; within the areas assigned the fire support ships, the known military targets had been conspicuously marked, and only these were to be fired on without air spot and positive identification.

Slowly the waters rose again. By 1300 the transports and the LSTs were standing in, and as afternoon wore on they began to boat their troops. At sea Task Force 77 had been reinforced by *Boxer,* that veteran oceanic commuter, who after delivering her load of Air Force F–51s had returned to the west coast, embarked an air group which had been flown across country from the Atlantic Fleet, and again recrossed the Pacific. Having fought her way through Kezia, *Boxer* now arrived, accompanied by *Manchester* and two destroyers, in time to launch for the beach preparation strikes. But three fast ocean crossings had taken their toll, the long-promised yard period had been indefinitely postponed, and that very morning a reduction gear failure had limited the carrier to steaming on three shafts.

At 1615 the strike groups from the fast carriers reported in and began the beach preparation work. By 1700, as the bombardment was about to begin again in earnest, more than 500 landing craft were churning the waters of Inchon harbor. Rain squalls drifting across the water mingled with smoke from fires in the city to diminish visibility as the armored LVTs with RCT 1 started in for Blue Beach, the faster LCVPs with RCT 5 headed north past Wolmi Do to the Red Beach boat lanes, and the DUKWs with two artillery battalions moved toward Wolmi Do. Then at H minus 25 the three rocket ships once more came into action. *LSMR 403,* with a load of 2,000 rockets, fired on Red Beach and the flanking area to the left while the others, with similar allowances, bombarded the tidal basin, Blue Beach, and the right flank area. Here the LVTs were set northward by the flooding tide, and *LSMR 401* was forced to fire over some of the boat waves, an operation both impressive and discomforting to the embarked Marines. At 1725, as scheduled, the bombardment ceased, the strafing planes came down, and the boats went in.

At Red Beach the two battalions of the 5th Marines got ashore on schedule to be opposed by scattered rifle, automatic weapon and mortar fire. Enemy resistance delayed clearing the beach area for a time, but in little more than an hour it had been overcome, the Marines were working their way in through the town to the dominating high ground, and tanks and

South of Wolmi Do, Amtracs cross the line of departure for Blue Beach. (USN 420024)

201

troops from Wolmi Do were crossing the causeway to join in. At Blue Beach vigorous mortar fire had greeted the approaching LVTs, and before being silenced by *Gurke* and the rocket ships had destroyed one LVT by a direct hit. Congestion caused by the difficult entries to the landing areas converted the first wave into a column, while diminished visibility from smoke, rain, and approaching sunset caused some confusion in the follow-up waves and some dispersion along the shoreline. But here too the landing force advanced inland without serious difficulty.

As the Marines disappeared from the beaches into the darkening city they were not forgotten by the supporting arms. Air spot remained available for an hour or more, and call fire in direct support of the landing force was provided by the gunnery ships. For post-landing gunfire support *Toledo*'s batteries were at the disposal of division headquarters, the 5th Marines controlled *Rochester* and the 1st Marines *Jamaica,* while each battalion was assigned a destroyer with which it was in direct communication. Night illumination fire, which had proven extremely valuable during the Pacific War, was limited on D-Day by the configuration of the harbor: the destroyers were too close in for satisfactory employment of star shell and the cruisers too far out. But on subsequent nights this situation did not obtain, and illuminating missions were most successful.

Within the city fighting continued through the hours of darkness, but by midnight the landing force had reached its initial phase lines. The 5th Marines controlled the hills commanding Red Beach, and thus the source of their logistic build-up, and had advanced southward as far as the tidal basin; the 1st Marines had reached the designated high ground north of Blue Beach and commanding the main road to Seoul. The price of D-Day was 174 casualties, including 20 killed in action, 1 missing, and 1 dead of wounds.

As had been expected, Inchon was not strongly garrisoned. Enemy strength within the city amounted only to some two thousand men of the 226th Marine Regiment, a comparatively new and ineffective unit. Weak to begin with, the forces defending the objective area had been further weakened by their southward displacement in response to Operation Lee and the ROKN landing on Yonghung Do. This move culminated, on the day of the Inchon landings, in a classic blow in the air, as a North Korean force was landed on that island and the outnumbered ROK garrison was taken off by *PC 701.* Next day the Communists woke up to what was going on to the northward, and departed hastily for the mainland.

With the Inchon assault successfully accomplished the problem of the Attack Force was to maintain momentum for the advance inland, and this was inevitably a matter of logistics. Armies still march upon their stomachs; problems of supply, though often hidden by the smoke of battle, are always governing; at Inchon their impact was more than usually immediate. To support the landing force during the intertidal darkness LSTs had to be

Over the walls: 1st Lieutenant Baldomero Lopez USMC leads his men up and over and on to Red Beach.
(USMC A–3190)

203

brought in; to bring in LSTs the landings had to be made at the height of the spring tides; to protect these ships Red Beach had to be cleared with all possible speed. An estimated six LST loads of ammunition, water, rations, vehicles, and fuel were needed; eight had been provided in the hope that six would survive. Recently recommissioned, outfitted with pick-up crews, in poor material condition and prone to breakdown, all eight had nevertheless reached Inchon, and beginning at H plus 60 went in at five-minute intervals. On Red Beach rifle and machine gun fire still continued, and the LSTs came in shooting, not always accurately; one had a minor collision with an ROK PC during the run in, and some were hit and holed by enemy fire. But all eight made it, and four more were put up on Green Beach on Wolmi after the DUKWs had landed the artillery and withdrawn.

Historically, some of the most vexing problems of amphibious warfare had been those concerned with the organization and administration of beachhead areas, and with the handling of assault supplies. In the course of the Second World War the employment for these purposes of details of combat troops, and of sailors from the amphibious shipping, had early proved unsatisfactory. The result had been the organization of commissioned Naval Beach Groups, and of Marine Shore Party Battalions, which while exacting the costs of specialization in terms of administrative overhead and shipping space had by now developed a considerable expertise. At 1840, H plus 70, Commander Naval Beach Group 1, Captain Watson T. Singer, landed in *LST 883* and set up his command post on Red Beach. All through the night his men and the Marines of the 1st SPB labored to empty the LSTs so they could retract with the morning tide and make room for others to be brought in. At the same time another all-night exercise was taking place on Wolmi Do, where the Beach Group's construction battalion was installing a pontoon dock, and where the supplies from the Green Beach LSTs were being unloaded for further delivery by way of the causeway. No effort was made to put important amounts of cargo in through Blue Beach owing to its inferior hydrography and intractable approaches; there material for immediate consumption only was sent in by small craft, and the beach was closed at 2100 on D plus 1.

Despite all geographic and hydrographic complications, the logistics of the assault phase turned out well. The early morning tide of the 16th saw all first echelon LSTs retracted and nine more run up on Red Beach; on the evening tide seven more were withdrawn and six put in; by 2100 almost 15,000 personnel, 1,500 vehicles, and 1,200 short tons of cargo had been put ashore. On D plus 2 Rear Admiral Lyman A. Thackrey, Commander Amphibious Group 3, who had just arrived from San Diego in the AGC *Eldorado,* was put in charge of port operations, and moved ashore with members of his staff. There his presence proved helpful in coordinating the efforts of the undermanned Beach Group in its three non-contiguous unloading zones, in setting up an unloading schedule, and in getting the inner harbor into operation. Here speed was essential, for with the end of the spring tides on D plus 3 the beaches would become inaccessible to LSTs, and here speed was obtained. On the 16th heavy cranes were landed on Wolmi Do, and moved across the causeway to the tidal basin, where unloading began on D plus 2, far sooner than had been anticipated.

All first echelon shipping had been emptied by D plus 4. Three days later 53,882 persons and 6,629 vehicles were ashore, and the 25,512 tons of cargo unloaded more than doubled the X Corps target figure for that date. Figures like these doubtless make arid reading; it takes an act of the imagination to translate tonnage into ammunition, water, rations, and plasma; but figures like these also make for victories. By the time the Army's 2nd Engineer Special Brigade assumed control of the Inchon port area the limitations on the supply of the front, far from being hydrographic, were a function of the availability of motor transport.

There were, of course, logistic problems afloat as well as ashore. The movement of the Attack Force to Inchon and the extended and extensive activities of the other units of Joint Task Force 7 placed new loads upon the Service Force organization. In the weeks prior to the invasion the resupply of combatant ships had been increasingly concentrated at Sasebo, which by now had taken on the characteristics of a major fleet base. But with the transfer of so large a portion of theater naval strength to the west coast of Korea, the job of backing up at Sasebo was turned over to Captain Wright's Service Division 31, and Servron 3, which had moved up from Okinawa in early September, was deployed forward to the objective area.

Four task groups had been created for the logistic support of "Chromite." To meet the needs of Task Force 77 a Mobile Logistic Service Group with two oilers, a reefer, and *Mount Katmai*, still the only ammunition ship in the Far East, was on station in the Yellow Sea. For towing and salvage work the tug *Mataco* and the salvage vessel *Bolster* were ordered up to Inchon, along with the oiler and five cargo ships of the Objective Area Logistic Group with fuel, ammunition, food, and stores. For follow-up resupply and maintenance ComServron 3 brought forward the Logistic Support Group: one oiler, one gasoline tanker, two destroyer tenders, two repair ships, two more cargo types, and a reefer. In-port nourishment of the Attack Force was complicated by the crowding of the anchorage, the tides and currents which made alongside loading of ammunition risky, and the shortage of lighters which made transfer by boat a time-consuming affair. Hard work was required of both the givers and the receivers, but everything necessary was accomplished and nobody went short.

From D plus 1 the campaign for Seoul moved rapidly forward. By the end of this day the Force Beachhead Line, some seven miles inland from the landing points, had been secured. In Inchon the Korean Marines were

Beachhead logistics: LSTs dried out on Red Beach on D plus 1. At the left the causeway to Wolmi Do; in the right distance L. K. Swenson in her fire support station. (USN 420027)

206

mopping up the last defenders. On the main road to Seoul five oncoming enemy tanks had been destroyed, two by Corsairs from *Sicily,* three by the 1st Marines. The transfer of control from ship to shore was underway: an observation plane strip was in operation, shore tactical air control parties had begun to take over some of the business previously handled by the Tactical Air Direction Center in *Mount McKinley,* and at 1800 the division command post displaced forward from Wolmi to Inchon and General Smith assumed control of operations ashore. Marine casualties for the first two days totalled 222, of whom 22 were killed in action, 2 were reported missing, and 2 had died of wounds; as against these figures, far below those anticipated by the medical planners, some 300 prisoners had been taken and an estimated 1,350 additional casualties inflicted on the enemy.

Although the North Koreans were by now reacting vigorously, D plus 2 was also a day of rapid progress. After repelling heavy early morning counterattacks the 1st Marines, supported by Corsairs from *Sicily,* pushed eastward along the Seoul highway toward the village of Sosa. Four tanks were destroyed during the advance, but resistance continued strong, and at 1415 the tactical air people put out an emergency call for all possible support. *Badoeng Strait* was fuelling destroyers, but with *Sicily's* aircraft already committed she turned to, cast off her customers, and had all planes airborne by 1558. By evening the 1st Marines were within 1,500 yards of Sosa, while the 5th Marines had gained a great strategic prize. Turning left off the main highway behind the 1st Marines, RCT 5 had barrelled up the road toward Kimpo airfield, with support from the air and from cruiser gunfire, and by nightfall had occupied the high ground east of the field and had pushed troops out onto the landing area itself.

Behind the front, reinforcements were beginning to arrive and transfer of control ashore continued. At Inchon the 32nd Infantry, first of the 7th Division's units to reach the objective area, arrived on D plus 2 and at once began its administrative landing. At 1800 that evening the shore-based TADC assumed control of all close air support, and next day the division Fire Support Control Center took over responsibility for the integration and control of air support, artillery, and naval gunfire.

For the next three days the 1st Marines pressed eastward against stubborn opposition. At Sosa, on the 18th, there was more heavy fighting, but the objective, a commanding hill northeast of the town, was gained with the help of the escort carriers' aircraft and of the cruisers' guns. Here was the half-way mark between Inchon and Yongdungpo, the industrial suburb of Seoul which lies on the south bank of the Han, and here enemy organization began to improve and enemy artillery was first encountered. Nevertheless the advance continued: by morning of the 20th the regiment controlled the high ground overlooking Yongdungpo and the Seoul-Suwon corridor, and had swung left to reach the banks of the Han, while the 32nd Infantry was moving up along the right flank.

For some reason the enemy had chosen to defend Yongdungpo in force. Air strikes from *Badoeng Strait* and artillery fire were called down upon the town, but when the attack was launched on the 21st the Marines met heavy resistance. Forward elements, finding themselves overextended, were forced to disengage under cover of strafing and bombing by *Sicily*'s Corsairs, some of which was directed within 30 yards of the front lines. But Communist counterattacks were beaten off, and the end of the first week of fighting found the 1st Marines 16 miles inland from their landing point, with one company deep in Yongdungpo making trouble for the city's defenders, and with the rest of the regiment preparing for the final assault into the town.

While RCT 1 was advancing on Yongdungpo the 5th Marines were preparing for the attack on Seoul. Having overrun Kimpo airfield, RCT 5 fanned out on the 18th and 19th, sending patrols along the banks of the Han and eastward toward Yongdungpo, and clearing terrain features overlooking the river. An attempted night surprise crossing of the Han aborted when the first swimmers encountered enemy forces on the far shore, but early on the morning of the 20th the 3rd Battalion crossed in LVTs against only light resistance. Covered by Marine aircraft from *Sicily,* the other battalions followed apace, and the regiment moved southeast along the railroad track toward Seoul. By the 21st the 5th Marines had reached within a mile and a half of the capital, and were approaching the ridges that guard its western border.

The seizure of Kimpo airfield on the evening of D plus 2 had been promptly exploited. On the afternoon of the 18th, with enemy artillery still within range and with enemy dead still unburied, the engineers reported the field ready to receive aircraft. On the 19th General Cushman, the X Corps Tactical Air Commander, set up his headquarters at Kimpo; the Corsairs of VMF 212 and the F7FNs of VMFN 542 were flown in from Japan; the aircraft of FEAF's Combat Cargo Command began a notable effort in lifting in aviation gasoline and ammunition. Thus within four days of the landing the air strength of X Corps had been increased by two new squadrons, one with a night capability, handily based within ten miles of the front lines on the best airfield in Korea.

Air support, air strikes against approaching enemy columns, and air cover for shipping were still being provided by the carriers, and the Kimpo-based squadrons began operations on the 20th. The only enemy air reaction in the entire operation had come on D plus 2 in a dawn attack by two Yaks directed against *Rochester* and *Jamaica,* anchored in their fire support positions south of Wolmi Do. One 100-pound bomb bounced off *Rochester*'s aircraft crane and failed to explode, and seven others were near misses; one

The transport area from Inchon. Souvolmi Do in the foreground; Rochester, flagship of JTF 7, center; Mount McKinley, flagship of the Attack Force, is the nearest of the three bunched ships at the left. (USN 420481)

man on board *Jamaica* was killed by strafing, and one of the Yaks was shot down by the British cruiser.

With the artillery in full operation, and with air support increasing, naval gunfire had begun to decline. By D plus 3 the destroyers had been outranged, and while the cruisers had supported the fighting around Sosa, the crossing of the Han and the advance toward Yongdungpo had taken the Marines beyond the range of 8-inch guns. But both cruisers and destroyers continued to provide support for operations against bypassed enemy units on the Kumpo peninsula, north of Inchon, which were being pressed by an Army airborne battalion and by one of Korean Marines.

Unloading of 7th Division and of corps troops meanwhile continued steadily. The 32nd Infantry Regiment had landed on the 18th, the 31st Infantry came ashore on the 20th, and the 17th Infantry, earlier designated as the floating reserve at Pusan, was soon to follow. At 1700 of D plus 6, with the 1st Marines entering Yongdungpo, the 5th Marines on the western borders of Seoul, and with units of the 7th Infantry Division advancing on the southern flank, General Almond assumed control of the land campaign and Joint Task Force 7 was dissolved. At Inchon, their various travels completed, the 7th Marines were coming ashore from transports and cargo ships which a month before had been part of the Atlantic Fleet, and were moving forward to the Kimpo area. With this arrival the 1st Marine Division at last acquired its full complement of three regimental combat teams. The deployment begun with the July sailing of General Craig's brigade had been completed.

3. 12 September–7 October: The Clearance of South Korea

Within the perimeter, 140 miles to the southeast, the tide had turned. The invading army, already suffering from serious logistic difficulties brought on by unexpected opposition and by attacks on its supply lines, now found the supply spigot turned hard off. The weeks of Air Force and naval effort had taken heavy toll; the occupation by the aircraft of Joint Task Force 7 of the airspace over the main Korean transportation nexus had pretty well brought things to a halt; the Inchon landing demanded the local concentration of all available Communist strength. If the effect of supply shortages on this hand-carrying austerity-type Oriental army was less immediate than it would have been upon a western force, the end result was nevertheless the same. Having come close to triumph, the North Korean People's Army now faced irredeemable disaster.

Behind the Naktong front phases one and two of the Korean campaign, strengthening the defense and building up for the counterattack, had proceeded concurrently, aided in the final stages by Kezia, whose rains had flooded the Nam and Naktong and isolated the North Korean spearheads from their support west of the rivers. As the enemy threat subsided, the Eighth Army, now composed of two ROK and two U.S. corps, and with the latter including both British and Korean troops, made ready to take the offensive. The attack was scheduled to begin on D plus 1.

Despite the great naval investment in the Inchon landing some fire support remained available for the flank forces in the perimeter. On 12 September, pursuant to a suggestion from Admiral Sherman, the various task groups operating under ComNavFE had been consolidated, and the Korea Support Group, Task Group 96.5, upgraded into Task Force 95.

TABLE 10.—NAVAL OPERATING COMMANDS, REORGANIZATION OF
12 SEPTEMBER 1950

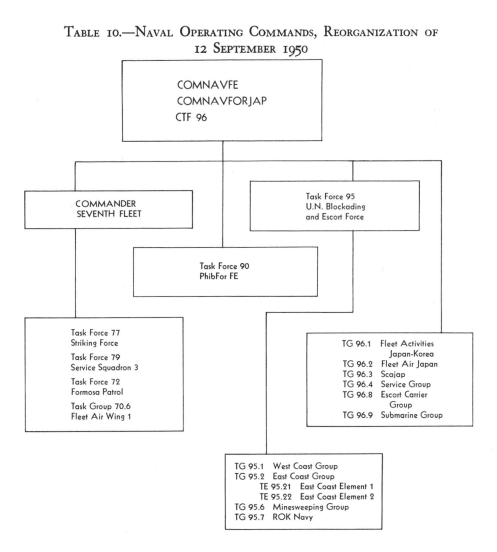

Overall command of the United Nations Blockading and Escort Force was assigned Rear Admiral Allan E. Smith; the West Coast Support Group, now Task Group 95.1, continued under control of Admiral Andrewes, and east coast operations under Admiral Hartman. In preparation for Eighth Army's offensive, and as a diversionary move coordinated with the Inchon landing, Hartman's ships bombarded Samchok on 14 and 15 September, where on the latter date *Helena* and *Brush* were joined by *Maddox* and by *Missouri,* first battleship to reach Korean waters. Five years before, as one of 23 active battleships in the U.S. Fleet, *Missouri* had lain in Tokyo Bay to receive the surrender of an empire; five weeks before, the single active unit of her class, she had been lying at Pier 88 in the North River with a load of midshipmen on a summer training cruise. Now in a different hemisphere she was demonstrating the demolition capabilities of the 16-inch gun, and with the expenditure of 52 HC shells destroyed one Samchok railroad bridge and damaged another.

In anticipation of the impending offensive ROK Army units below Pohang had been again provided with fire control parties. But help from the sea was curtailed during the first days of the operation as a result of an abortive amphibious landing independently undertaken by Eighth Army. An attempt on 15 September to land ROK guerillas at Changsadong, behind the enemy lines, went awry: the Korean merchant marine LST broached and was holed while landing; the troops, after seizing their first objective with the help of extemporized fire support from *Endicott,* retired upon their stranded vessel and called for help. Not until the 19th could rescue ships be obtained from Pusan, and to prevent the destruction of this force in the interim required a considerable bombardment effort from Admiral Hartman's force.

On the 16th, as planned, Eighth Army attacked all along the line. The North Korean radio had been conspicuously silent on affairs at Inchon, but the U.N. Command made every effort, by leaflet drop and otherwise, to give the enemy the word. Early progress, however, was negligible, and Communist resistance remained strong. On D plus 2, fearing that "Chromite," despite its tactical brilliance, had failed in its strategic purpose, General MacArthur directed Admiral Doyle to begin planning for a second landing at Kunsan. But if CincFE's mercurial temperament was for the moment cast down, the southern offensive soon began to roll, and as things turned out the only naval consequence of this order was a beach reconnaissance, carried out by *Bass'* UDTs on the 22nd, at the mouth of Chonsu Man north of Kunsan.

On the east coast, on 17 September, ROK troops crossed the Hyongsan River south of Pohang with the help of 298 16-inch persuaders from *Missouri,* captured the city, and pressed onward toward Yongdok. Two days later Struble began morning and evening air reconnaissance of the roads south of Seoul, and alerted Task Force 77 to the possibility of a big strike

Landing that went awry: In distance, center, stranded ROK LST; left, fast minesweeper Doyle; *right, a second LST and rescue vessel* Bolster; Helena's *whaleboat coming alongside. 19 September 1950. (USN 420836)*

against forces retiring northward from the perimeter. On the 20th, D plus 5, the North Korean II Corps, which manned the northern sector of the perimeter, began its retirement. By the end of the first week the pursued of July had become the pursuers of September as the 24th Division forced the Naktong and started up the road to Seoul. On the south coast, by this time, U.N. forces had advanced halfway to Chinju, and the Chinhae fire support destroyer had finally been released. On 25 September, D plus 10, orders were issued by the enemy for a general withdrawal.

In the north, however, resistance to the advance of X Corps had been stiffening, as Communist reinforcements were rushed down from Wonsan, Chorwon, and Sariwon. Despite all efforts at interdiction some six or seven thousand troops had reached the capital by the 20th, to reinforce an original garrison of perhaps 10,000. And although these newcomers lacked much of their heavy equipment, hard and costly fighting was taking place in Yongdungpo and in the outskirts of Seoul.

Appropriately enough, despite its situation in the western lowlands and on the estuary of the Han, the capital city of Korea is surrounded by its country's omnipresent hills. From a peak five miles to the northward a ridge descends to the 2,000-foot level, then divides east and west to end in wooded 1,000-foot outcroppings which cover the northeastern and northwestern approaches to the city. From the northwestern foothills broken ridges, some 300 feet in height, run south to the Han, guarding the city against intrusion from downstream. On the southeast, between the city and the river, South Mountain rises to an altitude of 1,000 feet. Within this eastward-facing amphitheater the ancient city arose, protected by walls connecting peak with peak and enclosing an area about five miles by three. But by the latter 19th century these ramparts had been outgrown, and Seoul had begun to sprawl outward, southward between the western ridges and South Mountain and eastward between South Mountain and the northern hills.

By 22 September the 5th Marines had reached the western ridge line and were knocking at the back door to Seoul. Here the enemy had established his main line of resistance, and here heavy opposition was encountered. Despite close support from the escort carriers and the Kimpo-based Marine squadrons, the advance was slow and costly. Progress through the ridges was measured in yards, the enemy fought bitterly and launched numerous counterattacks, and heavy air and artillery concentrations were replied to by artillery, phosphorus, and mortar fire.

The 1st Marines, in the meantime, were battling their way through Yongdungpo. Having reached the banks of the Han opposite the capital, they were ordered on the 23rd to throw two battalions across the river in the rear of RCT 5. This movement, accomplished by midday of the 24th, was followed by the crossing of two battalions from RCT 7. By afternoon the 1st Marines were moving southeastward, to a position on the right flank between RCT 5 and the river, while the 7th Marines were deploying on the left.

On the 25th, with this accretion of force, the enemy's main line of resistance was broken. Attacking into the southwestern corner of the city, the 1st Marines gained a mile and a half in house-to-house fighting; in the center RCT 5 broke through the ridge line, killing almost 2,000 of the enemy in the process; in the north the 7th Marines patrolled the covering hills to prevent the arrival of enemy reinforcements; to the southward the noose was tightened as the 32nd Infantry crossed the river and climbed South Mountain. For this attack the close support effort was carried to a high pitch: *Badoeng Strait* was loading ammunition in Inchon harbor, but *Sicily* provided five aircraft on station every two hours, and VMF 212 at Kimpo set a new record for combat sorties. But the 25th was a bad day for the

Missouri bombarding Pohang in support of the ROK crossing of the Hyongsan River. 17 September 1950. (USN 420651)

215

X Corps TAC: three squadron commanders were shot down and one, Lieutenant Colonel Walter E. Lischeid, USMC, of *Sicily's* squadron, was killed.

On 26 September the advance inside the city continued against house-to-house resistance. An evening order from X Corps directed a night attack against enemy forces thought to be fleeing Seoul, but the presumption proved erroneous: the darkness was fully occupied in repelling strong enemy counterattacks backed up by self-propelled guns and tanks which had been brought down from Wonsan. By morning, however, these had been disposed of, and the Marines pressed on through road blocks and sniper fire deep into the burning city. Although progress remained slow the enemy was noticeably weakening, and the city had been declared secured by X Corps. On the 28th organized resistance in the capital was finally broken, although small pockets of enemy troops remained to be dealt with and enemy counterattacks continued on its outskirts.

The 7th Division, in the meantime, had moved forward on the right flank to Osan, where 12 weeks before Task Force Smith had engaged the invading army. There on the 27th it made contact with a small force of the 1st Cavalry which had raced northward along the main road. On the 29th General MacArthur turned the capital back to President Rhee. All that remained was to seal Seoul off from the north, and this was done in the early days of October as the 1st and 5th Marines took blocking positions northeast and northwest of the city, and as RCT 7 was advanced northward to Uijongbu.

By this time the ground situation was both fluid and favorable in the extreme. The last days of September saw the collapse of enemy resistance in South Korea, as Communist troops were herded into prisoner of war pens or dispersed into the hills. As the U.S. I Corps moved northwest toward Seoul, the IX Corps crossed the peninsula from east to west, driving a column to Kunsan, where cut-off enemy troops had been shelled by *Athabaskan* and *Bataan*. In the central mountains the ROK II Corps was moving northward; in the east the ROK I Corps pressed rapidly up the coastal road. Here the advance was paced by Admiral Hartman's fire support ships, but their efforts were seldom required and then only against minor resistance. Paying the fire support group the ultimate compliment, the enemy had abandoned the shore road and was retiring along inland tracks: in its move north to the parallel the ROK I Corps bypassed three North Korean divisions.

Throughout this period the Korean Navy remained active along the coastline. In the west, following the Inchon landing, Operation Lee had continued. From Kunsan in the south to the Sir James Hall Archipelago on the 38th parallel, the clearance of islands was pressed, with the result that when on 2 October higher authority got around to implementing Operation Comeback for the recovery of these positions, the job had in effect been done. On the south coast ROK naval forces cooperating with Eighth Army took

Namhae Island on the 27th and Yosu on the 29th, and on 3 October a landing at Mokpo, supported by *PC 703* and some smaller units, secured that important port.

North of the parallel in Communist country the east coast naval units were also busy. On 23 September the submarine *Segundo* carried out a special mission in Area 7 on the northeast coast. On the 25th the submarine transport *Perch* sailed from Japan with its force of British Commandos to conduct demolition raids on enemy communications in this zone. But with the ground war in the exploitation phase, the sea war became suddenly costly as the enemy's countermeasures began to take effect.

On 26 September the destroyer *Brush,* patrolling in company with *Maddox* off Tanchon, hit a mine; 13 members of the crew were killed, 34 wounded, and the ship was badly damaged. Two days later the ROK *YMS 509* was mined off Yongdok, with 26 killed or missing and 5 wounded. Two more days had gone by when *Mansfield,* nosing her way into the harbor of Changjon in search of a downed Air Force pilot, struck a mine which blew off most of her bow and wounded 28 of her men. While sweeping near Yongdok on 1 October the AMS *Magpie,* recently arrived from Guam, hit a mine, blew up, and sank with the loss of 21 of a crew of 33. On the 2nd the Korean *YMS 504* was mined at Mokpo.

The loss of one ship and heavy damage to four, not to mention the casualties to personnel, made this the most costly week of the war for the U.N. naval forces. For the enemy it was profitable well beyond the damage inflicted. Serious problems were raised regarding future operations, the East Coast Support Group was instructed not to operate inside the 100-fathom curve, and *Perch,* en route to strike the North Korean line of communications, was ordered to stay outside of 50 fathoms and to limit her efforts to a single raid.

This attack was carried out on the night of 1–2 October. With the destroyer *Thomas* bombarding an adjacent target as a diversion, and with *Maddox* backing up, *Perch* sent her raiders against a section of the railroad line in 40°21′, where two tunnels adjoin. Some enemy resistance was encountered, and one Royal Marine was killed by rifle fire as the landing party was reembarking, but a culvert was destroyed by demolition charges and both tunnels were mined.

At Inchon Joint Task Force 7 had been dissolved on the 21st, as control of the land campaign passed from Admiral Struble to General Almond. Original plans had then called for Seventh Fleet units to revert to their normal organization, and for the reconstitution of remaining naval strength into the Naval Support Force under Admiral Doyle. But Struble, reluctant for reasons of interservice comity to seem hasty in departure, decided to assume the job himself, and as Commander Support Force remained in the objective area until 1 October. Naval effort in this period continued intense, with heavy movements of X Corps supplies into Inchon, logistic support of the fleet, fire support of such friendly troops as remained within range, and air operations from the carriers offshore.

Missouri had reported in from the east coast on the 19th, and next day was moved as far as possible upstream, to a berth from which her 16-inch guns could interdict the Seoul-Wonsan road, some 28 miles away. But the front was moving so fast that her effort was limited to 11 ranging rounds in four days, and the principal activity of the gunnery ships was by this time taking place elsewhere. ROKN units had reported a concentration of enemy troops on Tungsan Got, the peninsula west of Haeju Man, and on the 27th a bombardment of this region, designed to encourage belief in the imminence of another landing, was carried out by *Manchester* and four destroyers, assisted by a strike from *Boxer's* air group. Two days later the British cruiser *Ceylon* put a landing party ashore on Taechong Do, in the Sir James Hall group, only to find that the reported enemy garrison had packed up and departed.

Offshore the carrier air effort had remained vigorous throughout the month. *Triumph* had worked over targets in southwestern North Korea until 25 September, at which time she was relieved by her sister ship *Theseus* and departed the area. While replenishing at intervals from Servron 3 in Inchon harbor, Admiral Ruble's escort carriers continued until 2 October to contribute to the work of X Corps Tactical Air Command. Since the arrival of *Boxer* Admiral Ewen had been able to keep two fast carriers active in daily flight operations, while the third moved south to take on food and drink from the Mobile Logistic Service Group; with the capture of Seoul Task Force 77 switched from deep support of X Corps to attacks on enemy lines of communication which continued until its withdrawal on the 3rd.

By 4 October no targets remained within gunnery range, all gunfire ships were released by X Corps, and Admiral Higgins sortied the last of his Support Group from Inchon. With customers running short Captain Austin sailed in *Hector* on the same day, leaving behind a reduced logistic force. On the 5th the Fifth Air Force took over from General Cushman's Tactical Air Command, and on the 7th the last X Corps troops were relieved by units of the Eighth Army. The campaign was over.

Admiral Doyle had already departed. This officer, who with his staff had done so much to prove that "Inchon is not impossible," had been relieved by Admiral Thackrey on the 27th, the day of the ground force link-up south of Suwon, and had sailed for Tokyo to start work on the next operation.

CHAPTER VIII

On to the Border

1. 27 September–15 October: Planning the Wonsan Landing

THE TRIUMPHANT events of September had changed the entire Korean picture. With the reconquest of Seoul, the northward sweep of Eighth Army, and the collapse of North Korean resistance, unification of the peninsula, long the aim of the United Nations and even longer the hope of the Koreans, seemed imminently possible. There were, it was true, certain legal questions to be answered and certain policy decisions to be made by the United Nations and the United States before the armies could go north, but so far as one government was concerned the decision was not in doubt. During the dark days of July President Rhee had announced his intention of unifying his country by military action, and four days after the landing at Inchon he affirmed that with or without the assistance of the United Nations his forces would continue the battle.

The objectives heretofore assigned CincFE had been more limited in scope. In August, when General Collins and Admiral Sherman had come out to talk about Inchon, General MacArthur's goal had been the destruction of North Korean armed forces. But it had also been agreed that pursuit of this aim would not necessarily be limited by the 38th parallel. In mid-September permission was granted by the Joint Chiefs of Staff to plan for operations in North Korea, and on the 27th CincFE was authorized to carry out such operations in order to complete the destruction of the armed forces of the aggressor.

This permission reflected the view of the government in Washington that the Security Council resolution of June provided a sufficient legal authority for crossing the parallel. Equally, however, the message from the Joint Chiefs demonstrated the government's determination to keep the conflict localized, both to prevent a world-wide shooting war and to avoid, within the framework of the existing world-wide war of maneuver, an over-commitment of forces to the Far East. If Chinese Communist units were encountered south of the parallel, CincFE was instructed to continue action so long as success seemed probable. But the authorization to go north was qualified by the proviso that no major Soviet or Communist Chinese forces should have entered North Korea, or have announced their intention of entering North Korea, or have threatened military action. Under no circumstances were U.N. forces to violate the Manchurian or Russian borders; none but Korean ground forces were to be employed in the border region.

One day before this authorization was received, General MacArthur instructed his planners to come up with a concept for future operations, modeled on that of "Chromite," in which Eighth Army would make the main effort on one coast while X Corps carried out a second amphibious envelopment on the other. The request found the planners prepared. Dusting off some earlier staff studies, they produced on the 27th, the day of the U.N. link-up south of Suwon, a tentative operation plan. In mid-October, as soon as the necessary logistic build-up could be accomplished, Eighth Army would move northwestward from Seoul against Pyongyang, the North Korean capital. X Corps, in the meantime, would reembark and sail for Wonsan on Korea's eastern shore, 115 miles north of Seoul and 95 miles east of Pyongyang. There, following an assault landing, General Almond's units would attack westward across the narrow Korean waist, link up with Eighth Army, and encircle enemy forces retreating from the south. This operation was christened "Tailboard."

Although this plan involved the occupation of half of North Korea, and the better half at that, it also reflected the caution so evident in the Joint Chiefs' message of the same date. Occupation of territory was incidental to the liquidation of the enemy's remaining strength; the assumption that neither Communist Chinese nor Soviets would intervene, openly or covertly, was explicit; a restraining line was drawn below the 40th parallel, from Chongju in the west to Hungnam in the east, beyond which no non-Korean forces would advance. On the 28th a brief of the plan was sent the Joint Chiefs, accompanied by the comment that there were no present indications of the entry into North Korea of major Soviet or Chinese Communist forces.

On 29 September, the day of liberation ceremonies in Seoul, General MacArthur outlined the new plan to the commanders of Eighth Army, X Corps, NavFE, and FEAF. Shooting was still going on in the capital and Eighth Army had not arrived, but CincFE was still driving his people: the D-Day of 20 October which he set for the Wonsan landing was but three weeks away, and left even less time for preparation than had been available for Inchon.

Over and above the shortage of time, the idea of another two-coast operation raised some serious difficulties. The capacity of Pusan and Inchon, the only major ports available, remained critical, and the mounting out of "Tailboard" was to require remarkable feats of planning and preparation. Despite the obstacles of nature, X Corps had succeeded in getting in through

Inchon, but the competition of incoming supplies for Eighth Army made it harder to get out. In this situation it was decided to transfer some of this competition ashore, and to send the 7th Infantry Division south by road and rail for embarkation at Pusan, while the Marines went aboard ship at Inchon. But even this division of effort required further modification, for the 7th Division's tanks and heavy equipment could not be moved overland, and had to be loaded at Inchon and sent down by LST.

Even with the decision to send the 7th Division south by land, the preparations for the Wonsan landing put Eighth Army and the Fifth Air Force in a serious logistic bind. General Walker was scheduled to attack northward before the landing at Wonsan took place, and had to accumulate supplies for this new movement; in order to support these forward operations Fifth Air Force was struggling to bring up its squadrons and supporting organizations. But road and rail communications north from Pusan, attacked throughout the summer by U.N. aircraft, were not what they used to be, and were also carrying southbound 7th Division traffic; the embarkation schedule required that the Marines be given priority in the use of Inchon's limited facilities. To top it all, the pressure of time was increased to an almost ludicrous degree as General Almond attempted to move the Wonsan D-Day forward to the 15th.

These complications raised the question of an overland approach to Wonsan. Some Army commanders preferred this route, although General Almond was firm in his belief in the superior economy of water lift. Admiral Joy and some of his senior officers opposed the amphibious operation, although this time on grounds of necessity rather than of feasibility. But the case, if debatable, does not appear clear-cut: the corridor from Seoul to Wonsan is narrow and mountainous, there were hostiles in the hills, and the idea of supporting a two-pronged advance on Pyongyang and Wonsan from the Inchon-Seoul area raised a whole new set of logistic problems. And in any event it appears that none ventured to dispute the matter with CincFE.

With acceptance of the new concept by the Joint Chiefs, things began to happen. As October opened the mimeographs were whirring and the plans were flowing forth. ComNavFE issued his operation plan on the 1st; the U.N. Command's overall operation order appeared the next day; on the 5th Joint Task Force 7 was reactivated and Admiral Struble published his orders for preliminary operations. Elsewhere in the world other statements of intention were also beginning to multiply. General MacArthur had been authorized to call upon the enemy for surrender; on 1 October the message was broadcast, but answer came there none. One day earlier Chou En-lai, foreign minister of Communist China, had observed that his government would not tolerate the crossing of the 38th parallel, and "would not stand aside" if North Korea were invaded. On the 3rd Chou was reported by the Indian Ambassador at Peking as stating that if non-Korean forces crossed the parallel the Chinese would send in troops.

This thunder out of China was of no effect. In the U.N. General Assembly a debate on Korean policy ended with a vote that since "unification . . . has not yet been achieved" all appropriate steps should "be taken to ensure conditions of stability throughout Korea." If the language was a little vague this resolution was of great importance, for it signalled a change in the mission of the U.N. forces from repelling aggression, and inferentially destroying enemy forces even if north of the parallel, to one of uniting Korea by force of arms and ensuring stability by territorial occupation. The point was emphasized by General MacArthur's statement that if cooperation in establishing a unified Korea was not forthcoming from the north, military action would be taken "to enforce the decrees of the United Nations." And on the 9th the Joint Chiefs went some distance to qualify their earlier caution concerning threatened Soviet or Chinese intervention. The threat, it would appear, had now been made, but a message of the 9th merely rephrased previous instructions concerning possible contact with the Chinese: should such forces now be met with "anywhere in Korea," CincFE was to continue the action so long as success seemed probable.

For the amphibious half of the new encirclement, the responsibility again fell upon Admiral Struble, as Commander Joint Task Force 7. For the Wonsan landing the planned course of events was very similar to what it had been at Inchon. As in September the arrival of the Attack Force in the objective area would be preceded by the activities of the patrol planes, of carrier aviation, and of the gunfire and minesweeping units. Once again Joint Task Force 7 had its own organic air force, both afloat and ashore, and its private theater of air operations. Within a line run inland from Kosong at the southern end of the Korean Gulf, north along the mountain spine, and eastward to enclose Hungnam, the carriers of JTF 7 and the shore-based aircraft of X Corps Tactical Air Command would operate without disturbance from FEAF, except for air transport and specially requested missions.

But while the externals were similar, the internal organization of the joint task force was considerably modified. The upgrading of the mine menace, following events at Inchon, made it essential to extend the preparatory period of the operation, and to send the sweepers and their supporting ships in well ahead of the Attack Force. A jelling command structure and the diminution of enemy pressure made more commanders and staffs available for the planning phase. The consequence was the separation of the Advance Force and of the Escort Carrier Group from the Attack Force, in conformity with more usual practice, and a sharing of the planning load. While Doyle and his staff concentrated on the landing itself, the directives

Table 11.—JOINT TASK FORCE 7: WONSAN

JOINT TASK FORCE 7.	VICE ADMIRAL A. D. STRUBLE.
TASK FORCE 90. ATTACK FORCE.	REAR ADMIRAL J. H. DOYLE.

2 AGC, 2 APD, 4 PF (1 RN, 2 RNZN, 1 French), 1 PCEC, 9 APA, 15 T-AP, 10 AKA, 5 LSD, 1 LSM, 3 LSMR, 48 LST (30 Scajap), 20 LSU, MSTS shipping as assigned.

TASK FORCE 92, X CORPS.	MAJOR GENERAL E. M. ALMOND, USA.
TASK FORCE 95. ADVANCE FORCE.	REAR ADMIRAL A. E. SMITH.

Task Group 95.2. Covering and Support Group.
Rear Admiral C. C. Hartman.
3 CA, 1 RNCL, 6 DD (1 RN, 1 RAN, 1 RCN).

Task Group 95.6. Minesweeping Group. Captain R. T. Spofford.
1 DD, 1 APD, 2 DMS, 3 AM, 7 AMS, 1 ARG, 1 ARS, 8 JMS.

Task Group 96.2. Patrol and Reconnaissance Group.
Rear Admiral G. R. Henderson.
1 AV, 1 AVP; 3 USN, 1 RAF Patrol Squadrons.

Task Group 96.8. Escort Carrier Group. Rear Admiral R. W. Ruble.
2 CVE, 6 DD.

TASK FORCE 77. FAST CARRIER FORCE. REAR ADMIRAL E. C. EWEN.
4 CV, 1 BB, 1 CL, 16 DD.

TASK FORCE 79. LOGISTIC SUPPORT FORCE. CAPTAIN B. L. AUSTIN.
Units assigned from Service Squadron 3 and Service Division 31.

for the Covering and Support Group were written by Admiral Smith, and the minesweeping plan was worked up in Tokyo under the supervision of Admiral Struble.

The new objective of Joint Task Force 7, the city of Wonsan, occupies one of the most important strategic positions on the Sea of Japan. This location had long made it an object of international interest, a fact reflected in the more than oriental splendor of place-name confusion which afflicts the charts and sailing directions for the area. Of this problem in geographic nomenclature, a hazard both to military planner and to historian, the following may serve as example.

The approach to Wonsan leads through the Japan Sea and into the Korean Gulf, once Broughton Bay, then Chosen Kaiwan, and now known as Tongjoson Man. At the southwestern extremity of this body of water lies Yonghung Man, sometime Yunghing Bay or Eiko Wan, the northern entrance point of which is Taegang Got (ex-Nan Kaku, ex-Desfosses Point) at the end of the Nakhimova Peninsula (later known as Koto Hanto and now as Hodo Pando). South of this point two islands obstruct the mouth of Yonghung Man: of these Ung Do (or Ko To, or Kuprianova Island) should be left to starboard, and under no circumstances confused with Yo Do, formerly Rei To, which may be passed on either hand (or indeed with Song Do, or An Do, or Sa Do, or Worhyon Am [also Woreniru To, Getsuken Gan, and Orupyon Pao] which lie immediately beyond). Once past these obstacles to sanity and navigation, the mariner may head north to anchor in capacious but shallow Port Lazaref, subsequently Shoden Wan and now Songjon Man, or southward to Genzan Ko, now known as Wonsan Hang, the objective of the X Corps planners.

Seen from the sea, the Wonsan shore appears precipitous. But although the coastal plain is small there does exist, in the delta of the Namdae River east of the city, a sufficient area for an amphibious lodgment. The port itself is perhaps the best on Korea's eastern coast. Silting between a harbor island and the southern shore had led to the formation of Kalma Pando, a two and a half mile long peninsula with a rocky head and a flat body, which protects a harbor three miles wide at the mouth with the city at its southwestern corner. Despite the bombings of the summer the Wonsan docks remained to all intents undamaged, and these facilities, protected by Kalma Pando on the east and by a breakwater to the north, included a 900-foot concrete wharf with sheds, railroad sidings, and cranes, and with four fathoms or more alongside, as well as piers for smaller vessels. The town had rail and road connections with the east coast route, with the Seoul corridor, and with Pyongyang. And as a final bonus the base of Kalma Pando held an excellent airfield, originally developed as a Japanese naval air station. Taken together, the facilities of Wonsan constituted a prize that any military planner would value.

At Uijongbu, on the far side of the peninsula, the last units of the Marine Division were relieved on 7 October and moved to the Inchon assembly area. There they began loading on the next day, under the direction of Commander Amphibious Group 3, Rear Admiral Thackrey, and while embarkation progressed planning was expedited. A scheme of maneuver was worked out which called for a landing on the seaward side of Kalma Pando, where there was an excellent beach handicapped only by a shallow gradient which placed the two-fathom curve some 300 yards offshore. No help in beaching could be expected from the tides: in notable contrast to Inchon, the tidal range at Wonsan is about one foot.

For the Wonsan landing planning was both concurrent and dispersed. The troop commanders were in Korea, but Struble, Doyle, and Smith were working up the naval side of things in Japan. Once again much of the problem involved the rapid assembly of the necessary shipping: before Admiral Doyle could concern himself with routing and loading of ships these had to be procured from Scajap and MSTS by way of NavFE headquarters. On 30 September a first call was made upon MSTS for 20 APs and 25 AKs; by D-Day the requirement had been increased to a total of 66 vessels which, with the

Amphibious Force units and the Scajap LSTs, proved sufficient to do the job. But no sooner was the X Corps lift provided for than a further transport problem arose: CincFE had originally designated the 3rd Infantry Division as theater reserve; now a decision to employ it in eastern North Korea brought instructions to CTF 90 to employ his shipping, once unloaded at Wonsan, to bring this reinforcing unit in from Japan.

Beginning on 4 October the lift for the Wonsan invasion was assembled at the two Korean ports of embarkation. At Inchon the Marines embarked in assault shipping, APA and AKA types, LSTs and LSDs, filled out with six time-charter vessels. At Pusan the 7th Division was loaded in transports and cargo ships while its heavy gear—tanks and the like—was brought down from Inchon by sea in Scajap LSTs. Although Admiral Doyle was still at work in Tokyo, he had sent his flagship *Mount McKinley* back to Inchon to embark the headquarters staff of the Marine Division. On the 11th he followed by air and relieved Admiral Thackrey of his Inchon responsibilities, whereupon the latter proceeded to Pusan to oversee the 7th Division movement.

By this time the question of D-Day had settled itself. General Almond had based his choice of the 15th on the assumption that X Corps would be relieved on the 3rd, but although the 7th Division had started south to Pusan by that time, the Marines had been held in the line until the 7th. Subsequent preparations were handicapped by shortages of maps and other intelligence material, by a shortage of motor transport ashore created by the requirements of the overland movement to Pusan, and by the complications of embarking the Marines while unloading high-priority incoming cargo in a port where activity was restricted to short bursts at periods of high tide. In the event, therefore, although pressure for speed continued, the best that could be done was to stick with the original date, and to schedule the assault for the 20th.

But just as the date was settled, the objective became uncertain and the entire concept of the operation became subject to review. Although three North Korean divisions had survived the debacle in more or less organized form, their respect for U.N. naval gunfire and air activity had led them to hole up in the mountains south of Wonsan and make no attempt to dispute the coastal road. ROK forces on the east coast consequently moved forward almost unhindered, crossed the parallel on 1 October, and by the 7th were within a few miles of Wonsan.

This development led CincFE to propose changing the objective of the Marine Division from Wonsan in the southwest corner of the Korean Gulf to Hungnam in the northwest. But while this scheme promised to catch more enemy troops, it also modified the original strategic concept by placing the division further from the intended junction with Eighth Army. This was, of course, a problem for the highest level, but there were other difficulties of immediate naval concern. Maps, intelligence material, and time were critically short for so considerable a change; there were insufficient minesweepers to clear two harbors at once; the 7th Division was loading in large transports which could not be accommodated at the Wonsan docks, and its landing plans had been predicated on the availability of the amphibious craft which accompanied the Marines. Although these difficulties were expounded by Struble and Doyle to ComNavFE, and by ComNavFE to General MacArthur, they were at first of little effect. CincFE was always a hard man to argue with, but in this instance Joy persisted, and on the 10th the decision to land the entire X Corps at Wonsan was confirmed.

These revolutionary last minute propositions were still being put forward and evaded as the operation entered its preliminary stages. East coast activity had begun, even before the relief of the Marines, with two night raids on the northeastern coastal railway by the fast transports *Bass* and *Wantuck* with their Royal Marine Commando, supported by the destroyer *De Haven*. The first of these attacks, on the night of 6–7 October, was directed against a tunnel in Kyongsong Man, less than 20 miles south of Chongjin; the target of the second was a tunnel and bridge four miles below Songjin. Both were apparently successful, and the demolition charges were seen by the retiring raiders to explode.

While the raiding group was approaching its first objective the minesweepers of JTF 7, Task Group 95.6, departed Sasebo with a scheduled arrival off Wonsan on the 10th. On the 8th the PBM patrol planes which had been hunting mines in the Yellow Sea shifted their activities to the east coast. On the 9th the carriers *Leyte,* Captain Thomas U. Sisson, and *Philippine Sea,* the former a recent arrival from the Mediterranean by way of Norfolk and the Panama Canal, sortied from Sasebo in company with *Manchester* and 11 destroyers, and headed north to provide air support. On the 10th Admiral Hartman departed with *Helena, Worcester,* and *Ceylon,* and on the next day Admiral Struble sailed in *Missouri,* accompanied by *Valley Forge* and screening destroyers.

Early on the morning of the 10th the Minesweeping Group reached the objective area and began its work. From their operating area a hundred miles offshore, *Leyte* and *Philippine Sea* sent in a combat air patrol for the sweepers and aircraft for interdiction strikes and preparation of the objective. Possible military installations on the island of Yo Do in the harbor entrance were worked over repeatedly, and some useful support was provided the advancing ROK troops, who entered the city this day and who captured the airfield on the 11th.

On the 12th Admiral Struble arrived off Wonsan in *Missouri,* joined up with Admiral Hartman's cruisers, and headed north for a bombardment of Chongjin. With a screen composed of one Canadian, one British, and one Australian destroyer, and with combat air patrol and air spot provided by the fast carriers, *Missouri* and the cruisers conducted a deliberate and sustained bombardment of warehouses, rolling stock, and marshalling yards. Although the spotting provided by the carrier pilots was less than wholly satisfactory, owing to a lack of common grid charts, an absence of specialized training, and some serious communication difficulties, the bombarding ships reported the results as excellent.

The offensive naval strength deployed off Korea's eastern coast, three carriers, a battleship, some cruisers, and numerous destroyers, had by now reached a very respectable level. Of the Far East Air Forces and of the Army in the peninsula, the same could be said. Taken together with the collapse of the North Korean People's Army, this prosperity raised the question of how to end the war without redundant fighting. To this question, one of the most difficult of modern times, World War II had offered no apparent answer, and the war against the Axis had been fought out to its destructive conclusion. No ready answer was apparent in Korea either, and here the problem was still more difficult: where the Axis nations had been led by irresponsible dictators, the enemy in Korea was a dictator's front man only doubtfully possessed of authority to treat.

FEAF, in its approach to this problem, had wished to give authority to CincFE's call for surrender by burning down Pyongyang, the enemy capital, in an all-out early morning incendiary attack. But the proposal was rejected by higher authority, and this approach to the problem of surrender seems in any event to reflect a misunderstanding of the anatomy of Communist society. Even assuming they were masters in their house, the North Korean bosses could be presumed to be comparatively indifferent to burning citizens, yet it was on the bosses that pressure had to be exerted.

A more specifically military effort to bring pressure on the enemy was, however, carried out by CTF 95. Admiral Smith had recommended that the Chongjin shoot be followed by public announcement of the next day's targets, and on Friday the 13th the list was attacked as scheduled. In the Yellow Sea Admiral Andrewes' ships bombarded Haeju while *Theseus* flew strikes against the city of Chinnampo. On the east coast Admiral Hartman's group, joined by *Toledo* and the destroyer *H. J. Thomas,* separated to shoot up five coastal targets along a 120-mile stretch south from Chongjin. Together with the work of the aviators of the U.N., this seemed a sufficient demonstration of the fact that while the Communists might still control some mountain real estate, their writ no longer ran along their coasts or in the air above. But the political impact, so far as could be told, was nil.

Although the Attack Force had not set sail, and although minesweeping had barely begun, the capture of the Kalma Pando airfield by ROK troops had opened a door to Wonsan. On the 13th, therefore, Major General Field Harris, USMC, the X Corps Tactical Air Commander, flew in, and after looking things over ordered up two Marine fighter squadrons. These arrived the next day and at once began operations in support of the ROK I

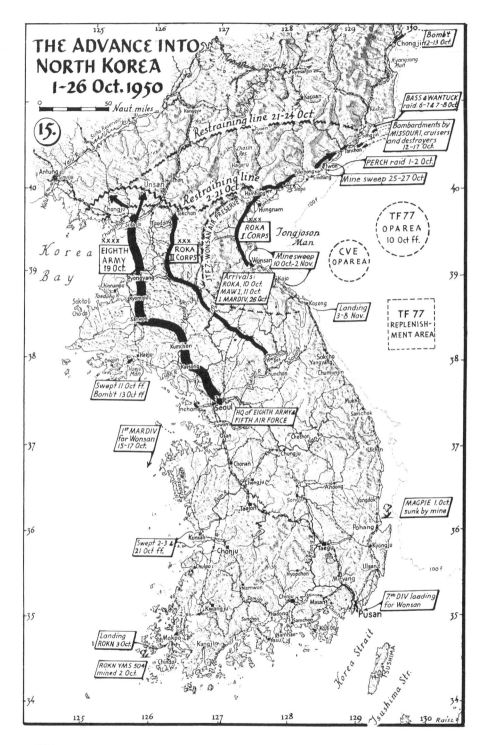

Corps, while being themselves supported by Marine transport aircraft, by the planes of FEAF's Combat Cargo Command, and by a USO troop led by Bob Hope. At sea as well as on shore the air strength available for east coast operations was increasing: *Valley Forge* had arrived on the 12th, and two days later, after docking at Yokosuka to have her frozen propeller removed, *Boxer* also reported in. For the first time since 1945 four *Essex*-class carriers were operating in a single force, and on the 15th Admiral Ewen celebrated by sending forth 392 sorties to press the northern offensive and harry the enemy in the hills.

In the west, in the meantime, Eighth Army had begun its advance, and had crossed the parallel north of Kaesong. Enemy resistance in the hills beyond that town, together with continuing logistic difficulties, slowed progress for a few days, but by mid-month the jam was beginning to break. At Inchon, at the same time, the problems of outbound traffic had been surmounted, and the LSTs of the Wonsan Attack Force sailed on the 15th. By 0800 of the 17th the last transport was clear and *Mount McKinley,* with the big brass embarked, was getting underway. If the departure seemed anticlimactic, in view of the previous capture of the objective, it was still necessary. The need for an assault landing no longer existed, but the need for X Corps in eastern North Korea was undiminished.

2. *11 September–30 November: The Opening of Wonsan and Chinnampo*

The campaign of October, like that of the previous month, involved large-scale operations by both Eighth Army and X Corps. But unlike the period of the Inchon landing and the breakout from the perimeter, the obstacles to movement were now primarily those of space and time, geographic and logistic rather than military. The sporadic resistance of the remnants of the NKPA was never dangerous, but problems of resupply at times seemed well-nigh insurmountable. All supplies for Eighth Army and Fifth Air Force had to pass the bottlenecks at Pusan and Inchon, and the restrictions of port logistics were compounded by those of land transport. Korean roads, never good, had been made worse by war, and throughout the summer rail and highway bridges had been favored objects of air attack. North of Seoul important bridges were down, and everything sent forward by rail had to be trucked around these breaks in the line.

These difficulties of land transport reemphasized the need for seaborne supply, and the extent to which war in the peninsula depended on the use of the surrounding sea. For although the North Korean Army had penetrated far into South Korea without benefit of coastal traffic, such an advance was much more difficult for the forces of the United Nations. Over and above the problems of victualling and munitioning, the complex requirements of the highly mechanized American contingent imposed a heavy load, and the tremendous demands for movement of heavy equipment, petroleum products, electronic gear, spare parts, ice cream, and comic books were reinforced by the national disinclination to walk when riding was possible.

Theater naval forces were consequently faced with an urgent requirement for expansion of the available port facilities and for the opening, on both coasts, of new ports to the northward. But at the same time the events of September had signalled a new problem: the discovery of contact mines in the Inchon entrance channel had been followed by the discovery of magnetic mines ashore, and between 26 September and 2 October five ships had been mined. As both ComNavFE and Commander Seventh Fleet noted in their operation plans for Wonsan, it seemed highly probable that the Communists had worked to deny their ports to the U.N. by a vigorous mining campaign.

Historically it was wholly appropriate that the Korean conflict should have come to involve mine warfare, for it was in Far Eastern waters that the submarine mine, an American invention, was first used with significant success. In the Russo-Japanese War the navy of the Czar lost important vessels to sea mines; that of the Mikado lost two battleships, four cruisers, and three other ships. These successes, in effect their only successes in that war, were not lost upon the Russian Navy, which whatever its politics had in the following half century placed heavy emphasis on mine warfare.

But however apt historically, the circumstance was operationally awkward for the United Nations' naval forces. Although in the First World War the United States Navy had conceived and largely executed the enormous project of the North Sea mine barrage, in the interwar period the problems of oceanic conflict with Japan had relegated mine warfare to a position of unimportance. During most of the Pacific War the mine was little used, although the seeding of Japanese home waters, with mines provided by the Navy and dropped by Army Air Force B–29s, had proven extraordinarily effective.

In the European theater it had been otherwise. There the belligerents were in close proximity, the British Isles depended wholly on overseas supply, and the Germans ran a considerable coastal traffic along the shores of occupied Europe. In this context, not dissimilar to the Korean situation, the mine had from the start proven a devastating weapon. German mining forced Great Britain to sustain a very large minesweeping effort; the British, for their part, employed mine warfare with conspicuous results. Of this success one example will suffice: in the first half of 1942 the RAF sank three times the enemy tonnage by mining as it did by direct attack on ships, and this with 40 percent of the sorties and at 40 percent of the cost in aircraft. Impressive as these statistics are, they by no means show the total impact of the mining campaign, for such an effort, even if it sinks no ships, dislocates maritime transport, overloads alternative routes, and imposes a requirement for costly and complex countermeasures.

Like all American military activities, and indeed more than most, the mine warfare branch of the Navy had suffered from the postwar stringencies. The type command, Mine Force Pacific Fleet, had remained in existence for a year and a half after V–J Day, with a flagship and a reduced force; among its commanders was Rear Admiral Struble. This situation was ended by the budget for Fiscal 1948, which forced dissolution of the type command and further decrease of active minecraft. The lack of a coordinating authority and the strategic dispersion of the remaining minesweepers had adverse effects on readiness, and materiel and training fell below par. In the fleet at large, paravanes had been abandoned; degaussing, the method of reducing to a minimum the magnetic field beneath a ship to guard against magnetic mines, had not been kept up to date; there was no degaussing range west of Pearl Harbor.

The minesweeping force available to ComNavFE on the outbreak of war in Korea consisted of the six wooden-hulled AMS of Mindiv 31 and of the four steel-hulled AMs, one in commission and three in reserve, of Mindiv 32. These ships were grouped in Minron 3, Lieutenant Commander D'Arcy Shouldice, a unit which enjoyed a high state of training and readiness as a consequence of the mine situation in Japanese waters. Other than these units the Pacific Fleet contained a dozen active minesweepers, of which the two AMS of Mindiv 52 were stationed at Guam and the remainder were divided between Pearl Harbor and the west coast.

Activation of the AMs in reserve in Japan had been approved early in the conflict. Nothing could be done about *Mainstay,* owing to unavailability of replacement parts, but by mid-August *Pirate* and *Incredible* were in operating condition. Ordered out from the west coast, the destroyer minesweepers *Endicott* and *Doyle* had reached Far Eastern waters in late July, but in the absence of enemy mining they had been diverted to other duties, in the first instance as screen for Cardiv 15 and subsequently in fire support. In August Admiral Joy had asked for a further increase in minesweepers, but the request was denied on the ground that other types had higher priority.

With the discovery of enemy mines all this was changed. On 11 September CincPac started the three AMS of Mindiv 51 west from Pearl Harbor. Four days later the Chief of Naval Operations revised the schedule for activation of mothballed ships to include nine AMS. From Guam, on the 16th, *Magpie* and *Merganser* of Mindiv 52 were sailed for Korean waters, where the former was promptly mined and sunk and the latter incorporated into Mindiv 31. On 2 October *Thompson* and *Carmick,* the two remaining DMS of the Pacific Fleet, were ordered west from the continental United States, and the remaining three AMS of Mindiv 53 were sailed from the west coast for Pearl Harbor. In late October these reinforcements would reach Sasebo, and in time the ships ordered for activation would become available. But the immediate need for assault sweeps and harbor clearance placed a heavy overload on theater forces, while the emergency reinforcement of the Far East had brought the transfer of every available active unit, and had denuded Guam, Pearl Harbor, and the west coast of all protection.

There were, it is true, an estimated 213 minesweepers in Asiatic waters belonging to other member nations of the U.N. But almost half of these, including 50 ex-U.S. motor minesweepers, belonged to the Soviet Navy, whose current role was as provider of mines rather than of sweepers; as for the others, no offer of their services was received. Still, there did exist one ray of sunshine from an outside source. The mining of Japanese home waters, so successful as to keep the Japanese sweeping ever since, now paid an unexpected dividend as ComNavFE obtained authority from General MacArthur, in his capacity of Supreme Commander for the Allied Powers, to employ 20 contract Japanese sweepers (JMS) for work in Korea, initially below the 38th parallel.

Faced with the need to open North Korean harbors, Admiral Joy now found his force increased by the two activated AMs, by one AMS from Guam, and by two DMS from the west coast. For the opening of Wonsan these units had been assigned to Joint Task Force 7 and organized into Task Group 95.6, the Minesweeping and Protective Group, with *Diachenko,* the repair ship *Kermit Roosevelt,* and eight contract Japanese sweepers. Command of the task group, to which four U.N. frigates and some ROKN YMS would in time be added, was assigned to Captain Richard T. Spofford, who had relieved Shouldice as ComMinron 3 in August, and who was embarked in the destroyer *Collett.*

In addition to the units of Spofford's own task group, a considerable amount of supporting force was at hand. Admiral Higgins was offshore with *Rochester* and some destroyers to provide gunnery support, and *Rochester* had a helicopter available; the aircraft of the fast carriers were on call; the mine search efforts of the PBMs had been shifted to the east coast, and the seaplane tender *Gardiner's Bay* was preparing to establish an advanced seadrome at Chinhae. But the coordination of these diverse forces had not been wholly solved by the time the sweep began, and a considerable amount of time was consequently to be expended in trial and error.

The nature of the situation at Wonsan remained unknown. Clearance of an approach from the 100-fathom curve to the beaches on Kalma Pando called for the sweeping of a 30-mile lane, and of an area of more than 50 square miles. ComNavFE's operation plan had noted the "strong probability" that North Korean ports and landing beaches had been mined; on 1 October he had called for the sweep to begin on D minus 5. Struble's estimate of the situation, which assumed the existence of fields of moored Russian mines, possibly supplemented by more modern types, envisaged the possibility of clearance within five days; alternatively, if bad weather were encountered, or if influence mines had in fact been laid, postponement of the scheduled D–Day might prove necessary. On the 6th he advanced the date for beginning the sweep to D minus 10.

The first problem which faced the minesweepers was to select the route. Six miles out from the landing beaches the sentinel island of Yo Do guards the harbor entrance. Although the Sailing Directions permit Yo Do to be left on either hand, it was known that Russian practice had been to use the northern entrance, and some thought was consequently given to conducting the sweep in that channel. But the final decision was to take the direct route south of the island, and on the morning of 10 October work was begun, with the three AMs in the lead, the AMS buoying the swept area astern, and *Rochester*'s helicopter searching ahead. By late afternoon good progress had been made, a ten-mile channel had been swept to the 30-fathom curve, and 18 mines had been destroyed. But the general feeling of satisfaction was suddenly dashed when the helicopter reported first one, then two, and finally five lines of mines directly ahead of the sweepers.

This discovery cancelled out the whole day's work and raised again the possibility that the sweep could not be completed within the allotted time. In an effort to turn the flanks of the mine lines the direct route to the beaches was abandoned, and on the 11th work was begun in the Russian channel, with a new emphasis on the search function. Overhead a PBM from VP 47 circled, seeking out the mine locations, which were then plotted and communicated to the forces below. From *Diachenko,* UDT personnel were sent in to Yo Do and Ung Do to scout for evidence of controlled minefields. Personnel in Wonsan were urged to seek out charts of the minefield and individuals who had assisted in the lay. Arrangements were made with Task Force 77 for a countermining effort by bomb drop from carrier aircraft. Sweeping went well on the 11th, and a lane was cleared and buoyed to within about four miles of the entrance islands.

Early on the next morning the attempt at countermining took place, as 39 carrier planes, armed with 1,000-pound bombs fused to explode at a depth of 20 feet, flew in to bomb a five-mile lane past Yo Do. For the pilots the exercise was a novel one: proper spacing of the bombs proved difficult owing to lack of control procedures and malfunction of smoke floats, and the results, although spectacular in the amount of water thrown up, were only briefly encouraging. Following the drop, the sweepers headed on through the bombed area for the turn around Yo Do toward Kalma Pando. In the lead, echeloned to port in normal sweep formation, were *Pirate, Pledge,* and *Incredible.* No paravanes were streamed since there were none to stream, there had been no small boat exploration ahead of the sweep, and the searching helicopter could communicate with the sweepers only by relay through the DMS *Endicott.* At 1112 unswept waters were entered; as the sweepers

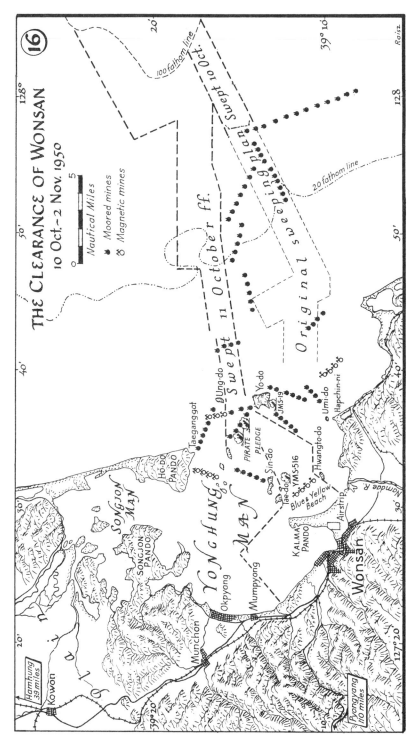

THE CLEARANCE OF WONSAN
10 Oct.–2 Nov. 1950

Nautical Miles

• Moored mines
⊗ Magnetic mines

16

234

came left around Yo Do many mines were cut and bobbed to the surface; at 1200 as the helicopter reported three lines ahead, underwater contacts were obtained on *Pirate's* sound gear.

Then came the blow. At 1209 *Pirate* hit a mine, blew up, capsized, and sank in four minutes. *Pledge,* the second ship, slowed and stopped, cut loose her gear, and lowered a boat to pick up survivors. In this awkward situation fire was opened on the sweepers from previously undetected batteries on Sin Do, and was replied to by *Pledge* and *Endicott.* As rescue operations were pressed the gunnery duel continued, while overhead the circling PBM spotted the gunfire and called on Task Force 77 for an air strike. Ten minutes had gone by when at 1220, in an attempt to turn back into cleared waters, *Pledge* came left out of the swept lane, and in her turn hit a mine and began to sink. Two ships had been lost, 13 men were missing or dead, and 79 wounded. The rest of the day was spent in picking up the pieces and trying to decide what to do next.

When news of the sinkings reached the bombardment forces off Chongjin it brought impressive reinforcement, as Admirals Struble and Smith boarded the destroyer *Rowan* and steamed southward at best speed. But admirals cannot do the work of minesweepers, and with no replacements for the lost ships, safe sweeping had become essential. Further emphasis was laid on searching, by patrol plane and helicopter, to permit a route of approach that would turn the mine lines. Mine disposal was accomplished by strafing and by UDT personnel from *Diachenko,* assisted by the inhabitants of Ung Do, who were rewarded for their enthusiasm by the issue of rations and by medical assistance. In this wise, progress continued, the channel was cleared of contact mines, and on the 14th magnetic sweeping was begun. How long this would take was anybody's guess.

By 18 October, D minus 2, the sweepers had reached the beaches of Kalma Pando. The only further incidents had been the loss of one JMS off the southern shore of Yo Do, and damage to a small ROK freighter which took an unauthorized shortcut through the minefields. Although four days of magnetic sweeping had brought only negative results, information from prisoners ashore on the 16th indicated that ground mines had been laid. Next day this report was contradicted, but on the 18th confirmation was gained both by land and sea. Ashore a sample coil was recovered from the railroad station master; off the beaches two detonations arose astern of the minesweepers, and then, in a great explosion, the ROK *YMS 516* disappeared in a cloud of water and smoke. Faced with this proof of the presence of influence mines, and with further sweeping obviously necessary, Admiral Struble recommended postponement of D-Day, and his view was concurred in by higher authority. Although it proved possible, beginning on the 19th, to beach landing craft with urgently needed supplies for the

Wonsan: Off the beaches of Kalma Pando the ROKN YMS 516 is blown up by a magnetic mine. 18 October 1950. (USN 423625)

236

Marine squadrons on Kalma Pando, it was another week before the channel could be declared clear for the Attack Force.

One must credit the Russian naval personnel who had been assigned to mine Wonsan with the achievement of a considerable success. Prior to their departure in early October, these gentlemen had not only held mine school for the North Koreans but had assembled the magnetic mines, planned the minefields, and supervised their planting. The effort had been an extremely economical one. Barges towed by motor sampan had been employed as minelayers, and local labor used both to load the barges and to roll the mines off the stern. With this negligible investment in training, equipment, and personnel, more than 2,000 of a planned 4,000 mines had been planted in the harbor, four ships had been sunk, and a delay of six days imposed upon the Attack Force.

Arduous though it had been, the opening of Wonsan was but part of the job which faced the minesweepers. Other east coast ports demanded clearance, while in the west the need for seaborne supply was urgent. There the advance of Eighth Army, although only lightly opposed, had been carried out under circumstances of considerable logistic difficulty. Daily requirements were on the order of 1,500 tons; the rail and truck shuttle above Seoul could produce only half that figure; and as the best efforts of the airlift could not make up the deficit, every mile of northward movement increased the troubles of the overworked quartermasters.

So far as capabilities permitted, efforts to open west coast ports had already begun. Returning from Inchon in early October, one AM and six AMS had stopped by at Kunsan, and in the course of a sweep to the docks had destroyed four mines and located another two score. In mid-October, as Eighth Army was moving on Pyongyang, the Japanese contract sweepers were ordered to clear the entrance to Haeju, an operation which would make available a 2,000-foot quay with four fathoms alongside and with road and rail connections to the north. By 1 November the work was done, but by this time the front had reached the Chongchon River, and with the Army's needs increasing, the effect was marginal. Autumn comes suddenly in North Korea: at Pyongyang the monthly mean temperature drops from 40° in October to 23° in November, and the nights are cold. Short of rations, short of fuel, and with both men and machinery urgently in need of winterizing, Eighth Army was under heavy pressure from CincFE to expedite its advance. In this situation, and in the absence in the north of suitable LST beaching sites, anguished cries arose from EUSAK for the opening of the port of Chinnampo.

Situated ten miles up the tidal Taedong River, Chinnampo is to Pyongyang as Inchon is to Seoul. Like Inchon it suffers from the disability of its location on the eastern shore of the Yellow Sea. For 30 miles or so islands and drying mud banks line the approach; inside the headlands the channel shrinks to a mere quarter of a mile in width in the narrows of Pido Sudo; tidal currents in the river reach three and a half knots on the flood and four a half on the ebb. The port itself had a dredged basin which could accommodate a few ships, along with railroad spurs and some unloading equipment; there were beaches which could take a few LSTs. But damage had been suffered from air strikes, there was an extreme shortage of lighterage, and the maximum capacity of the port was less than half that of Inchon. Still, with all its faults, Chinnampo was unique. No alternative existed. Its opening was mandatory.

The appeals from Eighth Army for the opening of Chinnampo were sympathetically received by Admiral Joy. But his slender force was fully committed at Wonsan, and although on 21 October he promised to commence the clearance at the earliest possible date, his estimate of the time required for completion was a pessimistic three weeks. But, even if forces are unavailable, orders can always be issued, and ComNavFE had already ordered Admiral Smith relieved of his duties at Wonsan in order to prepare plans for the earliest possible sweeping of Chinnampo. On the afternoon of the 22d, CTF 95 was so released.

Although the disposable force immediately available to Smith consisted of himself, it was soon to be augmented. Two visiting officers, Commanders Stephen M. Archer and Donald N. Clay, who had come out from CincLantFleet and CincPacFleet headquarters to look over the mine situation, were put to work. Clay was at once constituted an intelligence team, and sent off to Chinnampo to investigate the enemy lay; Archer was ordered to Sasebo, where CTF 95 was attempting to scrounge a sweeping force.

In point of fact prospects were not as bad as they seemed at first sight. On the 22d the two remaining Pacific Fleet DMS, *Thompson* and *Carmick*, reached Japan, to be followed on the next day by the three AMS of Mindiv 51 from Pearl Harbor. These were at once ordered forward to the Yellow Sea: *Thompson* and *Carmick* sailed on the 27th, to be shortly followed by the AMS and by the destroyer *Forrest Royal*, a new arrival from the Atlantic Fleet which Smith had obtained as Archer's flagship. Together with various later acquisitions these units made up Task Element 95.69 which was to do the job.

With Wonsan open the PBMs were switched back to west coast mine hunting, assisted by the RAF Sunderlands. Efforts in the Yellow Sea were complicated by the many large jellyfish, four feet or more in diameter, gray in color, and floating a few feet below the surface, which gave rise to numerous false alarms. But despite this distraction good work was done. Three days of search brought 34 mine sightings, and 16 sinkings by strafing, and a subsequent attempt to blow magnetic mines by depth charging met with some slight success, although at a considerable cost in ordnance. On 29 October the air effort was strengthened by *Worcester*'s helicopter, tem-

Chinnampo: A bucking LCVP in the well of Catamount; in the background the destroyer Forrest Royal, *flagship of the West Coast minesweeping group.* (USN 422837)

porarily based on the British carrier *Theseus* which also provided combat air patrol. And in due course the work of the patrol planes was simplified, and more time on station made possible, with the reestablishment of the Inchon seadrome by *Gardiner's Bay*.

Since the entire Yellow Sea is of mineable depth, the point of origin of the sweep was arbitrarily located some 30 miles off the channel entrance and 69 miles from the docks. The approach sweep was begun on the 29th, as *Thompson* and *Carmick* headed in from the west and turned south inside the outer mine line to reach the channel entrance near the island of Cho Do. On the 31st Commander Archer arrived in *Forrest Royal;* on 1 November the three AMS turned up, along with *Bass* and her UDT detachment, two ROK YMS, and a Scajap LST which would relieve *Theseus* as helicopter base. By 2 November Commander Clay and Lieutenant (j.g.) Hong, ROKN, had discovered the pattern of the minefield: 217 moored and 25 magnetic mines were reported to have been laid, with five lines across the main channel north of Sok To and one across the passage south of that island. Although this southern channel, Sok To Myoji, is a shallow draft affair with a least depth of two and a quarter fathoms at low water, its lighter protection made it for the moment the channel of choice. Here the effort was pressed.

The predominant lesson of the Wonsan experience had been to search before you sweep. At Chinnampo, where this lesson was faithfully followed, the hunt was simplified by the tidal characteristics of the Yellow Sea, which tended to expose mines at low water. Searching at low tide by patrol plane, helicopter, small boat, and swimmers was emphasized; sweeping was done at high tide with the aim of clearing a not too devious route around rather than through the fields; on 3 November a Korean YMS made a safe passage into Chinnampo. Two helpful arrivals took place on the 4th and 5th in the form of high winds, which shook loose some of the moored mines, and of the LSD *Catamount,* which after unloading Marines at Wonsan had been loaded at Sasebo with small boats and extra gear and sent west to act as mother ship. On the 6th an ROK YMS took a convoy of tugs and barges in the Sok To channel, five small *Marus* were put through the next day, and with the arrival on the 10th of a Scajap LST the western approach and southern entrance could be considered clear.

With Sok To Myoji opened, Commander Archer's force shifted its effort to the deep water entrance and to Cho Do Sudo, the coastal route of approach from the southward. A dozen Japanese sweepers had by now arrived, accompanied by two mother ships, and were checksweeping the already opened channels. By 17 November 14 ships had reached Chinnampo; three days later 40,000 tons had been unloaded and the opening of the deep channel celebrated by the arrival of the hospital ship *Repose*. Already the Army's logistic situation had been greatly improved, and Gen-

Chinnampo: Near the mouth of the Taedong River a PBM detonates a mine by strafing. (USN 422817)

eral Walker was looking forward to a resumption of the northward advance. By month's end unloading had reached a rate of 4,800 tons a day, and the sweepers were working north along the coast to clear a channel for possible use by fire support ships or by LSTs supplying the northern front.

Like so many things in human life the opening of a mined harbor is easier the second time. At Chinnampo, in contrast to the events at Wonsan, no lives had been lost and no ships damaged. Of the 80 moored mines swept or destroyed, 36 were credited to patrol planes and 27 to the underwater demolition personnel; 12 had been broken loose by storms; only 5 had been cut by sweepers. Better and earlier intelligence, different tidal conditions, and experience had all been helpful.

Yet if the sweep had been successful, so once again had been the mining; as at Wonsan, considerable delay had been imposed. Shallow draft shipping had been put in to Chinnampo within ten days, but for larger vessels Com-NavFE's estimate of three weeks had proven accurate. The result of these experiences, and of the promise of more trouble in the future, was to give mine warfare, for the first time in years, a high priority in U.S. naval thinking.

The continuing shortage of sweepers now brought a speed-up in their activation: on 16 October the Chief of Naval Operations gave overriding priority to the nine AMS previously scheduled for recommissioning, and added four AMs to the list. The history of the Wonsan sweep, begun in one channel and completed in another, and carried out first by large sweepers, then by small boats and swimmers, and finally by the minesweepers again, showed the need both for improved tactical organization and for better procedures in mine location and mine clearance. In the United States a research and development program was begun. In Japan steps were taken to provide a suitable mother ship by conversion of an LST to carry supplies, accommodate small boats, and serve as helicopter platform. In the administrative sphere ComNavFE in late October had recommended the reestablishment of the Mine Force type command, and had urged that pending this step a flag officer be assigned to administer mine warfare in the Far East. These recommendations were approved, and on 11 November the Minesweeping Force Western Pacific was activated under the command of Admiral Higgins.

3. 19 October–20 November: Operations in Eastern North Korea

"The neighborhood of Wonsan," says the old guide book to North China and Korea, "heavily forested and with mountains rising from the sea, is extremely picturesque. To the southwest lie the Diamond Mountains, whose watercourses, forests, and famous monasteries have earned them the appellation of the Jewel of Korea. Here tiger, leopard, bear, wolves, and wild boar may still be found, as well as various species of deer, pheasant, and bustard. The natives, hardy in the chase, employ falcons in their pursuit of small game."

Having prepared for their assault into this tourist wonderland, the Marines, embarked in the ships of Task Force 90, had left Inchon in time to make the 20 October D–Day. But the capture of Wonsan by ROK forces made the assault landing unnecessary, and eased the problem of introducing X Corps into northeastern Korea. Although the forests hid more dangerous game than tiger or bear, in the form of sizable North Korean units moving along the inland mountain tracks, no really serious opposition was anticipated, while the Kalma Pando air strip and the decks of the carriers at sea held larger and more lethal birds than falcons.

While the dangerous and tedious work of minesweeping went forward, the ships of the Attack Force were moving south through the Yellow Sea and east through the Korean Strait. At Pusan the 7th Division and corps contingents were preparing to sail. But on the 18th the discovery of influence mines off the Wonsan beaches brought the decision to delay entrance until a thorough magnetic sweeping could be accomplished. Admiral Thackrey was instructed to hold the later echelons in port, and the projected movement of the 3rd Division from Japan to Korea was postponed.

On the afternoon of 19 October the Transport and Tractor Groups arrived in the Korean Gulf. The flagship *Mount McKinley,* with the Attack Force and Marine Division staffs embarked, moved in and anchored in the swept channel, but the rest of the force was ordered to reverse course and so maneuver as to return at daylight of the 21st. Further delay brought repetition of these instructions, and until morning of the 25th the Attack Force steamed back and forth, first south and then north again, through the Sea of Japan. This evolution, designated Operation Yo-Yo by the crowded and disgruntled Marines, had some serious implications: food threatened to run short; ideal conditions were presented for the spread of epidemic disease. Only a few days earlier, dysentery had hit the crews of two cruisers of the Formosa Patrol; during "Yo-Yo" it broke out in epidemic form on the MSTS transport *Marine Phoenix,* afflicting 700 of the 2,000 embarked troops and a like proportion of the crew. But terms in purgatory are by definition limited, and "Yo-Yo" in due time came to an end. Beginning at 1500 on the 25th the ships of the Attack Force moved in column through the swept channel to drop anchor in southern Yonghung Man.

Five LSTs were beached at once with engineer and shore party materiel, and at daylight on the 26th general unloading began. In accordance with the original assault plan the 1st Marines went in across Yellow Beach and the 7th Marines across Blue Beach, with RCT 5 following on the next day. As a result of the shallow gradient, landing craft grounded some distance offshore, personnel had to wade the last few yards, and the rapid

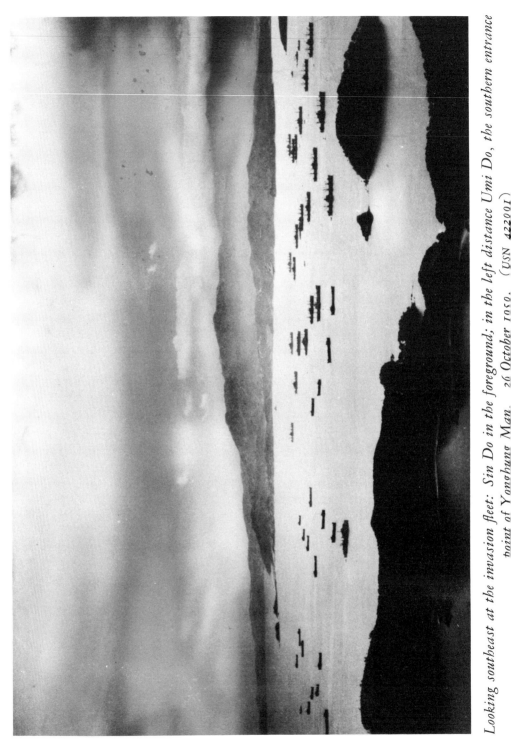

Looking southeast at the invasion fleet: Sin Do in the foreground; in the left distance Umi Do, the southern entrance point of Yonghung Man.   26 October 1950.   (USN 422001)

244

handling of inanimate objects waited on the construction of ramps and causeways. But work was pushed: of the more than 25,000 men in the division and attached units, well over half were ashore by evening of the 26th, along with more than 2,000 vehicles and 2,000 tons of cargo, and five days later the operation was completed. While the Marines were coming ashore over the Kalma Pando beaches and deploying outward, the mine-sweepers had moved on into the inner harbor. Although local information indicated that this had not been mined, nobody wanted to take chances. But the informants proved correct, and by 2 November the port was pronounced clear.

The landing had been delayed six days. First on to so many beaches, the Marine Division had this time been preceded by its Aircraft Wing and by a USO troop. But except by the mining effort and the Sin Do batteries, the operation had been unopposed, and so economical. A major port had been seized and opened, an important force was ashore in eastern North Korea, and more was on the way. For the Marines the only casualties were those 84 dysentery victims who had to be hospitalized, and even when the losses of the minesweeping force were reckoned in, the bill in military terms was small.

Throughout the period of Operation Yo-Yo Eighth Army had been advancing in the west. In the central mountains the Korean II Corps had continued northward. Moving onward from Wonsan, ROK troops had entered Hamhung and Hungnam on 17 October; by the time the Marine Division came ashore the front was more than 50 miles to the northward, and was still moving. On the 17th *Helena* and *Worcester* had bombarded transportation targets at Songjin, but from that time on the work of the gunfire ships was largely limited to standing by. Since its preinvasion strikes in the Wonsan region Task Force 77 had been sending its flights northward, in support of the South Koreans and in attacks against a diminishing number of targets beyond the bombline; soon the fast carriers would be withdrawn to port. On the entire coast the only really busy units were the minesweepers and the ships of the Amphibious Force, on whom devolved responsibility for opening new ports, bringing in more forces, and providing logistic support for X Corps as it sprawled out over eastern North Korea.

In these circumstances General Almond's force found its mission changed. The speed of advance into North Korea had obviated the need for a westward thrust by the units of X Corps; the U.N. resolution of early October had shifted the emphasis of the campaign from the destruction of the enemy army to the pacification of North Korea. A new scheme of maneuver had consequently been developed by GHQ, and five days before the Wonsan landing X Corps received orders to advance to the north.

On 25 October, with Wonsan at last open to the invasion fleet, Struble, Almond, and Doyle met to consider the implications of this change for the operations of the Joint Task Force. To speed the northward movement it was decided to land one or more of the regiments of the 7th Division at Iwon, 90 miles to the northeast, on the coastal strip which had been the summer target of NavFE surface forces. North and south of this small administrative center the bombardment ships had carried out their work, and landing parties from *Juneau, Bass,* and *Perch* had gone ashore to raid the railroad. But Iwon, and its port town of Kunson, had remained undisturbed, and between 25 and 27 October *Endicott, Doyle,* and one AMS swept an 18-mile channel and an anchorage area without discovering any mines.

The landing of the 7th Division at Iwon was entrusted to Admiral Thackrey. Having supervised the operation of the port of Inchon and the early stages of the reembarkation of the Marines, ComPhibGroup 3 had since 11 October been administering the loading of 7th Division and corps troops at Pusan. On the 26th he arrived at Wonsan in *Eldorado,* and next day sailed for Iwon, where debarkation began on the 29th. The lack of amphibious craft in the 7th Division convoys, the absence of local lighterage, and the need to improvise a beach party made the operation a slow one; everything in the transports and cargo ships had to be offloaded into LSTs and smaller craft, a process which resulted in considerable superficial topside damage owing to swell in the unprotected anchorage. But by the 30th one regiment had landed all its personnel and vehicles and much of its gear. By 8 November the entire lift of 29,000 men had been put ashore, and the division was backtracking down the coast in preparation for its move to the north.

Although it too was shortly to move northward, the Marine Division, following its landing at Wonsan, found itself for the moment involved in blocking and protective missions. One battalion was moved in over the mountains to cut off enemy troops retiring up the Imjin valley road, while a second was ordered to Kojo, some 30 miles back down the coast to the southeast. The assignment to the Kojo area, where the situation map showed a patchwork of North Korean and ROK units, was not wholly unexpected. On the 21st, while the Marines were still cruising the Sea of Japan, General Almond had asked for the immediate landing of a battalion there to ensure the protection of an ROK supply dump. The request had been denied by Admiral Struble, owing to the possibility of unswept mines, but on the 24th the task was reassigned to the Marine Division. Since a Marine air strike in this region had discovered and attacked an estimated 800 enemy troops, the idea seemed a reasonable one.

On the 24th, in preparation for this move and to ensure the possibility of support from the sea in the event of an enemy descent upon the coastal road, the fast minesweepers *Endicott* and *Doyle* swept and buoyed a channel into Kojo, and two days later a battalion was sent down from Wonsan by train. At Kojo all seemed peaceful on arrival: the sea was blue, the town undamaged. But on the night of the 27th the battalion was surprised and hit

One U.S. and eight Scajap LSTs beached on Kalma Pando. In the left distance Hwangto Do; right center, Umi Do. 26 October 1950. (USN 707996)

hard by troops of the North Korean 5th Division, and a call for helicopter evacuation of casualties, for air and gunfire support, and for tanks quickly brought forth a miniature example of standard amphibious support procedures.

Sicily and *Badoeng Strait* had arrived off Wonsan on 18 October and had been covering the minesweeping operations. Now, in concert with the squadrons on Kalma Pando, they stepped up their sorties against enemy troops, and heavily attacked the town of Tongchon, reported to contain the enemy headquarters. Helicopters were provided to fly out the more seriously wounded, and the fast transport *Wantuck* was ordered down from Wonsan with a surgical team. The destroyers *Hank* and *English* took the enemy troops under fire, *LST 883* got underway from Wonsan with a load of tanks, a reinforcing battalion was sent down to Kojo by rail, and the situation was soon under control. The whole affair was a somewhat confused one, for the supply dump which provided the rationale of the operation turned out to have been removed before the first contingent of Marines arrived. But in any event the Kojo effort was shortly terminated: on the 31st a battalion of Korean Marines arrived from Samchok by LST to take over the job of policing the area.

As the Koreans were relieving at Kojo a second minor amphibious operation was getting underway. Sixty miles below Wonsan, at the southern end of the Korean Gulf, sizable and aggressive guerilla forces were reported operating in the hills behind Kosong. Under the supervision of Captain Robert C. Peden, Commander Tractor Group, Korean troops were loaded into two LSTs, and sailed on 1 November for this area. The two destroyer minesweepers made a sweep which discovered no mines, and on the morning of the 3rd an unopposed landing was successfully executed. A few days bushwhacking brought the situation under control; on 8 November two LSTs were sent down to bring the Koreans back again, and by the 10th they had been returned to Wonsan.

There more strength was now arriving to take over the responsibility for local defense and to relieve the Marine Division for its move to the north. With the Wonsan landing completed, and with the 7th Division going ashore at Iwon, Admiral Doyle had sent six ships to Pusan to bring back one of the regiments of the 3rd Infantry Division. Units of this group began returning to Wonsan on 5 November, and by the 8th the movement was completed and the regiment was ashore. In the meantime a larger task element, composed of nine transport and cargo types, some MSTS shipping, and some LSTs, was formed and ordered to Moji, on Shimonoseki Strait, to lift the balance of the 3rd Division.

All troop movements were now provided for, but there was still work for the Navy, for the northward reorientation of the campaign required both a reshuffling of forces already ashore and the opening of another port. Gen-

eral Almond had selected the city of Hamhung as the site of X Corps Headquarters, the Marines were moving north from Wonsan, and the new problem for the minesweepers, who had opened Wonsan to the southward and
Iwon to the north, was to clear the neighboring harbor of Hungnam in
anticipation of a consolidation of east coast logistic activities there.

The city of Hungnam, manufacturing center as well as seaport, lies
in the northwestern corner of the Korean Gulf near the delta of the Songchon
River. Although Hamhung, its inland satellite, is an important road and
railway center, Hungnam is the larger of the two, with a population in 1950
a third again that of Wonsan. The bay on which the city lies is open to the
south, but the inner harbor is protected by a 2,200-foot wharf with four
fathoms of water and by a breakwater. Other smaller wharves existed, as
did heavy loading equipment, developed to handle the products of the city's
chemical industry. As at Wonsan, the 100-fathom curve runs 30 miles
offshore, and the approaches are easily mined.

Since intelligence reports indicated that over a hundred moored mines
had been planted at Hungnam, a serious sweeping effort was required. A
destroyer minesweeper, seven AMS, and supporting units were made available, and on 7 November clearance was begun. Small boat and helicopter
search was employed to the utmost; an approach was chosen which would
detour the minefields by passing close under the eastern point; so successful
was the reconnaissance that the only mines swept were well clear of the
entrance lane. A sweep was made for magnetic mines, but none was discovered, and the port was declared open on the 11th. On the 14th Admiral
Doyle turned affairs at Wonsan over to Commander Transport Group, Captain Samuel G. Kelly in the attack transport *Bayfield,* and sailed for Hungnam in *Mount McKinley*.

One more harbor clearance was necessary to provide the desired ac-
cessibility to eastern North Korea. To simplify the logistic support of ROK
troops advancing up the coast, General Almond on 3 November had requested the opening of Songjin, 35 miles beyond Iwon. On completion
of the job at Hungnam the sweepers were ordered onward, and between
16 and 19 November the seven AMS swept a channel and an anchorage area
at Songjin without discovering any mines. This, for the moment, completed the minesweeping task. In time, it is true, the continuing northward
progress of Korean troops would bring a call for the opening of Chongjin.
But for reasons beyond the sweepers' control this request would not be implemented.

For the ships of Task Force 90 and for Captain Spofford's sweepers the
weeks following the Wonsan landing had been busy ones. Three divisions
had been put into North Korea through two ports; support had been provided for two small operations against remnants of the North Korean Army;
five harbors had been swept for mines. By mid-November pressure was

decreasing, but there remained some chores to be performed. Although the personnel of the Army's 2nd Engineer Special Brigade, which was to operate the port of Hungnam, had been moved down from Iwon by rail, some of the heavy equipment could not pass the tunnels and had to be reloaded and brought down by sea. A considerable amount of X Corps cargo, initially landed at Wonsan but now needed at Hungnam, also required water transport, and this movement was accomplished by LST shuttle service in the closing days of the month. So far as the movement of forces into eastern North Korea went, however, a terminal date could be assigned, for on 20 November the final elements of the 3rd Infantry Division reached Wonsan from Moji. This day was also made memorable by the landing on the Wonsan airstrip of the Secretary of the Navy and an inspection party. Apprised of this prospect, Admiral Doyle had sailed down from Hungnam the day before to meet the distinguished visitors and to welcome them aboard his flagship. There, in the course of a short speech delivered to the ship's company, the Secretary observed that this was the first visit he had ever paid to any ship of the U.S. Navy.

Much game has been made by later writers of the incumbent of this office during the Grant administration, who was said to have been surprised by the discovery that ships were hollow. The events of the 20th on *Mount McKinley* should perhaps also be recorded as a footnote to history, and as memorializing a Secretary who, in office for more than a year and a half, had never bothered to find out.

4. *15 October–24 November: New Plans and New Problems*

For all but the minesweeping crews afloat and those with logistic responsibilities ashore, October had been a happy month. On land, at sea, and in the air it was a harvest time, a period of exploitation of a great victory, in which the steady advance of U.N. forces brought visions of a speedy end to hostilities. On the 15th, having found time to fly to Wake Island for a conference with the President of the United States, CincFE opined that organized resistance would end by Thanksgiving. The likelihood of Russian or Chinese intervention, a matter of concern at Washington and Lake Success, was very small; if the Chinese did attempt to enter Korea it could only be with comparatively small forces which would be "slaughtered" by U.N. air strength. With the war over by Thanksgiving, Eighth Army could be withdrawn to Japan by Christmas, while X Corps remained as an occupation force for the month or two necessary to prepare and hold elections throughout Korea.

The military situation, as of the moment, went far to bear out CincFE's optimistic picture. Resistance on the ground, steadily decreasing, had by mid-month practically ended.   On 19 October, as the Marine Division was rounding the Korean peninsula, Eighth Army entered Pyongyang, to the pleasure of the acquisitive American soldiery who liberated quantities of red flags, portraits and busts of Stalin, and other desirable impedimenta. Entrance into the capital was followed by a parachute drop in regimental strength 30 miles to the northward, and the drop by a CincFE statement to the press that the war was coming to an end.   Shortly the forces of the U.N. pushed on across the Chongchon River, and on 26 October ROK troops reached the banks of the Yalu.

While the armies advanced almost at will, the navies of the United Nations cruised undisturbed along the Korean coasts.   Across the vast Pacific transports and cargo ships steamed without let or hindrance, bringing the necessities and luxuries of war.   Step by step, as sweeping progressed and ports were opened, the ends of the seaborne supply line closed up on the advancing front, to lighten the burdens of the logisticians.

In the air, too, the war was uncontested, and U.N. air strength was moving forward.   At Wonsan, 70 miles above the parallel, Marine squadrons were ashore; at Yonpo, near Hungnam, a second modern airfield was available; in the west Fifth Air Force had advanced its JOC to Seoul and was preparing to activate northern airfields; in the Yellow Sea and in the Sea of Japan the carriers still sent forth their planes.   But increasingly the airmen of all services found themselves hard up for targets, and as the month wore on the sortie rate diminished.

Already the cheerful prospect of an imminent end to the fighting had been reflected in the activities of Naval Forces Far East.   This change was first apparent in the activities of the planners, whose working day embraces future time, and even before the Wonsan Attack Force sailed, Admiral Joy's staff had turned its attention to post-war redeployment.   Estimates were made of desirable post-hostility force levels in the Far East, and of the size of the shore establishment in Japan; planning was undertaken for future assistance to the ROK Navy and Marine Corps.   So far indeed had things progressed that Operation Plan 114–50, which listed naval missions in support of the pacification of North Korea and contained an annex on the homeward movement of forces, was issued on 19 October, the day of entry into Pyongyang, and plans for the redeployment of the Marine Division reached General Smith while he was still en route to Wonsan.

Nor were the operating forces unaffected.   Although the minesweepers were working overtime, and although Task Force 90 still had plenty to do in getting X Corps ashore, elsewhere the tempo of the campaign diminished. With less and less to shoot at, some of the fire support ships were returned to port, while the functions of the remainder were reduced to patrolling and covering operations.   From the west coast the British carrier *Theseus,* with no more targets in hand, was sailed for Sasebo for onward routing to Hong Kong. Off Korea's eastern shore a major redeployment of naval strength was begun.

More carrier strength was now available than could be profitably employed. With elimination of the Joint Task Force's Wonsan objective area by advancing ROK troops, there again arose the question of the assumption by FEAF of operational or coordination control of carrier air. The always present possibility of a new intervention from the north posed questions as to the readiness of antisubmarine forces. To meet or minimize these problems a reduction and modification of theater naval strength seemed desirable: on 22 October *Philippine Sea* and *Boxer* left the operating area for Yokosuka; one week later *Valley Forge* and *Leyte* retired to Sasebo. On her arrival in Japan *Boxer* was routed onward to the continental United States for navy yard overhaul; *Valley Force* was scheduled to return to the west coast in late November; plans were made to withdraw the escort carriers from Korean waters, and to send *Sicily* to Guam to reembark her antisubmarine squadron. On 28 October Admiral Struble forwarded his appreciation to ComNavFE: recent experience showed that the Seventh Fleet should not revert to the status of a one-carrier force, but should remain a balanced fleet with amphibious and minesweeping capabilities; to emphasize the mobility of naval forces, and to strengthen the impact on the doubtful of the United Nations' success in Korea, he proposed at the earliest moment to take his command to southeast Asian waters to show the flag and to conduct training exercises. Three days later Joint Task Force 7 was dissolved, and the flagship group retired to Sasebo.

Only Admiral Higgins' minesweeping groups and the Military Sea Transportation Service continued to grow in strength. Reinforcements for the former were still arriving as November came, while the latter had not yet reached its peak. Having entered business on 1 July as the proprietor of 25 small ships, Captain Junker's command had undergone an explosive expansion, until by the time of the Wonsan landing it controlled 243 vessels. The requirements of the advance to the north brought a further slight increase, and the week of 8 November saw 263 ships under MSTS WestPac control. But then, with X Corps well established ashore, the decline began, and by mid-month the total would be down some ten percent. Similar considerations affected the Amphibious Force, but by mid-November Admiral Doyle could contemplate a redeployment of his hard-worked shipping for respite and training in Japan.

The diminishing activity of Naval Forces Far East was quickly reflected in reduced expenditure of important commodities. Naval consumption of aviation gasoline, which had reached a peak of 187,000 barrels in August, was down in October to 130,000. Ammunition expenditure, more than 2,100 short tons in the week of 19 September, had declined by October's end to less than a sixth of that amount. Navy cargo lifted from the west coast, POL excepted, had fallen radically from the 107,000 measurement tons of the week of 21 August; in October it dropped steadily from 29,000 tons per week to a mere 11,000. What the naval effort had amounted to in terms of transfer of force may be seen from the extraordinary expansion of NavFE-supported personnel, U.S. and U.N., which from a mere 11,000 in June had reached 40,000 by early August, 69,000 in late September, and 79,000 by mid-October. But there it stopped, homeward deployment was begun, and the coming of November saw the total naval population down to 75,000.

Not only had intensity of effort diminished, following the defeat of the North Koreans, but the entire concept of operations had been changed. The late September plans for the encirclement of retiring enemy remnants had called for a landing at Wonsan, followed by a westward thrust of X Corps to a junction with Eighth Army in the neighborhood of Pyongyang. Completion of this movement would have resulted in control of the Korean waist south of the restraining line, and of the Pyongyang-Sinanju-Hungnam-Wonsan quadrilateral. Here the axial range is lowest, the mountains rarely rise above 3,000 feet, and here are found the best transverse communications in the entire peninsula. Harbors on both coasts are useful to a force sustained by sea, and the area's industrial towns are linked by a road net of considerable density in Korean terms, and one at least marginally adequate for western forces.

But the successes that had crowned his arms, and the U.N. mandate for Korean unification, had caused General MacArthur to lift up his eyes unto the hills. On 17 October, following his return from Wake, CincFE had issued orders that if Pyongyang fell before the Wonsan landing was completed, X Corps should no longer strike westward across the peninsula, but instead continue on to the north. The restraining line, beyond which non-Korean forces were not to pass, would be swung to the northwest, and parallel zones established, separated by the central mountain range, through which Eighth Army and X Corps would advance. With the capture of Pyongyang, entered by Eighth Army on the 19th and declared secure two days later, these new orders became effective.

With this change the forces of the United Nations faced the task of occupying a very different geographical province. The new restraining line, moved forward in the east some 60 miles, now lay in the watershed of the Yalu, beyond the northern divide, and in its course from east to west crossed mountains towering above 8,000 feet. In this sparsely populated high and craggy country planners could draw lines on maps, but implementers could not man the lines. Indigenous forces, lightly armed and durable, might perhaps maneuver here with some facility, but for motorized armies it was another matter. Only a handful of north-south routes existed; except in the western lowlands only narrow columns could push forward through the twisting defiles. Mutual support under such conditions was hardly a possibility, and even radio communication would be made difficult by the intervening mountains.

For a scant week this concept stayed on the books, and then on 24 October, with the bulk of Eighth Army stalled above Pyongyang by shortage of supplies and with X Corps still awaiting the clearance of Wonsan, the restraining line was abolished altogether and more trackless wastes and frozen peaks were marked for conquest. Since the September authorization of operations above the parallel had stipulated that "no non-Korean ground forces will be used in the northeast provinces . . . or . . . along the Manchurian border," this action caused some stir in Washington. But General MacArthur's reply to a query from the Joint Chiefs described the decision as based on "military necessity," and stated that "tactical hazards might even result from other action." And once again CincFE had his way.

Whatever the nature of the "military necessity" that General MacArthur had in mind, the proposal to push through to the border with the forces available seems explicable only on the assumption that no serious resistance was anticipated, a view reflected in the diaspora now imposed on X Corps. In its entire zone only three routes led to the northern border, the coastal route by which Korean forces were advancing, and two roads through the inland mountains. Of these the eastern route, from Sinchang north through Kapsan to Hyesanjin, was assigned the 7th Division; the other, 50 miles to the westward, from Hungnam over the mountains and down the Changjin Valley to the Yalu, was given to the Marines. As if this were an insufficient dispersion, the Marine Division came ashore with orders to prepare for a move to the Manchurian border, to make ready a battalion for a possible landing at Chongjin, and at the same time to provide local security in the Wonsan region and at Kojo.

Such was the situation when, in the last week of October, there came sudden signs of increased enemy activity. Large concentrations of fighter planes were reported on the airfield at Antung, on the Manchurian side of the lower Yalu, and Air Force pilots flying down the valley reported antiaircraft fire from the far shore. ROK troops which had reached the Yalu in the Eighth Army zone were roughly handled and driven back. At Unsan the 8th Cavalry Regiment was hit hard by a force which ominously included Chinese. Thirty miles above Hamhung, in the X Corps sector, ROK troops suffered a check in an action in which they captured Chinese prisoners. From Marine night fighters flying out of Kimpo came reports of extensive enemy vehicular traffic across the Yalu bridge at Sinuiju. Soon the available Chinese prisoners were talking freely, affably describing the units to which they belonged and the story of their movement into Korea. On 1 November Fifth Air Force had a tentative report of Russian MIG-15 jet fighters, a report which would soon prove only too true. Two days later

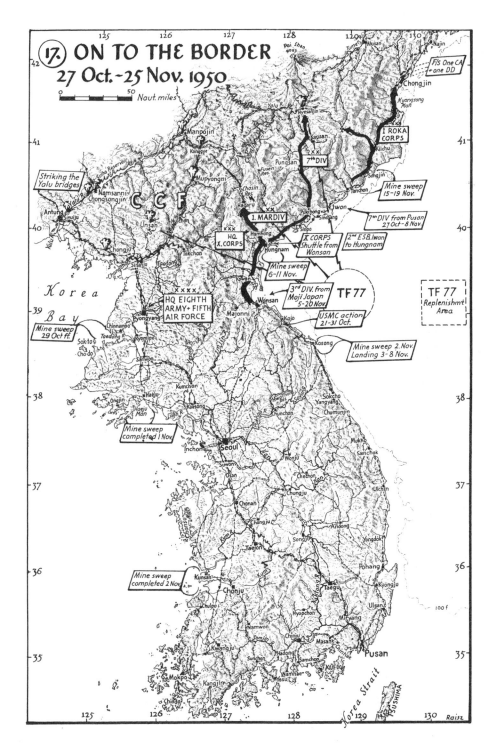

ON TO THE BORDER
27 Oct.-25 Nov. 1950

0 ___ 50 Naut. miles

125   126   127   128   129   130

42

Pai Shan
9003

Tumen Musan

Najin

F/s One CA
+ one DD

Chongjin

Kyangsong
Man

41

Manpojin

Kanggye

Hyesanjin

Kapsan

Pungsan

XX
7th DIV

Kilchu

I ROKA
CORPS

Songjin

Mine sweep
15-19 Nov.

Suiho Reservoir

Mupyongni

Chosin
Res.

Tanchon

Striking the
Yalu bridges

Namsanni
Chongsongjin

Pusen
Res.

Hagaru

Pukchong

Iwon

7th DIV from Pusan
27 Oct - 8 Nov.

C C F

Antung
Simuju

Unsan

Huichon

XX
1. MARDIV

Sinpo

Sinchang

Hamhong

2nd ESB. Iwon
to Hungnam

40

Chongju

Yalu

Tokchon

XXX
HQ.
X. CORPS

Hungnam

X CORPS
Shuttle from
Wonsan

Chongchon

Sinanju

Taedong

Kowon

Mine sweep
6-11 Nov.

3rd DIV. from
Moji Japan
5-20 Nov.

TF 77

TF 77
Replenishmt
Area

K o r e a

39

B a y

Mine sweep
29 Oct ft.

Pyongyang

XXXX
HQ EIGHTH
ARMY + FIFTH
AIR FORCE

Majonni

Wonsan

Kojo

USMC action
21-31 Oct.

Chinnampo

Taedong

Kyemipo

Sok-to
Cho-do

Samwon

Kosong

Mine sweep 2. Nov.
Landing 3-8 Nov.

38

Haeju
Haeju
Man

Ongjin

Kumchon

Kaesong

Hwachon

Soyang

Sokcho
Yangyang

Chumunjin

38

Han R.

Chunchon

Mukho

Mine sweep
completed 1 Nov.

Inchon

Seoul

Wonju

Samchok

37

Suwon

Osan

Chechon

Ulchin

37

Chonan

Chungju

Han R.

Chongju

Andong

Yongdok

100 f

36

Mine sweep
completed 2 Nov.

Kunsan

Chonju

Kum R.

Taejon

Songju

Taegu

Pohang

Kyongju

36

Chulpo

Hyopchon

Ulsan

Miryang

Kwangju

Namwon

Chinju

Masan

Pusan

35

Mokpo

Sunchon

Hadong

Samchon

Kojedo

Namhae

Yosu

Korea Strait

TSUSHIMA

35

Kangjin

Chindo

125   126   127   128   129   130   Raisz

a Nationalist Chinese source reported that the level of military activity in North China and Manchuria indicated an imminent all-out effort, and expressed fears that the forces of the U.N. were in grave danger. On the 5th a PBM patrol plane disappeared in Formosa Strait. Suddenly it seemed as if the party might be getting bigger.

In the X Corps zone the Chinese captured by the ROK forces were seen on 31 October by a Marine patrol, whose report constituted the first information on the new intervention to reach Washington. Queried at the request of the President as to his assessment of the situation, CincFE observed on 4 November that it was as yet impossible to appraise the "actualities of Chinese Communist intervention," put forward a variety of possible explanations, discounted the probability of a full-scale effort, and suggested the avoidance of hasty conclusions. But the reassuring tenor of this message was in contrast to the action undertaken in Korea.

In the west, where Eighth Army's logistic deficiencies still waited on the opening of Chinnampo, the discovery of Chinese soldiers was taken seriously. General Walker at once recalled his probing columns and formed his army up along the south bank of the Chongchon River, there to remain until the general offensive became possible. On the east coast, on 7 November, Admiral Doyle issued orders to expedite the movement of the 3rd Division from Moji to Korea by sailing ships independently as soon as they were loaded.

While these precautions were being taken on the ground, General MacArthur called upon FEAF and NavFE for their best efforts in the air. On the afternoon of 4 November CincFE's headquarters instructed Admiral Joy to apply the "immediate maximum air effort of your forces . . . in close support of ground units and interdiction of enemy communications, assembly areas and troop columns." Although the escort carriers were still at sea, supporting the 7th Division's northward advance, this unexpected order found the fast carriers in port in Japan. Action was immediate: Cardiv 15 was transferred from Admiral Doyle's control to that of Admiral Struble; the prospective return of *Valley Forge* to the United States was cancelled; task force personnel were rounded up from the pleasure spots of Japan, and on the morning of the 5th, with Commander Seventh Fleet in *Missouri* in company, Admiral Hoskins sortied *Valley Forge* and *Leyte* from Sasebo. Although winds to 50 knots were met en route, the next day found them back at work in the Sea of Japan, where they were joined on the 9th by Admiral Ewen in *Philippine Sea* from Yokosuka. They were to be there a long while.

A similar maximum effort was called for from FEAF, which on 5 November was instructed to fly its crews "to exhaustion if necessary" in a two-week effort "to destroy every means of communication and every installation, factory, city and village" below the Yalu River, the hydroelectric complex only excepted. So important was this effort deemed to be that the prohibition of incendiary attacks on inhabited areas, effective since the beginning of the conflict, was now rescinded.

Faced with the requirements of this offensive, and with the increasing probability of jet opposition, General Stratemeyer on 7 November urgently requested reinforcement of his fighter strength by something with higher performance than the F–80. On the next day he was promised a wing of F–84s and one of F–86As; on the 14th these began loading at San Diego on the escort carrier *Bairoko* and the light carrier *Bataan*. By 6 December some of these high-performance fighters were flying Korean missions, and once again the availability of carrier decks had made possible a demonstration of the "inherent mobility" of air power.

In Washington the news of the maximum air effort and of a projected B–29 attack against the Yalu bridges had caused another flurry. An order from the Joint Chiefs to suspend attacks within five miles of the border was coupled with a request for the reasons behind the air offensives. The reply elicited by this dispatch was couched in very different terms from CincFE's message of the 4th, which had discounted the likelihood of full-scale Chinese intervention. Now on the 6th General MacArthur reported "men and material in large force" pouring across the Yalu bridges and threatening "the ultimate destruction of the forces" under his command. Cancellation of the bridge strike might "well result in a calamity of major proportions"; the sole means of preventing enemy reinforcement was destruction of these bridges and of "all installations in the north area supporting the enemy advance."

Next day, however, the alarm was muted. In response to a request for an estimate of the situation, CincFE on 7 November struck an average of his previous messages. While emphasizing the importance of Communist air operations from beyond the Yalu, and requesting instructions which would permit him to deal with this development, General MacArthur observed that his early belief that the Chinese were not intervening on a major scale had been confirmed. In reply to these dispatches the Joint Chiefs authorized attacks against the Korean ends of the Yalu bridges, and against other targets up to the river's bank, while reemphasizing the necessity of avoiding violation of Manchurian territory or airspace.

Winter had now reached the Sea of Japan. There, back on location, Task Force 77 was maneuvering to avoid snow storms, sweeping and drying the carrier decks with the blast of jet engines, and putting forth its best efforts in interdiction of the area east of 126°40'E and south of a line five miles below the Manchurian border. At mid-day on the 8th a new priority target was added, as a flash message from ComNavFE informed Admiral Struble that CincFE had determined to destroy the first overwater span on the Korean side of all bridges leading to Manchuria. Since FEAF's

Bomber Command was fully committed to attacks on the downstream bridges at Sinuiju, those at Chongsongjin at the lower end of the Suiho Reservoir, where Air Force pilots had reported heavy vehicular traffic, had been assigned the Navy. Consistent with instructions from Washington, these strikes were to be carried out under restrictive ground rules: the target was the first over-water span, and that only; Manchurian air space was not to be violated; the hydroelectric plants and associated facilities were to remain untouched. Two days later the assignment was generalized by instructions to Task Force 77 to destroy the seven major bridges from Sinuiju eastward, through Chongsongjin, Namsan-ni, and Manpojin, to Hyesanjin at the headwaters of the Yalu.

These were extremely difficult targets. Since the approach had to be made either up or down stream, all attacks had to be carried out through predetermined airspace and subject to unimpeded antiaircraft and fighter opposition from the Manchurian side. To hit a single span, while crossing the narrow dimension of the bridge, was difficult for horizontal bombers owing to the intervals within their sticks of bombs; since crossing the bends in the river was forbidden, it was difficult for the B–29s to get a satisfactory aiming run. For the dive bombers this approach meant that any error in range, normally greater than that in deflection, would ensure a miss, while the attacks involved flights of over 220 miles, across high mountains and through winter weather, which called for the most accurate navigation.

Nine B–29s attacked the Sinuiju bridges on 8 November, while 70 more destroyed 60 percent of the town; next day the carriers flew strikes against the bridges there and at Chongsongjin. Three more days of carrier plane attacks were followed by a day of rest; on the 13th and 14th both B–29s and Task Force 77 returned to the fray. The week of the 15th brought four more carrier strikes, and in the last ten days of the month seven B–29 raids were mounted against the bridges.

The bridge attacks by carrier planes were made by groups of upwards of eight ADs, armed with one 2,000-pound bomb or two 1,000-pound bombs apiece, accompanied by Corsairs with VT-fused bombs and rockets to discourage antiaircraft fire from at least the Korean side of the river. For top cover, necessitated by the newly invigorated Communist air opposition, eight or more Panthers accompanied the attack planes. From their launching point in the Korean Gulf the piston-engined aircraft crossed the mountains at 10,000 feet with the Corsairs on top, climbed to 13,000 feet for a high-speed approach, and then, overhauled and joined by the jets some 60 miles short of the target, started their run in. At the objective the Corsairs went down first, to strike the defending gun emplacements, and were followed by the heavyweight ADs, while the F9Fs stepped down to protect against attacks from the rear.

This protection was needed. The enemy jets were real. On the 8th, in the first all-jet air battle of history, an Air Force F–80 fighter pilot had destroyed a MIG; on the 9th, during the attack at Sinuiju, a Navy pilot duplicated the feat, as Lieutenant Commander W. T. Amen of *Philippine Sea* chased one from 4,000 to 15,000 feet and down again before the enemy spun in. No more than the Air Force F–80s could the Navy fighters match the agile MIG in speed, maneuverability, or rate of climb, but training and gunnery worked to outweigh these adverse factors.

Faced with the double problem of aerial opposition and of antiaircraft gunfire from the sanctuary across the river, Admiral Ewen recommended that members of the U.N. Korean Commission, together with representatives of the Soviets and of the Communist Chinese, be sent up in a transport plane to orbit over and observe the border, and that permission be obtained for hot pursuit of unfriendly aircraft and for attacks on Manchurian batteries which opened fire. Nothing was to come of these suggestions, but the problems which gave rise to them remained, and on the 18th two more MIGs were shot down by pilots from *Valley Forge* and *Leyte*.

So far as it went the result of these engagements was encouraging, but the purpose of the strikes was to destroy the bridges, and here the bombing was spotty and the results disappointing. The carrier pilots succeeded in dropping the highway bridge at Sinuiju and in taking out spans at Hyesan-jin; the B–29s broke one or two more. But the Communists demonstrated great vigor and ingenuity in improvising repairs, and as November wore on the Yalu ice was thickening to the point where even heavy equipment could be moved across it.

As the airmen in Korea were flying against the bridges, and as the capitals of the world were considering the implications of Chinese intervention, headquarters estimates of Chinese forces in Korea were on the rise. On 2 November the estimated total was 16,500; by mid-month, when 12 divisions had been identified, it was of the order of 100,000. Total enemy strength, including North Koreans, was estimated at about 145,000 as of the 15th, a figure which was adhered to with little change until the 23rd when it developed a considerable spread, postulating either a minimum of 142,000 or a maximum of 167,000. Whether one accepted the minimum or the maximum or struck an average, this still implied a lot of Chinamen, and their presumed presence in the mountains of central North Korea brought further modification to the mission assigned to General Almond's forces.

These, since early November, had been pressing forward toward the Manchurian border. After concentrating in the neighborhood of Hamhung, the Marine Division had moved out to the north along the narrow road which leads to the Chosin Reservoir. One brisk fight with Chinese forces took place at Sudong, following which, as in the west, the opposition

The bridges at Sinuiju: Photograph of Leyte strike shows three spans out on the highway bridge, but the railroad bridge still stands. Across the Yalu, the Manchurian town of Antung. 14 November 1950. (USN 423495)

had disappeared. By the 10th the Marines were over the pass and had reached the headwaters of the Changjin River at Koto-ri; five days later they had gained the reservoir at Hagaru. To the eastward the advance had been still more rapid. ROK forces moving up the coast were approaching Chongjin. The 7th Division had captured Kapsan on the 12th and was moving toward Hyesanjin on the Yalu; although narrow mountain roads and subzero temperatures made progress arduous, no Chinese had been encountered.

Here in the northern mountains, 90 miles above the Wonsan-Pyongyang corridor, the concept of X Corps assistance to Eighth Army was revived by a directive of 15 November, which instructed General Almond to reorient his attack to the westward so as to facilitate the advance of General Walker's force. Instead of continuing north to the Manchurian border, the Marines were to strike west for 40 miles against the enemy's supply line. In the works for ten days, the orders for this flattering operation, in which one division was to clear the way for an army, were issued on the 25th, and required the Marine Division to move west from the reservoir to Mupyong-ni, and thence north through Kanggye to the Yalu.

By this time Admiral Doyle had finished off his east coast job. The harbors were open, the logistic situation was satisfactory, and the X Corps rear, firmly based upon the sea, was secure. Rather less, however, could be said for the advanced units, for the Yalu River towns of Manpojin and Hyesanjin, the ultimate objectives of the Marines and of the 7th Division, are 120 miles by air, and perhaps half as much again by mountain road, from the Hungnam base. The concept of the operation is a puzzling one, for while the reorientation of the Marines' thrust was predicated on the need to help Eighth Army, its extent implied an expectation of non-resistance, and seemed based less on assumptions regarding Chinese capabilities than on assumptions of intent which, if correct, would make the effort hardly necessary.

In the west, since first contact with the Chinese, Eighth Army headquarters had entertained serious doubts about the future. Early in November Admiral Joy had begun to fear that the war would last out the winter; by mid-month he had come to feel that the Chinese had the manpower to expel the U.N. from Korea, and was keeping his fingers crossed against a third World War. Dubious of this winter campaign, General Smith had earlier suggested holding merely the territory covering Hamhung and Wonsan, and even the ever-sanguine Almond had been concerned. But at GHQ, where the strategic art was cultivated in its pure form, optimism appeared to have returned, and lack of contact with the Chinese to have brought the belief that they would fade away. On 18 November General MacArthur concluded that the all-out air effort had isolated the battlefield and restricted enemy supply; this and the logistic improvement which had followed the opening of Chinnampo led him to fix the 24th as the date for Eighth Army's offensive.

At sea, as on land, this was a period of contradictions. Following the strikes against the Yalu bridges the airmen had again found targets short: on the 18th the escort carriers were withdrawn; on the 19th *Valley Forge* and two destroyers were detached and ordered to the United States for overhaul. On the 22nd, as the day for the advance approached, Commander Weymouth flew to Seoul to confer with Fifth Air Force on the desired employment of the air groups of the remaining two fast carriers. This was not much. No close support was wanted, whether for Eighth Army or for X Corps. Seventh Fleet aircraft, with those of FEAF's Bomber Command, were to concentrate their efforts on bridges and communications within a 15-mile strip along the Yalu.

To Commander Task Force 77 the proposal for interdiction flights in western Korea from carriers in the Sea of Japan seemed uneconomical. As a better employment of available force, he suggested that he assume responsibility for supplemental close support of X Corps. But the proposal was turned down.

On 19 November, Moscow broadcast promises of a great offensive which would destroy the U.N. armies. On the 20th CincFE issued orders regarding the etiquette for U.N. forces at the border. Its sanctity was to be meticulously preserved; only small elements would be advanced to its immediate neighborhood; the hydroelectric plants, which served both North Korea and Manchuria, would be kept in uninterrupted operation. On the 24th the opening of the offensive was announced in confident terms. Again it appeared to some that the war was about to end, if not by Thanksgiving at least by Christmas.

CHAPTER IX

Retreat to the South

1. 24 November–6 December: Defeat in the West

IMPORTED, sustained, brought forward, and now at last supplied by sea, the multinational ground forces of the U.N. made ready for the final offensive. On 24 November, as Chinese Communist representatives were arriving at Lake Success to complain of American aggression in Formosa, Eighth Army attacked north from the Chongchon River. On the left the II Corps moved forward through the coastal plain; in the center the IX Corps, with the 2nd Infantry Division on its right, advanced northward up the valleys of the Kuryong and the Chongchon; at Tokchon in the central mountains the ROK II Corps, under General Walker's command although not part of Eighth Army, was under orders to establish contact with X Corps to the northeast. The advance of the Army was supported by Fifth Air Force, while aircraft of Bomber Command and Task Force 77 patrolled a 15-mile strip below the Manchurian border. Progress on the 24th was satisfactory all along the line.

Across the peninsula to the northeast, supported by the fighter squadrons of the 1st Marine Aircraft Wing and by an Air Force fighter-bomber group, General Almond's X Corps was again preparing to act as the right arm of the pincer. Up in the high country, 65 mountainous miles from Tokchon, the 7th Marines were moving west from Hagaru to Yudam-ni, where they arrived on the 25th after meeting only light opposition, and where next day they were joined by RCT 5. No more than their predecessors did the 5th Marines have trouble on the road, although interrogation of Chinese prisoners and information from local inhabitants indicated that three Chinese divisions had reached the area. In compliance with the revised plan for X Corps operations General Smith intended to pass the 5th Marines through RCT 7, and to attack westward from Yudam-ni on the morning of the 27th.

But while operations at the reservoir were of a routine nature, things were happening in the west. There on the 25th heavy pressure had developed on the right at Tokchon, and the 2nd Division had been engaged by Chinese Communist forces. By the next day the ROK II Corps had broken before the CCF assault, the right flank was exposed, and the Turkish Brigade and the 1st Cavalry Division were ordered up to bolster the threatened IX Corps.

Before the westward thrust from Yudam-ni was scheduled to begin, Eighth Army's offensive had been stopped.

On the morning of the 27th, following a night of zero temperature and high winds, the 5th Marines nevertheless led out to the west. But the advance was limited to less than a mile by strong Chinese forces entrenched in the hills overlooking the road. With darkness very heavy attacks were launched by two Chinese divisions against the 5th and 7th Marines, while east of the reservoir three Army battalions were assaulted by a third. At Yudam-ni, where violent fighting continued throughout the night and into the morning, the enemy was ultimately repelled. But casualties were heavy, and in the rear, between Yudam-ni and Hagaru, the Chinese controlled the road, and had cut off and surrounded two companies. Further advance was out of the question, and in the afternoon General Smith issued orders halting the movement to the west.

Across the peninsula in the western lowlands things were even worse. On 27 November, as enemy pressure increased, advanced forces on the coastal plain were ordered back across the Chongchon. By the next day Eighth Army was in full retreat and the 2nd Division was desperately trying to extricate itself from a position of the gravest peril. With evening of the 28th Generals Walker and Almond were summoned to Tokyo for a conference with CincFE who, after authorizing Eighth Army and X Corps to withdraw, reported to Washington that the U.N. Command had met "conditions beyond its control and its strength," that he had gone over to the defensive, and that "we face an entirely new war."

Subject only to the deletion of the adjective "entirely," the statement appears correct. Once again an intervention from outside had changed the scale of the Korean conflict, and had removed control of their destinies still further from the inhabitants of the peninsula. The original elder brother had returned, and his forces, it was now sufficiently clear, were not limited to a sprinkling of volunteers but included important components of two field armies. Shortly some 30 Chinese divisions would be identified in North Korea, totalling perhaps 250,000 men, and the imaginative expansion of the NKPA remnants to a strength of 180,000 which was quickly accomplished by GHQ intelligence was not necessary to the proposition that the enemy was once again formidable. In the air the situation had also changed, and fighter planes of very advanced design were operating from the Manchurian fields across the Yalu River. Unlike the situation in June the prospect of U.N. reinforcement was dim: the commitment of very considerable forces to the theater of action had left practically nothing in reserve; the greater part of the Pacific Fleet was in the forward area and Army strength in the continental United States was down to a single division.

Yet not everything was new and different; in some respects the pattern was familiar. The new enemy, like the old, was based on the Asiatic mainland; the forces of the United Nations were still sustained by sea. Again intelligence had been available, again there had been surprise. As had been the case five months before, rapid enemy successes brought rapid retirement by the ground forces of the U.N. At sea, where enemy strength was still conspicuous by its absence, Naval Forces Far East retained the responsibility for any necessary evacuation of friendly nationals, a responsibility now greatly enlarged. As before, enemy offensive efforts in the air were negligible; as before, the full employment of U.N. air strength was hindered by circumstance. In July the problem had been one of range, and the lack of advanced airfields had placed a premium on available carrier strength; in November a dearth of identifiable targets had limited the effectiveness of Air Force and naval aviation alike; in December the forced abandonment of forward bases would bring the range problem back to the fore. Once again a period of emergency would raise problems of Navy-Air Force coordination. New war, in many respects, was just old war writ large.

Even before General MacArthur had reported his shift to the defensive, the Navy had begun to react. At Admiral Joy's headquarters, where the possibility of a general emergency had been kept steadily in mind, the first appearance of the Chinese had caused concern. Planning had been expedited, and Operation Plan 116–50, laying down procedures for an emergency evacuation of U.N. forces from Korea, had been issued on 13 November. Enunciating the concept that any such operation "should be based upon the principle of an 'assault in reverse,' " this plan provided detailed hydrographic and loading information for Korean and Japanese ports, gave figures on troop capacity of both commercial and combatant shipping, and established a command structure in which CTF 90, supported by other theater naval forces, would control naval and air operations in evacuation areas. Rarely, it would seem, have the routine precautions of the planners proved of such immediate value. At 1534 on 28 November ComNavFE alerted Admiral Doyle for a possible general emergency which would require redeployment of the ground forces from Korea to Japan.

On receipt of this dispatch CTF 90 and his staff at once worked out preliminary plans for the deployment of half the Amphibious Force to west coast operations under Admiral Thackrey and half to the Wonsan–Hungnam area. Next day the operation order was promulgated, all ships were alerted to the possibility of air attack, Task Force 90 was placed on six-hour notice, amphibious shipping in Korean waters was held there, and all units at Yokosuka were ordered down to Sasebo.

As the first steps were being taken to prepare for the ultimate emergency other action was underway to prevent its development. On the 28th, in response to a Fifth Air Force request, Task Force 77 had expanded its area of armed reconnaissance southward, and throughout the day *Philippine Sea* and *Leyte* had kept eight Corsairs and six ADs over the newly enlarged border strip. But reports of the apparent crisis which confronted EUSAK led Admiral Ewen to feel that more could and should be done, and that circumstances called less for armed reconnaissance than for support of troops. On conclusion of operations on the 28th he proposed to Admiral Struble that the six flights scheduled for the next day be routed to check in with the Fifth Air Force Tactical Air Control Center and offer their services in close support before proceeding to the border zone, and that consideration on the highest level be given the assignment to EUSAK of Marine tactical air control parties for the handling of available naval aircraft. In the evening Commander Seventh Fleet passed the first of these suggestions to Fifth Air Force.

For the present this offer of assistance by the two Seventh Fleet fast carriers was all that could be done to provide increased support to the armies in the peninsula. For the future, despite the heavy deployment to Far Eastern waters, some further accretions of force could still be called for. To the British at Hong Kong went an urgent call to hurry back, and on 1 December Andrewes sailed for Sasebo in *Theseus,* to be shortly followed by *Kenya.* From Formosa Strait the cruiser *Manchester* was ordered up to Korean waters. Destroyer Division 31, en route to the west coast for overhaul, was ordered to reverse course. The sailing of the APA *Bexar* for the United States was cancelled. *Sicily* and her antisubmarine squadron had just reached Japan from Guam; once again she was directed to unload in order to embark Marine fighter planes. The light carrier *Bataan,* with her load of high-performance Air Force jets, was just arriving at Yokosuka, and the escort carrier *Bairoko* was on the way; shortly ComNavFE would request permission to retain these ships so as to have decks available for more Marines should the Wonsan and Yonpo airstrips be overrun. First of the carriers to see action in the summer war, *Valley Forge* was now halfway across the Pacific on her way home; she was instructed to expedite her movement to the United States, exchange her air group for that of *Boxer,* and return at once.

This evolution, however, would take time, and for the moment Task Force 77 contained only two carriers. That earlier reinforcement would prove possible was due to the existence of the mothball fleet, and to the reactivation program previously begun. On 25 July the Chief of Naval Operations had ordered the activation of the fast carrier *Princeton,* then in reserve at Bremerton. Recommissioned on 28 August, under command of Captain William O. Gallery and with a crew largely composed of recalled reservists, *Princeton* had completed her period of shakedown training, had embarked Rear Admiral Ralph A. Ofstie, Commander Carrier Division 5, and had sailed from the west coast in early November. On the 25th she departed Pearl Harbor for the Western Pacific; on the 27th, on orders from CincPacFleet to proceed at maximum safe speed, she went up to 30 knots; on the 30th ComNavFE instructed her to proceed directly to the operating area.

On 29 and 30 November Eighth Army continued its retreat across the Chongchon River. On the left disengagement proceeded without great difficulty, but there was trouble in the center, and on the right the situation was very bad. The Turkish Brigade, moved forward following the ROK collapse, was roughly handled, while the 2nd Division, after a difficult crossing of the Chongchon, became entangled in a five-mile roadblock north of Sunchon. Cut off and cut up, swept with fire from the hills along the road and blocked by its own vehicles, the division became disorganized, and in a two-day ordeal lost some 40 percent of its personnel and most of its guns and gear.

That these losses, great though they were, were not still greater, was due in considerable part to an all-out effort by Fifth Air Force against the attacking Chinese, an effort to some degree assisted by the air groups of the fast carriers. On the morning of the 29th, pursuant to his suggestion of the previous evening, Admiral Ewen sent seven Corsairs and five ADs across the peninsula to offer their services in close support. Passed from hand to hand for a time, they were finally instructed to circle Kunu-ri in the 2nd Division trouble zone; there, after a 25-minute wait, they were directed onto a troop concentration north of the town. This qualified success, together with Air Force acceptance of his offer of the 28th, led CTF 77 to route all armed reconnaissance flights for the 30th through a point in 39° 30′ N 126° E, near the big bend in the Taedong and just east of the pass in which the 2nd Division was engaged in dubious combat, to offer their loads for close support to any controller they could reach. But by the time these instructions were issued new claims on the fast carriers had developed.

Up on the plateau, following the attacks of the 27th and 28th, comparative quiet reigned, but the enemy controlled the roads and Marine and Army units had been separated into a series of isolated perimeters. In this situation General Harris, the Marine air commander, had strongly recommended to ComNavFE a sustained effort by the fast carriers in the X Corps zone, and had stated that Fifth Air Force concurred in this proposal. But an evening dispatch from FAFIK on the 29th indicated that such concurrence applied only to that day's operations, and asked, in view of the "critical condition" in the EUSAK area, a divided effort for the next few days. And a message from ComNavFE, confirming that close support had priority over all other commitments, prescribed such distribution of carrier air effort.

The sorties of the 30th were consequently so divided, and the schedule of operations stepped up by the addition of five jet flights of four planes each. Thirty-nine sorties were sent up to the reservoir while 74, including 23 jet sorties, were dispatched on armed reconnaissance with instructions to report en route to any available Air Force control agency. As always in emergencies there were difficulties. In X Corps zone, communications were overcrowded and radio discipline poor, but the coherence of Marine units had not been broken and most flights found control. In the west, by contrast, the state of affairs was chaotic: the Fifth Air Force had already been forced out of its forward staging fields at Sinanju on the Chongchon, some advanced control parties had been overrun, irreplaceable control equipment had been lost, and evacuation of the Mosquito control planes from the Pyongyang airfields was in progress.

The effects of this situation were apparent in difficulties of aircraft control. Of four jet flights to the EUSAK zone three made no contact. Of the heavily-armed strike groups of Corsairs and Skyraiders that were dispatched to the west, one was weathered out, one failed to find a controller, and one found good control. There were delays, and when one flight came across to the west, after failing to make contact in the X Corps area, the ADs were incomprehensibly detached from attack to road reconnaissance. But control once gained was fair to excellent: the two propeller strikes which did make contact put 14 Corsairs and 5 ADs with more than 14 tons of napalm and 5 of bombs onto troop concentrations in the crucial 2nd Division area; the jet flight, after being directed against entrenched troops south of Tokchon, ran the roads north to Manpojin.

Considering the conditions under which advanced Air Force units were working this was not too bad a performance, but to Admiral Ewen, lacking detailed information on the state of affairs in the west, it seemed that the situation of early September was repeating itself. At 2230 on the 30th he informed Commander Seventh Fleet that while all missions sent to X Corps had been successful, about two-thirds of the effort in the EUSAK zone had been wasted, and asked him to pass the word to Fifth Air Force. This Struble did in a midnight emergency dispatch in which he reiterated his desire to help, stated that in view of unsatisfactory control in the west he would adjust his distribution of effort, and asked to be advised when the situation improved.

By now the successes of the Chinese had ended all possibility of coordinated effort by Eighth Army and X Corps, and in the two theaters of action very different types of operations were developing. In the west, as December opened, the remnants of the 2nd Division had at last reached Sunchon, and Eighth Army was disengaging and moving south toward Pyongyang. But in the X Corps zone, where the Marine Division had been fragmented and cut off, the situation was one of beleaguered strong points. On the plateau maximum air support was needed; across the peninsula, movement requirements took precedence over those for firepower.

These conditions governed the distribution of Task Force 90. On the 30th, with the ground situation steadily deteriorating, Admiral Doyle put all ships in port on two-hour notice and began to deploy his shipping to Korea. Transports were divided on a 50–50 basis, with four APAs and two AKAs being ordered to Inchon and a like number to Wonsan. But the apparently more critical situation of Eighth Army, together with the problems of handling large ships in west coast ports, led to the assignment of two-thirds of other amphibious types to Admiral Thackrey's Task Group 90.1. Thackrey himself had flown to Inchon with General Walker on the 29th to inspect and advise on port operations. On the next day two members of his staff went up to Chinnampo to look things over, and the APA *Bexar,* the LSD *Catamount,* and two LSTs were added to his command. On 1 December, as Thackrey reported aboard *Mount McKinley* at Hungnam to confer with Admiral Doyle and to plan for the future, his flagship *Eldorado,* two more LSDs, and the fast transport *H. A. Bass* were ordered west, along with ten Scajap LSTs.

In eastern North Korea, where the ground battle was still developing, X Corps on 1 December ordered a retirement upon Hungnam. Since only the forces on the plateau had been engaged, the concentration of the other units from such widely dispersed points as Wonsan, Hyesanjin, and Chongjin would be successfully accomplished by routine land and sea movement. But while no requirement for emergency evacuation as yet existed, the situation of the Marine Division and of the Army battalions at the reservoir was such as to cause the greatest concern. The division which had been moved forward to aid the advance of an army was now surrounded, and the army was in no position to return the favor. With the MSR cut, with supplies running short and casualties accumulating, air supply, air evacuation, and the maximum possible air support were urgently required.

Although retirement rather than advance was now the order of the day, the Chinese attack had put X Corps back in the kind of beachhead situation that had existed at Inchon and had been planned for at Wonsan. The collapse in the west had forced Fifth Air Force back to fields at Seoul and beyond, and local air support depended upon the two east coast air strips and upon embarked aviation. Recognizing this situation, FAFIK on 1 December cut existing red tape, gave General Harris autonomy in the conduct of air operations in support of X Corps, and instructed him to proceed without reference to Fifth Air Force except when reinforcements were needed. And the first days of December saw a steady shift of the fast carrier effort toward complete concentration in the X Corps zone.

Commander Seventh Fleet's relay of Admiral Ewen's complaint had elicited an emergency reply. On the morning of the 1st, Fifth Air Force reported that many of its TACPs appeared to have been lost to enemy action in the fluid situation then prevailing, that every effort was being made to provide replacements, and that instructions had been issued to give naval flights priority of employment. And as had been proposed by someone in one or another service in every crisis since early July, the Air Force now suggested that for better coordination CTF 77 should provide a representative at the JOC and should establish a direct radio link.

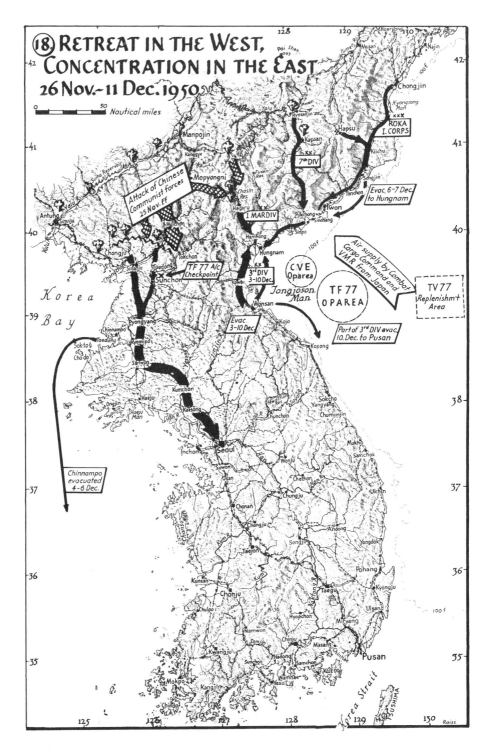

In part for technical reasons, in part because of the complex structure of the U.N. Command, communications between Fifth Air Force and the fast carriers had long presented a problem. But somewhere, in some corner of the JOC, there did in fact exist a direct CW radio circuit, activated on 6 November at the persistent urging of the task force communication officer, over which for two days drill messages had passed with gratifying speed. What was wanted by the Air Force, however, appears to have been a voice circuit rather than a manually-keyed one, and this was provided a few days later, by which time Commander Weymouth had once again been flown in to the JOC. And once again, under the lash of necessity, coordination began to improve.

On 1 December the weather over eastern Korea was very bad. Morning flights from the carriers met a solid overcast over the plateau and were diverted to the EUSAK area, where three missions totalling 23 aircraft found satisfactory control, successfully attacked large concentrations of enemy troops and abandoned friendly equipment, and blew an ammunition dump at Sinanju. But the weather which had altered their employment also prevented their return to base, for the task force had been obliged to cease flight operations late in the morning. Unable to get home, the aircraft landed at Wonsan, were kicked out again owing to rumors of a deteriorating ground situation in the neighborhood, and finally spent the night at Kimpo.

Next day the fast carriers again split their efforts, sending 28 sorties to EUSAK and half again as many to the Chosin area. In the west two flights with 10 aircraft had good success, while three totalling 18 found no controllers. But these were the last sorties sent to the western front, where EUSAK had by now disengaged, and where fears of being outflanked and forced back upon Chinnampo had ended all thoughts of holding a line at the waist along the Pyongyang-Wonsan road. On 3 December, as the Fifth Air Force was completing the first stage of its redeployment to South Korea and to Japan, General Walker's command post displaced from Pyong-yang to Seoul, and service units began packing up for the move south. Two days later the North Korean capital was abandoned to the enemy.

The rapid southward movement of Eighth Army, which threatened momently to leave Chinnampo uncovered, called urgently for the evacuation of that port. The urgency was nothing new, for in five months of war in Korea emergencies had become routine. Surprisingly, however, the sequence of planning and execution, although often greatly condensed, had not pre-viously broken down; the organizational framework had remained intact, and operations had tested the technical competence of juniors in the execu-tion of orders rather than their initiative in crisis when orders failed to come. Now for the first time the collapse in the west, and the short interval between defeat on the Chongchon and retirement from Pyongyang, put the job up to those on the spot.

In the course of the movement of amphibious shipping to Korea, Transport Squadron 1, Captain Kelly in *Bayfield,* had been assigned to Task Group 90.1 and ordered to Inchon. On 30 November and 1 December these ships—the APAs *Bayfield, Bexar* and *Okanogan,* and the AKAs *Algol* and *Montague*—had sailed independently from Japanese ports. On the afternoon of the 3rd, while heading northward into the Yellow Sea, Kelly intercepted a message from ComNavFE to CTG 90.1 which reported an urgent EUSAK request for the dispatch of these ships to Chinnampo, but which expressed doubts as to the possibility of loading and protecting so many large units there. But Admiral Thackrey was still on his Korean travels, his flagship was at sea, and his staff was slow to act. For five hours, as *Bayfield* steamed northward, Captain Kelly puzzled over the tone of ComNavFE's message and the lack of implementing instructions. At 2200 he decided to wait no more but to sail to the sound of the guns, and ordered his dispersed units to join him off the Chinnampo swept channel in the morning.

Others were swinging into action too. At 0330 on the 4th *Bayfield* intercepted a message from Admiral Smith to Thackrey which reported that the six west coast destroyers of TE 95.12, Captain Jeffrey V. Brock, RCN, in *Cayuga,* were available to protect the transports, and that *Ceylon* was being started from Sasebo for the west coast. Unknown to Kelly, still more help was on the way, for Admiral Andrewes, after a hasty return from Hong Kong to Sasebo, was preparing to sail with *Theseus* and four destroyers for the Yellow Sea.

Naval units already at Chinnampo consisted of the DE *Foss,* Lieutenant Commander Henry J. Ereckson, which was providing the city with electric power, and a small Korean naval base command with three motor launches; off the mouth of the Taedong River the minesweeping group was still at work. These too were standing to their posts. Offshore the sweepers took station to guide incoming ships along the tortuous channel. At 0236 of the 4th Ereckson reported that the situation in Chinnampo was shaky, but that he would keep the power on as long as possible, evacuate Eighth Army personnel, and then at the last, if still senior officer, would form a convoy and get the shipping out. Shortly the Korean base commander advised his superiors that EUSAK had ordered him to redeploy at once, and that with 100 sailboats and 50,000 refugees on hand he would try to send 30,000 out by sea and the remainder overland.

Through the night the transport group steamed on. By 0425, when orders to proceed to Chinnampo were finally received, Kelly's initiative had gained him more than six hours, and by 0930 all but *Bexar* had reached the outer end of the 84-mile swept channel and were standing in. Despite requests for information no word had been received on the size and shape of the units to be evacuated, the tactical situation ashore, the availability of ground or air support, or on who was to command the operation. But they had their orders, they believed that beleaguered army units were awaiting them, so on they went. At noon Kelly issued his operation order: man all guns, lower all boats, commence loading at once, keep steam up to the throttles. And then, at last, dispatches began to arrive: Brock's destroyers were heading his way; *Theseus* would have air cover there next day; he was in charge.

The anchors went down, the boats were launched. The call for help had been answered. Having thrust their heads into the lion's mouth it was discouraging to the transport crews to discover that the only EUSAK units in the Chinnampo area were the 1,700 men of the port logistics group, that these had their own shipping on hand, and that while perhaps 6,000 Koreans—wounded soldiers, government workers, military and political prisoners, police and boy scouts—had some official claim on transportation, the number was hardly enough to fill the transport group. There was no need for *Bexar,* who had reached the entrance channel at 1830, but it was too late to stop her: her commanding officer had smelled powder too, so single screw, low power, and all, in she came through the dark and snow.

All transports were now in and loading was in progress. The remaining problem was to get out. Quite apart from the hazards of navigation, Chinnampo is a poor place to be caught in, for the reverse slopes of the hills that front the harbor are within mortar range of the anchorage. Word from the Army ashore indicated an 80-mile gap in the lines to the north, the enemy was reported in Pyongyang and heading for Chinnampo, no combat forces were available, and the service troops manning the road blocks were to be withdrawn at midnight. In this situation a dispatch from Captain Brock, inquiring as to the state of affairs and offering to come in in the dark if needed, was very welcome, and the offer was accepted. Off the mouth of the Taedong the destroyers got the word at 2100 and started in at once, and this time the passage took its toll. *Warramunga* grounded but got off later with little damage; *Sioux* fouled a screw in a buoy cable and turned back; but by 0240 of the 5th *Cayuga, Athabaskan, Bataan,* and *Forrest Royal* were anchored with their guns trained on the Chinnampo waterfront.

With the destroyers on hand things looked better. Throughout the morning, as loading continued, sailboats packed with refugees slipped down the river. *Foss* kept the power on, the ROKN shore party guarded the docks while their small boats patrolled the harbor, and in the afternoon aircraft from *Theseus* appeared overhead. Beginning at 1230 the transports were sailed independently, and by 1430 the beach was being cleared. A late influx of refugees had left 3,000 at the docks, but their problem was providentially solved by the unexpected arrival of an MSTS vessel which had failed to receive notice of its diversion to a safer destination. *Ceylon,* now standing in the entrance channel, was ordered to stay outside, and at 1730 *Bexar,* last of the transports, headed downstream escorted by *Foss.* In the harbor the LSTs with the port logistics personnel anchored for the night, and the destroyers bombarded oil storage, harbor cranes, and railway equipment. One final emergency developed when *Bexar,* having made both inward and outward voyages in darkness, grounded north of Sokto. But she got herself off without damage, and with morning the destroyers and LSTs made an uneventful downstream passage to reach Cho Do at noon and anchor in a blinding snowstorm.

As in the first days of the summer war, a west coast port had been evacuated. As in July the armies were retiring and the situation was a gloomy one. General MacArthur had earlier planned to remove Eighth Army from Korea by Christmas, leaving X Corps as an occupation force, and in an unanticipated fashion it seemed that much of this plan was coming true. Eighth Army was almost clear of North Korea, and consideration was already being given to the abandonment of Seoul and the fortification of the Naktong River line; the X Corps area of occupation, however, was a diminishing one, and the Marines were still outnumbered, surrounded, and far from the sea. Again, as in the summer, visibility was poor, and none knew what would happen next. On 29 November CTF 95 had warned west coast units of the possibility of air attack from across the Yellow Sea; on the next day a special antisubmarine patrol had been instituted off Sasebo. At NavFE headquarters the intervention of the Chinese had expanded planning responsibilities from matters of postwar redeployment to problems of more pressing concern, and from Korean waters to the entire coast of Asia. Momentarily an invasion of Formosa seemed imminent as a Navy patrol plane reported a fleet of junks heading eastward from the mainland. An unconfirmed intelligence report indicated that the Soviets were preparing an all-out air attack against Japan. On 6 December, in view of possible contingencies, the Joint Chiefs of Staff sent out a general alarm to American forces throughout the world.

2. *14 November–10 December: The Campaign at the Reservoir*

Fifty miles north of Hungnam, at an altitude of 3,400 feet, lies the Chosin Reservoir. For 13 miles from north to south and 8 from east to west its narrow arms extend into the mountain valleys. At Yudam-ni at the western extremity there are a few square yards of flat land; at Hagaru at the southern tip there is rather more; but in general the shores are steep, and the hills which rim the water's edge are ringed at a distance of five or ten miles by mountains rising 3,000 feet above the reservoir. The country is barren and sparsely populated; the vegetation a none-too-plentiful mixture of fir, aspen, and brush. Between Hungnam at the sea and Hagaru, where the Marine

Division had established its advanced base, a single road, narrow, twisting, inadequate to heavy traffic, and with bridges of only light construction, provided the MSR.

On their way up-hill the Marines had encountered two new enemies, the Chinese and the cold. Between 2 and 7 November vigorous resistance had been offered in the neighborhood of Sudong by CCF units with tank and artillery support; there was evidence that two more Chinese divisions were operating to the westward; a further build-up was suggested by pilots' reports of troops approaching from the northwest and north. But with air support the Chinese roadblocks were broken, Koto-ri was entered on 11 November and Hagaru on the 14th, and aerial reconnaissance indicated that the enemy was straggling to the northwest. Yet if the Chinese had for the moment gone, winter had come. Intermittent snowfall, encountered during the advance up-hill, had by now blanketed the plateau. As early as mid-November canteens were freezing and bursting, while by December night temperatures would at times reach 25° below zero. Climatically, at least, the Marines did face a new war.

Through this extreme cold, which brought frostbite and respiratory disease to personnel, adversely affected the operation of weapons and equipment, and made foxhole digging in the frozen earth a six to eight-hour affair, the northward advance had continued. By late November the entire Marine Division was strung out along the 75 miles of road from Hungnam to Yudam-ni. Two regiments were in the Yudam-ni area, division headquarters and an infantry battalion were located at Hagaru, while on the MSR the villages of Koto-ri and Chinhung-ni were garrisoned by something more than two battalions. A total of about seven days' supply had been dumped on the plateau. Against this force, divided and far from base and with a strength of slightly more than 25,000, there would be committed during the next two weeks eight divisions from three Chinese Communist armies whose strength totalled some 60,000 men.

Chinese movement into Korea had begun in mid-October, as the Eighth Army was approaching Pyongyang, with the passage of the Yalu by leading elements of the Fourth CCF Field Army, General Lin Piao. As he deployed to oppose General Walker's advance, Lin had detached his 42nd Army to cover his left against the intrusions of X Corps; this unit had been the source of the opposition against which the Marines had run up at Sudong. Following the movement of the Fourth Field Army, the 9th Army Group of General Chen Yi's Third Field Army had crossed over into Korea to oppose X Corps; Lin's units had retired to the westward, and had been replaced at Yudam-ni by four divisions of the 20th Army. The intention of this force, according to prisoners, was to bypass the advancing Marines and cut the MSR to the east and south.

Other Chinese movements were also in progress. As the 20th **Army** approached from the northwest, two divisions of the 27th Army moved down on the reservoir from the north and there divided, with one moving onward against Yudam-ni and the other coming down the eastern shore. With completion of these movements in the last days of November the two Marine regiments at Yudam-ni found themselves engaged by two divisions, one from the 20th Army and one from the 27th; a second division from the 27th Army had attacked the three battalions of the 7th Infantry Division east of the reservoir; bypassing the American forces, the three remaining 20th Army divisions had moved onward to cut the road east of Yudam-ni, to attack the advanced base at Hagaru, and to operate against the Hamhung road in the neighborhood of Koto-ri.

On the plateau, as in the west, Chinese tactics were to permit, indeed to encourage, a maximum extension of U.N. forces, and then to cut the MSR, press against the column from all sides, fracture, fragment, and destroy it. Such procedures had been effective on the Chongchon River, but although the Marines were far deeper in enemy country, and had a far more precarious line of communications, the success was not to be repeated. Rather than extending itself along the road, the Marine Division formed the modern equivalent of the square and, with firepower maintained through air supply and multiplied by air support, accomplished the extrication of its units and the destruction of its enemies. By night the Marines, concentrated and dug in in tight perimeters, presented heavily-armed strong points on which the Chinese impaled themselves in the attack. By day, with close support aircraft on station and with flanking forces clearing the heights along the road, they formed moving fortresses which brushed the Communists aside, while over the hill, beyond artillery range, the extension of fire power by Marine and Navy aircraft kept the enemy down.

The coming of the Chinese onslaught had found the fast carriers still committed to armed reconnaissance. On 28 November the forces available to General Harris consisted of MAG 12 with two fighter and one night fighter squadrons at Wonsan, MAG 33 with one fighter and one night fighter squadron at Yonpo and a fighter squadron in *Badoeng Strait,* and the Air Force's 35th Fighter-Bomber Group at Yonpo. There were plenty of calls on the services of these units. At Chinhung-ni, in the southern sector of the MSR, Chinese probing attacks had begun on the 26th; west of Koto-ri, next day, Marine patrols had encountered the new enemy; on the night of the 27th heavy fighting had broken out in Yudam-ni and east of the reservoir. On the 28th liaison pilots reported that the enemy controlled the road between Yudam-ni and Toktong Pass, between the pass and Hagaru, and between Hagaru and Koto-ri, and in addition to thus segmenting the Marine Division into four groups had surrounded the Army forces east of the reservoir. In all these areas enemy pressure continued, but the central problem, on which the future of all units on the plateau depended, was the defense of Hagaru.

At Hagaru there were located three irreplaceable commodities. There the Marine Division had set up its command post, there supplies had been laid down for the developing campaign, and there, on one of the few flat pieces of ground in North Korea, was an incipient airstrip, begun on the 18th with the intention of providing facilities for twin-engined transport aircraft, which by the 27th was about a quarter completed. But the defensive force available for the protection of this investment was very limited, and consisted merely of one rifle battalion, two batteries of artillery, and service and division troops. General Smith had ordered reinforcements up from Koto-ri, but the Chinese did not await their coming and on the night of 28–29 November committed two regiments against the perimeter. Violent fighting continued throughout the frozen darkness and the line was more than once broken, but the enemy proved unable to exploit his gains. Although pressure remained heavy on the 29th the first crisis had been surmounted.

With Hagaru still holding out, the second phase of the campaign began. Control of the Army forces at the reservoir was passed to General Smith, who was directed to concentrate all units at Hagaru in anticipation of a further move to the southward. Pursuant to these instructions the forces at Yudam-ni were ordered to fight their way back, and on the afternoon of 1 December, after a day of preparation, the 5th and 7th Marines disengaged and started south for Hagaru.

Orders from X Corps had contemplated the employment of one of these regiments to bring out the beleaguered 7th Division units from Sinhung-ni on the eastern shore of the reservoir. But some time would elapse before this would be possible, and no other forces were available for this task. The reinforcements ordered up from Koto-ri had had a difficult time of it on the road, only a part had managed to get through, and the night of 30 November brought further heavy attacks at Hagaru and against the Army battalions. On the morning of 1 December, therefore, the Army troops were ordered to break out to the southward at the earliest possible time, and were advised that while no troop assistance could be given, owing to the situation at Hagaru, maximum air support would be provided.

The air strength available for the support of X Corps had by this time been considerably increased, as a result of the eastward shift of the fast carrier effort. On the 30th, following General Harris' first request for carrier air, Task Force 77 had sent 39 sorties to the reservoir, of which 14 struck at Chinese troops surrounding the isolated Army units while 25 attacked the enemy in the hills about Hagaru. By bad luck, however, the next day brought bad weather both at the reservoir and in the Sea of Japan. Although aircraft from *Badoeng Strait* and Marine shore-based squadrons got through to napalm the Chinese enemy, the early flights from Task Force 77 were weathered out of the reservoir, and in late morning the force was obliged to cancel operations. At midday the Army troops began their southward movement with 20 fighters overhead, but in the course of the afternoon a combination of heavy attacks and enemy roadblocks fragmented the column, most officers and key NCOs became casualties, and as darkness fell the force dissolved. It had almost made it in: the disintegration took place only four and a half miles from Hagaru; but although a number of stragglers was brought in across the frozen reservoir, total casualties reached almost 75 percent.

Tragic though it was, this was to be the last such enemy success. It was not only in the eastward movement of carrier effort that the support situation was improving A plan on the part of the patrol squadrons to provide air supply and evacuation by flying boat had been abandoned when the first flights disclosed that the reservoir was frozen solid. But air drops had been begun on the 28th by Marine and Air Force transport planes, and Combat Cargo Command, by notable efforts, had by 1 December increased deliveries from 70 to 250 tons a day. Despite the violent Chinese attacks, work on the Hagaru airstrip had been pressed around the clock; almost half-completed by the 1st, it was consequently declared operational, and four Air Force C–47s flew in with supplies. On the same day MAG 12's three fighter squadrons moved north from Wonsan to Yonpo, thus concentrating nearer the area of action. On the 3rd the Fifth Air Force would offer its entire light bomber effort for the support of the campaign.

The 2nd of December was the last day on which the carriers split their effort between eastern and western theaters. As the 5th and 7th Marines continued their move toward Hagaru, Task Force 77 put two-thirds of its sorties into the reservoir area, attacking troop positions at Toktong Pass and to the southward, and providing fighter cover to transports flying supplies into Hagaru. Although hampered by excessive radio chatter, and by a difference in scale of grid charts held by controllers and controlled, the day's work seemed generally successful. Following a Marine request for night hecklers over the Yudam-ni road, where many thousands of Chinese were reported active, the work was continued on into the darkness.

Chinese attacks on the moving column continued heavy throughout the night and into the next day, but without disorganizing the advance. The Marines, by contrast, had a considerable impact on their enemies, as did the very large amount of air support provided. Throughout the 3rd, observation planes circled over the column, warning of enemy positions ahead; a total of 117 sorties flown by the five Marine squadrons at Yonpo and the sixth in *Badoeng Strait* were devoted to support of the movement; Task Force 77 put an additional 80 sorties into the reservoir area. The 45 flights of 197 aircraft made available to the close support section of MTACS 2 at Hagaru were parcelled out as needed among the various control agencies,

Table 12.—Aircraft Employment and Control in X Corps Zone During the Passage of Toktong Pass, 3 December 1950

Total effort handled by Air Defense Section, MTACS 2, Hamhung:
Flights 140
Aircraft 359
    Average number of aircraft per flight. 2.6
Portion assigned to Close Support Section, MTACS 2, Hagaru:
Flights. 45 (32%)
Aircraft. 197 (55%)
    Average number of aircraft per flight. 4.4
Source of aircraft assigned to Close Support Section, Hagaru:
VMF 117 (59%)
TF 77 . . . . 80 (41%)
Assignment of flights by Close Support Section, Hagaru:
To close-in search and attack in the Yudam-ni-Hagaru area. 17
To close support of the movement from Yudam-ni. 18
    Controlled by:
        3d Bn RCT 5, leading the advance, then center column. 4
        2d Bn RCT 7, in forward part of column. 1
        RCT 5, in Toktong Pass. 2
        3d Bn RCT 7, covering right flank, then rearguard. 3
        2d Bn RCT 5, rearguard until passed through 3/7. 8
To support at Hagaru, controlled by 3d Bn RCT 1. 2
To support at Koto-ri, controlled by 2d Bn RCT 1. 8
                                            —————
                                              45

most of them at the battalion level. Of the carrier aircraft involved 32 attacked the enemy near Yudam-ni and in the rear of the column, 23 struck targets along the flanks from Toktong Pass to Hagaru, and 25 worked over Chinese forces east of the reservoir and south of Hagaru. Once again excessive radio chatter was reported, but despite this, and despite snowstorms in the objective area, the desired results were obtained, and by evening the lead elements of RCT 7 were inside the Hagaru perimeter. On the 4th the weight of air support increased still further as 68 flights of 238 aircraft came up to the reservoir. By afternoon the entire Yudam-ni movement was in.

The first step in the concentration had thus been successfully accomplished, but the campaign had hardly begun. Others beside the Marines were heading for Hagaru. On 4 December a morning flight from *Leyte* sighted and attacked an estimated thousand troops at the northern end of the reservoir; in the same area, later in the day, another *Leyte* flight reported troops moving south on all trails. But whatever these newcomers might intend, it was reasonably clear by now who was in charge. General Almond had earlier authorized General Smith to destroy any equipment which would delay his withdrawal, but the Marine commander had observed that he intended to bring out all that he could. On the 5th, Major General William H. Tunner, USAF, whose Combat Cargo Command had done such vital work in air supply and casualty evacuation, flew into Hagaru with an offer to lift the troops out, only to discover that the Marines held different views and had been flying in replacements. If movement was not impeded by anything more than Chinese forces, and if air support and air supply continued as before, the Marine Division could operate at will. Still, it was a long and slippery downhill road that stretched from Hagaru to Hungnam.

General Harris had flown up to Hagaru on the 4th and had watched the Yudam-ni Marines come in. That night, in a dispatch to Admiral Ewen, he observed that they could not have made it without air support, and asked for all possible help in covering the downhill march, front, flanks, and rear. Next day MAW 1 brought out its air support plan designed to accomplish these ends. From dawn to dark, 24 close support aircraft would be on station over the column, while the surplus worked the hills flanking the roads; through the hours of darkness, night hecklers from the carriers, from Marine F7F squadrons, and from Fifth Air Force, would harass the enemy.

By this time the concentration of fast carrier effort in the X Corps zone had been made official. FEAF, on 2 December, had asked a resumption of attacks against the Yalu bridges, but the request had been turned down by Admiral Struble in view of the pressing need for air support on the plateau. In effect, if not in form, this marked the end of fast carrier support to Eighth Army's withdrawal, for although two flights were instructed to proceed to the EUSAK area if not urgently required at the reservoir, all were in fact employed in the north. On the 3rd, as ComNavFE confirmed that close support remained the primary responsibility of Task Force 77, General Harris made another try, and "urgently" recommended the assignment of the main carrier effort to the support of the Marine Division. On the 4th FEAF concurred in this recommendation.

In other ways supporting strength continued on the rise. Although the Air Force fighter-bomber group had redeployed south from Yonpo by air and by LST, General Almond had put in a bid for B-29 strikes against command posts and troop concentrations in towns outside the immediate zone of action. *Sicily* was expected momentarily, and on the morning of 5 December an important reinforcement took place as *Princeton,* escorted by four destroyers, joined Task Force 77 and began launching aircraft. The result was a record 248 sorties controlled by the close support section of MTACS 2 at Hagaru.

As quantity was important, so was quality. The presence of the fast carriers provided types of force not otherwise available. Only the carrier air groups operated the heavily-armed AD whose load, greater than that of the World War II Flying Fortress, made it the outstanding attack plane in

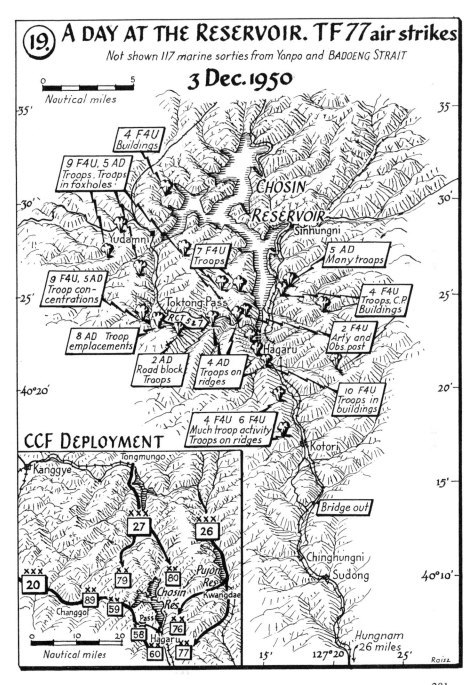

A DAY AT THE RESERVOIR. TF 77 air strikes

Not shown 117 marine sorties from Yonpo and BADOENG STRAIT

3 Dec. 1950

19.

0 ——————— 5
Nautical miles

35'
35

4 F4U
Buildings

9 F4U, 5 AD
Troops, Troops
in foxholes

CHOSIN
RESERVOIR

30'
30'

Yudamni

Sinhungni

7 F4U
Troops

5 AD
Many troops

9 F4U, 5AD
Troop con-
centrations

25'
25'

Toktong Pass

4 F4U
Troops, C.P.
Buildings

8 AD Troop
emplacements

RCT 5 & 7

2 F4U
Arty and
Obs. post

2 AD
Road block
Troops

4 AD
Troops on
ridges

Hagaru

40°20'

10 F4U
Troops in
buildings

20'

4 F4U 6 F4U
Much troop activity
Troops on ridges

Kotori

CCF DEPLOYMENT

Tongmungo

Kanggye

15'

XXX
27

XXX
26

Bridge out

Chinghungni

XXX
20

XX
79

XX
80

Pujon
Res.

Sudong

40°10'

89

XX

Chosin
Res.

Kwangdae

Changgol

59

Pass

76

0 —— 10 —— 20

58

Hagaru

77

Nautical miles

60

15'

127°20

Hungnam
26 miles

25'

Raisz

281

Korea. Defensively, too, the Seventh Fleet's contribution was unique: with no Marine jets yet in Korea, and with the nearest Air Force squadrons 200 miles away at Kimpo, only the fast carriers could attempt to provide a jet combat air patrol over the area of operations. This CAP, a precautionary measure of some importance in view of the MIG concentration across the Yalu, had been earlier discontinued in the interest of fuel economy and sustained flight operations, but with the arrival of *Princeton* it was reinstituted.

On 6 December the Marines started south over the winding road. Disengagement at Hagaru required hard fighting, for the troops previously sighted to the northward had now arrived, and two divisions of the Chinese 26th Army had taken up position on the eastern side of the MSR. Morning air operations were prevented by a ground fog, but this in time lifted, and the hundred offensive sorties sent up by *Princeton, Leyte,* and the Marine squadrons provided strikes against troops in ridges along the road as well as a jet CAP. All day and throughout the night the march continued; in mid-morning of the 7th, as the rearguard was preparing to move out from Hagaru, the lead elements entered Koto-ri. For a brief period the convoy extended over the entire 11-mile distance between the towns, but air support kept the Chinese under control until the movement was completed.

By now the exigencies of the situation had led to innovation in the form of an airborne close support control center. At the suggestion of the MTACS personnel with the Marine Division, whose work would be made difficult with radios packed for march and shielded by the surrounding hills, a Marine R5D had been hastily modified for this task. An extra radio, a chart board, and a situation map were installed; extra oxygen and cabin fuel tanks gave both personnel and plane the required endurance; three controllers were flown out from Hagaru to man the aircraft. From dawn to dusk from 6 to 10 December this very large Mosquito orbited over the moving column to provide, in addition to the basic necessity of reliable VHF communications, the bonus of sustained visual observation of the entire area of action.

On the 7th the three fast carriers continued operations, and *Badoeng Strait* was joined by *Sicily.* In the course of the day, and despite bad weather in the afternoon, *Philippine Sea, Princeton,* and *Leyte* put 125 offensive sorties into the Koto-ri area, more than half the day's total of 216. Of the 49 flights handled by the airborne control center, one was assigned to the 3rd Infantry Division and eight to the control parties of the 5th Marines, notably to the 2nd Battalion, rearguard during the disengagement at Hagaru. The remaining 40 were employed on search and attack missions against troops in the hills along the road, troops and horses east of the reservoir, and villages in the hills near Koto-ri.

These villages had by now become prime targets. The discrepancy between infrequent air sightings of the enemy and persistent reports from

Up on the hill: On the road south from Hagaru napalm clears the way. (USMC A-5440)

283

local inhabitants of vast quantities of Chinese had been resolved by the discovery that the CCF soldiers had been crowding by day into all available housing for shelter both from air attack and cold. Reports from the dispossessed Koreans of this invasion of their homes had been followed by requests for the destruction of their villages, and thus of the invader. Once begun, these attacks produced eruptions of surprising numbers of Chinese soldiery, and bombing and frostbite multiplied enemy casualties.

The Marines had reached Koto-ri on the 7th. But the roughest stretch was still to come, in the march across the divide and down to Chinhung-ni. On this route, described by General Shepherd as "a defile through which no military force should ever have to fight," cliff sides are steep, with drops of more than a hundred feet from the road's edge; the road itself abounds in hairpin turns; opportunities for road blocks are unsurpassed. Midway through the gorge there was a bridge, three times blown by the enemy and twice restored by Army engineers, on whose further replacement depended the division's ability to bring out its vehicles. On the 6th a request for air-dropped treadway bridge material had been made to Combat Cargo Command, and the next day this unprecedented operation was successfully accomplished.

The move south from Koto-ri began on 8 December, while a battalion of the 1st Marines attacked up-hill from Chinhung-ni to gain control of the lower half of the road. The bad weather which had limited carrier operations on the afternoon before had now really arrived: the attacks were begun in a swirling snowstorm, throughout the day zero visibility prevailed, the carriers were unable to operate, and of 5 flights of 15 aircraft which got off the ground at Yonpo only one reached the zone of march. But on the 9th, with the fast carriers back at work, X Corps sorties mounted to a record 479, half of which were assigned to the airborne control center. This abundance of riches permitted large diversions to search and attack; a wide area east and north of the reservoir was covered, and in addition to numerous troop concentrations the bag of targets included such unlikely items as switch engines and a horse corral. On the ground the chasm was successfully bridged: by great good fortune the enemy had blown only the bridge and not the road, and by afternoon of the 9th the division trains were leaving Koto-ri.

On 10 December, two weeks to the day after the Chinese onfall at Yudam-ni, the leading elements of the Marines reached Chinhung-ni and the command post was flown down to Hungnam. At a cost to the enemy immeasurably greater than that to itself, the Marine Division, under its canopy of Marine and naval air, had been extricated from an impossible situation. The Chinese were still hovering on the flanks, and there were minor reverses in the rear that night; but from Chinhung-ni it was all downhill, and on the 11th all units reached the staging area at Hungnam. After reaching the sea, according to a later chronicler, the Marines set up a trophy and sacrificed to Hermes. Doubtless some of them did, if only metaphorically, but they might better have devoted their offerings to Poseidon. The division had received harsh treatment from the god of roads, but once again in touch with the friendly sea all things were possible.

3. 30 November–13 December: Concentration in the East

The 2nd Division was still in the gantlet, the Marines were still up on the hill, and the deployment of Task Force 90 to Korea was just beginning, when on 30 November General Almond's headquarters issued orders for a retirement upon Hamhung. For the next ten days, while Eighth Army retired southward and the Marines fought their way down from the reservoir, the concentration of X Corps in the Hamhung-Hungnam area continued by land and by sea.

The instructions of 30 November found Almond's command widely dispersed. Three battalions of the 7th Infantry Division were with the Marines at the Chosin Reservoir, while the rest of the division was stretched out along the road to Hyesanjin. From its base at Wonsan the 3rd Division was expanding its holdings westward across the narrow part of Korea. On the eastern flank the ROK I Corps had a division at Hapsu and another on the coast, near the outskirts of Chongjin, where its advance was being supported by Commander Cruiser Division 1, Rear Admiral Roscoe H. Hillenkoetter, in *Saint Paul,* with the destroyer *Zellars.*

Implementing orders went out the following day. At the same time that the Marines were instructed to concentrate at Hagaru, the 3rd Division was ordered to reassemble at Wonsan, and the 7th Division to withdraw southward from the Manchurian border to Hamhung. Up the coast to the northeast the ROK I Corps was ordered to retire on Songjin, and to prepare for further movement by land or sea. On 2 December, after firing night harassing missions north of Chongjin, *Saint Paul* and *Zellars* moved south to Kyongsong Man to support the withdrawal of the ROK Capital Division.

No serious pressure was to be exerted against the ROK corps. Except for the battalions at the reservoir the retirement of the 7th Division was unhindered by the enemy. But at Wonsan apprehensions of enemy attack had prevented the aircraft from Task Force 77 from staying the night of 1 December, and X Corps reported that road and rail communications with Hungnam had been cut. Since here, if anywhere, it seemed that an emergency evacuation might be necessary, Admiral Doyle requested Commander Seventh Fleet to order *Saint Paul* and *Zellars* down for fire support. The message got a rapid response, and although the destroyer was held in the north until a relief could be provided, Admiral Hillenkoetter at once headed southward. By mid-day of 3 December *Saint Paul* had anchored in the harbor of Wonsan.

There she was shortly joined by a transport group of four APAs, two AKAs, and an APD, Captain Albert E. Jarrell in *Henrico,* which had previously been ordered forward from Japan. On the afternoon of the 3rd, Doyle instructed Jarrell to commence loading the 3rd Infantry Division on arrival, advised Admiral Joy's headquarters of his estimate of shipping requirements for the lift, and himself sailed for Wonsan to supervise the outloading. But the emergency had been somewhat exaggerated: loading had begun by the time CTF 90 arrived on the 4th, but no enemy pressure was in fact being exerted; most of the division was already moving north to Hamhung by road and rail, and only an estimated 4,000 men and 12,000 tons of gear remained to be removed.

This situation permitted a downward revision of the Wonsan requirements and freed some shipping for use elsewhere. On the 5th Captain Michael F. D. Flaherty in *Noble* was detached from the Wonsan group with a couple of merchantmen and ordered to Songjin to outload elements of the retiring ROK I Corps. Unlike the harbor at Iwon, Task Force 90's previous farthest north, the mineral and lumber export center of Songjin had reasonable loading facilities: behind a sheltering peninsula an 1,800-foot quay with depths of more than 27 feet permitted large ships to lie alongside. At Songjin the transports were joined by one Scajap and one Korean LST, everything went according to the book, and on the 9th, as the destroyers *Moore* and *Maddox* arrived to cover his departure, Flaherty finished loading up his task element and sailed his ships for Pusan.

At Wonsan, in the meantime, embarkation of the 3rd Division remnants continued, assisted by a Marine shore party battalion. On the 5th one Army battalion and two of Korean Marines formed a defensive perimeter, and *Saint Paul, Zellars, Hank,* and *Sperry* fired a short mission against a reported enemy troop concentration. But although the ships continued throughout the operation to provide night harassing and interdiction fires, little opposition developed. While loading was in progress Captain Jarrell carried out a search for enemy installations on the principal harbor islands; on Yo Do an observation post was destroyed, while Sin Do produced four 76-millimeter guns and a couple of ammunition dumps.

Except for one ROK Marine battalion, assigned to cover the removal of MAG 12 equipment from Kalma Pando, all friendly forces were clear by the 7th. There remained one empty Victory ship, and into this, during the day, Korean refugees were jammed to a total far in excess of normal capacity. With covering fire from *Saint Paul* and the destroyers, the final withdrawal took place on the evening of the 9th, and by 2215 the beach was clear. Everything had been taken out, no destruction of supplies or gear had been necessary, and the total Wonsan lift—3,800 troops, 7,000 refugees, 1,146 vehicles, and 10,000 tons of cargo—exceeded that removed from Chinnampo. On the morning of the 10th, as the last transport cleared the harbor, Admiral Hillenkoetter headed *Saint Paul* and *Hank* back to the northward, to provide fire support at Hungnam. All that remained at Wonsan was a salvage group in the outer harbor working over the hulks of *Pirate* and *Pledge*.

For ten days divers from the rescue ship *Conserver* had been attempting to remove classified gear from the sunken minesweepers. But the work had been hampered by heavy swells, by the bottom mud which partially covered the hulks, and by water temperatures in the cool low 50's. On 5 December *Diachenko* was placed in charge of the operations, and next day the decision was taken to demolish what remained of the minesweepers. Covered by *Zellars* and *Sperry* the work continued, depth and demolition charges were used to dismantle the wrecks, and on the 13th the job was done.

Two east coast evacuations had by now been completed, and a third was shaping up. General MacArthur's first reports of the emergency created by the Chinese intervention had limited themselves to a description of the "new war" and to a request for Chinese Nationalist reinforcement, but on 30 November he had forwarded to Washington his strategic concept for dealing with the altered situation. As was perhaps natural for a commander whose devotion to a maritime strategy had forced through the Inchon and Wonsan landings, this called for the retirement of Eighth Army on Pyongyang and Seoul, and for the concentration of X Corps in the Hamhung-Wonsan region, where it would present a flanking threat to a Chinese southward movement.

At Tobruk, in the North African campaign of 1941, the British had for eight months held a lodgment against heavier metal than the Chinese could be expected to bring forward. During his withdrawal from the reservoir General Smith had expected that a perimeter would be formed and maintained in the Hamhung region; General Almond felt that a position on the coast could be defended throughout the winter; Admiral Doyle and others held similar views. But this possibility seems to have fallen victim to the larger scene. The usefulness of such an advanced position depends largely on the moves in prospect for supporting forces, and these were for the moment retrograde. Impressed by CincFE's description of the emergency, oppressed by their world-wide responsibilities, the Joint Chiefs on 1 December had pointed out the dangers of the central mountain gap, and had instructed General MacArthur to withdraw X Corps and coordinate it with Eighth Army. And a second dispatch from CincFE, in which he declared himself unable to hold the line at the waist of Korea, brought orders to consolidate his forces into beachheads.

The crisis in Korea had by this time produced another trans-Pacific migration of the high command. General Shepherd had come out from Pearl, and on his arrival on the 6th had found CincFE's demeanor "not optimistic;"

General Collins had been flown out from Washington. On the 7th discussions were held in Tokyo between Generals MacArthur, Collins, and Stratemeyer, Admirals Joy and Struble, General Shepherd, and others, concerning the proposed new U.N. plan, which called for holding Seoul as long as possible prior to retirement upon Pusan, and for ferrying X Corps back south and integrating it into Eighth Army.

Since General Walker's command had already reached the area of Seoul, action was for the moment required only of X Corps. Following the Tokyo discussions the responsible conferees adjourned to *Mount McKinley* at Hungnam, where Joy, Shepherd, Struble, Doyle, and Higgins considered both the problem of defending a perimeter and the more probable alternative of withdrawal. But the uncertainty was ended on the 9th by JCS approval of General MacArthur's revised plan, and by announcement of the decision to redeploy to the southward. On his arrival from Koto-ri next day, General Smith learned that the Marines would go out first, and embarkation was begun.

For the previous week CTF 90 and his staff had been preparing for contingencies. To enlarge usable harbor space and to provide lanes for fire support ships a second minesweeping operation had been undertaken at Hungnam. Plans had been sketched out both for the defense of a perimeter and for the evacuation, not only of X Corps, but of west and south coast ports as well. Now, with the decision to withdraw, Admiral Doyle had to halt all operations in support of X Corps, put his organization into reverse and accelerate again. A shift to seaborne logistics was at once commenced: floating dumps of POL and ammunition were established, along with a floating evacuation center and a floating prisoner of war camp. A large order was put in for life jackets, cargo and floater nets, debarkation ladders, and the like, and once again a redeployment of Amphibious Force shipping was begun. Admiral Thackrey was directed to send all available APAs and AKAs together with one LSD from Inchon to Hungnam; Admiral Joy was requested to provide ten empty cargo ships daily at Hungnam until further notice; the instructions of the Wonsan and Songjin evacuation groups were altered.

At Wonsan Captain Jarrell had originally been ordered to sail his ships to Pusan for unloading. On the 9th, however, this directive was modified by orders to transport Marine shore party and MSTS shipping control personnel to Hungnam for service in another evacuation. Some reloading was required to consolidate these units in a single LST, but this was accomplished in routine fashion. At Songjin the situation was more complicated.

Captain Flaherty had also been directed to send his ships to Pusan, and had done so on the afternoon of the 9th. But as midnight approached, nine hours after his two LSTs had departed for the south and six hours after the transports had got underway, a message was received changing the destination to Hungnam. Ordering his merchant ships to proceed there independently, Flaherty began to search the ocean darkness for the vanished LSTs, and in time managed to find one by radar and to raise the other on 500 kcs. On arrival at Hungnam one ROK RCT and the Capital Division's artillery were offloaded to strengthen the defenses of the perimeter, and the task element then continued to Pusan.

The events of 9 December marked the beginning of what later became known, following the concept of ComNavFE's operation plan, as an amphibious operation in reverse. The image is a useful one, and one can envisage the proceedings in terms of a film run backward. On shore, supplies are packed up, moved down to the beach, and lifted out to the anchored cargo ships; from the steadily shrinking perimeter the troops retire on the embarkation points; the landing craft return to the transports; the transports put to sea. But in two ways, at least, one of which complicated and one of which facilitated the operation, things were different.

On the debit side this backwards operation involved great problems in the compression of space and time. Troops and supplies that had reached the theater through three ports and troops that had arrived overland now had to be funneled out a single harbor; personnel and gear that had come in over a period of two months were to be removed in the space of two weeks. With a winter campaign in prospect, General Almond had been authorized a 30-day supply level for his forces, and while this had not yet been achieved, X Corps was considerably oversupplied for an evacuation. The extension of operations from Wonsan to the Manchurian border had led to a dispersal of supply dumps; some tergiversation regarding the employment of the 3rd Infantry Division had complicated administrative procedures; air operations at Wonsan and Yonpo had brought the accumulation of large stocks of gasoline and aviation ordnance. Initial estimates of the task at hand called for the removal of between 110,000 and 120,000 men, some 15,000 vehicles, and about 400,000 measurement tons of cargo. No such lift had been required since Okinawa, and although here the distances were fortunately shorter, the limited amount of available shipping necessarily called for multiple turnarounds.

On the credit side, however, there are advantages to the amphibious departure. In contrast to an arrival from the sea, control organizations can be established before work is begun, and without the complications of enemy action. At Hungnam the problem of matching outgoing troops and supplies with incoming ships was accomplished by two such organisms, one ashore under Colonel Edward H. Forney, USMC, Deputy Chief of Staff of X Corps, and a special organization set up in Task Force 90 by Admiral Doyle.

As control officer, Colonel Forney, with his staff, selected the units to be loaded on the basis of available tactical and administrative information, and assigned shipping in consultation with the operations section of Task Force

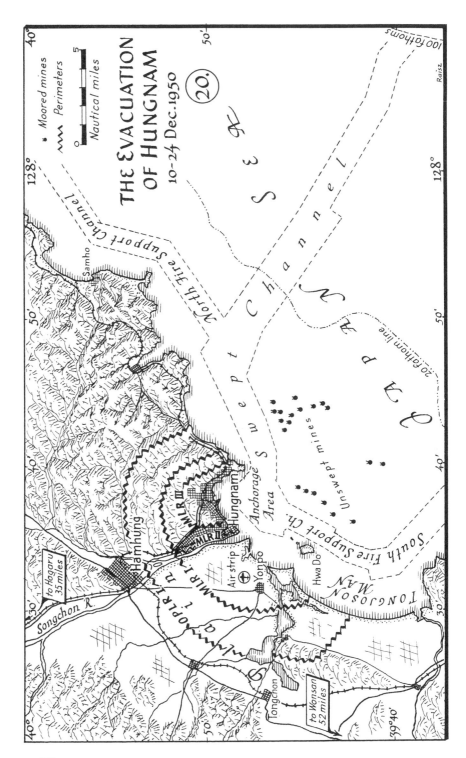

THE EVACUATION OF HUNGNAM
10–24 Dec. 1950

⟨20⟩

Moored mines
Perimeters
Nautical miles

JAPAN SEA

North Fire Support Channel

Swept Channel

South Fire Support Ch.

Unswept mines

20 fathom line

100 fathoms

Raisz

128°   128°   128°
40°   50'   50'   40'   30'   39°40'

Samho
Hamhung
to Hogaru 35 miles
Songchon R.
Hungnam
MLR II
MLR II
MLR I
Air strip
Yonpo
Anchorage Area
Hwa Do
Tongchon
to Wonsan 52 miles
TONGJOSON MAN

290

90. Port operating units were then advised of dockside requirements, the loading section ground out its plans, the movement section got the traffic down to the water, and the rations people laid down these useful items alongside.

While the outbound units were moving to the docks, shipping from over the horizon was being put in to meet them by the Task Force 90 control group. Two frigates in the offing guided vessels through the swept channel to the control ship near the harbor entrance. There they were boarded and their characteristics ascertained for relay to the operations section, and there they were instructed, as conditions warranted, either to anchor in the outer harbor or to continue in. Here too shipping was separated by category: APA and AKA types from the Amphibious Force were anchored close in for loading by small craft from the beach, while merchant ships and LSTs were sent on into the inner harbor.

Inside the main pier and breakwater there were beaching slots for 14 LSTs, while four concrete wharves provided seven workable alongside berths. Bad winter weather, which restricted lighterage outside the sheltered area, brought the expedient of double-banking cargo vessels and loading the inboard one from the wharf and the outboard one by lighter. The result was that twice as many ships could be worked, whatever the state of the sea, the run from the loading beaches was greatly reduced, and men could be marched from the wharves across the inboard vessels to those on the outside.

At the docks and on the beaches outgoing soldiers and incoming shipping met. The port was operated by the Army's 2nd Engineer Special Brigade, reinforced by elements of the Marine shore party battalion which had been brought up from Wonsan. Winch operators were provided by the ESB and stevedoring by 1,200 Japanese, who had arrived in late November and who were housed in the mother ship *Shinano Maru*. It would be hard to imagine a more joint or combined operation: Army, Navy, Marine Corps, and Merchant Marine, Americans, Koreans, and Japanese worked expeditiously together and to excellent purpose. During the Second World War there had been some unedifying exhibitions on the part of merchant mariners in forward areas, but none developed here, and the performance of the crews of the time-charter vessels was uniformly excellent.

Administrative arrangements had been pretty well completed by 10 December, when the Marines began to arrive, and although no corps operation order was as yet available, the Marine Division began to load at once. In planning for the evacuation General Almond had been faced with the problem of whether to conduct a simultaneous withdrawal of elements of all units from their pie-shaped sectors of the perimeter, or a retirement by divisions which would require side-slipping the remaining units to fill the emptied gaps. But the choice turned out to be largely illusory; the decision was forced upon the corps commander, both by his instructions, which called for the earliest possible outloading of the ROK Corps, and by the battleworn condition of the Marines. As promulgated, therefore, the plan called for the immediate evacuation of the Marines, followed in order by the Koreans, and by the 7th and 3rd Divisions. And step by step, as troops were taken out and the perimeter diminished, responsibility for the foothold would be transferred to the Navy.

With embarkation planning under control, it remained to erect defenses against possible enemy attack. Unlike the amphibious entrances into Korea which had preceded it, this amphibious exodus was conducted without the organization of a Joint Task Force, and indeed the command arrangements, derived from the NavFE Op Plan of 13 November, were rather odd. The possibility that Soviet intervention would follow upon that of the Chinese, which had already led Admiral Joy to reinstitute the submarine patrol of La Pérouse Strait and to intensify his air search, made him feel that the Seventh Fleet should be kept free to move upon an instant's notice. The result was to place Commander Seventh Fleet in a supporting role: Admiral Struble was to provide air and gunfire support as feasible, while continuing carrier operations against the enemy in coordination with Fifth Air Force. Admiral Doyle's instructions, by contrast, were very far-reaching, and charged him not only with the responsibility for Korean redeployment, but for control of air and naval gunfire in embarkation areas, gunfire support of friendly units, protection of shipping, and maintenance of the blockade. And a final complication was provided by the presence of General Shepherd, Commanding General Fleet Marine Force Pacific, as ComNavFE representative "on matters relating to the Marine Corps and for consultation and advice," and, as he later described the situation, with oral instructions from both CincPacFleet and ComNavFE to take command of the naval phase of the evacuation should he consider it desirable. But if the possibilities for confusion here were infinite, the individuals involved were fortunately able to make things work.

At sea the enemy remained quiescent. No submarine threat developed, and shipping was sailed independently in steady procession from Hungnam to Pusan and back again. But on land, as from the beginning, and now also in the air, the enemy had capabilities which deserved consideration. The attentions of the supporting naval units were consequently focused on the perimeter, on the mountainous hinterland behind Hungnam, and on the airstrips beyond the Yalu.

Large numbers of high-performance jets were now operating from these Manchurian fields; quite possibly advanced types of attack planes had also been made available to the Chinese. The large quantities of troops and shipping concentrated at the Hungnam beachhead offered an inviting target, and it was at least conceivable that the enemy's success on land might tempt him to offensive action in the air. Against this threat X Corps and its supporting naval forces were on their own; no help could be expected from Fifth

Air Force, whose nearest fighter group at Kimpo was as far away as were the Antung MIGs. So long as Yonpo airfield remained operational the Marines would provide combat air patrol, and on the 10th this defensive effort was strengthened as the first Marine jets to reach the Orient flew in from Japan. But shrinkage of the perimeter would uncover the airstrip and force their departure three days later, from which time Admiral Ewen's F9Fs would form the mainstay of the defense against air attack.

Table 13.—Hungnam Task Organization

Task Force 90.	Rear Admiral J. H. Doyle.
Task Element 90.00. Flagship Element.	Captain C. A. Printup.
1 AGC	
Task Element 90.01. Tactical Air Control Element.	Comdr. R. W. Arndt.
Tacron 1.	
Task Element 90.02. Repair and Salvage Element.	Comdr. L. C. Conwell.
1 ARG, 1 ARL, 2 ARS, 1 ATF.	
Task Element 90.03. Control Element.	Lt. Comdr. C. E. Allmon.
2 APD,[1] 1 PCEC.[1]	
Task Group 90.2. Transport Group.	Captain S. G. Kelly.
Task Element 90.21. Transport Element.	Captain A. E. Jarrell.
3 APA, 3 AKA, 2 APD,[1] 1 PCEC,[1] 3 LSD (9 LSU embarked), 11 LST, 27 Scajap LST, plus MSTS shipping assigned.	
Task Group 90.8. Gunfire Support Group.	Rear Admiral R. H. Hillenkoetter.
1 CA, 4 DD, 3 LSMR, plus 1 CA and DD from TG 95.2.	
Task Group 95.2. Blockade, Escort, and Minesweeping Group.	
	Rear Admiral J. M. Higgins.
1 CA, 4 DD, 6 PF, plus DMS, AM, AMS from TG 95.6.	
Seventh Fleet.	Vice Admiral A. D. Struble.
Task Force 77. Fast Carrier Force.	Rear Admiral E. C. Ewen.
Task Group 77.1. Support Group.	Captain I. T. Duke.
1 BB, 1 CL, 1 CLAA.	
Task Group 77.2. Screening Group.	Captain J. R. Clark.
17–22 DD.	
Task Group 77.3. Carrier Group.	Rear Admiral E. C. Ewen.
3–4 CV.	
Task Group 96.8. Escort Carrier Group.	Rear Admiral R. W. Ruble.
1–2 CVE, 0–1 CVL, 3–8 DD.	
Task Group 79.2. Logistic Support Group.	Captain B. L. Austin.
Units assigned from Service Squadron 3 and Service Division 31.	

[1] Units assigned to two task elements.

In the absence of an overall commander, the air plans were drawn up in consultation by representatives of Task Force 90 and Task Force 77, and Commander Seventh Fleet was advised of what was required of his carriers. Air support duties imposed upon the escort carriers called for four fighters on station throughout the day for close support, and for the provision of tactical air observers and airborne controllers. The fast carriers were assigned responsibilities in air defense, deep support, and interdiction, and for night heckler missions and night combat air patrol. This last requirement amounted to something of an overload, but as congestion in the harbor area and the all-night air traffic at Yonpo made defense by antiaircraft gunfire undesirable, the task force undertook to do what it could. Since air control was complicated by the hills north of Hungnam, which blanketed the radars of ships in harbor, the destroyer *Duncan* was assigned as radar picket ship and stationed 50 miles to seaward. All arrangements were completed by the 11th, at which time Admiral Doyle assumed responsibility for air defense of the Hungnam embarkation area.

Estimates of enemy capabilities indicated that the Chinese could throw between six and eight divisions against the perimeter, all of which, however, were thought to have been seriously weakened in their encounters with the Marines. Against this threat Task Force 77 would fly offensive strikes up-country, and in emergency would augment the escort carrier effort in close-in work. The embarkation plan was designed to leave as much artillery on shore as long as possible. Fire support ships were assigned to reinforce the corps and regimental guns, and their efforts, with those of the close support aircraft, were tied in through the Corps Fire Support Coordination Center, a dominantly Marine-staffed outfit with a naval member as gunfire officer.

Fire support planning was also tidied up on the 11th, in a conference between General Almond, Admiral Hillenkoetter, and a representative of Task Force 77. Stations for the fire support ships were established in the swept channel, which by now extended ten miles on either side of the port; the defensive positions ashore were laid out to permit naval gunfire to bear upon an attacking force; control of gunfire was assigned to Anglico and Marine personnel attached to the 3rd and 7th Divisions. In addition to his flagship *Saint Paul,* and the destroyers and LSMRs of Task Group 90.8, Admiral Hillenkoetter had the services of *Rochester,* Admiral Higgins' flagship, and of two destroyers from Higgins' group. On the 16th the planned total of two cruisers, six destroyers, and three rocket ships was met, as *Zellars* and *Sperry* reported in from Wonsan.

Although the ship in which he hung his hat was doing duty in the fire support group, Admiral Higgins' responsibilities lay elsewhere. Upon him and upon the remaining units of Task Groups 95.2 and 95.6 lay the multitudinous responsibilities of blockade, control, escort, and minesweeping, which among other tasks involved maintaining two destroyers on coastal blockade to the northward, a frigate patrolling off the Wonsan swept channel, and three more handling traffic in and out of Hungnam.

The directives for these supporting operations, originally issued separately, were consolidated on the 13th in Admiral Doyle's Operation Order 20–50. The arrangements had been made, the forces deployed, the evacuation was already underway. That these defensive preparations were in the end hardly required would seem to prove their wisdom. No serious effort was made against the perimeter by the Communist enemy, whose casualties had been very great, and at Hungnam, as on other occasions in history, the availability of arms made their employment largely unnecessary.

4. *11 December–24 December: The Evacuation of Hungnam*

By 11 December, when the Marines reached Hungnam, amphibious and MSTS shipping had begun to arrive. Having off-loaded at Pusan following his evacuation of Chinnampo, Captain Kelly had been ordered back to Inchon; no sooner had he reached that port than new orders flowing from new decisions directed him to Hungnam, where he arrived on the 11th to take charge of the movement of the Marine Division. By the 14th the Marines had loaded in one APA, one AKA, 3 APs, 13 LSTs, 3 LSDs, and 7 time-chartered merchant ships, and next morning Kelly sailed his convoy for Pusan. As soon as the Marines were clear the loading of the 7th Division was begun, to continue through the following week.

While these evolutions were in progress Admiral Doyle and his staff found themselves faced with a requirement for a small amphibious landing. In order to block the east coast route General Almond had requested that the ROK I Corps be put ashore in the area of Samchok, 40 miles below the parallel, where *Juneau* had carried out the first bombardment of the war. The undertaking was accepted, and on the basis of corps' estimates shipping was assigned to lift 12,000 men and a few trucks, an allocation which in the end had to be more than doubled as 25,000 ROKs and 700 vehicles turned up. Preparation for the operation involved intelligence studies and photo reconnaissance; the port of Mukho, just north of Samchok, where breakwaters enclose a small harbor area, was selected as the landing site. Between 15 and 18 December Captain Spofford's ships swept and buoyed a channel in from the 100-fathom curve, and on the 16th the operation was turned over to Captain Jarrell, who had by now returned from Pusan. In addition to *Henrico,* one APA, one AKA, three chartered merchantmen, and two LSTs were included in the movement group, while reports of Chinese penetrations south of the parallel brought the assignment of the DMS *Endicott* and the destroyer *Forrest Royal* for fire support. At noon of the 17th Captain Jarrell sailed for Mukho, the landing was uneventful, and this important position was quickly secured. By the 20th the destroyers were back on station at Hungnam.

There loading had continued day and night, hindered only by the vagaries of nature. Bad weather inland on the 16th, which limited fast carrier offensive sorties to a mere 41, reached Hungnam on the following day; the temperature dropped below freezing and the sea worked up. As westerly winds reached 40 knots, four LCMs went adrift and were blown out into the minefields, and from 1700 until after midnight small boat traffic had to be halted. This was the worst day, but throughout the operation the continuing cold created problems for materiel and personnel alike: working around the clock and exposed to cold, spray, and wind, many of the coxswains had to be carried aboard their ships after returning from long trips.

It was the hope both of those ashore and of those afloat to get everything out; not just personnel and loaded vehicles, but everything, and they very nearly did. To deprive the enemy of salvage possibilities even broken-down vehicles were outloaded, a lift of inoperative machinery which in the end filled four Liberty ships. In the bulk categories of POL and ammunition Colonel Forney found his responsibilities steadily increasing: an original count of 5,000 drums of POL ended up in the outloading of 29,500 drums, with 200 left behind; almost 9,000 tons of ammunition was taken out, and of the 1,000 tons remaining, half was frozen dynamite too dangerous to handle. Ultimately, in any event, these left-over commodities were put to use in the final demolition of the port.

On water as on land, salvage problems presented themselves. Considering the amount of traffic at this small port, at all hours and in all weathers, mishaps were extraordinarily few, but three which did occur well illustrate the importance of the salvage organization. Standing out of harbor late on the night of 10 December the *Enid Victory,* a chartered MSTS vessel, cut the eastern point too close and ran aground. Here the one-foot tide of the Sea of Japan, otherwise so agreeable, proved disadvantageous, but by next afternoon the ARL *Askari,* the fleet tug *Tawakoni,* and two harbor tugs managed to get her off, and she continued to Pusan. A more intractable proposition had been presented a few days earlier when *Senzan Maru,* a Japanese time-charter laden with 50,000 bags of flour, missed the entrance channel in the morning darkness and hit a mine. Damage was serious, but although flooded forward, eight feet down by the head, and with only two feet of freeboard remaining, she made it in, whereupon divers from *Askari* investigated the damage and the ship doctors prescribed. The flour paste was jettisoned from the forward hold and the rest of the cargo shifted, bulkheads were shored up and flotation provided by filling the hold with empty oil drums, and after ten days work *Senzan Maru* was sailed in company for Moji where she arrived safely.

Last and most difficult of these problems was that presented by a Korean LST, which fouled a shaft with manila line and was unable to retract from

Hungnam: Troops embarking.   (DAVID DOUGLAS DUNCAN—LIFE)

the beach. The snarl was cleared and repairs to the main engines were provided by personnel from the rescue ship *Conserver,* after which the LST docked again and on her second attempt to get underway fouled both shafts. By this time her troubles were snowballing: more engine repairs were needed and the gyrocompass had broken down; there were eight turns of 1⅛-inch wire around the port shaft and many of 8-inch manila around the starboard one; a food and water shortage had developed, which was the more serious in view of a reported 7,400 refugees on board. Despite difficulties from the cold, the port shaft was freed by divers from *Conserver; Askari* contributed 26,000 gallons of water; 1,500 loaves of bread and a quantity of cooked rice were procured from other ships in harbor, and eight tons of food from Army sources ashore. There was no time to do more, and on 19 December the invalid was sailed for Samchok, accompanied by *Diachenko* and another Korean LST, both rigged for towing. She got there.

As in all overseas operations, but more visibly than in most, the key problem at Hungnam was the availability of shipping. Here the time of turnaround was crucial. At Pusan, where scant notice had been received of the impending arrivals, unloading capacity proved for a time unable to match the rate of outloading in the north, and the resulting congestion brought diversions to Japan, where progress was even more leisurely. In this situation, and as reports from Eighth Army indicated that evacuation of Inchon might become necessary before Hungnam was cleared, Admiral Joy twice found himself obliged to call upon CincFE to prevent ships being sent east of Moji for unloading, to order port authorities to work ships 24 hours a day, and to have idle shipping in Japan emptied to provide reserve.

There was also, as in any amphibious operation, the special problem of the availability of LSTs. These for a time were scarce. Counting Scajap and Korean vessels, a total of about 40 ultimately became available, but some were slow in arriving, 13 had sailed with the Marine Division, and 2 more had been committed to the ROK lift to Mukho. Bad weather and congestion at Pusan had delayed the return of those which had lifted the Marines, and the resultant shortage had slowed the outloading of engineer troops and gear. But by the 18th they were beginning to arrive again, within two days a score had been loaded and sailed, and again the problem of availability arose. With an estimated 22 needed to lift the last elements from the beachhead, and on the basis of an assumed five-day turnaround between Hungnam and Pusan, Forney began stockpiling LSTs on the evening of the 20th. By this time the port of Pusan was operating in high gear, unloading was also in progress at Masan and Ulsan, and Liberty and Victory ships as well as LSTs were being emptied in time for a second run. In the end enough LSTs became available, and indeed there were a couple to spare.

In the air the defenses of Hungnam grew steadily stronger. Through the period of concentration and outloading, the Marine squadrons were con-

LST with oil drums. Looking northeast from Blue Beach across the inner harbor; harbor entrance control frigate in the right distance. 14 December 1950. (USN 423913)

299

ducting a complicated series of redeployments and more carriers were mustering offshore, with the remarkable result that air strength in the Hungnam area, far from diminishing as the evacuation progressed, actually increased. On 1 December the three fighter squadrons at Wonsan had moved up to Yonpo. On the 3rd the Air Force fighter-bombers left for the south, and next day one of the Corsair squadrons was flown out to Itami for embarkation on the light carrier *Bataan,* but these deficits were more than made up by the arrival of *Princeton* on the 5th. On the 6th *Sicily* reached Hungnam, loaded the personnel and gear of VMF 214 in an all-night evolution, and took the planes aboard in the course of the next day's operations. On 10 December the Yonpo air garrison was reinforced by a squadron of Marine Panther jets, which had come out along with Air Force fighters in the escort carrier *Bairoko,* and which operated from the shore strip until the 13th, when they were flown south to Pusan. After unloading her cargo of Air Force fighters at Yokosuka, *Bataan* proceeded to Kobe, embarked VMF 212, and sailed for the Sea of Japan where she joined Task Force 77 on the 16th.

On the 14th the three Marine squadrons still at Yonpo were flown to Itami. Following this departure CTF 90 relieved the Marine Aircraft Wing of air control within a 35-mile radius of Hungnam, and General Harris' headquarters moved aboard an LST, to assume on the 17th the duties of standby Tactical Air Direction Center. On 22 December *Valley Forge* arrived from the United States and the evolution was complete.

The virtues of the movable floating air base and of carrier training for Marine pilots had again been demonstrated. Where embarked aviation had

Table 14.—Hungnam Air Deployment

U.N. SQUADRONS ON HAND

	At Yonpo			Embarked			Total
	F9F	F4U	F7FN	F9F	F4U	AD	
1 December	0	3	2	3	5	2	[1] 15
10 December	1	1	2	4	9	3	20
16 December	0	0	0	4	10	3	17
23 December	0	0	0	4	14	4	22

AIRCRAFT ON HAND (Computed on the basis of complements: CV 80, CVL 30, CVE 24, VMF 24, VMFN 12)

	Shore Based	Embarked	Total
1 December	[1] 96	184	[1] 280
10 December	72	288	360
16 December	0	318	318
23 December	0	398	398

[1] Plus 35th Fighter-Bomber Group (2 USAF, 1 RAAF F–51 squadrons).

at first been limited to two fast carriers and one escort carrier, much more was now on hand, and the total of Navy and Marine squadrons operating in the X Corps area had risen from 15 on 1 December to 22 as the evacuation was ending. For a brief moment Task Force 77 reached a peak strength of 4 attack carriers, one battleship, 2 cruisers, and 22 destroyers, and except for snow on deck and ice on the forecastle it began to look like old times.

Throughout the period of embarkation carrier air operations continued. Over Hungnam the jet combat air patrol was maintained, but with gaps: owing to the limited endurance of the F9F and the spacing of task force launching times it proved impossible to relieve patrols on station. For the rest, the focus of air operations narrowed steadily from the northern hills to the embarkation area. In mid-December, as outloading was begun, attacks were being flown against troops and horses along the reservoir road, abandoned equipment in the Songjin area, and targets near the Fusen Reservoir. A tunnel on the narrow gauge railroad leading up to Hagaru was hit with 11-inch Tiny Tim rockets; to the westward armed reconnaissance flights struck at enemy troops moving south across the Wonsan-Pyongyang road. Ten days later, as the date of final departure approached and with a perimeter which covered only the city of Hungnam, the situation was very different. Although lacking in armor and artillery, enemy troops had reached the suburbs in sizable numbers; and while perhaps a third of the sorties were still employed upcountry, the greater part was used within the 35-mile circle. Troop movements on the roads approaching the town were hit; fuel drums and a rocket dump, overlooked in the sweeping-up process, were attacked and destroyed; an enemy command post in Hamhung and buildings on the western edge of Hungnam were bombed. And by this time the guns of the fire support ships had come into play.

Admiral Hillenkoetter began shooting on the night of the 15th, as *Saint Paul* commenced 8-inch call fire for deep support and for interdiction of enemy movements. On the 17th *Rochester* took the 8-inch duty, and nightly thereafter cruisers and destroyers delivered prearranged harassing and illumination fire, while responding to requests from ashore by day. To supplement the flat-trajectory fire of the cruisers and destroyers, and to put plunging fire on reverse slopes, the three rocket ships had been maintained on station; on the 21st they let go their first barrage against a reported troop concentration in the hills along the eastern flank.

Gunfire support more than met all tests, although these, it should be said, were not severe. There was some difficulty with control arrangements resulting from an unfortunate choice of radio channels, and from intervention by X Corps in the assignment of missions to specific ships. The success of the departing artillery battalions in using up the local ammunition oversupply had imbued commanders ashore with large ideas; the resultant pressures led to an extravagant volume of fire, and this in turn, given the limited capacity of ships' magazines, to a replenishment problem. But the needs were met by the Logistic Support Group, which kept an AKA and an LST loaded with ammunition on station in Hungnam harbor, with delivery to the firing ships accomplished by off-loading into the AKL *Ryer,* one of the small cargo vessels which MSTS had inherited from the Army. By these expedients the impressive total of 18,637 rounds of 5-inch and 2,932 of 8-inch was fired during the evacuation phase, an increase respectively of about 70 and 27 percent over expenditures in the Inchon landing. The investment was perhaps excessive, in view of the paucity of targets, but it was written off as a contribution to troop morale.

By now the perimeter had diminished to a radius of about 5,000 yards from the center of town, outposted for another thousand yards, and the evacuation was entering its final stage. On 18 December Captain Kelly returned from the south, and was placed in charge of the shore-to-ship movement of the remaining corps and 3rd Division troops. Early on the afternoon of the 19th Major General Robert H. Soule, USA, commander of the 3rd Division, took charge of the ground defenses; General Almond and his staff moved aboard *Mount McKinley;* and responsibility for the defense of Hungnam passed to Admiral Doyle. Next day the 7th Division completed embarkation, and at first light on the 21st was sailed to the southward. On shore there remained three RCTs with their tanks, six battalions of artillery, and three antiaircraft battalions. Loading of corps and division troops was being pressed; the tempo of naval gunfire was going up as artillery began to be withdrawn; and D-Day had been tentatively set for the 24th.

One aspect of the operation which had by now developed wholly unanticipated proportions was the problem of the Korean refugees. In a sense this problem was not new. In July, as the North Korean armies pressed southward, the countless civilians fleeing before them had created grave difficulties for the U.N. forces. In late October the combination of ROK and Marine forces at Kojo, and of Communist units in the hills, had produced a similar if smaller phenomenon, as thousands of Koreans had descended from the hinterland upon the port. With the intervention of the Chinese and the reverses of the U.N. the spectacle of displaced masses of humanity again developed.

In the first week of December thousands of North Koreans, fleeing the Chinese armies, had sailed from Chinnampo. At Wonsan, where Captain Jarrell had arranged a screening of civilians so that those whose lives would be endangered by the Communists could be removed, an anticipated thousand refugees had multiplied beyond belief. With 7,000 aboard, and with the ships filled to capacity, the transport crews had been confronted with the tragic sight of another 20,000 trying to break through the barbed wire barriers, and had concluded that about twice the population of Wonsan had gathered there in the hope of escape. At Hungnam it was still worse.

Refugees on Green Beach: The bullock cart stops at tidewater and the LST takes over. In the background a merchant ship alongside Dock 4. 19 December 1950. (USN 424096)

303

For the inhabitants of North Korea the miseries of war had been compounded by the arrival of an alien army from across the Yalu. Villagers on the Chosin plateau, their houses taken over by the Chinese, had requested the Marines to call down air strikes upon the invader; their wishes had been granted them, and their villages had been burned from the air. Thus twice dispossessed, and preferring the invader from overseas to the invader from the north, the tide of humanity flowed southward toward Hungnam. As the Marines moved down from Hagaru the thousands of civilians followed, huddling outside the perimeter by night and moving onward when the march resumed, presenting both tragic spectacle and military menace.

At Hungnam an original estimate of 25,000 refugees requiring evacuation had quickly to be abandoned. Early in the operation Colonel Forney found himself with 50,000 in hastily constructed camps and more pouring in; at Hamhung more than 50,000 had attempted to board the last refugee train for Hungnam. In the light of these numbers the few vessels furnished by the Republic of Korea were wholly inadequate, and other shipping had to be committed at an early date. The exodus involved an incredible packing of humanity: LST loads were never less than 5,000, and in one case reached 10,500; a total of about 14,000 was taken out in the chartered *Meredith Victory*. On the 23rd, as preparations to close down were being completed, a temporary surplus of shipping developed, and Forney brought in three Victory ships and two LSTs on which he loaded 50,000 Koreans. In the end the record showed 91,000 taken out, not counting children in arms, in knapsacks, or *in utero*. If this was a remarkable accomplishment no one congratulated himself overmuch, for, as the report concludes, "at least that number had to be left behind for lack of shipping space, and riot among these was only prevented by subterfuge."

Heavy Chinese pressure had been expected from about the 20th, but although from time to time night probing attacks were reported, the perimeter remained generally quiet to the last. With loading ahead of schedule, and with sufficient shipping on hand, 4,000 tons of ammunition and 13 boxcars were added to the scheduled lift. On the 22nd the 3rd Division began loading everything but the infantry and artillery, while excess transport from these units was put on board during that day and the next. As zero hour approached, air support was increased, and the offensive sorties from Task Force 77 went up from 105 on the 21st to 161 on the 23rd. General Almond had repeatedly suggested bringing in *Missouri* from Task Force 77, and Struble had planned to do so for the final phase. So in she came on the 23rd, as the last battalion of corps artillery was being taken off. That night naval gunfire increased by a factor of three.

The 24th of December dawned clear, and by 0800 all was in readiness. To lift the remaining 9,720 personnel, LVTs had been put up on the flanking beaches, and seven LSTs along the Hungnam waterfront. During the morning the gunfire ships maintained a zone barrage covering a mile-wide area outside the 3,000-yard perimeter. At 1100, as the troops began to pull back, embarkation was begun. Everything went as planned. The enemy made no appearance. The only difficulties were caused by an accidental explosion of an ammunition dump, which destroyed some landing craft and resulted in a number of casualties. By 1405 all beaches were secured. At 1410 Admiral Doyle ordered the UDT personnel to blow the place, demolition charges were set off, and the piers, cranes, and walls of the inner harbor disappeared in an eruption of smoke and flame.

By 1436 all hands were off and Captain Kelly was preparing to sortie the amphibious shipping. Overhead in the cold sky there orbited the last combat air patrol from the fast carrier task force. Along the docks the explosions had stopped, but fire was licking at the ruins, and from the harbor of Hungnam, briefly one of the world's busiest ports, a column of smoke rose high into the air. Three miles inland, as the gunfire ships were getting underway, some Chinese troops were observed coming over a hill, and a few Parthian salvos were let go at these individuals, who by their temerity thus achieved the distinction of receiving the last rounds of the campaign.

The statistics of the evacuation are worth noting: 105,000 U.S. and Korean military personnel, 91,000 refugees, 350,000 measurement tons of cargo, 17,500 vehicles. The available shipping had proved sufficient, although most vessels had to make two trips, some made more, and the loads involved totalled 6 APAs, 6 AKAs, 13 T-APs, 76 MSTS time-charters, 81 LSTs, and 11 LSDs. As for comparisons with other operations, none seems very fruitful. Dunkirk comes first to mind, but circumstances there were very different: 338,000 troops were taken out, but many remained behind, hardly any equipment was saved, and the ships involved suffered grievously from air attack. But such questions concerning the degree of enemy opposition and the size of the lift tend to obscure the central point, that freedom to come and go depends upon control of the sea. The Athenians at Syracuse, Cornwallis at Yorktown, the Axis forces in North Africa lacked this control. In those armies no one escaped captivity.

5. *7 December 1950–25 January 1951: The Second Chinese Offensive*

Evacuations, doubtless, can hardly be counted victories, but the conduct of the December campaign in northeastern Korea was nevertheless impressive. Despite the suddenness of the Chinese onslaught, the extraordinarily exposed position of the Marine Division, and an enemy numerical superiority of more than two to one, the situation never quite escaped from control, and from the time the Yudam-ni Marines reached Hagaru there was little question as to who held the initiative. Under the severest possible conditions the march to

Blow and go: The last LCVPs leave the western side of the harbor as the docks go up. 24 December 1950.

(USN 424299)

the sea was successfully accomplished; only the barest minimum of equipment and supplies had to be destroyed; the evacuation, with no air or submarine opposition and with little pressure on the ground, was a deliberate, orderly, and controlled process.

This is not to say that the campaign was cheap. With a strength slightly exceeding 25,000, the Marine Division between 27 November and 11 December suffered 556 killed, 182 missing, 2,872 wounded, and 3,648 non-battle casualties, the last largely from frostbite. But for the Chinese Third Field Army the campaign was a disaster. The 60,000 men of the eight divisions committed by the 9th Army Group were later estimated by the Marine Corps to have suffered 37,500 combat casualties, a little over half inflicted by the ground forces and the rest by air attack. Of estimates such as these everyone must be his own judge, but the order of magnitude appears not far from the mark. Total casualties, indeed, would seem to have been still greater, for the Chinese had been engaged not only with the Marine Division and with naval and Marine aviation but had also had to fight the cold, and for them General Winter proved a more redoubtable enemy than for the Americans. Poorly clad, poorly fed, without hospitalization or air evacuation, the Chinese froze to death in quantities: the CCF 27th Army, which had put in two divisions at the opening of the campaign, alone complained of 10,000 non-combat casualties.

Whatever the precise figure of their losses, doubtless also unknown to them, it seems fair to say that in forcing the Marine Division down off the plateau the 9th Army Group committed military suicide. Much concern, following the evacuation, was evinced in U.N. command circles over the possibility that Chen Yi's divisions might move south to reinforce the Fourth Field Army, and on 2 January Commander Seventh Fleet and CTF 95 were urgently instructed to report all information on the location and movements of this force. But not until mid-March, three full months later, was the 9th Army Group again identified in action.

In the west, in contrast to the campaign at the reservoir, action had been brief. Contact with the Chinese was broken in the first days of December, as Eighth Army retired rapidly on Seoul; for more than three weeks the ground forces were out of touch; and the only war in progress was that carried on by Fifth Air Force, whose attacks inflicted heavy casualties and soon forced the enemy to confine his movement to the hours of darkness. But the fact that Communist success against Eighth Army was limited to the first days of combat, and that the march to the sea and the evacuation of X Corps were handled in masterly fashion, should not operate to conceal the effects of the Chinese onslaught. Strategically and psychologically the enemy's success was great. In the long run Chinese intervention would entail abandonment of the objective of Korean unification, and a return to the original U.N. aim of repelling aggression; for the moment, however, it seemed that it might force the evacuation of Korea. Since a concern for the integrity of China had been a major plank in American foreign policy for more than half a century, and a fundamental reason for the embroilment of the United States and Japan, this accomplishment of the new Chinese regime ranks high among the ironies of history.

Throughout December the planning of the U.N. Command was retrograde to a degree; having suffered one reverse it prepared rapidly for more. The plan of 7 December had envisaged resistance in the area of Seoul, with subsequent retirement upon Pusan, and the results of this concept were manifest in efforts to fortify the Naktong line and in the assignment of Navy underwater demolition teams to a survey of beaches in South Korea, Tsushima Island, and western Japan in preparation for an emergency withdrawal. At Inchon Admiral Thackrey was scouting the Tokchok Islands as a possible refuge in an emergency redeployment; on 6 December, with the evacuation of Kimpo in prospect, he had asked Admiral Struble for carrier air support; on the 7th, two days before X Corps was ordered to redeploy south from Hungnam, he was instructed to start the removal of Army supplies from Inchon. Soon Eighth Army would pose a requirement for naval gunfire support along the entire western coast of South Korea.

On 8 December there came an astonishing report from EUSAK of a 20-ship Chinese convoy en route from Shanghai for a landing in Korea; by the 12th this had grown to a fleet of 100 ships headed for Ongjin; on the 14th *Theseus* was held back from replenishment by a report of 20 AKs approaching Sinanju. But these shortly shrank to fishing boats, and the convoy never appeared. By midmonth air raid alarms were a daily occurrence in the Seoul area; on the 14th a Navy helicopter was attacked by MIGs which had ventured south to within a few miles of Haeju. Four days later FEAF closed down its electronic navigational installation on Tokchok To, and men and gear were taken out by LSU. As yet there were no positive indications that the Chinese would cross the 38th parallel; equally, there was little evidence of a firm intention to defend the capital. President Rhee and his government had refused to leave for the southward, but by the 20th Eighth Army headquarters had been withdrawn to Taegu, where it was joined by Fifth Air Force on the 22nd.

In these gloomy circumstances General Walker was killed in a road accident, like General Patton before him, and Lieutenant General Matthew B. Ridgway, USA, was ordered out from Washington to take over Eighth Army. Both in the capital from which he departed, and in the peninsula which was his destination, it might have seemed that Ridgway was being appointed receiver in bankruptcy: CincFE's early dispatches had produced an atmosphere of depression in Washington; the Truman-Attlee talks of early December concerned themselves, among other things, with the question of seeking a cease-fire; and U.N. efforts in this same direction ended only with Chinese rejection of the terms proposed. Efforts to increase the nation's armed strength were redoubled, and on 15 December the President declared a state of national emergency. But results would take time, and the available reserve within the continental United States remained at one Army and one Marine division.

Unable, in the circumstances, to honor General MacArthur's request for reinforcements for the defense of Japan, the Joint Chiefs began to consider withdrawal from Korea to the Japanese islands. These deliberations resulted in a new directive of 29 December, which may be taken as a measure of the Chinese Communist success. The safety of the U.N. Command and of Japan were given precedence over support of the Republic of Korea, the enemy was conceded the capability of forcing a U.N. evacuation, and instructions now called for defense in successive positions and for the infliction of maximum damage on the Communists.

Of this estimate of Chinese capabilities, as seen through the dark glass of CincFE's dispatches, time would be the test. But if General Ridgway had indeed been nominated as receiver in bankruptcy, he acquired upon his arrival in Korea certain welcome assets. The Fourth Chinese Field Army, victor in the battle of the Chongchon, was suffering in its southward progress from logistic inadequacy and from the efforts of the Fifth Air Force. Completion of the Hungnam evacuation had provided a considerable Christmas bonus, and the land and naval forces which had demobilized the Chinese 9th Army Group were now available for the defense of South Korea.

On Christmas Day the command of Task Force 77 changed as Admiral Ewen, after four months of strenuous operations, was relieved by Admiral Ofstie, and sailed with *Philippine Sea* and *Leyte* for Japan. Fifty days had passed since CincFE's alarm had summoned the Seventh Fleet from port, and throughout that time, in bitter winter weather, an intense air effort had been maintained, without return to port, and with all needs cared for by the mobile replenishment groups. Two fast carriers now remained on the line, voice and CW communications with the JOC were at last functioning effectively, and on the same day Admiral Struble advised Fifth Air Force that his ships would resume air operations on the 28th, and would provide from 75 to 100 Corsair and Skyraider sorties daily. On the 27th, in a conference between FEAF and NavFE, it was agreed to use the carrier aircraft in support of the eastern front, with pilots pre-briefed for armed reconnaissance should no CAS targets be available. On the next day operations began as scheduled, directed principally against troops and troop shelters in the central mountains along the 38th parallel.

On 26 December, as General Ridgway arrived in Korea, X Corps was integrated into Eighth Army. At Pusan the last of the Hungnam forces were going ashore. On the east coast the sweepers were hard at work clearing an inshore lane for the destroyers, now back at their summer's task of

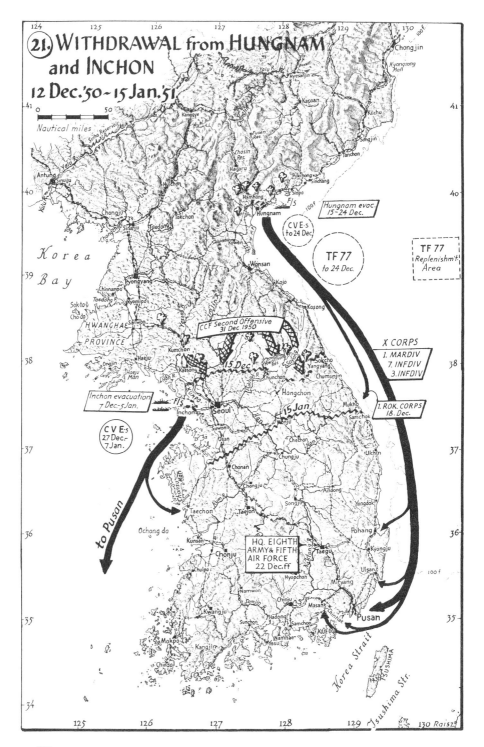

21. WITHDRAWAL from HUNGNAM and INCHON
12 Dec.'50 ~ 15 Jan.'51

0   50
Nautical miles

Chongjin
Kyongsong Man
Kapsan
Kichu
Kanggye
Songjin
Fusen Res.
Chasin Res.
Hagaru
Sinchang
Pukchong
Tanchon
Antung
Sinuiju
Huichon
Hamhung
Sinpo
Hungnam
Hungnam evac. 15-24 Dec.
C.V.E.s to 24 Dec
Chongju
Tokchon
TF 77 to 24 Dec.
TF 77 Replenishm't Area
Kowan
Korea Bay
Wonsan
Pyongyang
Kyomipo
Kojo
Chinnampo
Sok-to
Cho-do
Taedong
Sariwon
Kosong
HWANGHAE PROVINCE
CCF Second Offensive 31 Dec. 1950
Kumchon
Ongjin
Haeju
Haeju Man
15 Dec
Kaesong
Hwachon Res.
Sokcho
Yangyang
Chunchon
Chumunjin
X CORPS
1. MARDIV
7. INFDIV
3. INFDIV
Hongchon
Inchon evacuation 7 Dec.-5 Jan.
Seoul
Inchon
15 Jan
Mukho
Samchok
1. ROK. CORPS 18. Dec.
Suwon
Wonju
Chechon
C.V.E.s 27 Dec.- 7 Jan.
Osan
Han R.
Chungju
Ulchin
Chonan
Chongju
Andong
Yongdok
Taechon
Taejon
Songju
Pohang
Ochong do
Kunsan
Kyongju
HQ. EIGHTH ARMY & FIFTH AIR FORCE 22 Dec. ff
Taegu
Chonju
Ulsan
100 f
to Pusan
Hyopchon
Miryang
Namwon
Chinju
Masan
Chimhae
Pusan
Kwangju
Hadong
Samchon
Sunchon
Mokpo
Namhae
Yosu
KOJE DO
Kangjin
Korea Strait
Chindo
TSUSHIMA
Tsushima Str.
130 Raisz

supporting ROK units on the coastal road. At the western end of the line, where an enemy drive on Seoul was momently awaited, reinforcements from Hungnam were also arriving. In response to earlier requests from Admiral Thackrey, *Sicily* and *Badoeng Strait* had started west on Christmas Day; on the 27th they relieved *Theseus* in the Yellow Sea operating area and began to fly missions in support of Eighth Army. On the 29th Admiral Hillenkoetter arrived at Inchon with *Rochester,* to join *Ceylon* and the Australian destroyers *Warramunga* and *Bataan* in the support of forces on the Kumpo peninsula.

As yet, however, the Chinese had not resumed the attack, a situation which raises some interesting problems in relative motion. The Fourth Field Army had entered Pyongyang on 5 December while the Marine Division was still up on the hill at Hagaru. By the time the Chinese had covered the ninety miles from Pyongyang to the parallel, X Corps had been concentrated, evacuated, and relanded in South Korea, and ships which had covered the evacuation had rounded the peninsula to help confront the expected western offensive. These facts say something about floating weapons systems, most notably perhaps in the case of embarked aviation, for while the Air Force was shortly to be forced out of Kimpo and Suwon, and by 5 January would have no operating base forward of Taegu, the carriers were now working off both ends of the battle line. They say something also about the rudimentary nature of Chinese logistics, the effectiveness of Fifth Air Force's December effort against the advancing enemy, and the validity of the estimates which conceded to the Chinese the ability to throw the U.N. armies into the sea.

With orders to defend important positions, inflict maximum damage, and preserve its major units, Eighth Army awaited the enemy on a line running from the Han Delta up the Imjin, and eastward through the razorbacked mountains of central Korea, to Yangyang on the Sea of Japan. Here, in the northern basin of the Han, strategic virtue lies not in the western coastal plain but in the valley routes of the interior. With the water barriers of the Yesong and the Imjin, the road from Pyongyang is easy to defend, but to the invader from the north all streams flow onward to the Han and all roads lead to Seoul. Once at the headwaters of the northern tributaries, movement is all downhill: south from Chorwon to the capital, southwest from Chunchon to the Pukhan Valley, through Hongchon to the Han Valley road, west from Wonju to take the capital in the rear. In the presence of so many flanking routes, the defense of Seoul depends less on holding the west coast road than on plugging the valleys to the northeast; failing in this the position becomes untenable.

The enemy arrived with the New Year. On the left three Chinese armies pushed down the northern approaches to the capital; in the center another heavy thrust was delivered north of Wonju. Further retirement seemed necessary, and on 4 January Seoul was abandoned, the Han bridges were blown, and the army started south again. At Inchon all ships were put on one-hour notice, and on orders from ComNavFE the destruction of the port was begun.

There, as the enemy offensive broke, Admiral Thackrey had at his disposal his flagship *Eldorado,* one AKA, two APAs, two LSDs, one APD, two U.S. Navy and nine Scajap LSTs; in Japan MSTS was holding 15 empty Victory ships and transports as a reserve. Although Eighth Army intended to retire by land rather than redeploy by sea, the staff of Task Group 90.1 had worked up plans for all contingencies, including an emergency outloading of up to 135,000 troops by shuttle service to the off-shore islands. But these precautions proved unnecessary, and the principal withdrawal from the Seoul area was carried out, as planned, by road.

The sea lift from Inchon was nevertheless a sizable one. The original estimates from EUSAK, which had called for the sailing of between 3,000 and 5,000 personnel, had been surpassed by 18 December, and the total lifted out during the month amounted to 32,000 troops, more than 1,000 vehicles, and 55,000 tons of cargo. Completion of the Hungnam evacuation brought six more Scajap LSTs together with some MSTS vessels, and the advent of the Chinese speeded the work. On 5 January port facilities were blown, somewhat purposelessly, it would seem, in view of U.N. control of Korean waters, and as the Chinese entered the town Thackrey sortied his shipping. In these last five days a few hundred more vehicles, a few thousand more tons of supplies, and another 37,000 military personnel had been taken out. In vehicles and cargo the Inchon evacuation was far smaller than that at Hungnam; in personnel, however, the addition of 64,200 Korean nationals to the 69,000 military yields a not unimpressive figure. But the accomplishment had to be its own reward: of the large number of press correspondents currently accredited to the U.N. naval forces, all but one had elected to cover Hungnam.

As in the previous summer, major ports were now in short supply. With Inchon gone only overloaded Pusan remained, and there the larger ships were sailed. But there was still the problem of supporting the western flank without overwhelming the Pusan port organization and the rail and road systems, and this time it was met by the opening of a seaport where none had existed before. Twenty-five miles north of Kunsan, at the mouth of Chonsu Man, the town of Taechon lies at the head of a drying bay; from Taechon a road and single-tracked railroad run northeast, joining the main line at Chonan, behind the new-formed front. Here in September CincFE's momentary apprehensions about Inchon had brought the UDTs from *Bass* to seek a second landing place; here in December, as a precautionary measure, Thackrey had swept a major anchorage area; here in January, following a check-sweep by *Carmick* and *Swallow,* the Inchon LSTs were beached and

Thai frigate Prasae aground behind enemy lines. In the distance destroyers and a helicopter from Task Force 95.
January 1951. (USN 432568)

their men and stores unloaded.   On the 8th, a convoy came up from Ulsan with artillery and tanks of the 3rd Division, and between the 9th and 12th this support was continued by 13 Scajap LSTs, which brought POL and other urgently needed cargo from Pusan to Taechon and Kunsan.

Throughout the period of retirement the naval forces of the U.N. did what they could to help stem the Chinese tide.   On the east coast the destroyers worked to help the ROK defenders, while Admiral Ofstie's carriers flew strikes against enemy concentrations in the central mountains and westward to the area of Seoul.   At Inchon *Rochester, Kenya,* and *Ceylon* supported the withdrawal across the Han and the evacuation of the port, and bombarded Kimpo airfield.   From the Yellow Sea the Marine fighter pilots embarked in *Sicily* and *Badoeng Strait* flew in to provide protective patrols, strike the advancing enemy, and burn quantities of abandoned supplies at Kimpo.   On 1 January EUSAK's wish for more support brought a request for increased carrier strength, and two days later *Bataan* arrived to join the west coast group.   For a brief period, from 30 December to 3 January, the possibility of a diversionary landing at Haeju was under active consideration.

In the Sea of Japan on 7 January *Philippine Sea* and *Leyte* returned to action; but while *Princeton* retired to Sasebo for upkeep, such was the magnitude of the Communist offensive that *Valley Forge* was held on station.   For the next two weeks three carriers were kept on the line, working in the triangular pattern which permitted daily operations by two while the third replenished.   But their effectiveness, as indeed that of all supporting forces, was severely limited by the January foul weather, which on 12 days brought winds exceeding 30 knots.   On the 7th, in a snowstorm, the Thai frigate *Prasae* went aground on the east coast, behind the enemy lines, and despite prolonged attempts at salvage had ultimately to be destroyed.   From 6 to 10 January low clouds and heavy snow prevented carrier operations; on the 10th things were so bad that all land-based aircraft were grounded; and from the 11th to the 13th Task Force 77 was forced to operate south of the peninsula where the visibility was somewhat better.

The coming of the bad weather coincided with a shift of enemy pressure to the central front.   In the west on 7 January U.N. patrols had moved north without opposition to the neighborhood of Inchon, but in the center very heavy fighting continued, infiltrating Chinese forces reached south to the 37th parallel, and reviving North Korean guerrillas raided supply lines inside the Naktong Basin.   On 9 January the Marine Division was ordered out of Army reserve and moved up to prevent enemy penetrations south of the Andong-Yongdok road.   On the 11th, with clearing weather, aircraft from Task Force 77 attacked large troop concentrations southeast of Wonju, at Kangnung on the east coast, and as far south as the headwaters of the Naktong.

Weather at sea: Water over the flight deck of Valley Forge. (USN 440889)

315

As snowstorms swirled through the mountains of central Korea, where the battle for Wonju was in progress, the weather was bad in other high places as well.   To a CincFE message of 29 December, which had posed the alternatives of expanding the war or evacuating Korea, the Joint Chiefs on 9 January replied with a repetition of earlier instructions to defend, inflict maximum damage, and withdraw if the safety of the command and of Japan so required.   On the next day CincFE reiterated that lacking either reinforcement or an expansion of the war the position in Korea was untenable, and urged, in the absence of overriding political considerations, as rapid a withdrawal as possible.   This view, together with his observations that his troops were embittered and that the defense of a beachhead would be costly, led to more gloom in Washington and to a new directive.   On the 12th, while emphasizing their desire for time to permit military and diplomatic consultations, the Joint Chiefs accepted the view that holding for a protracted period was infeasible.   At Lake Success a second effort at a cease-fire was begun on the basis of a plan which, in exchange for a U.N.-approved administration of a unified Korea, would include the government of Communist China in an agency designed to settle the issues of Formosa and of Chinese membership in the United Nations.   But in turn the Chinese now overreached themselves, and insisted that admission to the United Nations and the commencement of Korean negotiations precede any cease-fire.

By the time this diplomatic fumble took place the Korean balance was beginning to tilt the other way.   On the west coast, behind enemy lines, carrier aircraft had reported ROK flags flying in the coastal villages, and the governor of Hwanghae Province had asked for ammunition; on 13 January CTF 95 recommended to ComNavFE the arming of the estimated 10,000 patriotic volunteers in this area.   At EUSAK, far from looking over his shoulder toward Pusan, General Ridgway was directing his gaze northward.   On the 16th a reconnaissance in force had penetrated as far as Suwon; soon diminished contact in the center would bring more ambitious efforts. By the 20th General MacArthur was demonstrating a qualified optimism. By the 23rd ground fighting was limited to bushwhacking in the south, where the Marines were rounding up guerrillas.   On 25 January the northward movement of Eighth Army began against only slight resistance.   Ten days later the Chinese commander had decided to retire beyond the 38th parallel.

CHAPTER X

The Second Six Months

1. *February, 1951: Back to the Han*

B Y LATE JANUARY the immediate crisis was over, but as the armies started north again it was still a new war. Not only had the arrival of the Chinese made it difficult to see the conflict as a mere police action against a minor league aggressor; it had also forced the United Nations and the United States back to the original aim of repelling aggression, and in doing so had changed the nature of the fighting. Avoidance of defeat at the Pusan perimeter had been followed by a resort to an amphibious strategy and to larger goals, and by four months of rapid movement up and down the peninsula. But this was history. By January the objectives had been revised, no plans for great amphibious operations existed, X Corps had been integrated into Eighth Army, a more or less continuous front now stretched from sea to sea. Although the focus of action had always been on land, the campaign in Korea in the first half of 1951 was more than ever a ground war.

Depending upon one's preconceptions, one could look at the Korean War as a land campaign with amphibious aspects or as an amphibious war with resemblances to a continental struggle. Whatever the precise nature of this hybrid conflict, which indeed varied with the passing of time, it posed difficult problems of marrying the divergent histories of the Pacific and European theaters of operations, and of coordinating forces which postwar military doctrine had attempted to separate. These difficulties had been briefly apparent during the defense of the perimeter in the previous August; inevitably, with the coming of a stabilized front, the question of how to integrate a naval force into a land campaign again arose. This question had implications for almost all the subdivisions of Naval Forces Far East.

The fate of the Marine Division, designed, trained, and so far largely employed as a force to bridge the gap between control of the sea and large-scale operations ashore, was paradoxical. The postwar years had seen the Marines repeatedly accused of trying to develop a "second army," and much effort had been expended within the Defense Department to reduce the corps to guard functions and to prevent its again developing a force of the size and sort so useful in the war against Japan. Now, however, in the

317

existing stringency of Army units, the Marines were integrated into Eighth Army along with the rest of X Corps; after a period devoted to guerrilla-chasing in the neighborhood of Andong they would find themselves committed by higher authority to sustained land combat. Although there was no question of their competence to perform such duty, this continued employment on inland work made it difficult to maintain their special skills, divorced as they now were by distance from the Amphibious Force and naval gunfire support, and by doctrine from their Aircraft Wing.

In July CincFE had promised General Craig that the integrity of the Marine air-ground team would be preserved. But circumstances alter cases, and this situation did not outlast the Hungnam evacuation. With a single front in existence, and with ground commanders eager to share the benefits of Marine close air support, MAW 1 was absorbed by the Fifth Air Force and employed in accordance with Air Force doctrine. The wing's commanding general found himself bypassed in the operational chain of command, and efforts by the division to have their own planes assigned to their support were turned down. The long history of cooperative training and the great fund of recent experience acquired at Inchon and at the reservoir were to a considerable degree sacrificed, and so far as air support in the line was concerned the Marines now had to take pot luck with everyone else.

The Amphibious Force, perhaps the most important single weapons system of the war so far, and the one whose capabilities had governed both advance and retreat, was still on hand, but commitment of the landing force to the ground front had greatly limited its future possibilities. As the new year opened, the principal activity of Admiral Doyle's units was in preparation for a possible large-scale emergency evacuation of the Korean peninsula. Surveys of Korean and Japanese beaches, begun in anticipation of a forced and hasty departure, were continuing at a rapid rate, and by June would have provided essential information on some 40 miles of strategically located shore line. The single untoward incident to mar this operation occurred on 19 January, halfway between Kunsan and Mokpo and far south of the battle-line, when some apparent civilians, previously engaged in conversation with *Bass'* survey party, produced concealed weapons, killed two, and wounded three.

This hydrographic work, however, required the participation of but a fraction of the force. The greater part of Task Force 90 was consequently divided into three roughly equal groups, and an employment schedule worked out which assigned one to amphibious training of Army troops in Japan, and one to upkeep and maintenance at Yokosuka, while the third remained on call for services to the forces in the peninsula. On 15 January the job of transporting refugees and prisoners to Koje Do and Cheju Do was assigned CTF 90, and five days later an AKA lifted the first load of refugees from Pusan. This was the last task imposed upon Admiral Doyle. At Pusan, on the 24th, he was relieved by Rear Admiral Ingolf N. Kiland, in a ceremony which numbered CincPacFleet, ComNavFE, and Commander Seventh Fleet among those present.

Along the coastline matters were less changed, and in both Yellow Sea and Sea of Japan the Blockading and Escort Force continued to perform its duties. If fire support of amphibious operations was no longer required of the gunnery ships, the blockade remained important, and there were coastal targets to bombard. In the east, where the enemy had been checked at Mukho, the front was still susceptible of support by naval gunfire. But the fighting was less intense than in the previous summer, and as both sides increasingly concentrated their weight of effort in the central mountains, the pace of action on the coastal road diminished.

For the minesweepers, however, nothing had altered. Their work continued as before, and their tasks remained arduous, uncomfortable, and dangerous. The short winter daylight hampered operations; the winter weather, with high winds and freezing spray, made small ship work particularly uncomfortable. There was always the chance of new minefields or of the replenishment of those previously swept; the continued possibility of influence mines increased the load; intelligence reports indicated that the enemy was preparing a new mining campaign. Minesweeping capabilities, nevertheless, had been increased, and something better than the shoestring force of the previous autumn was now on hand. The four DMS, oversized for their task, had proven only marginally useful, and two were shortly to be returned to the United States, but 13 AMS and 2 AMs were now available, and 2 more of the latter were en route. Although the LST conversion to headquarters ship and helicopter base was still in the works, the force was profiting from the support of the LSD *Comstock*. In the naval establishment at large the efforts in updating and improving mine warfare, begun following the unpleasant experiences at Wonsan, were being pressed. Technological development was being expedited, and the coordinated tactical employment of patrol plane and helicopter search and of underwater demolition teams was moving forward. With the reestablishment early in the year of the Mine Force Pacific Fleet, and the appointment of Admiral Higgins as type commander, the sweepers at last acquired a home of their own and an administrator who cared.

In January, in addition to routine checks of vital areas like the Chinhae entrance channel, the main effort of the minesweeping forces was devoted to the clearance between 36° and 38° 40', of an inshore lane, for the east coast fire support ships. This work, which permitted more effective support of the ROK I Corps on the coastal road, was completed by early February, but again at a cost. On 2 February the AMS *Partridge* hit a mine about a mile off Sokcho, just north of the parallel, and sank in ten minutes with a loss of ten killed or missing and six severely wounded.

With the completion of this sweep, fire support activities were stepped up. Along the eastern coast four of the eight destroyers of Task Group 95.2 were continuously on station, with one pair patrolling the 100-fathom curve north to the limit of the blockade, while the second provided fire support to the Korean troops. At Mukho, and at Yongchu Gap to the southward, ROKN forces had established minor operating bases, from which their small craft sortied to collect intelligence from behind enemy lines, and to tighten the blockade through control of North Korean junk traffic and of South Korean fishing.

Although the hydrography of Korea's western shore greatly limited the possibilities of naval gunfire, Task Group 95.1 was also active. In the west the prevalence of islands permitted the establishment of useful advanced bases, and the advance of 1950 had brought possession of holdings off Inchon and Haeju, of the Sir James Hall Group near the 38th parallel, of Cho Do and Sok To off the Taedong estuary, and of islands in the Yalu Gulf. Most of these islands were informally controlled by guerrilla groups, and employed as bases for intelligence activities and for raids behind enemy lines. But responsibility for three of them—Ochong Do off Kunsan, Tokchok To in the Inchon approaches, and Taechong Do off the Ongjin peninsula—had been assigned to Admiral Andrewes' West Coast Group, and these islands had been given ROKN garrisons in January. Inshore patrol of the shallow coastal waters was provided by four groups of Korean ships, supported as necessary by Andrewes' surface units, which otherwise continued to maintain their designated blocking points, patrol northward into the Yalu Gulf, and bombard targets of opportunity.

For the carriers of Naval Forces Far East the deployment of January was little changed. With stabilization of the front and the passing of the emergency a reduction of Seventh Fleet strength from four carriers to three seemed feasible, and arrangements for regular maintenance desirable. *Leyte,* present in the Far East on loan from the Atlantic Fleet, was consequently headed homeward late in January, and a rotational schedule established which would send a third of the force at a time to Yokosuka for a ten-day stay. Taken together with the similar deployment of the ships of Task Force 90, this made for a considerable eastward shift in the logistic center of gravity, and for a corresponding reorientation of Service Force effort from Sasebo to Yokosuka.

The departure of *Leyte* left the Pacific Fleet with four fast carriers, *Valley Forge, Philippine Sea,* and *Princeton* in Korean waters, and *Boxer* under overhaul at San Francisco. But the reactivation of mothballed ships was proceeding apace, and more were coming. *Bon Homme Richard* and *Essex* were on the way, with arrivals in Far Eastern waters scheduled for May and August; shortly *Antietam* would be removed from the Reserve Fleet for arrival in October. By autumn the Pacific Fleet would contain seven operational fast carriers, compared with the three of the preceding June, and units on duty in the forward area could be rapidly and heavily reinforced.

Although *Badoeng Strait* and *Sicily* had left the Yellow Sea following the evacuation of Inchon, and had subsequently off-loaded their squadrons and sailed for the United States, west coast carrier operations did not lapse. The work of *Triumph* and *Theseus* had shown the need for carrier aircraft to enforce the blockade, to provide air strikes, aerial photography, and close support, and to spot gunfire for west coast surface units. On 7 January, as the escort carriers departed, *Theseus* again assumed the load, and following representations by Admiral Andrewes a continuity of effort was assured. The CVL *Bataan,* which had operated with the escort carriers during the critical period of the Inchon evacuation, was assigned by Admiral Struble to Task Group 95.1, and began to alternate ten-day periods of duty with *Theseus* as the principal unit of Task Element 95.11.

Something new had by now been added in the field of embarked aviation with the activation of an antisubmarine warfare task group, established by ComNavFE in view of the possibility that the intervention of new armies might be followed by an intervention of new weapons. An antisubmarine squadron was embarked in *Bairoko,* the escort carrier which in December had brought Air Force and Marine jet fighters to the Far East, and two destroyer divisions were added to make up Task Group 96.7, operating out of Yokosuka under the control of ComNavFE. Since enemy submarines did not in fact appear, this Hunter-Killer Group confined itself to training duties with the destroyers that were rotated through it from the other forces in Far Eastern waters.

Yet while the deployment of carrier strength remained the same, the problem of optimum employment was again much to the fore. Having been used first in long-range interdiction and emergency close support, and then in two landings and an evacuation, Task Force 77 now found itself faced with the long haul. In January its work had been principally in support of the battleline and in attacks on southward moving Chinese forces, a function of great importance in view of the withdrawal of shore-based squadrons to Japan. But as the ground situation stabilized, and the move back north began, the question of the relative usefulness of close support and interdiction arose once more.

For both these types of operation Task Force 77 had certain advantages not shared by other U.N. forces. Historically, naval aviation had been more sympathetic to close support than had the Air Force; the tradition was reflected in pilot training and doctrine, in tendencies in aircraft design which permitted heavier loads and more time on station, and in techniques of accurate dive bombing derived from a generation of training for attack on maneuvering ships. Although the communications problem, central to the close support difficulties of the early months, still remained, the Army's situation was so far improved that the normal air request net worked adequately in periods of relative inactivity, if not in time of crisis. Coordination of the carrier effort with that of Fifth Air Force had also shown some progress: daily by noon the air plan for the morrow was passed to JOC, while problems arising from crowded radio channels and last minute changes were reduced by the dispatch of a communications relay plane ahead of each strike, to shop for a controller and then brief the strike leader on a clear channel. All things considered, air support was going reasonably well.

Yet in interdiction, which in the context of the moment meant primarily the destruction of rail and highway bridges, the carrier air groups also had solid advantages. Even when based in Korea and modified by tip tanks, the F–80 Shooting Star, for the moment the standard Air Force fighter-bomber, lacked sufficient range and lift to accomplish much north of the Pyongyang-Hungnam radius, while from Japanese bases its load rarely exceeded two rockets and a tank of napalm. The F–51 Mustang had excellent lift and endurance, but was considered too vulnerable to the increasing threat of jet fighters for employment far to the north. The B–26 and B–29 had the lift and range, but were unsuited to attacks on small targets and were vulnerable, respectively, to antiaircraft and fighter opposition. Such opposition, of course, presented problems to the carrier planes as well, but approach routes and attack tactics were more flexible than those of horizontal bombers, the movable base and the built-in range of its aircraft permitted escorted strikes to the uttermost ends of Korea, and the load and accuracy of the AD made it uniquely effective against bridge targets.

As to the choice of employment one could find all opinions in all services. Although as a result of the earlier campaigns there had developed a strong Army school, particularly within X Corps, which favored the Navy-Marine system of close support, Admiral Struble's Christmas Day offer had elicited a request from EUSAK for interdiction of the northeastern transportation network. Doubtless a doubled carrier force, with half assigned each function, would have suited the Army best, but the postwar military establishment had not been designed with an eye to this. In its absence, and as operations went on, there ensued a period of debate and discussion which lasted through February.

In December, following the Chinese intervention, FEAF had prepared a new interdiction plan; in January, reports of rail activity in the northeast had led General Stratemeyer to inquire about the capabilities of the fast carrier task force in this regard. If the effort in close support were not to be diminished these capabilities were limited: only in the presence of *Valley Forge,* whose lack of jet squadrons was made up by a surplus of F4Us, could a two-carrier force take on the added load; with *Valley Forge* present, or with all three carriers in the line, two strikes a day could be sent northward on interdiction missions without prejudice to the support of the battleline. In response to FEAF's inquiry such an effort was begun, although both ComNavFE and Commander Seventh Fleet reaffirmed their view that given only suitable control facilities, close support was the most effective contribution the carriers could make, and urged that it remain the primary function. But in reply FEAF again put forward the need for interdiction to forestall a renewed Chinese offensive.

On 18 January the issue was discussed in a meeting at Taegu between Admiral Struble, the other major commanders in Korea, and the Army and Air Force Chiefs of Staff, out once again from Washington. Whatever the views of the other services, the Navy remained on the side of close support. After conferring with his carrier commanders, following his return to the fleet, Admiral Struble observed that an assignment to armed reconnaissance would be executed to the best of his capability, but reiterated his opinion that support of the line was more effective, and was punishing the enemy more severely, than was generally realized.

By this time the Chinese had broken contact and, following the reconnaissance to Suwon, General Ridgway had ordered a two-divisional advance toward the Han River. To assist this operation, known as "Thunderbolt," Yellow Sea forces were strengthened by the dispatch of *Saint Paul,* escorted by two destroyers, to provide 8-inch gunfire at Inchon. On both coasts, as the armies moved forward, the carrier air groups continued to contribute to the support of troops in the line.

With planning for the future still in flux, with the Marines chasing guerrillas in the southern mountains, and with Task Force 90 dispersed, there was no possibility of a flanking amphibious operation. Yet intelligence indicated an extreme Chinese concern with the landing in the rear, and if no such stroke was possible one could always pretend. As Eighth Army advanced and as ROK forces on the eastern shore were also moving forward, Admiral Smith conceived the notion of assisting their progress by an amphibious feint in the Kansong-Kosong area, some 50 miles beyond the front lines, where a slightly expanded coastal plain and a road through the mountains to the central front provided a logical objective for an assault from the sea. For this enterprise, Operation Ascendant, CTF 95 borrowed two AKAs, two LSTs, and a couple of rocket ships from the Amphibious Force, secured a promise of assistance from the fast carriers, and set sail on 29 January in his flagship, the destroyer tender *Dixie,* with his gunnery ships in company.

At 0700 on the 30th the bombardment group, *Missouri, Manchester,* and their screening destroyers, opened a vigorous fire on the Kansong area, and throughout the day the minesweepers, landing craft, and rocket ships went through their paces. After retiring seaward during the night, the force reappeared next morning off Kosong to repeat the bombardment effort. If the effectiveness of these maneuvers on enemy troop dispositions was largely unassessable, the operation was at least unique in the presence of a destroyer tender as flagship and participant in beach bombardment. Since such an event may never recur, let the record show that at 1400 on the 31st *Dixie* commenced firing on the beaches at Kosong, and expended 204 rounds.

At Inchon, where *Saint Paul* had arrived on 25 January, a second deceptive operation was scheduled to follow. There Admiral Hillenkoetter had been greeted by some short salvos from Wolmi Do, but with the assistance of an air strike from *Theseus,* and gunfire from *Ceylon* and some destroyers, the Wolmi batteries were neutralized and the Kimpo-Kumpo area subsequently kept under intermittent bombardment. On 6 February Admiral Andrewes sailed from Sasebo in *Belfast* to administer the pretended landing, and two days later, after some shooting in support of ROK troops at Kangnung, *Missouri* was started west.

Captain Kelly reached Inchon on the 8th, with two AKAs and an LSD, to simulate pre-landing operations; on the next day *Missouri* arrived and began to bombard enemy positions; a demonstration involving two transport divisions was planned for the afternoon tide of the 10th. But the affair was cancelled as a result of successes ashore: enemy resistance in the west, which had stiffened at the start of the month, gave way suddenly on the 9th, and the Chinese retired from the area; on the afternoon of the 10th Inchon was occupied by a party of ROK Marines from Tokchok To, and by nightfall American troops had reached the banks of the Han.

The reoccupation of Inchon was more than welcome. For the past month, as in the previous summer, Pusan had been a madhouse, as the difficulties of supplying the armies through a single port were compounded by the need to plan a complete and to accomplish a partial evacuation of Korea. Unfortunately, however, the advantages of a second port could not at once be realized. Not only would operations necessarily remain limited until the security of Inchon could be assured, but the demolitions of the previous month had to be cleared, a situation which raised some questions as to the wisdom, for the side which enjoyed command of the sea, of the policy of "blow and go" which had governed the evacuations. To accomplish the necessary restoration of facilities, and to get the port in working order, Admiral Thackrey had sailed from Yokosuka on 10 February with an amphibious task group carrying the Army's 2nd Engineer Special Brigade. He arrived on the 15th just as a new emergency was developing.

The advance to the Han and the recovery of Inchon had been followed by hard fighting in the center. There the move north from Wonju had begun on 5 February, and there, while giving way in the west, the enemy had reinforced his defenses. On the 11th the Chinese pushed a heavy attack down the valley north of Wonju, punched a hole in the ROK lines, and brought about a local collapse in which for four days large gaps existed in the front. One river valley to the eastward, similar difficulties arose from a

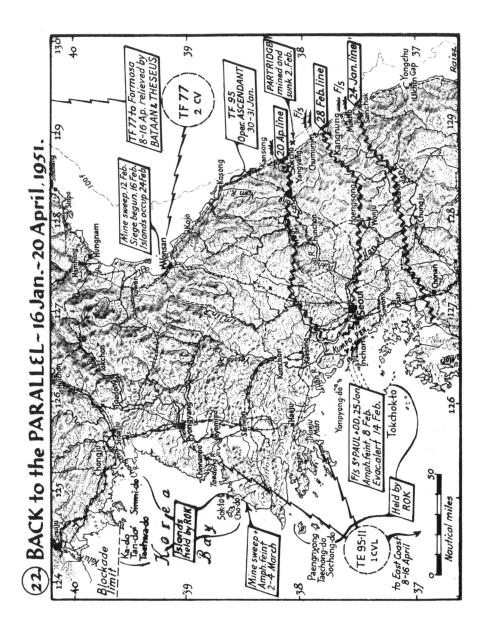

22 BACK to the PARALLEL ~ 16 Jan.~ 20 April. 1951.

Blockade limit

Korea Bay

Islands held by ROK

Mine sweep + Amph.feint 2-4 March

Paengnyang Taechong-do Sochong-do

TE 95-11 1 CVL

to East Coast 8-16 April

Held by ROK

F/s S'PAUL+DD, 25 Jan. Amph.feint 8 Feb. Evac.alert 14 Feb.

Tokchok-to

Yonpyong-do

TF 77 2 CV

TF 77 to Formosa 8-16 Ap. relieved by BATAAN & THESEUS

Mine sweep, 12 Feb. Siege begun, 16 Feb. Islands occup. 24 Feb.

TF 95 Oper. ASCENDANT 30-31 Jan.

20 Ap. line

F/s

F/s

PARTRIDGE mined and sunk 2. Feb.

28 Feb. line

24 Jan. line

Wonsan

Kansong

Kangnung

Mukho

Samchok

Chumunjin

Hoengsong

Wonju

Usan

Chonan

Seoul

Inchon

KUMPO PEN.

Han R.

Suwon

Nam R.

Yongchu Uichin Gap 37

Raisz.

Nautical miles

50

325

thrust aimed south at Chechon, while between Wonju and Seoul an enemy column struck southwestward toward Suwon. Such was the pressure in the center that on the 14th the Marine Division was relieved of its anti-guerrilla efforts in the south and ordered up to Wonju, while in the west the threat to Suwon brought an alert from Eighth Army for a possible evacuation of Inchon.

As a result of this alert, received just as the effort to open the port was beginning, Admiral Thackrey decided to avoid drying out LSTs on the mud-flats, and to limit his rate of unloading so that no more would be put ashore than could be packed up inside of 12 hours. With time the situation improved, but for the rest of February a truck shortage limited EUSAK's acceptance of cargo to a mere 500 tons a day, while a 48-hour withdrawal notice remained in effect for a full month. Considerable congestion resulted, as the ships of Task Group 90.1 being used to work the port and those held against the possibility of evacuation were joined by new arrivals with supplies for Eighth Army, and by early March, Thackrey was crying "Hold, enough!"

Prompt reinforcement of the menaced sectors checked the mid-February threat, and by the 18th the Communists had given up and were retiring. General Ridgway now resumed his advance with Operation Killer, a move forward by IX and X Corps in the center which would bring them abreast of the line in the west, and would clear the Wonju-Kangnung road. On 21 February the Marine Division led out from Wonju, and for the remainder of the month Eighth Army moved forward against varying resistance and through abominable terrain, its movement hindered by the beginning thaw and by heavy rains which turned all roads into mudholes. By the end of the month, however, the Marines were approaching Hoengsong and the objectives of "Killer" were in hand, while on the Sea of Japan the maritime flank had been pushed forward in a great bound.

There Admiral Smith had had his eyes on the strategic islands north of the parallel, and in his concept of operations for February had noted that their occupation would be "of inestimable value," both for control of enemy junk traffic and minelaying and to provide potentially valuable staging areas. In order to undo, at least to some extent, the effects of the abandonment of northeastern Korean footholds, he proposed a heavy bombardment of Wonsan, to take place with or immediately after that at Inchon, and to be accompanied if possible by seizure of the islands of Yo Do and Ung Do which guard the harbor entrance. The idea seemed good and the execution proved better, when enemy reaction to the bombardment stimulated the seizure of an island even further in.

At sea February was a rough month, and on 13 days the blockading ships found their operations seriously hindered by foul weather. On the 12th, nevertheless, the minesweepers went in to check the Wonsan channel, and

The Wonsan siege begins: Paricutin *rearming* Manchester; *in the background LSTs and minesweepers anchored in the lee of snow-covered Yo Do.* March 1951. (USN 427259)

four days later two destroyers entered to bombard the port. On the 18th, in a return engagement, the destroyer *Ozbourn* was hit by artillery fire, apparently originating from the island of Sin Do, two miles off the tip of Kalma Pando. The result of this impudence was an air strike from Task Force 77 that very day, a bombardment by *Belfast* on the 19th, and the appearance on the morning of the 24th of two destroyers, a frigate, and an ROK LST with an assault party of 110 Korean Marines. Lacking a shore fire control party, the arrangements to support the Sin Do landing were somewhat complex: the Koreans had been given a portable radio, but the only interpreter was on the cruiser *Manchester* offshore, and messages to the supporting destroyers had to be relayed; *Manchester's* helicopter, which provided aerial observation, was in communication with the destroyers but not the landing party. But all went well: two hours of bombardment were followed by an unopposed landing, and the island was soon declared secure. United Nations forces were back at, if not in, Wonsan.

With these February operations the tempo of naval gunfire began a rapid rise. Where ammunition expenditures in December at Hungnam had set a new record, those of January had plummeted. But with clearance of the coastal fire support lane and with seizure of the Wonsan islands there came a radical increase, and by March the expenditure of 5-inch ammunition had become phenomenal. That this fluctuating consumption imposed heavy problems upon the logistic agencies may be seen from the statistics in Table 15.

Table 15.—Ammunition Expended in Bombardment

Caliber	December	January	February	March
16-inch	162	0	997	994
8-inch	3, 357	651	2, 395	1, 577
6-inch	0	159	3, 290	6, 050
5-inch	15, 357	3, 468	13, 385	43, 360

For the Seventh Fleet carriers February was a period of transition. Close support of the battleline continued, as did intermittent strikes against transportation targets, but the generalized nature of FEAF's basic request for interdiction led to duplication of effort with Bomber Command. Yet the problem remained and, following repeated reports of heavy movement on the Hoeryong-Wonsan line, FEAF directed Fifth Air Force to attack a group of bridges in the northeast. But to ask this was to ask too much. On 15 February General Stratemeyer advised Admiral Joy that the withdrawal from forward air bases had made operations in northeastern Korea difficult for Fifth Air Force, occupied as it was by commitments to the support of Eighth Army, to bomber escort, and to interdiction in the northwest. Stating that "naval air could greatly assist interdiction" by covering the northeastern route, he requested a ten-day effort against important bridges and proposed, if this were agreeable, to reschedule the work of Bomber Command, both to prevent duplication in the northeast and to improve coverage in the northwest. The proposition was accepted by ComNavFE, and Commander Seventh Fleet was instructed to apply his principal effort for the next ten days to the Hoeryong-Wonsan railroad.

As this work began the Chinese again disappeared from the front, and Eighth Army resumed the advance. The generalized chaos and the very large number of dead that U.N. troops discovered on their way north from Wonju went far to bear out Admiral Struble's feeling that close support had hurt the enemy more than was generally appreciated. On the other hand the altered ground situation emphasized the desirability of cutting the flow of supply and reinforcement, so as to prevent Communist recuperation. On

20 February Admiral Joy moved to coordinate the efforts against the east coast transportation line by providing the carriers and gunnery ships with a list of rail and highway bridges accessible to naval gunfire, 13 in the Wonsan area, 23 in the north on the shores of Kyongsong Man, and 25 in the region south of Songjin which had been the target of earlier attacks by raiders from *Juneau, Bass,* and *Perch.* As the dispatch went forth it was already being implemented, for *Missouri,* now returned from her west coast bombardment duties, was dispensing 16-inch shells against the multiple bridges which span the double river at Tanchon. On the 22nd and the 23rd this enterprise was continued, and the expenditure, with helicopter spot, of an average of 166 rounds a day effectively subdivided these overwater structures.

The assignment of the fast carriers to rail interdiction had originally been scheduled to run through 25 February; on that date ComNavFE ordered it continued; by month's end it had become the primary task. To Admiral Ofstie it so commended itself, in view of the preoccupation of Fifth Air Force in the northwest and of the greater effectiveness of Bomber Command in attacks on marshalling yards and supply areas; on 28 February he proposed that his force apply its main effort to interdiction, set up a schedule for future operations, and made recommendations for more effective coordination with the work of the bombardment ships.

Essentially this shift from close support to interdiction was the result of differential capabilities, deriving in large measure from the existing air base situation. For the United Nations, at this time, Korea formed a large beachhead, in which inward or outward deployment followed the fortunes of war. The retirement of the armies from North Korea and the redeployment of the greater part of land-based air strength to Japan had returned the peninsula to the stage which, in a normal amphibious operation, precedes the introduction of garrison air. In these circumstances Fifth Air Force found itself obliged to abandon the interdiction function, and on 26 February, as Task Force 77 began its extended stint in the northeast, the responsibility for northwestern Korea reverted to the B–29s of Bomber Command.

Difficult though the situation still remained, it was about to improve. The Army had started north the latter part of January; as March opened, the objectives of "Killer" were in hand and the U.N. line, both stable and relatively straight, extended eastward from the lower Han through Hoengsong, and thence northeasterly to Chumunjin. In these circumstances it was possible to return evacuated air units to Korea: in early February the Marines had moved three fighter squadrons in from Japan, and by month's end Fifth Air Force squadrons and supporting units were preparing to return. At Wonsan in the east, and from Inchon to the Yalu in the west, U.N. forces held islands off the enemy shore. Along both coasts, from the battleline to the northern limits of the blockade, the surface units of Task Force 95 patrolled and bombarded. The effort of the fast carriers had shifted northward, and was focussed on the rail lines leading down from Manchuria. Eighth Army was preparing a new offensive.

2. *March–April 1951: On to the Parallel*

On 2 March the Marine Division, spearheading the drive up the center, captured Hoengsong. With the aims of "Killer" accomplished, EUSAK now planned a further advance, Operation Ripper, which by pushing onward through Hongchon to Chunchon would outflank Seoul, and gain a line in the neighborhood of the 38th parallel. This new move would take General Ridgway's armies through the region of the enemy's January offensive, and as it had for the Communists, so now for the United Nations the topography of the area would pull the armies to the right and away from the axis of the peninsula. As Eighth Army moved onward through the central hill country the valley roads would lead not toward Pyongyang but north through the mountains to Kansong, Kojo, and Wonsan on the eastern coast. In this situation, and as the battleline had now acquired a national compartmentation with U.N. and Chinese forces in the west and center, and with the eastern flank remaining an all-Korean affair, it was hoped to split the Chinese off from their indigenous subordinates. Finally, as in the operations of February, General Ridgway intended to inflict maximum attrition on the enemy, and by keeping the pressure on to inhibit his preparation of a new offensive.

To assist the planned advance EUSAK had again asked for an amphibious demonstration in the Yellow Sea. Feeling that the speed of earlier efforts had not given the sluggish enemy sufficient time to react, Admiral Andrewes now planned for deliberate fraud. Beginning on 27 February the air activities of *Bataan* were increased and localized; for two days the DMS *Carmick,* the frigate *Alacrity,* and two Korean YMS swept northward along the coast and into the mush ice of the Taedong estuary; there followed a cruiser and destroyer bombardment. On 3 March the amphibious element of three APAs and two AKAs appeared, escorted by two destroyers, to steam northward along the shore. Half way to Cho Do the transports reversed course and retired to Inchon, whence they made an ostentatious departure on the 5th to continue the effort at mystification.

After a heavy artillery preparation, Operation Ripper was launched on 7 March, and began a steady progress up the center of the peninsula. Seoul this time was captured not on the beaches of Inchon but on the Pukhan: as the 25th Division forced the Han near its junction with that river and moved on to the north the capital was outflanked, and on the 15th was reoccupied without a fight. But two conquests and two liberations had taken a frightful toll, and hardly a tenth of the city's original population still skulked amid the ruins.

On the east coast, as "Ripper" began, the destroyers continued to provide fire support; at Inchon the heavy cruiser *Saint Paul* remained on station, her 8-inch guns closely tied in with I Corps artillery. But with the flanks holding and the center advancing, and with Task Force 95 concentrating on the disruption of enemy transport and supply, gunfire support was for the moment of secondary importance and the trend of naval activity continued northerly. Task Force 77 was working over east coast transportation targets; east coast bombardment efforts were centered at Wonsan and Songjin; in the northwest *Belfast, Kenya,* and associated light units shot up enemy positions at the mouth of the Taedong estuary.

Since 16 February Wonsan had been under siege, and of the 31 days of March found itself subjected to gunfire on 31. As April opened, all important harbor islands had been occupied by the U.N., the record for continuous naval bombardment, established at Vicksburg almost a century before, had been surpassed, and a long and uninterruptedly difficult future lay ahead of the town. Enemy response to these operations involved a build-up of artillery and garrison forces, and a persistent if small-scale effort to remine the harbor: of the 28 mines swept in March—some of them new and shiny—20 were swept at Wonsan. Despite frequent and increasing artillery opposition, the sweepers worked persistently to enlarge the bombardment lanes, while the gunnery ships, beneficiaries of the effort, supported them by counterbattery fire and bombardment. On 1 March Korean agents reported that the enemy was unloading Soviet mines at the Kalma railroad siding, and on the 7th a bombardment of this target by the light cruiser *Manchester* brought a gratifying high order detonation of a boxcar full.

The precaution of arranging for east coast intelligence sources proved rewarding in other ways. On 15 March, in response to reports from ashore of enemy troop concentrations, a special event was laid on. Rapid fire bombardment of reported assembly areas in the neighborhood of Wonsan by *Manchester* and the destroyer *Lind* brought reports of 6,000 and 2,000 casualties respectively, and follow-up information from agents ashore indicated that the civilian population had fled the city and that morale among the military was not good. Pressure from the sea nevertheless continued undiminished: an enemy effort to land by sampan on ROKN-occupied Tae Do, off the end of Kalma Pando, was repelled; on the 24th a fire control party was put ashore on Tae Do by the destroyer *English,* with beneficial results in the spotting of bombardment.

At Songjin, 120 miles to the northeast and halfway to the Siberian border, a similar if less intensive siege had meanwhile been commenced. Mine reconnaissance of Songjin, carried out in the first days of March, was followed by daily bombardment of the port and of rail bridges neighboring the town, and in the first week of April a major minesweeping effort was undertaken to provide increased maneuvering room for the firing ships.

In addition to the work at the bombline, and at Wonsan and Songjin, intermittent bombardment of bridge targets was conducted in Kyongsong Man to the northward. On three days in mid-March, from the 14th to the 16th, *Missouri* was in action against east coast transportation targets in the Chongjin area, after which she moved southward to fire on the coastal rail line in the neighborhood of 40° and to shoot up Wonsan.

By this time the efforts against enemy transportation targets were beginning to develop into a concentrated and coordinated campaign. The Communists, of course, had long since lost the use of the sea; seaborne import of useful objects from Vladivostok or from China ports had been eliminated, along with coastal traffic, in the first days of war. Enemy logistics therefore depended on the two principal land transport nets, the western rail and road complex, in which the lines from the lower Yalu and from Manpojin joined in the area north of Pyongyang, and the eastern route, in which the tracks south from Hoeryong and southeast from Hyesanjin met at Kilchu and continued down the coast to join the transpeninsular line below Hungnam. In the west the mission of interdiction had been assumed by Bomber Command; the eastern rail and road lines, more distant from U.N. bases, became the responsibility of the Navy.

These tasks would of course have been far simpler had only the position at Wonsan been maintained. Given the topography of east central Korea, and the resulting configuration of the rail and road net, such a foothold would have blocked enemy supply of the eastern front, while Marine fighter-bombers based on Kalma Pando would have had the entire transpeninsular line and a major portion of the western transportation system within the 100-mile circle. As it was, however, the evacuation of X Corps, the result of fears for Eighth Army rather than of doubts as to the feasibility of holding a perimeter, led to the imposition for the remainder of the war of a heavy and continuing burden upon the carrier and gunnery forces.

In the circumstances, however, it was fortunate these forces existed. With them, in the continued absence of air and submarine opposition, targets 400 miles from the nearest U.N. airstrip could be kept under dive bomber attack, and coastal targets 300 road miles behind the lines subjected to naval gunfire. The importance of such action had been emphasized in early 1951 by intelligence of a strenuous impending enemy logistic effort on the east coast route, by the knowledge that some reorganized North Korean divisions were scheduled for rail movement south from Hoeryong, and by expectations of an important secondary traffic from Manpojin through Kanggye by rail, across to the Chosin Reservoir by truck, and thence down to Hamhung. It was in the context of this intelligence that ComNavFE had accepted FEAF's request to put the fast carriers on interdiction, and had moved to shift the efforts of Task Force 95 from control of the sea approaches to the interruption of land transport by providing the list of rail and highway bridges.

Such target information was most helpful, but for a number of reasons effective interdiction of Communist supply lines remained extremely difficult. This was so in the first instance because of the enemy's logistic austerity. As compared with a figure of 50 pounds per day for the individual in the U.S. Eighth Army, and of 64 pounds per man-day with the Fifth Air Force in Korea's heavy logistic requirements figured in, the best available estimates indicated that the Communists subsisted on a supply basis of ten pounds per man per day. Measured against this requirement, which worked out at about 50 tons per day per division, the North Korean transportation net was more than adequate, although its peacetime capacity had been gravely diminished by damage to rails and rolling stock and by limitation to night movement. In early March the capacity of the west coast rail line was estimated at between 500 and 1,000 tons per day, and that of the east coast railroad at about 500, while highways in the west and east were capable of transporting 1,000 and 500 tons per day respectively. In these circumstances it appeared that the enemy could support half a million troops, with something over a third dependent on the east coast rail and road nets.

Interdiction of these routes depended, at least in the first instance, upon bridge demolition, and modern reinforced concrete bridges, hard to hit and hard to destroy, requiring the hitting power of battleship or heavy cruiser main battery fire, or of the AD attack plane. Experience gained as the campaign progressed showed force requirements of about 60 rounds of 16-inch gunfire or of 12 to 16 AD sorties per bridge destroyed, so that for battleship and carrier alike, two a day was the average capability. Knocking down the bridges was therefore well within the realm of possibility, but while the rail net could be thus fragmented the effect on highway travel was less decisive: a truck can be detoured more easily than a train, and the supply of trucks from north of the border was a continuing one.

In his dispatch of 28 February Admiral Ofstie had proposed to rotate the efforts of his force between the area north of Hamhung, the complex south and west of Hamhung-Wonsan, and the route between Hamhung and the Chosin Reservoir, and had observed that better coordination with the gunnery ships would be helpful to the enterprise. The proposed procedure for Task Force 77 was approved by Admiral Struble; with reference to the comments on naval gunfire, however, Commander Seventh Fleet somewhat sourly observed that coordination between Task Force 77 and Task Force 95 was in the hands of ComNavFE. Passing upward through the chain of command, CTF 77's plan received the blessing of NavFE headquarters; arrangements for exchange of information between Bomber Command and the carriers were worked out; and the force set to work in the area east of a line drawn south along 127°E, and thence through Yangdok to Kumwha. Ultimately the coordination with Task Force 95 would also come.

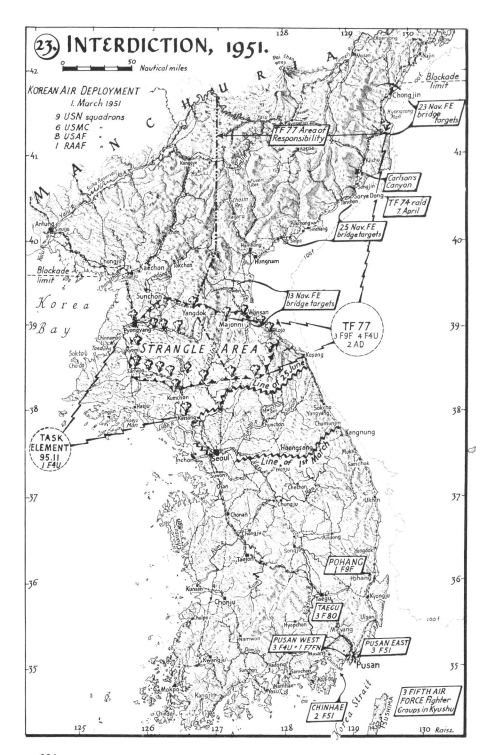

23. INTERDICTION, 1951.

0   50   *Nautical miles*

KOREAN AIR DEPLOYMENT
    1. *March* 1951
     9 USN squadrons
     6 USMC "
     8 USAF "
     1 RAAF "

Korea Bay

STRANGLE AREA

Line of 25 June

Line of 1st March

TASK ELEMENT 95.11 1 F4U

TF 77 3 F9F 4 F4U 2 AD

TF 77 Area of Responsibility

23 Nav. FE bridge targets

Carlson's Canyon

TF 74 raid 7. April

25 Nav. FE bridge targets

13 Nav. FE bridge targets

POHANG 1 F9F

TAEGU 3 F80

PUSAN WEST 3 F4U + 1 F7FN

PUSAN EAST 3 F51

CHINHAE 2 F51

3 FIFTH AIR FORCE Fighter Groups in Kyushu

Blockade limit

Blockade limit

334

Within the carrier task force the campaign was carefully planned. Since the 395 major bridges in eastern North Korea afforded a surplus of targets, a research effort was undertaken which cut the list to 48 "key bridges," structures in difficult terrain which were hard to bypass, and which once destroyed would have to be rebuilt. Attack on these key bridges was to be supplemented by track breaking, by destruction of minor bridges in areas where no key structure existed, and by surface gunfire at specific points along the coast, of which Kyongson Man, Songjin, and Iwon were of primary importance. The backbone of the striking force was provided by the ADs, lifting three 2,000-pound GP bombs apiece, and accompanied by F4Us for fighter cover and flak suppression, each with a 1,000-pound bomb for added striking power. The entire campaign was backed up by a comprehensive and continuing program of aerial photography. Maximum economy of effort was derived from careful briefing, and no pilot was sent off without one or more photographs of his target.

Through March and into April the carrier planes ranged over northeastern Korea, covering the four degrees of latitude from the 38th parallel north to beyond Chongjin. As the three complexes named by CTF 77 were attacked in regular succession, the box score grew and the impact upon the enemy became severe. The effectiveness both of the bridge strikes and of Communist efforts to undo the damage may be seen in the history of the most famous of east coast structures, the bridge below Kilchu, where the railroad crosses what came to be known as Carlson's Canyon.

Of the valley named in his honor, Lieutenant Commander Harold G. Carlson, commanding officer of VA 195 in *Princeton,* was the Vespucci rather than the Columbus, exploiter rather than discoverer, for the bridge that crossed it was first sighted by a shipmate, Lieutenant Commander Clement M. Craig, while flying homeward on the morning of 2 March from a strike on Kilchu. Eight miles southwest of that town the rail line, tunnelling through the hills, emerges briefly to span a gully and then disappears again underground. Twin tunnels had been dug in preparation for double tracking, and two sets of piers erected, but only a single track had been thrown across the chasm on a six-span bridge, 650 feet long and 60 feet high. The tunnels made it difficult to bypass; its height made it difficult to repair. That afternoon a strike was flown off which damaged the southern approach.

Next day Commander Carlson led a second flight of ADs against the bridge. As a result of this event one span was dropped, a second damaged, two more shifted out of line, and the site rechristened by Admiral Ofstie in honor of the strike leader. Four days later, on 7 March, a follow-up attack dropped the northernmost of the previously shifted spans.

The attacks on the railroad bridges quickly resulted in pile-ups of supplies at breaks in the line, in concentrations of vehicles to truck material past the choke points, and in energetic efforts at repair.   By 8 March the Corsairs were loading with 100 and 250-pound bombs for employment against these accumulations of supplies and vehicles, while the ADs and the heavy ordnance were reserved for the interdiction targets proper.   At Carlson's Canyon the vigor of the enemy effort was revealed on the 14th by photo plane inspection which showed rough but effective repairs in the form of wooden cribbing, built up to replace the missing spans.   Strike 4 followed the next day, knocked down all new construction, dropped another span at the southern end, and damaged the northern approach; but within two days large piles of wooden ties had been assembled in the gully preparatory to re-reconstruction. The extraordinary persistence of this engineering effort, paralleled at all important broken bridges, testified to the importance of the east coast rail net, demonstrated the availablity of repair crews and materials, and imposed upon the task force the requirement of rephotographing all key targets at four-day intervals.

Following the strike of 15 March Admiral Ofstie recommended to ComNavFE that Bomber Command be asked to inhibit repair activity by seeding the gully with long-delay bombs.   In spite of JOC concurrence FEAF's first reaction was adverse, but a study of photographs provided by the task force showed the site to be a prime objective for this combination of naval and Air Force capabilities; on the 24th a B–29 was sent out with a bomb load fused for long and varying delays, and three days later the effort was repeated.

Despite this useful contribution, the enemy continued to press the work with great determination.   On 20 March photographs again revealed large piles of construction material.   By the 30th, cribbing of the four central spans and the northern approach had been completed, transverse members had been installed, and only the rails were lacking.   On 2 April, therefore, Admiral Ofstie sent off Strikes 5 and 6 which destroyed the whole works, knocking down all rebuilt cribs and spans and leaving only the concrete piers.

If it did not discourage the enemy, this destruction at least forced him to change his plans.   Reconstruction of the bridge was abandoned and the labor force put to work on the building of a four-mile serpentine which would bypass bridge and tunnels alike.   This bypass required eight new bridges of its own, but all were short and low; although a number were knocked out in April, the new simplicity of repair made the site no longer an attractive one, and the attention of the force was shifted southward to the area of Songjin. There, after first breaking some low bridges north of the city, CTF 77 turned to the area south of the town, where the bridge-tunnel-bridge sequence was three times repeated close to the water's edge, and where gunfire from the besieging destroyer could delay the rebuilding of structures taken out by air attack.   Already once destroyed and once repaired, these bridges began to

AD in a glide-bombing run. A broken rail bridge, a newly-constructed bypass, and breaks in the new line. In the background the shore of the Sea of Japan. October 1951. (USN 435044)

receive the concentrated treatment on April Fool's Day, and here through June the same sequence of destruction, cribbing, destruction, and bypassing would take place.

On 4 April, after 38 days of concentrated effort in interdiction, Admiral Ofstie turned over tactical command of the force, and *Princeton* sailed for Yokosuka for an overdue period of rehabilitation and maintenance. In this period 54 rail and 37 highway bridges had been rendered inoperable, 44 more had been damaged in varying degree, and the railroad tracks had been broken in more than 200 places. For much of the Korean War, pliots' claims are difficult to assess, and statistics of attacks against such evanescent targets as personnel, rolling stock, and guns must be taken as approximations only. But of these bridges it is possible to speak with some confidence, for in Task Force 77 "inoperable" meant that photographs showed one or more spans destroyed.

*Table 16.—*Task Force 77 Rail Interdiction, February–April 1951

Area	Rail bridges inoperable 4 April 1951
Hoeryong south to Chongjin	3
Chongjin south to Pukchong	23
Inland from Tanchon, Songjin, and Kilchu	3
Pukchong south to Wonsan and inland to the Chosin and Fusen Reservoirs	12
Wonsan west to Yangdok	4
Wonsan south to Chorwon and Kumwha	9

Enemy response to this extremely destructive campaign was not limited to the effort in reconstruction. Antiaircraft defenses of key points were rapidly increased, and there developed an extraordinary increase in truck traffic which brought April air sightings of vehicles to more than four times the January total. Since trucks and antiaircraft, unlike bridges, were available on requisition from the north in practically unlimited quantity, it was soon apparent that interdiction could hardly be absolute, and that to maintain its effectiveness would require continuous effort. Nevertheless the work of the fast carriers had been fruitful: the east coast rail system, which had carried two-thirds of North Korean traffic in February, in March moved less than half the total and in April less than a third, and east coast enemy road transport was likewise proportionately reduced.

*Table 17.—*GHQ United Nations Command Analysis of Enemy Transport, January–April 1951

Daily average sightings	January	February	March	April
Railroad cars	147	155	199	179
Vehicles	236	398	633	1,048
Estimated percent of total enemy rail or road traffic, transpeninsular route excluded:				
East coast rail	55	64	49	29
East coast road	37	38	36	29
West coast rail	35	23	46	59
West coast road	37	59	59	61

Despite the virtues of modernity, as exemplified in bombing and bombardment, it remains true that the surest way of getting explosives where you want them is the old-fashioned one of putting them there by hand. With this sometimes forgotten truth in mind, ComNavFE in mid-March had conceived the idea of assisting the interdiction of the east coast rail line by a commando raid. A special task organization, Task Force 74, was set up under Admiral Hillenkoetter; 250 men of the Royal Marine Commando were embarked in the LSD *Fort Marion* and a UDT detachment in the APD *Begor*. Following rehearsals at Kure these ships set sail for Sorye Dong, eight miles south of Songjin, with a somewhat elaborate supporting force composed of *Saint Paul,* two destroyers, and six minesweepers.

The operation took place on 7 April. Owing in part to the directive, and in part to limited communications facilities in the participating ships, command arrangements were rather unorthodox. The landing itself was the responsibility of Captain Philip W. Mothersill, commanding officer of *Fort Marion* and Commander Amphibious Group, and Admiral Hillenkoetter controlled only the supporting ships. Instead of awaiting an expression of readiness on the part of the landing force commander, transfer of control ashore was to take place automatically the moment the troops hit the beach, although, oddly enough, fire support and air control personnel were to remain subordinate to the Amphibious Group. Shore fire control personnel from a Marine Anglico had been offered but declined; the SFCP, composed of ship's company from *Saint Paul,* was inexperienced in troop fire support and lacked direct communications with the landing force.

To the distress of the landing force commander, who felt that it would reveal intentions and gain him a warm welcome ashore, a conspicuous minesweeping effort had been arranged. The landing itself, scheduled to take place in the pre-dawn darkness, was to be preceded by UDT beach reconnaissance, but pea soup fog frustrated the latter and delayed the former until 0800. Beach intelligence, based on few photographs and faulty interpretation, had promised a sandy shore with suitable exit for tracked vehicles; in fact no exit existed and the beach was fouled by boulders which, but for the fortunate absence of swell, would have ripped the tracks off the LVTs.

In these circumstances it was well that opposition was negligible. Operations proceeded deliberately, the demolitions were satisfactorily accomplished, and by 1600 the landing force had reembarked. But the whole comedy was labor lost: the point of attack was just south of some of Task Force 77's favorite bridges, the rails were red with rust, and local inhabitants reported that for 40 days and 40 nights no train had passed through Sorye Dong.

By this time the ships, the commanders, and the crews who had carried the burden during the early months of the war were being rotated homeward. Hoskins, Hartman, Higgins, and Doyle had already moved on to new commands, and as spring came more and more new faces blossomed in Korea. Naval reservists, who had earlier come forward in drafts and as individuals, now began to arrive in organized units: the first weekend-warrior aviation unit, a PBM patrol squadron, had reached Japan in mid-December; in late March the first reserve air group arrived when *Boxer,* her long-delayed overhaul at last completed, returned to relieve *Valley Forge.* Also embarked in

The raid at Sorye Dong: LVTAs leaving the well of Fort Marion with the Royal Marine raiding party. 7 April 1951. (USN 428316)

Boxer was Rear Admiral William G. Tomlinson, Commander Carrier Division 3, whose impending arrival at last permitted Admiral Ewen to go home. But *Philippine Sea,* his long-time flagship, remained, and her flag quarters were taken over on 25 March by Vice Admiral Harold M. Martin, who three days later relieved Admiral Struble as Commander Seventh Fleet.

This shift in the principal naval operating command was followed, in early April, by changes in subordinate echelons and by a major structural revision of Naval Forces Far East. Admiral Andrewes, who following promotion to vice admiral earlier in the year had for six weeks commanded Task Force 95, was relieved by Rear Admiral Alan K. Scott-Moncrieff, RN, and command of the Blockading and Escort Force reverted to Admiral Smith. Service Force units, previously organized in separate Seventh Fleet and NavFE groups, were consolidated into Task Force 92; with the departure of Captain Austin, who had run the logistics for Inchon, Wonsan, and Hungnam, command of this force devolved upon Captain Wright, formerly ComServDiv 31. And with these changes Admiral Martin got something that Struble had repeatedly sought without success, when on 3 April Task Force 92, Task Force 95, and all U.S. Navy destroyers in the Far East were assigned to his operational control.

With this consolidation only the patrol planes, the submarines, the Hunter-Killer Group, and the Amphibious Force remained directly under ComNavFE, and these would be assigned to Seventh Fleet as need arose. One result was a considerable simplification of command relations and of the associated communications problem as between Eighth Army, Fifth Air Force, and theater naval forces; another was an improved coordination of carrier and gunnery units in the east coast interdiction campaign. Admiral Ofstie had earlier commented on the economy of effort to be derived from such coordination, then requiring action at the NavFE level, and while exchange of information had been improved the results were not yet wholly satisfactory. Following the reorganization of 3 April, however, Commander Seventh Fleet assumed responsibility for the interdiction campaign. All heavy ships were absorbed into Task Force 77, while Task Force 95, composed of two U.S. destroyer divisions, the ROK Navy, and units of other U.N. member nations, became in fact as in name the Blockading and Escort Force. Shortly Admiral Martin would delegate responsibility for east coast interdiction, gunfire as well as air, to CTF 77, and by instructing him to make recommendations for supplementary commando raids ensure that there would be no more Sorye Dongs.

Through March, while the aviators were breaking down the bridges, Operation Ripper had continued, with U.N. forces pressing onward through the razor-edged mountains and precipitous valleys of central Korea. Although winter had ended, the spring thaws and heavy rains continued to make movement difficult, while to the delays imposed by nature were added the delaying operations of small enemy groups. Only in mid-month was variety provided by a singular operation in which the remnants of the North Korean 10th Division, which the Marines had earlier been chasing through the upper Naktong Basin, moved northward, fought their way through the ROK lines from the rear, and disappeared into the distance.

The escape of these people was regrettable, but was compensated for by more important developments. The advance of IX and X Corps in the center had freed the flanks for rapid movement, and in the west, following the reoccupation of Seoul, the I Corps moved raipdly to the Imjin River. There by month's end the line had been pushed forward to the 38th parallel, while on the east coast ROK forces had again crossed into North Korea.

In the west, too, the logistic situation was easing. At Inchon, by mid-March, the MSTS representative had opened his office ashore, and on the 17th EUSAK lifted its 48-hour evacuation notice. On the 25th, with the Army engineers ashore and with unloading proceeding at a rate of over 3,000 tons a day, Admiral Thackrey closed down his operations and departed. Although the delay had been considerable, it was less than that in exploitation of the neighboring strategic prize, for Kimpo did not become fully operational until May.

With the armies of the U.N. astride the 38th parallel, the question of how far to press the advance again presented itself, this time to be answered on tactical grounds. For some time intelligence had indicated that the Chinese intended to hold at the dividing line, while preparing for a major offensive in May. Since there was plenty of evidence, not least the Communist diligence in bridge repair, to show that these preparations were being earnestly pressed, this intelligence was taken seriously. To hinder the enemy build-up and to maintain pressure on the Communist armies, EUSAK had planned a further move. The Imjin River would remain the western anchor, but the remainder of the front would be advanced across the parallel, to shorten the line and to provide a labor-saving ten-mile water frontage at the Hwachon Reservoir. This movement, Operation Rugged, began on 5 April.

In the air, too, the enemy was growing stronger. In late March Communist air strength was estimated to have reached a total of some 750 aircraft of all types, and B–29 attacks on northern targets were meeting heavy MIG opposition. Ominously, on 29 March, a twin-jet bomber was sighted over central North Korea; equally ominously, efforts were underway to rehabilitate the North Korean airfields.

This threat found the forces of the United Nations in an extremely vulnerable position. Nine months of exemption from the dangers of air attack had taught bad habits. On shore, camouflage discipline was non-existent, housing and equipment were disposed in orderly rows about the Korean landscape, stockpiles were open and conspicuous, aircraft were parked in close formation on unrevetted airfields. Along both coasts blockading ships operated without air cover, which in any event could hardly have been provided, and skills in air defense had rusted. For the naval forces the danger was emphasized on 15 April, when the ROK frigate *Apnok,* straggling in somewhat undisciplined fashion from a force returning from the Yalu Gulf, was attacked by three enemy propeller-driven aircraft. *Apnok* fought back well, and shot down one of her attackers, but her topsides were chewed up by strafing and near misses, and there were numerous casualties among the crew.

FEAF, in the meantime, had been watching the Communist airfield reconstruction, and on 13 April began a neutralization campaign which, for the balance of the month, would see a dozen B–29s sent off daily to crater the runways and seed them with delayed-action bombs. As a further precautionary measure, an agreement had been concluded between FEAF and NavFE which provided that in the event of an emergency the air defense commander would have control of all shore-based naval and Marine fighter planes. For the Air Force, still desirous of gaining operational control of naval air, this seemed little enough, and the exemption of embarked aviation as "an integral part of the fleet" from this prior commitment was disappointing. But reasons for retaining this freedom of action shortly became apparent.

The commitment of the Marine Division to the mountain front had limited the offensive capabilities of the Amphibious Force to the conduct of feints and demonstrations. This, however, was a game at which two could play, and resurgent Communist activities in the Formosa area now had impact on Korean naval operations. Since the summer of 1950 the Formosa Strait patrol had been continued by long-range search planes and by a small destroyer force. But with the new year intelligence of troop and junk concentrations in mainland ports suggested the possibility of an invasion attempt when the April good weather came. In mid-February Struble had again visited Formosa, and an improved and expanded Formosa defense plan had been prepared. Late in the month ComNavFE took cognizance of the situation, and inaugurated a series of experiments to determine the optimum choice of weapons against a junk fleet.

In warfare between forces of radically different technological capabilities the advantages are not all on one side. In Korea the virtues of primitivism in conflict with technology had been clearly demonstrated in the difficulties that had beset Eighth Army, mechanized, heavily equipped, and road-bound, when locked in combat with the lightly armed, ridge-running levies of North Korea and Communist China. The difficulties of successfully interdicting the supply lines of an army whose logistic requirements per man were about a sixth of those of U.S. forces had reinforced the lesson, which promised also to apply to action between naval air and gunnery forces and fleets of wooden junks.

Such fleets present numerous small targets, hard to hit, impossible to sink, and whose destruction may prove excessively costly in ammunition expenditure. On 24 February, therefore, with the Formosan question in mind, ComNavFE directed Admiral Thackrey to provide some samples at Yokosuka for practice purposes. Eight 60-foot Korean junks were salvaged at Inchon and brought across in the LSD *Tortuga;* a sunken Chinese 100-foot 600-tonner presented more difficulties, but in time was floated, beached at Wolmi Do, and embarked in the LSD *Colonial* for delivery to Japan. In March and April extensive tests were conducted under the direction of Rear Admiral Edgar A. Cruise, commander of the Hunter-Killer Task Group. But his report on ordnance selection was not completed until May, by which time the Communist build-up in Formosa Strait had already had strategic effect.

The intelligence from the south and the coming of the invasion season made a show of force appear in order. On 8 April, therefore, with Admiral Martin in *Philippine Sea* and Admiral Tomlinson as OTC in *Boxer,* Task Force 77 left Korean waters and steamed southward through the East China Sea. On the 13th Admiral Martin flew in to visit the Generalissimo at Taipei, and an air parade was flown over Formosa to strengthen Nationalist morale; two days earlier a similar demonstration had been made along the three-mile limit off the Chinese mainland *pour encourager les autres;* on both days high-altitude photography of selected coastal staging areas was carried out. On the 14th the force again headed northward and on the 16th resumed its efforts in interdiction of the northeastern transportation net. But while the demonstration may have had value in Formosa, it had proven costly in Korea: although *Bataan* and *Theseus* had been shifted from the Yellow Sea to the east coast, their weight of effort had proven insufficient, and the eight-day hiatus in fast carrier operations had left the interdiction program almost out of hand.

Important though they were, these workaday problems were for the moment overshadowed by events on a higher level, for following a series of public and private disagreements concerning Far Eastern strategic aims President Truman on 11 April relieved CincFE of his commands. Where the military had already had to adjust to an Amphibious Force without a Marine Division, to a Marine Division without its Aircraft Wing, and to a United Nations force shorn of its amphibious capability and limited in strategic aim, the world now faced the problem of adjusting to a Far East Command without General MacArthur. "New war" had required a new commander.

The manifold responsibilities of Supreme Commander for the Allied Powers, Commander in Chief United Nations Command, Commander in Chief Far East Command, and Commanding General, U.S. Army, Far East, now devolved upon General Ridgway, who was in turn relieved at Eighth

Army by Lieutenant General James A. Van Fleet, USA. Having been concerned with the implementation of the Truman Doctrine in Greece, a country also in large part surrounded by sea and troubled by visitors from beyond the northern mountains, General Van Fleet found himself in a not unfamiliar strategic situation. Under its new commander Eighth Army continued its northward advance, while preparing, in anticipation of a CCF offensive, for a fighting retirement which would inflict maximum punishment on the enemy. By the third week of April the Hwachon Reservoir had been reached, and from the Imjin to the Sea of Japan the line ran some ten miles north of the parallel.

At sea as on land, operations continued in routine fashion. On the east coast the sieges of Wonsan and Songjin went on, with daily bombardment and daily minesweeping. For the sweepers, life had been eased by the arrival of *LST 799,* whose conversion to minesweep tender and helicopter base had been completed; her presence also proved a boon to U.N. pilots, who could now ditch damaged planes in Wonsan harbor in confidence of expeditious rescue. In early April a new technique was developed by the Wonsan besiegers when an Air Force night intruder pilot employed his previous experience in the artillery to coach ships' gunners on to targets they could not see. This happenstance was followed by a visit of the Task Force 95 gunnery officer to the pilot's parent squadron, and by a developing coordination of gunfire illumination with air bombardment, strafing, and spotting, which was limited in its prospects only by the number of available intruder aircraft.

In the northeast, where the interdiction campaign was now the sole responsibility of Task Force 77, the fast carriers had resumed their effort, and while the rotating emphasis on different sections of the transportation net continued, the focus, with Carlson's Canyon bypassed, was on the bridges south of Songjin. In the Yellow Sea the carrier element worked over western Hwanghae Province, the surface ships continued their missions of bombardment and patrol, and guerrilla raiding forces were put ashore. In all services all hands had been alerted to the impending attack, which indeed the enemy had advertised, in his press and on his radio, as one designed utterly to destroy the forces of the U.N. This time, at any rate, there would be no surprise.

3. *April-May 1951: The Communist Spring Offensive*

The enemy offensive broke on the evening of 22 April with a thrust down the center by the Chinese 20th Army. South of Kumwha the ROK 6th Division collapsed under the weight of the attack, and as the enemy poured through the gap between the Marines and the 24th Infantry Division, General Van Fleet ordered a withdrawal. Four days went by before the assault was checked, and in this interval, with the enemy out in the open and moving, more than a thousand close support sorties by Fifth Air Force and carrier-based aircraft inflicted very heavy casualties.

The attack in the center and the U.N. retirement which followed had opened the valley of the Pukhan and the Chunchon-Seoul road. On the 26th, therefore, the Communists launched their main effort in an attempted double envelopment of Seoul, in which one prong was pushed down the Pukhan valley, while in the west an attempt was made to ferry troops across the Han onto the Kumpo peninsula. Both moves failed. The eastern threat to the capital was checked by the 24th and 25th Divisions, while on the Han a busy day of strafing by aircraft of the West Coast Carrier Element limited the arrivals to a number easily dealt with by the ROK Marine battalion defending the Kumpo peninsula. In the end the enemy advance in the west central sector reached a maximum of about 30 miles; east of the Hwachon Reservoir the Communists captured the town of Inje on the Hongchon-Kansong road; on the east coast they moved forward some five miles. But despite casualties estimated at ten times those of the U.N. no decisive advantage had been gained, and by the 29th the front was stabilized once more.

Once again the enemy offensive brought an immediate response from U.N. naval forces. On 23 April Task Force 77 began a ten-day sustained effort in support of the battleline. On the next day the first of a series of amphibious feints was carried out. On the 26th the threat to Seoul brought another evacuation alert at Inchon: cruiser *Toledo* was sent in to provide 8-inch gunfire support and once again Admiral Thackrey was ordered up to take charge. By the 1st of May, as redeployment shipping was beginning to arrive, some 200,000 refugees had clustered in the Inchon area.

The Chinese breakthrough in the center posed urgent requirements for air support, but the Korean airbase situation remained difficult. In April, in addition to the 5 Marine squadrons in Korea, only 3 of the 18 Air Force groups committed to the conflict could be based in the peninsula; in May runway difficulties at Taegu forced the closing of that field and the return of its F-80s to Japan. Over and above the airbase problem the operations of both carrier and land-based squadrons were complicated by the seasonal bad weather. Fog was reported at sea on 17 days in May, rain and low ceilings were prevalent, and visibility in the combat area was further restricted by smoke haze from brush fires set by the enemy for protection against air attack.

These circumstances called for the immediate shift of fast carrier operations from interdiction to close support, and for the greatest possible weight of effort. To avoid the loss of a day in four in refueling and rearming, Admiral Ofstie on 24 April began a schedule of daily replenishment. For ten days the force joined the logistic ships in late afternoon to load until midnight, and while this made for a long working day, it also made it possible to keep pace with the high rate of expenditure of aviation gasoline and ordnance.

To this shift in carrier employment and this intensification of operations there was also added an increase in strength. On 1 May, as *Boxer* returned from Yokosuka, the retirement of *Philippine Sea* was delayed, and for three days three carriers were kept on the line. On the same day, as the result of pressure in the west, *Bataan's* replenishment period was cut short, her pilots were recalled from leave, and she was sailed from Sasebo for the Yellow Sea. There she joined HMS *Glory,* recently arrived as relief for *Theseus,* and there from 2 to 6 May the two ships worked together to strengthen the west coast effort.

Although close support was for the moment the primary task, the most striking carrier operation of the period was the attack on the Hwachon Dam, which by impounding the waters of the upper Pukhan both provided a barrier to movement and held back water usable for tactical purposes. In January, in the hope of impeding enemy progress, Eighth Army had asked FEAF to hole the dam, but an attack by a couple of B–29s with 6-ton guided bombs had failed of success. On 9 April, as Eighth Army was moving northward, the enemy had turned the trick, and by opening the gates had flooded the Pukhan and decommissioned some bridges . Two days later a small and hastily organized force of cavalrymen and rangers failed in an attempt to capture the dam; on 21 April the KMC Regiment had seized it, only to be ordered back as the Chinese broke through the line on the left. Now at April's end, as the Chinese lunge expended itself, EUSAK again developed the desire to break the dam, wet down the Communists, and prevent them from using the water as a weapon.

On the afternoon of 30 April Admiral Ofstie received a photograph of the dam, with a notation requesting that two or more sluice gates be knocked out, and was informed that EUSAK was the requesting agency and wanted it done at once. At 1600 six ADs were flown off with two 2,000-pound GP bombs apiece, accompanied by five Corsairs for flak suppression, and a dive bombing attack was carried out which produced a hole in one gate. A request from EUSAK for another try and a night's consideration led to a change in ordnance selection: on the next day eight ADs were launched with torpedoes set for surface run, and at 1100 the Skyraiders went in on this now unfamiliar mission. One torpedo was a dud and one erratic, but the remaining six ran true. One flood gate and the lower half of a second were removed, the dam's western abutment was holed, and the enemy deprived of control of the waters.

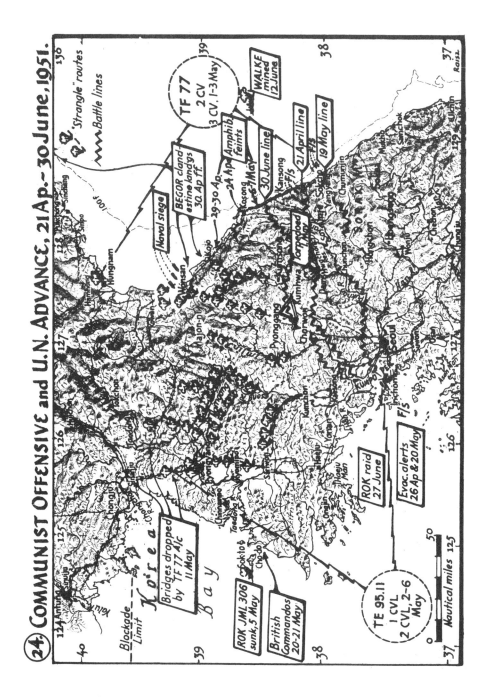

24. COMMUNIST OFFENSIVE and U.N. ADVANCE, 21 Ap.~30 June, 1951.

348

By April's end the offensive had been contained, and in the first two weeks of May, as Eighth Army probed northward and the enemy prepared for a second try, U.N. aircraft renewed their efforts in interdiction. This interlude brought a temporary expansion of the work of the fast carriers as the result of a request from the Joint Operations Center for help in the interdiction of the western rail lines. In response Rear Admiral George R. Henderson, who had just relieved Admiral Ofstie as CTF 77, advised the JOC that on 11 May he would strike railroad bridges in the triangle which connects Pyongyang, Sunchon, and the transpeninsular line to the east. On the morning of the 11th 32 ADs carrying two 2,000-pound bombs apiece, and accompanied by 32 F4Us for flak suppression and 16 F9Fs for top cover, attacked four of these bridges and dropped spans in three. This success elicited a further request from Fifth Air Force for the destruction of bridges in the rail quadrilateral which links Pyongyang with Sinanju, Kaechon, and Sunchon.

In reply to this message Admiral Henderson observed that while he would be glad to help out from time to time, existing obligations prevented his assuming any permanent responsibility. But the request for such a "substantial and continuing commitment" of the fast carrier effort brought ComNavFE to his feet, and on 16 May he informed Commander Seventh Fleet that such proposals should pass through appropriate service channels for action by higher authority. But by the time this dispatch was on its way the enemy was on the move again: on the 18th, EUSAK called for maximum effort in close air support, and when interdiction again came to the fore the situation had changed.

The failure of the Communists' first attack, and their evident intention to try again, raised the question of the possible employment of new weapons and brought steps to guard against surprise. Where the first five months of war had produced 80 reports of possible submarine contacts, the second five months had brought a mere 16, a change which could be interpreted as either a threat or a promise. In the air, by contrast, there was no question as to the magnitude of the Communist build-up across the Yalu, nor as to the earnestness of the effort to rehabilitate North Korean airfields. Although no air commitment had accompanied the April offensive, the possibility remained, and on the 29th Commander Seventh Fleet again warned of the chance of surprise air or submarine attack.

For the carrier force, which could operate from beyond MIG range and fight off attacks from other aircraft types available to the enemy, the submarine presented the major hazard, but for the units of Task Force 95 the air question was the serious one. Admiral Smith had alerted his force in April; now on 10 May he advised his ships that the next ten days would be critical with regard to enemy commitment of air strength, credited the Communists with a capability of 300 offensive sorties a day, issued instructions as to procedures to be adopted under attacks of varying weight, and instructed replenishment vessels to avoid anchoring in forward locations.

In the event, although subsequent evidence indicated that the Chinese had hoped to provide their armies with air support, neither menace developed. FEAF's attacks on North Korean airfields had kept the rehabilitation effort down, and on 9 May, following reports that 40 fighter planes had been sighted at Sinuiju, on the Korean side of the Yalu, Fifth Air Force sent up 250 Air Force and 56 Marine aircraft to deposit more than 40 tons of bombs on the airfield. In the air, despite promises to his troops, the launching of the second spring drive found the enemy no better off than had the first.

The weight of the April thrust toward Seoul had led General Van Fleet to bolster his forces in the western lowlands. Contrariwise, while this movement was in progress, the Chinese were shifting eastward to the central mountains, where on the night of 15 May they attacked in strength. On the Soyang River, southeast of the reservoir, the brunt of the attack was again borne by ROK divisions; again these dissolved, and in the exploitation phase the Communists advanced 25 miles down the valley and across into the upper waters of the Hongchon. To the eastward, in the Sorak Mountains, enemy units overran the ROK III Corps and filtered down to the southeast; on the coast the ROK I Corps withdrew south to Kangnung. In the west Chinese divisions crossed the Pukhan below Chunchon, and on the 17th opened a drive down the valley toward the Han.

As the ground forces struggled to check the attack the supporting arms again stepped up their action. Fifth Air Force increased its effort in close support; on the 17th, after being weathered out for two days, Task Force 77 began another stint of operating by day and replenishing by night; following an appeal from EUSAK for all possible support, *Princeton* delayed her departure for Yokosuka to permit another period of three-carrier operations. At Inchon, where the enemy was again within range of *Toledo*'s guns, the drive down the Pukhan brought another redeployment alert, and Admiral Thackrey, who had retained some Scajap LSTs for such a contingency, put in a request for further shipping against the chance that he would have to evacuate the city and the Kumpo peninsula.

This precaution proved unnecessary. In the center the 2nd Division, which had come a long way since the hard times on the Chongchon River, did what was necessary: although under pressure on three sides it maintained its integrity, held while so instructed, reopened its supply line, and retired on order, with minimum casualties to itself and maximum to the enemy. Three days of violent fighting in the Pukhan Valley saw the Chinese thrust turned back by the 25th Division. In the Sorak Mountains, some 20 miles below the parallel, the enemy was checked at Soksa by the 3rd Division, rushed eastward from Army reserve. By 21 May the Communists had been stopped all along the line. Despite a gain of 30 miles in the eastern mountains, and a considerable penetration in the Pukhan valley, nothing decisive had been accomplished, and the price had been higher than before. On the 23rd Admiral Thackrey began to release shipping from Inchon; on the 25th the evacuation alert was ended, all restrictions on stockpiling ashore were removed, and *Toledo* was at last relieved of her fire support duties.

The Communist spring offensive had brought about a sudden spate of simulated pre-landing operations by units of Task Force 90 and Task Force 95. The first of these, carried out on short notice on 24 April, consisted of a two-hour bombardment of Kosong by *St. Paul, Helena, Manchester,* and four destroyers. Five days later, on the 29th and 30th, *Helena, Manchester,* four destroyers, two attack transports and an attack cargo ship made a demonstration in the Kojo area, in the hope of taking pressure off Eighth Army. On the evening of 4 May General Van Fleet asked for another such affair on the 6th and 7th at Kansong; ComNavFE passed the word to Seventh Fleet to do what it could on short notice, and on the 5th Kosong was added as a target at the request of CincFE. On the desired date *Helena* and four destroyers bombarded as requested; fortuitously, their arrival coincided with a heavy enemy attack, and the bombardment, according to KMAG's flatteringly redundant description, saved the ROK forces from "complete annihilation." On the 13th Eighth Army called for another demonstration at Kosong on the 18th and 19th; this request was cancelled two days later, but a west coast event already underway continued to its conclusion.

Feeling, as had his predecessor, that previous demonstrations had been too short and too transparent to produce the maximum reaction, Admiral Scott-Moncrieff planned this with some finesse. Rumors of an impending landing were spread by agents of Leopard Force, a west coast guerrilla organization, and so successfully that aircraft from *Glory,* flying cover for the minesweepers, reported a large sign near the landing area which read "Welcome, U.N. Army." By 20 May the preliminaries had been completed and *Toledo* and Commonwealth ships were on hand to provide fire support. In the afternoon a dozen LCVPs, three loaded with Royal Marines and the others empty, were put up on the beach opposite Cho Do, and the Marines made a brief unopposed excursion inland prior to reembarking.

The popularity of these small demonstrations with Army commanders, and the frequency with which they were requested, led to some study of their actual effectiveness and of measures which might make for greater realism. That the enemy, after the events of the previous autumn, was fully aware of the amphibious capabilities of the United States Navy was unquestionable: information from various sources indicated that special pains were taken to keep track of the movements of the Marine Division. But with the Marines in the line, and given the slow reaction time of the Communist armies, there remained the question of whether much was

Naval gunfire support: A shore fire control party from Toledo at an observation post overlooking the Han. May 1951. (USN 432346) actually accomplished. Admiral Andrewes had been skeptical; after the operation of 20 May Admiral Scott-Moncrieff remained dubious, feeling that enemy communications were so poor that two or three days might pass before headquarters got the word. EUSAK, on the other hand, estimated that the Inchon feint in February had fixed two Communist divisions, and that the March operation off the Taedong had moved one; following the Cho Do affair in May reports were received of troop movements across the Taedong River into previously undefended areas of Hwanghae Province. Although it seems unlikely that enemy response to any particular demonstration was very impressive, their repetition did serve to emphasize existing possibilities, and to reinforce a real concern about a possible major assault in the Wonsan area. With the passage of time it also brought an increasing concentration of defensive force along the coasts, opposite Cho Do in the west and between Kojo and Hungnam in the east.

This concentration was heaviest at Wonsan, where day after day the siege continued. Uninterrupted bombardment and frequent air attack had obliged the Communists to commit large numbers of personnel to defense and to repair work and had curtailed enemy transport, but although the railroad had been stopped road traffic was harder to inhibit, and some 500 trucks were thought to pass through nightly. Attempting to take the pressure off, the enemy moved in increasing amounts of artillery and the Wonsan garrison stepped up its shooting; in late April an unsuccessful attempt was made to recapture one of the ROK-held harbor islands. Whether this enemy reaction amounted to a good return on the effort invested was another matter. CTF 95 had earlier advocated emplacing artillery on the harbor islands, but no such step had been taken and the responsibility for dealing with the shore batteries remained entirely upon the ships; additionally, the original offensive purpose of the siege had been undercut by the decision not to attempt a return to Wonsan. The absence of any very clear objective and the size of the commitment proved disturbing to Commander Seventh Fleet, who felt the entire concept of the operation needed some rethinking. Pending such clarification the cruiser previously assigned the Wonsan task unit was withdrawn, and the garrison situation rationalized by the assignment of a Marine officer to Yo Do as commander of the island's defenses.

As the enemy's second offensive slowed, the harassment of his seaward flanks was stepped up, and the Cho Do raid was followed by activity in the east. At Wonsan, following vigorous efforts by enemy artillerists which had damaged a destroyer and bounced a shell off one of the turrets of the recently arrived *New Jersey,* the rocket ships were sent in for two night bombardments of known gun emplacements. Plunging fire of 7,700 rockets delivered by *LSMR 409* and *LSMR 412* on 23 and 25 May had impressive results: intelligence agents reported that the enemy was clearing the harbor area of personnel; for three weeks the batteries remained silent. In the north, too, the pressure was maintained: in an interval between bridge bombardments in Kyongsong Man the destroyer *Stickell* destroyed a 70-foot motor junk, and followed up by putting a landing party ashore to blow three more with hand grenades.

Even before the second Chinese push was halted General Van Fleet was preparing his reply. On 18 May he ordered all forces from the Marine Division westward to prepare to attack to the north; next day, with the situation in the eastern mountains improving, he included X Corps in this planned general advance across the parallel. On the 22nd the battle of the Soyang River entered its offensive phase as the Marines and the 2nd Division attacked to the northeast against vigorous resistance. In the west, at the same time, I Corps moved steadily northward toward the so-called Iron Triangle, the important and heavily defended area bounded by the towns of Chorwon, Kumwha, and Pyonggang. Since seizure of the Iron Triangle would open the corridor to Wonsan, this movement held great possibilities.

The advance up the Soyang valley toward Inje threatened to cut off the Chinese in the Sorak Mountain salient, and opened the possibility of a thrust through the mountains to Kansong which would trap the enemy forces on the coastal strip. To provide logistic support for such a move some Scajap LSTs, released from Inchon, were assigned to meet the advance at Kansong and establish an advanced supply base. But the threat at Inje made the operation unnecessary, the enemy pulled back, and on 29 May, with minesweeping completed and gunfire about to begin, ROK forces regained control of the Kansong area. By the end of the month the armies of the U.N. were back at the Hwachon Reservoir, and in firm possession of the line from which they had been dislodged by the attacks of April.

The two Communist thrusts and the U.N. counteroffensive had brought the enemy out into the open, and had provided profitable targets for air attack. The response to this opportunity had been vigorous: Fifth Air Force had stepped up its sorties in support of Eighth Army; Task Force 77 had shifted to continuous operations and daily replenishment; in times of crisis all three fast carriers and both light carriers had been put on the line. The statistical results were impressive: the Air Force claimed 21,536 enemy personnel "destroyed" in April and May; Task Force 77 aircraft claimed 1,400 killed on 29 May; on 4 June, following attacks by carrier planes, the advancing ground forces counted more than 1,000 dead.

Whether all this effort, indubitably severe in its effects on the enemy, amounted to efficient close air support was another matter. In his report for this period Admiral Martin observed that while three fast carriers had been employed at Army request, the calls for close support had never exceeded the capacity of two, the controllers had once again been swamped, and much ordnance had been dumped. Nor were the Marines more satisfied. In the later phases of the battle of the Soyang River the division, advancing at a rate of three miles a day against continuing stiff resistance, wanted and needed support from the air, and on two days requested all available aircraft. But advance requests, submitted on the previous day conformably with Air Force practice, were only about half-fulfilled. And while the use of special emergency requests produced a sortie total approximating that originally called for, processing delays were such that time from request to receipt of aircraft averaged 95 minutes.

Such delays, varying unpredictably from one to two hours, have obvious effects on the momentum of attack and on the health of the attackers. To those accustomed to getting strikes in 10 to 20 minutes from aircraft orbiting on station, they were unacceptable, and led to loss of confidence in air support on the part of front line commanders. On 31 May the division commander made the inadequacies of the situation the subject of an official report to X Corps, and such was the feeling within the division as to bring an investigation by the Commanding General, Fleet Marine Force Pacific, once again in Korea on an inspection tour. After working through the numerous and sometimes contradictory allegations, and attempting to separate fact from fancy, General Shepherd concluded that the JOC processing time, the remoteness of airfields from the front lines, the struggle between Mosquito aircraft and ground parties for control of strikes, and the unwieldy nature of the Army-Air Force system, which forced communications to parallel the chain of command all the way to the top and back again, added up to excessive and unacceptable delay. In March he had raised the subject with Fifth Air Force, but to little purpose; now he went to the top, and on 24 May discussed the close support question with CincFE. With General Ridgway's view that it was improper for Marine air to support the Marine Division exclusively, General Shepherd concurred; for this problem, inevitable when a division with a private air force specializing in troop support was operating in company with air-starved Army units, no other answer was possible. But the basic difficulty was less the identity of the aircraft than the nature of the system, with all its built-in delays.

In June, as the Marine Division continued on the offensive east of the Hwachon Reservoir, two changes were made. Permission was secured from Fifth Air Force to keep four Marine aircraft on alert at an advanced airstrip, and to notify them of requirements by messages paralleling those to JOC. But direct communication with the airfield remained prohibited, the policy of scrambling and reporting was not permitted, and takeoff still had to await word from JOC. At the same time, in view of the radical discounting of routine requests in May, the Marines adopted a policy of submitting special requests only. But this proved self-defeating, as the resultant saturation of JOC communications facilities tended to offset other efforts to diminish delay time. This indeed was decreased in June to an average of 81 minutes, but the percentage of requests fulfilled dropped from 95 to 74 in good weather, and to 65 for the month as a whole, and nobody was much the happier.

4. *June–July 1951: North to Kaesong*

By the 1st of June the ground forces had regained the line of the Hwachon Reservoir. Only in the eastern mountains, where the desired front turned sharply northward, were the Marines still fighting hard for their objectives, and there the drive up the valley of the Soyang was completed in mid-month. Since instructions from the Joint Chiefs had by now limited the advance to the neighborhood of this line, although permitting local action to gain more commanding terrain, General Van Fleet prepared to fortify his positions while at the same time pushing forward I and IX Corps into the Iron Triangle.

This operation continued throughout the first half of June. By the 11th both Chorwon and Kumwha at the base of the triangle had been taken, and two days later Eighth Army briefly entered Pyonggang at the northern apex. Northeast of Kumwha IX Corps units moved up to Kumsong, where the enemy was attempting to establish defensive positions, and in mid-month attempted to outflank the town on the east, a move which in the absence of JCS limitations might have opened the Wonsan road and liquidated enemy forces to the eastward. Given these restraints, however, the effort was not pressed, and Kumsong remained in enemy hands. Except on the shores of the Sea of Japan, where ROK divisions moved onward to the outskirts of Kosong, this June advance to Pyonggang and Kumsong marked the farthest north for the remainder of the war.

As before, operations on the east coast were assisted from the sea. As the forward movement of the ROK I Corps took it into the difficult hill country at the mouth of the Nam River, gunfire support became extremely active. On 4 and 5 June the heavy cruiser *Los Angeles,* a recent arrival in the theater, provided support at the bombline; on the 6th, joined by *New Jersey,* she bombarded enemy positions in the vicinity of Kosong; on the 7th, as the result of an emergency call from the KMAG party ashore, received while she was replenishing, she had the interesting experience of loading 8-inch ammunition from an AKA over one side while unloading it out the guns over the other.

In the east as in the west, the long Korean coastline invited efforts to make trouble in the enemy rear. For some time the APD *Begor* had been putting agents ashore by night along the northeastern coast, and while security was imperfect—on one occasion the ship's departure from Pusan was announced by the North Korean radio the same evening—all the landings were successful. These nocturnal enterprises ranged from Chongjin in the north to Kojo, south of Wonsan, where on the night of 2–3 June *Begor* and her UDT complement landed 235 ROK guerrillas on an islet less than half a mile from the northern arm of the harbor. But this cloak and dagger business was a two-way street: 30 miles back down the coast, at the same time that the guerrillas were going in at Kojo, an ROK intelligence team, surrounded and hard-pressed by the enemy, was departing Kosong under cover of gunfire from an ROK PC and the destroyer *Rush*.

As the end of the U.N. offensive approached and the intensity of ground action diminished, the attentions of the gunnery forces shifted northward and fire support again gave way to bombardment. The communications centers of Wonsan and Songjin remained daily on the receiving end of gunfire from everything from LSMRs up to the battleship *New Jersey*. Far in the north the blockade of Chongjin was maintained, and the road and rail bridges leading south from that city subjected to frequent bombardment. On 8 June the efforts of the light ships were supplemented as Task Force 77 sent in *Helena,* now on her second tour of Korean duty, for three days work on transportation targets in the Songjin, Iwon, and Kyongsong Man areas, and ten days later *Toledo* gave Songjin a repeat performance.

In the operations of Task Force 77, where *Bon Homme Richard* had relieved *Philippine Sea* on the 1st of the month, a similar shift was apparent. Although support continued to be provided for the Marines east of the reservoir and for Army forces in the Iron Triangle, interdiction again became the primary task. A sufficient effort was committed to the northeastern rail bridges to keep them broken down, and an ambitious new interservice effort, Operation Strangle, was begun.

Admiral Ofstie's spring campaign had pretty well stopped the eastern railroad. But despite the efforts of Navy, Air Force, and Marines alike, truck traffic had continued to increase, and the daily average of North Korean vehicle sightings had risen spectacularly from 236 in January to 1,760 in May. Analysis of these sightings indicated that the enemy possessed some 20,000 trucks, a tenth of which arrived nightly in the combat zone, and suggested the difficulty of interdicting this logistic effort; it also brought a request from General Van Fleet to Fifth Air Force and to Task Force 77 to make the attempt. The importance of the problem was emphasized in early June by a GHQ announcement of the record vehicle sightings of the preceding month and, despite some skepticism within the Air Force as to its feasibility, the program was accepted on an experimental basis.

In the planning for "Strangle" the main north-south road routes behind the enemy lines were identified and parcelled out among the services. Three routes south and southeast of Pyongyang were taken by the Air Force; the two central routes, from Yangdok down the upper Nam and from Majon-ni south along the upper Imjin, went to Task Force 77; the Marines were assigned the roads running down from Wonsan and Kojo. Where defiles or watercourses made bypassing difficult, "Strangle Areas" were set up for cratering and for seeding with delayed-action and antipersonnel bombs.

From the very start the task was difficult, owing to the greater ease of bypassing by truck than by train, and to the fact that while almost all enemy movement was now night movement, all services were very limited in night capability. All hands nevertheless did their best, although the force requirements to keep the "Strangle Areas" strangled turned out to be somewhere between twice and five times those necessary to maintain an equal number of rail cuts. Dawn and dusk sorties were flown by the carriers, in addition to their normal daytime load, and the Air Force kept its B–26 intruders busily on the job. Best of all, perhaps, was the ingenious system evolved by the Marines, which teamed their night fighters with flare-dropping Navy patrol planes, and although these operations were extremely hazardous, owing to the restricted maneuvering room inside Korean valleys and the effect of the flares on night vision, good work was done. But in mid-June, after 13 days of "Strangle," a preliminary Air Force assessment indicated that while movement past the cut-points had been almost entirely stopped, and the enemy inconvenienced by being forced onto secondary roads, total north-south vehicle sightings remained about the same and arrivals in the front line area showed little ascertainable change. The conclusions were hardly encouraging, but as no obvious alternative presented itself "Strangle" was continued on into the summer.

Naval operations during the period of the enemy spring offensive and the United Nations advance to the north had not been without cost. The increasing strength of enemy antiaircraft was being felt: combat losses from April through June totalled 3 F9Fs, 8 ADs, and 19 Corsairs, and on 18 May Task Force 77 had its worst day of the war thus far when 6 planes failed to return. Enemy coastal batteries were also increasing in number, and not only in Wonsan. On 7 May the frigate *Hoquiam* was hit off Songjin, and on 14 June the DMS *Thompson* met trouble in the same area: having closed to 40-millimeter range of the beach and slowed to search for targets, *Thompson* was surprised when the enemy suddenly wheeled four guns out from under cover, opened fire, and scored 13 hits before the ship got clear.

The continuous efforts of the sweepers had by now largely conquered the minefields, but the threat remained, and on 5 May the first loss since February took place when the ROK *JML 306* was sunk off Sok To. More serious than the anchored fields was the problem of drifting mines: not only were the Russian moored mines fused to remain armed after breaking loose, but many had apparently been launched as drifters, to take advantage of prevailing southerly currents. Increasing reports of floating mines came in from the Sea of Japan and from the North Pacific; in June the destroyer *Walke,* steaming some 60 miles offshore as part of the carrier task force screen, ran upon a floater which exploded on the port side aft, inflicting serious damage and killing 25; by autumn more than 300 mines would have been recovered on Japanese shores.

For the U.N. divisions in Korea the bill had of course been higher, although ground force casualties in April and May were less than half those of November and December, less even than those of January and February. But for the armies of Communist China the spring offensive had proved disastrous. United Nations' estimates of casualties inflicted on the enemy claimed 70,000 for the April push, 90,000 for the week ending 23 May, and 147,000 for the two-week period from 20 May to 3 June; GHQ intelligence summaries estimated a total for April and May of 283,000, with 72,000 more in June. Figures like these do not, perhaps, inspire complete confidence, but unquestionably Communist losses were extremely severe, and while the impact of this bloody attrition on the manpower of China was minimal, its impact on the available total of trained military personnel was not. There was also a perceptible effect on morale, and prisoners began to surrender in unprecedented numbers: 3,000 Chinese were taken between 16 and 22 May and another 10,000 in the following week.

As the defeated Communists retired northward, with Van Fleet's armies hard on their heels, command changes continued throughout the forces of the U.N. Subsequent to the attack on the Hwachon Dam, Admiral Ofstie had been relieved of command of Task Force 77 by Admiral Henderson, and on 17 May had taken over as Chief of Staff to ComNavFE. In April Major General Gerald C. Thomas, USMC, had relieved General Smith in command of the Marine Division; late in May General Cushman, who had come out with the brigade, succeeded General Harris in command of the Aircraft Wing, to be himself relieved two months later. With the ending of the threat to Inchon Admiral Thackrey went home; in June, Task Force 95 got a new commander in the person of Rear Admiral George C. Dyer. In the other services the same was true: the Army command had changed in April; in June command of FEAF was assumed by Lieutenant General Otto P. Weyland, USAF, previously vice-commander for operations; at Fifth Air Force, General Partridge was replaced by Major General Frank P. Everest, USAF. Of major force commanders present in the Far East when the troubles began, only Admiral Joy remained, and he was shortly to receive some temporary additional duty which would occupy his whole attention.

At home, meanwhile, the United States had resumed its peculiar custom of conducting foreign policy by congressional hearing. In 1949 the unification investigation had demonstrated, through its exposition of military capability and strategic intent, that the only war contemplated by the United States was a big war in defense of Europe, and had opened the door to aggression by proxy in Asia. Now in the MacArthur hearings the details of strategic planning were again spread upon the public record, to reaffirm beyond a shadow of a doubt that the United States, unwilling to become fixed in a secondary theater, neither intended to expand the war in Asia nor to attempt the forcible unification of Korea. This separation of the political aim of Korean unification from the military objective of repelling aggression was reaffirmed by the President in May, and by the Secretary of State and the Secretary General of the United Nations in early June.

Since the United States did not propose to advance farther into North Korea, and since the Communists were in no condition to advance southward, an agreement to disagree seemed possible, which, while leaving the world and Korea divided much as before, would at least liquidate the fighting. On 23 June the Russian representative at the Security Council, whose fortuitous absence a year before had permitted U.N. action, made a radio address in which he indicated that the chief string-pullers would look favorably upon negotiations for an armistice.

Soundings in Moscow confirmed the official nature of these views, and the offer was taken up. General Ridgway was instructed to invite the Communists to meet with U.N. delegates on board the Danish hospital ship *Jutlandia* in Wonsan harbor for discussion of an armistice. With the selection of Admiral Joy as senior delegate for the United Nations, Admiral Ofstie took over in Tokyo as acting ComNavFE, and Naval Forces Far East were alerted to support the armistice discussions. On 30 June the invitation was broadcast to the enemy.

The reply came the next day: while agreeing to meet for talks, the Communists suggested that the location be changed to the city of Kaesong, 35 miles northwest of Seoul. This counterproposal doubtless reflected the symbolic difference between a meeting in one of Korea's historic cities, within Communist lines yet south of the 38th parallel, and one at sea on board a United Nations ship. Since the progress of negotiations would impede military action in the immediate neighborhood, it may also have indicated a desire to block the main road to Pyongyang. Possibly the Communists merely wanted the last word. The suggestion was quickly accepted, presumably in anticipation of an expeditious settlement, but in time the U.N. Command would regret this easy complaisance. On 8 July, following further communications, there was a meeting of liaison officers, and on the 10th, ComNavFE and his delegation confronted the Communists at Kaesong.

To the peoples of the non-Communist world the commencement of armistice discussions was heartening. Although Syngman Rhee went at once on record against all compromise, and demanded a continuation of the war for unification, elsewhere the hope that rational solutions would be quickly found produced a lifting of the spirit. These hopes were doubtless highest among the Americans, with their inbred belief in the value of the spoken and written word and their congenital distrust of the gloomy lessons of history. But even in the United States there were perhaps some whose experience encompassed negotiations with the Communists, and who could see the omens in the meeting at Kaesong.

The presence at the conference table of Chinese generals and an American naval officer called to mind the earlier discussions between Shufeldt and Li Hung-chang concerning the future of Korea, a future which intervening decades had done little to clarify. The antiquity of American concern with the welfare of the Koreans was recalled in the persons of the American interpreters, Lieutenants Horace G. Underwood, USNR, and Richard Underwood, AUS, grandsons of that Underwood who 66 years before had founded the Presbyterian mission to Korea. If these echoes of the past did not sufficiently suggest the intractability of the Korean question, and a likelihood that no speedy settlement would be reached, a contemporary incident, passing almost unnoticed, could have served as evidence that wars do not end all at once. On 30 June, on a little island in the northern Marianas, 19 Japanese soldiers and sailors, who for six years had refused to believe that their war was over, finally surrendered to the U.S.S. *Cocopa*.

CHAPTER XI

Problems of a Policeman

1. The Unexpected Face of War

IN A SMALL bronze shrine in the forum of ancient Rome the image of Janus, god of beginnings and endings, looked both east and west. It was the custom of the Romans, upon the outbreak of war, to throw wide the doors of this temple, and to shut them up again with the return of peace. In the summer of 1951 the commencement of Korean armistice talks seemed to promise an imminent end to the fighting, and a return of the struggle to the diplomatic plane. It seems a propitious moment to emulate the two-headed god, and to look, before the doors are closed, forward and backward in time, and east and west toward distant horizons.

In a year of Korean fighting the forces of the United Nations, with those of the United States in great preponderance, could be said to have won two wars. Successively, following initial surprise and early reverses, the armies of North Korea and of Communist China had been defeated. But the policy adopted following the second victory differed strikingly from that of the autumn before: rather than press on to the northward, and to possible involvement with yet another previously uncommitted force, it was decided to stabilize the situation, and to abandon the aim of a military unification of Korea. Yet though success was therefore limited, and though the cost had not been cheap, fulfillment of the original aim of repelling invasion made the enterprise worthwhile. Those mindful of earlier unchecked Axis aggressions who had taken the momentous decision to intervene could properly feel themselves justified, the more so in view of the implications of the fall of an undefended South Korea.

That so much had been accomplished, given the unexpected nature of the conflict, appears remarkable. If war, as someone has said, is a matter of surprise and movement, the first year of fighting in Korea certainly qualifies. The invasion of South Korea had come as a decided and unpleasant surprise to the United States; the intervention of the Chinese surprised the U.N. Command. Equally, it may be presumed, the rapidity of American diplomatic and military reaction in the summer of 1950 surprised the enemy, as did the recovery of the Eighth Army after the low point of the winter campaign. Most surprised of all, perhaps, were the members of the prevailing school of American military thought, with their emphasis on single-weapon single-theater strategy. War had come but not in Europe, nor, at least formally, with the "one possible enemy." Despite the view that held the assault from the sea to be a thing of the past, the pattern of the conflict had been shaped, not by the heavy bomber with its atomic weapon, but by the Amphibious Force and its projectile, the Marine Division.

For this there were a variety of reasons. The agreed and publicized strategic plan had found, hardly surprisingly, an enemy intelligent enough to circumvent it. Despite the impact of budgetary considerations on defense planning there remained, if narrowly, enough conventional force to permit a descent from fancy to fact and the conduct of a land war supported by sea and air. The nature of the theater, the ground rules which came to govern the campaign, and the importance of collective action all militated against employment of the atomic bomb and in favor of rational warfare. And lastly, the choice between accepting defeat and employing nuclear weapons was never finally posed.

In any event the atomic art, in those far-off days, was still somewhat primitive. Only eight nuclear explosions had been set off by the United States, and none since 1948. There had been no development of low-yield tactical weapons. In the Air Force the delivery of the bomb still rested on the capabilities of piston-engined aircraft: the first production B–47 only took the air the day the North Koreans crossed the parallel. In the Navy only the three large carriers—*Coral Sea, Franklin D. Roosevelt,* and *Midway*— had any kind of atomic capability, and all were assigned to the Atlantic Fleet.

The Russian explosion of the previous year had, it is true, expedited work on both the hydrogen bomb and tactical weapons, and the coming of war in Korea spurred the effort. Preparations for new tests at Eniwetok were underway at the time of the invasion of South Korea, and 1951 saw 16 U.S. explosions which, with two more by the Soviets, doubled the total of the preceding years. While the threat to the perimeter was at its height, and again in the dark days of December 1950, there was some talk of tactical use of existing atomic devices; some training runs were carried out in the course of the war by the Air Force, and by the Navy after the arrival in 1952 of the converted *Oriskany* and *Kearsarge*. But that was all. The war was fought to its end with conventional weapons. The Strategic Air Command turned out to be the shield rather than the sword of strategy, and as a limiting rather than an expanding agent wholly justified, if in an unexpected manner, its great cost.

As things worked out, therefore, the war in Korea developed as a classic exercise in sea power reminiscent of earlier times. The similarity, it is true, was to some extent concealed by differences in the society that supported the campaign, for to Americans of the mid-20th century the struggle was confusing and at times distressing. If a war, it was one which had never been declared by Congress; if a police action, it was of a magnitude without precedent since the affair with Tripoli; for those whose lives had spanned periods of presumed peace punctuated by world-wide conflict, the concept of limited war took some getting used to. At home, life went on as usual, with no restrictions on civilian consumption, with no apparent all-out national effort, and with administration policy subjected to increasing criticism. But however limited the war, for the individual in the armed forces—regular, recalled reserve, or draftee—there was no limit on the strain, hazard, or boredom of the conflict. Although mitigated by a purposeful program of rapid rotation, this situation, acceptable in 19th century wars fought by regulars, inevitably created problems of morale for those on the fighting line, as shown by conduct after capture by the enemy. Inevitably, too, it created serious tensions at home, which were not diminished by the cooperative nature of the U.N. effort, with its incumbent need to defer to allies whose contribution at times seemed minimal.

Back of all this, however, the historic pattern remained. As in earlier days the entire enterprise rested on control of the ocean highway, by which the troops were transported from the metropolis to the theater of action, and there supplied, supported, and assisted by the Navy. But here too time had wrought its changes. Where in the expeditions to Mexico and the Crimea, to the Sudan and South Africa, free use of the seas had been the prime enabling factor, in Korea the nature of the theater and the development of modern weapons gave the Navy important influence throughout the conflict. For the first year of war, above all for the first six months when the elements of surprise and movement were most apparent, this influence was so great as to be almost described as controlling.

The maritime aspect of the campaign first showed itself in the concentration of forces to meet the unexpected emergency, a concentration so rapid as to surprise friend and foe alike. To MSTS lifts of Army units from Japan, Okinawa, and the continental United States, to the Amphibious Force's management of the Pohang landing and the trans-Pacific movement of the Marine Division, to the high-speed delivery of Air Force fighter-bombers by aircraft carrier, and to logistic support of the entire U.N. effort, there was added a rapid and extensive reinforcement of naval fighting strength.

Table 18.—Growth of Western Pacific Naval Strength

Type	U.S. only June 1950	U.S. and U.N. October 1950
Fleet Carriers	1	4
Escort and Light Carriers	0	4
Battleships	0	1
Cruisers	2	9
Destroyer Types	16	54
Submarines	4	6
Minecraft	10	16
AGC/APA/AKA	3	22
APD	0	3
LST (including Scajap)	50	75
LSD	0	5
T–AP/Merchant Ships	0	75
	86	274

U.S. Navy Personnel, Western Pacific

June 1950	10, 990
August 1950	33, 465
October 1950	59, 375
January 1951	66, 930
April 1951	70, 315
July 1951	74, 335

This speed of concentration was vital, given the shortage of force which in the summer of 1950 affected all services alike. Although the Army was to commit almost everything it had to the narrow Korean front, and although numerically large ROK contingents were available, it was necessary to employ the Marine Division as an infantry force throughout the war. From beginning to end the Air Force felt itself operating on a shoestring, with limited strength, obsolescent types, and a very marginal supporting organization. For the naval forces of the U.N. the situation was the same. While the speed and size of reinforcement were impressive, base facilities in the the Far East were marginal; and while all available ships were committed to the Korean theater, these proved no more than sufficient for the war that did develop. Delayed deployment would have meant the loss of the Korean foothold; further opposition would have meant a very different war.

So speed of movement to a large degree made up for shortages, and weakness on the ground was counterbalanced by supremacy at sea and in the air. Together with the work of the Air Force, the northern strikes by Task Force 77, the close support provided by both fast and escort carriers, the blockade of the Korean coast, the bombing and bombardment of enemy transportation facilities, and the gunfire support of the ends of the perimeter made it possible for Eighth Army to stabilize a chaotic situation. This done, the forces of the U.N. assumed the initiative, and with the landing at Inchon commenced three months of rapid movement up and down the peninsula. The two landings and the evacuations of this period of triumph and tragedy demonstrated that in a theater of combat washed by the sea the forces of the West possessed a flexibility, a sped of movement, and a strategic freedom for which the enemy had no answer. Yet while this rapid movement derived entirely from naval capabilities it should be noted that the Navy, skeptical of the proposed amphibious operations, sailed somewhat reluctantly to glory.

Of the decision to invade Inchon, pushed through by General Mac-Arthur in the face of generalized doubts, it seems profitless to inquire whether it was in fact strategically sound. A success of such a magnitude would seem to justify even unjustifiable risks, and in any case once the decision had been made the risks, as always, began to seem smaller. But regarding the argument that the landing was unnecessary and that a better solution would have been for Eighth Army merely to shove against the perimeter, some comment may be in order. Doubtless this unimaginative strategy would have worked in time, but a victory so won would have been more costly, less elegant, and less decisive, and America at that moment had great need of a decisive victory. One should, it would seem, play from strength: so long as the U.N. fought its own kind of war, and used its advantages at sea and in the air, in sophisticated control systems, and in more efficient transport, the enemy was at a disadvantage. When these factors were neglected, and the North Koreans and Chinese given time to play it their way, the consequences were less happy.

Criticism has also been directed against CincFE's decision for a second amphibious landing. Both at the time and since, the overland movement by way of the Seoul-Wonsan corridor has been urged as the preferable alternative, and the anticlimactic nature of the Wonsan operation has seemed to lend weight to this view. But the fact that South Korean forces got there before the Marines appears less an indictment of "Tailboard" than testimony to the extraordinary effectiveness of "Chromite." If some in both Army and Navy urged the overland route, it was still true that the road was a difficult one, and that, as the affair at Kojo showed, there were enemy forces in the flanking hills. It is, of course, undeniable that the reembarkation of X Corps wrought considerable confusion in the logistic sphere, and slowed the preparations of Eighth Army and Fifth Air Force for the advance on Pyongyang. Equally, however, the problem of supporting both X Corps and Eighth Army through Inchon and Seoul would have been far from child's play. And whatever the decision as to the route, the harbor of Wonsan, strategically essential, had to be swept and opened to shipping before further moves could be undertaken.

As X Corps was floated up first one side of the peninsula and then the other, and as Eighth Army pressed on to seize the enemy capital, none foresaw the impending disaster. Yet it was in their response to the Chinese onslaught that the forces under Admirals Joy and Struble made perhaps their greatest contribution. The size of the attacking Chinese forces, the collapse in the west, and the widely dispersed condition of X Corps combined to bring about a major emergency and to return the initiative to the other side. But the crisis was met, and previous conscientious staff work was implemented with zeal and competence, to assist the retreat of Eighth Army, to help the Marines down from the hill, and to accomplish the redeployment of X Corps. Indeed the work of the Marine Division, of the Marine and naval aviators, of the gunnery ships and of the Amphibious Force may well have done still more, for one may wonder whether in the event of a major tragedy in northeastern Korea the war could have been kept limited. It is at least conceivable that the enemy, as well as the U.N., had in this instance cause to be grateful for the capabilities of the United States Navy and Marines.

Thus in the space of six months a scheme of maneuver made possible by rapid overseas deployment and based on the maximum use of naval capabilities had halted one invasion, defeated one enemy, and saved the day when a second intervened. But the period of a dominantly maritime strategy ended with the old year. The numerical strength of the new enemy required the retention of all ground forces in the line, and when the armies of the U.N. again moved north it was without benefit of the amphibious encirclement.

Yet while land operations henceforth held the center of the stage, the strategic situation was little changed. Korea was still a peninsular war, and supporting naval action was still of prime importance. On both coasts the blockade continued, while the lessons of history were brandished before the enemy in a series of amphibious feints. In the east, as it had from the beginning, naval gunfire continued to support the movements of ROK troops. In the interdiction of enemy transportation routes and along the battleline the work of naval air remained essential. Pusan port was still the basis of the campaign; the reopening of Inchon had greatly eased logistics in the western lowlands; in forward coastal areas and on the offshore islands, ground forces were supplied by LST. Underlying all was the Pacific Ocean supply line, by which rations, rounds, and gaiter buttons reached the free world's Asiatic toehold. Whatever the specific reasons for his selection, the choice of Commander Naval Forces Far East as chief of the U.N. Armistice Delegation was symbolically wholly appropriate.

2. Operating Problems

Seen in the large, therefore, the struggle in Korea greatly resembled the classic overseas campaigns of previous times. But within this framework the Korean War, like all wars, was unique, and the questions that faced those charged with its prosecution were questions of the moment. Daily, as is always the case in war, problems presented themselves, their nature governed by the immediate situation, and were faced, solved, evaded, or lived with as the ingenuity of man permitted.

In Korea the collective nature of the effort to repel the aggressor led, in notable contradistinction to most small wars of the 19th century, to the development of international forces on land, at sea, and in the air. Although the United States provided by far the largest part of the U.N. naval contingent, and although the second contribution derived from Britain and the British Commonwealth, units from the navies of Colombia, France, the Netherlands, and Thailand also took part. And special notice should be taken of the accomplishments of the ROK Navy and Marine Corps in developing, in circumstances tragic for them and amidst almost indescribable difficulties, into forces of considerable size and efficiency.

Within the structure of the U.N. Command the Korean Navy remained a separate task group. All other foreign units were assigned for administrative purposes to Rear Admiral Andrewes' West Coast Group, and at an early date that commander was confiding to his war dairy his need for the gift of tongues, as described in the Acts of the Apostles, and his relief at not having acquired, at least as yet, any recruits from Phrygia or Pamphilia. Inevitably some "very original problems" arose owing to language difficulties, the absence of common codes, varying degrees of training and expertise, and differing dietary preferences. Yet to the credit of all participants no insoluble difficulties developed, workable solutions were invariably thrashed out, and command relations remained excellent.

The rapid assembly of sufficient strength made the waging of a campaign possible. The nature of the campaign was largely governed by that of the assembled force. For the navies of the U.N. the lack of new construction, the limited funds available for modernization, and the restricted aircraft procurement programs made it inevitable that the war would be fought with ships, gear, and personnel largely left over from World War II. This situation, generally applicable to first-line units, was emphasized with time, as aging ships were removed from the mothball fleet, hastily refurbished, and deployed forward manned by aging reserves.

In all areas of naval operations, although in varying degree, problems of obsolescence presented themselves. Radar capabilities had not kept up with advances in aircraft performance; the limitations of World War II sonar were becoming critical; the unloading rates of APA and AKA types had fallen behind the needs of the times; everywhere maintenance was becoming an increasing problem. But it was in the carrier forces that the pressures of change and progress were most acute.

There the march of events was dramatized in the operation, side by side and throughout the war, of the first jet fighters, the last and finest of the piston-engined attack planes, and the F4U Corsair, in active service ever since the campaign in the Solomons. Continued dependence on this ancient aircraft was made possible by the existence of large numbers of preserved leftovers; in the circumstances prevailing in Korea it gave excellent service, eased the problems of transition, and made possible the useful work of escort and light carriers throughout the war.   Yet even with the F4U, operational requirements pressed against the limits of the capabilities of these smaller ships: the low wind conditions of summer in the Yellow Sea made the speed limitations of the escort carrier critical; although the CVL had the speed, its limited bunker capacity restricted the fuelling of screening ships and limited endurance. And in the fast carriers, despite the cushioning effect of the presence of these old friends, the advent of new types presented difficulties.

The takeoff and landing characteristics of the newer aircraft posed needs for more powerful catapults and for improved arresting gear. The advent of the jet fighter, essentially a flying gasoline barrel which paid for increased performance in phenomenal fuel consumption, raised difficult logistic problems, as did the great lifting capacity of the AD: each jet sortie cost the parent ship a minute in replenishment alongside a tanker; each three-ton bombload that left the deck meant a couple of minutes alongside an AE. And month by month these difficulties became more pressing, for as the efficiency of carrier operations increased, as the jet complement grew from one squadron to two, and as the jets in turn began to be launched with bombs, full-scale operations could exhaust certain types of ammunition in a day and use up the aviation gasoline of a non-converted carrier in less than two.

Thus the problems consequent to the introduction of new aircraft, while impinging directly upon the carriers and their crews, radiated outward to affect the work of their replenishment and screening ships. A more general difficulty, particularly apparent in the carriers owing to the complex nature of their operations but affecting all ship types, was the congestion brought about by new equipment: larger catapult machinery and magazine spaces in the carriers, more elaborate electronic and communications gear in all ships. Such installations take up space, but shipboard space is finite; their operation calls for personnel; with less space and larger crews comes undesirable crowding, or a diminution of military capabilities, or both. For this generalized tendency of modern war toward greater and greater complication the obvious theoretical answer was newer and larger ships; a more immediately practical one was the modification of existing hulls. This, for the fleet carriers, took place in stages: a first modernization of units of the *Essex* class brought various improvements, most notably more powerful catapults and larger fuel capacity, but at the cost of space for five aircraft; the second stage, reached late in the war, produced the "converted" *Essex* carrier with additional aviation fuel capacity, reinforced flight decks, and other new developments. There remained the angled deck, which began to appear after the Korean armistice, but this marked about the limit of what could be done with old hulls, and further progress waited upon new construction.

These tendencies toward specialization, elaboration, size, complexity, and cost, apparent throughout the fleet, placed a great premium upon versatility, and emphasized the value of any multipurpose instruments that might come along. Two of these, one new and one old, were of such importance as to deserve special mention. These were the helicopter and the LST.

The helicopter, here receiving its first test in combat, proved of transcendent value as plane guard for carrier operations, as platform for observation and for gunfire spotting, in the location of underwater mines, in providing courier and transport service between ships at sea and across difficult terrain ashore, in the rescue of pilots down behind enemy lines, and in the rapid evacuation of the wounded. The aging and awkward LST, with its ability to beach where ports were lacking and to load and discharge by the bow without the need of winchmen and stevedores, was wholly indispensable. In addition to filling their primary amphibious role, and so greatly speeding both advance and retreat, Scajap and Amphibious Force LSTs provided logistic support across the beaches to units dispersed along the length of the peninsula and among the outlying islands. In December 1950, in a report to the Chief of Naval Operations, Admiral Joy expressed his belief that the 38 Scajap ships had made the difference between holding and losing the Pusan beachhead, and observed that "the LST has possibly made the greatest single contribution to the success of the U.N. forces in Korea."

Within the operating forces the demonstrated versatility of both helicopter and LST led quickly to insatiable demands. For the minesweeping groups the marriage of these two instruments produced an unmatched combination of reconnaissance base, headquarters, and small boat mother ship. From all ships of sufficient size arose appeals for the installation of helicopter landing platforms. From numerous commands came urgent recommendations for the construction of new and improved LSTs.

Interacting with these problems of technological change and suitability were those posed by the nature of the theater and the actions of the enemy. Of these, one never before encountered on any scale and looked forward to with some apprehension, was that of cold weather carrier operations. But

Winter at sea: Snow scene on the flight deck of Essex. (USN 437710) winter in the Sea of Japan proved no great obstacle, and despite low temperatures, stormy seas, and snow and ice on the flight deck, the carrier force continued as before with but a slight reduction in sortie rate.

Night carrier operations, however, were another matter, for in the air, as elsewhere, western-style war had been generally unable to adapt to the hours of darkness. In the war against Japan no permanent solution had been found, and the Pacific Fleet had wavered between employment of special night detachments and the assignment of individual carriers to night work only. In Korea the enemy's predilection for night attacks, and his dependence on nightly truck convoys for logistic support, raised the problem in an acute form for the aviators of all services.

In the Navy the handful of specially-configured carrier aircraft soon proved inadequate, and from the beginning of the conflict carrier commanders commented on the lack of night capabilities. At home, by early 1951, the Chief of Staff of the Operational Development Force was urging the assignment of a fleet carrier to night work. In April 1952 Admiral Ofstie observed that "until effective techniques for night attacks are available, interdiction will be at best only marginal." But since carrier decks were in short supply and techniques left much to be desired, the deficiency remained for the duration, in embarked as in shore-based aviation.

With the single exception of the mining campaign the enemy made no effort at sea. But this stroke hit where economy had been compounded by disinterest, and the difficulties at Wonsan demonstrated the outstanding naval deficiency of the conflict. Despite all efforts to improve the situation the mine remained a most effective weapon, costly in time and effort, and one which would have been more so had the Soviets chosen to commit advanced types. As it was, the lessons of previous wars were reaffirmed, the importance of the mine reemphasized, and a research program of considerable magnitude undertaken for the development of efficient methods of detection and removal.

Two other areas of potentially serious trouble went untested by the enemy. Without question a Communist submarine offensive would have changed the entire nature of the war. Harbor defense installations had enjoyed a low priority in planning and were but tardily completed; destroyers and frigates were in short supply. Although the early efforts to provide minimum cover for convoys in Tsushima Strait were soon terminated, and the escorts assigned to blockade duty, the total number of antisubmarine types was never more than sufficient to provide a minimum sound screen for the carrier task force and to meet the requirements of blockade. No effort was ever made at trans-Pacific escort of convoy, and this was perhaps just as well, for the half-dozen oilers and escort carriers and the hundred-odd escort types needed for such an enterprise were nowhere to be found.

Almost equally, a determined enemy air offensive would have raised grave problems, at sea as well as on shore. Here too the destroyer shortage was important, limiting as it did the strength of antiaircraft screens for major vessels and the employment of radar picket ships. Against propeller-driven attack planes the fast carriers could doubtless have given a good account of themselves, but operation within the range of enemy jets was complicated by various factors. Since the World War II electronic identification devices were known to the Russians, and since newer systems were only gradually becoming operational, there was a serious recognition problem. Shipborne radar capabilities were inadequate, owing both to postwar concentration on resolution rather than range, and to the concurrent arrival of the jet airplane, in which higher speeds and operating altitudes accompanied a reflecting surface greatly diminished by absence of a propeller. To cap all there was the lack, at the outset not peculiar to the Navy, of a plane which could meet the MIG on anything approaching even terms. But although in late 1950 the Air Force received, in the F–86 Sabre, a fighter of comparable performance, no such carrier-based jet was to appear in Korea.

The questions thus far considered have been principally of a technological nature. But armaments themselves are neutral, only their users give them meaning, and among the complex problems posed by war in Korea was that of personnel. In June 1950 the Pacific Fleet was manned slightly below peacetime level, and the naval population of the Western Pacific was of the order of 11,000; within the space of six months this total was to be multiplied by six, and the need for so rapid an increase raised pressing questions of where to find the men.

Finding them involved a series of emergency actions. All hands were recalled from leave, overseas tours of duty and enlistments were indefinitely extended and ship-to-shore rotation halted, shore stations were stripped of all that they could spare and more. But despite all, the situation in the early weeks was often critical, especially in the Amphibious Force. Both at Inchon and at Wonsan ships were manned well below operational requirements, and in some cases even below peacetime allowances; some of the LSTs for Inchon were recommissioned a bare two weeks before the event with but 30 percent of complement on board, and with the majority of the crews and even some of the commanding officers lacking previous experience with this type.

Great difficulties also developed in providing the staff personnel needed to direct the operations of the expanding naval force. ComNavFE's staff had been designed for occupation duty, Admiral Higgins' was tailored to show the flag, and others were in a similar fix. In some areas nothing existed and drastic action was necessary, as when the need for a shore-based air command brought the shanghaiing of Captain Alderman and the borrowing of Admiral Ruble. Most dramatic of the staff problems was that which afflicted Admiral Smith upon his arrival from the United States to assume command of Task Force 95: on 12 September 1950 Smith broke his flag on a tender in Sasebo with no staff at all, a condition of lonely splendor in which he continued for two weeks before anyone reported in, and for more than a month before his principal assistants were all on board.

Over and above the resources made available by emergency measures the only personnel stockpile lay in the Naval Reserve. This was immediately levied upon, both to increase existing complements and for fleet expansion. Here again, in another context, the timing of the Korean War may be said to have been fortunate: a few more years and the capabilities of the dominantly World War II Reserve would have been very doubtful.

Selective recall of reservists was at once begun, but the remedy, as always, brought its own problems. However willing to take part in a major national emergency, those recalled could hardly avoid a feeling of double jeopardy while some of their fellows, and others who had never served in uniform, remained uncalled upon. Like the population at large, the Reserve doubtless contained a handful of the politically disaffected: at one point a suspicion of sabotage on one of the fast carriers brought an investigation and the precautionary transfer of a few hands to other duty. But no serious problems ever developed, and despite the strains imposed by prosperity and lack of interest at home, morale remained generally excellent.

By the end of 1950 the personnel situation was satisfactory in total numbers, but the distribution of regulars and reserves, hastily accomplished, was extremely unbalanced. The training of many reserves was below standard. There were acute shortages in certain categories of commissioned personnel and in a number of crucial ratings. The selection and detail of those recalled to active duty suffered from the nature of mobilization planning, where once again the concept of the one big war had proven costly. In the years after 1945 an emergency service rating structure had been set up, predicated on prospective full mobilization, which divided the normal ratings into specialized subcategories to which individual reservists were assigned. But since Korea did not qualify as a general emergency no shift to the new structure was made, and reservists were called up in their general service ratings. Within these larger groupings there was ample room for misassignment, but while some of the results were sufficiently dramatic to excite attention the situation never reached gross dimensions.

Most of these difficulties could be cured in time, but in some areas famine was endemic: certain rates were short throughout the war; with the release of reservists in 1952 the shortage of reliable and experienced petty officers became increasingly acute. In November 1951 CincPacFleet warned of this impending scarcity; in February 1952 both ComServPac and Cinc-

PacFleet felt the situation presented a serious threat to combat readiness. By the end of the year it was expected that allowances would on the average be only some 40 percent filled, and would drop as low as 25 percent in those crucial specialties—yeoman, radarman, radioman, and electrician's and machinist's mate—in which the armed forces were competing directly with American industry.

Dangerous though these shortages were, they seem never to have seriously affected combat readiness. A questionnaire circulated among ships in the Western Pacific, inquiring if damage or casualty had resulted from personnel shortage, produced a majority of negative answers, although a number of replies reported minor maintenance difficulties and a continued shortage of deck watch standers and of radiomen. This rating, indeed, despite the establishment of a special school at Sasebo, remained most critical of all, and these people were perhaps the real heroes of the Korean War: in many ships, particularly destroyers, a six-hour watch-and-watch schedule was the rule for weeks on end. It is, of course, a truism that burdens are never equally distributed in time of crisis, but the effect of loads like this on the inclination to reenlist needs no elaboration.

3. Logistic Support

No one can fight unsupported. Without timely and adequate logistic backing the finest strategy is only a paper plan. In Korea, as in any overseas theater, land strategy was a function of port facilities, and the campaign developed as a series of movements based on Pusan, Inchon, Wonsan, Hungnam, and Chinnampo. At sea, as always, the capabilities of the fighting forces were similarly dependent on the effectiveness of the supporting organization. The importance of seaborne supply to the war in the peninsula has already been touched on; it remains to consider the administration of naval logistics.

Here too affairs were complicated by the absence of plans for other than major hostilities, and by the resultant need to improvise. In the Far East the lack of a naval logistic command, the general shortage of staff personnel, and the pressure of operations hampered logistic planning. Since most Pacific and Far Eastern base facilities had been either inactivated or reduced to an austerity level, support for the Korean effort had to be projected in one bound from the west coast. Lacking both high-level guidance and detailed requests from the theater of operations, Admiral Denebrink's Service Force had, at the start, to fight its war intuitively.

With the outbreak of war the immediate problem was to provide a flow of consumer's goods for the expanding Western Pacific naval force, a problem calling both for estimates of needs and for action to fulfill them. In such items as rations, clothing, and small and general stores, where usage is closely related to population, prediction is simple enough, and in any case fleet units can live off their fat for a time. In these categories all that was required was a rapid expansion of overseas shipments. But in ammunition and petroleum products, where usage varies unpredictably with the tempo of operations, more complicated questions arise.

The first steps in ammunition supply have been noted earlier. Until late August, when the pipeline from the United States became filled, ammunition was hurried forward from stocks at Guam and Pearl Harbor. By mid-November some 66,000 tons had been delivered to NavFE and Seventh Fleet, of which only about 15,000 tons had been expended, and except for intermittent and unpredictable spot shortages this problem was under control for the duration.

In petroleum, the lifeblood of modern war, the situation was less satisfactory. Jurisdiction over POL had been centralized in Washington in the Armed Services Petroleum Purchasing Agency, and overseas in the theater commanders. In July, as consumption skyrocketed, Service Force oilers and gasoline tankers were pressed into duty and MSTS expanded its contract tanker fleet. In the Pacific Area, despite the drain from increased transoceanic sea and air movement, petroleum stocks were adequately maintained, but in the Far East there developed a series of potentially dangerous shortages.

Although adequate storage capacity was available in the theater, the supply on hand in the summer of 1950 was not what it should have been, and the planners failed adequately to anticipate the increase in demand. In the grade of aviation gasoline used by the Navy, stocks remained relatively constant, but by October increased consumption had brought local shortages which had to be made up by shipments from the Pacific Area and from the Philippines. In Air Force grade aviation gasoline and in Navy fuel oil the situation was worse: supplies of the former declined steadily from the start of the war, and monthly from August to November there came periods of crisis; in black oil, increased usage coupled with inadequate requests produced a serious December shortage which required rapid transfers from the Pacific Area. Except for some restrictions on airlift, the fighting forces were fortunately never affected, but the margin was too close for comfort. No safety factor existed, and the loss of a single tanker from whatever cause would have seriously curtailed operations.

In two other areas of fleet support, shortages and delays developed, although again happily without ill effect. Plans for emergency establishment of harbor defenses were lacking, and materiel was in short supply: the laying of an antisubmarine net at Sasebo, although stimulated by a submarine alarm within the harbor in mid-August, was begun only on 3 October.

Similar troubles affected the provision of degaussing facilities, where construction of a range at Yokosuka, begun as a routine project, was raised to the highest priority with the first evidence of enemy mining. But here fate intervened: en route to the California port of embarkation a truck loaded with instruments for this installation rolled off the highway, outloading was not completed until 9 November, and not until eight months after its authorization did the Yokosuka range become operational.

As supplies and gear were hurried west, and as the Service Force moved to assume its administrative responsibilities, service units were deployed forward to provide the maximum in floating support and to minimize the need for expanded shore facilities. The establishment in July of Service Squadron 3 and of Service Division 31 eased planning problems and implementing responsibilities for both Seventh Fleet and Naval Forces Far East. In the following weeks the expansion of Service Force strength in the forward area was expedited to provide underway replenishment of operating forces, salvage services, and in-port replenishment and maintenance at Sasebo and at amphibious objectives. By September, when this procedure received formal ratification in an exchange of dispatches between CincPacFleet and the Chief of Naval Operations, its implementation was well underway. Its dimensions may be appreciated from the tabulation of supporting units present in the theater.

Table 19.—Service Force Deployment to the Western Pacific
(Yard Types Omitted)

Type	29 June 1950	1 August 1950	15 September 1950
AD	1	2	2
AE	0	0	1
AF	1	2	2
AK	0	1	1
AKA	0	1	4
AKL	0	1	3
AN	0	0	1
AO	1	3	5
AOG	0	1	1
ARH	0	0	1
ARS	0	1	2
ATF	1	3	4
LSD	0	1	0
LST	0	1	0
	—	—	—
	4	17	27

Appreciable though it was, to those involved this reinforcement seemed only marginal, as did the projected growth of Service Force strength as a whole. The plans for naval expansion which developed over the summer called for an increase of service vessels from 46 to 67, a growth of less than 50 percent, while the active strength of the Pacific Fleet was slated to rise from 259 ships to 492, thus nearly doubling. With more than 90 fighting ships in the Western Pacific this allowance of repair vessels and tenders promised to be adequate only so long as battle damage remained small, while in other logistic types day-to-day requirements threatened to exceed the capacity of deployed units. The availability of oilers was marginal: despite the proximity of the operating area to the Japanese base, the demands of underway replenishment were such that in-port fuelling was dependent upon British and Scajap tankers. The lack of ammunition ships forced early recourse to the use of AKAs with specially sheathed holds, an expedient which fortunately worked out acceptably. And of course there were never enough LSTs.

Despite the shortage of oilers and ammunition ships, replenishment at sea was quickly begun. Unavoidably, in the first days of action, naval units refueled and rearmed in port, the Seventh Fleet at Buckner Bay and Sasebo, NavFE ships at Sasebo and at Pusan. But the need to keep the carriers on the line brought a shift to underway resupply at the earliest possible date, and on 23 July Task Force 77 first fueled at sea to the south of Cheju Do. For the rest of 1950, the expansion of the carrier force and the high rate of consumption at Inchon and in the December crisis kept this a shoestring operation. By year's end, nevertheless, ComServron 3's fleet oilers, in 72 meetings, had accomplished 100 carrier, 11 battleship, 50 cruiser, and 546 destroyer fuelings at sea, while *Mount Katmai,* the reactivated *Paricutin,* and the sheathed AKAs had rearmed the force on 54 occasions. Transfers during these exercises were not limited to the 1,750,000 barrels of fuel oil, the 171,000 barrels of aviation gasoline, and the 7,665 short tons of ammunition which were delivered, but included numerous passengers and an infinite variety of miscellaneous commodities and fleet freight. And the supply of urgently needed items had been speeded by the institution of a daily air delivery service from Japan to Seventh Fleet carrier decks carried out by war surplus TBMs.

For the rest of the war the deployment of underway replenishment ships remained largely unchanged. One oiler was maintained at Keelung to fuel the Formosa Strait patrol; Yellow Sea units were serviced by independently sailed ships; to meet the larger needs of forces in the Sea of Japan two tankers and one or two ammunition ships were kept on station, joined as necessary by storeships and reefers. By 1952 it had become possible to replenish the entire fast carrier task force in the space of nine hours, and the impact of logistics upon operations was being further diminished by resort to the hours of darkness. Night-time replenishment, once

Continuing operations need continuing replenishment: Ashtabula fueling Boxer and a destroyer in breezy weather. (USN 435050)

considered so dangerous as to be impracticable, now became increasingly routine as a realistic appreciation of the possibilities of radar detection brought a relaxation of darken-ship requirements and the use of screened lights. By 1952 this evolution had become standard to the extent that the first ships were alongside the tankers before daybreak. In the last months of war nightly replenishment became the rule, and the force was meeting requirements which would have seemed wholly visionary in the war against Japan, or indeed in the summer of 1950.

At no time did the underway replenishment force have much leeway. The lifting ability of the ADs and the fuel consumption of the jets strained the capacity, not only of the parent carriers, but of ammunition ships and oilers as well. One result of these steadily increasing requirements was a variety of ingenious improvisations and modifications to the equipment for transfer of POL and ammunition. Another was a vigorous debate on the future of the art, which centered on the need for replenishment vessels with more speed and longer hulls, to keep the force moving and improve handling characteristics alongside, and on the desirability of developing composite replenishment ships which could issue more than one commodity at a time.

In-port logistic support, by contrast, remained comparatively routine once the early period of improvisation was over. Replenishment and repair were handled as practicable by the floating base at Sasebo and by its smaller sister at Yokosuka, while overload requirements were contracted out to Japanese shipyards. Of the 640,000 items of material required to support a modern naval force, some 83,000 high-demand articles, enough to supply 90 percent of fleet needs, were stocked by the Service Squadron; supplies of very large items such as propellers and radar antennae were maintained ashore; more exotic objects were procured on special order, locally or from the United States. The use of Japanese sources of supply, encouraged both by price differential and by elimination of shipping costs and time, rapidly became extensive; for the Navy this reached a peak of over $1,750,000 in June 1951, and although subsequently diminishing, owing to Japanese inflation and to some instances of poor quality or delayed delivery, remained of importance throughout the war.

The value of the Japanese base, indeed, went far beyond the opportunities it afforded for offshore procurement. Although floating support was employed to the utmost, some things, inevitably, had to be done ashore. At the outbreak of hostilities ComNavFE had been faced with the immediate need to convert Sasebo from stand-by status to major operating base, and to provide some airbase facilities in Japan. The first of these requirements called for a rapid expansion of ammunition and cargo-handling capacity and of storage space; the second, urgent in view of the needs for cargo, mail, and passenger services, for carrier aircraft replacement pools, and for patrol plane bases, was solved in the early weeks through negotiations with FEAF.

But such growth tends to snowball. These new and expanded supporting activities came in due course to require support of their own, in expansion of the supply department of Fleet Activities Sasebo and of the Naval Supply Depot at Yokosuka. And in time further steps proved necessary, as needs developed for the enlargement of NavFE headquarters, of naval hospital facilities, and of ship repair capacity.

That these requirements did not make the personnel problem wholly unmanageable was owing to the availability of Japanese labor. At Sasebo, by mid-November 1950, more than 100,000 man-days of Japanese stevedoring had been used in ammunition handling alone, a contribution equivalent to that of a thousand-man labor battalion; at Inchon, Wonsan, and Hungnam, Japanese stevedores were also employed. At Fleet Activities Yokosuka, and elsewhere, nine-tenths of the jobs in the supply and similar organizations were filled by Japanese civilians. In the course of time the staffing of the Yokosuka Ship Repair Facility came to involve about 3,900 Japanese, with some 350 U.S. naval personnel engaged in supervisory work.

In all aspects of logistic support the early days were unavoidably hectic, but from November 1950 quality and quantity improved steadily, both afloat and ashore. Indeed there were triumphs: the possible need for cold weather clothing was anticipated in midsummer, and prompt procurement and shipment met all requirements of the winter campaign. There were also, of course, crises: the embarkation of X Corps in December pretty well stripped the Far East of tobacco, candy, and writing paper and required, among other things, an emergency order for a million candy bars. But by spring of 1951 the situation was well under control: underway replenishment was meeting all demands, floating support in Japan had been expanded by the arrival of reactivated repair ships, shore-based activities were running smoothly. If it had required almost ten months to assemble a well-rounded logistics command, no major crisis had developed at any point in the chain. The affair had been so managed that support of Central Pacific trust territories and preparations at Eniwetok for the forthcoming atomic tests had suffered only minor delays. And once the basic military requirements had been satisfied the American standard of living came to attract the solicitude of supply officers, and a growing proportion of correspondence to be devoted to requisitions for beer, baseballs, boxing gloves, phonographs, pinochle sets, and the like.

What this surplus implied in operating terms became apparent in August 1952, following a hangar deck fire which caused major damage to *Boxer*. Although no great military urgency existed, it was decided to make repairs locally rather than sailing the ship ahead of schedule to the United States. Needed material was ordered by dispatch and assembled at Yokosuka or flown out from the United States while *Boxer* was returning from the operating area. Following an all-hands evolution by the Yokosuka Ship Repair Facility, the repaired and refurbished carrier was back on the line 19 days after the fire, and completed five more days of flight operations before heading homeward.

Thus far the discussion has concerned only the naval side of the war. But before leaving the subject of logistics some notice should be taken of the work of the Military Sea Transportation Service in providing the trans-Pacific lift on which the entire campaign depended. With the decision to intervene in South Korea the expanding needs of Army, Navy, and Air Force brought an immediate doubling of the load for MSTS Pacific: in contrast to a westward lift of 812,000 measurement tons and 71,000 passengers in the second quarter of 1950, the period from July through September saw 1,984,000 tons and 136,000 passengers carried forward. But to double the lift, in view of the length of the supply line, the time required for the round trip, and the need for simultaneous increase of intratheater movement, required far more than a doubling of assigned shipping: the 25 MSTS vessels in or en route to the Western Pacific on 1 July had increased to 117 by 1 September and to 263 by 1 November.

Such an expansion inevitably had its growing pains. In Japan the recently opened Western Pacific headquarters of MSTS was acutely short of personnel, and the first weeks were rough ones. In the San Francisco Bay area the recruitment of merchant marine crews for contract vessels suffered some delays, while an overestimate of requirements by continental commands resulted for a time in idle shipping. Some administrative inefficiency developed in the Far East when CincFE, having failed to assign Army and Air Force personnel to the MSTS Joint Space Assignment Board, complicated communications and planning by interposing a GHQ staff section between Captain Junker and his customers. The peak loads which accompanied the Inchon, Wonsan, and Hungnam operations strained the capacity of MSTS to the utmost.

Some questions were also raised in the course of 1950 concerning the efficiency of utilization of MSTS shipping by the Far East Command. Here speed of cargo handling at destination is the crucial factor, and here, despite the best efforts of theater port commands, the first months saw considerable delays. Where estimated required port time was of the order of two weeks, the average ship reaching the Far Eastern theater spent almost a month in harbor, and the cumulative losses worked out to such considerable equivalents as an entire month's lift to Korea, 32 ships assigned to the trans-Pacific run, or $8,000,000 in time charter hire. But this wastage seems ascribable more to tactical and geographical factors than to ineptitude in the Far East Command: port time analyses for Japan, and for Pusan, Wonsan, and Iwon, show a utilization close to maximum; the big losses came in the autumn at

Inchon, where tidal and other limitations of the harbor were compounded by the mounting out of X Corps units for Wonsan.

With time these difficulties were overcome, and with time operations became routine. They were also impressively large, for the Korean War absorbed the major portion of the activity of MSTS, by now the largest shipping organization in the world. What is needed to support a modern transoceanic war of even limited dimensions may be indicated by a few figures. For World War II the average monthly Pacific outbound cargo came to 1,085,000 tons; in 1953 it fluctuated between 880,000 and 1,400,000 tons. In World War II the monthly average of westbound passengers was 49,200; in 1953 this figure varied between 39,000 and 58,000. As for the shipping requirements which such loads impose, it may be noted that MSTS operated more than three-score ships within the Far Eastern theater, moving 626,000 tons and 74,000 persons a month, while the trans-Pacific figures, in "notional" ships of standard types, reached the totals indicated in Table 20.

Table 20.—MSTS Trans-Pacific Shipping Requirements

Cargo	Required monthly quantities	Required monthly arrivals	Required ships in the pipe line
Provisions	78,000 tons	9.7	24
General cargo	381,000 tons	38	95
Ammunition	103,000 tons	17.7	44
Aircraft	50,000 tons	1.6	3
Personnel	39,000	16	24
Fuel oil	1,663,000 bbls.	17	29
Diesel oil	675,000 bbls.	6	11
Gasoline	1,419,000 bbls.	11	21
Shipping required		117	251
Grand total			368

Beyond these problems of logistic administration two factors in the Korean situation deserve attention. The first relates to the problem of petroleum procurement, and to the extent to which the ability to make war may be subject to developments independent of the belligerent's control. The second concerns the nature of the theater of operations, and its influence upon the magnitude of military effort.

Although the POL to support the Korean campaign came, in the first instance, from American stocks, the passage of time brought increasing reliance on the Middle East. Beginning in 1952 a considerable proportion of the jet fuel used in the Far East originated in the Persian Gulf. At a fairly early date the procurement of motor gasoline was divided between U.S. and Persian Gulf sources, while at intervals recourse was had to Aruba in the Dutch Antilles. From the latter half of 1951 the sources of both diesel oil and Navy standard fuel oil were almost entirely Middle Eastern. In the last months of conflict the Persian Gulf provided the United Nations with all its black oil, about a third of the jet fuel, a quarter of the motor gasoline, and more than half the diesel oil; aviation gasoline alone remained a wholly American product. This Middle Eastern procurement afforded a considerable economy in tanker turnaround time as compared to the U.S. Gulf coast, but it also gave hostages to fortune. In the disturbed political state of the area, emphasized in these years by the quarrel between Britain and the Mossadegh regime in Iran, there was little assurance from one month to the next that this source would remain open.

While the ability to prosecute the war thus depended in uncomfortable degree upon the continuity of Middle Eastern oil supplies, the size of the military effort was in large part a function of port capacity. Throughout the war, despite the opportunities offered by the long Korean coast line, United Nations forces remained heavily dependent upon Pusan and Inchon. Such dependence placed a rigid if theoretical limit on the size of the forces that could be supported: a study of the shipping situation in 1951 demonstrated that, in view of the physical limitations of these ports and of Yokohama, a doubling of shipping assigned the Korean run would augment deliveries by a mere 31 percent, and an infinite increase by only 37 percent.

The implications of the study are of interest, applying as they do not only to Korea but to the Indo-China crisis that followed, and indeed to any theater of operations where ports are few. It may be granted that the use of a few large ports is more efficient than a resort to many small ones. But the multiplication of forward unloading sites provides offsetting advantages in economy of land transport, as shown by the difficulties of the post-Inchon advance, and in spreading of risk, as illustrated by the beach surveys of the winter of 1950–51, motivated in part by the possibility of nuclear attack against Pusan.

This whole question of the support of a campaign in a coastal area where ports are few and communications primitive would seem to pose heavy contingent responsibilities upon the Navy. Had it been desired to increase the effort at the front beyond the capacity of Pusan and Inchon, certain steps were theoretically possible. A reallocation of resources to the ground forces might have been accomplished by the shift of Air Force units to island sites, Ullung Do in the east and Tokchok To in the west, for example; an increase in the proportion of embarked aviation, which carries its own port facilities in the form of the Service Squadron, would have had similar results; an expansion of over the beach supply would have been helpful. But none of these solutions was easily available. The rugged topography of the Korean islands was uninviting, and the islands themselves lacked ports: indeed, a Fifth Air Force desire to set up a Tactical Air Direction Center on Paengnyong Do went unsatisfied owing to presumed logistic impossibility. As for an increase in embarked aviation and in over the beach supply, such measures would have required more carriers and more LSTs, and these were not available.

These questions, however, are speculative. So far as needs and desires dictated, maritime logistics appear to have been well handled. For all forces MSTS did its job; for the Navy the system of mobile logistic support, backed by limited base development in Japan, proved adequate to all demands while obviating the need for extensive construction ashore. If the outbreak of this unexpected war had imposed sudden and sizable logistic problems upon the armed forces of the United States, the impact had not been wholly one-sided. Reports from the submarine patrols in La Pérouse Strait indicated a volume of traffic inbound for Vladivostok which greatly exceeded previous estimates, and which was on the increase.

4. Interservice Coordination and the Air Problem

Throughout the Korean War, routine interservice problems were solved with little difficulty. The evacuation of casualties and the allocation of air and sea lift crossed service bounds. Joint planning for amphibious operations was effective. Logistic cross-servicing was generally satisfactory, as Marine aviation was provided with scarce engineering talent by the Air Force, deficiencies in Marine transport were made up by the Army, and aviation materiel was traded back and forth between the Air Force and the Navy. But there was one great exception to this generally harmonious picture.

The exception, of course, concerned the question of the proper employment of tactical aviation, a problem of very long standing and one for which no agreed solution had ever been developed. In the United States a generation of impassioned doctrinal controversy and the experiences of the Second World War had resulted in a reorganization of the armed forces in which the Army was shorn of its aviation and the Army Air Force transmuted into a separate service, while the Navy and Marines retained their organic air components. This reorganization, and the conflicting philosophies and practices which it embodied, met its first test in Korea.

Less than a year before, in the congressional hearings on "Unification and Strategy," the ancient controversy between the schools of separate and of integrated air war had reached its moment of greatest bitterness. With the invasion of South Korea the dollar aspect of the problem disappeared, but in place of budgetary pressures there developed those exerted by an enemy apparently unimpressed with air theory. The locus of tension between the services shifted from Washington to the theater of operations, where difficulties reappeared in conflict between Navy and Air Force over the control and employment of aircraft, and in controversy between Army and Air Force as well.

Given the history of the air question the reappearance in Korea of controversy and tension was hardly surprising. Nor, indeed, should the importance of these conflicts be overestimated. So much, in recent years, has been blamed on service rivalries as to raise the suspicion that some of the talk is used by civilians, whether taxpayers or administrators, to camouflage their own derelictions. And it should be remembered that equally vigorous if less publicized controversies exist within the individual services. In the Navy there was friction between surface and air, and disagreement as to the proper structure of the command organization. In the Air Force such matters as the control of airlift, the coordination of Bomber Command, and authority over service units provided bones of contention for FEAF and Fifth Air Force. Doubtless the Army had its problems too. Nevertheless the interservice difficulties deserve some comment, if only because the greatest tactical surprise of the Korean War was its demonstration of the limited effectiveness of "air power."

The argument that strength in the air is the sufficient precondition of victory, and that an air force which commands the skies inevitably commands all below, had in the years since World War II commended itself to many. Yet although in some respects persuasive, this argument had been less than wholly substantiated by the experience of the wars with Germany and Japan, to say nothing of the Italian campaign. In Korea it was to be quickly refuted.

In the first six months of war, although enjoying almost complete command of the air, the aviation of the U.N. was unable to prevent reverses on the ground, deny the enemy the use of his own territory, isolate the battlefield, or detect the assembly of large enemy forces. The defense of the perimeter had been a very close thing; in the disastrous battle of the Chong-chon and the subsequent retreat to the south every aircraft in the sky was friendly; in the later stages of the war a costly and sustained effort to isolate the battlefield by the interdiction of enemy supply lines was to fail of its anticipated success.

Yet where proper control procedures were available the employment of aircraft in direct support of troops had tremendous military effectiveness, as was amply demonstrated by the operations of the Marine Brigade along the Naktong, by the campaign for Seoul, and by the movement of the Marine Division from the reservoir to the sea. In a different context the essential interdependence of air and surface activity was reaffirmed when the failure of interdiction was attributed by air commanders to the diminished enemy consumption which followed stabilization of the front. Paradoxically indeed, the first test of the new service concerned with air war pure resulted in a striking reaffirmation of the great degree to which, in a non-nuclear environment, success in the air depends on events below.

For this lesson the services were unequally prepared. The divergent histories of Air Force and naval aviation had by 1950 produced very different patterns in training, equipment, and control mechanisms. The geography of the plains of North Africa and Europe and the ideology of independent air power had made that "inherent flexibility" of which enthusiasts prated a macroflexibility. For the conduct of the air campaign, control was centralized at the highest possible level and preplanned operations were the rule, with the result that while a large effort could be switched from day to day along an extensive battle front, control at the target had been neglected. From this structure had developed a communications system with large capacity for routine transmission of orders and reports between central command post and operating air bases, but with limited provision for tactical communications at the scene of action.

The Navy and Marines, by contrast, accustomed to attacks against such easily defined targets as fleets and airbases, and to operations within the constricted beachhead, tended to rely on doctrine supplemented by brief orders, and on delegation of control to those on the spot. Provision of tactical aviation in ground warfare was looked upon as a service to the forces involved rather than as part of a separately controlled campaign, as an *à la carte* rather than a *table d'hôte* proposition. The consequence was a command communications system of high reliability but comparatively small capacity, lacking in such automated devices as the radioteletype, but balanced by an emphasis on discrimination at the objective expressed in liberal provision of ground controllers and in the design of tactical communications equipment. As compared to the four VHF channels in the radios of Air Force fighter-bombers, the sets in naval and Marine aircraft had ten.

The incompatability of these systems was forcefully demonstrated in Korea. As in the Southwest Pacific in the war against Japan, Air Force verbosity in communications swamped the less capacious naval circuits, and indeed, at times, FEAF's own: an extreme example was the grandfather of all radio messages, received by Task Force 77 in November 1950, which took 8,000 encrypted groups to set forth the air plan for one day, and which required over 30 man-hours for processing. Contrariwise, scene of action requirements for precise and deliberate control of aircraft in situations tightly packed in the air and fluid on the ground went far beyond the capacity of Air Force tactical communications. Both services, in a sense, were right in this matter, and both wrong: the land campaign, if only from problems of target description, is unavoidably wordier than war at sea; the compression of space and time brought about by the speed and power of modern weapons has made all tactical situations increasingly approximate the tightly-packed beachhead.

In the months before the war some efforts at improvement of joint communications had been made by Seventh Fleet. With an eye to the need for cooperation in a possible emergency, a series of drills and exercises with Western Pacific Air Force units had been attempted. But success had been only moderate, and the reports had emphasized the "real and urgent" need for action at the Washington level in the interest of efficient interservice communications. Somewhat similar conditions existed in Japan, where Air Force efforts at joint exercises and Air Force tentatives toward establishment of a Joint Operations Center had met little response from the Army. The whole situation points up a failure at Department of Defense level to place sufficient emphasis on joint matters, a failure apparently consequent not only to budgetary pressures and to the primacy in planning for war in the North European plain, but also to the well-meant efforts to prevent "duplication" by writing down exclusive rather than cooperative roles and missions.

With the arrival of the Seventh Fleet in Korean waters the problems of coordination assumed immediate practical importance, and on 8 July General Stratemeyer asked CincFE for operational control over all naval aircraft operating from Japan or over Korea. But this request, which involved authority to select carrier operating areas as well as targets, was resisted by Admiral Joy. Quite apart from the echoes of Air Force imperialism and from technical questions of capability, the felt hazards of Communist submarines and the contingent responsibility of Seventh Fleet for the defense of Formosa made the proposal undesirable, and after a meeting of interested parties the phrase "coordination control" was substituted. Although the term had enjoyed some use in prior planning for analogous situations, the Air Force was later to profess itself unsatisfied with such limited authority. But difficulties deriving from phraseology were less important than those arising from the structure of the Far East Command, and from incompatabilities of doctrine, equipment, and training.

While the early employment of Task Force 77 on northern strikes posed few problems, the air situation, as General Shepherd noted in July, was full of paradox. As a result of the pressures of the moment, B–29s were employed on tactical targets to the dissatisfaction of all concerned; jet fighters, with a fuel restriction limiting them to 15 minutes in the combat zone, were assigned to troop support; despite a wealth of close support opportunities carrier aircraft were committed against semi-strategic objectives. With the passing of time, however, the imperative needs of the perimeter brought a steady southward displacement of carrier operations which culminated with CincFE's order of 8 August to put everything on close support. This development made necessary the coordination of Seventh Fleet operations, not only with FEAF, but with the Air Force and Army commands in the peninsula as well. On paper the question was dealt with by FEAF and NavFE representatives in the 3 August memorandum on "Proposed Target Arrangements with Navy." In actuality it had hardly been faced.

Arriving in circumstances of great emergency to lend a hand, the carrier aviators found themselves faced with difficulties which frustrated their best efforts. Common maps and common grids were lacking, so that location and designation of targets on an interservice basis was almost impossible. The command structure, presided over by the distant genius of the Dai Ichi Building and overcentralized in Tokyo, made no provision for a field commander charged with the coordination of forces, and little for direct dealing between Eighth Army, Fifth Air Force, and Seventh Fleet. But perhaps the greatest problem was that of communications.

In the first days of fighting, requests for air support had gone through GHQ and FEAF; only on 7 July did Stratemeyer gain CincFE's permission to have the Army in Korea call directly upon Fifth Air Force. The entry of the carriers into support of the perimeter led to further complications, and in late July, in the hope of bringing order into chaos, Admiral Hoskins sent a representative to Taegu to establish communications with the Joint Operations Center. But incompatibility of facilities limited the success of this effort, as did the command structure, since direct dealing was authorized only for "coordination of air operations previously scheduled by higher authority." What this meant, in terms of emergency calls for close support, was that a dispatch originating at battalion level was supposed to travel normal infantry channels to Army at Taegu, thence to JOC, thence by relay to FEAF in Tokyo, and there from FEAF to NavFE for broadcast to Commander Seventh Fleet.

Under such restrictions it seems unlikely that the most elaborate communications system could have done the job, and the net that actually existed was rudimentary. On 15 July FEAF set up a circuit linking its Tokyo headquarters with FAFIK and with Seventh Fleet; ten days later Admiral Struble was still having difficulty in direct communications with FEAF; on 4 August, as a result of the pressure of other needs, FEAF was obliged to secure this circuit, thus further complicating an originally marginal situation. And even in the autumn, when circuits had been successfully established, slow internal handling of messages on the part of shore-based commands continued to impose delays.

In the air over Korea communications also presented difficulties. Confronted by the requirement of converting a defensive fighter force into one which could participate effectively in the land battle, Fifth Air Force had begun an heroic effort in improvisation. Two tactical air control parties were in the field by the end of June; a small combat operations section reached Taejon in the first week of July; late in the month a Joint Operations Center of sorts had become operational at Taegu. But by this time attrition of the TACPs had forced resort to airborne control of support strikes, while saturation of inadequate Army communications had encouraged the relaying of requests for air support through the orbiting Mosquito control planes.

This practice made a bad situation worse. Of the four VHF channels to which most Air Force planes were limited, only two were common to the various types of aircraft in the theater and to the jeep-mounted radios of tactical air control parties. Since Air Force procedures required incoming flights to report to JOC for assignment, and then to be passed through division to a regimental TACP or Mosquito, a considerable amount of talk was involved. As a result of this insistence on the part of JOC on acting as control as well as scheduling center, channels were so jammed that to drown out competing chatter a reporting aircraft had to come within 10 or 15 miles, a situation which at times imposed as much as 200 extra flight miles on carrier planes coming in from the west. Over the lines, meanwhile, the passage of information between attacking aircraft, Mosquito control plane, and ground party was confined to a single channel on which more than a dozen controlling centers were talking simultaneously, all this against a background buzz of conversation between the JOC and other flights. When to these circumstances was added a general indiscipline in voice communications, the difficulties encountered became quite understandable.

Both at command and tactical levels, therefore, the communications system proved inadequate to effective joint operations. One result was uncertainty in Task Force 77 as to the real nature of the emergency when calls for help came in, and in commands ashore as to its availability for support; a second was the frustrating inability of aviators to gain adequate control over the battleline. In time this situation would lead to attempts to break away from the perimeter, and to find more constructive employment for the air groups of Seventh Fleet; more immediately, it brought a number of unsuccessful efforts to short-circuit the established system. On 23 July an urgent plea from EUSAK for carrier support led to protests from Fifth Air Force, which had failed to receive its copy of the message. Two days later an attempt by Admiral Struble to bypass the Tokyo echelon and operate in consultation with EUSAK and the Joint Operations Center brought reproaches from ComNavFE. In early August a move by the commanding officer of *Sicily* to avoid the communications jam and gain more time over target by sending flights directly to the front was slapped down as "not acceptable." Late in the month, in an effort to reduce direct calls for naval air and gunfire from the forces in the field, ComNavFE got CincFE to remind all hands that any request involving changes in naval planning, or action against Bomber Command targets, had to be arranged through Tokyo.

In this situation effective control of close support proved impossible to attain. While the forces defending the perimeter could hardly have managed without the support they got, its quality, judged by any serious standard, was generally poor.   The exception to this generalization, which shone the brighter in contrast to the general confusion, was in the support of the Marine ground forces by Marine and naval aviation, where the complexities of integration of ground and air were competently solved.   In the southern spoiling offensive and in the battles on the Naktong the Marine aircraft from the escort carriers, exempted from the requirement of reporting in through JOC, checked in directly with their own people and did the job they had been trained to do; in the operations of Joint Task Force 7 at Inchon and of X Corps in northeastern Korea a similar situation prevailed. Much of the credit for these successes was due to pilot training based on a long history of air-ground cooperation; still more, perhaps, to effectiveness of control.

Here some statistics may be in order.   Of 668 "close support" sorties sent in from the fast carriers between 26 July and 3 September, 28 percent were not controlled; for 299 such sorties at Inchon the proportion was 2 percent.   In the crisis of 1 September some 280 sorties were put into the Naktong front between Tuksongdong and the south coast, an effort beyond the capacity of the JOC control system and which resulted in its collapse.   On D-Day at Inchon, by contrast, the Tactical Air Control Squadron in *Mount McKinley* handled 302 Navy and Marine sorties without difficulty.   On 3 December, with a daylight working period three and a half hours shorter than that of early September, X Corps' Marine controllers at Hungnam processed 359 sorties; of these 197 were passed on to the tactical control section at Hagaru, where four-fifths were employed in the ten-mile sector between Hagaru and Yudam-ni under the direction of six ground parties.   On 23 December the *Mount McKinley* Tacron handled 247 sorties in close and deep support of the shrunken Hungnam perimeter.   If none of these figures matches the amphibious set-pieces of the latter part of World War II, in which upwards of 60 aircraft an hour were fed into restricted beachhead areas, they nonetheless reflect the virtue and the necessity of sophisticated and decentralized control systems.

The failures of air support in the summer of 1950 had sizable repercussions.   The operations of the Marine Brigade and of Marine and naval aircraft had shown Eighth Army some of the possibilities in this area; in the campaign for Seoul and in northeastern Korea the Army units assigned to X Corps had their education continued; within the Air Force there was considerable soul-searching.   In Korea this led to an influx of dignitaries from Washington to study the situation, to the convening of various boards of investigation, and to a discussion of the proper relationships between air and ground forces which lasted throughout the war.   In the United States the Tactical Air Command reappeared as a major functional unit of the Air Force.   In the Defense Department rumors were afoot that General Collins was contemplating an attempt to recover Army control of tactical aviation, a possibility which, in view of the nature of the earlier Collins Plan for reorganization of the armed forces, was not devoid of humor.

In the end this ferment was to have certain constructive results. For the short term, however, and under the tension of the campaign, the effects were exacerbating. In late August the troubles reached the press, with publication in the Baltimore *Sun* of a news story supported by editorial comment based on the views of the frustrated aviators of Task Force 77. One result was a dispatch from the Chief of Naval Operations and a memorandum from ComNavFE adjuring naval personnel to keep their criticisms inside the family and out of the newspapers. Another was a rejoinder from a nationally syndicated columnist who alleged that, far from being of superior effectiveness, the Navy and the Marines had been lying down on the job in Korea, and that their air support system was good only for butchering friendly troops.

This last effusion brought a letter from General Stratemeyer, expressing his regret for such unwarranted criticism and assuring Admiral Joy that the staff of FEAF was not responsible; earlier, in the flurry caused by the *Sun* articles, he had inquired of ComNavFE whether, in his opinion, the derogatory allegations about the Air Force were true. In reply, while regretting that accounts of "these deficiencies" had reached the press, Admiral Joy observed that with regard to air-ground cooperation he thought they were, but that allegations that the Air Force was unreceptive to suggestion were wholly false; to Stratemeyer's expressed desire that problems be thrashed out between the two of them, ComNavFE replied that tactical air was a difficult problem and that perhaps they should have got together sooner on it.

With this conclusion we may leave the subject. While the failure to provide adequate support for the Army in the perimeter was undeniable, it would seem that more help might have been given by the Navy. The analyses of the situation by Struble, Hoskins, and Ewen, and the remedies that they proposed had been perceptive, but despite an apparently hospitable attitude on the part of FEAF toward naval participation in close support and the use of Navy controllers, their implementation was never pressed. Requests from the Army in Korea and recommendations from the Seventh Fleet for the commitment of the Anglico and of the Tactical Air Control Squadron from *Mount McKinley* were denied; assignment of Navy planes to share in the control function was the exception rather than the rule; although all services would have benefited from strong naval representation in the JOC, and although the visits of Weymouth and others had proved helpful, no serious attempt to make this a truly joint enterprise took place.

To some degree the atomistic nature of the Tokyo command, where General MacArthur had retained his World War II structure despite directives to establish a unified staff, can be held responsible; to some degree instructions from Washington limited the freedom of action of local commanders in all services. Within the forces afloat there seems to have been insufficient understanding of the appalling difficulties under which Fifth Air Force labored, not all of which were due to faulty doctrine, and some failure to give credit where credit was due, as in the rapid increase of jet fighter bombloads. Not fully appreciating the necessarily deliberate nature of close support, the pilots of Task Force 77 were at times overly impatient of delay. And finally, there existed at certain levels of the naval command a distrust of the Air Force and a desire to keep at a distance not wholly explicable by the submarine problem and the Formosan responsibility, and this defensive attitude, however understandable, was perhaps the saddest consequence of the interservice battles of the preceding years.

With the movement to Inchon and the separation of naval and Air Force operations, relations became easier, and by early 1951 things had improved. Communications between Task Force 77 and the JOC were at last working effectively; air group commanders from the fast carriers were being sent in in rotation to handle the liaison function; in due course a permanent assignment would be made. With the passage of time and the discounting of the submarine, Task Force 77 had taken permanent station in the Sea of Japan and was no longer puzzling Air Force officers by its mobility. From this time on division of labor was to be largely geographical, with operations coordinated by JOC on the basis of daily submission of the task force air plan. In this favorable situation cooperation developed by natural growth: by war's end the installation of radioteletype had enabled the carriers to master the communication load, while the replacement at JOC of the naval liaison officer by a full-fledged naval member, the so-called NMJ, confirmed the joint nature of the enterprise.

In the controversial question of close support doctrinal differences remained. Overcentralization at JOC, where aircraft allocation was controlled and where all requests had to be approved, kept the system vulnerable both to enemy action and to communications saturation at times of peak activity. Air Force unwillingness to assign forward air controllers below the regimental level left this function largely in the hands of the Mosquitos, most effective in the stable situations in which least needed. But with calls for close support diminished by the static nature of the front, and with the carriers committed to interdiction, the problems inherent in the system could be ignored, and only in the final weeks of war did there develop a repetition of the confusion of August 1950.

In August 1953, 12 days after the signing of the Korean armistice, an interservice board assembled at Seoul to consider the problems of joint air-ground operations. The conclusions of the board reflected adversely on the rigid administrative procedures which in Korea had limited the effectiveness of air in fast-moving tactical situations. The need for better communications, both in the request net and at the scene of action, was emphasized. The excessive delays resulting from reliance on ground alert aircraft for attack against fleeting targets were noted; the employment of flights orbiting on station or diverted from preplanned missions was urged; and it was made clear that the Mosquito was no substitute for ground control of strikes against targets close to the MLR. For effective joint action in future comparable situations the establishment of a Joint Operations Center, 1953 model, was recommended, and the proposal, dating back to the summer of 1950, that the Navy provide a quota of forward air controllers was revived. This report marked a real step toward a meeting of minds in this complex and vital area: only in the question of providing air controllers at battalion level did the Air Force members disagree with the representatives of the other services. And all hands agreed on the "urgent requirement" for an established joint air support doctrine and procedure.

But Korea was far from home, and the victories of peace are different, if no less renowned, than those of war. Pursuant to the urgent recommendation of the conference the job of developing an agreed joint doctrine for air support of ground forces was quickly undertaken. On 28 August, only a week after adjournment of the Seoul meetings, this task was assigned the Joint Tactical Air Support Board "as a matter of priority," but with the proviso that if "inter-service divergent views" were encountered, these should be referred to the Chief of Staff of the Air Force for resolution at department level.

The hint, if hint it was, was quickly taken. The Air Force members of the board broadened the discussion to discover areas of difference, insisted that joint action take place on the highest rather than the lowest echelon, and looked with disfavor upon joint activities below the level of the area commander. The separateness and co-equality of air was stressed at the expense of integrated action, the need for joint task force organizations for airborne or amphibious operations was denied, the concept of joint planning conferences was evaded, and heavy emphasis was placed on the necessity of adhering to "the operational procedures which have worked with outstanding success in World War II and in Korea."

The Army, Navy, and Marine Corps members, for their part, while attempting to keep the discussion on the track, expressed some doubt as to the "outstanding success" of existing methods, and urged that development be not restricted by a blind adherence to the past. But agreement between the representatives of these three services was of no avail. In December 1953 the split report was forwarded to Washington for resolution at department level and there, presumably, suitably interred. In any event there is still no joint doctrine.

5. The Larger Picture

Despite its violence and drama the struggle in Korea was but one aspect of a larger whole. While the tide of battle flowed up and down the peninsula, the war of maneuver, diplomacy, and subsidy continued all along the frontiers of the divided world. Unquestionably there were great differences between the operations in the Korean sector and the course of affairs elsewhere: as General MacArthur, who felt this most keenly, observed, "here we fight Europe's war with arms while the diplomats there still fight it with words." But words are weapons; the aims and stakes were everywhere the same; Europe remained of primary importance and the boundaries of the shooting war subject to change.

For the armed forces in the Far East, most of all, perhaps, for the Navy, the existence of Communist nations on both flanks, the commitment to defend Formosa, and the international nature of the high seas obscured the borders of the conflict. Of the possibilities inherent in the conduct of operations in an area flanked by unfriendly powers, both possessed of military air forces and one with a sizable submarine fleet, the most dramatic example had been the destruction of the Russian bomber in September 1950. But while the chance of similar incidents was ever present, it was with regard to the submarine that the question of when properly to engage an unidentified intruder was most puzzling.

Early in the conflict Admiral Joy had advised his forces that "unidentified submarines may be attacked and driven off by any means available in self-defense or when offensive action against our forces is indicated," and that "continued submergence of an unidentified submarine in position to attack . . . is considered to indicate offensive action." Since submarines can detect an approaching surface force before being themselves discovered, and so enjoy a period of time in which to make their presence known, "continued submergence" was narrowly interpreted and sound contacts were invariably attacked at once. Such attacks were frequent in the first months of fighting, both in Korean waters and in the Ryukyu—Formosa area, but most targets were ultimately evaluated doubtful and some as positively non-submarine.

The air action in the Yellow Sea was not repeated, and no submarine attacks developed. But there remained, most notably in the Formosa area and along the patrol plane tracks in the Yellow and Japan Seas, the possibility of chance encounters with Chinese Communist or Soviet forces. In the Yellow Sea, except for the loss of a patrol plane to North Korean antiaircraft, no incidents took place until summer of 1952, when two PBMs were attacked and damaged by Communist jets. In the Sea of Japan, however, in November 1951, a P2V failed to return from a northerly search, and subsequent information indicated that it had been shot down off Cape Ostrovnoy by Soviet fighters. Here in the north the Air Force also engaged in reconnaissance, and with similar results: in October 1952, a year after the loss of the P2V, a B–29 was shot down off Hokkaido by Soviet fighters; in March 1953 an RB–50 was attacked, although without damage, over the sea to the east of the Kamchatka Peninsula.

In Formosa Strait, the region of Seventh Fleet's contingent responsibility, the situation remained generally quiescent. The alarm of late July 1950 had brought the hasty diversion of *Helena* and a destroyer division from Korea, followed within a few days by *Juneau*. Early in August Admiral Struble formed *Juneau*, two destroyers, and an oiler into Task Group 77.3, based at Keelung and shortly to be reinforced by *Worcester* and another destroyer from the Mediterranean. By month's end Rear Admiral Thomas H. Binford, who in 1942 had commanded the old four-stackers in the Java Sea fighting, had arrived from the United States in the heavy cruiser *Saint Paul* to assume command of the Formosa Patrol. Although the crisis of December brought the surface units north the task group was shortly reconstituted, and throughout the war surveillance of the strait was continued by Seventh Fleet surface units and by patrol planes.

Here, too, as in the north, long-range naval aircaft working the area from their bases in the Pescadores, at Buckner Bay, and on Luzon, had intermittent brushes with the Communists. As early as 26 July 1950 a P4Y was attacked by fighters in northern Formosa Strait, but escaped without damage; ten days later a PBM was fired on by antiaircraft batteries in the neighborhood of Amoy. On 5 November a PBM failed to return from southern Formosa Strait, and although searches were persistent they were also negative and the cause of loss remained unknown. Two generally peaceful years followed, but in the autumn of 1952 there developed a number of antiaircraft actions with shore batteries and small warships, and on two occasions patrol aircraft were attacked by MIGs. But no plane was lost until January 1953, when a P2V was shot down by gunfire from a coastal island and a Coast Guard PBM, sent to rescue the crew, itself crashed and sank while attempting takeoff in heavy seas.

So despite all hazards the war remained circumscribed. Although planning for larger things had followed the intervention of the CCF, the blockade of mainland China was never implemented and mainland target folders stayed on the shelf. The intensity of action diminished rapidly with distance, and except for minor incidents shooting was limited to Korea and to Korean waters. In the northern Sea of Japan the units of the Soviet Far Eastern Fleet maneuvered, undisturbed and undisturbing. Through the waters of the Western Pacific, Soviet and Chinese Communist merchant ships continued on their way, subject only to the photographic efforts of search planes and submarines. But while the area of actual combat remained small, related events of great importance were taking place throughout the world.

In the United States, in September 1950, a controversial career ended as Louis Johnson, in part the architect and in part the victim of the Truman administration's defense policies, departed Washington, and General Marshall, again recalled from retirement, reigned in his place. Already, however, the policies had changed. With the invasion of South Korea the $14 billion ceiling vanished overnight, and budgeting and planning officers labored to keep up with administration willingness to approve and congressional readiness to appropriate. In the fiscal year 1949–50, the year of interservice quarreling and the B–36 hearings, naval appropriations, originally voted at slightly over $5 billion, had been cut by the Johnsonian ax to less than $4½ billion. For 1950–51 they totalled more than $12 billion, and in the following fiscal year monies appropriated for the Navy alone would exceed the earlier three-service ceiling, while the total defense budget would approach $60 billion.

It is, of course, easier to appropriate than to spend, and the events of immediate significance were less the dollar votes than the recall of reserves, the expansion of selective service calls, and the reactivation of fleet units and base facilities. But with the passing of time expenditures also rose dramatically: the $14½ billion spent by all services in fiscal 1950 rose to $38½ billion in 1952; for the Navy alone the increase was from $4.1 billion to almost $10 billion. The effects on the national economy were not disastrous.

For the Navy's operating forces two principal consequences followed this dollar flood: an immediate expansion of the fleet through reactivation of mothballed ships, and its subsequent strengthening by conversion of existing units and by new construction. Reserving the latter subject for later treatment, it may be noted here that fleet expansion took place in all categories from attack carriers of the *Essex* class down to yard craft and liberty boats. The extent and speed of this expansion may be inferred from a tabulation of major combatant ships in active service in June and October 1950.

Table 21.—Distribution of Major Combat Ships

	June 1950			October 1950		
Type	*Atlantic Fleet*	*Pacific Fleet*	*Total*	*Atlantic Fleet*	*Pacific Fleet*	*Total*
Fleet carriers	4	3	7	4	5	9
Light carriers	3	1	4	4	1	5
Escort carriers	2	2	4	3	3	6
Battleships	1	0	1	1	1	2
Cruisers	7	6	13	8	8	16
Totals	17	12	29	20	18	38

The 50 percent expansion of the Pacific Fleet, while sufficiently impressive, is perhaps less remarkable than the fact that the Atlantic Fleet should have expanded at all, while at the same time contributing heavily to the increase of Far Eastern naval strength. From this Fleet, by way of the Suez and Panama Canals, there came in the early months a battleship, a fleet carrier, a light cruiser, a destroyer squadron and an escort destroyer division, a hospital ship, three attack transports, three attack cargo ships, and two LSDs. This was no inconsiderable contribution, yet it was dwarfed by that of the Fleet Marine Force Atlantic, which for a time almost disappeared as a result of the need to reinforce the 1st Marine Division for Inchon. In the period between June and mid-August, when FMFLant hit its low point, onboard personnel, officer and enlisted, diminished from 18,470 to a mere 3,196.

Notable as was this westward shift of force, it was controlled and limited. Great though they were, the exigencies of the Korean situation were not permitted to overthrow the broad lines of accepted strategy. The defense of Europe remained the primary task; the larger portion of the Navy remained in the Atlantic. And as a precautionary measure, since none could read the future, the outbreak of fighting in Asia was soon followed by a forward deployment on the other side of the world.

In the Mediterranean Sea, where geography affords the opportunity to reach behind the Iron Curtain and to sustain the independence of the nations of Southern Europe and the Near East, the Navy maintained its Sixth Fleet. This fleet, lineal descendant of the Naval Forces Mediterranean of World War II days, had received its current designation in early 1950. Its existing deployment dated from the previous year, at which time the Atlantic Fleet had organized three carrier task forces, one of which was at all times kept on station in the Mediterranean, along with an amphibious element embarking a Marine battalion and miscellaneous supporting units. Spring of 1950 had seen this force, built around the carrier *Leyte* and the cruisers *Salem* and *Worcester,* engaged in routine exercises. With the invasion of the Republic of Korea its strength was to be more than doubled.

Escorted by a division of destroyers, the large carrier *Midway,* which already enjoyed a limited nuclear capability, was speedily sailed for the Mediterranean, where she arrived in mid-July and where she was joined shortly by her sister *Coral Sea.* With the striking force thus strengthened, *Worcester* and a destroyer division were detached to the Far East by way of Suez, followed in mid-August by *Bexar* and *Montague* with the Marine battalion, while *Leyte* was returned to the United States for further transfer to the Far East by way of Panama. There remained in the Sixth Fleet the 2 large carriers, 3 cruisers, and 14 destroyers, and in September the force was further strengthened by an antisubmarine group formed about the escort carrier *Mindoro.* But with the period of triumph in Korea the crisis seemed to have been surmounted, tension diminished, and Sixth Fleet was cut back to normal size.

The reduction, like the triumph, was to prove short-lived. As the emergency which followed Chinese intervention in Korea brought a second hasty reinforcement of the Far East, so too it governed movements in the Atlantic. In January a new augmentation of the Sixth Fleet was begun, as a light carrier, a destroyer division, and two fast minesweepers were ordered forward. With the apparent imminence of a major spring crisis the scheduled May relieving group of one large carrier, 11 destroyers, and ancillary units was sailed to reach the Mediterranean in March; at the same time an amphibious task element with a Marine battalion was sent forward to provide, for the first time since the previous August, a limited amphibious capability. Following the arrival of these reinforcements the ships already on station were kept on through early May, with the result that these months saw the largest concentration of American naval power in the Mediterranean since the end of World War II.

The expected crisis did not come, but little relaxation resulted. Over and above the necessity of strengthening its striking force in Mediterranean waters, and of contributing to Far Eastern naval strength, manifold responsibilities weighed upon the Atlantic Fleet. During the warm months resupply convoys had to be sent up to the Arctic. Spring of 1951 brought the need to transport and land the newly established Iceland Defense Force. An arduous and continuing schedule of training in convoy work, mine warfare, amphibious operations, and air defense had to be maintained. The strains of rapid expansion, brought about by reactivation of mothballed ships and the activation of new aviation units, imposed a heavy load in personnel training and administration as on-board complement expanded in the space of two years from 107,575 to 235,426. Nor was non-shooting war without its costs: the greatest single tragedy of the period of the Korean conflict took place in the Atlantic, when in April 1952, in the course of night air operations, the DMS *Hobson* got in front of the carrier *Wasp* and was run down and sunk with a loss of 176 lives.

So war in Europe, if still in CincFE's phrase only a war of words, absorbed large quantities of naval strength. And in diplomacy, as in the military establishment, the sense of urgency deriving from aggression in Korea was employed to strengthen the defenses of the West. This process was most notable in the fleshing out of the North Atlantic Treaty Organization, where the treaty of April 1949 had been followed by requests for American military assistance and these, in October, by the Mutual Defense Act. More paperwork and negotiation followed, but in March of 1950 shipment of materiel began with the sailing of a load of naval aircraft on the French carrier *Dixmude,* a vessel of appropriately international background which, begun as an American merchant ship, had been converted to an auxiliary aircraft carrier, lend-leased for wartime service to Great Britain, and ultimately transferred to the French Navy.

The NATO powers had by now agreed on broad strategic concepts, and the wheels of implementation were grinding. The pace, however, remained leisurely: Russian forces in the satellites outnumbered those available for the defense of Europe by perhaps five to one, and the latter, of widely varying quality, were maldeployed, malsupported, and without a coordinating command structure. But Korea changed all this. In the new atmosphere came new effort, and on 15 September, as the Marines were going over the seawalls at Inchon, the North Atlantic Council voted to create an integrated force under centralized command. In December the call went out for General Eisenhower to return to the scene of his earlier triumphs; in January the organization of a headquarters was begun; on 2 April 1951 SHAPE assumed operational control of NATO forces.

Although much remained to be done, General Eisenhower's hand had already been strengthened by the arrival of new Army and Air Force contingents, as well as by expansion of the Sixth Fleet. Following the invasion of South Korea an increase of jet fighters and B–50 bombers had trebled Air Force strength in the United Kingdom. In the course of 1951 the Air Divisions there and in Germany were expanded into Air Forces, the southern flank was strengthened by acquisition of North African airbases, and four more Army divisions reached Europe to join the two already there. There was also reinforcement from within: in Europe as in America defense expenditures rose steadily, and while the American contribution continued to predominate, the outlays of European NATO members more than doubled between 1949 and 1952.

While the defenses were going up in Europe the right flank was pushed forward through the Mediterranean. Here geography and naval power permitted both the development of advanced airfields in Tripoli and Saudi Arabia and the extension of NATO planning to include Greece and Turkey. These were hardly Atlantic states, and their accession was consequently opposed by some, but the sea road that connected them with the Atlantic made possible their support against pressure from the north. These facts of life were emphasized and western power made tangible in the summer of 1950 by the appearance of the Sixth Fleet at Phaleron Bay, just east of the Piraeus; by amphibious exercises in Crete; and by an aerial demonstration staged over Lebanon at the request of the Lebanese government. Late in the year Greece and Turkey were invited to associate themselves with NATO planning, and in early 1951 the Sixth Fleet again called at Phaleron Bay. In May the United States proposed formal NATO membership for these countries, and in July *Coral Sea* and her attendant ships dropped anchor at Istanbul. In the fall the formal invitation to accede was issued, and early in 1952 the transaction was consummated.

Naval diplomacy was by this time in full swing, and the fleet was showing the flag in a new area. The adherence of Greece and Turkey to the North Atlantic Treaty Organization greatly emphasized the importance of Yugoslavia and the Yugoslav Army. Here cooperation had been facilitated by the end of civil war in Greece and by Tito's break with Russia. Subsequent to these developments crop failures had forced this Communist country to turn westward and, despite many protestations to the contrary, to start edging into the position of a constructive member of NATO. By early 1951 Yugoslav preparations to receive assistance were in progress and in February food and credits began arriving. In April former German military equipment was provided by France and Britain, to be followed, with poetic justice, by Russian gear captured in Korea. Before the year was out military missions had been exchanged with the United States, and in December Sixth Fleet units visited a Yugoslav port. In 1952 this developing cordiality brought a task force built around *Coral Sea* to Split, finest of Adriatic harbors, where Marshal Tito was himself embarked and edified by a demonstration of flight operations.

By early 1952 the NATO naval command structure had been completed, and arduous efforts in the coordination of multinational forces were beginning to flower in large-scale naval exercises. In November a six-nation operation was carried out; in the following March a large NATO maneuver was held in the Western Mediterranean; in the autumn of 1953 the Sixth Fleet would sortie to the North Atlantic, to join the forces of that ocean in the greatest combined exercise to date.

So in Europe, as in Korea, the line was held, and even slightly improved. As always the imperfect world contained sufficient difficulties: despite SEATO and the Baghdad Pact, the unsettled conditions of Southeast Asia and the Near East continued to resist treatment. Still, it could be said that the events set in train by the invasion of South Korea had reacted, on balance, to the detriment rather than the advantage of the Communist world. The North Korean People's Army had been destroyed and the forces of Communist China heavily punished. Japan had been protected; the Republic of Korea had been liberated; Formosa had not fallen. In Europe NATO had been built up. The United States, keystone of the entire structure, was to a considerable degree rearmed.

All this, of course, had been accomplished by way of reaction. That so much had to be credited to the North Koreans rather than to the conscious and purposeful initiative of the West was perhaps cause for philosophical regret. But the response, for the moment at least, had been a notable one.

6. Into the Future

The fighting in Korea was accompanied, for those who had ears to hear, by ominous rumblings offstage, as the nuclear powers labored to perfect and expand their arsenals. The explosions of 1951 marked but the start of a period of accelerated development in which tests were carried out by the United States at Eniwetok and in Nevada, by the British in Australia and in the Pacific, and by the Soviets within the Asiatic land mass. Before peace came to the embattled peninsula a whole new spectrum of weapons had been developed: at one end there lay the hydrogen bomb, with its appalling implications for victim, neutral, and user alike; at the other the need for an explosive return proportionate to the rising costs of delivery was bringing warheads for missile, artillery, antisubmarine, antiaircraft, and infantry use.

The possibilities of the world struggle and the actualities of Korea, so important in forwarding the nuclear research and development programs, had important results in other spheres. The shock effect of the North Korean mining campaign gave mine warfare an unaccustomedly high priority, both in research and in the Navy's building program. The immediate response to the emergency involved the installation of underwater search gear in a number of infantry landing craft, to permit their use as mine locators, and the conversion of four motor launches to shoal-water sweepers. But these expedients, like the many World War II minesweepers, had been largely obsoleted by the magnetic mine. Subsequent development of the mine-hunters involved the conversion of wooden-hulled YMS and the construction of wooden-hulled minesweeping boats, while the need for larger sweepers led to the construction of new non-magnetic types. Of these, three were developed: the MSO, an ocean minesweeper, 171 feet in length and of 750 tons full load displacement; the MSC, a somewhat smaller coastal minesweeper, 144 feet overall; and the MSI, a 112-foot inshore minesweeper.

The building of truly non-magnetic ships is no simple matter, involving as it does, in addition to wooden hull construction, the design and procurement of much special equipment including engines of non-magnetic stainless steel alloys. Yet, despite the complexities of the task, production was not inconsiderable. Of the MSOs, which began launching in 1952 and commissioning in the next year, more than 100 were projected, while almost 150 MSCs and about 50 inshore sweepers were planned. Such quantities, of course, were more than enough for the U.S. Navy, but the United States was now supplier to the whole free world. With the anti-Communist alliance dependent on the uninterrupted use of the seas, and with a mine threat which knew no geographical limitations, something more than half this new construction was slated for transfer, under the Mutual Defense Assistance Program, to countries along the entire maritime arc from Norway in the west through the Mediterranean and Indian Ocean to the Western Pacific and Japan.

In amphibious warfare, too, the Korean experience had consequences for new construction. The extraordinary usefulness of the LST resulted in an immediate program for 15 of the *1156* series, a development of earlier experimental types, longer (384 as compared to 328 feet), faster (15 as opposed to 11 knots), and of larger capacity than their elder sisters; these began launching in mid–1952. The next step came two years later with the laying down of the first of seven *Suffolk County* class LSTs—442 feet overall, 7,100 tons full load displacement, 17 knots—which would carry 20 amphibious vehicles and 700 troops in air-conditioned spaces.

This, it appeared, was about as far as the type could go, despite the enthusiasm of some officers who, on the basis of Korean experience, appealed for clouds of these ships to replace rather than supplement the APA and AKA types. Since problems of design placed unavoidable limits on beaching ability, further progress tended toward the elaboration of the dock landing ship, also of great use in Korea. Eight new LSDs of the *Thomaston* class were undertaken and these, like all new construction, were larger (11,270 tons full load as against 8,700 tons) and faster (24 knots as compared to 15½) than their World War II predecessors. The direction this development was taking became apparent a few years later with the completion of plans for the LPD, a transport designed on the *Thomaston* hull, in which the increased troop and cargo space gained by the use of a smaller well gave a capacity approximating the AKA or APA.

Other than the LST, the most prominent all-purpose workhorse of the Korean War had been the helicopter. So necessary had these contraptions suddenly become that landing platforms sprouted throughout the fleet and were designed into all possible new construction, while their further implications for amphibious warfare attracted the interest of the Marines. As the tactical possibilities of vertical envelopment were clarified, there came proposals for the conversion of escort carriers to helicopter work and the projection of the helicopter amphibious assault ship (LPH), which would carry a Marine battalion, its supplies, and the helicopters necessary to land it. And a final contribution to the welfare of those who have to land on beaches came in late 1952, with the laying down of *Carronade,* the first rocket ship specifically designed for the purpose.

While the virtues of flexibility of movement over the beaches and over the hills were being worked out, through development of LST and LSD types and of helicopter employment, concurrent advances took place in more conventional areas. Since in addition to the problems of minefields and beaches the Korean War had emphasized those of supply, a share of new construction was allocated to logistic support units. Early in the conflict three 20-knot passenger ships, already building for the American President Lines, were taken over and completed as troop transports for MSTS, which also acquired some new cargo types with roll-on roll-off loading systems and with hulls strengthened for use in ice.   Under the stimulus of war the Maritime Commission undertook the construction of a number of 20-knot Mariner class cargo ships, of which one was early acquired by the Navy for conversion to an AKA and others in due course for conversion to attack transports.   The shortage of reefers in Korea brought the inclusion of two 18-knot vessels in the post-Korean construction program.   The problems of underway re-plenishment and of accelerated consumption of fuel and ammunition led to experimental work with an ex-German U-boat supply ship to test the theory of one-stop replenishment, and to planning for a composite type which would carry ammunition, petroleum products, and miscellaneous cargo as well.   But this development would take time, and more immediate help came from the construction of six new 20-knot fleet oilers, 100 feet longer than any previously available, of which the first was launched in late 1953, and from the five new ammunition ships of the *Suribachi* class, built from the hull up for this purpose, and providing higher speed, new methods of storage, and new and faster handling machinery.

Essential though they were, these advances in mine and amphibious warfare and in logistic support of overseas operations were overshadowed by developments in the striking forces.   In carrier aviation the lessons of Korea, the availability of more money, and the implications of the future led to a dramatic reversal.   In July 1951, only two years after cancellation of the supercarrier *United States,* a contract was awarded for the first of six vessels of the *Forrestal* class, ships more than 1,000 feet in overall length and with a full load displacement almost twice that of the *Essex* carriers.   On these colossal hulls, in addition to machinery for speeds upwards of 33 knots, the new class of carrier provided larger fuel capacity, larger hangars, more powerful catapults, more elevators, and an angled deck layout which would permit the handling of almost 100 of the larger and higher performance aircraft soon to become available.

As construction of these behemoths was getting underway an extensive conversion program for existing aircraft carriers was begun.   Here the most significant new step was the incorporation of the angled deck, a British development, which permitted simultaneous launching and landing and at the same time removed the hazards of the barrier crash.   With success of an experimental installation on *Antietam,* other *Essex*-class ships were put into the works to emerge in due time with the new deck configuration, modernized elevators, new steam catapults, and other improvements, and in 1954 similar modernization of the three *Midway*-class carriers was begun.

What all this implied in terms of aircraft performance may be seen by a few comparisons.   For the Korean war the best available Navy fighters were the Grumman F9F Panther and the McDonnell F2H Banshee with maximum speeds of something over 600 miles an hour; the AD attack plane, last and finest flower of the piston-engined line, lumbered along at a mere 365 miles an hour. But as the war was ending the Douglas F4D Skyray, a supersonic fighter capable of speeds up to about 750 miles an hour, was commencing its fleet trials. The A3D twin-jet heavy attack plane, with a top speed roughly equivalent to the F9F, was already in production. The prototype of the still faster A4D light attack plane was building and a contract had been let for the Chance Vought F8U-2, an advanced fighter which on completion would set some records with speeds exceeding 1,000 miles an hour.

Paralleling these advances in fighter and attack aircraft, the continuing trend toward complexity of equipment and size of vehicle was bringing multi-engined antisubmarine aircraft to the fleet. These larger planes required larger decks: in 1953 half the *Essex* class was assigned to antisubmarine warfare, and with this step the light carrier and the escort carrier reached the end of the road. After a short period in training duty the last CVL followed her sisters into inactivity, while those CVEs not destined for the scrap heap were reclassified as aircraft transports or as helicopter carriers.

The advent of new high-performance aircraft and the proliferation of nuclear weapons inevitably revolutionized the air defense problem. To increase the range of radar detection, early warning aircraft and radar picket submarines were given high priority. In fighter planes the machine gun gave way to the target-seeking missile, while aboard ship the antiaircraft gun began to disappear. Although the first group of post-Korean destroyers—one of which was to be christened *Turner Joy*—mounted new 3-inch automatic antiaircraft batteries, this was but a brief transitional phase. In 1955–56 the heavy cruisers *Boston* and *Canberra* were modified to carry two twin launching mounts for Terrier, a beam-riding antiaircraft missile with a ten-mile range. The next step was the conversion of the destroyer *Gyatt* to carry a Terrier mount, and of six *Cleveland*-class light cruisers, three to carry Terrier and three Talos, a larger missile with a slant range of up to 65 miles. And in due course there followed a program for guided missile destroyers of new design.

Although in Korea the submarine had been only a threat, new developments promised it a considerable future. In the years before 1950 some new construction and conversion had been undertaken with an eye to increased submerged speed, and some of a specialized nature for antisubmarine work. But the great developments came in the course of the Korean conflict, with the construction of *Albacore,* a wholly streamlined boat which compensated for awkward handling on the surface by extraordinary speed and maneuverability in the depths, and with the laying of the keel of the nuclear submarine *Nautilus.* Marriage of the speeds possible with the new hull form and the almost unlimited endurance bestowed by nuclear propulsion was to give wholly new dimensions to undersea warfare, while with the advent of the offensive guided missile the submarine gained awesome potentialities for action against land targets.

Naval development of the surface-to-surface guided weapon, begun shortly after World War II, first took operational form in 1951 with the flight of Regulus I, a subsonic missile with a range of 575 miles. Designed originally for launching by submarine, Regulus proved versatile, and in the course of time was embarked in aircraft carriers and cruisers as well. By 1958, when production ended, a supersonic longer-range successor was on the way, and submarines specifically designed for missile work were under construction.

While much had been said of push-button warfare in the years after World War II, all this, when war came to Korea, was still largely talk. But before the decade had ended changes of a truly revolutionary nature had indeed developed. Nuclear-powered submarines were in operation and more were building; nuclear-powered cruisers and frigates were in contemplation; surface ships as well as submarines were carrying long-range missiles; as an outgrowth of the *Forrestal* class an even larger carrier was under construction.

This was *Enterprise,* 1,100 feet long and with a flight deck 252 feet wide, displacing 85,000 tons full load, defended by missiles, powered by eight nuclear reactors. This new dispensation in propulsive machinery would give her a maximum speed of 35 knots and an estimated endurance of *five years;* by eliminating the need for oil storage and stacks it would provide twice the aviation fuel capacity of her largest predecessors and permit the installation, on the sides of the island structure, of fixed radar antennae of advanced design. This astounding vessel marked the culmination of the Navy's development of shipboard aviation, a development begun within the service lives of many still on active duty with the conversion, in 1922, of the old 15-knot collier *Jupiter* into the *Langley* as an experimental aircraft carrier. But *Enterprise* was not alone in manifesting the possibilities of the new technology, for work was simultaneously going forward on a series of nuclear-powered ballistic missile submarines, whose displacement would approximate that of a small light cruiser and whose armament had a projected range of 1,500 miles.

What these developments of Promethean man promised for the future of warfare was by no means clear, least of all for the kind of limited war that had taken place in Korea. Despite a change of administration at home and ultimate agreement on a Korean armistice, military policy was to continue much as before. At the Pentagon the bad old chiefs departed and the good new chiefs came in, a change chiefly significant for the promulgation of the "New Look" which, with its emphasis on the size of the bang, harked back to pre-Korean days. On the level of higher policy the concept of "massive retaliation," with its promise of converting all small wars into big ones, seemed a denial of all Korea had stood for and a return to the position of 1949. With the end of the Korean fighting, the Bureau of the Budget regained its ascendancy in military affairs, dollar problems returned to harass and divide the services, and the only difference was that this time it was the Army, which had borne the heat of the day in Korea, that suffered most.

Yet however predestined, all this was in the future in July of 1951 as the delegates gathered for the commencement of Korean armistice talks. At 1100 on the morning of the 10th Admiral Joy led his colleagues into the teahouse at Kaesong to confront the emissaries of the enemy. Among the correspondents present to observe proceedings, bets were being made on how long it would take to close the gates of the temple. The pessimists thought six weeks.

Chapter XII

Two More Years

1. July 1951–February 1952: Stabilized Front and Peripheral War

AT KAESONG the first few days of talk were not auspicious, occupied
as they were by U.N. efforts to control Communist propaganda activity, by argument over the administration of the neutral area, and by procedural disputation. Nevertheless, in the course of little more than two
weeks, an agenda was adopted and the delegates proceeded to address themselves to the question of a cease-fire.

Although hostilities were to continue until agreement had been reached,
the commencement of negotiations made for optimism, and ComNavFE
thought it necessary to warn of possible acts of treachery. Ground action,
nevertheless, continued to diminish: six months of grinding frontline warfare had ended, the battleline had been stabilized on favorable ground, and
except in the Iron Triangle and on the Soyang River, United Nations activity
was limited to patrolling and to the improvement of defensive positions.
But since the enemy was busily engaged in bringing down new units to
replace those chewed up in the spring offensives, and was bending every
effort to improve his logistic position, interdiction perforce continued. For
the next two years, as hopes of peace continued to be frustrated, the burden
of offensive action was to lie principally upon the Air Force and the Navy.

The prospect of an early armistice had already been reflected in the movements and composition of the Amphibious Force. With the departure of
Admiral Thackrey in June the number of Amphibious Force flag officers
in the Western Pacific dropped from two to one; at the end of the month
a recommended reduction in the Far Eastern deployment of larger
PhibPac ships to one AGC, seven APAs, and two AKAs had been approved
by CincPacFleet; in time the allowance of LSTs would also be cut down.
Concurrent with this diminution of strength, however, there arose the
requirement of supporting the U.N. armistice delegation, and a special task
element of one AGC, one APA, and an LST helicopter base was formed
and stationed at Inchon to provide logistic and communications services.
And at the same time other units of Task Force 90 were assisting in a special
operation to the northward.

This affair, of the greatest importance for technical intelligence, involved the recovery of a downed Russian MIG. For although U.N. aviators were by now well acquainted with this high-performance fighter, Communist reluctance to engage in combat far from base had prevented acquisition of a specimen for closer examination, and a previous search by west coast ships for one reported on the sandbars of the Yalu Gulf had proved fruitless. On 9 July, however, word was received from JOC that a MIG was down in shoal water off the mouth of the Chongchon River; *Sicily,* back again in the Far East as relief for *Bataan,* was ordered to search, and the American officers in charge of west coast underground activities, "Leopard" on Paengnyong Do and "Salamander" on Cho Do, were instructed to alert their people. But the reported position was 15 miles in error, the weather was foggy, and the aircraft, awash only at low water, was hard to see; not until the 11th did planes from *Glory* find the MIG a couple of miles offshore and 33 miles north of the Taedong estuary.

This location, less than 10 minutes flying time from the enemy's Antung airfields, was both risky and navigationally difficult. But photographs indicated that recovery might be practicable, every effort was ordered by ComNavFE, and the commanding officer of *Ceylon* worked out a plan. On 18 July an LSU equipped with a special crane was borrowed from CTF 90 and sent up to Cho Do in the LSD *Whetstone*. The next day's effort ended with the LSU fast on a sandbar, but on the 20th, with air cover from *Glory,* with *Belfast* stationed to warn of air attack, and with *Cardigan Bay* on hand for fire support, a U.S. Navy helicopter operating from the British carrier buoyed the site and *Glory* aircraft led the LSU through the sandbars. By evening the engine had been recovered and the major portions of the airframe located; next morning the pieces were loaded on the LSU. In the afternoon *Sicily* pilots sighted 32 MIGs heading for the area, but foggy weather prevented contact, no trouble ensued, and on the 22nd the LSU and its precious cargo were embarked in the LSD *Epping Forest* and the MIG brought back to Inchon.

Along both coasts, as talks began, action continued. On the western shore British Commonwealth, ROK, and U.S. units carried out a number of small bombardments and raids. At Wonsan in the east, activity increased as the enemy worked to expand his truck traffic and to develop his coastal defenses: reports from agents within the city made frequent mention of the presence of Soviet advisors, of the massing of troops, of possible shore-based torpedo firing facilities, and of the installation of batteries of impressive size, including a "Stalin gun" said to have been hauled out to Hodo Pando by 12 horses. Sufficient credence was placed in these reports to produce the "Wonsan Special" of 5 July, in which Task Force 77 helped out the bombardment group by devoting its entire day and 247 sorties to the city. And further confirmatory evidence was soon forthcoming.

Rocket-carrying F9Fs over Wonsan. On the right the railroad curves inland before turning north to Hamhung; on the left the Kalma Pando airstrip, the Namdae River, and the valley route to Seoul. July 1951. (USN 431907)

At 1637 on the afternoon of the 17th, shore batteries opened on the destroyers *O'Brien, Blue,* and *Cunningham* from three sides of the Wonsan swept area. The ships at once went into the War Dance, an evasive maneuver originated in May by *Brinkley Bass* and *Duncan,* steaming in an ellipse at 22 knots and firing on batteries in each sector as their guns came to bear. As enemy fire continued heavy, Task Force 77 was called upon for air support; at 1650, and again an hour later, an LSMR was brought in from the outer channel to deliver a long-range rocket barrage against enemy gun positions. By 1830 the batteries on Hodo Pando, Umi Do, and the tip of Kalma Pando had been silenced or had checked fire, but a new group of emplacements at the base of Kalma Pando presently opened up. By this time *Helena* and *New Jersey* had been started in from Task Force 77, and HMS *Morecambe Bay,* en route to Songjin, had been diverted to Wonsan. At 2000 in she came to join the dance, and for another hour, until darkness descended, shooting continued. Despite many very near misses no ship had been hit, and the single casualty was treated by the application of a Band-Aid, but the more than 500 splashes observed and the far larger number of rounds returned made the so-called "Battle of the Buzz Saw" a very respectable engagement. Late that night *Helena* reached the outer channel, to be followed by *New Jersey* in the morning, and since something heavier than 5-inch gunfire seemed needed, both ships stayed on for two days of heavy-gun bombardment.

Prospects nevertheless seemed warm, and future policy deserving of consideration. To the Seventh Fleet staff the value of the Wonsan foothold seemed dependent on the future intentions of CincFE, a view which was communicated to the higher levels for comment. But there, owing to the commencement of armistice talks, planning was largely in abeyance, and answer came there none. In the absence of guidance from above, Admiral Martin decided, as an interim measure, to hold the harbor islands for bargaining purposes. It was to prove a long interim.

Offshore, despite the hindrance of the July fogs, Task Force 77 continued to provide aircraft for close support, armed reconnaissance, and interdiction. Since requests from JOC for support of the battleline seldom exceeded 30 sorties a day the main effort was invested in a continuation of Operation Strangle, the attempt to cut truck traffic between 38° 15′ and 39° 15′, and in a return to bridge breaking. Here foggy weather, increased antiaircraft, and the recent emphasis on close support had worked in favor of the enemy; the bridge cuts south of Songjin had been eliminated, and few breaks existed in the line. But by month's end things were again under control, and a new program of systematic photography was underway to provide information for a new key bridge list.

At Kaesong, following agreement on the agenda, the delegates in late July took up the question of a demarcation line. Here the Communists, who by now had suffered a net loss of territory, insisted on the 38th parallel. But since an armistice would bring an end to the blockade, and to air and naval action against enemy territory, the U.N. negotiators, for their part, sought compensation in a line north of the existing front. From this discussion there soon arose the question of who in fact controlled the territory of the Yonan and Ongjin peninsulas, south of 38° and west of the Imjin River.

Largely untouched by war, and but lightly held by the enemy, the coastal parts of Hwanghae Province were subject at any time to descents from the sea, or to raids by partisans operating from the offshore islands. At the end of June ROK guerrillas with naval support had landed south of Yonan to destroy two ammunition dumps; in the following weeks raids were carried out against the mainland opposite Cho Do. On the evening of 24 July, as the question of the demarcation line arose, CTF 95 received a message from Admiral Joy asking for a show of strength in the Han River estuary as close as possible to Kaesong. Admiral Dyer at once committed all but one of his west coast frigates to this operation, *Glory* was ordered from Sasebo to join *Sicily,* and a check sweep of the entrance to Haeju Man was undertaken to permit the entry of heavy bombardment ships.

Two-carrier operations were carried out from 26 to 29 July; from the 27th to the 29th the heavy cruiser *Los Angeles* shot up targets on the western shore of Haeju Man; in the Han the Commonwealth frigates bombarded the northern bank. For these operations in the estuary the finest kind of sea-manship was necessary: U.S. and British charts of the area differed widely, and none showed any very reassuring depths; the liquid medium in the Han, brown soup rather than clear water, was lined with rocks; currents reached eight to ten knots, and so poor was the holding ground that on one occasion *Comus* dragged while steaming to both anchors.

Although targets for bombardment, obtained from JOC and from the Leopard organization, were generally unprofitable, and although enemy reaction was for the moment nil, the demonstration was more concerned with capabilities than with accomplishments. By early August, despite intermittent groundings, the bombarding ships had succeeded in penetrating upstream to fire on Yonan from the southeast and northward up the Yesong River; on the 17th three of the frigates found 400 enemy troops along the river bank and gave them a thorough shelling. Late in the month, on the urging of Admiral Scott-Moncreiff, a survey of the river was begun by a UDT detachment in the APD *Weiss,* and the channel was buoyed by the fleet tug *Abnaki.*

By this time the optimism which had accompanied the opening of armistice talks was dead. In early August negotiations had been briefly suspended by General Ridgway in protest against Communist violations of the neutral zone; late in the month, following an incident apparently fabri-cated to suggest that U.N. aircraft had bombed the conference site, the Com-munists in turn refused to talk; only in late October, with transfer of the

The Han River patrol: HMS Comus, riding to both anchors, fires on the northern bank. August 1951. (USN 436391)

413

conference site to Panmunjom, were plenary sessions resumed. These events governed the progress of the fighting. In mid-August General Van Fleet launched a limited offensive on the eastern coastal strip; with the breakdown in negotiations he ordered a larger effort east of the Hwachon Reservoir in X Corps zone.

Once again fire support was needed on the coastal road. On 17 August a special bombardment group, Task Group 95.9, was formed to assist the ROK advance into the difficult hill country south of Kosong; composed initially of *New Jersey, Toledo,* and two destroyers, this group continued through various changes of ships and of designation to support the eastern end of the battleline through August and into September.

Once again, also, an amphibious demonstration was called for to assist the forward movement. On 27 August a minesweeping group composed of three AMS and the LSD *Whetstone* moved into the objective area at Changjon, to be followed in due course by *Helena,* three destroyers, and an LSMR, and on the 30th by *New Jersey* and another destroyer. On the 30th and 31st the beach and adjacent troop and gun positions were bombarded and subjected to air strikes; offshore, where the transport group lay to, the boats were lowered, formed into waves, and headed for shore, before being recalled and hoisted in. But although the demonstration was more elaborate than its predecessors, it remained questionable what diversionary impact had been created, or whether anything over and above the bombardment damage had been accomplished.

The main effort, however, was inland, and there on the 31st the attack began as the Marine Division, fresh from a six-week rest, pushed northward up the Soyang Valley, while the 2nd Division pressed forward on its left. By 18 September the Marines had reached their objectives, as did the 2nd Division in mid-October. West of the Hwachon Reservoir, IX Corps was also pressing forward, and by 21 October was looking down upon Kumsong. Seventh Fleet planners had by this time produced a follow-up plan, known as "Wrangler," which involved withdrawing the Marines from X Corps, embarking them at Sokcho, and landing them in assault at Kojo to link up with the advance of IX Corps. But on 24 October, after a month of haggling by liaison officers, the Communists asked that talks be resumed, and "Wrangler" never came off.

The northward advance of the Marines since their February commitment to the Wonju front had brought them steadily closer to the Sea of Japan. Late September found the division on the upper waters of the Soyang River where its right, though still west of the Korean divide, was less than ten miles from the sea. This proximity to tidewater raised possibilities of naval gunfire and maritime logistics which were quickly embraced.

In this extremely mountainous country the enemy, deeply entrenched on the reverse slopes, was hard to reach. Since artillery could not touch him, and since air support was in short supply and unpredictable in quality, resort was had for the first time in a year to naval gunfire. On 20 September *New Jersey* was sent in to provide support; on the 23rd, after liaison officers had been sent out by helicopter and radio communication had been established, ranging rounds were fired; on the next two days, and again on 2 and 3 October, 16-inch fire was called down upon the backsides of the enemy with destructive and demoralizing effect. On 17 October *New Jersey* returned to the task, and for five days late in the month support was provided by the heavy cruiser *Toledo*. Intermittently throughout the winter this work continued, with the ships firing at ranges of 11 to 16 miles, their shells sailing over 2,000-foot mountains and across the Nam River valley to embed themselves amidst the enemy's supply concentrations and command posts.

The proximity of the sea also held logistic promise. In contrast to the ROK I Corps on the coast, always largely supported by sea, the Marines in September were dependent on their railhead at Wonju, 91 bad road miles away, a situation which required greatly increased allowances of motor transport, communications gear, and heavy engineer equipment. Now, however, encouraged by the prospect of "Wrangler," a road was cut through the mountains to the sea, Sokcho in the ROK zone was pressed into use as a supply port, and an adjacent airstrip was employed as division airhead. The impressive consequence of this shift to seaborne supply was the addition to the division's monthly potential of an estimated 8,000 to 10,000 combat man-days.

In somewhat similar manner Marine air units attempted to base themselves on the sea. MAG 12, with its main base at Pusan West, had been increasing its output and decreasing commuting time by staging through a forward field near Wonju; in July this field was closed, and in August forward operations were shifted to a coastal strip near Kangnung. But Kangnung has no harbor, and although use of this strip greatly improved the sortie rate, the exposed nature of the coastline complicated logistics. Original plans to bring supplies in across the beaches foundered when the broaching of an LST showed the beach to be unsatisfactory. Resort was next had to unloading at Chumunjin, but at the cost of a 17-mile trucking requirement over inferior roads. In early September the construction of a pontoon causeway near Kangnung eased the situation until its destruction by winter weather necessitated further recourse to Chumunjin.

Still, if the complications of beach logistics forced the working hands to a variety of expedients, the support provided by MAG 12's neighbors was unsurpassed. The broaching of the LST, with its vital load of POL and ordnance, brought an immediate response from the population of nearby fishing villages. Sampans were lashed together to form a causeway, and then overlaid by pierced steel planking across which the cargo was man-handled ashore. Twenty-four hours of continuous effort finished the job,

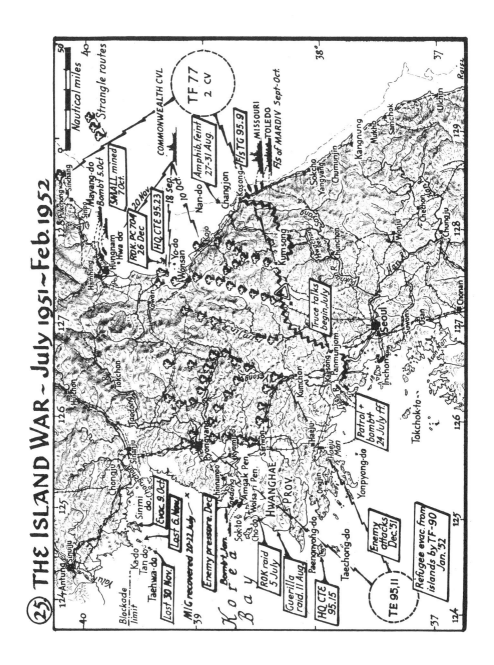

㉕ THE ISLAND WAR ~ July 1951~ Feb. 1952

Nautical miles

Strangle routes

COMMONWEALTH CVL

TF 77
2 CV

MISSOURI
TOLEDO
Fls of MARDIV Sept-Oct.

TF/sTG 95.9

Amphib. feint
27-31. Aug.

Nan-do

Changjon

Kosong

Kojo

Wonsan

Yo-do

10 Oct.

18 Sep.

HQ.CTE 95.23

ROK-PC 704
26 Dec.

SMALL mined
7 Oct.

Wayang-do
Bombt 5 Oct.

20 Nov.

Sinchang

Hukchong-ni

Sinpo

Hungnam

Hamhung

Hwa-do

Kowon

Tokchon

Hungnam

Truce talks
begin.July

Kumsong

Seoul

Inchon

Suwon

Osan

Chonan

Kaesong
Panmunjom

Kumchon

Haeju

Kumchon

Patrol +
bombt
24 July ff.

Yonpyong-do

Haeju
Man

Ongjin

Paengyong-do

Taechong-do

Enemy
attacks
Dec.'51

Refugee evac. from
islands by TF-90
Jan. '52

TE 95,11

HQ.CTE
95.15

Guerilla
raid. 11 Aug.

ROK raid
5 July

Wolsa'ri Pen.

Cho-do

Soktok

Amgak Pen

Chinnampo

Bombt Jan.

Enemy pressure. Dec.

Chongju

Sinanju

Sinmi
do. 6 Oct.

Evac. 9 Oct.

Lost 6. Nov.

Tan-do

Kado

MIG recovered 20-22 July

Lost 30 Nov.

Taehwa-do

Blockade
limit

Antung

Sinuiju

Yalu

Pyongyang

Ryongho

Sariwon

HWANGHAE
PROV.

K o r e a
B a y

Tokchok-to

Seoul

Seoul

and as no pay would be accepted by the Koreans the best the Marines could do was to set up a fund for the families of fishermen lost at sea.

Day after day throughout the summer the fast carriers continued the effort at interdiction. On 22 August a new face appeared in the Far East with the arrival of *Essex,* first of her class to enter World War II and first also to reach Korea following modernization to provide more powerful catapults, larger elevators for planes and bombs, and most importantly a larger gasoline capacity and an improved fueling system to cope with the insatiable demands of jet aircraft. Embarked in *Essex* was Air Group 5 with one squadron of ADs, one of F4Us, one of F9Fs, and one of the McDonnell F2H Banshee, an excellent twin-jet fighter, larger, heavier, and superior in performance to the F9F, although still, like all U.S. aircraft except the F–86, inferior to the MIG in speed and maneuverability.

Essex's first month in the theater was one of developmental progress. Operationally a new first in interservice cooperation was effected when 23 F9F and F2H fighters escorted 35 B–29s in a strike against Najin, a Communist storage center on the northeast coast beyond the range of Air Force fighters and but 17 miles from the Soviet boundary. In materiel also an advance took place, following a serious accident in which a damaged F2H floated over the barriers and into parked aircraft, causing a gasoline fire which destroyed 4 planes, killed 7, and injured 27. Lacking propellers to catch the barricades, floating jets had always been hard to stop, and the ultimate solution of the angled deck was still some years away; but the *Essex* incident brought an effective interim measure in the installation of a ten-foot barrier of wire and nylon tape as a last-resort midships arresting device.

For the most part, however, the work went on, day after day, in routine fashion. "Strangle" operations against the North Korean road net continued into September, as did attacks on key rail bridges. Across the peninsula Fifth Air Force also continued its efforts against road traffic, but with a progressive tendency to shift to a new concept, still under the rubric "Strangle," which called for the destruction of railroad trackage in the optimistic hope that this would force the enemy to wear out his motor transport. In this effort, officially begun on 19 August, the carriers soon joined; a month later, on orders from CincFE, all close support was halted to permit full concentration on interdiction; on the last day of September, following a conference between Air Force and Navy commanders, it was decided to emphasize rail cutting supplemented by the destruction of a small number of key bridges. The Navy's part began fast with 131 track cuts in the first three days of October, and as the enemy's repair parties were poorly deployed to meet the new tactic, both Air Force and carrier airmen managed to stay ahead while the flying weather remained good.

At intervals throughout the fall the work of the fast carriers in the Sea of Japan was augmented by the Commonwealth light carrier. On 18 and

Fire at sea: Essex burning after an F2H jumped the barrier. A second F2H in the landing circle and two ADs in the distance. 16 September 1951. (USN 435079)

19 September, at the suggestion of Commander Seventh Fleet, CTF 95 put on a special two-day air, gun, and rocket effort against Wonsan, in which the air strikes were provided by HMS *Glory*. On 10 and 11 October a similar operation against the Kojo area, with air strikes from HMAS *Sydney*, and with a mixed U.S., British, and Canadian screen, was carried out by Rear Admiral Scott-Moncreiff in *Belfast*. Late in November Scott-Moncreiff returned again with *Belfast* and *Sydney*, and with a screen still further internationalized by the addition of a Dutch destroyer, to spend two days in banging up Hungnam.

In the east, along the 300 miles of enemy coast, the ships of Task Force 95 continued to provide fire support, to patrol and bombard, and to besiege the cities of Wonsan and Songjin. In July the Royal Marine Commando, whose varied experiences had taken it under the sea in *Perch*, up to the reservoir with the Marines, and into enemy country near the mouth of the Taedong River, had arrived at Yo Do for a six month's tour of duty; after some practice raids against the Wonsan mainland the Royal Marines began a series of autumn operations, landing from an APD to attack targets along the northeastern coast. On 5 September, on orders from Seventh Fleet, CTF 95 instructed the minesweepers to clear a lane between Wonsan and Hungnam to bring the western shore of the Korean Gulf within gunfire range. One month later, as the job was being finished, *New Jersey, Helena,* and some destroyers bombarded the Hungnam area for the first time since the X Corps evacuation, destroying an oil refinery and some ammunition dumps. But although the clearance of Hungnam had been successful not everyone had heard the details, and on 7 October the destroyer *Small* got outside the swept area and was mined with considerable damage and heavy casualties.

The efforts at interdiction by Fifth Air Force in the west and Task Force 77 in the east, together with surface ship bombardment of accessible coastal pressure points, had placed a heavy load upon the Communists. Their Department of Military Highway Administration, charged with road repair, had grown to a total of some 20,000 men, and the railroad repair organization was estimated of equivalent size. But despite all, it still seemed impossible to cut the flow of supplies below the enemy's requirements. Persistence and diligence in repair, a determination to get supplies through, and the small logistic requirements of Communist forces had resulted in continuous improvement of the enemy's front line logistic situation: his soldiers were better fed than ever before, his number of tanks had increased, and his expenditure of artillery ammunition had risen from 8,000 rounds in July to 43,000 in November. For one side, at least, negotiation had proven profitable.

Not only were supplies getting through, but some 500 heavy anti-aircraft guns and almost 2,000 automatic weapons had by now been emplaced in North Korea, and U.N. aircraft were suffering increasing losses. The increase in coast artillery, first noted at Wonsan, had extended along the shore, with the result that U.N. vessels could no longer move close in or lie to while firing. At sea the possible submarine threat continued to preoccupy naval commanders, while in the air enemy strength continued to grow.

Steadily increasing totals of MIG sorties were being reported by Air Force fighter pilots on northern patrols—180 on 2 October, more than 300 on 29 November—while the availability of light bombers and propeller-driven attack planes was no longer a matter of question. Following an Air Force query as to carrier jet capabilities in the northwest an F2H sweep was sent off to MIG Alley; no contact was made, and this maximum-range effort was not repeated, but the menace remained. Noting the increase in Communist air strength and the concurrent effort to activate North Korean airstrips, ComNavFE in early November informed his command that enemy aircraft had been sighted south of Pyongyang, and directed heavy ships not to operate north of Wonsan without air cover. On 27 November a flight from *Bon Homme Richard* was attacked by MIGs near Wonsan, and on subsequent occasions contrails were sighted high overhead. In early December, as the Amphibious Force began an interchange of Army units between Hokkaido and Inchon, CincFE instructed FEAF and the West Coast Carrier Element to provide cover for all troop movements in the Yellow Sea.

Nevertheless, despite the enemy's increasing material prosperity, the movement of the battleline had continued northward, the U.N. retained command of the air over most of North Korea, the U.N. navies controlled the coasts, and bombardment at Wonsan, Songjin, and in the Han River estuary remained a daily affair. On 28 September CTF 95 made an inspection trip up the Han in the Australian frigate *Murchison,* only to be opened on by mortars, small arms, and light field guns. Contemporaneously with this first instance of the long-awaited enemy reaction, indications that the Communists were about to abandon their insistence on the 38th parallel brought requests from the U.N. delegation and from EUSAK for more gunfire.

Admiral Dyer at once ordered the Han River operation intensified. The Yellow Sea carrier was directed to bomb the northern banks daily and to provide air spot and CAP for the bombarding frigates. On 3 October *Black Swan* steamed up the river to draw enemy fire, whereupon 13 F4Us from *Rendova* attacked the gun positions; and for the balance of the month, as carrier aircraft burned off the cover on the northern bank, the noise of the bombardment was wafted to the negotiators at Kaesong. By October's end an effort originally scheduled for a few days had lasted a hundred, and like the destroyers at Wonsan the frigates in the Han estuary had become fixed.

F2H Banshees over Hungnam on their way back to base.   Upper left, the mouth of the Songchon River.   July 1953.   (USN 630625)

On 25 October, as the enemy returned to the truce table, the U.N. negotiators proposed the establishment of a four-kilometer demilitarized zone based generally on the existing line of contact.   On 5 November the proposal was accepted, together with a U.N. proviso that the line be that existing when final agreement was reached.   A week later General Ridgway directed Eighth Army to cease offensive operations and commence an active defense of existing positions.   By the 27th the front had been mapped and accepted by both sides, and a bait provided for the Communists by a U.N. undertaking to accept this line should the armistice be concluded within a month.

With this agreement, frigate bombardment in the Han River was terminated and ground action again diminished.   Along the entire front, from the Imjin to the sea, the Communists pressed the fortification of defensive positions.   But as the ground battle tapered off into patrolling, the enemy commenced an offensive effort in a new sphere, and the seat of war was transferred to the offshore islands.

These islands, acquired during the U.N. advance in late 1950, had since that time been employed as bases for raids and for intelligence activities. On the eastern shore the picture was a fairly simple one: except for those in Wonsan harbor only four islands of importance lie along this coast, and of these the two largest, Mayang Do on the 40th parallel and Hwa Do off Hungnam, were enemy controlled. Northeast of Songjin, however, the Yang Do island group, two miles offshore, accommodated intelligence personnel moving in and out of North Korea, and in time would become an ROKN PT operating base; off the bomb line on the 39th parallel the little island of Nan Do was employed as a base for Task Force Kirkland, a EUSAK unconventional warfare organization.

In the west the situation was more complex. On Tokchok To, off Inchon, the Air Force navigational equipment evacuated in December had been reinstalled in February, and similar gear had been emplaced on Paengnyong Do on the 38th parallel. Along the southern shore of Hwanghae Province, from the Han estuary to Korea's western tip, numerous coastal islets were employed as bases by partisan groups, of which Leopard Force was the most notable. Off the Chinnampo approaches, the important islands of Sok To and Cho Do supported guerrilla and clandestine operations, and an Air Force desire to install radar facilities and rescue helicopters on Cho Do waited only on improved security. To the northward in the Yalu Gulf a group of islands, seized by the ROK Navy in November 1950, contained numerous anti-Communist guerrillas.

The number of independent agencies on these islands led at times to situations of considerable complexity. In August 1951 one observer noted that Yo Do in Wonsan harbor was crowded with uncoordinated delegations from nearly every organization operating in Korea, and that the masses of amateurs commuting to and from the mainland created hazards for the skilled agents. In the west a FEAF outfit which operated its own private navy, and the organizations controlled by Leopard at Paengyong Do and by Salamander at Cho Do, cooperated well with the blockading force. But other groups, too mysterious to mention, were less considerate, and when NavFE headquarters proved unable to influence the state of affairs, Admiral Scott-Moncreiff ordered the apprehension and detention of all unidentifiable travellers. By autumn this particular situation had improved, but by this time the enemy was showing interest in the islands, while the armistice talks had adversely affected the morale of anti-Communist North Korean guerrillas.

Giving thought to their future status in the event of a cease-fire, many of these now became double or triple agents, or went over to the Communists. At Sok To a mutiny of the garrison and landing force was caught in the nick of time by Leopard, and 300 prisoners were removed to the southward. On 30 August Royal Marines and stokers from *Ceylon* made a descent upon a west coast target designated by Leopard Force; Leopard himself accompanied the raiders and no trouble was expected, but someone had leaked and the opposition was waiting. On Cho Do, in early September, an attempt on the life of Salamander was made by one of his own ex-agents. But not all developments were adverse. On 24 September, supported by gunfire from *Comus,* Leopard's Sok To agent led a small raid against the Amgak peninsula, and returned with nine prisoners including a North Korean colonel and his concubine. The colonel, recently transferred from Wonsan, reported that he was fed up with the war; the comments of his lady have unfortunately not been preserved.

In this situation of tension and uncertainty the enemy, in early October, began to exert pressure. On the 9th, 600 invaders from the mainland landed on the large Yalu Gulf island of Sinmi Do, and although the garrison held for a time with support from *Cossack* and *Ceylon,* reinforcements arriving across the tidal mud flats forced withdrawal on the 12th. On the 30th *Cayuga* reported receiving a hundred rounds of artillery fire from the Amgak peninsula opposite Sok To; in the Yalu Gulf the island of Taehwa Do, where friendly forces had concentrated, was attacked by aircraft on 6 November in the first confirmed enemy employment of light bombers in Korea. That night Ka Do and Tan Do, two of the smaller northern islands, were seized by the Communists in a night amphibious attack.

Since the U.N. delegation hoped to use the islands as counters to trade off against the Kaesong area, these events served to stimulate some interest. From Commander Seventh Fleet came a request for an inventory of west coast islands, and from EUSAK a hope that Taehwa Do would be held. Although he felt the northern islands were not worth the effort required to defend them, Admiral Scott-Moncreiff on 9 November ordered a destroyer to patrol the area during the hours of darkness. Shortly Commander Seventh Fleet appeared in the Yellow Sea on an inspection tour; on the 12th, with air spot from HMAS *Sydney,* his flagship *New Jersey* fired her final Korean bombardment and her 3,000th 16-inch round of the war at troop concentrations reported by Leopard Force.

Winter by now had come again bringing strong winds, cold, and the first snows to the northern Yellow Sea. Nightly, nevertheless, ships of the blockading force went up to Taehwa Do; in the course of the month guerrilla raids supported by naval units were conducted against enemy-held islands in the Yalu Gulf; but the proximity of these positions to enemy airfields prevented daylight surface support or carrier air patrol. On 27 November the subject of the offshore islands came up for discussion at Panmunjom, and at once the Communists stepped up their efforts.

Although the enemy carried out a successful raid against Hwangto Do in Wonsan harbor on the night of the 28th, his principal effort was in the west. On 30 November, as CincFE warned that the islands had become

critical to the negotiations and adjured his island commanders to make preparations for defense, Fifth Air Force fighters intercepted a formation of 12
twin-engine bombers heading for Taehwa Do with an escort of 16 propeller
fighters and 50 MIGs, and destroyed the greater part of the bomber force.
Nevertheless the island was lost that night to a well-planned amphibious
assault supported by artillery from Ka Do, and of some 1,200 guerrillas and
inhabitants only about a quarter got out. This affair was followed almost
immediately by further enemy shore-to-shore attacks which seized six small
coastal islets in Haeju Man, and by reports of extensive troop movements
in Hwanghae Province. These events brought a review of the island situation.

Responsibility for island defense was at this time somewhat obscure.
Tokchok To and Paengnyong Do had for almost a year been charges of CTG
95.1; other islands where U.S. intelligence activities or equipment were operative were under the control of CincFE; the Korean-occupied islands were
pretty much on their own. The loss of Taehwa Do had brought increased
patrolling by west coast ships and a request for reinforcement of the Cho
Do, Sok To, and Paengyong Do garrisons; on higher levels various proposals for the institution of small boat patrols, reinforcement of the islands
by air, and the like, were bandied about; in the south ROK Marine units
were alerted for movement to the threatened islands. On 7 December Admiral Dyer received the loan of *Manchester* from Commander Seventh Fleet,
and followed by *Ceylon* proceeded west at speed to Cho Do. But the attitude of higher echelons remained obscure, no reinforcements were available
from EUSAK, and Commander Seventh Fleet was reluctant to become too
deeply involved.

At Cho Do and Sok To, Admiral Dyer found morale improved by
the news that the islands would be defended, but the situation was still
precarious. Island commanders, intelligence officers rather than Marine or
Army line, were inexperienced in organizing defenses; since the guerrillas
were all natives of North Korea, security was inherently poor; conversation
with Leopard indicated the great desirability of getting the refugees out
and the ROK Marines in as fast as possible. An LSD and some AMS were
brought in to keep the Sok To anchorage swept and to strengthen the small
craft patrol, and arrangements were made for the LSTs bringing up the
ROK Marines to remove the refugees. With this much accomplished, and
with an apparently growing small boat menace to the Wonsan harbor islands,
CTF 95 proceeded to the east coast.

Hardly, however, had he reached Wonsan when word was received
of attacks on two small islands inboard of Sok To, and between 16 and
18 December, despite support from U.N. ships and aircraft, an enemy force
of about 600 overran these positions. With the situation apparently still
deteriorating, CTF 95 again headed west, and on the 18th took over as officer
in tactical command on the west coast. By the 20th the ships on anti-

invasion duty near Cho Do included *Manchester, Ceylon,* and two destroyers, and the question of responsibility for island defense was at last beginning to jell.

Despite the fact that all islands north of 38° were conceded by the U.N. negotiators on 21 December, failing an armistice agreement the defensive requirement remained. On 6 January responsibility for the overall defense, local ground defense included, of designated islands on both coasts, was assigned the Navy and delegated to CTF 95. So far as east coast islands were concerned only Nan Do, off the bombline, had not previously been a naval responsibility; in the west, however, Sok To and Cho Do in the Chinnampo approaches, Taechong Do in the Sir James Hall group, and Taeyongpyong Do south of Haeju were added to the list. On the 9th an Army-Navy-Air Force island defense conference was held aboard *Wisconsin,* following which the West Coast Island Defense Element was organized with a U.S. Marine officer in command, with headquarters on Paengnyong Do, and with two battalions of ROK Marines distributed among critical islands.

Already the LSTs of Task Force 90, which had brought the defenders in, had begun to evacuate refugees: by 22 December about 9,000 had been lifted out and by late January some 20,000 had been transported south to Kunsan. Constant patrolling of the threatened areas was undertaken, and an LST with armed small boats was provided for inshore work. In mid-January, in an effort to suppress the artillery effort against Cho Do and Sok To, CTF 95 went north in *Rochester* to bombard the Amgak peninsula in coordination with a Marine air strike from *Badoeng Strait.* By early February the enemy had retired from a number of the captured islets in Haeju Man and off the Ongjin peninsula, in part apparently owing to bombardment by rocket ships, in part to inability to support his forces. By March these islets were being reoccupied by anti-Communist partisans and a number of enemy efforts to attack across the mud flats had been thrown back by naval gunfire.

The period following naval assumption of responsibility for island defense brought two actions of some importance. On the northeast coast, after a month of careful preparation, the North Koreans mounted a raid on the Yang Do group by some 250 troops boated in sampans. Shortly after midnight on 20 February the New Zealand frigate *Taupo,* the DMS *Endicott,* and the destroyer *Shelton* were patrolling to the northward when an emergency dispatch reported Yang Do under fire from the mainland and invasion apparently imminent. Steaming at flank speed the ships reached the islands to discover bombardment continuing and fighting in progress ashore, but by this time radio contact had been broken. With daylight, however, the island commander came back on the air: all invaders on Yang Do had been either killed or captured, those on East Yang Do were departing for the mainland. There followed a spirited engagement in the two-mile strait in which *Taupo* and *Endicott* engaged some 15 sampans, destroying 10 and damaging the rest, and were themselves engaged by artillery from the mainland, while *Shelton* put up counter-battery fire. This was all very well, but on the west coast the enemy fared better, and in a successful assault on the night of 24 March seized a small island between Cho Do and Sok To and eliminated its defenders.

Although reports of enemy offensive plans continued to come in, and although artillery fire was persistently directed against Cho Do, Sok To, and their supporting ships, as well as against the islands at Wonsan, the enemy island offensive was limited in its success to the elimination of the foothold in the Yalu Gulf. At Cho Do improved defensive arrangements were followed by the installation of radar and antiaircraft weapons in February, and in March by a helicopter detachment; these facilities, together with naval patrol of the surrounding waters and a rescue B–29 which orbited overhead, made the Cho Do area a useful bail-out and rescue zone for pilots from the Yellow Sea carrier and from the Fifth Air Force. Elsewhere the offshore positions continued to provide bases for intelligence and guerrilla activity, while at Wonsan possession of the harbor islands paid an unexpected dividend. Some concern had been caused the U.N. Command by events such as the Sok To mutiny, and by reports that guerrillas were surrendering in response to an enemy offer of amnesty. But at Wonsan, on 21 February, reassurance was gained when at 0630 in the morning Brigadier General Lee Il, NKPA, reached Tae Do in a stolen sampan, with a briefcase full of top secret papers, a head full of top secret plans, and a strong desire to make himself useful.

As the war continued among the islands, along the coasts, and in the air over North Korea, so did the talks at Panmunjom. There, with agreement on the demarcation line, discussion had turned to arrangements for a cease-fire and to the question of prisoners of war. December and January brought abandonment by the U.N. of the northern islands, of the right to air reconnaissance over North Korea, and of a previously proposed limitation on Communist rehabilitation of airfields. But with the New Year the sticking point appeared in the question of forced repatriation of prisoners. Despite further U.N. concessions all progress ceased, while continued enemy pressure against the islands was indicative of no speedy peace.

Through the winter cold and winds and snow, naval and air operations went on. The Amphibious Force was engaged in further troop lifts between Korea and Japan. The units of Task Force 95 continued as before, the monotony interrupted only by a brief resumption of the Han River patrol, by rumors of a Soviet submarine in the northeastern coastal area, and by the loss with all hands of an ROK PC, presumably by mining, at Wonsan. On the east coast the detachment of the ROK Capital Division to chase guerrillas in the southern mountains imposed additional burdens at the bombline, but the assignment of a heavy ship and of another destroyer to duty there enabled the remaining forces to hold the road while the extermination campaign went on. The load of the minesweepers was increased by the decision of CTF 95 to sweep the east coast from Kansong to Songjin every two weeks. As for the aviators, they were still working on the railroad.

Table 22.—COMMUNIST AND U.N. TRANSPORT, WINTER 1951–52

	Vehicles	*Locomotives*	*Rolling Stock*
North Korea	6–7,000	275	7,700
South Korea	22,000	486	8,314

In the north the frugal and ant-like enemy continued to accumulate supplies and, as the table shows, to maintain with roughly half the logistic means of the U.N. a larger military establishment. At year's end total U.N. strength in Korea was of the order of 600,000, and that of the Communists a third as much again, while EUSAK credited the enemy with the ability to launch a general offensive with a force of more than 40 divisions.

So spring came.

2. *March 1952–February 1953: Stalemate*

Watch after watch, day after weary day, the war went on. The cold of winter passed, to be followed by the thaw and rains of spring, the haze and fog and steaming heat of summer, and the clear days of early autumn. In steady succession carriers and their air groups crossed the Pacific to take their tour of combat and depart; from the west coast of the United States destroyers crossed the ocean and from the Atlantic coast the world, operated for their allotted period, and returned again. In the Atlantic and Mediterranean the larger half of the U.S. Navy was also working on an accelerated schedule in a situation that was neither peace nor war. Throughout the establishment and on both sides of the world effort was called for from all hands, and particularly from the career personnel, laboring to accomplish an acceptable minimum of training while watching the steady disappearance of rated men and qualified reserves into the welcoming arms of American industry.

Stalemate existed, but stalemate brought no rest. Readiness had to be maintained; crews had to be trained; the enemy, ensconced in the northern half of the peninsula, had to be harassed, and if possible brought to terms. Day after day the F–86s went up to the Yalu, Air Force fighter-bombers and carrier aircraft ranged over North Korea, the gunnery ships continued on patrol, mines were swept.   But month after month went by, and increasingly the question of what leverage to employ upon the enemy became more puzzling and more frustrating.

For the supporting forces and for the NavFE shore establishment, as well as for those on the line, life continued arduous under the twin pressures of operational load and Parkinson's Law.   The hazards of the sea continued to manifest themselves in run-of-the-mill casualties and breakdowns calling for the attention of the Service Force, while April brought a major tragedy when an explosion in *Saint Paul's* forward 8-inch turret took 30 lives.   In some areas, however, appropriate savings were effected: to economize on pilots and aircraft, pull-out altitudes were raised and passes over a target limited; to economize on fuel and ammunition Commander Seventh Fleet would soon restrict speed in transit and unobserved gunfire.   Expenditure of aviation ordnance, however, continued apace, aided by the load-carrying characteristics of the AD, with the surprising result that by May 1952 Navy and Marine usage in Korea equalled their total for the entire war against Japan.   In communications, too, economy was hard to come by, and multiplied circuits and augmented personnel struggled bravely but vainly against the loquacity of the human animal.   The message count of late 1950, when great operations were afoot, was up by half again in 1952 though all remained routine; in the autumn an amphibious feint would double the peak reached during the amphibious strokes of two years before.

For the enemy, too, the war went on, the seasons passed.   To a country hardly worth more devastation, and to men whose lives held little value for their rulers, U.N. aircraft and ships and artillery brought destruction and death.   What the Communists thought they were accomplishing remains unknown.   Their inability to deal with the situation in constructive terms, either for themselves or for the world at large, remained unimpeachable.

Once more in 1952 the coming of spring brought changes to the Far East.   In Europe General Eisenhower gave up his command at SHAPE, and returned home to begin a career in politics.   Summoned to succeed him, General Ridgway was in May relieved of his commands by General Mark W. Clark, USA, who had struggled in Italy with the problems of peninsular war and in Austria with those of negotiating with the Communists.   This change at the top of the U.N. Command was paralleled throughout the echelons of Naval Forces Far East: the Marine Division and the Marine Aircraft Wing received new commanding generals; with the arrival of Rear Admiral Burton B. Biggs the Logistic Support Force got a flag officer at its head; in April the first of a new generation of carrier division commanders arrived in the person of Rear Admiral Apollo Soucek; in May Vice Admiral Joseph J. Clark become Commander Seventh Fleet and Rear Admiral Frederick W. McMahon, for four months ComCarDiv 5 in *Valley Forge,* relieved Admiral Ofstie as Chief of Staff of Naval Forces Far East.

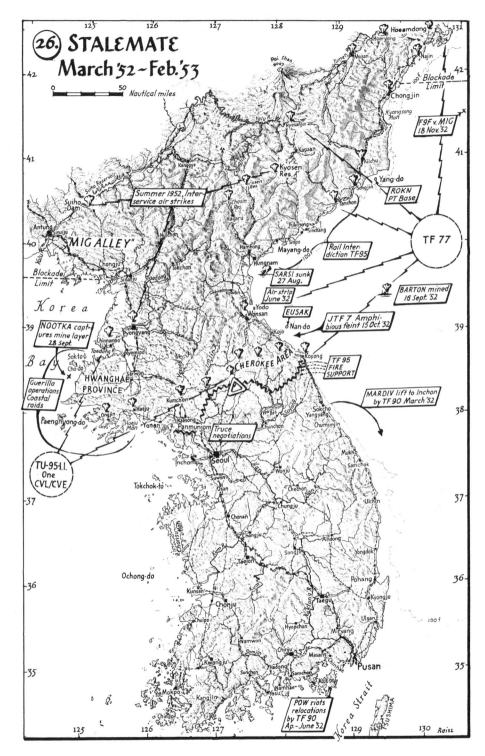

Although rotation and relief had brought multiple changes in most Far Eastern billets there remained two commanders who had seen it all. Now, at long last, replacements for these veterans arrived. On 1 June Commander Luosey, who since the earliest days had administered the ROK Navy, was relieved. In May, after ten months of negotiations, Admiral Joy was succeeded as head of the truce team by Major General William K. Harrison, Jr., USA; in June, after nearly three years in peace and war as Commander Naval Forces Far East, he turned over his Tokyo command to Vice Admiral Robert P. Briscoe.

As the faces changed so did the problems faced. In mid-March the command structure of the Western Pacific was modified by presidential order, and military responsibility for the Philippine-Formosa-Marianas area transferred from CincFE to CincPac; local responsibility, however, remained with Commander Seventh Fleet, in his capacity as Commander Formosa Defense Force, and standing orders dating from Struble's time, to proceed to Formosa at best speed in the event of a serious invasion threat, continued in effect. In April the Japanese peace treaty became effective and that war, at least, was formally over. For Naval Forces Far East this had a variety of implications. Along with their sister services in Japan they had to transmute themselves from occupation forces into guests, a process facilitated by war in Korea which both demonstrated the virtues of available force and provided a sizable infusion of dollars for the Japanese economy. With the peace treaty came also the disestablishment of Scajap, the Navy-administered Japanese-manned shipping concern which had performed such yeoman service in support of the Korean campaign, and the transfer of its LSTs to MSTS contract operations. For the future, ComNavFE acquired new responsibilities in helping the Japanese to organize a Coastal Security Force, and in supervising the transfer of frigates and landing craft to Japanese control.

Within Korea, spring of 1952 brought a change of some importance in the move of the Marine Division from the Soyang River sector to the Imjin front. On the tactical level this shift was occasioned by concern at EUSAK for the defenses in the west; strategically, it reflected the final abandonment of plans for an east coast amphibious envelopment. For most of the troops this 160-mile movement across everyone else's supply lines was carried out between 18 and 25 March by road, but the tanks, amphibian tractors, and much of the engineering equipment were lifted out from Sokcho by two AKAs, three LSDs, and ten LSTs from Task Force 90. The arrival of the Marines west of the Imjin, where they relieved the ROK 1st Division, made it for the first time possible to hold this position against determined attack, while their transfer to a coastal sector produced an extra dividend as an amphibious retraining program, conducted throughout the summer in the Tokchok Islands, was apprehensively observed by the enemy.

Support of the line: Napalm drops by Marine F4Us in the Imjin River sector. October 1952. (USN 447567)

The continuing amphibious threat, together with U.N. occupancy of islands off the enemy's shore, had by now brought the assignment of three North Korean corps and three CCF armies to coast defense. In March and April, enemy raids across the mud flats of Haeju Man against Yongmae Do were repulsed by gunfire from Commonwealth naval units; on the east coast enemy batteries on Mayang Do fired on minesweepers and patrolling ships. U.N. forces, for their part, continued to exploit the islands for their opportunities in evasion and escape, and as bases for guerrilla operations. Attacks by APD-borne detachments against the east coast rail line were resumed, but with diminishing dividends; in the west, coastal raids and incursions into the Haeju area were supported by the Yellow Sea carrier and by gunnery ships.

At Cho Do and Sok To, which with their valuable radar, weather, and helicopter detachments had become the Wonsan of the west, a series of intermittent engagements took place between ships, carrier and Fifth Air Force aircraft, and enemy coastal batteries. In July there was a brief flurry in the Yellow Sea as an island close to the tip of the Ongjin peninsula was invaded by a North Korean force embarked in junks and outboard motorboats. As *Belfast* and *Amethyst* converged to assist the defenders, and as Marine fighter planes from *Bataan* answered the call, other west coast ships manned anti-invasion stations off Cho Do and Sok To; within two days only 5 of the 156 invaders were missing and unaccounted for. More troublesome than the enemy were outbreaks of typhus on Cho Do and Paengnyong Do, but the epidemics were quickly controlled by a naval medical unit.

With the front remaining relatively quiet, the most conspicuous ground action of early 1952 was the campaign of Koje Do. On this island, 30 miles southwest of Pusan, camps had been erected to hold the more than 100,000 prisoners of war. Early in the year a screening program, intended to separate civilians from bona fide soldiers, had culled out some thousands of the former, who were then lifted by LST to mainland ports; it had also been violently resisted by organized prisoner groups. With the commencement of a second screening cycle, designed to separate those desiring repatriation from those who would resist it, disorder and violence increased; within the Communist-controlled pens the prisoners reigned supreme, and by their riotous activity provided grist for enemy propaganda mills. In May the capture of the camp commander by his charges provided embarrassing evidence of a need for reinforcement.

Five ROKN small craft were ordered to Koje to prevent escape by water; elements of the 187th Airborne Regiment were hastily flown from Japan to Pusan and lifted out by LST, while the rest of the regiment with its heavy gear was brought across by sea. For Task Force 90 the sudden calls resulting from the crisis on Koje Do meant that scheduled maintenance had to be foregone and training schedules modified, but in due course the campaign was won. New island sites for camps were selected by aerial reconnaissance, beach surveys for LST slots were carried out by the UDTs, Army engineers and equipment were lifted to the new locations to construct new compounds. On 10 June a new camp commander imposed control upon his intransigent wards, and in July Task Force 90 carried 37,000 prisoners to their new decentralized homes.

At Panmunjom no progress remained the order of the day. Enemy insistence on freedom to reconstruct the North Korean airfields, on a limitation on rotation of forces in Korea, and on crippling restrictions for the proposed Neutral Nations Supervisory Commission sufficiently impeded agreement. But the insuperable barrier to progress, which no concession could apparently move, was the reluctance of Communist prisoners to return home and the insistence of their governments on forced repatriation.

Behind his fortified front, his stubbornness in negotiation, and his vigor in propaganda, the enemy continued to increase his strength. In March, interrogation of prisoners indicated that great operations were impending. On 1 April the biggest air battle of the year occurred when 186 F–86s took on some 350 MIGs. Late in the month piles of construction material at the Pyongyang airbase evidenced continued intentions of rehabilitation. In May an unparalleled 4,000 vehicle sightings a night betokened an extremely active logistic effort. In the weeks that followed, increased aggressiveness brought the MIGs south as far as Sinanju.

On the east coast, as well, the growth in enemy capabilities was apparent. There, where the ships of Task Force 95 continued to patrol, bombard, and besiege, enemy gunfire steadily increased. From Kojo north to Chongjin the installation of radar, together with such devices as anchored ranging buoys, led to continued improvement in Communist fire control. March brought the heaviest shooting since the previous July, and April's fall of shot was double that of March. Reports from captured and defecting personnel, which suggested that an assault against the Wonsan islands was in preparation, gained at least superficial confirmation from the discovery that the boatbuilders of the area had been mobilized, and that the bays west of Hodo Pando contained a large and increasing number of small craft.

By June the greatest troop and supply accumulations of the war were in evidence behind Communist lines, and intelligence indicated the imminence of a general offensive. There was also a rumor circulating, derived from POW interrogation, that the enemy proposed to kidnap the U.N. armistice delegation on the 25th, the second anniversary of the outbreak of war. No one can feel very safe when dealing with such people: as far back as April the Marines had formed a covering force to protect the truce team should the talks break down, and the new rumors brought further preparations. But June passed without difficulty and the anticipated offensive never came.

The naval siege of Wonsan was now well into its second year. Begun in order to take some pressure off Eighth Army and to get the gunnery ships on the offensive, it had by now become institutionalized: the officer in tactical command afloat enjoyed the additional honorific title of Mayor of Wonsan, and with changes of command there passed also a large gilt key to the city. But here too the passage of time, the size of effort, and the difficulty of damage assessment led inevitably to questioning. Certainly the extensive installation of shore batteries and antiaircraft, and the reported presence in the neighborhood of almost 80,000 troops, gave evidence that the effects had been considerable. On the other hand a sizable force was required to maintain the siege, defend the islands, and prevent remining of the harbor: in addition to four or five minesweepers, their tender and a tug, two or three destroyers were maintained permanently on station, and the expenditure of ammunition, much of it unobserved and unspotted, had been heavy. Demonstrable damage to the enemy hardly made up for this investment, which could only be justified by the argument that it held down large enemy forces, and by such incidental advantages as the flow of information gained through the infiltration of agents. Some now came to argue that the siege should never have been undertaken, but its long history made it difficult to abandon without apparent admission of defeat.

But the enemy, too, was concerned about Wonsan. One indication of the extent of his worries was provided by captured records of a war game conducted by North Korean division commanders in early 1952. This problem was concerned with a defense against a four-divisional assault at Wonsan, accompanied by subsidiary landings at Kojo and Hungnam, and by a northward thrust of Eighth Army through the Iron Triangle and the eastern mountains. Against this hypothetical maneuver, which bore a not too remote resemblance to U.N. planning, there were available to the North Koreans the two mobile artillery brigades which manned the Wonsan shore, three infantry divisions in the near neighborhood, and Chinese forces further inland. Interestingly, the exercise conceded inability to prevent a U.N. lodgment, and the scheme of maneuver emphasized an all-out counterattack on D plus 4. Interestingly also, and showing that spies are everywhere, the problem included among the assaulting units the 40th and 45th Infantry Divisions which, at the time the exercise was prepared, had just finished amphibious indoctrination in Japan and were preparing to be lifted to Korea.

Since the Navy, like it or not, appeared to be committed, steps were taken to improve the position at Wonsan. Island fortifications were strengthened; a clear statement from CTF 95 defined the primary mission of ships at Wonsan, as at Yang Do and Nan Do, as the defense of those positions; construction of an emergency airstrip on Yo Do was undertaken. This enterprise had been suggested the previous autumn, when the increased effectiveness of Communist antiaircraft had forced a number of damaged planes to ditch in Wonsan harbor. In the absence of a regular naval construction unit in the area the proposition had been put up to the Army and Air Force, in whose custody, in view of the continuing hopes of an armistice, it had languished for six months. In May 1952, however, permission was secured for the employment of Task Force 90's Amphibious Construction Battalion, and ComNavFE obtained the approval of CincFE. On 9 June a detachment of 3 officers and 75 men from ACB 1 was landed by LST, and began work under intermittent bombardment from Hodo Pando and Umi Do. The planned 2,400-foot runway had been estimated to be a 45-day project, but the Seabees did better than the planners, and in 16 days the strip was finished. The commanding officer of the construction battalion had predicted that salvage of one plane would more than offset the expense of the project, and if his cost accounting was correct the dividends were enormous: eight Corsairs from Task Force 77, damaged or low on fuel, were brought in safely in July, and in time twin-engined transports would arrive bringing the sinews of war and lady war correspondents. This success stimulated jealousy in the west, where the condition of the emergency beach strip on Paengnyong Do was such as to cause frequent damage in landing, and from the commanding officer of *Badoeng Strait* came a request for the provision of separate but equal facilities.

Along the familiar stretch of coast from Hungnam to Songjin the campaign against the east coast rail line continued. The effort had been simplified, early in the year, with the designation of 16 target areas, 5 of which were to be dealt with initially by carrier air and then kept out by surface gunfire, while the rest were assigned to heavy gun bombardment. As before, the targets were principally bridges, vulnerable tunnel entrances, embankments, and slide areas along the precipitous shore. As previously, the effort was comparatively successful: in the first half of 1952 less traffic passed along this stretch of railroad than along any other line north of Pyongyang-Wonsan. With time, however, and as the employment of Task Force 77 shifted from interdiction to strikes against strategic targets, the responsibility devolved increasingly upon the gunnery ships, while in the interest of economy in ammunition expenditure the shooting up of trains replaced the shooting up of track.

By now, indeed, the interdiction campaign had become the despair of all concerned, and at Air Force headquarters the publicity given the code name "Strangle" was bitterly regretted. Rails could be broken, trains shot up, bridges knocked down, and truck formations harassed, but the enemy continued, largely through night movement, to accumulate supplies in the forward areas. In this situation the inadequacies of U.N. night air capabilities rose again for discussion, and new efforts were undertaken to improve night work.

In May, Task Force 77 put on a series of night attacks, Operation Insomnia, in which six aircraft were launched at midnight and six more at 0200; for a time this tactic permitted unopposed attacks on heavily defended areas; on one occasion 11 locomotives were trapped for later destruction by day strike groups.   By July, in an effort to provide all-night operations without overloading ships' companies, three teams of hecklers were being launched at dusk, of which one worked until midnight while the others landed ashore for later takeoff.   But by autumn the lack of personnel to man key posts on a 24-hour basis, and the view of Commander Seventh Fleet that unless a special night carrier could be provided the emphasis should be on daytime operations, had led to diminished effort.   Owing to the world situation and the shortage of operating carriers no such ship was ever made available, although an abortive attempt was to be made at war's end to do this locally, and the lack of night capabilities remained a major U.N. deficiency.

Through the spring of 1952 Task Force 77 had drifted slowly away from rail interdiction.   Although in March the force was still averaging 133 rail cuts per operating day, increased attention was being given to small boat demolition so as to inhibit attempts to recapture offshore islands.   In April a series of coordinated air-gun strikes on coastal cities was begun: at Chongjin on the 13th, 246 sorties from *Boxer* and *Philippine Sea* deposited 200 tons of bombs while *Saint Paul,* escorted by three destroyers and with spot from the carrier planes, kept up a daylong bombardment.   In May a three-day effort, equally divided between Chongjin and Wonsan and supported by *Iowa,* was conducted in two installments when the original plans were frustrated by sea fog.   But deserving targets were limited, and in June the work of the carrier air groups was shifted inland beyond gun range.

Diminishing and discouraging returns from interdiction and disillusion with the progress at Panmunjom had also led the staff of FEAF to seek alternative employment.   Since the enemy was now amply supplied for offensive action, and since any offensive would bring him into the open and subject him to heavy damage, FEAF's planners proposed to concentrate on maintaining air superiority in MIG Alley while maximizing the cost of war to the other side.   In May, therefore, in a move somewhat parallel to the air-gun strikes by Task Force 77, Fifth Air Force sent large fighter-bomber attacks against concentrations of supplies, facilities, and equipment in the enemy rear.

This attempt to maximize enemy costs inevitably raised the question of the hydroelectric complex, the one important untouched target system in North Korea.   These generating plants and their related distribution facilities had been brought to high development during the period of Japanese occupation.   At Suiho on the Yalu River the world's fourth largest hydroelectric plant, with an output of some 300,000 kilowatts, supplied power both to Korea and Manchuria; up in the mountains, in what had once been X Corps territory, the Chosin, Fusen, and Kyosen Reservoirs together produced an even larger quantity for the cities of the eastern coast. In the summer of 1950 proposals to attack the power complex had very sensibly been turned down on the ground that the bill for reconstruction would fall upon the American taxpayer; subsequently, in the effort to avoid Chinese intervention, the importance of the Suiho plant to Manchurian industry had led these targets to be placed off-limits. But as the armistice negotiations stretched out into 1952 the question was again raised by FEAF, as on a lower level by CTG 95.2, who was desirous of turning off the lights at Wonsan by shooting up the substation.

The timing was appropriate. In late April, in an effort to compose remaining differences at Panmunjom, Admiral Joy had offered to waive restrictions on airfield rehabilitation if the Communists would accept voluntary repatriation of prisoners and the exclusion of the U.S.S.R. from the Neutral Nations Supervisory Commission. But this offer was violently rejected, all progress ceased, and the meetings degenerated into propaganda about POW riots and bacteriological warfare. In this situation, comparable to the period in World War II when water barriers separated the principal belligerents, a turn to attritional bombardment, the slowest of all methods of war, was almost inevitable.

Early in June, FEAF put the proposition up to General Clark, and was given permission to plan the destruction of all hydroelectric plants except Suiho, which was still off-limits without JCS approval. But with the Chinese carrying the burden of the war for the enemy, the earlier rationale had disappeared, and since damage to Suiho offered a method of making trouble in Manchuria without crossing the border, approval from Washington was forthcoming. In Tokyo a date was selected which would permit the maximum carrier contribution and on 18 June FEAF alerted Fifth Air Force for strikes on the 23rd or 24th, weather permitting.

Since late January, four fast carriers had been present in the theater, working in teams of two. For the power plant attacks, arrivals and departures in the operating area were overlapped to provide, for the first time since December 1950, four on station at once. In another way the situation was a reminiscent one, for not since the strikes on the Sinuiju bridges in November of that year had the carrier attack planes crossed Korea to hit targets in MIG Alley. Joint planning between Task Force 77 and Fifth Air Force was begun at JOC on 21 June; on the 22nd flight schedules and ordnance plans were made up and navigational details worked out. The Suiho strike was to be a joint operation in which the carrier pilots had the place of honor; the 1st Marine Aircraft Wing was given the two Chosin installations; the Kyosen plants were assigned to other task force strike groups; those at Fusen were divided between the Navy and Air Force. Since

Suiho, where heavy MIG opposition was expected, was the critical target, the other attacks were timed to follow it by a few minutes.

Early on the 23rd *Boxer* and *Princeton* were joined by *Bon Homme Richard* and *Philippine Sea*. Preparation for the launch was halted when the Air Force put off the strike owing to anticipated adverse weather. But in the course of the day the operation was rescheduled, H-Hour was set for 1600, and at 1410 the force began launching 35 ADs with 4,000 and 5,000-pound bombloads for the Suiho attack. Forming up at 5,000 feet, the Skyraiders crossed the coastline at Mayang Do and then, keeping low to the mountains to avoid radar detection, headed straight for the target. Fifty miles from Suiho they were overhauled by 35 F9Fs which had taken off 50 minutes later. Eighteen miles from the target the group commenced a climb to 10,000 feet, with one jet squadron going up to 16,000 feet as combat air patrol. Two miles from the target a high-speed approach was begun.

At 1600, precisely on schedule, the first squadron of Panthers dove on the gun positions on the Korean bank, closely followed by the ADs and by the other flak-suppression jets. Release altitude was at 3,000 feet and pull-out at 1,000; within a space of two and one half minutes the attacking aircraft delivered 81 tons of bombs. At the power house which was the main target red flames filled the windows, secondary explosions were reported, and photographs taken by the last ADs to drop showed smoke pouring from the roof. The antiaircraft batteries had opened as the attack began, heavy weapons and automatic fire was moderate and machine gun fire intense, but the defenses were overwhelmed. No plane was lost, and the only Skyraider to suffer serious damage made a successful wheels-up landing at Kimpo. Everyone else was back aboard by dinner time.

As the carrier group departed the attack continued with interservice cooperation of a high order. Beginning at 1610, 79 F–84s and 49 F–80s of Fifth Air Force, which had come up from the south to continue the pummeling, added a further 145 tons of bombs. Downstream, between Suiho and Antung, a total of 84 Sabre jets gave top cover against enemy MIGs. But while the Antung field is only 35 miles from Suiho, none of these gentlemen put in an appearance, and of 250 reported on the ground by Air Force pilots, two-thirds disappeared into interior Manchuria during the attack, a tactic for which, on the U.N. side at least, no firm explanation was ever devised.

While the attacks at Suiho were in progress the Chosin plants received the attentions of 75 aircraft from the Marine Aircraft Wing, a second group of 90 planes from Task Force 77 hit the Fusen plants along with 52 Air Force F–51s, and 70 carrier aircraft went in on Kyosen. These efforts were followed up the next day by carrier, Air Force, and Marine attacks on all three complexes, and on 26 and 27 June the Air Force returned to Chosin and Fusen. Then the picture taking and the photo interpretation began, but in North Korea and Manchuria the lights had already gone out.

The results appear to have been first-class. Something in the neighbor-hood of 90 percent of North Korean power production had been disabled; for two weeks there was an almost complete blackout in enemy country; even at year's end a power deficit remained. But if liaison between the Air Force, Navy, and Marines was well nigh perfect, on the upper levels some-one had forgotten to pass the word. The British had not been advised of the contemplated attacks, and in Parliament some ructions developed among the opposition.

Admiral Briscoe had requested a detailed breakdown of the strikes, and ten days later his operational intelligence officer provided it. The extent of the naval contribution revealed by this tally was such as to give ComNavFE cause for pride. Total Task Force 77 sorties against the plants on 23 and 24 June exceeded those of Fifth Air Force and Marines together, as did the weight of bombs dropped. On a service basis breakdown, Navy and Marine sorties were of the order of 700, as compared to some 400 by the Air Force, and Navy and Marine bomb tonnage amounted to more than two-thirds the total. These figures, however, are in a sense delusive, for they take no account of the F–86 top cover provided at Suiho, nor of the later Air Force attacks at Chosin and Fusen. Since FEAF had performed the preliminary planning, and since final preparations had been joint, it seems proper to conclude that all hands had done a good job to excellent purpose.

In the course of the summer of 1952 three more large interservice air oper-ations took place. On 11 July 822 Air Force, Marine, and Navy planes, led by 106 from *Bon Homme Richard* and *Princeton,* struck Pyongyang gun posi-tions, supply and billeting areas, and factories. Although weather prevented the carriers from launching more than one strike group and hindered shore-based operations, the demolition of designated targets was extensive, and encouraging reports were received of direct hits on a Communist brass hat air raid shelter. On 20 August a sizable combined Navy-Marine-Air Force effort was conducted against a large west coast supply area, and nine days later the enemy capital was subjected to the largest air attack of the war.

The seven weeks since the first joint strike on Pyongyang had seen renewed movement of troops and guns into the North Korean capital. To get these targets, as well as to provide food for thought in Moscow where Chou En-lai was conferring with the Soviets, another attack was laid on. On 28 August warning leaflets were scattered over Pyongyang, and on the next day 1,080 aircraft descended on the luckless city. Everyone and his cousin got into the act this time, for in addition to aircraft from Fifth Air Force, Task Force 77, and the Marine Aircraft Wing, the British carrier and the ROK Air Force also took part.

Over and above these cooperative efforts, the work of the fast carriers during the summer consisted principally of maximum-effort strikes against targets in eastern North Korea. These, insofar as possible, were directed against objectives which, like the hydroelectric system, had importance on both sides of the North Korean border. In July strikes against the small Funei complex near Musan, the smallest grid in North Korea, finished off the power plants within the Navy's zone. Late in the month the Sindok lead and zinc mill, reportedly a considerable exporter to Iron Curtain countries, was three-quarters destroyed, and the magnesite and thermoelectric plants at Kilchu heavily damaged by *Princeton* strike groups.

The course of the war by this time had brought a northward displacement of remaining North Korean industrial facilities, and a concentration of new development along the Manchurian and Russian borders. In early August Rear Admiral Herbert E. Regan, ComCarDiv 1, had commented on the build-up of new industry near Aoji in the far northeast, and had urged attack upon these targets. One month later, in response to this request, the Joint Chiefs suspended for a single event their rule against air operations within 12 miles of Soviet territory. On 1 September, in the biggest all-Navy strike yet, morning and afternoon deck loads from *Essex, Boxer,* and *Princeton* went up to the north, and while the jets worked over oil storage and an iron mine at Musan and targets at Hoeamdong, the attack planes destroyed synthetic oil production facilities at Aoji. Other attacks in the far north followed at the border town of Hoeryong, at the Yalu bridge town of Hyesanjin, and on a munitions factory near Najin. On three days in October task force aircraft teamed with B–29s in strikes against North Korean objectives. By winter most known targets had been eliminated.

Taken in connection with the increasing boldness of enemy fighter pilots, the northward movement of carrier operations raised the prospect of collision. On the west coast, during the summer, aircraft from the British carrier and the American CVE had clashed repeatedly with MIGs; during the west coast strike of 20 August *Princeton* F9Fs had an inconclusive skirmish south of Sinanju; on 10 September a Marine flyer had made history by becoming the first pilot of a piston-engined aircraft to shoot down an enemy jet. On 13 September a two-carrier strike against Hoeryong, though unopposed, produced large numbers of bogeys orbiting 50 miles to the eastward over the Siberian border. On the 26th MIGs were sighted over eastern Korea, and in the first week of October two Corsairs were lost in the course of a series of engagements south of Hungnam.

This situation led to some excitement on 18 November as *Kearsarge* and *Oriskany* were again striking Hoeryong. The force was operating in 41°30′, about 100 miles south of Vladivostok, with the cruiser *Helena* and a destroyer on search and rescue station halfway in to Najin. During the morning *Helena* tracked numerous high-speed radar contacts to the northward, which seemed to be flying a barrier patrol under ground control. At 1329 Raid 20, estimated at 16 to 20 aircraft, was approaching from the north, distant 35 miles. This contact or a part of it, estimated at eight aircraft, was also detected by *Oriskany,* and a four-plane division of F9Fs, which had descended to 13,000 feet owing to fuel pump failure in the leader's aircraft, was vectored out with instructions not to engage unless attacked.

Having overshot its mark the patrol was turned back to the southwest while the bogey, in its turn, reversed course to close. At 1336, 45 miles north of the force, Lieutenant E. Royce Williams, leader of the second section, reported seven vapor trails high overhead and identified the aircraft as MIGs. As the jets passed over to the northeast they turned, split, came down below the contrail level, and were lost to sight; ordered upstairs by *Oriskany* controllers, Williams' section of F9Fs reversed course to the northeast and began a full-power climb. Turning again at 26,000 feet, the section leader sighted four aircraft approaching from ahead and to port; as they opened fire he rolled into them in a hard turn, came out to find the trailing MIG in his sights, fired, and saw the adversary smoke and spiral downward.

All seven MIGs had now joined the fray, the two Americans had become separated, and from below a third Panther was climbing to join them. But just as help was arriving Williams' plane was hit: with a MIG on his tail and able to maneuver only by zooming, diving, and popping his brakes, he headed for an undercast ten miles to the southward while his partner, ammunition exhausted, flew wing on the enemy in the hope of scaring him off. Coming out of a turn the pilot from the section below sighted this extraordinary procession and dove toward it, was engaged by another head-on attacker, and after a brief engagement saw a plane going into the water. Far below a flash of silver indicated another target, and he dove, only to find a parachute which he orbited and reported to base.

Williams, by this time, had reached cloud cover. The MIGs had broken off. Return to base was uneventful. But within the force, which was now at general quarters, some tension had apparently developed, for as the section leader brought his cranky plane in over the screen one of the destroyers briefly opened fire on him.

Considering the disparity in aircraft performance and number, and the fact that the Americans allowed themselves to indulge in an uncoordinated melee, the results of the engagement—two MIGs down and one damaged in exchange for damage to one friendly aircraft—were highly gratifying. Control and communications in the force were adjudged good, although with less justification: *Helena*'s attempts to report the approaching raid had been unsuccessful; the effort to fix the parachuting pilot met with no success; two divisions of airborne CAP were not vectored into the fight. For the next hour the force had almost constant radar contacts in the northerly quadrant at ranges down to 40 miles, and at 1510 a slow-speed bogey in the general area of the engagement suggested the presence of a rescue plane. Twice again fighters were vectored out as contacts closed; one sighting was made but the MIGs turned away; by 1625 the screen was clear.

In addition to the strikes against northern industrial areas, some routine attacks on seacoast cities, and a minor continuing interdiction effort, summer and fall of 1952 brought a few operational novelties. In the latter half of July Admiral Soucek took *Philippine Sea* and *Essex* to the Formosa area for air parades over the island and along the China coast, and for some high-altitude photography. In North Korea the expansion of the enemy radar net stimulated efforts by the carrier airmen to locate and demolish these installations. Some experiments were run with guided missiles in the form of war-surplus F6F drones, explosive-laden and guided by television, which were flown against a variety of targets in an inquiring frame of mind. In the west the Yellow Sea carrier took steps to salt up the rice paddies by bombing sluice gates on the Yonan peninsula. In September a new technique of rail interdiction was introduced in which, after a full deckload had beaten up a mile or two of track, a two-plane CAP was employed by day and ship's gunfire by night to inhibit repairs.

Like the earlier interdiction programs, the maximum-effort strikes soon reached the stage of diminishing returns, and with the approach of autumn the activities of Task Force 77 returned gradually to the bombline. No support of ground forces had been provided by the fast carriers in the first six months of 1952. By August, however, an average of 12 sorties a day was being flown in support of X Corps and the ROK I Corps on the eastern front, and with increasing ground action this contribution was to grow. Midsummer had seen some enemy raids, September brought assaults on U.N. outposts and increased artillery expenditure, and with October came the hardest fighting in more than a year. On the 6th the Chinese commenced a week of heavy pressure in the area west of the Iron Triangle, the next day brought 93,000 rounds of artillery and mortar fire into U.N. positions, and the last half of the month saw bitter action in the hills above Kumwha. With these developments what had originally been undertaken as a training exercise gained operational importance, and by October the effort was averaging 22 sorties a day. With the emphasis on support of troops there came again complaints about inadequate control, and the situation was further obfuscated by the development of the so-called Cherokee Strike.

This operation, the brain child of Commander Seventh Fleet, and so christened in celebration of Admiral Clark's descent from that civilized tribe, was developed to fill the vacuum left by the abandonment of interdiction and the elimination of industrial targets. Having observed exposed U.S. supply dumps, and reasoning that the enemy must be similarly vulnerable, Clark, on 5 October, put his main effort on the destruction of supplies, artillery, and troops behind the enemy lines. Four days later, after arrangements with X and IX Corps, 91 aircraft were launched against troop and supply areas just beyond artillery range. They could not have come at a more confusing time.

Ground force discontent with Air Force support procedures had been simmering since the early days of the Korean conflict. Following a request by General Almond in June 1951 for a reexamination of the system, General Van Fleet had attempted to persuade Fifth Air Force to place fighter-bombers under corps control, and had subsequently asked CincFE to explore the advantages of decentralization of air. With the departure of General Ridgway these problems were inherited by his successor, with the result that on 11 August 1952 there appeared a CincFE discussion of air-ground operations in which, at one and the same time, criticism of the system was described as inadequately justified, current doctrine was upheld as sound, and numerous methods of improving matters were put forward, including some non-doctrinal experiments in delegation of control after the Marine fashion. To these proposals, as to Van Fleet's earlier request, the reaction of the Air Force was strongly adverse, and the debate was further complicated by the development of the Cherokee Strike, a method of supporting the battleline which differed from Air Force techniques in that arrangements were made directly with corps, from the Navy and Marine system in being pre-briefed and remote from the line of contact, and from both in being uncontrolled. The touchy question, however, was that of direct negotiation with corps, and there followed a minor eruption.

By November, however, agreed procedures had been worked out which pushed these strikes back beyond the bombline and into the category of deep or general support. From late autumn through January the Cherokee Strikes absorbed more than a third of the Seventh Fleet air effort, concentrated in heavy blows against enemy supplies and equipment. A large bomb tonnage was ferried in, many explosions resulted, and as one carrier division commander observed, the strikes "can't help but be doing a lot of damage." Doubtless not, but target selection and damage assessment were difficult, and any verdict as to the results was largely a matter of faith. It was a strange type of warfare in which naval aviation was now engaged. The close support control system could not handle a large effort in proximity to friendly forces; the enemy's antiaircraft strength made deliberate individual attacks costly; interdiction had been tacitly abandoned by its most ardent protagonists; industrial targets were now notable by their absence. For want of something better to do the carrier air groups were hauling explosives in and dumping them in the general neighborhood of the front. Volume had been substituted for accuracy, and the only indisputable dividends were the approval with which the Army greeted the effort, and the morale boost provided the frontline troops by the noise and smoke which rose from the enemy's back yard.

Elsewhere at sea patrolling, minesweeping, and bombardment continued in arduous but monotonous routine. The number of ships damaged by enemy action diminished from 23 in the first half of 1952 to 19 in the second six months. But in August, for the first time since February 1951, a U.S. ship was lost when *Sarsi,* a fleet tug, was mined and sunk at Hungnam, an event followed by discontinuance of the bombardment unit off this marginal target port. Three weeks later the problem of armed drifters was again emphasized when the destroyer *Barton,* steaming in Task Force 77 some 90 miles east of Wonsan, hit one which blew a five-foot hole in her side, killed five, and wounded seven. No further losses to this agency would be sustained, but with war's end the feeling that the floaters were no accident, strong since the first sightings in September 1950, was confirmed. In contrast to frequent reports of loose mines while fighting was in progress, the five months following the armistice produced but one.

One exception to the tedious routine came in September when HMCS *Nootka* captured an enemy "naval vessel," a 25-foot sampan propelled by oarsmen, which had been laying magnetic mines in the swept channel south of Cho Do. Another, which brought together in momentary reunion the gunnery ships, the Amphibious Force, and the aircraft carriers, was a major amphibious demonstration. Conceptually an outgrowth of "Wrangler," and staged off Kojo in mid-October, this affair was the last and biggest of the war, and stemmed from the suggestion by CTF 90, Rear Admiral Francis X. McInerney, that routine troop movements between Japan and Korea might be employed for training and deception. With approval of the scheme by General Clark, Commander Seventh Fleet was designated Commander Joint Amphibious Task Force 7, and in mid-September planning was begun. Two alternative assault plans were worked up, one for a landing by two divisions in column and one for an attack by a single RCT. The wide discrepancy in scale complicated the paperwork, and as only the highest echelons knew that a bona fide operation was not intended, the troubles of the planners were real. In little over a month, nevertheless, all was in readiness, and the amphibious ships carrying the 8th Cavalry Regiment sortied from Hokkaido. On 12 October, D minus 3, a rehearsal was carried out at Kangnung, hampered by winds of 25 knots which led to the loss of four LCVPs after broaching on the beach.

While the rehearsal was going on, the Advance Force, similarly handicapped, appeared off Kojo to sweep and to bombard. One battleship, two heavy cruisers, and a batch of destroyers worked over the landing area; four fast carriers operating in the Sea of Japan provided air strikes, including a remarkable 667 sorties on D minus 3; *Sicily* and *Badoeng Strait* were both on hand, the former for air spot while the latter, as Hunter-Killer carrier, cruised the area in search of submarines and briefly thought she found one.

By this time the demonstration had become an interservice affair. FEAF and Fifth Air Force stepped up their operations, a mock parachute landing was set up, and on the night of 13–14 October Eighth Army launched a two-battalion attack near Kumwha. By dawn of D-Day, the 15th, more than a hundred ships were off the Kojo beaches, and control procedures were getting a serious test. The aerologists, however, had already failed theirs, for the weather had continued to degenerate: poor visibility and low clouds delayed the bombardment, while winds freshening to 50 knots kicked up high seas. At 1400, nevertheless, seven waves of landing craft were sent in from the transport area to pass the line of departure and then retire seaward. Owing to the heavy seas no troops were boated; owing to the skill of the coxswains no boats were lost or seriously damaged. But two mine-sweepers had been hit by shore fire and five carrier planes lost to antiaircraft.

So ended what some proclaimed to have been the largest-scale fraud in military history. Again a deception ended with a question as to who had been deceived. No troop movements of magnitude had been detected ashore, although in the weeks that followed some shifts were noted in the Kojo-Wonsan area. What was certain, however, was that most of the participants had been fooled, and when the true nature of the operation became known some were very angry. The feeling that at last the war was getting off dead center had produced a tension and degree of effort that made the let-down in morale the greater, and one carrier commanding officer strongly protested the internal secrecy which had led his pilots to take risks of a sort appropriate to a landing but not to an exercise. Of Kojo, as of earlier and smaller demonstrations, it seems proper to conclude that an enemy incapable of quick response cannot be very profitably hoaxed.

The Kojo feint had been planned prior to the enemy's October pressure, on which, indeed, it had little apparent effect. But this Communist ground activity proved both limited and temporary, and the war continued much as before. Since in the circumstances of the fighting in Korea neither side could inflict unacceptable damage upon the other, the locus of decision had long since come to lie elsewhere. At Panmunjom, following a summer of deadlock, the U.N. negotiators had declared the meetings indefinitely recessed. At the United Nations, efforts to break the stalemate were renewed, and the Indian government busied itself with the attempt to provide the Communists with a face-saving solution to their prisoner of war problem. In the United States an election campaign was underway which interacted with the campaign in Korea: in America the Republican candidate undertook to visit the scene of action; in the Far East electioneering seems to have motivated the enemy's autumn effort. In addition to heavy fighting in the area of the Iron Triangle, September and October brought an increase in incidents around the periphery, in a rash of antiaircraft actions between Chinese gunboats and Navy patrol planes in Formosa Strait, and in the loss of a B-29 to Soviet fighters off Hokkaido. But following election day the pressure decreased rapidly, and the record 93,000 rounds of artillery fired on 7 October had a month later diminished to a mere trickle.

In the United States the elections of November were followed by a change of administration in January. In the next month President Eisenhower "unleashed" Chiang Kai-shek, a measure of very limited effect on the Formosan situation and on the operations of the Formosa Patrol. No similar change took place in Korean policy, which remained one of willingness to settle on almost any basis that would not require forced repatriation. But as all other possible concessions had long since been made, deadlock continued, and again it was made clear that while one side can start a war it takes two to make a bargain. Progress toward such a bargain remained impossible pending another change in administration, which took place on 5 March 1953 with the death of Joseph Stalin.

3. March–July 1953: Progress, Crisis, Conclusion

Not since the war with Tripoli, a century and a half before, when year after passing year Dale and Morris and Preble maneuvered their squadrons off that other distant shore, blockading and bombarding an enemy they could not reach, had Americans fought a war like this. And as 1953 began, and stalemate still continued, it seemed increasingly possible that this war would outlast that one. In February, however, General Clark moved to break the jam on the repatriation question by proposing an immediate exchange of sick and wounded personnel. The answer was delayed, doubtless owing to difficulties in Moscow concerning the devolution of power, and the interval between letter and reply was marked by heavier than usual enemy pressure. But on 28 March an answer was received which both accepted the proposal and indicated a disposition to proceed further.

The enemy's March doings produced an increasing effort in troop support, both by the West Coast Carrier Element and by Task Force 77. There were, of course, diversions: *Oriskany* in mid-March put on a big effort against a mining complex up-country from Songjin; on the night of the 27th three volunteer Corsair pilots made a moonlight attack on the Hamhung highway bridge, one of the most heavily defended targets in Korea, and dropped the center span before the enemy could open fire; the Wonsan batteries, the city of Songjin, some residual power plant targets, and a number of militarized villages also received attention. Pilot morale was boosted by a strike on a North Korean rest camp, which reportedly accommodated heroes of the Communist forces credited with shooting down U.N. planes, and by the accomplishment of two night hecklers who chased two trains into opposite ends of a short and single-tracked tunnel, to be rewarded by gratifying amounts of steam from both entrances. A pleasant custom, instituted early in the year, involved the rotation of one carrier at a time to Hong Kong, to provide both a show of force to the southward and a new liberty port.

Late in April the force celebrated Boy-San Day, on which the airplane drivers picked their own targets without interference from higher authority.

Nevertheless the emphasis was on the bombline. In March almost half the offensive sorties were assigned to Cherokee Strikes and troop support, and while this figure dropped in early April it subsequently rose again. Repetition of Cherokee Strikes against the same area over a period of days was now the custom, a measure felt both to limit the effectiveness of anti-aircraft and to result in greater destruction of targets. As always, damage assessment remained the problem, but POWs reported results in excess of the pilots' estimates and Eighth Army officers were high in their praise.

For the Amphibious Force the early months of 1953 were occupied by routine training exercises, minor troop lifts, and logistic support work. For the gunnery ships, however, as for the soldiers in the line, March and April brought increased action. The number of mines encountered rose radically, from 14 in March to 31 in April, and as usual most were floaters. Increased artillery fire directed against the minesweepers required special attention to the employment and positioning of gunfire support ships. Interdiction of train traffic along the eastern shore continued. Off the bombline, destroyers and heavy ships continued to keep the enemy down and, through their ability to fire upon him from the rear, forced him to keep his targets defiladed both from artillery and from the sea. But the principal problem of the spring months was the need to keep the duty heavy cruiser or battleship on notice at all times for immediate movement to Wonsan.

There pressure against the harbor islands continued to increase. In December a CincPacFleet appreciation had foreseen a Communist attempt to recapture these positions, and this prospect was emphasized by the events of early spring. The record 523 rounds which fell upon the islands in March doubled in April, while another 553 were aimed at U.N. ships. The volume did not compare with the Battle of the Buzz Saw, but accuracy was up: from March through May five destroyers and the cruisers *Los Angeles* and *Bremerton* were hit, and casualties were incurred both by their crews and by the island garrisons.

In the west the situation was similar. The two rounds fired at Cho Do and Sok To in February by the Wolsa-ri and Amgak batteries, and the 16 rounds of March, increased in April to 440, while ships of the blockading force observed more work in progress on the Wolsa-ri cliff positions. Small-caliber counterbattery fire remained of slight effect; a strike from *Glory* and a series of Air Force sorties accomplished little more; and a moonlight attempt by the frigate *Cardigan Bay* to eliminate the guns after closing to within 1,000 yards of the shore proved unsuccessful.

These events brought further reconsideration of the island problem. At Wonsan the commanding officer of *Saint Paul* recommended an invasion of Hodo Pando, to eliminate the threat of gunfire from the north. At Cho

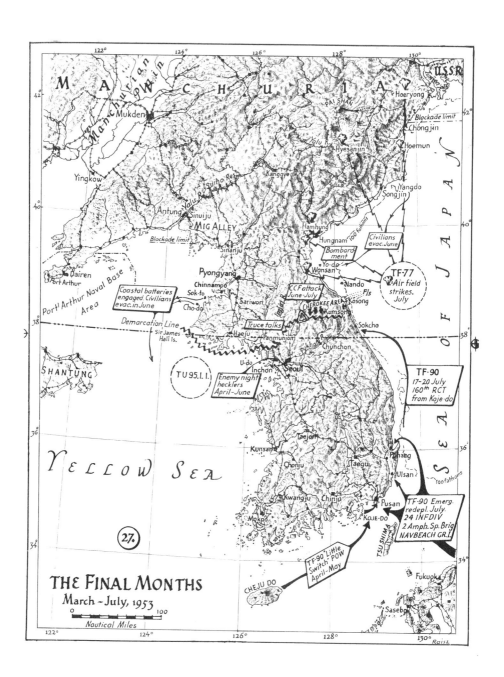

M A N C H U R I A

U.S.S.R.

PAI SHAN

Hoeryong

Blockade limit

Chongjin

Hoemun

Mukden

Yingkow

Kanggye

Yangdo
Songjin

Antung

Sinuiju

MIG ALLEY

Hamhung

Civilians
evac. June

TF-77
Air field
strikes.
July

Sinanju

Hungnam

Bombard-
ment

Wonsan

Yo-do

Pyongyang

Chinnampo

Sok-to

Sariwon

CC F attack
June-July

Nando

Kosong

Fls

Dairen

Port Arthur

Port Arthur Naval Base
Area

Coastal batteries
engaged. Civilians
evac. in June

Cho-do

CHEROKEE AREA

Kumsong

Demarcation Line

Sir James
Hall Is.

Truce talks

Haeju

Panmunjom

Pukhan

Chunchon

Sokcho

38°

S H A N T U N G

TU 95.I.I.

Enemy night
hecklers
April-June

U-do

Inchon

Seoul

TF-90
17-20 July
160th RCT
from Koje-do

Y E L L O W   S E A

Kunsan

Taejon

Chonju

Taegu

Pohang

Ulsan

100 fathoms

27.

Kwangju

Chinju

Pusan

TF-90 Emerg.
redepl. July.
24 INFDIV
2 Amph. Sp. Brig
NAVBEACH GR.I.

Mokpo

KOJE-DO

TSU SHIMA

THE FINAL MONTHS

March – July, 1953

0   100
Nautical Miles

CHEJU DO

TF-90 Little
Switch POW
April-May

Fukuoka

Sasebo

Raisz

SEA OF JAPAN

Do the commanding officer of *Cardigan Bay,* fearing that the Wolsa-ri batteries might force abandonment of the anchorage and relocation of the island's radar station, suggested a raid to seize the peninsula for 24 hours while guns were spiked and gun positions destroyed. Neither suggestion was approved by higher authority, but taken in conjunction with a proposal by CTF 95 to abandon Yang Do in the northeast, on the ground that the defensive investment was out of proportion to the profit from intelligence activities, they indicate the imminence of a crisis. But for whatever reasons the crisis never quite came.

On the west coast, April bombardments by the British cruisers *Newcastle* and *Birmingham* knocked down chunks of the Wolsa-ri cliffs and silenced the guns for a month, but the Amgak batteries overlooking Sok To continued lively. To counter this pressure 90-millimeter guns were brought in and emplaced on Sok To and on Cho Do, and in late May *New Jersey* was sailed around from the east coast to bombard. At Wonsan Communist artillery remained active, and with the coming of an enemy ground offensive in June the bombardment ships found themselves extremely busy. Between the bombline and Wonsan harbor ruts were worn in the sea, as the heavy ships steamed back and forth in response to emergency calls. Gun strikes by *New Jersey* and *Bremerton* in May were followed up in June by *Saint Paul* and *Manchester;* and although for a time it seemed that the destroyers might be driven out, the position was maintained. On both coasts, at the end of June, enemy harassment of the island footholds markedly declined.

For the islands, in any event, the days of U.N. occupation were numbered by the approaching armistice. The resumption of plenary sessions on 26 April, which followed the exchange of sick and wounded prisoners and ended a recess of 199 days, ushered in a period of progress which, in comparison with what preceded, could only be described as extremely rapid. By 8 June the thorny question of repatriation had been settled and hopes again rose high.

Since the armistice would prohibit further removal of the inhabitants of the northern islands, CincFE on 12 June directed the outloading of all civilians and all excess supplies from the Wonsan islands and from Yang Do. On the west coast, following the updating of plans, the evacuation of partisan forces, their dependents, and other refugees from islands north of the parallel was begun. In the east the dimensions of the problem were small, but in the Yellow Sea this last tragic displacement brought the departure, after their cattle had been slaughtered and their dwellings razed, of 19,425 persons from the islands above the demarcation line.

Although the line mapped and agreed to in November 1951 remained acceptable to the United Nations Command, the Communists insisted on renegotiation. Reasons for this attitude had for some time been evident in continued enemy troop and vehicle movement and in ostentatious stockpiling of supplies, and on 10 June anticipations were fulfilled as a heavy attack was pushed down the valley of the upper Pukhan against the ROK II Corps. The local collapse which followed required a considerable reshuffling of units on the part of Lieutenant General Maxwell D. Taylor, USA, who in February had relieved General Van Fleet at Eighth Army. But by the 18th the front had been stabilized, at the cost of a few miles of inhospitable terrain above the Hwachon Reservoir and of a little ground on the east coast. As the Chinese impetus declined hopes rose again, only to be dashed by an entirely unexpected development.

At Panmunjom General Harrison and his aides had for months been walking the knife edge between Communist obduracy and South Korean intransigence. Chinese and North Korean disinclination to admit reluctance on the part of their nationals to return to the Communist paradise found its counterpart in the unwillingness of the Rhee government to accept any armistice at all and so forego the last chance of forcible Korean unification. The signing on 8 June of the final agreement on repatriation had been followed by threats and fulminations from the ROK government, and by a period of tension in its relations with the U.N. Command.

In this crisis President Rhee found himself in a strong position. Not only did he control the territory of South Korea, the theater of U.N. operations, but he also controlled, in the ROK Army, the largest single contingent of anti-Communist forces, well-trained, well-equipped, 15 divisions strong, and manning two-thirds of the battleline. Given his fierce opposition to an armistice, the possibility that he might order these forces to attack, independently and in defiance of the U.N. Command, raised the specter of a three-cornered conflict within the peninsula, and of a situation of almost unimaginable complexity.

This he did not do, but on 18 June, without warning and despite prior assurances, the Korean government engineered a mass escape of upwards of 25,000 anti-Communist prisoners, in the apparent hope of causing a Communist break-off of negotiations. The result was an interruption of plenary sessions at Panmunjom, an embarrassing period of Communist harangues, uncertainty as to the security of U.N. forces in Korea, and apprehension as to what might happen next. Again, as on the outbreak of war three summers before, more strength was urgently needed. Again help came by sea.

To the normal commitments of Task Force 90, spring had added a variety of tasks. In April the exchange of sick and wounded prisoners had been carried out; in May two landing exercises had been held, beach surveys continued, preparations for island evacuation begun, and a lift of LCVPs made to the French in Indo-China, where another war was in progress and where, a year later, another demarcation line would be drawn. These responsibilities were increased in June as the result of floods in southern Japan, which imposed requirements for evacuation, relief, and for shipping to replace disrupted land communications. At the same time the apparent imminence of the armistice made it necessary to be ready on short notice to repatriate large numbers of enemy prisoners.

In preparation for the movement of almost 100,000 enemy personnel, a task group of 2 APAs, 6 AKAs, 20 LSTs, and minor units had been assembled, although at the cost of delaying the scheduled return of a number to the United States. On 12 June Task Force 90 was alerted for this operation, all units were placed on 24-hour notice, and ships were ordered to Pusan for installation of wood and wire cribbing which would permit the movement of fractious prisoners in manageable groups. Eleven LSTs and one AKA had been fitted with these cribs when there arose the wholly new requirement of a major emergency troop movement.

On 21 June, three days after the ROK release of prisoners, CincFE ordered the immediate airlift of the 187th Airborne RCT to Korea; two days later 2,100 soldiers and 1,500 tons of gear had been flown in by the Air Force and three LSTs and two LSMs were bringing in the heavy equipment. On the 26th orders were received to lift the equipment of one RCT of the 24th Infantry Division from Japan to Korea; shortly CincFE alerted the entire division for movement by air and sea; by 2 July some 4,000 troops had been flown across, other units had been added to the planned movement, and the emphasis had shifted from air to surface transport. In anticipation of instructions to redeploy the division, Rear Admiral Walter E. Moore, CTF 90, now ordered the removal of security cribs from his amphibious shipping; on 3 July, following receipt of orders, he dispatched three task units to Japanese embarkation ports.

These operations coincided with the centenary of a memorable event, for it was in July 1853 that Commodore Perry had entered Tokyo Bay to attempt the opening of Japan. For the Black Ships Festival, staged by the Japanese in celebration of the anniversary, Task Force 90 dispatched an AKA to Shimoda, long the residence of Townsend Harris, first American consul in Japan, and an APD to Kurihama, where Perry first set foot on Japanese soil. But even this limited representation was hard to spare, for the 14th of July, the centenary of Perry's reception at Kurihama by the Prince of Idzu and the Prince of Iwami, found his descendants in the gray ships of the Amphibious Force working under heavy pressure.

The movement of the 24th Division, so suddenly called for, required not only the diversion of all available amphibious shipping but the requisitioning of LSTs and cargo ships from MSTS; numerous modifications to CincFE's plan had brought confusion and a communications overload; weather and the lack of adequate harbor facilities forced some extemporization in loading; at one port difficulties with Japanese customs officials bizarrely delayed embarkation. By 9 July, nevertheless, one RCT was in Korea and the others were loading, when suddenly the situation was complicated by a whole new series of directives.

The double requirements of the Korean crisis and of the impending armistice, with its prohibition of further reinforcement, now produced an eruption of orders from Supreme Headquarters. On 13 July CTF 90 was instructed to transport the Army's 2nd Amphibious Support Brigade, an amphibious tank battalion, and elements of Naval Beach Group 1 from Japan to Korea. Two days later, as embarkation of these units was beginning, came orders for the movement of a regiment from Pusan to Koje Do. On the 16th, as this lift was commenced, as the last elements of the 24th Division were sailing for Korea, and as loading of other units was continuing in Japan, transfer of a second regiment from Koje up the coast to Sokcho was ordered. On the 17th there came an emergency call to move a battalion from Cheju Do to Inchon, and on the next day, to complete this planner's nightmare, there arose the possibility of further redeployment of elements of the 24th Division.

One day before the anniversary of Perry's landing, and while these hasty maritime movements were in progress, the Chinese attacked again, in greater strength than in the month before. Whether this second blow had been long planned, and coordinated with peace table procrastination, or whether it was an afterthought intended to chastise a belligerent Syngman Rhee remained obscure. Again the blow fell on ROK forces, this time in the area south of Kumsong and just west of the June breakthrough, where four divisions were thrown against the junction of IX Corps and the ROK II Corps. Again there came collapse, followed by the development of a fluid situation and accompanied by pressure on the east coast strip. In response to the new emergency General Taylor moved two American divisions into the gap and brought reinforcements forward from Pusan; by 17 July U.N. forces were counterattacking; by the 20th some lost ground had been regained and a new line established which would be held until the armistice. Again some miles of mountain territory had been given up, again Chinese casualties were thought to have been extremely heavy. But the weight of the attack and the temporary disorder which ensued had brought a final period of frantic activity on land, at sea, and in the air.

Fire support off the eastern shore had been stepped up in early June when Communist seizure of Anchor Hill, a key ROK position south of Kosong, ushered in a period of heavy fighting. Two destroyers and the heavy cruiser *Saint Paul* were busily at work, and *New Jersey* was sent in to provide, for the first time since February, 16-inch gunfire at the bombline. Although the war against the railroad continued, as did the operations at Wonsan, the center of action in the final weeks was at the battleline, where one destroyer remained permanently on station, backed up for

13 days by *New Jersey,* and at other times by *Manchester, Bremerton,* or *Saint Paul.* Ammunition expenditure off the bombline in July totalled more than 6,000 rounds.

So, as the end approached, the gunnery forces on the eastern shore were back where they had been at the beginning, and the task that fell upon Rear Admiral Clarence E. Olsen, CTF 95 for the last five months of the war, was the task that had faced Admiral Higgins. The emphasis on interdiction of supply and transportation, strong during the period of stalemate, had given way at the last to the requirement of again supporting ROK forces on the coastal road.

For the naval aviators, as well, a cycle had been completed, and war's end found them back at the job that had once confronted *Valley Forge* and *Triumph.* Again the enemy was attacking; again the carriers, now four *Essex*-class ships plus a light unit in the Yellow Sea, were supporting the ground armies under the control of JOC. Some differences had indeed come with the passage of time: representation at JOC had been institutionalized and communications improved; movement from coast to coast and retirement for replenishment had long since been given up; the risks of air and submarine attack had been accepted, the advantages of mobility and surprise forgone, and the force, with its replenishment ships, was operating as a permanent air base in $39°N$ $129°E$.

Upon this air base, upon its flying personnel, and upon the Logistic Support Force, the events of the final weeks imposed severe demands. Early in June Eighth Army called for 48 close support sorties a day, and for a large additional effort in Cherokee Strikes. On the 6th orders were received to put the entire piston-engined effort into the support of ground forces, while dividing the jets between Cherokee Strikes, road sweeps, and reconnaissance. Late in the month the lull between Communist attacks brought a limited revival of interdiction, but on 14 July Commander Seventh Fleet put all propeller planes back into support of the armies. In the last five days three very large raids were made against seven enemy airfields in the eastern half of North Korea.

With this final period of emergency there developed the most intense flight operations of the war. On 11 June, the day after the opening of the first Communist offensive, *Princeton* joined *Philippine Sea* and *Boxer* on the line, and two days later *Lake Champlain,* fresh from the Atlantic Fleet, reached the operating area. Four-carrier operations were continued through the 19th, and three carriers were kept on station until the 27th. On 14 July, with the second enemy breakthrough, a third carrier joined the force, and on the 17th the fourth, and so it continued until the end of the war.

Flight operations were hindered by the usual weather difficulties of the Korean summer. In the interior mountains the monsoonal air masses condensed into heavy fog and rain; at sea, fog and low overcast prevailed.

For Task Force 77 the period was marked by a continuous search for clear areas, and by the conduct of full-scale operations with ceilings down to 100 feet and visibility of only a mile and a half. Despite this remarkable performance a large proportion of scheduled sorties was weathered out; despite these cancellations new marks for carrier operations were repeatedly set. The June record of 554 sorties flown on the 13th went by the board in July, with 592, 600, and 746 on three successive days. Total sorties rose steadily from 4,343 in May to 6,423 in July; close support sorties went up from 256 to 1,690; aircraft ordnance delivery rose from 2,835 tons in May to 4,606 in the final month.

So massive an offensive called for hard work from all hands, and for an heroic effort on the part of the Logistic Support Force. On 9 June fueling days were abolished, and from that date nightly replenishment, carried out in a mixture of fog and darkness that often required the use of towing spars and searchlights, continued to the end of hostilities. Owing to the coming of the jet airplane and to the increased bomb-carrying capacity of carrier attack planes, the requirements far exceeded anything accomplished or even contemplated in World War II. The increased expenditure of ordnance strained the capabilities of the ammunition ships; the consumption of aviation gasoline, which for a time reached 9,000 barrels a day, forced the recall of an oiler from other scheduled operations. Yet somehow all needs were met.

On men and machinery alike the strain of these final weeks began to tell, until as time went on bad weather came to seem almost a godsend. For the aviators the working day was a long one: good weather or bad, flying or not, they were on the alert and under strain; when the weather was operational the average jet pilot spent some four hours flying and another five in preparation, while propeller-plane pilots were airborne almost seven hours a day. When twilight brought an end to the long flight schedule it was time to go alongside the waiting replenishment ships, pass lines and hoses, and fuel and load far into the night. Here the immediate impact was on the ships' companies, who after arduous days had to manhandle and stow large quantities of stores and ammunition, but the pilots suffered too, their sleep disturbed by the clanking of handling machinery on the hangar deck.

Under such pressure, maintenance suffered and gear began to fail. Electronic equipment became temperamental, *Lake Champlain* experienced breakdown of both catapults, *Princeton* was out for a few days with shaft vibrations, and *Philippine Sea* had similar troubles. These casualties to her sister ships made it necessary to hold *Boxer* on the line long after her scheduled date of departure, with the result that on 23 July she set a new fleet record with her 61,000th landing.

In this situation something had to give, and what gave was a plan for intensified night work which had been developed in May. At long last it had seemed possible to put air operations on a 24-hour basis, by transferring all night-configured aircraft to *Princeton* and providing her with a small screen for independent night operations. But the May casualty to her shafts forced postponement of the scheme, and the subsequent need for maximum effort prevented the assignment of a carrier to night work only. So heavy, indeed, was the daytime schedule, that ordinary night heckling was first diminished and then discontinued, and the hours of darkness were conceded to the enemy.

Nevertheless night brought one triumph. Beginning in April the Communists had cast further doubt upon the virtues of modern design by the employment of fabric-covered training planes—Po-2 biplanes, or Yak-18 monoplanes—in a series of night air raids against the Inchon-Kimpo-Seoul area. Employed either singly or in masses of a half-dozen or so, these ancient 80-knot floaters, too low for antiaircraft fire and too slow for jet interceptors, for two months flew with impunity through the interstices of the air defense organization, damaging parked aircraft, burning a fuel dump, shaking up the residences of the President of Korea and of the gentlemen of the press, and causing generalized confusion and frustration. But in June a detachment of Corsair night fighters was sent in from the fleet, and within a month Lieutenant Guy P. Bordelon had disposed of five of the intruders, to become not only the first ace in this particular category but the Navy's only ace of the Korean War.

The enemy offensive of June and July gave the close support control system its first real test since the beginning of the stalemate. As before, the system of pre-planning strikes proved useless in emergency; as before, requests for help could not be promptly answered. Although communications capacity far exceeded that of 1950, this improvement was more than offset by the vastly increased sortie capability: the close support request net clogged almost at once, and despite resort to extemporized and non-doctrinal direct communications, strikes followed requests by as much as 17 hours. Again, as in the summer of 1950, the control system collapsed as JOC duty officers, remote from the situation but wishing to help, rammed aircraft in large numbers into the threatened sectors. Once more the lack of forward air controllers below the regimental level put the main responsibility on the Mosquitos which, in the fluid situation, once more demonstrated their inability to keep track of friendly positions and important targets. Inevitably, therefore, rather than hitting troops in the open and on the move, close support and Cherokee Strikes attacked supply and billeting areas, gun positions, and trenches, and much waste ensued through jettisoning of ordnance.

These difficulties, experienced for the first time by the personnel involved, although not for the first time in Korea, were compounded by the adverse weather. Large-scale Cherokee operations, sufficiently problematical in themselves, were forced by reduced visibility to operate under ground radar control. In June 577 sorties, some 30 percent of Task Force 77's support effort, were so employed, bombing in level flight from altitudes between 10,000 and 15,000 feet, and by July this was the rule rather than the exception. In their turn the radar facilities became overloaded, and many flights had to be diverted to secondary targets, or directed to dump their loads somewhere north of the bombline.

This situation, which would have scandalized the explosive Ewen, surprisingly seems to have brought little complaint from Navy commanders. A year on interdiction had been followed by a time of only token close support, and this, taken with the rotation of carrier and air group personnel, had permitted interests to change and skills to wither. With strike results unavailable or unassessable, the magnitude of the effort tended to be emphasized, and maximum support of Eighth Army became a trucking operation in which, as often before in air warfare, statistics of sorties flown and ordnance dropped acted to conceal the central question of whether the drops hit anything worthwhile.

Only the Marines still chafed under a system, incapable of effective operation in the fluid situations where it was most necessary, whose failures were then used to support the doctrinal position that close support was an uneconomic use of air strength. But this chafing was largely theoretical. No very heavy attacks were thrown against the division which, with the bulk of its support supplied by the Marine Aircraft Wing and controlled at battalion level, found itself in a reasonably satisfactory situation, and good use was made of the final months in working out techniques for searchlight-directed night close air support.

For the Wing, too, the situation was improved. Relations between the Marine liaison officers and their Air Force colleagues at JOC had become exceptionally harmonious, and in February the Commanding General had at last regained operational control of his own squadrons. But the Marines' final views on the Korean situation made no bones about the inadequacy of prevailing concepts, the inferior quality of close support rendered the armies, and the unwieldy, inflexible, and unsatisfactory methods of control which resulted from over-centralization, inadequate communications, and the lack of forward ground controllers. Still, the Marine Aircraft Wing had done its best, and if it had been unable to make experience prevail over theory, it had solid accomplishments to show. Throughout the war the Army had demonstrated its great appreciation of such Marine support as it could get; Marine night fighters had proven in certain respects superior to all others in the theater; a Marine pilot on exchange duty with the Air Force had become a jet ace; following the armistice the MAG 12 softball team became the champions of the Fifth Air Force and subsequently, disguised in Air

Force uniforms, went onward and upward to become FEAF champions in September.

So, with the emergencies of the final weeks, the war had come full circle, and the ships and aircraft of Naval Forces Far East were back at the tasks of 1950. Within the naval service at large another cycle was also ending. In the expansion of the past three years, priority had been given the operating forces; the shore establishment had remained undermanned, and ComNavFE had long been hoping for an increased allowance of personnel. But here the truth expounded by Clausewitz, that war is but the extension of politics, was once again brought home. As the Chinese were mounting their last offensives, proposals were being made in Congress for reduction of the armed forces, and a May dispatch from CNO had directed a 10 percent reduction in complement for shore activities.

But at last the end was at hand. On 19 July, with the halting of their final offensive, the Communists again evinced a willingness for progress, and on the morning of the 27th the armistice was signed to take effect that evening. The final line of contact ran from west of the Imjin River northeastward through the Iron Triangle, east to the headwaters of the Soyang River, and thence northerly to the coast below Kosong. On both shores, according to the agreement, islands beyond the demarcation line were to be evacuated by the U.N., with the exception of Paengnyong Do and the others of the Sir James Hall Group, and of Yonpyong Do and U Do off the mouth of Haeju Man.

For Task Force 77 the final day involved strikes on northern airfields; at Wonsan *Bremerton* and *Saint Paul* fired the last missions; the Amphibious Force busied itself in preparation for the repatriation of prisoners. At 2200, as the troops came out of their holes across the Korean peninsula, the ships in Wonsan harbor turned on their lights. On the harbor islands, on Yang Do and Nan Do in the east, and on Cho Do and Sok To in the west, the garrisons began to demolish their installations and pack their bags. Three years, one month, and two days after the North Korean People's Army had burst south across the parallel the war was over. Aggression had been repelled; Korea, like the rest of the world, remained divided.

If armistice there was, it was an uncertain one. Communist violation of provisions regarding reinforcement commenced almost at once; beyond the demarcation line the Neutral Nations Supervisory Committee was frustrated in its activities; men's lives were still at hazard. Up by the Yalu on the last day of action an Air Force fighter pilot had destroyed a twin-engined transport. The aircraft turned out to have been Russian; the event shortly produced a diplomatic protest, and still more quickly a reaction in another sphere. At 0615 on the 29th an Air Force RB-50, flying an easterly heading over the Sea of Japan, was shot down by Soviet MIGs some 30 miles south

The long siege: 28 months after she started the siege of the city, Manchester engages enemy batteries at Wonsan. The island is Hwangto Do. June 1953. (USN 483203)

of Cape Povorotnyy. All but one of the crew parachuted into the sea, where during the afternoon several were sighted by low-altitude search planes, as were a number of Soviet ships and aircraft. In the afternoon Navy assistance was requested, and at 1745 Task Force 77 launched 13 aircraft to search to the northeast. At 1900 rescue ships were called for and a force composed of *Bremerton* and five destroyers headed north at speed. At 0300, as this group was approaching the area where survivors had been sighted, two night fighters were sent up from the carriers, to be followed by other aircraft throughout the day. Spread out in scouting line and with a helicopter on each flank, *Bremerton* and the destroyers swept the waters off the Russian doorstep throughout the 30th, covering an area of 3,300 square miles. But despite all efforts only a single survivor could be found.

So ended in a shaky truce America's first 20th-century war for limited objectives. To some in the armed services, Army, Navy, and Air Force alike, this ending, with little permanently resolved, was less than satisfactory. Something seemed to have been forgone when truce negotiations with a beaten enemy had been commenced; the repeated concessions at Panmunjom had appeared unnecessary; and while none, perhaps, could satisfactorily define the victory he would have liked to gain, the Communist employment of negotiations as a shield for reinforcement and a forum for vituperation seemed infinitely repugnant.

But for this too there was a precedent. To the first John Rodgers, the peace of 1805 which ended the war with Tripoli was so distasteful that he offered to ransom the prisoners with funds raised from the officers of the squadron, if only the war could go on. Yet it may be that such an attitude, whether in Korea or in Tripoli, reflects an excessive emphasis upon the paper provisions of a settlement and an underestimation of the more substantial factors which govern the relations among nations. Unsatisfactory the Treaty of 1805 may well have been, but throughout the 19th century the United States maintained, in its Mediterranean Squadron, a body of armed force appropriate to the situation, and little more was heard from the Bashaw of Tripoli.

A Note on Source Materials

THIS ACCOUNT of the Korean War is based largely on official records of the U.S. Navy, supplemented by those of the other armed forces and by published material. The most important sources are discussed below; there then follows a listing by chapter and section of items of particular relevance to any given phase of the campaign.

By all odds the most important single source for the history of naval operations in Korea is the series of six Commander in Chief, U.S. Pacific Fleet, "Interim Evaluation Reports," the product of an unprecedented effort in large-scale concurrent evaluation of naval operations. This project was conceived by Rear Admiral Ralph A. Ofstie in August, 1950; recruitment of personnel had commenced by early September, while U.N. forces were still struggling to hold the Pusan perimeter; the evaluation group was officially constituted by an order of 20 September from the Chief of Naval Operations to the Commander in Chief Pacific Fleet; by mid-October the group was at work in the Western Pacific under the direction of Rear Admiral Lucian A. Moebus.

Admiral Sherman's letter had directed CincPacFleet to conduct a continuing evaluation of combat techniques, weapons employment, and logistics; to submit conclusions and recommendations for current training and operations or for desirable new developments; and to prepare an analysis and record of naval and Marine combat operations. More specifically, the evaluation group was directed to concern itself with all types of air operations, antisubmarine warfare, blockade and escort work, gunfire support, amphibious operations, joint aspects of ground warfare, and logistic matters.

This was a large order. Interpreting this directive, Admiral Moebus' group set itself the task of recording in detail the happenings within the various operational and administrative commands, of identifying the various difficulties and problems as well as the successes which developed, and of undertaking detailed staff studies of functional components of the Navy and of naval weapons systems with a view to recommendations for improvement. The first result of its efforts, "Interim Evaluation Report No. 1," covering the period from 25 June to 15 November 1950, was completed in early 1951, and was described by Admiral Moebus as "awesome in size." So it was, ex-

461

tending to 3,292 pages, with 928 pages of project studies on various forms of naval action supported by more than twice that amount of narrative annexes from both operational and administrative commands. The results were doubly fortunate: without the prodding of the evaluation group it seems certain that much of the record of the early days of crisis would have never been set down; as a result of the wide net cast by the CNO directive, much material was included for which the normal naval reporting system makes no provision. Special note, in this connection, should be taken of the annexes to the first Report which deal with the operations of Commander Air Force Pacific Fleet, Commander Service Force Pacific Fleet, Commander Western Sea Frontier, the various Pacific MSTS offices, and the Marine Corps administrative commands, without which the narrative of the assembly and movement of force, so central to the entire campaign, would be almost impossible to develop.

The second Evaluation Report, covering the period from 16 November 1950 to 30 April 1951, was also sizable, but the format was considerably changed. Here the chronological narratives of the various commands have disappeared, to be replaced by extensive excerpts from action reports and from various special studies (notably of close air support and interdiction) by sundry groups and boards within the several services. By this expedient the work was reduced to 1,874 pages. By the time of the third Report, routine had been well established, procedures had been institutionalized, and from this time on the product, while still of first importance, becomes less interesting to the historian. But then, of course, so does the war. The end product of the enterprise, six Reports totalling almost 10,000 pages, remains a mine of information, preserving much that would otherwise be lost or inaccessible. As perhaps the only individual to have read the entire work, I owe a personal debt of gratitude to Admiral Moebus and his colleagues.

It might be thought that so sizable a compendium would prove a sufficient source for the history of the war. But since, except in the appendices to the first Report, the approach is analytical rather than narrative, resort is necessary for the chronology of day-to-day activity to the Operation Plans, Operation Orders, Command Reports, Action Reports, and War Diaries at all levels from CincFE and Commander Naval Forces Far East down to the single ship or squadron. These items, stored in the custody of the Director of Naval History, total something over 50 file-cabinet drawers.

This material suffers from two principal weaknesses. Owing to the pressure of operations on the undermanned ships and staffs, the record of the crucial early months is often scanty. Owing to the nature of the Navy's reporting system, these reports are too frequently arid and uninformative. This reporting system, in Korea as in World War II, called for the submission by all operating commands of a War Diary, a running account of day-to-day movements, supplemented after battle by an Action Report. But Korea was a War Diary war: there were no important naval engagements, and except for the landings and evacuations of the first six months, no large set-piece operations. In such a situation the instructions for preparation of the War Diary left much to the initiative of the individual commander, and while some rose to the situation, expanding and contracting their Diaries with the varying tempo of action, many did not. And the American tendency toward the depersonalized report (or, alternatively, the overwritten press release) leaves the historian to infer the atmosphere of any given period from a simple record of movements, orders, and ammunition expenditures. The sense of urgency, the rising hopes, the dashed anticipations of war rarely appear.

In this our British cousins appear to have the advantage of us, especially as regards the reports of commanders of task group level and above. In the Second World War no American reports from commanders of whatever service provide a satisfactory equivalent to those dispatches of British commanders published in the *London Gazette*. Similarly in Korea, the Reports of Proceedings by the Flag Officer Second in Command Far Eastern Station (Commander Task Group 95.1) are in many respects the most informative command reports of the war. This was noted by Admiral Dyer who, while commanding Task Force 95, forwarded FOSICFES' "Report of Proceedings" for September 1950–November 1951 with the suggestion that U.S. Navy procedures might be modified to approximate the British. The historian can but reiterate this recommendation.

The limited coverage of the early months, while wholly understandable, also presents problems. At the level of command reports, nothing was forthcoming from the hard-pressed staff of Commander Naval Forces Far East until nine months of warfare had gone by. Information on the course of events in Tokyo in July and August is limited to a scanty annex to the first CincPacFleet Evaluation Report. By March 1951, however, it proved possible to produce a report covering the previous December; this was followed by reports for the early months of 1951, and from May of that year to the end of the war regular monthly reports are available. But July and August 1950 remain unrecorded, while the report covering the crucial months of September through November 1950 was not prepared until 1954. These ComNavFE "Command and Historical Reports," on the order of 70 to 80 pages each, provide summaries of the month's air and surface operations digested from Action Reports and War Diaries, together with comments on personnel, logistics, aerology, communications, shore activities, and medical matters. Though rather cut and dried in nature, they are nonetheless useful for chronology and statistical information.

For Seventh Fleet, the principal command afloat, the story is much the same. Throughout the period of Admiral Struble's command, the staff was undermanned and overworked, and although by July 1951 Action Reports had been submitted for Inchon, Wonsan, and for the period of the evacuation of northeastern Korea, one could wish for more. For the latter part of the war the reports of Admirals Martin and Clark, which summarize the operations carried out under their command, are generally adequate.

On the next level down things were not quite so difficult. Since the operations of the Amphibious Force Far East were necessarily intermittent, time was available between events to write the story down. One useful result was the detailed historical narrative of events from 25 June 1950 to 1 January 1951, in ComPhibGru 1's "Report of Operations," included as Appendix AA to CincPacFleet "Interim Evaluation Report No. 1." The War Diary of Task Force 95, the Blockading and Escort Force, although of variable quality, is important for the period from late 1950 through into 1952.

But the early period is the bad period, for the historian as for those who were on the job. Most fortunately, therefore, the Carrier and Cruiser Division Commanders, whose work was so important in the first weeks, kept reasonably full and complete War Diaries, and in addition two notable documents were produced in widely different and complementary spheres.

The first of these is Commander Carrier Division 1 (Rear Admiral E. C. Ewen), "Report of Task Force 77 Operations During the Korean Campaign (25 June 1950 to 19 January 1951)." This report of 616 pages (also available as Appendix R (Vol. 13) of CincPacFleet's "Interim Evaluation Report No. 1") contains a narrative of operations, a detailed analysis of the close air support situation as seen from the sea, a discussion of communications problems, and 303 pages of appendices which reproduce dispatches, bombline maps, orders, memoranda, and reports for the entire period, few of which are easily available elsewhere.

The second document of particular importance is the War Diary of the Republic of Korea Navy (Task Group 96.7/95.7), which provides a careful and detailed narrative of the campaign as viewed from Pusan and Chinhae. Although primarily important as the single source of information on the ROK Navy and its inshore operations, this War Diary is also a unique repository of information on the organization of naval support of the perimeter, the arrival of ground forces, logistic arrangements, intelligence of enemy movements, and such matters.

Over and above the periodic reports of participating units, some other naval records have proven useful. The Office of Naval History has a considerable body of miscellaneous material from the files of the Chief of Naval Operations and of Commander Naval Forces Far East, which includes occasional material of importance. The personal papers of Admiral Joy and of Admiral Ofstie, deposited in the Office of Naval History, contain some useful items. Various summaries and statistics can be found in the OpNav publication "Combat Activity of Naval Aviation," which appeared monthly from October 1950 to June 1951, and quarterly thereafter. There are some scattered articles of interest in the monthly *Review* of the Office of Naval Intelligence.

The principal lacuna in the naval sources, and one which is reflected in the narrative, concerns the control and direction of the naval campaign. For Korea, as for the Second World War, information on such evanescent matters as the availability of intelligence, estimates of the situation, concepts of employment of own forces, and relations with the other services and with allies, must be sought in the dispatch traffic between the flag officers involved. But this remains an unexplored field. Although the availability of all pertinent naval sources was a condition of my undertaking this history, I have been unable to gain access to this material.

Doubtless it has never been possible to write naval history in isolation; certainly this is the case for the Korean War, where the various arms of the defense establishment were so intimately and continuously associated. Equally, however, the problem of unified history is a difficult one, and the attempt to produce a "Report from the Secretary of Defense to the President of the United States on Operations in Korea during the period 25 June 1950 to 8 July 1951," ultimately bogged down. This effort, nevertheless, did give rise to a "Secretary of Defense Committee Final Draft," a mimeographed document of 265 pages containing a large amount of usefully summarized information on all services. At the level of the U.N. command in Tokyo, I have made intermittent use of the CincFE-CincUNC monthly Command Reports, which have all the usual large-scale virtues and defects of major headquarters compilations. And GHQ Tokyo also produced a useful "History of the North Korean Army."

At the individual service level the following may be noted. The Office of the Chief of Military History, Department of the Army, has published two preliminary narrative volumes, *Korea 1950* (Washington, 1952), and *Korea 1951–1953* (Washington, 1956) on which I have relied heavily. A number of detailed studies are in progress, of which the first, Roy E. Appleman, *South to the Naktong, North to the Yalu* (Washington, 1961) was published while this book was going to press. To Stetson Conn and John Miller, Jr., Chief and Deputy Chief Historians of OCMH, I owe thanks for perceptive criticism and helpful suggestion.

For the Navy, two published works are available. Walter Karig, Malcolm W. Cagle, and Frank A. Manson, *Battle Report, The War in Korea* (New York, 1952), a continuation of the popularly written series of World War II, takes the story through the evacuation of Hungnam. A follow-up effort by the last two named authors, *The Sea War in Korea* (Annapolis, 1957), deals with the entire period of the Korean conflict. The files of the United States Naval Institute *Proceedings* are worth investigation.

Of a projected five volumes on Korean operations, the Marine Corps has published three. These volumes, *The Pusan Perimeter, The Inchon-Seoul*

Operation, and *The Chosin Reservoir Campaign,* by Lynn Montross and Nicholas A. Canzona, are detailed and painstaking studies, extremely useful for the period covered; surprisingly, however, in view of Marine organization and doctrine, they devote little attention to the operations of Marine Corps aviation and to its interrelations with the ground forces.

For the operations of the Air Force in Korea I have relied on the three volumes of *U.S. Air Force Operations in Korea* (U.S.A.F. Historical Studies 71, 72, and 127), publications of the U.S. Air Force Historical Division, Air University, Maxwell Field. From these basic studies the author, Robert F. Futrell, has distilled an unclassified history of Air Force operations, which I have been privileged to read in manuscript form. And I am under further obligation to Mr. Futrell for courteous and helpful response to requests for information and amplification. Various aspects of the Air Force experience in Korea have been discussed in the Air University *Quarterly Review;* some of these articles are reprinted in J. T. Stewart (ed.), *Airpower—The Decisive Force in Korea* (Princeton, 1957).

For the conduct of foreign relations in the period of the Korean War the two volumes of basic documents published by the State Department, *American Foreign Policy 1950–1955* (Washington, 1957) are useful. On military and diplomatic policy, the records of two congressional hearings are crucial. The tensions in the Defense Department, and the nature of military planning in 1949, are considered in the hearings of the House Committee on the Armed Services, 81st Congress, 1st Session, on *Unification and Strategy;* how it all turned out may be seen in the hearings of the Senate Armed Services and Foreign Relations Committees, 82nd Congress, 1st Session, *The Military Situation in the Far East.* In connection with the subject here at issue I have profited from the use of two draft studies of the 20th Century Fund Project on Civil-Military Relations: Paul Y. Hammond, "Missions of the Services" (to be published as "Super-Carriers and B–36 Bombers: Appropriations, Strategy, and Politics"), and Martin Lichterman, "To the Yalu and Back," which were most generously made available by Harold Stein, the project director, and by the authors.

So much for sources of a specialized nature. There exists, of course, in the public domain, a large literature on problems of current foreign policy, the cold war, and national defense, much of which is in one way or another germane to this study. Works of a historical nature are necessarily fewer, but some are of particular importance. For the unification of the armed forces, Walter Millis (ed.), *The Forrestal Diaries* (New York, 1951), is important. Material on the Korean War and on subsequent developments in the Department of Defense appears in Matthew B. Ridgway, *Soldier* (New York, 1956), James M. Gavin, *War and Peace in the Space Age* (New York, 1958), Maxwell D. Taylor, *The Uncertain Trumpet* (New York, 1960), and

John B. Medaris, *Countdown for Decision* (New York, 1960). Naval officers, it appears, do not commit themselves to paper on these matters; the pre-Korean views of the Air Force may be traced through the pages of the *Reader's Digest,* December 1948–April 1949. The historical background is well treated in Walter Millis, *Arms and Men* (New York, 1956); assisted by others, the same author has grappled with the recent scene in *Arms and the State* (New York, 1958). Robert E. Osgood, *Limited War* (Chicago, 1957) has some perceptive comments on the Korean experience.

The position of the Commander in Chief is set forth in the two volumes of Truman's *Memoirs* (New York, 1955–56). On General MacArthur one may take one's choice between Courtney Whitney, *MacArthur, His Rendezvous with History* (New York, 1956), and Richard H. Rovere and Arthur M. Schlesinger, Jr., *The General and the President* (New York, 1951); a reading of Louis Morton, *The Fall of the Philippines* (Washington, 1953), will develop historical parallels which offer food for thought. R. M. Poats, *Decision in Korea* (New York, 1954), is a good contemporary history of the Korean War. On the armistice negotiations, see C. Turner Joy, *How Communists Negotiate* (New York, 1955) and William H. Vatcher, Jr., *Panmunjom* (New York, 1958). For those concerned with recent military developments, Brassey's *Annual* is extremely useful; for those interested in naval matters, Jane's *Fighting Ships* and *All the World's Aircraft* are essential.

On the fighting in Korea, and how it seemed to those involved, six books come to mind: S. L. A. Marshall, *The River and the Gauntlet* (New York, 1953) and *Pork Chop Hill* (New York, 1956) are concerned with Army small unit actions; James M. Michener, *The Bridges at Toko-ri* (New York, 1953), is a saccharine treatment of carrier aviation; Andrew Geer, *The New Breed* (New York, 1952) takes the Marines from the Pusan perimeter up to the reservoir and down again, as do the photographs in David D. Duncan, *This is War!* (New York, 1951); Martin Russ, *The Last Parallel* (New York, 1957) is the personal narrative of a member of the 1st Marine Division.

CHAPTER I. TO KOREA BY SEA

Of the large bibliography concerning American relations with the Orient the following have been most useful:

Tyler Dennett, *Americans in Eastern Asia* (New York, 1922); C. O. Paullin, *Diplomatic Negotiations of American Naval Officers* (Baltimore, 1912); M. F. Nelson, *Korea and the Old Orders in Eastern Asia* (Baton Rouge, La., 1945); F. H. Harrington, *God, Mammon, and the Japanese* (Madison, Wis., 1944); G. M. McCune and J. A. Harrison, *Korean-American Relations* (Berkeley, Cal., 1951); L. M. Goodrich, *Korea: A Study of U.S. Policy in the United Nations* (New York, 1956). The account of the engagement with the Korean forts is derived from Rodgers' reports in "Letters of the Commanding Officer of the Asiatic Squadron to the Secretary of the Navy," National Archives.

Chapter II. POLICY AND ITS INSTRUMENTS

1. Divided Korea

Goodrich, *Korea;* Carl L. Friedrich, *American Experience in Military Government in World War II* (New York, 1948); E. Grant Meade, *American Military Government in Korea* (New York, 1951); Truman, *Memoirs;* Secretary of Defense, "Report to the President of the United States on Operations in Korea."

2. Unified Defense

Millis, *The Forrestal Diaries, Arms and Men, Arms and the State;* Truman, *Memoirs;* House Committee on the Armed Services, Hearings on *Unification and Strategy;* Hammond, "Missions of the Services." S. P. Huntington, "National Policy and the Transoceanic Navy," 80 U.S. Naval Institute *Proceedings* 483–93, has some interesting comments on the theoretical difficulties of the period.

3. The Estimate of the Situation

Secretary of Defense Report; CincPacFleet Evaluation Report, I (Vol. 7, Intelligence); Truman, *Memoirs;* Goodrich, *Korea;* Montross and Canzona, *U.S. Marine Operations in Korea* (hereafter USMC *Operations*), I.

Chapter III. WAR BEGINS

1. The Decision to Intervene

Secretary of Defense Report; Senate Armed Services and Foreign Relations Committees, Hearings on *The Military Situation in the Far East;* Lichterman, "To the Yalu and Back"; Truman, *Memoirs;* Department of State, *American Foreign Policy 1950–1955;* A. L. Warner, "How the Korea Decision was Made," *Harper's Magazine,* June 1951.

2. The Far East Command

Secretary of Defense Report; CincPacFleet Evaluation Report, I; Department of the Army, *Korea 1950;* USAF Histories; USMC *Operations,* I; War Diaries of CarDiv 3, CruDiv 5.

3. The First Days of Naval Action

Secretary of Defense Report; CincPacFleet Evaluation Report, I (Vol. 6, Surface and Covering Operations; Annex A, ComNavFE Staff History);

Department of the Army, *Korea 1950;* USAF Histories; NavFE Operation Orders 4–50, 5–50, 7–50, 8–50; Seventh Fleet Operation Order 6–50; War Diaries of ROK Navy, CarDiv 3, CruDiv 5, *Juneau, DeHaven, Mansfield;* Action Reports of *Juneau* (24 June–6 July), *Suisun.*

4. Air Strikes, Coastal Bombardment, Flank Patrols

Secretary of Defense Report; CincPacFleet Evaluation Report, I (Vol. 6, Surface and Covering Operations; Annex A, ComNavFE Staff History; JJ, ComSubPac Submarine Operations); Department of the Army, *Korea 1950;* USAF Histories; NavFE Operation Order 6–50; Seventh Fleet Operation Plan 1–50, Operation Orders 6–50, 7–50; War Diaries of CarDiv 3, CruDiv 5, *Juneau;* ComCarDiv 1, Report of Task Force 77 Operations During the Korean Campaign (hereafter ComCarDiv 1 Action Report); Action Report of *Juneau* (24 June–6 July).

Chapter IV. HELP ON THE WAY

2. Troops and Supplies

Secretary of Defense Report; CincPacFleet Evaluation Report, I (Annexes FF, ComWestSeaFron Narrative; GG, DepComMSTSPac Report; HH, DepComMSTSWestPac Report); Department of the Army, *Korea 1950.*

3. Fighting Ships

Secretary of Defense Report; CincPacFleet Evaluation Report, I (Annexes T, U, ComAirPac Reports; EE, ComServPac Evaluation); War Diaries of CruDiv 3, *Helena, Badoeng Strait, Sicily.*

4. Naval Logistics

CincPacFleet Evaluation Report, I (Vol. 7, Logistics; Annex EE, ComServPac Evaluation), II.

5. The Marine Brigade

CincPacFleet Evaluation Report, I (Annexes V, ComAdComPhibPac Narrative; Z, FMFPac Report; DD, 1st MarDiv Report); USMC *Operations,* I; War Diary of *Badoeng Strait.*

6. Air Transport and Air Reinforcement

Secretary of Defense Report; USAF Histories; CincPacFleet Evaluation Report, I (Annexes T, U, ComAirPac Reports; W, FlogAirWingPac Report; FF, ComWestSeaFron Narrative); *Boxer,* Overall Report of Activities, 1 July–31 December 1950.

CHAPTER V. INTO THE PERIMETER

1. The Korean Theater

In hydrographic matters, here and throughout the book, I have relied on *Sailing Directions for the Southeast Coast of Siberia and Korea* (Hydrographic Office Publication 122B, Washington, 1951) and on the relevant H.O. charts; for Korean topography I have used the maps of the Army Map Service, Corps of Engineers, to the scales of 1:1,000,000 and 1:250,000. Korean place names have been employed throughout, with but a single exception: up in the high country I have followed the Marines in referring to the Chosin (rather than the Changjin) Reservoir, and in calling the town Hagaru (instead of Changjin).

Secretary of Defense Report; Department of the Army, *Korea 1950;* USMC *Operations,* I.

2. East Coast Bombardment

Secretary of Defense Report; CincPacFleet Evaluation Report, I (Vol. 6, Surface and Covering Operations); War Diaries of CruDiv 5, *Juneau, Mansfield;* Action Report of *Juneau* (7–23 July).

3. The Pohang Landing

Secretary of Defense Report; CincPacFleet Evaluation Report, I (Vol. 5, Amphibious and Ground Operations; Annexes AA, ComPhibGru 1 Report; HH, DepComMSTSWestPac Report); USAF Histories; NavFE Operation Orders 9–50, 10–50; War Diary of PhibGru 1.

4. Seventh Fleet Operations

Secretary of Defense Report; CincPacFleet Evaluation Report, I (Vol. 3, Naval Air Operations; Annex B, ComSeventh Fleet Narrative); USAF Histories; NavFE Operation Order 10–50; Seventh Fleet Operation Orders 9–50, 11–50, and Operation Plan 9–50; War Diaries of ROK Navy, CarDiv 3, Fleet Air Wing 1; Action Reports of ComCarDiv 1, Carrier Air Group 5 (18–19 July).

5. Patrol Planes and Gunnery Ships

Secretary of Defense Report; CincPacFleet Evaluation Report, I (Vol. 3, Naval Air Operations; Vol. 6, Surface and Covering Operations; Annexes D, ComFairWing 6 Report; H, VP 47 Report; Q–2, ComCruDiv 3 History); NavFE Operation Order 12–50; War Diaries of ROK Navy, CruDiv 3, CruDiv 5, *Helena, Juneau;* Action Report of *Juneau.*

6. The Marines Arrive

Secretary of Defense Report; CincPacFleet Evaluation Report, I (Annexes B, ComSeventh Fleet Narrative; S, ComCarDiv 15 Narrative; CC, 1st

MAW Report; DD, 1st MarDiv Report); USMC *Operations*, I; NavFE Operation Order 14–50; War Diaries of *Badoeng Strait, Sicily; Boxer*, Overall Report of Activities (1 July–31 December).

Chapter VI. HOLDING THE LINE

1. The Perimeter Takes Form

Secretary of Defense Report; CincPacFleet Evaluation Report, I; Department of the Army, *Korea 1950;* USMC *Operations*, I, II; GHQ, FEC, "History of the North Korean Army;" War Diary of ROK Navy.

2. Coastal Bombardment, The Problem of Carrier Air, and the Southern Spoiling Offensive

Secretary of Defense Report; CincPac Fleet Evaluation Report, I (Vol. 3, Naval Air Operations; Vol. 6, Surface and Covering Operations; Annexes Q–2, ComCruDiv 3 History; DD, 1st MarDiv Report); USMC *Operations*, I; USAF Histories; Seventh Fleet Operation Order 13–50; War Diaries of ROK Navy, CarDiv 3, CruDiv 3, CruDiv 5, *Badoeng Strait, Sicily, Diachenko;* Action Reports of ComCarDiv 1, *Diachenko* (4–5 August).

3. East Coast Interdiction, Pohang, and First Naktong

Secretary of Defense Report; CincPacFleet Evaluation Report, I (Vol. 3, Naval Air Operations; Vol. 6, Surface and Covering Operations; Annexes JJ, ComSubPac Submarine Operations; Q–2, ComCruDiv 3 History); Department of the Army, *Korea 1950;* USMC *Operations*, I; USAF Histories; NavFE Operation Orders 11–50, 13–50; War Diaries of ROK Navy, CarDiv 3, CruDiv 3, CruDiv 5, *Badoeng Strait, Sicily, Horace A. Bass;* Action Reports of ComCarDiv 1, *Horace A. Bass* (12–16 August).

4. Coastal Operations and Carrier Strikes

Secretary of Defense Report; CincPacFleet Evaluation Report, I (Vol. 3, Naval Air Operations; Vol. 6, Surface and Covering Operations); Department of the Army, *Korea 1950;* USAF Histories; Seventh Fleet Operation Order 14–50; War Diaries of ROK Navy, CarDiv 3, CruDiv 3, CruDiv 5, *Sicily;* Action Report of ComCarDiv 1.

5. The Enemy's Big Blast

Secretary of Defense Report; CincPacFleet Evaluation Report, I (as above); Department of the Army, *Korea 1950;* USMC *Operations*, I; USAF Histories; War Diaries of CarDiv 3, CruDiv 3, CruDiv 5, *Badoeng Strait, Sicily;* Action Report of ComCarDiv 1. For the affair of the Russian bomber, ComCarDiv 1 (CTF 77) Special Action Report of 6 September 1950, and enclosures; War Diary of *Herbert J. Thomas;* New York *Times,* 5–9 September 1950.

CHAPTER VII. BACK TO THE PARALLEL

1. Preparing the Counterstroke

Secretary of Defense Report; CincPacFleet Evaluation Report, I (Vol. 3, Naval Air Operations; Vol. 5, Amphibious and Ground Operations; Vol. 6, Surface and Covering Operations, Mine Warfare; Vol. 8, Intelligence; Annexes B, ComSeventhFleet Narrative; AA, ComPhibGru 1 Report); NavFE Command and Historical Report, September–November 1950; Department of the Army, *Korea 1950;* USMC *Operations,* II; USAF Histories; Senate Hearings on *The Military Situation in the Far East;* NavFE Operation Plan 108–50; Seventh Fleet Operation Plan 9–50; Amphibious Group 1 Operation Order 14–50; War Diaries of Amphibious Group 1, *Badoeng Strait, Horace A. Bass, McKean;* Action Reports of Seventh Fleet (JTF 7), *Horace A. Bass* (20–25 August).

2. North to Inchon

Secretary of Defense Report; CincPacFleet Evaluation Report, I (Vol. 3, Naval Air Operations; Vol. 4, Marine Air Operations; Vol. 5, Amphibious and Ground Operations; Vol. 6, Surface and Covering Operations; Vol 7, Logistics; Annexes AA, ComPhibGru 1 Report; DD, 1st Mardiv Report); NavFE Command and Historical Report, Sept.–Nov. 1950; Department of the Army, *Korea 1950;* USMC *Operations,* II; USAF Histories; Flag Officer Second in Command Far Eastern Station, Report of Proceedings, 1–14 Sept. 1950; War Diaries of ROK Navy, Amphibious Group 1, Transron 1, Fleet Air Wing 1, LSR Division 11, *Horace A. Bass, Manchester, Sicily, Badoeng Strait;* Action Reports of Seventh Fleet (JTF 7), ComCarDiv 1, Advance Attack Group, Naval Beach Group 1, Tacron 1, Minron 3.

3. The Clearance of South Korea

Secretary of Defense Report; CincPacFleet Evaluation Report, I (Vol. 6, Surface and Covering Operations, Mine Warfare; Annexes Q–1, ComUN Blockading and Escort Force Evaluation; Q–2, ComCruDiv 3 History; AA, ComPhibGru I Report); NavFE Command and Historical Report, Sept.–Nov. 1950; Department of the Army, *Korea 1950;* USMC *Operations* II; USAF Histories; GHQ, FEC, "History of the North Korean Army;" Flag Officer Second in Command Far Eastern Station, Consolidated Report of Proceedings, Sept. 1950–Nov. 1951 (hereafter FOSICFES Report); War Diaries of U.N. Blockading and Escort Force, ROK Navy, CruDiv 3, Amphibious Group 1, *Horace A. Bass, Missouri, Manchester;* Action Report of Seventh Fleet (JTF 7); *Perch,* Report of Raid.

CHAPTER VIII. ON TO THE BORDER

1. Planning the Wonsan Landing

Secretary of Defense Report; CincPacFleet Evaluation Report I (Annexes B, ComSeventh Fleet Narrative; AA, ComPhibGru 1 Report); NavFE Command and Historical Report, Sept.–Nov. 1950; Department of the Army, *Korea 1950;* USMC *Operations,* III; USAF Histories; Senate Hearings on *The Military Situation in the Far East;* Lichterman, "To the Yalu and Back;" Goodrich, *Korea;* NavFE Operation Plan 113–50; Seventh Fleet Operation Order 16–50, Operation Plan 10–50; Amphibious Group 1 Operation Order 16–50; Commander D. N. Clay, Trip Report, 18 Oct. 1950; War Diaries of *Bass and Wantuck;* Action Reports of Seventh Fleet (JTF 7), ComCarDiv 1.

2. The Opening of Wonsan and Chinnampo.

Secretary of Defense Report; CincPacFleet Evaluation Report, I (Vol. 6, Mine Warfare); NavFE Command and Historical Report, Sept.–Nov. 1950; FOSICFES Report; War Diaries of U.N. Blockading and Escort Force, ROK Navy, Minron 3, *Forrest Royal;* Action Report of Seventh Fleet (JTF 7); *Pirate* and *Pledge,* Reports of Sinking.

3. Operations in Eastern North Korea

Secretary of Defense Report; CincPacFleet Evaluation Report, I (Vol. 5, Amphibious and Ground Operations; Vol. 6, Mine Warfare; Annexes AA, ComPhibGru 1 Report; DD, 1st MarDiv Report); NavFE Command and Historical Report, Sept.–Nov. 1950; Department of the Army, *Korea 1950;* USMC *Operations,* III; USAF Histories; War Diaries of U.N. Blockading and Escort Force, ROK Navy, Minron 3; Action Reports of Seventh Fleet (JTF 7), Amphibious Group 3, Tacron 3.

4. New Plans and New Problems

Secretary of Defense Report; CincPacFleet Evaluation Reports, I (Annex AA, ComPhibGru 1 Report), II; NavFE Command and Historical Report, Sept.–Nov. 1950; Department of the Army, *Korea 1950;* USMC *Operations,* III; USAF Histories; Goodrich, *Korea;* Truman, *Memoirs;* Senate Hearings on *The Military Situation in the Far East;* Lichterman, "To the Yalu and Back;" FOSICFES Report; War Diaries of ROK Navy, *Philippine Sea, Bataan, Badoeng Strait, Sicily;* Action Reports of Seventh Fleet (1 Nov.–26 Dec. 1950), ComCarDiv 1, *Valley Forge, Philippine Sea;* Joy Papers.

CHAPTER IX. RETREAT TO THE SOUTH

1. Defeat in the West

Secretary of Defense Report; CincPacFleet Evaluation Reports, I (Annex AA, ComPhibGru 1 Report), II; NavFE Command and Historical Report,

Dec. 1950; Department of the Army, *Korea 1950;* USMC *Operations,* III; USAF Histories; Senate Hearings on *The Military Situation in the Far East;* NavFE Operation Plan 116–50; FOSICFES Report; War Diaries of U.N. Blockading and Escort Force, ROK Navy, Amphibious Group 3, Transron 1, *Forrest Royal;* Action Reports of Seventh Fleet (1 Nov.–26 Dec. 1950), ComCardiv 1.

2. *The Campaign at the Reservoir*

Secretary of Defense Report; CincPacFleet Evaluation Reports, I (Annex DD, 1st MarDiv Report), II; NavFE Command and Historical Report, Dec. 1950; USMC *Operations,* III; USAF Histories; War Diary of CarDiv 1; Action Reports of Seventh Fleet (1 Nov.–26 Dec. 1950), ComCarDiv 1, Marine Tactical Air Control Squadron 2 (in Action Report of 1st Marine Aircraft Wing, Wonsan-Hungnam).

3. *Concentration in the East*

Secretary of Defense Report; CincPacFleet Evaluation Reports, I (Annex AA, ComPhibGru 1 Report), II; NavFE Command and Historical Report, Dec. 1950; Department of the Army, *Korea 1950;* USMC *Operations,* III; USAF Histories; Seventh Fleet Operation Order 18–50; War Diaries of U.N. Blockading and Escort Force, TransDiv 11, *Noble;* Action Report of Seventh Fleet (1 Nov.–26 Dec. 1950).

4. *The Evacuation of Hungnam*

Secretary of Defense Report; CincPacFleet Evaluation Reports, I (Annex AA, ComPhibGru 1 Report), II; NavFE Command and Historical Report, Dec. 1950; USMC *Operations,* III; USAF Histories; NavFE Operation Plan 116–50; Amphibious Group 1 Operation Order 20–50; War Diaries of U.N. Blockading and Escort Force, ROK Navy, Transron 1; Action Reports of Seventh Fleet (1 Nov.–26 Dec. 1950), ComCarDiv 1, Tacron 1.

5. *The Second Chinese Offensive*

Secretary of Defense Report; CincPacFleet Evaluation Report, II; NavFE Command and Historical Reports, Dec. 1950, Jan. 1951; Department of the Army, *Korea 1950, Korea 1951–1953;* USAF Histories; Senate Hearings on *The Military Situation in the Far East;* Lichterman, "To the Yalu and Back;" Truman, *Memoirs;* Whitney, *MacArthur;* Seventh Fleet Operation Orders 19–50, 20–50; FOSICFES Report; War Diaries of Seventh Fleet, U.N. Blockading and Escort Force, Amphibious Group 3, *Horace A. Bass;* Action Reports of ComCarDiv 1, Amphibious Group 3.

CHAPTER X. THE SECOND SIX MONTHS

1. Back to the Han

Secretary of Defense Report; CincPacFleet Evaluation Report, II; NavFE Command and Historical Report, Feb. 1951; Department of the Army, *Korea 1951–1953;* USAF Histories; FOSICFES Report; War Diaries of Seventh Fleet, U.N. Blockading and Escort Force, Amphibious Group 3, CruDiv 1, *Horace A. Bass.*

2. On to the Parallel

Secretary of Defense Report; CincPacFleet Evaluation Report, II; NavFE Command and Historical Report, March, April, 1951; Department of the Army, *Korea 1951–1953;* USAF Histories; Truman, *Memoirs;* Senate Hearings on *The Military Situation in the Far East;* NavFE Operation Order 3–51; FOSICFES Report; War Diaries of Seventh Fleet, U.N. Blockading and Escort Force, Amphibious Group 3, *Missouri;* Action Report of Seventh Fleet (28 March 1951–3 March 1952), CTF 74 (Sorye Dong).

3. The Communist Spring Offensive

Secretary of Defense Report; CincPacFleet Evaluation Reports, II, III; NavFE Command and Historical Report, April, May, 1951; Department of the Army, *Korea 1951–1953;* USAF Histories; FOSICFES Report; War Diaries of U.N. Blockading and Escort Force, Amphibious Group 3; Action Report of Seventh Fleet (March 1951–March 1952), *Princeton* (on Hwachon Dam).

4. North to Kaesong

Secretary of Defense Report; CincPacFleet Evaluation Report, III; NavFE Command and Historical Reports, June, July, 1951; Department of the Army, *Korea 1951–1953;* USAF Histories; FOSICFES Report; War Diary of U.N. Blockading and Escort Force; Action Report of Seventh Fleet (March 1951–March 1952); *Walke,* Report of Mining.

CHAPTER XI. PROBLEMS OF A POLICEMAN

2. Operating Problems

The functional organization and the systematic arrangement of conclusions and recommendations in the CincPacFleet Evaluation Reports make these the most useful single source; some of these reports have extensive special sections on personnel problems. The NavFE files and the papers of Admirals Joy and Ofstie contain relevant items.

3. *Logistic Support*

Logistic sections of CincPacFleet Evaluation Reports, I–VI; information from W. H. Marlow, Principal Investigator, Logistics Research Project, The George Washington University.

4. *Interservice Coordination and the Air Problem*

The most inclusive sources are the CincPacFleet Evaluation Reports, especially I (for close support), II (for interdiction), and VI; the classified and unclassified Air Force Histories; and the Action Report of ComCarDiv 1. The NavFE files contain a series of letters and memoranda on the close support question, as do the papers of Admirals Joy and Ofstie. The action reports of Tacron 1 for Inchon and Hungnam, and of Marine Tactical Air Control Squadron 2 for the Chosin Reservoir campaign are important. The end of the story may be investigated in: "Report on Joint Air-Ground Operations Conference held at Headquarters, Fifth Air Force, Seoul, Korea, 8–22 August 1953," and in Joint Tactical Air Support Board, Fort Bragg, N.C., "Special Report Pertaining to Project No. 2–53 'To Establish Joint Doctrine and Procedures Governing Command, Employment, and Control of Tactical Air Forces in Support of Ground Forces.' "

5. *The Larger Picture*

On the Formosa patrol: Seventh Fleet Operation Order 15–50; War Diaries of ComCruDiv 1, *Juneau,* Fleet Air Wing 1. For the submarine problem, see the CincPacFleet Evaluation Reports; the NavFE files contain reports of ASW actions and correspondence on this subject. For patrol plane operations see the relevant sections of CincPacFleet Evaluation Reports. On the other side of the world, Annual Reports of CincLantFleet; H. L. Ismay, *NATO, the First Five Years, 1949–1954* (Paris? 1954?); Cinc-NELM, Report of Operations, 1 July–1 November 1950. The Office of Naval History has compiled a chronology of Mediterranean naval operations subsequent to World War II.

6. *Into the Future*

Almost all this information on ship and aircraft development is available in unclassified sources, notably *Jane's Fighting Ships* and *All the World's Aircraft.* The Joy and Ofstie papers contain some correspondence on the implications of the Korean experience for new construction.

Chapter XII. TWO MORE YEARS

The important general sources for the entire chapter are the 4,612 pages of CincPacFleet Evaluation Reports, III–VI; the ten file-drawer inches of monthly NavFE Command and Historical Reports, July 1951–July 1953; and the Reports of the two Seventh Fleet commanders, Admirals Martin and Clark, covering the periods 28 March 1951–3 March 1952 and May 1952–July 1953. For the other services, Department of the Army, *Korea 1951–1953,* and the USAF Histories. For the armistice negotiations, Vatcher, *Panmunjom.*

1. Stabilized Front and Peripheral War

War Diaries of U.N. Blockading and Escort Force, ROK Navy, Transdiv 13, *New Jersey*; FOSICFES Report; 41st Independent Commando, Report of Proceedings; Ofstie papers; Joy notes on armistice negotiations. On the Battle of the Buzz Saw, Action Reports of ComDesDiv 132, *Blue, Cunningham, O'Brien* (17 July 1951).

2. Stalemate

The NavFE files contain a study of the interdiction question of 28 April 1952, made in response to a CincFE query of 12 March; material on interdiction also exists in the Ofstie papers. On the transfer of the Marine Division, War Diary of Amphibious Group 1; on the Kojo demonstration, Action Report of Amphibious Group 3; on the engagement with the MIGs, Action Reports of *Oriskany, Kearsarge,* and *Helena,* and an account in the ONI *Review,* February 1953.

3. Progress, Crisis, Conclusion

On the last minute redeployments, War Diary of Amphibious Group 1; on the loss of the B–50, War Diary of CruDiv 3, Action Report of ComCarDiv 3 (27 July–1 August 1953), Department of State, *American Foreign Policy 1951–1955.*

Glossary

1. Ships

The designations of the various types of U.S. naval vessels are derived by compounding an initial letter indicative of general category (thus A, auxiliary; C, cruiser; D, destroyer; L, landing; P, patrol) with one or more modifiers descriptive of the particular species (thus C, command or craft; D, destroyer or dock; E, explosive or escort; H, hospital or helicopter; O, oiler or ocean; P, transport (i.e., personnel); T, tracked, tank, or torpedo; V, aviation). Type designators employed in this book are as follows:

AD	Destroyer tender
AE	Ammunition ship
AF	Refrigerated stores ship
AGC	Amphibious force flagship
AH	Hospital ship
AK	Cargo ship
AKA	Attack cargo ship
AKL	Light cargo ship
AM	Fleet minesweeper
AMS	Motor minesweeper (formerly YMS)
AN	Net tender
AO	Oiler
AOG	Gasoline tanker
AP	Transport
APA	Attack transport
APD	Fast transport (destroyer escort conversion)
ARG	Internal combustion engine repair ship
ARH	Heavy hull repair ship
ARL	Landing craft repair ship
ARS	Salvage vessel
ASR	Submarine rescue vessel
ATF	Fleet tug
AV	Seaplane tender

AVP	Small seaplane tender
BB	Battleship
CA	Heavy cruiser
CL	Light cruiser
CLAA	Antiaircraft light cruiser
CV	Aircraft carrier
CVE	Escort aircraft carrier (merchant ship hull)
CVL	Light aircraft carrier (cruiser hull)
DD	Destroyer
DE	Destroyer escort
DMS	Fast minesweeper (destroyer conversion)
DUKW	Amphibious truck (manufacturer's designation)
JMS	Japanese minesweeper (YMS type)
LCVP	Vehicle and personnel landing craft
LPH	Helicopter amphibious assault ship
LSD	Dock landing ship
LSMR	Rocket ship (medium landing ship conversion)
LST	Tank landing ship
LSU	Utility landing ship
LVT	Tracked landing vehicle
LVTA	Armored tracked landing vehicle
MSC	Coastal minesweeper (non-magnetic)
MSI	Inshore minesweeper (non-magnetic)
MSO	Ocean minesweeper (non-magnetic)
PC	Submarine chaser
PCEC	Amphibious control vessel (patrol escort modification)
PF	Frigate (patrol gunboat or corvette)
PT	Motor torpedo boat
T–AP	Transport assigned to MSTS
T–APc	Small coastal transport assigned to MSTS
YMS	Motor minesweeper (World War II designation)

2. *Aircraft*

Aircraft of the U.S. Navy are designated by a first letter indicative of functional category and by a second which identifies the manufacturer; to distinguish second and subsequent designs in the same category by the same company an intervening number is employed. Suffixed numbers and letters indicate changes to the basic model and special uses and configurations. Important categories of aircraft are:

A	attack	P	patrol
F	fighter	PB	patrol bomber
H	helicopter	R	transport
U	utility		

Relevant manufacturer's designators are:

D	Douglas	S	Sikorsky
F	Grumman	U	Chance Vought
H	McDonnell	V	Lockheed (current)
M	Martin	Y	Consolidated
O	Lockheed (former)		

To illustrate, the AD is the first naval attack plane produced by Douglas after the Attack designation was set up by the Navy in September 1946; the F9F is the ninth Grumman-designed shipboard fighter; the F4U–5N is the night-configured version of the fifth modification of the fourth naval fighter plane designed by Chance Vought.

In the Air Force a different series of letter prefixes is used to indicate function (B, bomber; C, cargo and transport; F, fighter; L, liaison; R, reconnaissance, and so on); these letters are followed by numbers running consecutively in each category, and in the event of model changes by a letter suffix. Thus, for example, the F–86A Sabre is the first modification of the basic design of the eighty-sixth in the sequence of Air Force fighters.

Soviet aircraft, regardless of type, are referred to by the designer's model number: thus MIG for products of the establishment presided over by Artem Mikoyan and Mikhail Gurevich; Yak for Aleksandir Sergeivich Yakovlev.

3. *Miscellaneous*

ACB	Amphibious Construction Battalion (Navy)
ADCOM	Advance Command and Liaison Group (Army)
Anglico	Air and Naval Gunfire Liaison Company (Navy-Marine)
AP	Armor-piercing
BLT	Battalion Landing Team
CAP	Combat air patrol
Cardiv	Carrier Division
CAS	Close air support
CCF	Chinese Communist Forces
CincFE	Commander in Chief, Far East Command
CincLantFleet	Commander in Chief, Atlantic Fleet
CincPac	Commander in Chief, Pacific
CincPacFleet	Commander in Chief, Pacific Fleet
CincUNC	Commander in Chief, United Nations Command

CNO	Chief of Naval Operations
Com	Commander (in compounds), as
ComNavFE	Commander Naval Forces Far East
Crudiv	Cruiser Division
CTF	Commander Task Force
CTG	Commander Task Group
CW	Continuous wave
Desdiv	Destroyer Division
ECA	Economic Cooperation Administration
ESB	Engineer Special Brigade (Army)
EUSAK	Eighth U.S. Army in Korea
FAFIK	Fifth Air Force in Korea
FEAF	Far East Air Forces
FEC	Far East Command
FLAW	Fleet Logistic Air Wing
FMF	Fleet Marine Force
FOSICFES	Flag Officer Second in Command, Far Eastern Station (British)
F/S	Fire Support
GCA	Ground control approach
GHQ	General Headquarters
HC	High capacity
IFF	Electronic identification device
JapLogCom	Japan Logistical Command
JCS	Joint Chiefs of Staff
JOC	Joint Operations Center
JTF	Joint Task Force
KMAG	Korean Military Advisory Group (U.S. Army)
KMC	Korean Marine Corps
Lant	Atlantic (in compounds)
MAG	Marine Aircraft Group
MATS	Military Air Transport Service
MAW	Marine Aircraft Wing
MDA(P)	Mutual Defense Assistance (Program)
Mindiv	Minecraft Division
MLR	Main line of resistance
MSR	Main supply route
MSTS	Military Sea Transportation Service
MTACS	Marine Tactical Air Control Squadron
NAF	Naval Air Facility
NATO	North Atlantic Treaty Organization
NavFE	Naval Forces Far East
NCO	Non-commissioned officer

NKPA	North Korean People's Army
NMJ	Naval Member, Joint Operations Center
OCMH	Office of the Chief of Military History (Army)
OpArea	Operating Area
OPLR	Outpost line of resistance
OpNav	Office of Naval Operations
OpPlan	Operation plan
OTC	Officer in tactical command
Pac	Pacific (in compounds)
PhibGru	Amphibious Group
POL	Petroleum, oil, lubricants
POW	Prisoner of war
RAF	Royal Air Force
RAN	Royal Australian Navy
RCN	Royal Canadian Navy
RCT	Regimental Combat Team
RN	Royal Navy (Gt. Britain)
RNZN	Royal New Zealand Navy
ROK	Republic of Korea
ROKN	Republic of Korea Navy
Scajap	Shipping Control Administration, Japan
SEATO	Southeast Asia Treaty Organization
ServPac	Service Force, Pacific Fleet
SHAPE	Supreme Headquarters, Allied Powers Europe
SPB	Shore Party Battalion (Marine)
TAC	Tactical Air Command
TACP	Tactical air control party
Tacron	Tactical Air Control Squadron (Navy)
TADC	Tactical air direction center
TE	Task Element
TF	Task Force
TG	Task Group
UDT	Underwater Demolition Team
UNC	United Nations Command
USNS	U.S. Naval Ship ("in Service", i.e. non-commissioned vessel of MSTS nucleus fleet)
VHF	Very high frequency
VT	Variable time (radar-controlled) fuse
VMF	Marine Fighter Squadron
VMFN	Marine Night Fighter Squadron
VMO	Marine Observation Squadron
VMR	Marine Transport Squadron
VP	Patrol Squadron

Index

485

U.S. GOVERNMENT PRINTING OFFICE: 1962

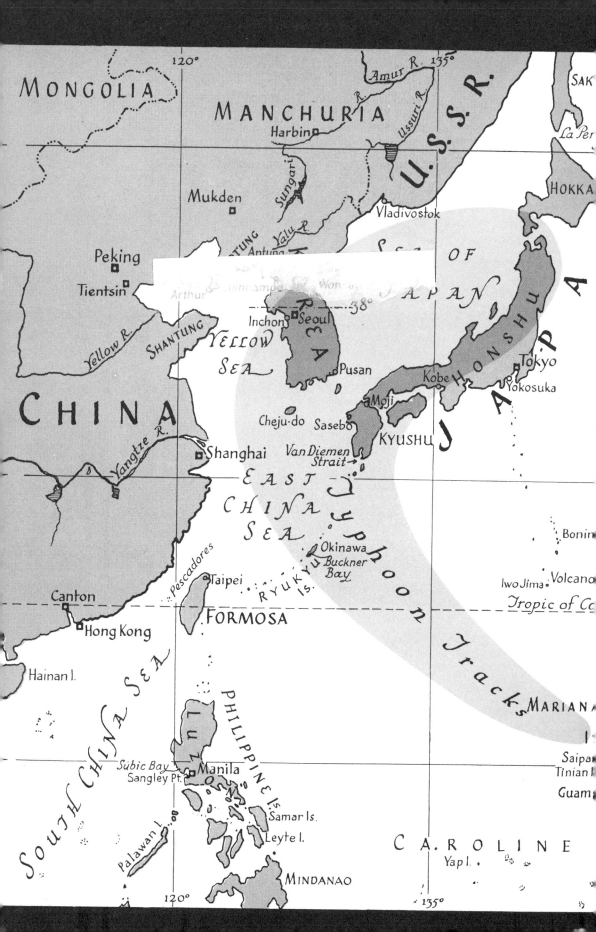